THE PEOPLE OF ARITAMA

THE PEOPLE OF ARITAMA

The Cultural Personality
of a Colombian Mestizo
Village

by

GERARDO and ALICIA
REICHEL-DOLMATOFF

THE UNIVERSITY OF CHICAGO PRESS

CONTENTS

Contents

PLATES

PREFACE

THE study of Aritama and its people, the basic results of which are incorporated in this report, was made possible by a grant from the Wenner-Gren Foundation for Anthropological Research, of New York. To this institution and in particular to its director, Dr. Paul Fejos, the authors express their sincere gratitude.

At the time this study was undertaken, official anthropology in Colombia was undergoing a crisis. The old Instituto Etnólogico Nacional had been dissolved and the new Instituto Colombiano de Antropología was founded, the consequence being the dispersal of many of the old staff members. Thanks to Father José Rafael Arboleda, S. J., Dean of the Faculty of Letters of Bogotá's St. Xavier's University, our initial project was taken under the sponsorship of that institution, and we are deeply indebted to the university's offer to back us in those critical times. When, several months later, after we had already left for the field, the new Instituto emerged, and we were honored to form part of its research staff, the directors, Drs. Francisco Antonio Vélez Arango and Antonio Andrade Crispino, kindly allowed us to continue our field work which was already well under way by that time.

In the planning and writing of this report several friends and colleagues gave us the benefit of their counsel and we are greatly obliged to them for the generous sharing of their knowledge. Father Arboleda read part of the manuscript and made many helpful suggestions and, with Dr. F. Ronnefeldt, of the World Health Organization, we were able to discuss many points relating to health and disease. Special thanks are due to Professor José de Recasens, of Bogotá, whose brilliant mind and deep insight were of immense help in all phases of our work. For the identification of plants and animals we are indebted to Dr. Armando Dugand, botanist; Dr. Roberto Jaramillo, botanist; and Dr. Frederik Medem, zoölogist, all three of the Instituto de Ciencias Naturales, of the National University of Bogotá. To Mrs. Lona Rawlins we owe a great debt for her painstaking work in correcting the grammar and style of our manuscript. To Mr. Alec S. Bright we are especially grateful for his generous co-operation in proofreading. To all these friends we express our sincere gratitude. The shortcomings of this report are, of course, our own.

Last but not least, we thank the people of Aritama, the anonymous informants, whose kindness and tolerance and endless patience made this study possible. To them our debt is greatest, for they taught us the most.

INTRODUCTION

I

THE present book is concerned with the life of a small Mestizo village in northern Colombia, with its people and institutions, its traditions in the past and its outlook on the future. Ever since anthropologists have applied their methods and concepts to the study of Latin–American peasant communities, it has become increasingly evident that the analysis of their structural and dynamic aspects throws an important light upon many little-known and little-understood fields of culture contact. This might prove to be of interest, not only for anthropological theory itself, but also for a better understanding of a large mass of peoples who are rapidly evolving into a major factor in shaping the future of Latin America. It is our hope that this report will contribute in some measure to the body of knowledge and understanding that anthropologists have accumulated on these problems during the last decade.

Colombia is a fruitful and practically untouched field for research in Creole peasant life in the tropics, especially of variables that can be observed in a wide range of different physical environments. There exists the widespread belief that Colombia is mainly an Andean country, the inhabitants of which dwell in the cool or cold sections of the northern Andes. But in reality only 23 per cent of the Colombian population live in the highlands, while 37 per cent live on the subtropical and temperate slopes of the mountain systems, and 40 per cent occupy the tropical lowlands. The cultural characteristics of this population, especially of its rural segments, are still very deficiently known, and only in recent years has the highland peasantry of some regions been the object of sporadic studies. Although we speak here of highlands, lowlands, and temperate zones, one must not think that these altitudinal divisions have a specific cultural significance in terms of homogeneous developments. It is true that the highlands are occupied mainly by a Mestizo population, while the coastal lowlands and the large inter-Andean valleys show a predominantly Negroid population with a tri-ethnic intermixture on the interfluvial plains and lower slopes, but historically (and prehistorically) many of these regions forming a climatic unit have quite different cultural traditions, and even within the same basic ethnic population groups there appear marked differences. There are regional subcultures, grown out of centuries of slow development, based upon varying combinations of different biological, social, and cultural heritages, different contact situations, or different forms of adaptation to similar environments. The common denominator is Spanish colonial culture, but the variety of its historical influence, its local interpretations, and its present forms, has created a wide range of variables. Similarities between them are often due not so much to spatial proximity and contact but to their occupying a similar synchronic level of development.

Among the larger subcultural units that can be isolated, stands the peasantry of the Caribbean lowlands, in northern Colombia. While the Negroid element predominates along the coast and the larger rivers, the wide interfluvial plains and the hill country are peopled by Mestizos. Culturally these, as well as the Negroid communities, represent different characteristics according to their relative isolation, the permanence of their local traditions, the influence of particular historical events, or the differential adaptation to a given environment. Next to these communities which, to a large but varying degree, are well incorporated into the Creole culture of the national whole, there still exist several Indian groups which, although nominally under government control, have maintained their tribal independence in the marginal territories. Even though all of these tribes have for centuries been in more or less close contact with the Creole peasants, they have conserved most of their aboriginal culture, together with their languages, and because most of these tribal groups are endogamous, there exists today little biological intermixture with the neighboring peasants. Near these tribal territories—often only a few hours distant—there are small villages of peasant farmers. Some of them are pioneer settlements which have advanced only in recent times toward the Indian-occupied regions, but others are old villages, originally Indian hamlets, which today find themselves in a transition from the native-oriented past to the nation-oriented present. Aritama is one of these.

Aritama (a pseudonym) is a small peasant community in the tropical mountain country of northern Colombia, in the foothills of the Sierra Nevada de Santa Marta. The village lies in the intermediate region between the rural and urban Creoles of the lowlands and the autochthonous Indian tribes of the mountains. Until the second half of the last century, Aritama, too, was an Indian village, although modified by its occasional contact with missionaries and traders, but in the years following, a peasant migration from the lowlands penetrated into the valley and occupied the village, introducing in the course of time many changes. The village became divided into an 'Indian' and a 'Spanish' *barrio*; subsistence agriculture was largely replaced by a cash-crop and livestock economy; religion-sanctioned monogamy changed into consensual concubinage and short-term unions. Color, class, and cultural differences became powerful status-defining factors. The struggle of prestige behavior increased individual and collective insecurity, and as higher formal control systems were lacking or unable to cope with the new situation, interpersonal hostilities spread and were openly expressed in malicious gossip and aggressive sorcery. This process has continued ever since. At present, this struggle dominates village life and the main ambition of all inhabitants consists in the desire to be accepted and respected, on an equal footing, by the general Creole population of the lowlands, which considers Aritama a backward Indian village. The tensions created by this quest for self-assertion are felt on all levels and in all dimensions of individual and community life. Paired with population increase and the mismanagement of resources, they have led to conflicts which begin to endanger survival and for which workable solutions have to be found by all. It is this struggle for physical subsistence and cultural recognition and identity, together with its failures and successes, which we have tried to describe in this report.

II

There are numerous reasons why we chose Aritama for the subject of this study. In the first place, years of field work among the neighboring Indian tribes and on the prehistory and early history of the general region had provided us with a time-perspective which led necessarily to an interest in modern peasant communities as a final phase of local cultural development. We had traced the archeological record back in time and, in some of its aspects, had followed it through into the colonial period and the modern surviving Indian cultures. It seemed logical to complete this historical vision with an evaluation of modern peasant life built, partly, on foundations laid in the remote prehistoric past, and partly shaped by a certain physical environment with which men had coped under different cultural conditions.

In the second place, under the influence of current anthropological thought, we had become interested in the problems of culture change and believed that Aritama would be a fruitful field for the study of its dynamics.

In the course of many years of travel among Colombian Indians and Creoles, we had observed that between the native territories and the peasant settlements there was always a cultural no-man's-land. From the advance post of the last Creole hamlet to the first Indian settlement there was a stretch taking hours or maybe days to traverse an area known to members of both cultures but usually uninhabited. Sometimes this border region was a feature of geography—a series of rapids in a

xiii

river, a mountain range, backswamps, or precipitous trails—but more often than not the land which formed this invisible frontier was merely uninhabited territory which had to be crossed to enter the habitat of the other culture. How, then, did culture contact develop? Could it be seen only in the slow change in a few Indian families which lived close to or within the Creole village and away from their own native community? Could it be observed only on the individual level—the level of the Indian who became a hired hand—and outside of its wider institutional context? So far we had observed this transition only in sporadic cases. We had seen individual Indians learn Spanish, adopt European clothing, trade with the Creoles, even settle among them. We had seen them become wage laborers who, out of shame, refused to speak their native tongue, while they still had not mastered Spanish; who accepted the rites of the Church, took part in politics, and eventually became peasants. But what we wanted to know was what contact meant in terms of changing institutions, motivations, values, and community attitudes. We thought of structural disintegration, of institutions breaking down and being replaced by new ones, guided by new goals. All this, we thought, should be observed on the village scene, within the functioning and living community. But such communities were apparently difficult to find because a no-man's-land separated both cultures and only individuals crossed it occasionally, changing *individually* but not affecting in any marked degree their communities. In Aritama, however, the situation was different. There, a compact village was situated in the middle of this no-man's-land and no matter from which side one approached—from the Creole territory of the lowlands or from the Indian territory in the mountains—one had to cross a shadowline that separated the village but, at the same time, linked it to both directions. While the neighboring Indians considered Aritama a Creole village, the neighboring Creoles considered it an Indian village. The hamlet itself showed this dichotomy by being divided into two *barrios*, each of which was associated with one of these cultural traditions.

Today, when we reconsider our original plan, we recognize its fallacies. We saw them soon after we began our study and we had to reformulate our theoretical premises. Instead of thinking in terms of 'disintegration', the 'breaking-down' of institutions and their underlying values, or the 'disorganization' of society, we realized that these concepts were value-loaded. What we saw in Aritama was change, sometimes accelerated and sometimes retarded, but more often simply change, such as will occur necessarily in any community of human beings. Of course, sometimes this change, when demanding an unaccustomed choice of action, affected profoundly an individual or a group or even the entire community, but it was never quite beyond ordinary human experience and there were always means to cope with it. Nothing 'disintegrated', nothing 'broke down'; a continuous shaping and reshaping of the relations between man and environment, man and society, man and the supernatural took place, but simply as a part of life, of anybody's life, anywhere.

It was because these and related thoughts were on our minds that we tried not to make of this study a 'problem-oriented' research within a rigid framework of inquiry but to approach the field as open-mindedly as possible. This, therefore, is not a problem analysis but a descriptive report in which we are concerned with factual details.

III

The fact that we have not used the traditional chapter headings of 'community studies' expresses a certain personal dissatisfaction with the tendency to subdivide and develop what should be a cultural whole. In the arrangement of our material we have tried to express the fact that the institutions, patterns, and mental attitudes which form the social and cultural life of the community have a time dimension. We have carried through a continuity, not given a static picture and we have meant to show full developmental cycles instead of mere cross-sections.

On the other hand, we have covered in this report several aspects that usually are not dealt with in much detail in anthropological monographs. In these chapters we present information on the health and nutritional status of the community, on formal education as taught in the local schools, and on certain sets of patterned attitudes, such as those which refer to work, illness, food, and hallucinatory experiences. Much space has been devoted here to disease and food, but we believe that these two features of existence are of importance if we wish to gain a better understanding of values and motivations. It seems evident that frequent disease and continuous fear of disease influence deeply many behavioral patterns of the individual and contribute thus to the shaping of group attitudes and the orientation of social institutions. Hunger, and the fear of hunger, are likely to do the same. But, above all, the inclusion of these aspects in our discussion was prompted by our belief in the inseparableness of the biological, the psychological, and the social being.

In this regard, therefore, the present report is essentially an exploratory study, and if not a well-rounded one, this is due partly to the fact that the community described is not well rounded itself. The problems of hunger and disease loom large on the village scene, and their obvious cultural significance seems to justify the amount of attention we have given to them.

Some observations on individual chapters are called for here. Several years of teaching and seminar work in the Department of Preventive

Medicine and Public Health of the Medical Faculty, University of Cartagena, have provided us with new perspectives, and the influence of this experience is reflected in the sections dealing with sanitation, hygiene, nutrition, and the specific problems of health encountered in the community. In the section on family structure the writers' debts are to the British anthropologists (Meyer Fortes, Raymond T. Smith, J. Goody, E. R. Leach) and their formulations of developmental cycles in household groups. In the chapter on religion and magic our field experience among the tribal Indians of the mountainous hinterland proved to be invaluable for a better understanding of many manifestations, especially of the ancestor cult. The section on hallucinatory imagery is, perhaps, the only one where an attempt has been made to outline a theory and which goes, therefore, slightly beyond the otherwise purely descriptive scope of the report.

IV

Before settling down in Aritama to undertake this study, we had known the village for many years and we had a fair knowledge of the neighboring Indian tribes and the cultural characteristics of the rural and urban lowland Creoles. Therefore, when we went there to live, we were already known and could count on friends and informants. We spent fourteen months in Aritama, and during this time we occupied a small wattle-and-daub hut in the Indian section, which we bought upon our arrival. During this time we had ample occasion to observe the full agricultural cycle, to take part in all yearly fiestas, and to observe individual and group activities of daily life. We saw birth, marriage, death, wake, and burial. We became godparents and members of the schoolboard. We traveled over the entire valley visiting the small satellite hamlets, the isolated homesteads, and the fields. We were allowed to study the records of the local authorities, the parish, and the schools, and in the neighboring lowland towns we were permitted to go over official and hospital records.

The main bulk of our material, however, was obtained during informal conversations with the villagers themselves. From the very beginning we decided not to limit our personal contacts to a few selected informants but to extend them over a large group of people with whom eventually the validity of individual informations could be checked. Therefore, we did not follow the traditional approach of working through a few main informants but gathered our data from a great number of sources—approximately eighty individuals of both sexes—all of whom contributed in some measure to our study. However, there were a few individuals who, because of their personal friendship, specific knowledge, and high intelligence, must be singled out as especially important sources. By lucky chance, among them there were a specialist in witchcraft, another in village genealogies, and several people with important specialized knowledge in various fields.

One aspect of our contacts with the villagers must be pointed out here specifically, as it provided us with a deeper insight into many of their vital problems. In view of the precarious health situation, we decided to help—whenever this seemed possible and professional service was unavailable—in attending to the sick. A well-stocked medicine chest and the generous contribution by the Lederle Company of Bogotá of several thousand vitamin capsules made it possible to alleviate and prevent suffering in some cases and even to cure minor afflictions. In this manner, a steady stream of people passed through our house and, although many times the cure of their ailments was far beyond our knowledge, the mere fact that we showed concern and tried to help created an atmosphere of understanding during which many barriers, evident at other moments, were removed.

To ask personal questions and to show interest in other people's lives is, according to local standards, one of the worst breaches of proper conduct. All inquiring is emphatically condemned, and it is therefore natural that our behavior conflicted at once with local values. At first we had been well received in the village but as soon as it became known that we were *preguntones*, i.e., inquisitive intruders, people were shocked, and during this period we gathered an amazing amount of misleading information. But after a few months people became accustomed to our ill-mannered insistence upon questioning and watching and developed a certain reserved tolerance toward us. In the final months even this resistance disappeared in most cases and spontaneous and free discussion became possible. What people resented most was our interest in the food situation and when, at the end of the year, we made a detailed survey of the exact individual food intake of a number of households, our relationships became rather tense. A complete household census also caused much unrest.

People in Aritama are not much given to friendly chatting and visiting. They are controlled and taciturn, evasive and monosyllabic. They are always afraid of giving themselves away somehow, of being ridiculed because of the things they say or do, or of being taken advantage of by persons of authority. This reserve, however, is not only displayed toward strangers but characterizes their own interpersonal contacts as well. There is a front of ready answers and expression, of standard affirmations and opinions, and there is always, in the last resort, the blank stare, the deaf ear, or the sullen *no sé*. Such behavior is, of course, to be expected among people who feel very insecure, but in the case of Aritama it leads frequently to a highly patterned type of confabulation. Individual and community life is explained by them in ideal, prestige-carrying terms meant to impress the outsider, but at the same time is so insistently stereotyped and so anxiously phrased that its stark reality becomes all the more evident behind this façade of complacency and conformity. In Aritama the make-believe of overt behavior and the flight from the misery of reality into an utterly imaginary world acquire striking proportions.

V

Finally we wish to point out that proper safeguards have to be observed before judging Aritama as typical of other regions of Colombia. In the details of structure and content Aritama is very similar to a dozen or so communities we know in other parts of the country, but it differs from the average Creole peasant society in that it represents an earlier time-level and an earlier stage in the current of cultural development. We believe that many other villages and towns all over the country have, in the course of their history, passed through a stage quite similar to the one observed at present in Aritama and that, therefore, an insight into Aritama's actual problems is significant to the proper evaluation in historical perspective of the much larger community. If the people of Aritama can teach us to understand this wider scene, their study will have been worth our efforts and the reader's indulgence.

PART I

Fundamental Conditions of
Individual Existence

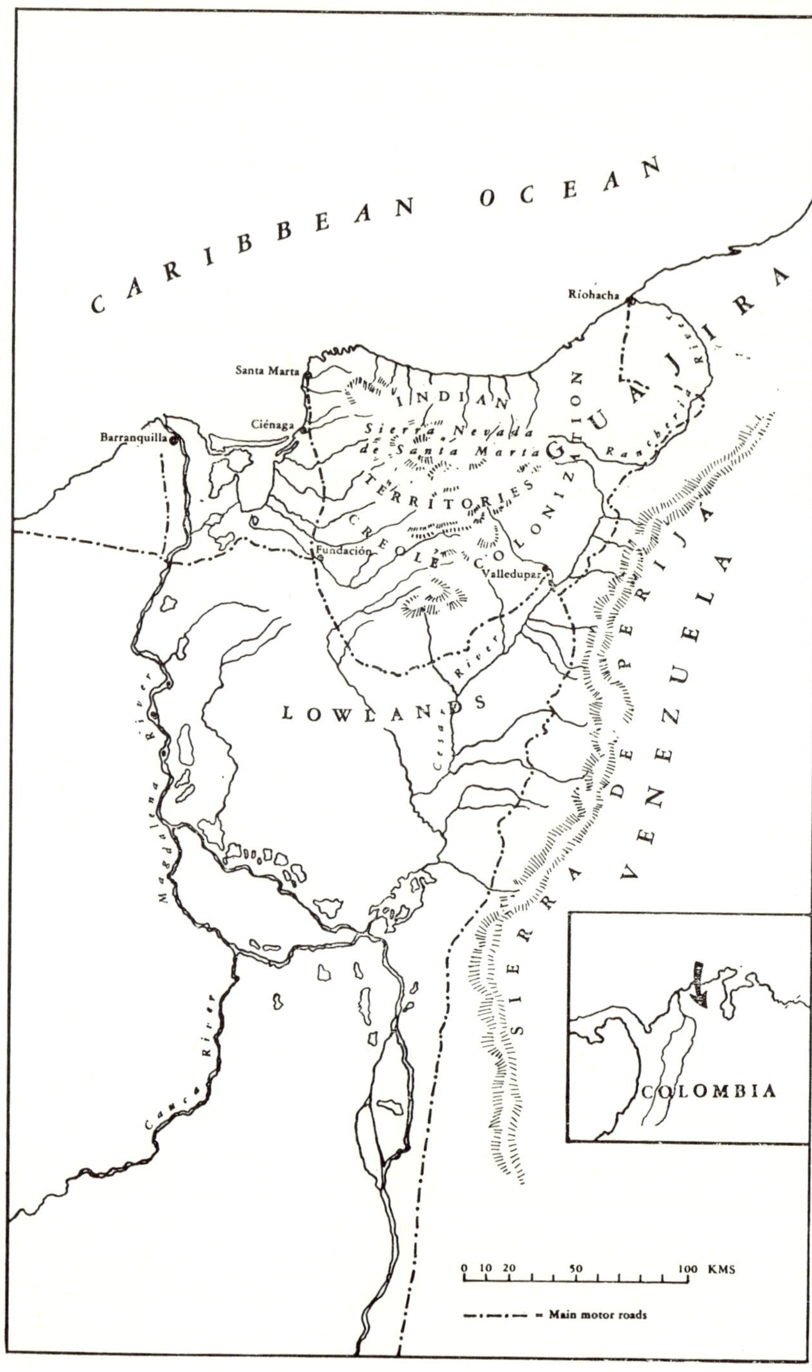

CARIBBEAN OCEAN
Riohacha
Santa Marta
INDIAN
Ciénaga
Sierra Nevada
de Santa Marta
Barranquilla
TERRITORIES
GUAJIRA
Rancheria River
CREOLE COLONIZATION
Fundación
Valledupar
SIERRA DE PERIJA
VENEZUELA
Magdalena River
Cesar River
LOWLANDS
Cauca River
COLOMBIA
0 10 20   50   100 KMS
Main motor roads

I

THE GEOGRAPHICAL AND ETHNO-GRAPHICAL SETTING

THE most outstanding physiographical feature of the Caribbean coast of Colombia is the Sierra Nevada de Santa Marta, an isolated mountain mass which rises abruptly from the tropical lowlands, between the delta of the Magdalena River and the northernmost extension of the Eastern Cordillera. Like a solitary island set between the dry deserts of the Guajira Peninsula and the green plains and swamps of the Lower Magdalena, this mountain massif covers approximately the third part of what is known as the Departmento del Magdalena, one of the twenty-four territorial districts which form the Republic of Colombia. With its highest peaks the Sierra Nevada reaches an altitude of 5,775 meters above sea level, which makes it the highest mountain in Colombia, but in proportion to its elevation its base is small, occupying an area, roughly triangular in shape, which measures not more than about 150 kilometers on each side.

Rising from the alluvial plains between the Magdalena River to the west and south, and the Ranchería and Cesar rivers to the east, this mountain is approximately pyramidal in shape. The steep northern slopes descend toward the Caribbean; the slightly less steep western slopes look toward the delta of the Magdalena River, and the gentle southeastern slopes face the Sierra de Perijá, a branch of the great system of the Colombian Cordilleras. The Sierra Nevada is separated from the Andes by the wide valleys of the Ranchería and Cesar rivers, both of which have their sources on the southeastern slopes, not far apart. But whereas the Ranchería River describes a wide curve toward the north and, at the end of its semicircular course, enters the sea near the town of Ríohacha, the Cesar River flows southward and joins the Magdalena near the town of El Banco. The watershed between the upper parts of the two rivers is hardly more than 200 meters high so that both drainages form a single, wide flood plain between the Sierra Nevada and the Cordillera of the Andes which, in this particular region, bears, from south to north, various names: Sierra de Perijá, Serranía de Valledupar, and Montes de Oca.

To the south of the Sierra Nevada there extend the wide lowland plains, interrupted here and there by low hills, reaching down to the immense, semiaquatic region which borders the Magdalena River, with its innumerable lagoons, backswamps, and oxbow lakes. To the same general region pertains the vicinity of the Ciénaga Grande, a large inland sea separated from the Caribbean by a narrow, sandy strip of land, the Costa de Salamanca, which extends between the mouth of the Magdalena and the little town of Ciénaga, south of the departmental capital, Santa Marta.

From these fertile alluvial plains abruptly rise the first foothills of the Sierra Nevada. Except for a stretch along the northern slopes where the forest reaches down to the coastline, the first elevations are covered with thorn scrubs. Then the 'dry forest', with a fringe of humid forest along the streams, reaches to about 500 to 700 meters altitude. From there on the humid forest extends to the lower limit of the *páramos*, the tundra-like summit plateaus which lie between 4,000 and 4,500 meters and above which the snow begins. This zonification can be observed best on the western slopes but it is not as clear in the southeast, where large extensions are covered with savannas, reaching sometimes to 2,000 meters altitude. These grassy savannas, interrupted here and there by small forests or fringes of dense vegetation, lend very special characteristics to this southeastern part of the Sierra Nevada, distinguishing it from the other slopes where there is denser forest. On the northern side the humid forest covers almost the entire extension from the seashore up to 3,000 meters, but here also occasionally appear small savannas which cover the principal valleys. The tropical zone covers the largest part of the total area, reaching in the Sierra Nevada to about 1,300 meters, an altitude which corresponds approximately to the upper limit of the low cloud layers. The subtropical zone follows, reaching to about 2,500 meters, where the temperate zone begins, which, in turn, is limited by the páramos at 3,500 or 4,000 meters. About 1,000 meters higher begins the snowline.

But climate and vegetation, and with them, the general aspect of the mountain, change not only according to altitude but also in relation to the geographical orientation of the slopes. The entire Caribbean coast of Colombia, between the Guajira Peninsula and the mouth of the Magdalena River, lies under the trade winds, which blow from the northeast during several months of the year, violently and continuously, reaching the Sierra Nevada after having passed over the sandy expanses of the Guajira desert. The southeastern slopes are, therefore, the most exposed to these winds, and so offer the characteristic aspect of grassy savannas and shrub-covered ridges and hills, wnile higher trees and small forests occur only along the streams or in the mountain folds which are protected from the trade winds. The northern slopes and, to a lesser degree, the western slopes, which are less exposed to the winds, are covered to a greater extent with true forest.

In the entire Caribbean lowlands of Colombia only two yearly seasons can be distinguished: the rainy season or 'winter' (*invierno*), which begins late in April and lasts through November or to the beginning of December, and the dry season or 'summer' (*verano*), which lasts from December to April. A short intermediate period of little rainfall in June and July is called 'little summer' or *veranillo*. During the rainy season heavy showers fall almost every day except in the semiarid regions of Santa Marta, Ríohacha, and some of the lower valleys in the southeast where precipitation is less marked and where occasionally weeks may pass without rain. During the dry season, on the other hand, the rains stop completely. The months of heaviest rainfall are May and October. Depending upon the orientation of the three slopes of the Sierra Nevada, precipitation varies considerably. The driest region is the southeastern slope, which is exposed to the trade winds, whereas the northern and western slopes are relatively wet.

The geographical isolation of the Sierra Nevada de Santa Marta imposes a certain biological and cultural isolation upon life, an isolation which can be observed to have existed since prehistoric times. Situated on a crossroad of aboriginal migrations, provided with permanent streams, arable land, abundant fish in both the sea and the inland lagoons, it is only natural that this solitary mountain, visible at great distances, should have caught the attention of migrating tribes and attracted them. Remains of their ancient cultures have been found everywhere, in hundreds of sites which dot the valleys and hills. Potsherds, remains of large architectural complexes built of stone, agricultural terraces, slab-paved roads, petroglyphs, and much other evidence of ancient cultures bear testimony to the Sierra Nevada's having been peopled since remote times by human groups who chose this mountain and its valleys for a temporary or permanent habitat. However, archeology has not yet succeeded in establishing a chronological sequence of these cultures, following them through time and space since their earliest beginnings. Most remains studied so far date from relatively recent periods and show a highly developed culture, the earlier phases of which are still largely unknown.

Although archeologists have hardly begun to decipher this abundant record of the past, many characteristics of a culture of Regional Florescent type are obvious. The ancient Indians lived in large nucleated villages of several hundred houses each, the foundations of which were constructed with carefully dressed or cut stone. A network of roads and bridges, stairs and trails, all built of stone slabs, covered the mountain folds, connecting these centers and allowing their inhabitants to travel easily from one valley to the other, from one slope to the adjoining, from the coast to the highlands. Agricultural terraces provided with irrigation ditches covered large areas. Society was stratified and directed by secular chieftains and priests, the latter beginning to exercise almost absolute authority. Two incipient 'states' had begun to take shape from alliances between numerous villages under the leadership of individuals. Metallurgy, pottery, and the stonecutter's craft had reached a level only rarely equaled by other pre-historic cultures of Colombia. This, then, was the aboriginal culture the Spaniards found when they first discovered the Sierra Nevada.

The first Europeans to see these mountain peaks rising over the plains of the South American mainland were the soldiers and sailors of Rodrigo de Bastidas, in 1501. Bastidas explored the coast between the Guajira Peninsula and Panama, visited several of the beaches at the foot of the northern slopes of the Sierra Nevada, discovered the Magdalena River, and established the first contacts with the natives. After him came other explorers and conquerors. Alonso de Hojeda, Rodrigo Hernández de Colmenares, Martín Fernández de Enciso, the expedition of Pedrarias Dávila—all followed this coast and took back the first news of the Sierra Nevada and its inhabitants. But they hardly ever left the safety of their ships, preferring to trade with the Indians for gold and pearls without trying to explore their hostile land.

But in 1521 the Spanish Crown decided to take possession of and explore this coast and Rodrigo de Bastidas, who by then had become a resident of Santo Domingo, was named by the Council of the Indies governor of the unknown lands lying between the Guajira and the mouth of the Magdalena. After long preparations, Bastidas landed in the Bay of Santa Marta in 1525, where he took formal possession of the land and founded what proved to be the first Spanish settlement, calling it Santa Marta. From here Spanish troops entered the valleys, penetrated to the highlands, explored the coast. The loot of gold and pearls, and the slave trade, which produced huge profits in the Antilles, were powerful incentives, but so was the zeal to convert the Indians to the Christian faith. The Spaniards quickly realized that a region which could sustain thousands of inhabitants in large villages, with thousands of men who were masons, agriculturalists, and navigators, was an excellent place for large-scale colonization. So the conquest of the fierce Tairona Indians, creators of this highly developed culture, was begun.

During their first encounters the Indians had shown little resistance and had received the Spaniards well. But soon this situation changed. The establishment of the first *encomiendas*, the abuses committed by their administrators and the soldiers, and the pressure brought to bear by missionaries who tried to suppress the aboriginal religion, began to cause serious difficulties. The Indians organized their resistance and practically the entire sixteenth century, from 1525 to 1599, was passed in bloody battle for possession of the lands to the east and south of Santa Marta.

In 1599 the governor, Don Juan Guiral Velón, led the Spanish forces in a war of extermination. Condemning all native chieftains to death at the stake or the gallows, the governor ordered their houses and fields burned, and their villages sacked by his troops. At this price peace was finally obtained, but the land had been devastated and the human element that had made it productive had been eliminated or dispersed. By the middle of the sixteenth century, many of the coastal villages had already been abandoned, their inhabitants having sought refuge in less accessible regions. The paved roads that in former times had been maintained by the communal labor of the villages they connected had become covered by the jungle. The villages themselves had fallen into ruins, because their inhabitants had fled, or had fallen victims to new epidemic diseases or to the blades of Spanish troops. The large maize fields which had been burned had overgrown with forest. When at last, at the beginning of the seventeenth century, Velón laid waste the Sierra Nevada, the Spaniards found themselves masters of jungle and ruins— the flourishing villages, with their fields, their roads, their numerous and active people, having disappeared.

And so the Sierra Nevada was abandoned again. Not a single Spanish village established in the mountains by force during the sixteenth century survived this war. The focus of colonization was transferred instead to the banks of the Magdalena River, to the littoral, and to the interior of the country. Even the town of Santa Marta almost disappeared. Burned to the ground by Indians and fugitive Negro slaves, sacked by English, French, and Dutch pirates, its inhabitants decimated by epidemics and isolated from other centers of Spanish colonization, the town barely survived the centuries of conquest and colonization and, in spite of its excellent harbor, lost its former importance. Not until the beginning of the twentieth century, with the advent of large-scale plantation and exportation of bananas, did there begin a new period of growth and development for Santa Marta. Even now for the most part Santa Marta continues its somnolent and provincial ways, overshadowed by the great commercial town of Barranquilla and the walls and fortresses of Cartagena of the Indies.

While the sixteenth century, which had seen the conquest of the Sierra Nevada with Spanish troops penetrating its most hidden valleys, is well documented, the seventeenth century remains almost a blank in the history of this region. Perhaps because of the wars that Spain was waging against her continental enemies or because of the Inquisition or for some other historical reason, there exist very few data on colonizing or missionary activity in this part of Colombia. It is known that there still existed a few *encomiendas* with a small number of Indians; that there were a few Indian parishes or villages whose inhabitants paid tribute to the Crown, but little is known of the processes and impacts of contact between the native culture and the Spanish overlords from 1600 to 1700.

For the eighteenth century, however, there is more concrete information. The archives and the Spanish chronicles of this period give many details on missionary activity among the surviving Indians of the Sierra Nevada and occasionally contain valuable data on colonization and aboriginal culture. From these sources it appears that during the eighteenth century the missionaries, mainly friars of the Franciscan community, again penetrated the valleys, establishing missions in several villages, building chapels, and baptizing the natives. By the end of the century, however, this development ceased. Many missionaries left. The great upheaval of the War of Independence, during the first decades of the nineteenth century, paralyzed the incipient colonization temporarily, while it contributed to its later revival by bringing to the region political refugees who hid in the mountain fastnesses. It appears that in those years some Negroes and Spaniards established themselves in isolated Indian villages, fleeing from the turmoil and danger of war and persecution.

During the sixteenth century the Spaniards had founded a number of towns at the foot of the Sierra Nevada, all of them situated in the tropical lowlands lying at the base of the mountain. After Santa Marta, founded in 1525, there had followed San Juan de Ciénaga, Ríohacha in 1545, Valledupar in 1550, Valencia de Jesús soon after, and Sevilla in 1592. On the old Spanish road between Ríohacha and Valledupar, today lost in underbrush and savannas, there still stand the ruins of the church of Badillo, a splendid example of colonial architecture. During the eighteenth century some new towns were founded, but none was established in the Sierra Nevada itself, except the small mission center now called San Sebastián de Rábago. This Indian village had been discovered in 1583 by the Spanish Captain Tapias and had been called San Sebastián de Taironaca by adding the name of the saint to its native name. But not until 1750 was a mission founded there. It flourished for some time but was abandoned during most of the nineteenth century, to be revived during the first decades of the present one.

At the beginning of the Spanish conquest, the region most densely populated by aborigines was the northern slope of the Sierra Nevada, but after the great defeat and dispersal of the natives by Juan Guiral Velón about 1600, not one of the flourishing villages survived, and this part of the mountains was practically uninhabited except for some small groups of Indians who had found refuge at the headwaters of some of the rivers. Many Indian villages on the western slopes had a similar fate, and on the southeastern slopes, where human occupation always had been rather sporadic, no population center of any importance is mentioned in the years following the conquest.

The northwestern spurs and foothills, near Santa Marta, had been colonized in the sixteenth century, as most of the agricultural products the town consumed were (and still are) grown there. However, this colonization established only a few small hamlets, which even today show little development. From this region the Indians had disappeared during the first years of Spanish penetration. The northern slopes were never colonized, but at the end of the nineteenth century a small group of Negroes from the coastal village of Dibulla founded the hamlet of San Antonio (now Pueblo Viejo) on the Ancho River. During the same period, the civil wars that devastated large areas of the lowlands brought about the migration of a heterogeneous element of Mestizos, Negroes, and a few foreigners toward the southeastern slopes, where they penetrated to the Indian villages of Marocaso, El Rosario, and Atánquez, all of them occupied by small groups of Indians who had had contact with the missionaries of the eighteenth century.

At present the state of Creole colonization of the Sierra Nevada is as follows: On the slopes and foothills of the northwest, near Santa Marta, the settlers reach an altitude of about 1,500 meters; on the western slopes they have penetrated to some of the valleys, especially in the general region of Ríofrío where they reach about the same altitude, but only 700 meters farther south; in the southeast where the slopes are considerably less steep and where, therefore, penetration roads are better, some small Creole settlements are scattered over the affluents of the Cesar and Ranchería rivers at about 700 or 800 meters altitude, while farther south a sporadic colonization is penetrating toward San Sebastián de Rábago and has reached 1,100 meters in Pueblo Bello.

But wherever Creole colonization has entered, it has not followed any plan. Individual families, or even lone settlers, in search of small subsistence plots or small cash crops of coffee or sugar cane, have penetrated many valleys, but rarely have they formed nucleated settlements. There is practically no motor or wheeled transportation, and only mule trails exist; there are no bridges and only miserable huts by the wayside where a traveler may spend the night.

So the center of the Sierra Nevada de Santa Marta has remained essentially Indian territory, occupied by the remnants of the groups the Spaniards found at the beginning of their conquest. At present the total Indian population reaches about 6,000 individuals, distributed among three tribes, the Ica, Cogui, and Sancá.

The Ica occupy mainly the southeastern slopes and the headwaters of the rivers which flow westward. Their principal center is San Sebastián de Rábago on the upper Fundación River, where, on the headwaters, in the region of El Mamón, there live numerous groups of these Indians. Toward the east they extend over the valleys of the Templado and Donachuí rivers, and toward the south they live in the region of La Cueva, on the headwaters of the Ariguaní River, a short distance from Pueblo Bello. Another group lives on the headwaters of the Aracataca River in the village of Seráncua, founded in recent times by fugitives from the mission of San Sebastián, and sporadic groups are found in the lower reaches of the Sevilla River. Their total number is about 3,000 or 3,500.

The second tribe, the Cogui, occupies the northern slopes, particularly the villages of Hucuméishi, Uluéishi, Santa Rosa, San Miguel, Taquína, Macotáma, and San Francisco. A migration that took place late in the nineteenth century founded San Andrés on the headwaters of the Río Frío, as well as Cherrúa and Mamaróngo on the Sevilla and Tucurinca rivers, respectively. Another migration of the same period crossed the páramos and founded the villages of San José and Chendúcua on the upper Guatapurí River, penetrating toward the lower Donachuí River. The total number of Cogui Indians is about 2,000. The Sancá occupy several valleys of the drainage of the Badillo and Cesar rivers, on the lower southeastern slope; they do not live in nucleated settlements but rather in scattered houses. There are only about 500 individuals left of this tribe.

Although these tribes, which in anthropological literature are generally (and quite erroneously) referred to as *Aruacos*, had established contact with Hispanic culture during the early sixteenth century, they are still far from becoming assimilated by the Creole peasant culture which surrounds them. The degree of influence varies from tribe to tribe and depends in part upon the accessibility of their habitat. For this reason the Sancá are at present the most Creole-influenced, their territory lying in the hot lowlands and being easily accessible. The Ica follow them, but there are still large segments of the tribe that reject contact. Some have fled from the mission center of San Sebastián, but others have begun to adopt part of the exterior trappings of rural Creole culture. The Cogui are the least influenced tribe. With the possible exception of one or two deviants, the tribe has not become absorbed by the rural culture of Hispanic tradition. Quite to the contrary, their highly integrated culture has maintained to a large degree its own heritage.

Linguistically, the tribes of the Sierra Nevada belong to the Chibcha stock, within which they form the so-called Chibcha-Aruac group. Culturally, they are classed within the general framework of sub-Andean culture, although Circumcaribbean and Tropical Forest traits are not infrequent.

The Geographical and Ethnographical Setting

ARITAMA: PREHISTORIC AND HISTORIC BACKGROUND

In one of the mountain folds, in a narrow and hidden valley formed by a small affluent of one of the larger rivers, lies the village of Aritama, or San Rafael de Aritama, as it is sometimes called in written records. Far from the roads that connect the large towns and villages of the lowlands, this small Mestizo community is rather typical of those isolated centers of colonization and missionary activity founded during colonial times in Indian territory and left afterward to their own devices.

Archeological remains are frequent in the valley of Aritama and from them it can be inferred that in times past the ancient inhabitants formed part of the complex known by the name 'Tairona'. As a matter of fact, architectural features such as stone foundations, terraces, and stairways can be seen here and there, and the ceramic and lithic artifacts unearthed near them leave no doubt that they represent an extension of this ancient and highly developed aboriginal culture. However, sporadic remains of different cultures, though contemporary with the Tairona, suggest that this was a contact area, a border region between the high culture of the Sierra Nevada and the less developed groups of the lowlands. It is evident that the bearers of this lowland culture also lived in permanent settlements, cultivated maize, and constructed small agricultural terraces, but otherwise they seem to have remained on a much lower level of cultural development than their neighbors of the mountain folds.

Although we know yet too little about prehistoric time-depth in the Sierra Nevada, about migrations, contacts, and successive phases of local development, we know that at the time of the rise of the Tairona culture, a widespread lowland culture was disappearing. The latter had occupied large extensions of the plains at the base of the mountains and had developed out of successive phases which date back considerably in time, but at some period in their history the development stopped without continuing itself in succeeding phases. Why this should have happened is still largely a matter of speculation. Archeological research in this area suggests that, at the time when this lowland culture was still thriving, physical conditions were very different from those encountered today in the same region. There is evidence that the rivers descending from the Sierra Nevada carried more water, that there were swamps and lagoons on their lower courses, that vegetation and animal life were far more abundant and the soil more fertile and humid. It is difficult to say what caused the progressive desiccation of the drainages of these rivers, but it seems probable that a major factor was the advent of an agrarian population in the mountains, a people who cleared and burned the forests on the headwaters and upper reaches of the rivers, causing them to dry up and opening the way to erosion. It seems quite possible that

11

the sterile savannas which cover many of the mountain folds were produced by such biological pressure in prehistoric times.

The valley of Aritama represents then a contact region between two archeological areas, the traditions of which were very different. In its territory there met two ways of life, two forms of adaptation to the physical environment. On the other hand, between these prehistoric and protohistoric cultures and the developments of historical times, there is a certain continuity that projects from the past into the present. In the first place, this continuity is established by the situation of the valley itself, which forms a gateway, however small, to the mountains and to the plains, participating in geographical, ecological, and cultural environments that differ greatly one from another. In the mountains there developed cultures of Andean type, advanced levels, characterized by a stratified society, a theocratic system, and an intensely agricultural foundation, while in the neighboring lowlands there lived the horticulturalists of the Tropical Forest, scattered groups with a simple social structure and a little-developed ceremonial life. But while the former occupied a privileged position of defense and refuge, the latter occupied a natural migration route, always exposed to contacts and aggressions from the coast, the banks of the Magdalena River, or the northern extensions of the Andes. The valley of Aritama found itself between these two regions and it must be supposed that this fact would have contributed to a certain degree in shaping its local cultural configuration.

On the other hand, the continuity is also expressed in the survival of many Indian tribes. The modern Indians of the Sierra Nevada are essentially the heirs of the ancient Tairona culture, and although most tribes of the neighboring lowlands have disappeared, the Indian element—as a biological and also cultural factor—is still present to a high degree. Thousands of Guajiro Indians live not too far off; the modern Yuko or Motilones of the Sierra de Perijá are, in part, the remnants of tribes that occupied the vicinity of the modern lowland towns as late as the nineteenth century. The Chimila, who still survive in the mountains and forests of the Ariguaní River, until recent times occupied the southern foothills of the Sierra Nevada.

It is true that all these tribes have retreated and live now in less accessible regions, at considerable distances, but this happened in relatively recent years. Near Aritama iron arrowheads of the Yuko have been found in a cave; the old people still remember marauding bands of Chimila Indians entering the valley. In reality, the lowland towns at the foot of the massif still form essentially an enclave in tribal territories, being surrounded on almost all sides by remnants of once-powerful tribes. And it is also evident that the Indian population did not retreat as a whole, but that a large part of it was absorbed by intermixture into the Creole peasantry.

In prehistoric times, when the lowlands were occupied by Tropical Forest tribes, the life of the Indians of Aritama was oriented toward the Sierra Nevada, toward the high culture of the Tairona. But since, in historic times, the lowland culture has changed into another form of 'high culture', now of Hispanic tradition, the village—by now already a Mestizo community—has come to change, too. Traditionally, there were close ties with the Indians of the center of the Sierra Nevada, but with the advance of industrialization, with population increase, new communications, and racial intermixture, the cultural orientation is now directed toward the lowlands, although there still continue certain local trends and traits that link the villagers to the prehistoric foundations of their Indian ancestors and to the Spanish colonial culture with which they had come in contact four centuries ago.

Although it seems very probable that the valley of Aritama was explored by the Spaniards during the sixteenth century, the village and its inhabitants are not mentioned by the chroniclers who tell of the events of that period. The name Aritama, however, is not an unknown one in the historical sources or aboriginal traditions of the Sierra Nevada. There was a village of that name near Santa Marta, and a legendary Indian shaman was also known by this name, but the village we are concerned with here seems to have had but little importance during the years of the Spanish conquest. The first reference to it is found in the chronicles of 1690, in the report of a Franciscan friar who by order of the bishop of Santa Marta visited the 'village of the Aritamas', the inhabitants of which had been accused of idolatry. The friar, accompanied by a Spanish captain and several soldiers, burned and destroyed ten large ceremonial houses and the wooden idols they contained, and baptized a large number of Indians. From his account it appears that the inhabitants even then spoke a few words of Spanish and had certain notions of Christianity. In any case, there was no opposition and the Spaniards left after having accomplished their mission. The next time we find Aritama mentioned is in 1787. In those years the increasing missionary activity made it desirable to gather the widely scattered Indians into permanent villages, and Aritama is mentioned as a small center of raw-sugar production, inhabited by Indians who of their own accord had settled in a compact hamlet. In a Spanish census of 1803, of all tributary Indians of the Sierra Nevada, the village appears for the first time with the name of San Rafael de Aritama.

According to these sources it seems that Aritama became a parish in the second half of the eighteenth century, much later than most neighboring villages, the names of which are found in earlier parish lists. The many local traditions and legends that have been preserved by the inhabitants seem to corroborate this. According to these traditions there existed from time immemorial only a small hamlet on the spot now occupied by the village. This hamlet was greatly augmented in the late eighteenth century when, by orders of the Spanish authorities, all Indians living in the surroundings had to establish themselves in a permanent settlement. The 'governor' or chieftain of the village then was an old Indian shaman who exercised a reign of terror over his subjects, destroying their fields with his magic and causing a period of famine. At last, according to the legend, the Indians revolted and killed him, freeing themselves of this tyrant. There remained five Indian shamans in the village and under their leadership the village flourished for several years, without maintaining any contact with the Spanish settlements in the lowlands. Sometime later, Spanish troops entered the village, bringing with them bloodhounds to hunt down all Indians who had refused to be baptized by the traveling friars who occasionally had been to the village. This was the 'Time of the Moors' (*el tiempo de la morisca*) when the *moros*, as the unbaptized Indians were called, were fleeing in the mountains. Most fugitives were brought back to the village, where a parish priest now took residence, and began the construction of a church. Tradition tells that the Spaniards brought Negro slaves from the lowlands, promising them their freedom on the day they finished the building. But others say that a rich Spanish nobleman, devoted to S. Rafael, had made the solemn vow to build this church in gratitude for the saint's blessings, bringing Spanish and Indian laborers to the village for this purpose. The church was finished late in the eighteenth century, of stonemasonry, with a wide nave and a low roof, but for some reason or other, it was destroyed soon afterward, perhaps by a fire or an earthquake. One of our informants, an octogenarian, claims to have known in his childhood an old woman, daughter of a famous local shaman, who told him the following story: When she was a child she once came to the village and saw a group of strange black-skinned people tearing down the old church and, at the same time, making adobe bricks and building it anew. The head mason was a Negro and the girl gave him a few plantains when she passed by. Shortly afterward, when the walls had reached about two meters in height, they fell down. This happened five times, every time the building had reached a certain stage of its construction. The head mason told the girl of this strange matter, and she in turn told her father, the shaman. After long divinations the Indian let it be known that while digging the foundations of the church, the bones of an ancient shaman had been disturbed, and that for this reason the shaman's spirit tore down the walls of the church, because no expiatory offerings had been made there. After consulting with the Indian priest, the mason made an offering and shortly afterward the building was completed.

Many local traditions are connected with the events of that period in the village's history. It was the custom then to bury the dead inside the church, a fact which greatly disturbed the local Indian shamans who always insisted on determining the place of their burial by divination. One of the shamans of that time, knowing that the Catholic Church refused to bury suicides on sacred ground, asked his relatives to tie a rope around his neck at his death, to pretend that he had hanged himself. Another shaman, when taken to be baptized, fled and committed suicide, and still another died the instant the missionary put salt to his lips in the baptismal rite. There are many such tales in the village, and with a pride tinged with anxiety people tell of the stubborn resistance with which the Indian shamans and many of their followers refused to accept Christianity. In many cases their names are still known and they are said to be the ancestors of families that still live in the village.

If we have mentioned here these apparently insignificant local traditions, we have done so, not because they have any special historical importance, but because they convey a general atmosphere of thought, a dimension of people's interest, which it is necessary to understand. Other, more Creole-oriented villages, may be proud of their participation in national Colombian history, but Aritama rather took pride in its non-participation. Even today the people still think and feel on an earlier level, the level of Indian persecution and missionary work, of first contacts with 'foreign' troops, and sudden flight into the mountains. It is the marginal and magical attitude that is important here, the belief in the 'just cause' of the Indians, and in their 'secret power' over their persecutors. Emotionally these traditions are Indian and not Spanish.

There is but little information about the life of the village during the first half of the nineteenth century. It does not seem that the people of Aritama took any active part in the War of Independence, and the few traditions concerning it indicate rather that they fled toward the mountains, living for some time in the neighboring Indian villages until the turmoil had pased. Independence from Spanish rule is not a living memory in the village.

But the civil wars, which during most of the nineteenth century devastated the country, are remembered in Aritama. As was mentioned earlier, fleeing soldiers and political outcasts came to the Sierra Nevada in search of refuge, sometimes living with the Indians, at other times hiding alone in the forest. Many episodes of these times are still told, but often they are confused with the War of Independence, with political strife in the twentieth century, and even with vague memories of violence and fear during Spanish colonial days. However, during one of the civil wars the people of Aritama took part in several campaigns, but this decision was due to very special circumstances. The commanding general of the Conservative party's army was said to be imbued with great magical powers which made him invulnerable to the enemies bullets. His fame spread to Aritama and, although the villagers had promised to be loyal to the opposing Liberal party, their admiration of the general's magic made them join the Conservative troops. But as soon as the general was killed by the countermagic of the enemy, the villagers deserted and returned to their mountains.

In the census of 1803, only four Spaniards are mentioned as living in the village, married to Indian women, while all other inhabitants are considered as tributary Indians, living under the administration of a Spanish *corregidor* and two Indian functionaries, one 'captain' and another 'alcalde'. It seems that until the middle of the last century Aritama was essentially an Indian village, isolated to a large degree from the lowland towns and hardly touched by the sociopolitical developments that took place during the first half-century of republican life in the rest of the Colombian nation. Of course, culturally the people of Aritama were influenced by Spanish colonial patterns; nominally they had adopted Christianity, many new food plants and their methods of preparation, house types, dress, metal tools, domestic animals, and many Mediterranean patterns connected with the interpretation and cure of disease, with childbirth, or with the belief in ghosts and witches. But other aspects continued Indian tradition. Religious concepts were mainly Indian, incorporating magical procedures; patterns of co-operative labor, child-training, some aspects of curing, recreation, or food preparation were largely indigenous; and many elements of material culture were hardly distinguishable from those used by the neighboring groups which still lived in a tribal system. Most people still spoke the native language, but many were bilingual; trade was based upon barter, not upon any monetary standard. Nobody pretended not to be Indian.

During the second half of the nineteenth century this situation changed entirely. In 1857 the General Government of the United States of Colombia, as it was then called, created the State of Magdalena (formerly called Province of Santa Marta), dividing it into five departments: Santa Marta, Padilla, El Banco, Tenerife, and Valledupar. In 1871 the State of Magdalena ceded to the central government two territorial sections to be administered apart: the Territorio de Nevada y Motilones and the Territorio de la Guajira. This concession was made for a term of twenty years, and its immediate object was to facilitate the colonization of these two Indian territories, which until then had not been exploited economically. The village of Atánquez, situated on the southeastern slopes, became the capital of the territorial division that included the Sierra Nevada and the Sierra de Perijá, and Aritama thus became one of the various villages exposed to colonization. At first, several government officials resided in the principal villages and as some of the settlements, because of their isolation, were also used as places of exile for political convicts, there were government soldiers and a police force. In Aritama, however, none of the newcomers stayed for more than a few months and there was hardly any contact between them and the villagers. The administrative personnel soon went to live in the lowland towns, all plans of colonization were shortly abandoned, the territorial subdivisions were again reincorporated into the state, and life continued as before. One important step, however, had been taken which had a far-reaching effect in the future: The prefect of the territory had introduced small coffee plantations in the Sierra Nevada, choosing valleys and villages where the climate was suitable, among others the valley of Aritama.

A high Church official who in these years visited the valley wrote that many Indians were already speaking Spanish, and he remarks caustically that the younger generation was ashamed to speak the old Indian language, 'which seems to them not in agreement with their Spanish dress'.

It was in these years, beginning approximately in 1860, that a migratory movement set in among the rural Creole peasants of the lowlands. The insecurity created by the civil wars, a plague of locusts that devastated the fields, and the threat of famine and epidemics induced many of the poorer peasants to abandon their native villages and to seek new land in the valleys of the Sierra Nevada. Some had sold their few belongings in the lowlands, but others were without any means. However, life in the isolated villages was inexpensive and the land promised profit if properly used. A considerable number of these immigrants arrived in Aritama between the years 1860 and 1880. They bought houses and built new ones, acquired land or cleared new fields, and settled down permanently in the village, where, at first, they were received with indifference.

With the liquidation of the Territorio de Nevada, Aritama had become a municipal district of the nearest lowland town, and in 1908 it became a *Corregimiento* within the municipality of one of the old Spanish towns founded in the sixteenth century. As an administrative unit, the Corregimiento is organized thus: The mayor of the lowland town designates the *Corregidor*, also called *Inspector de Policía* and his subalterns: secretary (*Secretario*), treasure (*Tesorero*), tax collector (*recaudador de rentas*), and caretaker of the pound (*celador del coso*). The Corregidor in turn appoints the deputies (*comisarios*) of the satellite villages, both Indian and Mestizo who, in the former, are assisted by a 'first corporal' (*cabo major*), two 'corporals' (*cabos*), and a substituting deputy (*suplente*). The Corregidor has the functions of judge and chief of police, and occasionally the municipality will send one or two policemen to live in the village for a few weeks or months.

17

THE VALLEY, THE VILLAGE, AND THE PEOPLE

The valley of Aritama covers only a small part of the Corregimiento. It rises, gently at first, more steeply later, from the hot plains toward the cool mountains, and at its far end lies the village, hidden from view until one approaches the first houses. Although the valley can be seen from the lowlands, at a distance it is impossible to tell that it is inhabited, because neither houses nor fields can be made out clearly in the monotonous shades of yellow and green of mountain grass and rocks and fringes of trees which border the creeks. The village occupies a series of small elevations and depressions formed among various minor affluents which descend from the upper part of the valley, some houses standing on the top or ridge of an elevation while others occupy the slopes and the little valleys. Behind the village rise the huge buttresses of the Sierra Nevada. In the morning the brilliant white peaks and snowfields seem to float in the air, while below them the bizarre cone- or tower-shaped mountains, topped with barren rock, rise from the dark-green forest. To both sides of the valley there ascend the steep grass-covered slopes so characteristic of the landscape. Innumerable small creeks, most of them carrying water only during the months of the rainy season, descend from their folds, interrupting the yellow monotony of the savannas with shades of green. In the other direction the valley opens toward the lowlands. There extends the wide plain, covered by a purple haze, fading away in the distance in the vibrating air of tropical heat and dust.

But most characteristic of the valley are the steep folds covered with grass and dark rocks—rocks blackened by centuries of field-burning fires. There is very little underbrush along the creeks that cross these slopes and only rarely a few large trees grow on their ridges, except maybe on the sides protected against the winds or in depressions where the soil is more humid. All these small valleys, rivers, creeks, and hills form a complex topography. There are depressions and caves, falls and swamps, small stretches of flat valley bottoms with patches of dense vegetation, eroded and sterile barrancos. Tortuous trails cross this landscape in all directions, visible for many kilometers as they wind up the grassy slopes, leading to neighboring valleys and villages, to the pastures, fields, sugar-cane or coffee plantations. And, of course, every spot has its name and every name its history, its tradition, its significance.

About ten small satellite hamlets called *retiros* (retreats), composed of a few houses and at an hour's walking distance or more from the main village (*la cabecera*) are scattered all over the valley, hidden away on creeks or behind hills, almost invisible from the main trail.

The climate of the valley varies with its elevations. The entire valley bottom, including Aritama, lies within the tropical zone, but the surrounding slopes have a subtropical climate, and halfway up the mountain there begins the temperate zone, followed by the cool or cold highlands. No official data are available on temperature or rainfall. The cycle of dry and rainy seasons that prevails in the entire northern section of the country is the same in Aritama except that the rains often begin late in May and December is sometimes a cloudy and humid month. But even in the rainy season precipitation is low. During the three months of April, May, and June we counted only twenty-six days of rainfall, but even then it never rained for more than one hour and the rapid showers were soon absorbed by the dry soil. On the upper reaches of the valley, behind the village, precipitation is considerably greater. There the dry season is short, covering hardly more than the months of January, February, and perhaps the first weeks of March. In Aritama, however, the dry season begins in November, and, although an occasional shower may still fall, the air has by then the transparency typical of summer in the Sierra Nevada, and the first cool breeze is coming up from the lowlands. The months of the dry season are cooler than those of the rainy season because of these winds. While during most of the year there is hardly a breeze to be felt, from December to March the trade winds enter the valley and then the nights are cool and even at noontime there is often a fresh breeze.

The inhabitants of the village insist that the climate, especially in the quantity of rain, has changed very much in the course of the last half-century, it being said that in former times it rained much more than at present. This could be true if one takes into account the progressive desiccation of the region caused by deforestation and periodic burnings, which have eliminated the denser vegetation that covered the slopes before the introduction of such cash crops as coffee and sugar cane. The population was much smaller then and put less pressure upon the land. But today total yearly rainfall evidently seems to be insufficient for the development of agriculture and cash crops. The torrential downpours of the rainy season, concentrated in only a few months of the year, do almost more harm than good, since the rush of water has no time to penetrate the soil, but instead erodes and damages the fields.

The vegetation of the valley is varied and zoned according to altitude. In the lower part of the valley, near the plains, there exists a semiarid zone, sterile and rocky, covered only by patches of brazil wood (*Hematoxylon Brasiletto* Karst.), *trupillo* (*Neltuma juliflora*) and some varieties of cacti. But slightly higher up this characteristic plant cover disappears and is replaced by underbrush and scattered large trees such as the *caracoli* (*Anarcadium excelsum*), the *higuerón* (*Ficus* sp.), and the *ceiba* (*Ceiba pentandra*), especially along the creeks and the river. On the low hill slopes there grow many *peralejo* trees (*Curatella americana*), which, with their gnarled trunks, lend a very typical aspect to the land-scape.

Between 500 and 2,000 meters altitude the mountain folds are covered by grass, and only on the creeks is there some underbrush and small trees. From 1,500 meters up there are frequent large outcrops of rock, often of bizarre contours, while from 2,000 meters on, the humid forest takes over. In some places, where it is not exposed to the trade winds, this forest begins at about 1,500 meters. Locally these different regions are called *loma* ('ridge', 'hill') and *monte* ('forest'), respectively, while the term *sierra* is used only with reference to the high mountains toward the center of the Sierra Nevada.

The lack of dense plant cover and, of course, the fact that the valley has been inhabited since prehistoric times, explain why the region is very poor in animal life. Rarely does one hear of a jaguar, mountain lion, tapir, or deer, and even wild boars are found only very seldom in the rain forest and at great distances from the valley itself. Small rodents such as the paca (*Coelogynis paca*) or the squirrel are sometimes hunted in the surroundings but are also rare, as are also marsupials (*Didelphis marsupialis*) and armadillos. Rats and mice, however, are abundant, although they never represent a real problem to the fields. There are a few snakes, such as the boa, rattlesnake, and several kinds of coral snakes, and many lizards, especially in the lower part of the valley where there are also iguanas and several species of land turtles. Birdlife is represented mainly by mawcaws and small parrots, hummingbirds, weaverbirds, buzzards, and owls. Fish are few and small, even in the main river. Aritama lies above the limit of the anopheles mosquito but mosquitoes of the *Culicidae* family, the yellow fever-carrying Aëdes, and the diminutive *jején* (*Simulidae*) are frequent, although they are not so bothersome here as in many other parts of the Sierra Nevada. Ticks, above all a very small kind that is found on the grassy slopes, are abundant. Carrying ants are very numerous and a major pest, causing considerable damage to fields, gardens, and fruit trees. Termites, large spiders, scorpions, as well as chicken fleas, common houseflies, and lice infest practically all houses, but there are no fleas, *niguas* (*Pulex penetrans*), or *nuches* (*Dermatobia hominis*).

It is evident then that the valley of Aritama forms by no means a homogeneous geographical or ecological area, but is extremely varied in its environmental aspects. This diversity is certainly not a local phenomenon but is characteristic of the entire Corregimiento, or indeed of the whole municipality.

The village itself is rather picturesque. Spread out over a series of ridges and depressions, crossed by several small creeks and eroded ravines, it occupies a triangle formed by the main river and one of its principal affluents, hidden deep between the grass-covered hill slopes which descend from the mountain. To this irregular terrain the houses are adapted as well as possible, some of them scattered over the slopes, some huddled together on ridges or in depressions, some forming a street front, others widely spaced and isolated. Near the main entrance to the village there is the plaza, a roughly triangular and relatively flat expanse, covered with grass and fringed with large trees. In one corner there is the church and next to it the priest's house shouldered by some other houses. In another corner there is the girls' school, the house occupied by the police inspector and the government post office, the village jail, and then a few houses belonging to the wealthier families. Near the third corner there are several stores and a few empty lots.

Beyond the plaza there are no streets, but only narrow, irregular thoroughfares and trails zigzagging between house fronts and back-yards, kitchens and fences, ravines and groups of trees. Large granite boulders, some of them several meters high, are scattered about, and around them or between them wind the trails. Here and there stand huge mango trees or coconut palms, while the houses and their small out-buildings climb over the adjoining slopes, perch high on barren ridges, or hide at the bottom of old barrancos. There are no straight lines in the village; everything is inclined, oblique, curved, as if ready to fall. The houses seem to lean toward each other, to slide down the slopes, to sink into the ground. Their walls are not vertical, nor are their door-steps, window sills, or ridgepoles horizontal. There is no uniformity in height or inclination, every house occupying a different level. One house might look down into the patio of its neighbor; others stand out like small towers or lookouts; and of still others hardly more than the roof can be seen, the whole structure being built in a deeply eroded pit.

Two houses on the plaza have a small fenced-in garden in front, but elsewhere shrubs and flowers are seen only in the backyards. However, there are many trees between the houses and near the creeks, among them the *jamanare* (*Cassia grandis*) with its red flowers, mango, hog plum, and calabash trees, and many plantains. On fences and all around the village the *matarratón* tree (*Gliricidia sepium*) is prevalent. The general picture, therefore, differs quite strikingly from that offered by most Colombian lowland villages, the barren and desolate aspect of which is caused by the systematic destruction of all trees which might grow in or near the settlement.

The whole village is divided into two *barrios*, the *Plaza* and the *Loma*, the former occupying the flat area adjoining the village square, while the latter consists of the section which occupies the slopes and ridges toward the more elevated rear part of the village. This division is of great importance in the life of the community, being both the conse-quence and cause of its social theory. The Plaza is the 'civilized' section of the village where the Creole-oriented *placeros* live, where the stores, the church, and the few public buildings are, while the Loma is the 'Indian' quarter. Owing to the extremely uneven terrain, the two barrios cannot be clearly delimited, some parts of the Plaza lying on higher ground than some of the Loma, and vice versa, but for the inhabitants there can never be any doubt about the line that separates these two main sections. Although the number of houses in the Plaza and Loma barrios is approximately equal, the Loma occupies a much larger area. In the Plaza section the houses are generally close to one another, apparently trying to maintain a certain order of fronts and streets, but the dwellings of the Loma are scattered and irregularly spaced.

Toward the east and the west the Plaza barrio is limited by two small creeks, while a third one descends approximately through the middle of the barrio. Toward the north, toward the Loma, there is no such natural limit; there the dividing line is marked by a trail which crosses the slope and parallels a fence which, although built by various individual houseowners of the Plaza, forms a continuous division all across the village from east to west. Although the inhabitants maintain that this fence has no particular significance and that its presence beside the trail is mere coincidence, the real dividing line between the barrios being only the trail, this seems to be doubtful. Within the village, fences are generally short and are built only around individual property such as houses, backyards, or empty lots; but in this case the fence has been continued from house to house, forming a veritable frontier. From the Plaza to the Loma there are few marked changes, and except for the fence and trail the newcomer would hardly know whether he was still in one barrio or had arrived in the other. To him the houses and their inhabitants look all very much the same. But to the people of Aritama there never can be any doubt; to them the fence and the trail divide two worlds, two ways of life: the 'Indians' and the 'Spaniards'.

This division into Plaza and Loma seems to be of rather recent origin. In the years between 1870 and 1880 the entire village of Aritama consisted of only some sixty houses, most of them located on or near the plaza and only a few on the adjoining slopes toward the north. What is today the Loma was then covered by dense underbrush and trees, with only seven or eight widely scattered houses belonging to the poorest inhabitants. 'Indians' as well as 'Spaniards' then lived near the Plaza, and only about twenty or thirty years ago were the former definitely displaced and relocated toward the upper part of the village where by then the new barrio had begun to take shape. Today the division is clear to all inhabitants and to be a *placero* or *lomero* means much more than merely to be a resident of a certain geographical area within the village. It implies differences in social scale, in economic activity, in religious participation. It means tensions, contempt, fear, and frustration, because, whereas the Loma stands for tradition and isolation, for the old accustomed ways of the mountain peasant of Indian orientation, the Plaza stands for 'progress' and for contact with the outside world.

With time, change, and population increase, the present division into two barrios, however, is in many respects an emotional one, devoid of much of its former meaning in terms of caste and race. New subdivisions are beginning to emerge. Because of its relatively large size, the Loma is being divided into several sections which, although they are not yet recognized as barrios in their own right, are sometimes referred to by certain names. These sections are La Piedra, Papayal, Villa Vieja, Musaca, La Mina, and Aguas Blancas. They have no well-defined limits and their names are derived from some topographical feature, such as a rock formation or a growth of trees. It is always understood that each section still forms part of the Loma barrio, but it is evident that new barrios are slowly being formed.

The population of the Corregimiento of Aritama consists of Spanish-speaking Mestizo peasants called generally *civilizados* ('civilized people'), and members of various Indian tribes, called simply *indios* or *chinos*. There are no official census data on the numerical distribution of these ethnic groups, and the following data were obtained by our personally conducted household census of the main village, and by our frequent visits to the satellite hamlets. According to our count the total number of inhabitants of the Corregimiento reaches about 4,000. Of these about 1,600 are Indians living in tribal villages, while 2,400 Mestizo peasants live in the main village of Aritama (1,400) and its neighboring hamlets (1,000). Geographically, the ethnic groups are distributed in an altitudinal scale, the Mestizos occupying mainly the lower part of the valleys, while the Indians live in villages or scattered huts lying generally above 1,200 meters altitude.

On the historical development of this population there are but few data. In a Spanish census of 1803 there appear a total of sixty-nine Indians, all males between eighteen and fifty years of age, each paying a tribute of 4 pesos a year to the Crown, while three Spaniards, married to Indian women, paid only 2 pesos. The total population of the entire valley at that time might be calculated at some 300 individuals. A census taken in 1879 of the population of the village (not counting the adjoining Indian territory) shows an increase to 515 inhabitants. In 1952 the census data gave a total of 1,345 inhabitants for the village, distributed as shown in Table 1.

Data on the birth, fertility, and death rates are very scarce. The records kept by the Corregidor are confused and incomplete, and as there is no permanent parish priest, the church records contain only sporadic information. We found records for only the years 1938, 1939, and 1940 with thirty, twenty-two, and eleven deaths registered, respectively, three deaths for 1946, four for 1949, and three for 1951. The

TABLE 1

Distribution of Population

Age Group	Male	Female	Total
Under 5 years	131	116	247
5–9	110	102	212
10–14	91	81	172
15–19	58	74	132
20–24	50	73	123
25–29	50	42	92
30–34	28	42	70
35–39	29	41	70
40–44	21	36	57
45–49	14	26	40
50–54	15	23	38
55–59	13	11	24
60–64	11	15	26
65–69	6	10	16
70–74	5	3	8
75–79	5	3	8
80–84	5	2	7
85–89	—	1	1
90 and over	—	2	2
Total	642	703	1,345

cause of death is given in terms like 'stomach' (*estómago*), 'suddenly' (*repentinamente*), 'annihilation' (*aniquilamiento*), 'of swellings' (*de hinchazones*), and the like. Baptismal records and registration of marriages are also of little use, because they make no distinction between tribal Indians and Mestizo peasants and because many people married or had their children baptized in neighboring villages or lowland towns. The records that are kept at the municipality in the lowlands are equally deficient and entirely useless for statistical purposes. Although theoretically all these registrations are required by law for all citizens, people do not comply and the local authorities do little or nothing to enforce these government regulations.

The genetic constitution of the villagers is very mixed, and in their phenotypes all shades of crossing can be observed. The predominant type is triethnic, Caucasian features blending with Amerind and Negro traits, but there are also many individuals who are almost pure representatives of the three racial stocks. Negroes, however, are relatively rare and such negroid traits as can be observed in shape of lips or noses, hair form, or a markedly dark pigmentation, are usually seen in combination with Caucasoid features. Because of this heterogenity, it is quite impossible to describe the inhabitants as a group. There are squat, coarse-haired Indians with high cheekbones and epicanthic eyefolds;

blond and blue-eyed people; long-legged and narrow-skulled negroids; and between these extremes there lies the whole range of racial mixture with all its endless recombinations of exterior characteristics.

All the people speak Spanish as their native language. Their long isolation has led to certain peculiarities of speech: archaisms with only locally understood meaning, words taken from the Indian languages, or details of intonation and pronunciation. Some—very few—still speak the old Indian language, but they will never do so in public and, when asked, are likely to disclaim any knowledge of it. Its function has become purely ceremonial, being used today almost exclusively in secret spells, formulas, or prayers.

At first view the casual visitor will notice hardly any difference between the villagers of Aritama and those of hundreds of other small rural communities in the Colombian lowlands. Only after some time will he come to note the subtle details in manner and bearing, in the way people walk or rest, work or play, talk or listen, which distinguish them from the inhabitants of the neighbouring villages. Perhaps the most notable difference from other Mestizo communities lies in the great self-control and artificialness people display. Even within the intimacy of their homes they behave in a self-conscious and somewhat aloof manner, always being careful not to betray any emotion, not to disturb, not to be obvious. There is a self-effacing quality about this behavior, quite in contrast to the outspoken and often rather noisy ways found among the neighboring Mestizos. People in Aritama are almost never noisy. They are quiet and slow, with few and vague gestures, monotonous speech, and a retiring manner of formal politeness.

But all these aspects of exterior appearance, language, and manner are far from being accepted by the people themselves as a heritage, cherished, integrated, accustomed. Quite on the contrary, his physical appearance is a subject of continuous worry to the individual; his manner of speech is considered by him to be a serious handicap; the behavior he displays in his everyday social contacts is determined by tensions and conflicts. The people generally are extremely self-conscious and critical of the impression they might make upon the outsider, always fearing that their appearance, speech, and behavior might be interpreted as backward, as 'Indian', as uncivilized. They are insecure. As long as Aritama was an isolated self-contained Indian community, a small hamlet practically independent of the outside world and not much interested in it, there was security and contentment, or at least indifference. Among the old people one may still find a degree of this equanimity and naturalness of the integrated personality. But since the village has come into closer contact with the lowland towns, with trade and commerce, with technology and politics since from its marginal position it has been drawn closer and closer into the orbit of national life, it has become increasingly conscious of its antiquated customs and old-fashioned ways, and with this consciousness has come insecurity—the insecurity consonant with accelerated change.

ROADS, TRANSPORTATION, AND COMMUNICATIONS

The roads of Aritama are hardly more than narrow mountain trails, over which progress on foot or on burro is necessarily slow; but these trails form a complex network which covers the entire valley and connects it with the neighboring hamlets or farmlands, with the Indian territory, the lowland plains and towns, the rivers and roads at the base of the mountain. Most of these trails seem to have existed from time immemorial and many of them might even go back to prehistoric periods. The Tairona Indians were competent road-builders who constructed stairs, paved uneven stretches with flat stone slabs or built bridges from large flat rocks. Some of these ancient features are still in use and can be seen here and there on the trails. The nearest lowland town lies at about 50 kilometers distance and can be reached on horse- or muleback in some seven or eight hours, but smaller lowland settlements lie nearer, at some 20 kilometers from Aritama, or right at the entrance of the valley, though still on the plains. The Indian territory can be reached in about four or five hours, and the *retiros* of Aritama—the satellite villages of the Corregimiento—are almost all within two hours walking distance. Cultivated lands, however, often lie at considerable distances from the main village, and it might take a man up to two days to reach his field or small coffee plantation high up on the mountain slopes.

Most people move only between their houses and their fields. Year after year they use only a certain trail and when asked about trails in another direction they are often ignorant or uncertain of them. They may know a few neighboring trails, those used by villagers who have their fields in the same general direction, but a man who owns a field on the slopes west of the village does not necessarily know how the slopes to the east of it can be reached. And there is little interest in knowing. The trail a man uses and knows is 'his trail' (*su camino*) because it leads from his home to his field, and other people's trails are not his concern. But to some people, mostly to the wealthier placeros, roads and trails are of a wider importance. To them they are a most important link between points where food or other goods are produced, sold, or consumed. They are the means by which a client, a friend, a relative, an authority, a physician, or a priest can be reached; to them roads are a vital utility and their general state, maintenance, and length are discussed almost daily. In the Plaza barrio any conversation will turn sooner or later to the problem of roads, to the necessity of building a bridge, to the neglect of roads by the authorities, the difficulties of travel, the lack of rapid communication. Such talk is hardly ever heard among the lomeros. By most of them the lack of communications is felt to be rather an advantage. Who, after all, wants to made it easy for the police, the revenue agents, the priest, or the wandering peddler to come to the village? Only a few people of the Plaza could be interested in that and then only for their personal benefit, but not for the good of the community. Opinions, then, are divided by the barrio fence; while the placero minority complains about the lack of roads and desires closer and more rapid contact with the lowlands, the lomeros are fearful and reluctant to improve them. 'Once a motor road comes up here,' they say, 'the village is lost. Then thieves and burglars, swindlers and policemen, truckdrivers and politicians will come here, to steal our chickens and our women.'

But the motor road is approaching steadily. During the dry season trucks can now drive across the shrub-covered plains to the entrance of the valley and can even penetrate a few kilometers toward the village, after crossing several streams. But the main river forms an obstacle at all times of the year, and from its banks to the village all transportation is only by foot or by pack animals, for a trip of several hours. In any case, there is only one truck—a rather broken-down vehicle at that— and this does not have a fixed schedule but travels at odd times, or whenever its owner thinks it fit to do so. Being an inhabitant of the nearest lowland village, the owner of this conveyance, Don Paco, has close commercial and kinship ties with some of the placero merchants but, at the same time, shows an ill-disguised contempt for the people of Aritama in general. Often sacrificing profit to his pride of superiority, he carefully selects passengers and loads, accepting some while rejecting others. He starts or stops whenever he pleases, so the trip sometimes takes two or three days. To travel in Don Paco's truck is a memorable experience that lately has begun to enliven the village talk. First, word will come to Aritama that on a certain day the vehicle is due to be at the river to take passengers and loads to the lowland towns. This news is denied and reaffirmed for some time but finally, on the day in question, those interested will leave at dawn on foot or on muleback to wait at the river for the truck to arrive. Sometimes it does, and after hours of loading and reloading, it leaves again, the anxious passengers perched high upon sacks and bundles amidst pigs, infants, and chickens. Whenever the road is reasonably clear the truck goes at top speed and once it reaches the plain the driver races toward his final goal for the last 30 or 40 kilometers. No man in his sober mind would ever take this truck, and so it is customary for each prospective passenger to leave the village with a bottle of rum. The initial anxiety is, therefore, soon dispelled and when the swaying truck races over the dusty plain the general exhilaration has already reached a point where all physical danger is forgotten. Of course, there have been accidents and several spots are pointed out on the road where a passenger fell off or where the whole truck turned over, hurting or killing those who 'had it coming to them'. Smashed bottle glass and the debris of broken containers mark such sites and constitute a challenge to the driver, who will race by faster than ever in order to prove that he 'made it this time'.

Under these circumstances this 'modern' way of travel has not become very popular yet. Some placeros will use the truck when going to the lowlands to sell their goods or to buy new merchandise for their stores, but the majority of those who have to travel still use the mule trail.

Most transportation is by donkey, and practically every household— even the poorest ones—owns at least one, with a common wooden pack saddle which carries loads up to 70 kilos. As most cultivated foodstuffs are bulky and heavy, such as the starchy tubers of manioc and yams, plantains or pumpkins, daily life without some such simple and ready means of transportation is hardly imaginable. Horses and mules are scarce in the village, but both are used more for transporting loads than for riding. Oxen are also used widely as pack animals all over the mountainous region, being the common means of transportation on steep and slippery trails where a donkey or even a mule would lose its footing. Also, heavy burdens are carried by people of both sexes on the back, and often for long distances. The load is put into a large wide-meshed carrying net provided with a tumpline, and even small children can be seen carrying firewood or food in this manner. Women often prefer to carry heavy loads on their heads, at least on open roads and in relatively flat country. The load—a bundle, a water jar, a large tin container, etc.—is balanced upon a twisted rag which lies on the head, and many people say that this way of carrying burdens is less tiresome than that of using a tumpline.

The loads people carry to and fro are mainly food, water, and firewood. Not a single day passes without most people carrying these things for some distance, either from their fields or from the river. Outside the village one hardly ever sees a person without some load, since, when visiting another village, a person will always carry something there and bring back something else. Anyone will collect firewood near the trail, wild-growing fruits, some bark fiber for a rope, and so no one is ever seen empty-handed when walking in the open country. Children, of course, are also a daily burden as long as they are small or yet unable to walk on stony trails. They are carried straddling a hip, only the very small being wrapped in a cloth and carried on the back.

The heaviest loads that have to be transported are the crops or manu-factured goods destined for sale, such as coffee, raw sugar, and straw hats. From the fields to the village these are sometimes carried on the back, but when they are ready to be sold in the lowlands their transportation becomes difficult and costly, especially for those who produce small amounts at irregular intervals. It is hardly worthwhile for a man to take two sacks of coffee or a donkey load of palm fiber products down to the lowlands, as the expenses of the trip of one or two days are greater than the small profit obtained. Most people prefer, therefore, to sell their products at small profit to the merchants and storekeepers of the Plaza, who then arrange for transportation to the next town, in truck loads or large mule-team loads at a worthwhile profit.

There is no electricity in the village and no radio receiving sets. However, since the end of the last century, Aritama has had a telephone service which connects it with the nearest large lowland town, an advantage which is pointed out with pride by all inhabitants. This telephone, combined with a telegraph service and a general mail office, occupies a small room next to the police inspector's quarters, and is attended to by a government employee who—theoretically at least—is assisted by another employee who is responsible for traveling once a week between Aritama and the lowlands with the mails. As there are no office hours or house-to-house delivery of mail, the usefulness of this service depends largely upon the personal friendship existing between the interested public and the postal agent, who will put through a call and accept or deliver a letter or message only as a 'favor'.

As is the custom over most of rural Colombia, letters and other messages are rarely entrusted to the government mail, but are by preference delivered personally by friends or relatives who happen to travel. In any case, in Aritama few people read or write, and in the whole year of 1954 the post office received only 38 letters from the outside and dispatched 28 from the villagers. However, 399 telegrams were received during the same timespan and 522 were sent. Usually the postmaster himself writes these messages upon the illiterate senders' requests and reads to them the answers when they have been received. The content of the messages sent by the villagers consist mainly of greetings to relatives and friends, inquiries about their health, and requests for medicines or a certain merchandise to be sent to the village. The date of departure or arrival of the above-mentioned truck is one of the main reasons for using the telephone or telegraph. Sometimes the line is down because of a falling tree or the breaking of a rotten pole; and then the village is isolated for days or weeks, without contact with the lowlands, but nobody feels this to be a serious handicap. Messages of any importance are readily transmitted by people who meet on the trails, and in this manner news travels fast.

About two or three newspapers arrive once a month and are read by three or four placeros. However, their interest is only in the local news, the price of coffee or cattle or some government project concerning the local scene, and national or international politics are never discussed. There is a vague consciousness that there are other countries—Venezuela, France, Mexico—somewhere behind the mountains and beyond the plains, that there are wars and revolutions, strange cities and powerful leaders of nations; but there is no interest in what happens outside of the valley itself, no desire to know more about the world. Life in the valley of Aritama is difficult as it is; why should one worry about what happens outside its limits? Some people who have visited a cinema in the lowland towns, or who have heard radios and loudspeakers or even taken part in a political gathering, come back disturbed and frightened. What they saw and heard had no meaning to them and all they felt was the threat of a violent and noisy world that was not theirs.

SOME ASPECTS OF MATERIAL CULTURE

The predominant type of house in Aritama is a square, constructed of wattle and daub (*bahareque*), with a grass-thatched, square, high-pitched hip roof. The average size of such a house is rather small, being 7 by 4 meters, with walls about 2 meters high. The peak of the roof is relatively high, measuring about 4·5 meters from the floor, in the middle of the house. However, the eaves of the roof often extend well below the height of the walls, so that even an average-sized person has to stoop a little when entering.

These houses are usually built by communal labor, the work proceding by the following steps: First, the house lot is cleared of trees, rocks, or underbrush. As the terrain of the village is very irregular and houses quite often have to be built on more or less inclined slopes, a considerable amount of leveling has to be done. If a large boulder cannot be moved, it is incorporated into the construction as part of the walls. Once the ground has been leveled and cleared, the main posts (*horcones*) are erected. Their number varies from twelve to sixteen, according to the size of the house, their lower ends buried superficially or simply placed upon flat stones. All are of the same length, there being no central post. No special plan is laid out beforehand, the construction simply being adapted as well as possible to the available space. The roof is built first. On the upper ends of the main posts there are cut semi-circular notches which receive the ends of the wall plates. On them are placed the tie beams (*tirantes*) and crossbeams (*vigas*) which support the roof. As a rule, four-sided hip roofs with a triangular slope at either end are used, making what is called a *casa redonda* ('round house'), but occasionally open-sided gable roofs are built, called *casa de cuchilla* ('knife-backed house'). The first timbers (*maderamen*) of the roof are the *varas* (common rafters), which are long and rather thin, round poles, the lower ends of which are supported by the wallplates and tie beams, while the upper ends come to lie crosswise over the ridgepole (*cumbrera*). Several pairs of principal rafters end in forks and support the ridgepole securely. On top of the crossed rafters an additional ridge piece (*sobrecumbrera*) is placed. A number of horizontal or oblique struts (*burros, varas de viento*), purlins (*cintas*), and several king posts (*pies-amigos*), which stand upon the crossbeams, give strength to this structure. On top, and parallel to the rafters, another series of thin cane rafters (*flechas*) are tied and are then connected by a large number of horizontal, parallel-lying roof-rods (*latas atravesadas*). Upon these poles which form a dense network, the grass thatch is placed. Once the roof is completely covered, a third ridge piece (*iguana*) is put on top of the thatch, where it covers the other two ridgepoles and presses down the grass. The lower end of the roof is often slightly lifted by tying a series of short sticks (*barraganete*) below and on top of two of the lowest purlins, thus breaking the steep pitch of the roof and forming a slightly out-flaring end slope. Although the village lies, as we have shown, in a region of little rainfall, most roofs are high-pitched (up to 65 degrees), though in the more recent structures the pitch is about 50 degrees.

The roof finished, the walls are next built. The process followed in the construction of the walls is similar to roof construction in that a series of poles (*flechas*) are first tied vertically on the outside of the main posts, and are then connected by closely spaced horizontal canes (*latas*). Another series of these canes is tied on the inside, forming a double grillwork as thick as the diameter of the main posts. This space is then filled with clay which is pressed into place by hand, smoothed inside and outside, and occasionally whitewashed. Dividing walls are constructed in the same manner.

A very characteristic feature of local domestic architecture in the Sierra Nevada is the *estribera*, which is a buttress-like thickening of the lower part of the walls. Made of heavy clay into which stones are pressed, the estribera, which is often twice as thick as the wall and about 60 or 80 centimeters high, gives the house considerable stability and helps avoid erosion of the walls at the ground.

Relatively few houses have gable roofs constructed in the same manner as the four-sided hip roof, except that in some cases the triangular lateral openings are closed with wattle-and-daub walls. Five per cent of all buildings have corrugated metal roofs, among them the church, the priest's house, the police inspector's office, the jail, all the stores, and a few privately owned homes of placeros. The average house (72·8 per cent) has two rooms, connected by a small door, or a curtain or mat. Only 39 per cent have windows, the rest having only small ventilation holes about 10 by 10 centimeters. In old houses one still can see doors hewn out of one solid block of wood, with peg-shaped knobs which work in holes cut in the door frame as hinges, but doors and windows are now made from fitted boards and are provided with metal hinges.

House types are matters of deep concern to most villagers. The common 'round house' is despised and criticized as an 'Indian' type of dwelling, and people are greatly worried by the appearance which the frequency of this house type gives to the village. Houses with a gabled roof are considered much more 'civilized', and lately a number of people have begun to imitate the architecture of the lowland towns by building brick or adobe houses with square rectangular façades behind which a lean-to or shed roof of iron slopes backward toward the yard. The front view of such a house conveys the impression of a two-storied building, or at least of solidity and large size, but behind the high parapet-like façade there lie only two or three low rooms. This type of house, with its imposing (although misleading) front, has become the ambition of all villagers as it carries the prestige of the 'civilized' lowland Creoles, but the high construction costs limit its use. Only well-to-do people, and very few of them, can afford to build this type of house. The large majority of the villagers have to content themselves with their old-accustomed dwellings, even though their low prestige is acutely felt.

Of course, the lowland style could certainly be successfully imitated in wattle and daub and with thatched roofs, but there seem to have arisen certain technical problems which the local builders have not been able to solve. As a matter of fact, house construction, in its small technical details, is so standardized a procedure that any structural change that might be suggested by the owner is likely to meet with disapproval and protest from the people engaged in the actual work. For example, the time-honored use of two sets of rafters where one would do for all purposes is an obvious waste of materials and labor, but although some people realize this and protest it, the technique of thatching has not been altered. The desire to change the prevailing architectural style is growing but technical skill is lagging behind; and so only people who can afford to import laborers and to build in brick or adobe are able to live in 'civilized' houses.

Another matter which must be mentioned here concerns the dress of the villagers. All inhabitants of Aritama, with very few exceptions, today wear costumes of conventional European design. By 1830 Indian men had already abandoned the hand-woven cotton tunic (*muquéca*) and had begun to wear trousers and shirts, although their women continued to use their toga-like garments of thick white cotton cloth. But during the last decades of the nineteenth century the majority of women also adopted European dress for use on holidays, in processions, and for Mass, although in their own houses they still wore their aboriginal costume. At present there are still some ten or twelve women who wear this native dress and who never use European styles.

During the second half of the last century and the first decades of the present one, male dress consisted of wide cotton trousers called *tapabalazos*, made of thick homespun cotton cloth and tied around the waist with cords by which the front could be closed crosswise. With these trousers a white, plaited, collarless cotton shirt was worn, wide-sleeved and without buttons, tied at the neck with two little strings. A *pesetero* straw hat, called thus because it cost one peseta, completed the male costume. Although many men continued to wear their own homespun cotton fabrics until the late nineteenth century, women by then already used commercial textiles, which they bought from the lowland traders. The common female dress (*traje*) of that time was a long, sacklike, long-sleeved garment of dark cloth.

With the arrival of the immigrants from the lowlands, these costumes were rapidly modified and replaced by others. The men adopted tailored trousers, occasionally made of dark cloth, with buttons and belts, wearing with them white tailored shirts with collars and cuffs, and a high-crowned straw hat (*pava*). From this developed the male fashion used today. At present, the following styles are distinguished: a *flux*, a suit consisting of a pair of trousers and a coat, both of drill; a *káki*, a pair of thick cotton trousers worn only with a drill shirt; a *saquito de trabajo* ('workday coat'), a pair of drill trousers and a flannel shirt over which a drill coat is worn; and a *vestido de paseo*, the best suit of clothes a man owns, which consists of drill trousers and coat, worn with a long-sleeved shirt, sometimes a tie, a belt of leather or plastic material, a felt hat and black shoes.

Women's dresses became far more varied. The different styles introduced by the lowland Creoles, most of which are still in use, are the following: *traje bajito*, a very wide, ankle-length frock of white cotton, with a high, horizontal neckline, short sleeves, closed in the back with two strings; *bata zamba*, a similar frock but long-sleeved, of any color, but always provided with a tapelike cotton belt or sash (*fajón*); *bata suelta*, a wide frock of any color, with two darts (*machetes*) in front and a sewed-in belt; *bata justa*, similar to the bata suelta but with a tailored waistline effect; *manigueta*, a long-sleeved frock of any color, adorned with a few ribbons in front, and with darts (*piquetes*) in the back of the waistline, and beltlike tie ends; *polonesa*, a wide ankle-length skirt over which is worn a long-sleeved blouse of the same fabric, with the back part being considerably longer and rounded; *basquiña*, a long skirt with a rounded apron sewed on its front, adorned with ribbons and bows, worn with a long-sleeved blouse (*saco*) and a wide petticoat (*pollera*). With these dresses low-heeled, open-toed leather slippers (*botines*) and a colored square shawl (*pañolón*) are worn.

These basic styles are still in use at present with only slight modifications. The older generation of women wear the *chambrita*, a garment derived from a combination of the *polonesa* and the *basquiña*, consisting of a long, wide skirt with many pleats, and a short, long-sleeved blouse with a high gothic V-shaped neckline, buttoned in front. The fabric is a thin cotton with a characteristic small, black-and-white print. The most common cotton dress (*traje*) for women of all ages consists of a skirt and a long- or short-sleeved bodice sewed together, sometimes with the effect of a tailored waistline but more often of a sacklike appearance. These dresses generally open at the back but sometimes have a lateral opening on the left hip, with buttons. High, rounded necklines and darts are the rule, and the hem reaches well below the knees. A dress with a very wide pleated skirt is called a *serpentina* or, if less wide, a *faldita suelta*, while a narrow, sacklike skirt is called a *faldita de medio paso*.

The aboriginal garment (*manta*), which is still used by some women, consists of two large rectangular pieces of thick white cloth, folded lengthwise, with the corners of one end sewed together. These corners lie over the shoulders and the folded part comes to lie under the other armpit, the body being thus enveloped in a wide floating dress that reaches the ground.

An important part of women's festive attire is the shawl, of which, apart from the now obsolete black *pañolón*, several types are distinguishable. The *rebozo* is of black silk, while the *chalina* can be of silk or of cotton but is also in black; the *abrigo* is of wool, of any color, and is adorned with fringes and tassels; the *tapijo* is a shawl or kerchief generally of black or white silk, and the *tapijo de felpa* is of plushy black silk, with many large tassels. Women's footwear consists of *zapatillos*, more or less low-heeled leather shoes; *medio-botines* ('leather slippers'), *botines*, a slipper with a low heel. *Guaireñas*, a kind of sandal with a woven cloth cover and a thick sole cut out of old rubber tire, were introduced only in quite recent times.

Children's dresses have also changed a great deal. The earlier aboriginal form consisted of a short tunic for boys, and a wrap-around skirt and blouse for girls, while all children under ten years of age generally went naked. At present the following types of children's dresses are distinguishable: Newborn babies are either wrapped in a towel or wear a *jaquecito*, a long shirtlike garment without sleeves, open at the back. Boys from three to seven years wear shorts (*bombachos*), usually with a bib or with sewed-on cloth suspenders (*pantaloncito de cargadores*), and those up to ten years wear similar shorts with a short-sleeved shirt (*pantaloncito suelto y camisita*). Girls until five years of age wear a knee-length dress (*vestidito*) of skirt and bodice sewed together, and from then until puberty a similar sacklike dress (*trajecito*), with short sleeves and buttoned at the back.

Men's clothes are now either bought ready made at the stores, or are made by the local part-time tailor. Women's dresses, however, are almost always made by a local part-time seamstress (*costurera*) or by the wearer herself. No measurements are taken nor are there any fittings necessary, the new garment simply being copied from an old one. Colors and prints are carefully chosen and are discussed at length with friends. For their suits men prefer white or a pale blue, sometimes a light brownish color. Shirts are either white or have thin colored stripes. Women's dresses are rarely white, but rather pale blue, rose, or light gray. In printed cotton dresses stripes of different colors are avoided, the preferred designs being large flowers, polka dots, or small geometric figures.

Personal ornaments are few. Men wear cheap gold or silver rings bought from traveling peddlers or in the neighboring towns. One well-to-do man was rather remarkable in that he wore three or four rings set with jewels on each hand, keeping them lifted with spread fingers in front of his chest, every time he talked to someone. Men's handkerchiefs always have an aesthetic function and are often worn in pairs, half protruding from the back pockets of trousers. Most girls have their ears pierced at an early age, wear small flower- or bubble-shaped earrings of cheap jewelry, and occasionally one ring on the first finger of the right hand. Small straight combs made of plastic material are seen occasionally. The use of cosmetics is very limited and can be observed only among the younger women of high status who sometimes employ perfumes, lipstick, and powders. Hair pomades, on the contrary, are liberally employed by both sexes of all classes.

Men wear their hair short, having it cut periodically by a competent friend or by the part-time barber, but those who have light-colored hair show a tendency to let it grow longer and take obvious pride in it. Practically all women wear their hair long, not parted, but simply combed backward and sometimes held together at shoulder height with a piece of ribbon. Some twist it into a knot at the back of the neck. Only a few of the younger girls have adopted a 'modern' hairdress, wearing it short, especially if they have curly or wavy hair.

Dress and ornament are the most important exterior manifestations of a person's status and are thus the center of constant preoccupation, discussion, and gossip. Any commodities are willingly sacrificed in order to save money for clothes, and some people will go to the limit of physical starvation only to be able to appear in public in new suits and dresses. The prestige value of clothes is taught to all children from infancy and represents the basic incentive for work. The system of award and punishment is to a very high degree conceived in terms of the acquisition of new clothes, and formal schooling continues to reaffirm the high prestige value of dress. All schoolteachers discriminate sharply between well- or ill-dressed pupils, favoring the former and exposing the latter to ridicule.

To be well dressed is the ambition of all villagers. In their opinion only a well-dressed person is respected. And to be respected—as we shall see farther on—is the main preoccupation of the individual. A person might live in a miserable hut, deprive himself of food, travel, or even of medicines, but he must present himself on all public occasions in good clothes. People who simply do not have the means to do so and who must wear old clothes for years, avoid being seen. They will never cross the village square, nor walk in the daylight in the streets, but will use back streets or leave their houses only after dark. Should they be seen, they are certain to be ridiculed, and much bitterness and despair is caused by their poverty. Some people of the Loma have not visited the Plaza barrio for years.

But those who can afford to buy new clothes at least once a year—and they form the majority, as much of their total economic production is spent in this way—also have their difficulties. Their choice of fabric, style, cut, color, or print is certain to be discussed by neighbors who will doubt the person's 'right' to use a certain kind of suit, a certain quantity of dresses, or who will criticize the occasion upon which they are worn. Of any new suit or dress in the village, it is known whether it was paid for in cash or bought on credit, and there is much malicious talk every time a person is seen wearing a new costume. On the other hand, the complexities of modern dress have not been fully mastered yet by many people, and the correct use of certain items has led, not to reinterpretation, but to outright confusion. Women can be seen stumbling along with new shoes put on the wrong feet, while others wear their dresses backward. Most men are unable to knot a tie but insist on wearing one on certain occasions, inventing then their own versions of knots. Felt hats that have a broad hatband often are worn with the bow in front, and some men can be seen carrying women's handbags of plastic or leather when traveling. Belts, kerchiefs, umbrellas, fountain-pens, and other details also cause confusion and are sometimes affected out of place and in a manner which hardly corresponds to their basic functions.

People who work in the fields often take along a good suit and change into it before re-entering the village. When they return with their working clothes on, they will generally use hidden trails and back-doors so as not to be seen in public in old and dirty clothes. We have seen people break out in tears or run away frantically when surprised in their working clothes. Doors are bolted and windows are closed as soon as a visitor arrives, and people will show themselves only after they have changed into new, or at least clean and mended, clothes.

The high-prestige value of clothes is very characteristic for most of Colombia, but in Aritama it reaches a point where it becomes a pre-occupation so charged with anxieties that it forms a very real problem to the people concerned. The reason, of course, consists essentially in the fear of being taken for a backward 'Indian', the humiliation felt to be associated with agricultural labor.

Under these conditions it is quite natural that the few women who still use native dress are a thorn in the side of the whole community. At first their very existence is concealed or ignored, but once it has to be admitted, they are severely criticized and ridiculed. They are blamed for bringing shame upon the whole village, for being 'enemies of progress'; they are accused of being witches or of practicing Black Magic. But these old women pay little attention to the village gossip. Their marked Indian phenotype has never allowed them to aspire to higher levels within their village structure, and so they continue to wear the old aboriginal costume and only their deaths will put an end to their 'shameless stubbornness', as other villagers denominated this habit.

Few people in the village own watches or clocks, and those that do exist are often out of order. Anyhow, a rapid glance at the sun is sufficient to tell the time of day and there is no real need to know the exact hour. The day is divided in the following manner: the *madrugada* ('dawn') is followed by the *mañanita* ('early morning') between about 5 and 6 A.M.; the *mañana* ('morning') includes the hours from 6 to 11 A.M.; the *medio dia* ('noon') from 11 A.M. to 1 P.M.; the *tarde* ('afternoon') from 1 to 4 P.M.; the *tardecita* ('little afternoon') from 4 to 6 P.M. The noon hour is fixed by observing that the shadow of one's head falls upon the feet. Night is divided into *primanoche* ('nightfall to midnight'), *primer gallo* ('first cock's crow') at about 1 A.M., *segundo gallo* ('second cock's crow') between 3 and 4 A.M., and *tercer gallo* ('third cock's crow') between 4 and 6 A.M. The old generation refers occasionally to the *hora de la oración* ('prayer-time'), meaning 6 P.M., and some people say that they can tell the hour by the chirping of certain crickets, or by certain constellations of stars.

The days of the week and the months of the year are referred to by the common Spanish terms, but, when asked, many people do not know the name of the month, much less the year they are living in. Certain dates in the past are established by reference to historical events of local importance. A frequently heard expression is *en aquel tiempo* ('in those times'), by which the past century is meant. The 'first smallpox' and the 'second smallpox', as well as the major Colombian civil wars provide also more or less fixed dates. But nobody will say that this or that happened 'in 1930', but will refer the event to the death or birth of a relative, to a bad harvest, or to the passing of the first airplane.

Distances are measured in Spanish leagues, each league (*legua*) being equivalent to five kilometers. Other measurements generally relate to the human body: a *yarda* ('yard') is measured from the nose, face away, to the fingertips of the laterally extended arm, and is divided into four *cuartas* ('quarters'), one quarter being the maximal distance between the tips of thumb and little finger. A *metro* ('meter') is measured from the suprasternale to the fingertips of the extended arm, while a *vara* (about 80 centimeters) is taken to be the distance between nose and extended fingertips, but turning the face in the direction of the laterally extended arm. A *braza* ('armlength') is the distance measured from the ground to the fingertips, with vertically extended arm. A *jeme* is the maximal distance between the tips of thumb and forefinger. Smaller measures are given in *dedos* ('fingerbreadth'), or in *pulgadas*, the length of the first joint of the thumb.

The most commonly used units for measuring land are the following: a *cabulla* ('string', 'rope') covers an area of 80 by 80 meters, and is divided into twenty *tareas* ('tasks'), 60 by 48 brazas in extension, one 'task' containing 24 'armlengths'. The term *banco* (bank), approximately equivalent to a *tarea*, is now almost obsolete, but some of the older people still use it. House lots are always measured in *varas*, a unit which is also used to indicate the size of any construction. For example, a 'seven-vara house' is a house seven varas in length. All textiles of cotton or silk are also measured in varas.

Liquids and fat are measured in *botellas* ('bottles)', the common beer bottle being the norm. Two bottles make a *frasco* ('flask'). The *libra* ('pound') is the unit for measuring the following items: maize, coffee, raw sugar, pigeon peas, palm fibers, rope, onions. An *arroba* is 25 pounds, and a *quintal* is 100 pounds. To measure maize in *quartillos* (10 pounds) is becoming obsolete. Coffee is also measured in *latas* ('tins'), each one containing 10 pounds when fresh, or 5 pounds when dry. The units for firewood are the *burro* ('donkey'), i.e., the wood that can be placed between four sticks each one braza high; and the *carga*, which consists of two *bultos* and constitutes approximately what a donkey can carry. House posts and cross-beams are measured in varas, but boards are always measured in meters, giving the breadth and thickness in *cuartas*, *jemes*, and *dedos*. Straw for thatching is measured in *bohotes* ('trusses'), one bohote being the quantity which can be tied with a braza of rope; twelve such bohotes are then called a *tarea*. Also, garlic is measured in bohotes, this unit being the quantity a woman can grasp between thumb and forefinger. Cooking bananas, manioc, yams, and similar tubers are measured in terms of *bultos* and *cargas*, and occasionally in *pilas* ('piles'), the price of which varies according to quality. The unit for palm fiber products is the *docena* ('dozen').

Although the Colombian *peso*, consisting of 100 *centavos*, is recognized by all as the only legal currency, the older people still use the *real* in the following manner: 1 *real* = 2 *quartillos* or *medios*; 10 *reales* = 1 *fuerte*; 8 *reales* = 1 *peso sencillo* ('plain peso'), while 10 *reales* = 1 *peso oro* ('gold peso'). Because of this, old people will often say '100 pesos' instead of 10 pesos.

As most units for measurements used in Aritama differ from those used in the lowland towns, there is often considerable confusion as to the 'correct' extension, weight, or length of the different items in question. Even the more sophisticated inhabitants have difficulties converting leagues into kilometers, cabullas into acres, or brazas into meters, and most people are quite unable to do so. There is doubt and insecurity with regard to the common units, and at the same time the local system is thought to be antiquated and somehow 'Indian'.

II

THE BIOPHYSIOLOGICAL FOUNDATIONS

LOCAL SANITARY AND HYGIENIC CONDITIONS

ARITAMA has a healthful climate, a fact which is often pointed out with a certain pride by the inhabitants. After the oppressive heat of the tropical lowlands, the cool, dry mountain air of the village offers indeed a pleasant change, and in many parts of the Department of Magdalena Aritama is considered to be a kind of health resort where an occasional visitor might spend a few weeks or months to restore his health impaired by years of living in the hot lowlands.

The village lies above the upper limit of the anopheles mosquito and there is no malaria, although this disease occurs with some frequency in the lower part of the valley. Running surface water is plentiful all year round, and there are but few stagnant or polluted pools in the surroundings. Nature herself, therefore, does not present a serious menace to human health, leaving only man-made conditions to form a threat to the physical and mental well-being of the inhabitants. These conditions can be condensed into three main categories: poor sanitation and hygiene, deficient nutrition, and inadequate treatment of disease. A fourth factor, concerning mental health, might well be added here, viz., certain patterns of child-training and interpersonal relations which tend to produce strong emotional unbalance, leading eventually to neurotic or psychotic phenomena.

Housing conditions and the general siting of dwellings depend to a large degree upon the existence and availability of suitable lots. The original nucleus of the village was constructed around a slightly dome-shaped space between two small creeks, but the later expansion and continuous growth of the population have made it necessary to adapt the new houses to the irregularly shaped and deeply dissected ridges between the numerous small affluents of the creeks. The settlement pattern became, therefore, one of several nuclei with dense agglomerations of houses, separated by ditches, creeks, or rock formations and connected by irregularly spaced or isolated houses. Because of the general sloping of the terrain and to the many small elevations and depressions in it, few houses occupy the same level.

Practically all houses are constructed in such a way that their longitudinal axes point east–west. This protects the interior of the house to a certain degree against the heat and glare of the sun, but is done, above all, to keep the prevailing breeze from entering the living and sleeping quarters. During the dry season the hot trade winds sweep through the valley from the northeast, and these are considered to be the magical bearers of illness and death. So there are few, if any, windows on the east walls of the houses, and the other sides are similarly protected against the supposedly disease-laden winds which descend from the highlands and the snow peaks at intervals. This popular belief that winds carry diseases has, therefore, a strong influence upon the local architecture and general settlement pattern, and ventilation of a house is certainly not considered a desirable factor. Windows, especially those of the sleeping quarters, are, if present at all, very small and are usually kept closed as a preventive measure. Even the main doors are likely to be closed during most of the day.

Ninety-six per cent of all houses are wattle-and-daub constructions and 95 per cent are covered with a thatched roof of dry mountain grass, the rest having iron roofs. Only 12·7 per cent of the houses are whitewashed on the inside walls and 61·1 per cent have only the outside whitewashed, while the inside of the living and sleeping quarters show the bare dry clay. The remaining 38·9 per cent are not whitewashed at all. Cement floors are found in 7·1 per cent of the houses but only in 3·4 per cent of all cases do such floors cover the entire area. Three and seven tenths per cent of all cement floors are limited to the living-room, while the sleeping quarters have a dirt floor. Prestige factors have a very considerable influence upon these aspects of housing, both whitewashing or the use of cement floors being interpreted locally as signs of high social or economic status, but certainly not as sanitary measures. Wooden doors or windows are only rarely painted and often only on the outside, while the inside is left bare. Most furniture is locally made and is never painted.

In a total of 291 houses, 14·4 per cent consist of only one room, while 72·8 per cent have two rooms and 12·7 per cent have more than two. The latter are all owned by placero families. The floor space of the average two-room house is about 28 square metres. As the rooms have no ceilings but are covered directly by the thatched roof, the maximum height is about 4·5 metres, while the minimum height, measured at the walls, is about 1·8 metres. The two main entrances always lead to the living-room, which is, therefore, relatively well ventilated and lighted, but the sleeping quarters are accessible only through a small door in the dividing wall between the two rooms and are, therefore, very dark and seldom ventilated at all. During the night the entire family sleeps in this dark recess, in hammocks, or on mats on the floor—rarely in beds—and all doors and windows are kept closed. Iron bedsteads or folding beds are hardly ever used for sleeping, being reserved for serious illness or childbirth, but their possession has a high prestige value.

Wherever the houses are built very close together there is very little space for backyards, and in the more densely populated sections of the Plaza these are frequently missing entirely. The individual houseowner will then have a small backyard across the street or on part of a vacant lot near by. Cooking houses are built in the backyards, often as a lean-to on the side of the house. The houses have no roof gutters, and, as there is no drainage, the rainwater falling from the roof often erodes the surrounding ground in such a manner that the houses seem to have been built upon raised platforms.

There are seven privies in the village, all of them belonging to placero families. They are always constructed in the backyard and are, therefore, in the immediate vicinity of the kitchen. They are rarely used but, like cement floors, have a high prestige value. Even their owners rather avoid them, as they believe that many diseases are transmitted by bad odours. As there is otherwise no privacy, a considerable degree of retention of elimination is practiced during the daytime, and people use the open backyards or the streets after dark. On the outskirts, however, people can often be seen eliminating in the daytime, and even carrying on conversations with passers-by during the process. Instead of toilet paper, dry corncobs are used (and reused). All human excrements are promptly consumed by pigs, dogs, and chickens.

The water supply of the village comes principally from the fast-flowing, permanent streams in the vicinity. As the streambeds consist of rocks and gravel and no large settlements are located near the rivers between this village and the headwaters, the water here is clear but certainly contaminated with organic matter. No sanitary precautions of any kind are practiced in its use. The river water is brought early in the morning by women and children, generally in 5-gallon tin cans, or in large, gourd containers, and this amount of water is all that is used by the household during the day. Although the act of carrying water certainly does not represent a great physical effort or an appreciable loss of time, people avoid making more than one trip a day to the river and can bring forth many reasons why additional trips should not be made. Before a meal one feels too weak; after a meal the effort might cause harm to one's health; during the day it is too hot and the sudden change of temperature when dipping the can into the water is thought to be particularly unhealthful; and after dark ghosts and apparitions might be encountered. In any case, the water brought in early in the morning is considered to be quite sufficient and is made to last all day, the people taking pride in their thriftiness and their ingenuity in seeing how often the water can be used over and over again. An average household of two adults and two children never consumes more than 5 gallons a day. These 5 gallons are used for drinking, cooking, washing, bathing infants, cleaning kitchen utensils, soaking fruits, and washing laundry, and are finally given to the pigs and dogs. Children are taught not to waste water and a child may be severely punished for washing his face or hands in the daily water supply, or for spilling any once-used water which might eventually be used for another purpose. Although, potentially, water is abundant, the female head of the household watches jealously over this meager daily supply, which is considered a treasure acquired laboriously by her and her children's efforts. Some of the water is poured into a large earthenware vessel (*tinaja*) which stands in a corner of the living-room, and from which people drink during the day by dipping a tin cup or gourd spoon into it. This vessel is occasionally washed and the evaporation on its porous surface keeps the water pleasantly cool. Water is never filtered or purified in any way, nor is the drinking water ever boiled. Very few people use the water that accumulates in some of the holes dug near the small creeks that cross the village, and rainwater is used only occasionally, being infrequently collected in cooking vessels as it falls from the roof.

When brought from the fields or from a store, food is deposited on the dirt floor and is not protected against flies, dogs, pigs, or children. As all kitchens are open, animals and children have free access to them and to the food supply, which is often contaminated with feces, urine, vomit, dust, or insects. Sooty spiderwebs or dry grass drop from the inside of the thatched roof upon the food, while mice and rats roam freely about the kitchen. Before preparing or consuming food, the people do not wash their hands, and often the food itself is prepared without being washed first to remove dirt and dust. Instead of washing a used kitchen vessel, people quite often merely place it on the floor so that pigs and dogs may lick it 'clean'. No kitchen utensils are protected against contamination by dirt, insects, vermin, or domestic animals.

Refuse in the form of solid wastes, such as garbage, sweepings, household rubbish, bones, etc., is not collected daily and disposed of systematically. Instead, it is occasionally thrown in a corner of the backyard, on to the street, or sometimes into the nearest ditch or creek. The accumulations, which are all breeding places for flies, are the favored playing grounds of infants and younger children. Pigs, dogs, and black vultures dispose of part of this debris but also help to scatter it again, and so the streets and backyards are always littered with refuse, the stench from which pervades the air. Dead animals are not buried but are left where they die until vultures and dogs dispose of them.

Personal hygiene is limited. Soap is used to wash one's clothes but seldom to wash one's body. While fetching water or while doing the laundry in the river, women and children will wash themselves occasionally, although always fully clothed. Rarely does a person go to the river just in order to have a bath. Inside the village and the house there is no place where a person might wash himself. There is no privacy, no large water container. Early in the morning a person may rinse his mouth and splash some water on his face and hair, but he will hardly go beyond that. We have observed placeros who did not wash themselves or comb their hair for several consecutive days. Toothbrushes are practically unknown even among the most sophisticated families, and combs are little used even by women.

Personal clothing consists mainly of trousers and shirts for the men, and simple dresses for the women. Work clothes are worn for days, even weeks, without being changed or washed. Other clothes are washed frequently, but not with great care. Few men use underwear. Dirty clothing is piled up in a corner of the room and is used to clean the furniture or to dry the kitchenware, until time is found to wash it in the river. Most people sleep in the clothes they have worn all day, only occasionally putting on some old discarded garment for the night.

In everyday conversation the theme of personal hygiene and environmental sanitation is often referred to, and people pridefully claim that the village and its inhabitants are particularly clean and tidy. There is much elaborate talk of projected bathing excursions, cleaning days, the washing of infants, laundry, or household objects, but in reality nothing of this sort ever seems to happen. People expectorate freely and consider this to be a healthy custom which 'keeps the mouth clean'. Belching and flatulence are uninhibited, both being considered healthy signs of good digestion. The idea that dirt, excreta, or animals might cause or propagate disease is totally absent even among the most educated, and no disgust is felt at the sight or touch of these matters. However, men often show a marked repulsion to unpleasant odors, either body odors or odors of filth, and frequently scold their women and children for it. In referring to the women of neighboring settlements the people are likely to claim that in the other village they smell of garlic, goats, cattle, and so on. Cleanliness is always judged by smell, never by visual impression.

In summarizing, it can be said that the general sanitary conditions are very poor, and the consequences of this situation are only too evident in the level of health of the inhabitants.

GENERAL HEALTH CHARACTERISTICS

Our appraisal of local pathological phenomena, including the incidence, prevalence, and etiology of diseases, is, of course, a layman's estimate and offers at best only a rough outline of the more outstanding aspects.

However, we have discussed this matter at some length with several trained physicians of the lowland towns who had firsthand knowledge of the villagers, and the hospitals of the nearest towns put at our disposal the records of patients coming from this village over several years. These records and our personal observations were discussed with the hospital staff, doctors, nurses, and health workers, who all had wide experience with people from the same area and many of whom knew the village of our study and the health problems of its inhabitants.

The following communicable diseases were observed in the village: measles, smallpox, chickenpox, whooping cough, mumps, diarrhea, typhoid fever, amebic dysentery, ankylostomiasis, ascariasis, diphtheria, pneumonia, cold, bronchitis, malaria, syphillis, gonorrhea, lymphogranuloma venereum, erysipelas, puerperal infection, food infections and poisoning. Infant mortality is due mostly to acute gastrointestinal diseases, respiratory infections, and, sometimes, such infectious diseases as whooping cough. Maternal mortality is caused mainly by septicemia and sometimes by hemorrhage or eclampsia. Nutritional disturbances and deficiency disease are apparently very frequent, and gastrointestinal infections are common ailments in all age-groups.

The principal health problems of the community are gastrointestinal diseases caused by parasites and deficiency diseases due to inadequate food intake. Intestinal parasites are probably the main single cause of infant mortality, which coincides frequently with early weaning, as then the infant is rather suddenly exposed to infection by contaminated food. Practically all adults, with the possible exception of a few well-to-do placero families, seem to suffer to a greater or lesser degree from ankylostomiasis, ascariasis, and frequent attacks of amebic dysentery, all of them caused by the poor sanitary and hygienic conditions: disposal of excreta; lack of cleanliness in housing, clothing, and personal habits; and the continuous contamination of food and water by flies and other vectors.

Nutritional deficiencies, mainly from a low protein intake, are apparently severe and seem to have developed in many cases into clinical syndromes. Some of the more general symptoms and significant physical signs we were able to observe, or which were stated by our informants, were as follows: chronic fatigue, general lack or loss of strength, lack of appetite, diarrhea, night blindness and burning of the eyes, occasional photophobia, pallor, rough and scaly skin with occasional cutaneous lesions, edema. In infants and children we observed a great number of cases of retarded sitting, standing, and walking; retarded growth; marked pallor; abdominal swelling; frequent respiratory infections; and rough skin. Such gross evidence of malnutrition as pellagrous dermatitis was observed in several adult individuals, generally over forty years of age. The nutritional status of infants, children, and adults is characterized by an excess of carbohydrates, which probably tends to interfere with the absorption of the vitamin B complex, and by a low protein level.

A few cases of tuberculosis in adults came to our attention and were treated in the nearest hospital. Venereal diseases seemed to be rather infrequent. A few individuals had contracted malaria during work or travel in the lowlands, and two cases diagnosed as typhoid fever were treated in the hospital of the nearest lowland town.

Tooth decay is common and toothache is a very frequent complaint. Few people after twenty years of age have conserved all their teeth and often the upper incisors are badly decayed or missing altogether. Decay commonly begins soon after puberty has been attained and popular belief attributes it directly to the coming of age. Traveling 'dentists' will extract decayed teeth and some people have healthy teeth removed also in order to avoid suffering in the future. Sets of false teeth are unknown, and only among the more educated are there a few who have gold teeth made by dentists in the lowland towns.

Among adults there are eight cases of dumbness, five women and three men, all from the Loma barrio. Although they show in other respects a fairly normal development, they are said to have suffered from this affliction since birth, and it is believed that witchcraft was the cause of their being born that way. Fourteen people under fifty years of age are found to suffer from acute deafness, two of them since childhood. About fifteen people under sixty years are partially or totally blind and several of them are said to have been born blind. Strabism is observed in six others. Severe speech disturbances are observed in eight men, seven women, and three children between six and ten years of age, all of them of lomero families, with the exception of one man. We are told that all these individuals have stuttered since childhood. Four adults suffer from continuous clonic spasms of the whole body, being able to walk only with great difficulty. Fourteen adults (ten men and four women), suffer from advanced mental diseases, probably schizophrenia of hebephrenic and catatonic type. Four of the male cases do not live in the village, but in its vicinity. Eight cases of nanism occur in otherwise relatively normal adults. There are six cases of polydactylia. Goiter was observed in nineteen women and four men. Eighteen people over forty years old (six men and twelve women), are considered sterile. Although all of these people except one woman have lived for years with partners of the opposite sex, they have no offspring and that they are sterile is believed by themselves and acknowledged by everybody else.

There are seven children under eight years of age who suffer from the following symptoms: great difficulty in walking, inability to speak except for making incomprehensible sounds, clonic spasms of the upper part of the body accompanied by rhythmic rocking of the head while sitting or lying, more or less pronounced idiocy. In three of these cases vision is impaired, the child being able to perceive moving objects at a distance of some 80 centimeters but no farther. All of these children are said to have been born with a blood-filled 'bladder' (*vejiga*) on their heads. This is believed to have been caused by the violent methods employed by the midwife.

There is much talk in the village about people who have *ataques* ('fits'), a condition which is generally attributed to sorcery. Although the same term is used for both sexes, in men these fits are always associated with *loquera* ('madness'), but in women this is not the case. From the cases we have observed personally or on which we have detailed information, it seems that there occur two different types of fits, epileptoid seizures and hysteroid phenomena, the first being manifest in both sexes, whereas the second is largely limited to women (thirty-two cases). About twenty people, among them two or three adolescents and four or five children between six and eight years, suffer from epileptoid fits. They all claim to know for hours and even days in advance when such a fit is about to occur, and it is said that their occurrence coincides with the phases of the moon. The symptoms are first of all a depressed feeling followed by strong pains in the back of the head, dizziness, and finally unconsciousness. The individual falls suddenly to the ground in violent convulsions, often in a fetal position; the eyeballs are turned upward and the closed fists are pressed against the chest while the forearms are twisted in a muscular spasm as if trying to break a stick or rope. During the first stage, these people often wander off and are found later in distant and lonely places where they have fallen unconscious. It is said that when the fit occurs inside the house or the backyard these people often fall into the hearthfire, where they burn themselves or hurt their heads against the stones which support the cooking vessels. Many people believe that the victims of these fits fall intentionally into the fire (*buscan la candela*). In all cases, without exception, people who suffer from such fits are said to have been born under great difficulties, birth having been delayed for hours, or even days, making it necessary for the midwife to 'extract' the child. However, people do not seem to think it possible that this might have been the cause of these ailments in later life, and believe instead that they are due to sorcery (*los pusieron así*). All the victims of such seizures were from the Loma barrio.

The fits which seize women have quite different symptoms. Melancholia and headaches are followed by a state of great excitement, screams, tears, and violent spasms of the whole body. The person does not fall uncontrollably, but throws herself upon the floor or bed, with the head bent far backward, arms parallel to the body in a tonic cramp, and hands clutching the bedcloth or the skirt. Often the entire body stiffens and bends in an arch and then begins to sway in a rocking motion which may last for hours. Many women say that they feel a 'ball' (*pelota*) wandering about in their abdomen. The patient never loses consciousness, although she often talks incoherently. While a man's fits are feared because the patient is likely to receive harm when falling, a woman's fits are never thought to be very dangerous. They always occur inside the house and, characteristically, in the presence of other people. Although never ridiculed, these fits in women are considered a nuisance, a 'vagary' (*vagabundina*), and in the opinion of men their only aim is to impress and frighten the husband. The women, however, say that they are suffering from 'tuberculosis of the uterus' (*tisis matricida*). Women who suffer from such fits are generally over twenty-five years old and have had several children. The immediate cause of the seizure is often a fight with the husband, jealousy, or fear of physical aggression when the man is drunk. Although women with these fits are most frequently from the Loma, there are also some cases among the inhabitants of the Plaza barrio.

Five women, all of them over forty years old and of native Indian stock, complain of still another type of fit. The first symptoms are asphyxia and the complete inability to speak or scream. One of them, however, said, 'I feel so ill I do not want to speak.' Unconsciousness follows, lasting from one to three hours, after which a violent headache in the back of the head sets in. Strong pains between the shoulder blades and in the neck muscles are also said to be characteristic. The victims of these fits claim that rage and resentment against their daughters or nieces are the immediate causes.

Cases of somnambulism are said to be quite frequent and many people, most of them boys and young men, were pointed out to us as sleepwalkers. The pattern most frequently observed in sleepwalking consists of the individual's taking up his tools, such as machetes, carrying bags, and the like, and leaving the house as if to go to work in the fields; or taking a spindle to the backyard as if to spin thread; or leaving for the river with a large gourd container for fetching water. Sometimes the sleepwalker talks or mumbles to himself, thus waking other members of the household. According to local belief, a sleepwalker is under the influence of an evil spirit who tries to lead his victim astray so he might get killed by falling over a precipice or into a pool. For this reason, one should never call a sleepwalker by his name when trying to call him back to consciousness, but by a holy name like Jesús, José, or María. Upon waking there is usually complete amnesia about the occurrence, but occasionally a person will remember certain actions and will claim to have been awake while performing them. It is quite possible that the frequency of sleepwalking is related to scoptophilic tendencies, and the fact that sleepwalkers are said to try sometimes to carry off sleeping women or girls as 'companions' on their walks proves the presence of a sexual component in local somnambulistic patterns. We shall keep these considerations in mind when, later on, we discuss a series of hallucinatory phenomena.

Sexual aberrations form part of the general picture of mental health of the community and must be mentioned here. A relatively large number of people, about one dozen males and an equal number of females, are said to be homosexuals and are publicly mentioned by name as such. With very few exceptions they belong to the poorer section of the village and are of Indian phenotype. Some of them, mostly the women, are said to engage also in heterosexual relations and most of the latter have children. While male homosexuals (*maricos*) never live together, females (*areperas*) are said to do so frequently, and we were told of several cases where two women were known to have lived together for several months or years in such a relationship. Homosexuals are ridiculed or ignored, and people are likely to shrug off the matter by saying that every human being has 'his own inclinations'. Several cases of incestuous relations were also pointed out to us. Mother-son relationships were said to be absent, but incest between father and daughter, or brother and sister is said to occur occasionally. From some of these relations offspring are said to have been born, but our informants claimed that all these children showed some marked physical malformation and were therefore immediately killed by their mothers. Public opinion does not seem to condemn infanticide under these conditions. Although considered abnormal and even punishable, incest itself is not thought to be a very serious matter and is condemned mainly because children born from such unions are thought to be deformed or crippled in some way. All our informants assured us that most teenage boys, and also many young men over twenty, have occasional sexual contacts with animals, generally asses, mules, or cows. Some men are said to claim that intercourse with animals is more gratifying than with women, and many informants volunteered the names of their acquaintances who usually engage in such contacts. Sexual relations with animals are not condemned or punished in any way, but they are ridiculed and there are many jokes about them, especially about offspring of animals known to have been used so. The frequency of this practice during adolescence was explained by our informants as being due to the fact that women reject boys and young men who are unable to pay for sexual favours because they are still dependent upon their families.

There were four cases of male transvestism in the village, a large number for so small a population. One had died shortly before our arrival; another had moved to a neighbouring village; but we met the remaining two cases. One of a man about forty years of age who since early childhood has worn female dress. He lives with his grandmother and several small children that she is taking care of for relatives, and the transvestite is the only economically active member of the household, being a hard-working farmer. As a matter of fact, he is well known for his tireless work in the fields and for his physical strength and is often employed as a hired laborer. The other case is a twenty-year-old youth who lives with his family (father, mother, and several siblings) and who also has habitually worn female dress since childhood. No physical malformation seems to be involved in either of these cases, both of which, according to all informants, have normal male sexual organs, but it seems that both are sterile. We were told that all had at one time or another lived with female companions but that in spite of apparently normal sexual relations they had never procreated children. However, their apparent sterility is certainly not the cause of their transvestism, because they all had worn female clothing during childhood. Parents and neighbors said that they had never tried to influence their behavior but had let them wear female dress as they wished. All transvestites wear long hair and are known by female names. In the village, they are not regarded as mentally deranged but, rather, enjoy a certain prestige as being good workers and providers for their families. Homosexual tendencies are not suspected of them and do not seem to be present. In personal contact the transvestites are shy but affable. Both speak in a high-pitched female voice which only betrays their sex when they are made to laugh. In our presence they always acted normally, i.e., in accordance with local patterns of conduct, except that they did both male and female chores in and around the house. It is remarkable that all cases of transvestism, including the one who had died recently, were of a definite Indian phenotype and were members of very poor families.

As is evident from the foregoing description, the overall quality of the health status of the inhabitants is deficient in many respects. How this situation affects cultural patterns we shall see in the following chapters, but first we shall have to discuss some aspects of food and nutrition.

THE AVAILABILITY AND ACQUISITION OF FOOD

Aritama has always been an agricultural community the members of which produced almost all the food they consumed. Until around the middle of the last century, the villagers seem to have been almost completely self-sufficient, much like the neighboring Indians are today, producing all they ate except salt, which was brought from the coast by occasional traders. During the second half of the nineteenth century, however, the new settlers introduced a new dietary pattern, characterized by the use of beef, rice, flour, fats, and oils. These immigrants monopolized cattle-breeding as well as shops and transportation, and they also controlled these new foodstuffs, which, although at first associated with race and class concepts, soon became an essential part of the local food habits. As a matter of fact, the serious lack of land available for agricultural purposes, together with the upsurge in population and the introduction of cash crops and a monetary economy, made the acquisition of commercial foods a necessity. People began to depend heavily upon rice and fats to supplement their inadequate local resources.

The basic incentives for food production in Aritama are manifold. (1) Food is a biological necessity which has to be satisfied by the individual at short periodic intervals. (2) Food is produced for social reasons, i.e., to acquire prestige. The producer's role in society as owner, provider, and distributor is a very important one. (3) The production of food can be evaluated in terms of economic gain, either indirectly as commercial cash crops or directly as food for daily family consumption. Thus, food is produced to satisfy individual needs in spheres other than the merely nutritional or societal, for it plays an important role in the maintenance of the individual's security system.

The quality and quantity of food depend upon several factors. On the one hand, they are determined by the natural resources of the vicinity and by the availability of imported goods. The very nature of the land (i.e., its arability, fertility, and location), and the climate (i.e., seasons, rainfall, altitude) influence, of course, the kind of crops grown. The fauna and flora native to this vicinity (i.e., game, fish, wild-growing fruits and other native food-producing plants) are important factors. On the other hand, they are culturally conditioned by a marked selectivity in use. Some foods are preferred to others. Certain potential foods are ignored, or used only sparingly. New foods are accepted reluctantly, their generalized use imposing itself very slowly. The commercially acquired foodstuffs are also highly subject to selection, their consumption depending largely upon the economic situation of the consumer, upon his prestige system, his health concepts, his individual preferences, and, above all, his empirical knowledge of them. These commercial foods are either brought in from the lowland towns where they are produced or are imported from industrial towns. This progressive and interrelated selection is determined partly by the merchants and shopkeepers, who buy only products they know they can sell, partly by the consumer, whose limited choice and taste tend to establish preferential patterns and definite buying habits.

The problems arising out of availability and biological necessity, out of economic possibility and prestige factors i.e., out of physiological concepts, as opposed to culturally conditioned reactions toward food, have led to the adoption of a complex pattern of changing attitudes, by which the social and individual aspects of food are adapted to the nutritional necessity.

Table 2 contains all the locally cultivated food plants, together with their common local names, and their botanical classifications.

TABLE 2

English	*Local Name*	*Latin*
Plantain, cooking banana	Plátano	*Musa paradisiaca*
Banana	Guinéo	*Musa sapientium*
Sweet manioc	Yuca	*Manihot dulcis*
Taro, dasheen	Malanga	*Xanthosoma* sp. ; *Colocasia* sp.
Sweet potato	Batata	*Ipomea batatas*
Arracacha	Arracacha	*Arracacia xanthorrhiza*
Yam	Ñame	*Dioscorea alata*
Potato	Papa	*Solanum tuberosum*
Arrowroot	Perico	*Marantha arundinacea* (?)
Maize	Maíz	*Zea Mays* L. var.
Pigeon pea	Guandú	*Cajanus indicus; Cajanus cajan* L.
Onion	Cebolla	*Allium cepa*
Shallots (?)	Cebollín	Indet.
Cabbage	Col	*Brassica oleracea* L. var.
Sugar cane	Caña de azúcar	*Saccharum officinarum*
Squash	Calabaza	*Cucurbita pepo*
Pumpkin	Ahuyama	*Cucurbita* sp.
Watermelon	Patilla	*Citrullus vulgaris* Schrad.
Tomato	Tomate	*Lycopersicon* sp.
Lettuce	Lechuga	*Lactuca sativa* L.
Sorghum	Maíz millo	*Sorghum vulgare* Pers. var.
Eggplant	Berenjena	*Solanum melongena* var.
Broad beans	Habichuela	*Vicia faba* (?)
Swordbean	Fríjol cacao	*Canavalia ensiformis* (L) DC.
Swordbean	Fríjol de arroz	*Phaseolus angularis* (*Willd.*) Wight.
Kidney beans	Fríjol negro	*Phaseolus vulgaris* var.
Kidney beans	Fríjol cuarentano	*Phaseolus vulgaris var.*
Kidney beans	Fríjol rojo	*Phaseolus vulgaris* var.
Kidney beans	Fríjol indio	*Phaseolus vulgaris* var.
Kidney beans	Juan Pobre	*Phaseolus* sp.
Beans (*Lablab bean*)	Fríjol macuío	*Dolichos Lablab* L.
Beans	Fríjol macuco	*Dolichos* sp. (?)
Beans	Fríjol mindoca	*Dolichos* sp. (?)
Beans	Fríjol subalo	*Vigna* sp.
Beans	Fríjol café	*Stizolobium* sp.
Hot peppers	Pimienta picante	*Capsicum frutescens* L.

TABLE 2 (continued)

English	Local Name	Latin
Chili peppers	Pimiento dulce	*Capsicum frutescens* var.
Anatto	Achiote	*Bixa orellana*
Ginger	Ajengibre	*Zingiber officinale*
Coriander	Cilantro	*Coriandrum sativum* L.
Coffee	Café	*Coffea arabica* L.

Table 3 lists the animals hunted or collected for food.

TABLE 3

English	Local Name	Latin
Deer	Venado	*Odocoilus virginianus*
Deer	Cauquero	*Mazama americana*
Collared peccari	Zahíno	*Pecari tajaçu*
White-lipped peccari	Manáo	*Tayassu pecari*
Paca	Guatinaja	*Agouti paca*
Agouti	Ñeque	*Dasyprocta variegata*
Armadillo	Armadillo	*Dasypus novemcinctus*
Opossum	Chucha	*Didelphis marsupialis*
Squirrel	Ardita	*Sciurus granatensis*
Tapir	Danta	*Tapirus terrestris colombianus*
Spider monkey	Marimonda	*Ateles belzebuth*
Porcupine	Puerco espin	*Coëndu prehensilis*
Rabbit	Conejo	*Sylvilagus floridianus* spp.
Iguana	Iguana	*Iguana iguana*
Tegu	Lobo	*Tupinambis nigropunctatus*
Basilisk	Passaroyo	*Basiliscus basiliscus barbouri*
South American tortoise	Morrocón	*Testudo denticulata*
Boa constrictor	Boa	*Boa constrictor imperator*
Snails	Caracoles	Indet.
Worms, larvae	Gusanos	*Calandra palmarum*
Fresh-water crab	Cangrejo	*Potamon fluviatilis*
Small river fish	Cheba	Indet.
Eel-like fish	Chebanguma	Indet.
Edible ants	Hormigas, dín	*Atta* sp.

The following domestic animals are consumed: cattle, pigs, goats, sheep, turkeys, ducks, chickens, cats.

Table 4 contains all wild fruits which are gathered occasionally, but which are not cultivated.

53

TABLE 4

English	Local Name	Latin
Avocado	Aguacate	*Persea americana*
Mango	Mango	*Mangifera indica*
Pineapple	Piña	*Ananas comosus* (L.) Merrill
Papaya	Papaya	*Carica papaya*
Custard apple	Chirimoya	*Annona cherimolia*
Hog plum	Ciruela de España	*Spondias purpurea*
Hog plum	Ciruela cueruda	*Spondias* sp. (?)
Tamarind	Tamarindo	*Tamarindus indicus* L.
Orange	Naranja	*Citrus sinensis*
Shaddock	Toronja	*Citrus grandis* Osbeck
Lemon	Limón	*Citrus limonia* Osbeck
Lime	Lima	*Citrus aurantifolia* (?)
Sapota	Zapote	*Matisia cordata*
Mamey, mammee	Mamey	*Mammea americana*
Guava	Guayaba	*Psidium guajava*
Bullock's heart	Guanábana	*Annona muricata*
Custard apple (?)	Anón	*Annona* sp.
Tuna	Tuna	*Opuntia* spp.
Carob tree	Algarrobo	*Hymenaea courbaril* L.
Guamo	Guama	*Inga* spp.
	Níspero	*Achras zapota* L.
	Reviacano	*Alibertia edulis* (L. Rich) A. Rich.
	Sazao	*Hirtella* (?)
	Uvita	*Cavendishia* sp. (?)
	Jamanare	*Cassia grandis* L.
	Palmito	*Sabal mauritiiformis*
	Jaguito	*Cenipa caruto* H.B.K.
	Caracolí	*Anarcadium excelsum*
	Mora	*Clidemia hirta* (L.) G. Don; *Rubus* spp.
	Curumuta	*Scheelea butyracea* L.
	Lagrimita	*Chiococca alba* (L.) Hitch.
	Granada	*Citrus nobilis* Lour (?)
	Granadilla	*Passiflora* spp.
	Cotoprix	*Talisia olivaeformis* Radlk.
	Corozo	*Palmaceae;* several spp.
	Tamaco	*Palmaceae*
	Perehuétano	*Moquilea* sp.
	Bessa	*Bromelia* spp.
	Piñuela	*Aechmea* sp., *Bromelia* sp.
	Batatilla	Indet.
	Manzana	Indet.
	Candunga	Indet.
	Salva real	Indet.
	Lata negra	Indet.
	Zapotillo amarillo	Indet.

Wild honey is collected occasionally and some people keep domesticated bees. Small green algae, called *lama* or *brama*, which appear in stagnant water, are also consumed at times.

The following foods, some of which may be produced locally, are available at stores: rice, cheese, macaroni and spaghetti, dried fish, flour, maize, butter, lard, oats, crackers, sugar, cornstarch, cooking oil, fat, canned goods (sardines, deviled meat, powdered milk). Some are manufactured for commercial purposes by individuals in their own houses, such as raw sugar, cheese, fat, butter, bread, tortillas, sweets (*chiricanas, quéques, almohábanas, merengues, panelitas, alfandoques, pandero, paletas*).

The following condiments are bought at stores: salt, clove, cumin seed, cinnamon, garlic. The following beverages are locally available: milk (cow's and goat's), coffee, herb teas, chocolate, coconut milk, fermented sugar-cane juice (*guarapo*), homemade rum (*chirrinche*). Imported commercial beverages bought at stores are beer, rum, carbonated soft drinks, tinned or bottled fruit juices, and sometimes wine.

Among food substitutes can be counted the following: tobacco (cigars, cigarettes, pipe tobacco) and chewing gum. Geophagy is frequent in children and some adults, as is also the consuming of rotten wood. Pieces of sugar cane are chewed, and the wax from candles, or a waxy substance called *entrechispe*, which is formed in certain subterranean honeycombs. Small amounts of ashes are eaten occasionally.

The availability of these foods is, of course, subject to seasonal changes, altitudinal influences, the quality of the yearly crops, and the economic resources of the consumer. Most people cultivate only a few staple foods, the exact choice depending upon the individual's preferences and upon the nature of his fields. The cultivation of crops of lesser importance is a highly individual matter. Some people 'like' to plant maize but others don't; some gather wild fruits whereas others prefer to buy them or to go without them. The amount of economic collaboration within the family unit determines to a high degree the kind of secondary crops planted. Adults will hardly ever gather wild fruits, while children do not hunt or fish; ants and grubs are gathered by women and children, while wild honey is collected only by men.

The basic staple foods most commonly cultivated are sweet manioc, taro, plantains, and bananas. These foods are found in practically all fields in the vicinity of the village and constitute the fundamental diet of the inhabitants. All others can be said to be relatively scarce. Many of them are available only on very rare occasions. Maize is always scarce in Aritama because it is best suited to lower altitudes. For sugar cane Aritama is the lower altitudinal limit. No sweet potato is planted in the vicinity of the village, but rather in the region bordering on the lowlands. The lower limit for arracacha is at about 1,200 meters, while potatoes are planted only by the neighboring Indians, at still higher elevations. The larger fruit trees, such as mango, avocado, or papaya, are found near the village, but smaller varieties have to be gathered at considerable distances. Vegetables such as beans, tomatoes, cabbage, etc., although planted in and near the village, are always scarce.

The monthly and seasonal availability of the most important foods is given in Table 5.

TABLE 5

Season	Dry			Rainy		Dry			Rainy			
Months	I	II	III	IV	V	VI	VII	VIII	IX	X	XI	XII
Sweet manioc	x	x	x	x	–	x	xs	x	x	x	x	x
Taro	x	x	x	x	x	x	x	x	x	x	x	x
Plantain	x	x	x	x	–	x	xs	x	x	x	x	x
Banana	x	x	x	x	–	x	xs	x	x	x	x	x
Arracacha	x	x	x	x	–	x	x	x	x	x	x	x
Yams	x	x	x	–	–	–	–	–	x	–	–	–
Sweet potato	x	x	x	–	–	–	–	–	x	–	–	–
Maize	–	–	–	–	–	x	x	x	–	–	–	–
Potato	x	x	x	–	–	–	–	–	–	–	–	–
Pigeon pea	x	x	x	–	–	–	–	–	–	–	–	x
Kidney beans	–	–	x	x	–	x	x	–	–	–	x	–
Mango	–	–	–	x	x	x	–	–	–	–	–	–
Avocado	–	–	–	x	x	x	–	–	–	–	–	–
Papaya	x	x	x	x	x	x	x	x	x	x	x	x
Pumpkin	–	–	–	x	x	x	–	x	x	x	x	x
Minor fruits	–	x	x	x	x	x	x	x	x	x	x	–
Hunting	x	x	x	–	–	–	–	–	–	–	–	–
Fishing	x	x	x	xs	–	–	–	–	–	–	–	xs
Iguanas	x	x	x	–	–	–	–	–	–	–	–	xs
Beef, pork	xs	xs	xs	x	x	x	x	x	x	x	x	xs
Dried fish	x	x	x	xs	–	–	–	–	–	–	–	xs

NOTE: x — available; xs — available but scarce; – — not available.

Table 5 calls for some additional comments. Sweet potato and arracacha are not grown in the vicinity but at considerable distance and are, therefore, hardly ever available in the village. The same can be said about maize, which generally is imported from neighboring settlements in the lowlands. Potatoes are practically unavailable, as the Indians sell only very small quantities. Hunting and fishing have hardly any importance, as very few people will spend their time in these pursuits; and the gathering of wild fruits, except avocados and mangoes, is mainly a pastime for children. Such fruits as papayas or pumpkins are not at all commonly available. Cattle are slaughtered several times a week, but there is never sufficient meat for all buyers. Pigs are slaughtered only rarely. Occasionally such foods as maize, pumkins, bananas, dried fish, or peas are stored by the shopkeepers to be sold at times when they become scarce or unavailable, but usually they are eaten immediately. Eggs and milk are consumed by most people in such minor quantities as to be insignificant in the dietary habits.

The two rainy seasons are periods of relative scarcity, and May is an especially difficult month for most people. However, during April and May there is generally cash from the last coffee harvest, and therefore food can be bought.

The basic foods available all year round, therefore, are taro, sweet manioc, plantains, and bananas. These are supplemented by a few vegetables and by commercial foods such as rice, cheese, raw sugar, and fats. The consumption of these commercial foods and the general quantity and variety of foods consumed depend largely upon whether or not the consumer owns cash crops, cattle, or a shop. Many families depend for cash entirely upon the weaving of fiber hats, the sale of which hardly furnishes them enough to buy additional food.

There is a considerable difference between the availability of food for the twenty-five more Creole-oriented placero families and for the rest of the inhabitants. The former buy most of their food, including such items as eggs, milk, or onions, which the poorer people prefer to sell for cash rather than eat. Meat, cheese, fats, and oils are also common foodstuffs in the Plaza barrio but are seldom eaten by the poorer inhabitants.

The general availability of food has changed considerably during the last hundred years. Although the soil never seems to have been particularly fertile, the slash-and-burn technique of agriculture has led to extensive deforestation and progressive desiccation of the land, reducing its productivity to the present minimum. The increasing population and the increased use of the limited agricultural lands for grazing or cash crops have necessarily decimated the food resources. Game and fish, although probably never very abundant, have been depleted seriously by the periodic burnings and the consequent drying-up of rivers and creeks. The lack of crop rotation and fertilizers and inadequate selection of seeds are also responsible for the poor yield of such important food crops as maize. Many foods have to be bought in order to supplement the poor diet offered by the locally cultivated crops.

At the same time, the dietary habits are changing slowly under the influence of the new contact situation. Some foods are beginning to be considered 'Indian', whereas others have a high prestige value as being 'civilized'.

Fundamental Conditions of Individual Existence

The majority of local foodstuffs are processed by the consumer, generally by the women and children, while men take charge of most commercial processing. As a rule, women and children help in harvesting activities, and during the week any member of the family may go to the field in order to bring back a few fruits which will last for the next few days. In the late afternoon people arrive from all directions, taking food to their houses, some carrying it on their backs, some driving burros or oxen loaded with carrying nets.

The vegetable foods need very little preparation. They are washed, shelled, skinned, or peeled, cut or broken into pieces, and after being boiled for a while are ready to be eaten. Meat bought at the slaughterhouse is hardly ever washed or salted, but simply cut into irregular slices and boiled together with the tubers and vegetables. The basic diet is, therefore, ready for consumption in less than an hour after being brought from the field, little time or effort having been spent on its preparation previous to consumption. The same can be said of most of the other foodstuffs that may be consumed occasionally. No foods are smoked, cured, or salted away, and no by-products such as flour, starch, oils, or fermented preparations are derived from the basic staple foods.

Cooking facilities are simple. Most houses have a 'cooking house' (*cocina*), a small outbuilding often devoid of walls, consisting only of a gabled roof on a few posts. However, some of the poorer families cook in the backyard, without benefit of roof or, in case of rain, inside the living quarters. The most common type of cooking hearth consists of three stones (*tacán*) placed on the floor in a triangle. The firewood is placed from three sides between the stones, and the cooking vessel is placed upon them. Some houses situated near a more or less vertical gully have a subterranean hearth. At a convenient altitude near the flat surface of the barranco, a horizontal cavity is dug into the wall, connected with a short vertical hole, on top of which the cooking vessel is placed. Braziers (*anafes*) are also used; they consist of a cylindrical container woven of strips of tin plate manufactured in the lowland villages. They are filled with glowing embers, and the vessel is placed over them. In the Plaza barrio many houses have a hearth on a raised platform (*hornilla*) constructed with adobe bricks. The flat surface is about 1 meter above the floor, and small cubicles are built on it with bricks, each to hold a cooking vessel. This type of hearth is found only in specially constructed cooking houses and occupies a square area of some 2 by 2 meters. Kerosene stoves are found in the houses of a few highly educated families. They are bought in the lowland towns, at one of the government agencies where inexpensive farming equipment is sold. A few baking houses are also found, mostly in the Plaza barrio.

They consist of a beehive-shaped adobe-plastered structure that rests upon a table-like support, all of it covered with a thatched roof, but without walls. They are used only for baking bread. The various hearth types are often found in combination. The most widely used, however, is the one formed of three stones.

Kitchen utensils show little variety. The only earthenware in use are large red subglobular jars with a thickened rim, which are imported from the lowlands and serve for storing water. These water jars (*tinajas*) contain only drinking water for daily use and are placed in a corner of a room. All cooking vessels are made of aluminum or cast iron. The most common form is a 3- to 5-gallon aluminum pot with a flat bottom, a basket handle of strong wire, and a flat, circular lid provided with a small D-shaped handle. Smaller vessels of the same type are used for preparing beverages, such as coffee. Low cast-iron frying-pans, with small lug handles through which a wire is drawn, are used for frying meat, eggs, toasting coffee, and preparing rice. Water for cooking or cleaning is carried, and stored, in square 5-gallon tin cans, originally used for commercially processed fats. The poorer people carry and store water in large pear-shaped containers made of the fruit of a calabash tree (*Cucurbita maxima*). The neck is either cut off, or laterally perforated, and closed again with a corncob or some folded leaves. Common aluminum washbasins are in general use in most kitchens, for storing cooked foods, washing dishes, or even for serving. A great number of vegetable containers (*totumas*) are used. They are hemispherical or elongated in shape and are made of the dried fruit of the *totuma* tree (*Crescentia cujete*). Most people use them as plates or cups for eating and drinking. Larger shapes (*bangañas*), used for storing cooked food during the day, are made from a calabash cut in half. Flat circular vessels of heavy wood (*bateas*) are used for shelling peas, storing cooked food, serving food, or washing other utensils. Old tin cans that contained powdered milk or oats are widely used for making coffee. Only in a few houses of Creole-oriented placeros is food served at a table in dishes or plates of cheap porcelain or enamel-ware. Most people use only the vegetable containers described, or eat from the cooking vessel.

A wooden mortar (*pilón*), a large, cup-shaped trunk about 1 meter in height with a double-headed pestle with thickened cylindrical extremes, is used for pounding maize, coffee, or cacao beans to remove the hulls. Flat stones of approximately circular shape are sometimes used for pounding meat or grinding corn, with an elongated, loaf-shaped muller. However, metal grinders, usually made in the United States, are found in most houses and are used for maize, coffee, cacao, and meat.

Only the placeros use metal forks, knives, or spoons, most people preferring to eat with their fingers, using a piece of totuma shell as a spoon for soup. To stir the soup, a long, straight, wooden spatular-shaped instrument is used, some of them adorned with laterally cut-out decorations. Quite often, however, a stick of firewood is used for the same purpose. For shelling or skinning fruits and tubers a piece of an old machete, a kitchen knife, or a sharp splinter of wood may be used. A bent piece of tin plate, covered with holes made with a thick nail, is used as a grater, while a similarly perforated totuma shell is used as a strainer or colander. A small perforated totuma shell of spherical shape, provided with a hole and a stopper and fixed to a handle, is used as a shaker for anotto (*achiote*). In about 20 per cent of all houses United States–made thermos bottles are found, but most of them are damaged and have only prestige value.

Most people eat in the living-room (*sala*), sitting in a semicircle on the floor. The cooking vessel of food is placed in the middle, and each person dips his spoon into it, or takes the food with his fingers. As mentioned above, in the Plaza barrio some people have their food served at a table and eat on plates, but even many of these prefer to eat in the kitchen from a wooden dish or a washbasin. There are no napkins or kitchen towels. After the adults have finished, the children scrape all leftovers from the vessels and dishes, and then some water is poured into them and they are left for the pigs and dogs to clean very thoroughly. Sometimes a vessel is scraped with leaves, ashes, or sand.

Very few foods are stored for long. Yams, taro, and pumpkins can be kept for some time without spoiling if a piece of the stem is left on them, but few people will bother to store these foods. Plantains and bananas can be sun-dried and strung on a thread or wire, but this is done only very rarely. The practice of preserving and storing food for future use is entirely absent. People eat whatever is available at the moment.

Practically all cooking is done by women, generally by the female head of the family, although her daughters may help her, or even replace her in case of illness or temporary absence. The first task in the morning is to make fire, either with a match, or by borrowing a few embers from a neighbor. First, boiled black coffee and then the first meal of the day are prepared. The woman crouches on the floor and takes the fruits or tubers from the carrying nets lying in a corner of the kitchen or cooking house. Plantains and bananas are skinned by making a longitudinal slit with an old knife and peeling off the skin. Tubers are never scraped. Instead, the skin is cut off with a knife, wasting a considerable portion of edible matter. Often the fruits or tubers are thrown whole into a vessel to be cooked, sometimes they are hacked or broken into pieces, or cut into slices. The pieces are put into a large wooden dish, and some water is added to them. If the food is to be fried, the slices are very thin, but as it is usually boiled, they measure about 5 centimeters in diameter. The pieces are then put into an aluminum vessel filled to the top with cold water to which some salt may have been added. After about half of the water has been absorbed or evaporated, the pot is taken from the fire, and the food is ready to eat.

According to their general dietary habits, the people of Aritama can be classified into three groups. The first, made up of about 90 per cent of the inhabitants, includes those whose basic diet consists of a stew (*sancocho*) of manioc, plantain and some green leaves. The remaining 10 per cent are divided between two groups: (1) the educated placeros, who, although they also eat this same stew every day, occasionally add to it some other foods such as rice, meat, tortillas, eggs, or sweets, and (2) a very small group composed of shopowners and a few other people of comparative wealth who eat such food regularly.

With reference to the composition of the meal, three basic types can be established. The first consists of one or several of the staple foods such as manioc, plantains, or taro boiled in abundant water in a single vessel. Only a little salt is added, and maybe some onion or a few green leaves. Rarely a piece of meat or fish is put into it. The water is consumed with the solid food. The second type consists of foods which are baked, roasted, or fried, little or no water being used in the process. Such a meal may consist of several dishes prepared individually, such as rice, roasted meat, fried plantains. The third type of meal, distinguished by the use of flour and sugar, includes bread, thick soups, and a number of sweet foods. The three types occur, of course, in combination, but correspond to a considerable degree to the three groups outlined above.

The people of Aritama classify their prepared foods into several categories. The common diet of boiled stew is designated as 'soups' (*sopas*), whereas the cooked, roasted, or fried dishes are called 'dry foods' (*seco*), as the watery part is not consumed and the food has absorbed most of the liquid. The next category is the 'sweets' (*dulces*), which are prepared with imported sugar or with locally manufactured raw sugar. A fourth category consists of the 'doughs' (*amasijos*), i.e., foods made of flour and prepared by baking. Beverages are classified into 'refreshments' (*refrescos*), which are unfermented fruit drinks, water sweetened with raw sugar, or commercial soft carbonated drinks. Beverages such as coffee, chocolate, milk, or any medicinal potion, are called 'doses' (*tomas*), while the so-called 'drinks' (*tragos*) refer only to inebriating liquids.

In Table 6 we have arranged all known food preparations according to this classification.

TABLE 6

Soups: (*a*) Without meat   *cunche* (stew)
sancocho de piedra (stew)
mazamorra de sal (corn soup)

(*b*) With meat   *sancocho* (stew)
viuda (steamed tubers)

Dry food: (*a*) Cooked   *arroz seco* (rice)
arroz con pollo (boiled rice with chicken)
arroz de leche con sal (boiled rice with milk)
bollo de maíz (boiled corn dough)
bollo de queso (same with cheese added)
bollo de mazorca (same of green corn)
mazorca cocida (corn on the cob)
pastas (spaghetti, macaroni)
pastel (tamal)
lomo relleno (stuffed beef loin)
hígado de res (beef liver)
frijoles de sal (boiled beans)
guandú de sal (boiled pigeon peas)

(*b*) Fried   meat
fowl
eggs
manioc
plantain slices
buñuelos de yuca (manioc doughnuts)
roscas de maíz (corn doughnuts)

(*c*) Roasted   meat
fowl
plantain
manioc
tortillas

Sweets: (*a*) With sugar   *dulce de toronja* (shaddock preserve)
dulce de tomate (tomato preserve)
dulce de leche (sweet condensed milk)

(*b*) With raw sugar   *guandú de dulce* (sweetened pigeon peas)
frijoles de dulce (sweetened beans)
arroz de leche (rice with sweetened milk)
arroz de coco (rice with sweetened coconut)
arroz de queso (rice with cheese)
mazamorra de maíz fresco (green corn gruel)
mazamorra de maíz dulce (sweetened corn gruel)

62

dulce de arracacha (mashed arracacha)
dulce de ahuyama (mashed pumpkin)
dulce de maduro (mashed plantains)
cocadas de panela (coconut brown sugar bars)
cocadas de leche (coconut milk bars)
cocadas de piña (coconut pineapple bars)

Doughs: (a) With sugar   *pan de dulce* (sweetbread)
cuques (cookies)
chiricanas (corn and coconut cookies)
almojábanas (curd cookies)

(b) With salt   *pan de sal* (bread)

Beverages   (a) Refreshments   *guarapo de piña* (diluted pineapple juice)
agua de panela (water with raw sugar)
limonada (lemonade)

(b) Doses   *tinto* (black coffee)
café con leche (coffee with milk)
chocolate (chocolate)
infusiones (herb teas)

(c) Drinks   *ron* (rum)
cerveza (beer)
vino (wine)

Table 7 groups together all known food preparations according to frequency of consumption. The 'Indian' (90 per cent) group is designated as A; the group of educated placeros as B, and the small subgroup of the latter as C.

TABLE 7

Preparation	*Normative*			*Optional*		*Festive*
Cunche	A	B	C			
Sancocho	A	B	C			
Sancocho de piedra	A	B	C			
Viuda	A	B	C			
Café tinto	A	B	C			
Agua de panela	A	B	C			
Queso (cheese)		B	C	A		
Leche (milk)			C		B	
Carne frita (fried meat)			C		B	
Huevos (eggs)			C	A	B	
Carne asada (roasted meat)			C	A	B	

Preparation	Normative	Optional	Festive
Arroz seco (boiled rice)	C	A B	
Bollo de maíz	C	A B	
Arepa de maíz (tortillas)	C	A B	
Tajadas de plátano (sliced plantains)	C	B	
Buñuelos de yuca	C	B	
Roscas de maíz	C	B	
Iguana	A	B	
Mazamorra de sal		A B C	
Bollo de queso		A B C	
Bollo de mazorca		A B C	
Pescado seco (dried fish)		A B C	
Fríjoles de sal		A B C	
Mazamorra de maíz fresco		A B C	
Mazorca cocinada		A B C	
Guandú de sal		A B C	
Chocolate		A B C	
Guarapo de piña		B C	
Dulce de maduro		B C	
Arroz de coco		B C	
Mazamorra de maíz dulce		B C	
Dulce de ahuyama		B C	
Plátano asado		B C	
Yuca asada		B C	
Pastas		B C	
Pollo, gallina (chicken)		B C	A
Chiricanas		B C	A
Cuques		B C	A
Pan		B C	A
Pasteles			A B C
Fríjoles de dulce			A B C
Guandú de leche			A B C
Arroz de leche			A B C
Arroz de queso			B C
Arroz de leche con sal			B C
Dulce de toronja			B C
Dulce de tomate			B C
Dulce de arracacha			B C
Dulce de leche			B C
Cocadas de leche			B C
Ensaladas (salads)			C
Lomo relleno			C

As can be clearly seen from the normative food category of group A (Table 7), representing about 90 per cent of the population, there are only four common food preparations, which are all very similar in their basic composition and which constitute the average diet of the inhabitants. The length of the list of optional foods is, therefore, really somewhat misleading if we take into account that only a few people of group A find them available. With the exception of cheese and rice, practically all these foods are taken on rare occasions, depending upon seasonal availability and upon the financial condition of the consumer. As a matter of fact, weeks or even months may pass when beef, eggs, beans, or bread are almost completely unavailable in the village. Milk is always scarce, and sweet desserts are for sale only at one shop, and there only occasionally. The different foods listed as festive are seen only once or twice a year and are used by only a very few people, the majority continuing to eat the everyday diet.

THE QUANTITY AND QUALITY OF FOOD

People in Aritama generally eat two meals daily, but some of the poorer families (about 20 per cent of the total population) eat only one meal a day or sometimes go without any formal meal for a few days each month. After rising in the morning, a cup of black coffee sweetened with raw sugar is taken and the first meal of the day (*desayuno*) is eaten between 8:30 and 9:30 A.M. The second meal (*almuerzo*) is eaten between 3 and 4 P.M. A small percentage of placeros, about ten families in all, eat three meals a day, the first (*desayuno*) around 7 A.M.; the second (*almuerzo*) about noon, and a third meal called (*comida*) at about 4 P.M. Between meals people often eat some fruit or chew a piece of sugar cane.

We selected six households and measured their daily food consumption during a ten-day period. This survey was made in September, a month fairly representative of the entire year. Of the families chosen, three were lomeros and three placeros, and each was considered to be representative of the barrio. Of all fruits or tubers consumed, the weights were taken both before and after peeling or shelling, and the figures stated in the following tables refer only to food actually eaten. Of practically all tubers, roots, or fruits, such as plantains and bananas, from 50 per cent to 60 per cent of the total weight is discarded as kitchen waste, but of some thin-skinned fruits such as pineapples, papayas, or onions, perhaps 70 per cent to 80 per cent is consumed.

There is reasonable certainty that the amounts shown for the three lomero families are realistic, but it seems very doubtful that the three placero families really have such a varied and plentiful diet as they would have us believe. Our interest in their food habits caused considerable unrest, and we are under the impression that the placero families added several foods during that special ten-day period in order to appear more prosperous and 'civilized'. However, the basic composition of the daily intake is pictured fairly accurately, if one discounts some of the prestige foods such as sardines, crackers, fowl, and some of the eggs.

Household A is a lomero family, and consists of a fifty-year-old woman and her two children, between ten and thirteen years of age. They own no land, but the children work in the fields of relatives and can take home some of the produce. All three individuals weave straw hats, which they sell at a store or exchange for commercial foods.

The total food consumption in ounces of Household A for the ten days is given in Table 8.

Household B, another lomero family, consists of an adult man, his wife, their adult unmarried daughter, and three children between six and twelve years of age. They own no field, but the house has a large backyard, where most of the foods used are raised. All members of the family weave straw hats, but the man is often sick and works very little, if at all. Their daily food intake in ounces is given in Table 9.

Household C is a very active lomero unit made up of an adult woman, two young men, and seven children between five and fourteen years of age. They own a small field at some distance from the village, and six members of the household weave straw hats. The food consumed by them is given in Table 10.

Household D is a fairly educated placero family composed of one man, two women, and three children two, ten, and eleven years old. The family owns a field but does not work it personally. They own a small shop, and only occasionally weave straw hats. Their dairly food intake, in ounces, is given in Table 11.

TABLE 8

Food	1	2	3	4	5	6	7	8	9	10
Coffee	2	2	2	2	2	2	2	2	2	2
Beef	—	8	—	—	8	8	8	—	4	4
Cheese	—	—	—	8	—	—	4	—	—	—
Eggs	1	—	—	—	—	—	—	—	—	—
Lard	—	—	—	8	—	—	4	—	—	—
Rice	—	—	4	—	4	—	—	—	—	1
Manioc	—	—	—	—	—	12	12	—	—	—
Plantains	20	16	—	—	—	32	—	20	32	36
Bananas	80	80	80	80	80	80	80	80	80	80
Shallots	—	1	—	—	2	3	1	—	—	—
Green leaves	—	—	—	—	1	—	—	—	—	—
Peppers	—	—	—	—	—	1	—	—	—	—
Raw sugar	5	5	5	5	5	5	5	5	5	5
Salt	1	1	—	—	1	—	$\frac{1}{2}$	1	$\frac{1}{2}$	1

TABLE 9

Food	1	2	3	4	5	6	7	8	9	10
Coffee	4	4	4	4	4	4	4	4	4	4
Beef	8	—	—	16	—	—	—	—	—	—
Fowl	—	—	—	—	32	—	—	—	—	—
Cheese	—	—	—	—	—	—	4	—	—	—
Lard	—	1	3	2	—	2	—	2	—	2
Rice	—	8	—	—	8	8	—	—	—	16
Manioc	10	8	—	48	—	—	24	32	32	24
Plantains	—	56	8	—	—	—	—	—	—	16
Bananas	48	48	120	56	32	40	64	84	72	32
Taro	12	—	—	—	—	—	—	—	24	—
Sweet potato	—	—	—	—	128	154	—	—	—	—
Kidney beans	—	24	—	—	—	12	—	8	—	—
Cabbage	—	—	—	16	—	—	—	—	—	—
Pumpkin	—	—	—	—	24	—	40	—	40	—
Tomato	—	—	16	8	8	12	—	16	—	16
Shallots	—	—	—	4	—	—	—	—	—	—
Raw sugar	3	3	3	3	3	4	4	2	2	2
Salt	1	1	½	1	2	1½	1	1	½	½
Vinegar	—	1	—	—	—	—	—	—	—	—

TABLE 10

Food	1	2	3	4	5	6	7	8	9	10
Coffee	4	4	4	4	4	4	4	4	4	4
Beef	—	40	32	—	16	4	48	—	—	20
Cheese	—	—	—	4	—	8	—	—	4	—
Eggs (number)	—	—	—	1	1	—	—	—	—	—
Lard	—	1	—	—	—	—	4	—	—	—
Rice	—	—	—	8	—	12	8	—	8	—
Manioc	64	24	—	—	—	32	—	—	24	—
Plantains	—	200	84	80	176	64	128	176	80	120
Bananas	128	—	192	112	144	32	—	112	32	128
Tomato	—	—	—	—	6	—	—	—	—	—
Pepper leaves	—	—	—	—	3	—	—	—	—	—
Shallots	—	1	—	6	—	—	—	6	—	—
Raw sugar	4	4	4	4	4	4	4	4	4	4
Salt	5	4	4	2	5	4	3	4	3	4

TABLE 11

Food	1	2	3	4	5	6	7	8	9	10
Coffee	6	4	4	4	6	4	4	4	6	4
Milk	32	40	20	20	24	30	50	40	40	40
Chocolate	2	2	—	—	—	—	—	—	—	—
Beef	32	32	8	48	16	40	—	32	8	24
Pork	16	—	—	—	—	—	—	—	—	—
Mutton	—	48	—	—	—	—	—	—	—	—
Fowl	—	—	—	—	32	—	—	—	—	—
Viscera	—	—	48	—	—	—	—	—	—	—
Cheese	8	—	—	—	8	—	12	—	8	—
Eggs (number)	4	6	2	2	4	4	7	—	4	4
Lard	10	8	8	9	8	4	6	6	8	11
Sardines	5	—	—	—	—	—	8	—	—	—
Rice	28	24	16	16	24	20	28	28	24	32
Wheat flour	—	—	—	—	—	8	—	—	—	—
Bread	—	—	5	6	6	—	6	6	—	6
Oats	—	—	—	—	—	—	—	4	—	—
Cornstarch	—	4	4	—	—	—	—	—	—	—
Crackers	4	3	—	—	—	—	—	—	—	—
Tortillas	32	40	32	32	—	32	32	—	32	—
Spaghetti	8	—	—	—	8	—	4	—	8	8
Manioc	68	18	24	24	—	8	12	—	8	—
Plantains	64	18	24	8	48	24	—	52	8	—
Bananas	66	30	32	—	—	—	—	—	—	—
Taro	—	10	24	—	—	—	—	—	—	—
Potato	—	—	24	4	8	—	—	32	—	—
Avocado	16	28	8	—	—	—	—	—	—	—
Tomato	4	12	6	4	—	—	4	—	—	—
Onion	4	2	6	4	2	—	—	4	4	—
Shallots	—	1	2	—	—	—	—	—	—	—
Green leaves	—	6	—	—	32	—	—	—	—	32
Peppers	—	6	—	—	—	—	—	—	—	—
Garlic	—	$\frac{1}{4}$	$\frac{1}{2}$	—	—	—	—	—	—	—
Raw sugar	6	14	6	4	4	4	4	6	4	4
Sugar	8	8	4	—	—	16	—	10	—	—
Sweets	—	5	3	—	—	1	—	2	1	—
Frozen fruit juice	—	6	3	3	2	—	2	—	1	—
Vinegar	8	—	—	—	—	—	—	—	—	—
Condiments	—	$\frac{1}{4}$	$\frac{1}{4}$	—	—	—	—	—	—	—
Salt	4	8	4	6	4	8	8	6	4	6
Beer (bottles)	12	—	—	1	—	—	—	—	—	1

Household E represents the wealthiest section of the Plaza barrio. The family owns cattle and fields, a shop, sugar mills, and several houses. It is composed of two men, five women, and one eleven-year-old child. Their food consumption during ten days is given in Table 12.

TABLE 12

Food	1	2	3	4	5	6	7	8	9	10
Coffee	8	8	10	8	10	8	8	8	10	8
Milk	16	16	16	16	16	16	16	16	16	16
Beef	72	32	32	56	48	56	—	56	—	56
Pork	—	24	16	—	—	—	—	—	—	—
Fowl	—	—	—	32	—	—	48	—	—	—
Cheese	28	32	28	—	16	16	32	16	16	32
Eggs (number)	4	3	5	7	7	4	10	4	3	5
Lard	16	12	12	16	12	16	4	21	16	16
Rice	40	40	32	40	—	32	40	32	40	32
Tortillas	48	48	48	48	48	48	32	32	32	48
Bread	6	—	6	5	—	6	5	5	5	6
Wheat flour	—	—	6	2	—	—	—	—	—	—
Crackers	—	—	—	—	8	—	—	—	—	—
Spaghetti	—	8	—	8	—	8	—	15	—	8
Manioc	—	89	52	55	54	—	37	32	32	32
Plantains	88	100	112	48	32	68	54	73	56	36
Bananas	56	36	54	—	24	74	38	34	38	56
Taro	24	24	20	20	21	19	32	32	32	24
Potato	12	8	12	12	8	8	12	—	8	12
Kidney beans	—	—	—	8	12	—	8	—	—	—
Raw sugar	8	8	8	—	9	8	12	8	8	8
Sugar	—	—	16	—	—	—	—	—	—	—
Onion	6	—	6	2	2	4	7	2	2	4
Shallots	7	—	5	2	2	6	3	5	3	5
Garlic	—	$\frac{1}{2}$	1	—	—	1	—	1	—	1
Tomato	11	4	3	4	3	6	3	7	3	4
Lentils	—	—	—	8	—	—	—	—	—	—
Peppers	$\frac{1}{2}$	$\frac{1}{4}$	—	—	$\frac{1}{4}$	$\frac{1}{2}$	—	—	—	$\frac{1}{4}$
Pineapple	—	56	—	19	—	41	—	40	—	40
Papaya	25	—	24	—	—	22	—	—	25	—
Canned fruit	—	—	16	—	—	—	—	—	—	—
Cumin seed	1	$\frac{1}{4}$	—	—	—	—	—	—	—	—
Salt	6	6	6	6	6	6	6	6	6	6
Vinegar	—	6	—	—	—	—	—	—	—	—
Sweets	—	10	—	9	10	—	—	—	—	—

Household F is less well to do but owns several fields, some cattle, and a store. It is a very active family, composed of three men, two women, and two children six and twelve years old. All are hard workers, but do not belong to the upper social class, They do not weave straw hats. Their food intake is given in Table 13.

TABLE 13

Food	1	2	3	4	5	6	7	8	9	10
Coffee	2	4	4	6	6	4	3	4	4	6
Milk	32	32	30	16	16	16	30	16	16	32
Chocolate	3	3	3	3	3	3	3	3	3	3
Beef	48	16	16	32	16	—	16	16	—	32
Pork	—	—	—	48	16	—	—	—	—	—
Fowl	—	48	32	—	—	38	—	—	—	—
Cheese	16	8	8	16	16	16	8	8	16	8
Eggs (number)	2	8	3	4	5	5	4	3	2	4
Lard	10	8	30	32	19	16	16	20	16	16
Rice	8	16	8	16	24	32	16	8	16	16
Tortillas	32	32	32	40	40	32	40	32	30	40
Bread	—	—	—	—	32	32	—	—	—	—
Spaghetti	8	16	8	8	8	—	8	16	8	—
Manioc	32	16	32	32	24	168	32	16	40	32
Plantains	128	96	138	128	144	118	120	88	132	122
Bananas	—	—	—	32	—	16	—	—	16	—
Taro	32	16	32	16	24	32	24	20	32	28
Potato	—	—	32	16	32	48	—	40	—	—
Kidney beans	—	—	16	32	—	16	—	—	16	—
Raw sugar	9	10	7	12	10	12	10	8	9	8
Sugar	16	—	—	—	—	4	—	—	—	—
Onion	2	—	—	2	2	—	—	2	—	2
Papaya	—	—	8	48	—	2	—	2	2	—
Green leaves	8	16	—	2	16	—	—	8	—	16
Salt	8	8	8	8	8	8	8	8	8	8
Sweets	—	—	16	8	8	16	—	—	—	—

Before we go into further details, each household's food intake as tabulated here needs a few additional notes. According to our experience, Household A is quite representative of a wide section of the village (from 80 per cent to 90 per cent). Among this group meat and cheese are eaten, as a rule, on alternating days; plantains and bananas every day; and two or three times a week a starchy root such as taro, manioc, arracacha, sweet potato, according to availability. Beans, pigeon peas, avocados, and small wild fruits are eaten when in season, and often the first three replace meat or cheese in the daily menu. As vegetable fat has to be bought, it is used very sparingly, but when buying meat people always choose a piece that contains a good amount of fat. Some green leaf such as cabbage (*col*) is eaten almost every day.

Household B's tomato consumption is rather extraordinary, as this fruit is not truly a common menu item in this house. On the other hand, peppers and shallots are actually eaten with more regularity than would appear from the table. Household C consumed two eggs. Knowing the family, we feel sure these were included for prestige reasons. The commonly consumed red peppers seem to have been unavailable at this particular period.

In the placero households (D, E, and F) the variety of items is certainly exaggerated, but the composition of the basic diet (milk, beef, fat, rice, tortillas, starchy tubers and fruits, raw sugar, and green leaves) seems to be truly represented. Eggs, refined sugar, spaghetti, fowl, tomatoes, and fruit juices are luxury items which are by no means consumed so frequently as is suggested by the tables.

As can be readily seen from the six tables, the food intake of the lomero and placero households differs significantly, in quality and quantity. Although the placeros daily eat a considerable amount of the common tubers and fruits, they supplement this starchy diet with meat, cheese, tortillas, bread, milk, and several vegetables, most of which are rarely or never present in the lomero diet. The latter buy meat or cheese, some fat, a bit of raw sugar, and salt only occasionally, whereas a large proportion of the placero diet is bought at stores or from individuals who prefer to sell their produce for cash.

The combination of menu items in the six households, is essentially as given in Table 14.

TABLE 14

	Loma	*Plaza*
First meal	Black coffee	Coffee with milk; tortillas
Second meal	Stewed plantains and bananas, sometimes with rice; green leaves	Meat broth or vegetable soup; cooked plantains and bananas; meat or cheese; rice; vegetables; fruits
Third meal (*if taken*)	Stewed plantains or bananas, optionally with a piece of cheese or meat	Cooked plantains, bananas or manioc; meat or cheese; rice; vegetables

This represents the average diet. Seasonal changes are, of course, important here, and at certain times of the year certain items are partially or entirely replaced by others. In December the importation of dried fish begins and meat is hardly to be found. The avocado and mango harvests, each lasting for two or three months, play an important part in the daily diet. The annual coffee harvest provides many people with ready cash with which to buy commercially processed foods.

The average total daily food intake of an adult person, has been determined as given in Table 15.

TABLE 15

Loma (from 80 to 90% of population		*Plaza (from 10 to 20% of population)*	
	gm.		gm.
Plantains	290	Plantains	290
Bananas	290	Bananas	58
Manioc	123	Manioc	164
Cheese, meat	77	Milk	116
Green leaf	5	Cheese	77
Red peppers	2	Meat	116
Shallots	3	Tortillas	145
Raw sugar	65	Rice	116
		Vegetables	58
		Cabbage	5
		Red peppers	2
		Shallots	3
		Raw sugar	29
		Broth	58

A short discussion of the average nutrient composition follows. Carbohydrates are derived mainly from tubers and fruits like plantains, bananas, manioc, yams, and also from raw sugar and tortillas. Maize is negligible in the village but some starch is supplied in cucurbits, bread, and spaghetti. Proteins are supplied by beef, pork, cheese, beans, eggs, and in a highly concentrated form, in dried fish. Some are present in tortillas and maize; and the ground pumpkin seeds which are consumed occasionally might provide some. Pigeon peas are certainly a major source, but their availability is subject to seasonal changes. Practically all other protein foods have to be bought, and, therefore, are available to most people only in small quantities. Among the lomeros especially, few animal proteins are available. The main sources of fats and oils are vegetable fats, fat meat, and avocados. Calcium is present in raw sugar and cabbage, and some is found in tortillas. The drinking water probably supplies a considerable amount also. Phosphorus is obtained from beans and pigeon peas, rice, milk, and a number of minor sources, while iron is supplied by beef, pork, dried fish, eggs, maize, and raw sugar. Beans and pigeon peas are also minor sources of iron.

Vitamin A is derived from eggs, tomatoes, and maize, which are relatively scarce, but green plantains and arracacha seem to have a high carotene content, as do pumpkins and mangoes. Peppers and coriander also provide carotene. The vitamin B complex is represented by thiamine, which is supplied mainly by taro, with yams, maize, beans, and pork as minor sources. Taro seems to be the only source of thiamine that is more or less regularly consumed. Riboflavin is obtained in beef, pork, milk, eggs, all of which are luxury items for most people, but some is present in beans and cabbage, which are more readily available. Niacin is supplied by beef, pork, chicken, maize, arracacha, peppers, beans, and coffee. Ascorbic acid is provided by mangoes, papayas, hog plums, cabbage, fresh corn, citrus fruits, and by a large number of wild fruits.

The nutritive values of the local foodstuffs were not determined, but the approximate values can be estimated by comparison with analyses made by the Colombian Institute of Nutrition (Instituto Nacional de Nutrición). These analyses[1] include practically all the foods used in Aritama. Although it is very probable that plants of the same species but from different regions vary considerably in their nutritive values, the data elaborated by the Institute of Nutrition provide an adequate basis for a general evaluation of the nutritional adequacy of the food consumed in Aritama.

Tables 16 and 17 show the approximate average intake of essential nutrients per person per day.

Let us consider now the nutritional adequacy of the lomero diet. There is, first of all, a marked deficiency in proteins. The only animal proteins available are derived from cheese, and the beef which is eaten on rare occasions. The latter has a relatively low protein value, and even a daily combination of both beef and cheese would hardly fulfil the minimum requirements. It is possible that the protein intake increases during the dry season, when sun-dried fish is available, but even then it is probable that a certain degree of protein deficiency exists. As to the apparent niacin deficiency, it must be pointed out that the corresponding nutrient intake data must be supplemented with black coffee, which probably guarantees an adequate niacin intake. The average intake of the other nutrients is adequate, but the total caloric intake is rather low. A few more plantains, a bit more cheese, and some more raw sugar can increase it considerably, and a certain amount of these foods is taken occasionally between meals by those doing hard physical work.

The placero diet is fairly well balanced. Here high-class proteins are available in sufficient quantities, but a slight deficiency in riboflavin and niacin might be present. Caloric intake is adequate, for this group of

---

[1] José Góngora y López and Norton Young López, *Tabla de composición de alimentos colombianos* (Bogotá: Ministerio de Salud Pública, 1953).

people do little or no hard physical work. The placero's diet is evidently far superior to the lomero's, a fact due mainly to their being able to buy animal proteins and rice regularly.

In trying to evaluate the general adequacy of the local diet, several additional factors must be taken into account. In the first place, it is to be expected that seasonal variations might modify greatly the nutritional status of the individual consumer. The marked instability of household groups also seems to be responsible for significant alterations in the individual food intake, especially of women and children who are abandoned by their male providers. In the second place, local techniques of food preparation probably alter the nutrient content of certain foods, leading to the loss of valuable vitamins. There can be no doubt that the nutrition of a large proportion of the villagers is suboptimal and that we are dealing here with a malnourished population group. How this situation expresses itself in the local patterning of cultural activities, in attitudes, values, and goals, will be described in the the following chapters.

TABLE 16

Loma Barrio

Food	Calories	Proteins (gm.)	Fats (gm.)	Carbohydrates (gm.)	Cellulose, etc. (gm.)	Ashes (gm.)	Calcium (mg.)	Phosphorus (mg.)	Iron (mg.)	Vitamin A (I.U.)	Thiamine (mg.)	Riboflavin (mg.)	Niacin (mg.)	Ascorbic Acid (mg.)
Plantains	406	3·5	0·3	108·5	2·03	2·6	14·5	90·00	1·45	2,900	0·2	0·9	1·74	58
Bananas	244	3·5	0·3	63·8	2·9	2·6	17·4	72·5	1·45	638	·1	·9	2·0	29
Manioc	179	0·9	0·1	43·6	1·1	1·1	33·2	43·00	0·5	12	·05	·04	0·6	37
Cabbage	2	0·2	0·02	0·25	0·06	0·11	22·8	2·6	0·07	160	·06	·01	0·05	6
Red peppers	1	0·04	0·03	0·2	0·08	0·02	0·58	0·13	0·02	92	·001	·004	0·03	2
Shallots	1	0·03	0·003	0·15	0·03	0·01	0·81	0·93	0·01	0	·001	·001	0·01	0
Cheese	298	19·00	24·0	1·5	0·0	0·8	616·0	426·00	0·6	1,232	·03	·4	0·1	0
Raw sugar	203	0·3	0·0	55·2	0·0	0·7	52·0	39·00	15·8	0	0·01	0·04	0·2	2
Total intake:	1,334	27·5	24·8	273·0	6·2	10·9	0·75	0·7	19·3	5,034	0·452	2·3	4·73	134
Required	2,600	65·0					0·8		10·0	1,800	0·4	2–3	20·00	40

TABLE 17

Plaza Barrio

Food	Calories	Proteins (gm.)	Fats (gm.)	Carbohydrates (gm.)	Cellulose, etc. (gm.)	Ashes (gm.)	Calcium (mg.)	Phosphorus (mg.)	Iron (mg.)	Vitamin A (I.U.)	Thiamine (mg.)	Riboflavin (mg.)	Niacin (mg.)	Ascorbic Acid (mg.)
Plantains	406	3·5	0·3	108·5	2·03	2·6	14·5	90·00	1·45	2,900	0·2	0·87	1·74	58
Bananas	49	0·69	0·05	12·76	0·58	0·52	3·48	14·5	0·29	127	·01	·02	0·4	6
Manioc	239	1·3	0·16	58·2	1·47	1·47	44·28	57·4	0·65	16	·06	·05	0·8	49
Rice	395	9·97	1·16	89·3	0·92	1·2	11·6	441·00	2·32	0	·29	·07	6·14	0
Tortillas	212	4·93	0·43	45·82	0·72	0·14	2·9	26·1	0·58	0	·03	·001	0·01	0
Beef	371	21·7	19·7	0·0	0·0	1·16	6·96	127·00	3·6	0	·07	·19	4·98	0
Cheese	298	23·87	1·54	0·0	3·85	616·00	462·00	0·61	0·61	1,232	·03	·38	0·15	0
Milk	69·6	3·94	3·82	5·33	0·0	0·81	139·00	110·2	0·23	174	·04	·02	0·1	2
Fat	504	0·0	55·15	0·0	0·0	0·29	0·0	0·0	0·0	0	·0	·0	0·0	0
Red papers	1·2	0·04	0·03	0·19	0·08	0·02	0·58	0·13	0·02	92	·001	·04	0·032	2
Shallots	1	0·03	0·0	0·15	0·03	0·01	0·81	0·93	0·01	0	·001	·001	0·01	0
Cabbage	2	0·2	0·02	0·25	0·06	0·11	22·8	2·6	0·07	160	·006	·01	0·05	6
Raw sugar	91	0·14	0·02	24·9	0·0	0·31	23·2	16·4	6·7	0	0·005	0·02	0·08	1
Total intake	2,639	70·31	104·7	346·9	4·9	624·64	8·8	1·3	16·53	4,701	0·753	1·842	14·492	125
Required	2,600	65·00					0·8		10·00	1,800	0·4	2–3	20·00	40

III

THE SOCIOPSYCHOLOGICAL FOUNDATIONS

INFANCY

THE basis of educational theory in Aritama is the beliefs in the genetic heredity of all 'good' or 'evil' character traits, in fate and pre-destination, and that man is born evil. Because of these beliefs, education itself is thought to be of little avail should an infant show undesirable traits, and it becomes only a feeble attempt to curb as far as possible this allegedly innate 'evilness'. A 'good' child proves by his behavior that his parents succeeded in 'educating' him, but a 'bad' child's behavior can never be blamed upon the parents, who simply claim that the child happened to be born with undesirable traits that were beyond their control.

Both lomeros and placeros claim that patterns of child-training differ greatly between barrios. In fact, however, hardly any difference can be observed, and it is remarkable how uniform these patterns actually are in all sections of the population. Stereotypes imputed by the placeros to the lomeros are that their children are dirty, that they sleep on the floor, that they are fed with goats milk sweetened with raw sugar. Lomeros, on the other hand, say that placero children are kept very clean, sleep in beds, and are fed with dehydrated milk sweetened with sugar. While people tend to emphasize these nonexistent 'differences' and believe that they are of the greatest importance, in reality all children are more or less dirty and usually sleep on the floor or in a hammock; as there are only six goats in the whole village, goat milk is a rare article and by no means a standard nourishment for lomero children. Any variations in child-training which might occur are due not to race, class, or economic status but rather to individual situations and preferences.

The general attitude toward children is strongly influenced by the local food situation and they are always considered a heavy economic burden, but there are marked differences between men and women in other details of their attitudes toward offspring. Multiple fatherhood is a goal aspired to by all men, partly to prove their virility, partly to be able to count upon their children's help once the latter become economically productive. Women are much less concerned with such considerations. To them, childbearing is an obligation, a duty they have to fulfil for the man who supports them. A woman who has been married or kept by a man and who perhaps has received a house or some other property from him, practically 'owes him a child'. But neither men nor women would say that children as such are desirable. They are assets, they are tools; thus they have value in relation to the use to which they may be put by their parents, but not as human beings in themselves. Society at large cares very little whether a couple has children or not, but simply takes it for granted that every man will procreate and that every woman is a potential mother.

Men wish to have sons and women, daughters, and a man will often bitterly reproach the woman if his hopes do not come true; some even go so far as to threaten a pregnant wife with denying his fatherhood should she give birth to a girl. Some women say to this: 'He should not complain; after all, he made the child'—and will often add: 'Why should I have a son? Only so the government might take him away from me?' This fear is quite exaggerated, as hardly any villagers have ever been obliged to serve in the army, and it is evident that these women project onto the 'government' their resentments against their husbands. During the previous generation, women definitely preferred to have male children and were proud to have sons, but with the changing economic situation and their increasing dependence upon the help of a daughter, they now prefer female offspring, much against the wishes of their husbands.

The birth of a child changes very little the daily routine of the family. If it is a boy, the father may buy a bottle of rum and a few cigars and invite a group of friends into the backyard for a little celebration, but if it is a girl there is no such public manifestation of joy. In either case, the household is dominated for a time by the womenfolk who come and go, either to see the child or to assist the mother and to help in the household duties. After some ten to twelve days anyone may touch the newborn child, may even lift him up and caress him; but men rarely do so, and even the child's father seldom touches the newborn baby. Except for the immediate relatives, few people come to visit. There are no gifts or congratulations, only a few questions concerning the mother's health or some joking remark about the baby. The sleeping quarters where mother and child are confined are kept almost hermetically closed by stuffing leaves, grass, or clothes into all openings, even between the walls and the roof, as it is believed that both mother and child are susceptible to any current of cool air.

Every day, for about one week after birth, the midwife comes and prepares infusions and baths for the mother, urging her to eat regularly but to avoid foods which might be difficult to digest. Few people can afford to pay for services beyond assistance at birth and, among the lomeros especially, the midwife hardly ever returns once the immediate danger is over. There are no restrictions on the father's food habits or daily activities. The woman begins to resume her daily chores and often forces herself to do so in spite of pain and weakness, because if she should rest any longer or resume her work only gradually, gossip is certain to criticize her 'laziness'. People will say: 'How will she be able to feed her child if she does not work?' and the fear of this criticism is often strong enough to make a woman resume her heavy work although she feels that she still needs rest.

The amount and quality of attention a mother gives to her newborn child depend little upon the economic situation of the household, but much upon her individual attitude toward the child. A first child does not necessarily receive more attention than a third or fourth. Even the many women who have to weave straw hats in order to support themselves and their children have plenty of time to care for a baby but frequently are negligent, claiming that work, illness, or fatigue do not let them give more attention to their infants. Mothers consider the first year to be the most difficult, and during it they frequently put high demands upon the infant's physical and mental capacities, quite beyond the biological rhythm. We have observed several mothers using both hands in weaving hats while nursing their four- or five-month-old babies, who clung with the greatest effort to the breast. All obvious deficiencies in the care of a baby are always blamed upon his father, who is accused of miserliness, laziness, and lack of responsibility toward his family. A mother never will admit that she herself is to blame for the neglect of her child.

In her arms the infant leaves for the first time the semidarkness of the sleeping quarters, but soon she puts him again to sleep in the darkened room, on a bed, a mat, or, more frequently, in a hammock. Only during the night does the mother suckle the infant in a prone position, next to her. During the daytime she will sit down on a chair, a box, or on the doorstep in order to give him the breast. Even during these first days, the infant is hardly ever supported with both hands or arms, but is held in only one arm or on the mother's lap. Often she will perform some other task while giving the baby her breast, such as shelling beans with one hand, stirring the fire, or arranging some clothes. Frequently the baby is handled rather roughly, with rapid and clumsy movements and with little regard to his comfort. No efforts are made to avoid letting the bright sunlight fall on his face or to protect his body from exposure to a draft of cool air. He is handled like a dead weight, devoid of all feeling, and hardly any thought is given to his being comfortable and safe. Although women admit that a baby sees, hears, feels, thinks, and remembers, they handle him as if his only need were food.

If the mother's milk should not have appeared during the first day after birth, the baby is given a few spoonfuls of lukewarm water containing some raw sugar, prepared and administered by the midwife or some other adult woman, but as soon as the milk begins to flow, the infant is breast fed. Among the more educated placeros women will take commercial drugs, such as calcium tablets, in order to increase their milk, but on the Loma and among the poorer people of the Plaza, large amounts of raw sugar water are taken by the mother to achieve this purpose. It is believed that the mother's milk is formed somewhere below the shoulder blades, and light massages are applied to this part of the body to increase the flow.

Practically all women who have milk nurse their babies, but among the poorer people there are many who are undernourished and cannot breast-feed them. If they can afford it, they will try bottle-feeding with powdered milk, but as this product is very expensive by local standards, they usually prepare sweetened rice water, or simply lukewarm sugar water, sometimes containing a bit of milk. Even if cow's milk is available, or if powdered milk can be bought, it is always diluted with water and heavily sweetened. Many women think that bottle-feeding is too complicated and time-consuming, and so prefer to feed their babies with a spoon. It is said, however, that bottle-feeding was common in previous generations, having been introduced by the immigrants late in the last century.

In certain circumstances nursing is believed to be harmful to the mother and/or to the baby. For example, if a woman is 'hot', in the sense that she has been walking in the sun or has been working near the hearth or has been ironing, the milk is believed to be altered by this condition and she will have to rest awhile before giving the baby the breast. In such cases, however, the mother might squeeze some milk from her breast upon a stone or upon her own umbilicus, believing that this will 'cool' the remaining milk in her breast.

Women consider suckling a very tiresome task and always complain of it. Nursing mothers worry a great deal about their own health, as they believe that their blood becomes 'weak' while feeding a baby, and they also complain that they lose valuable time while nursing. Some women fear that their breasts will be less attractive to men if they nurse their babies. However, neither prudery nor modesty influences nursing, and a mother will suckle her baby in public or in the presence of strangers as freely as at home.

The position in which a baby is held while being nursed is rarely a comfortable one for him, and during suckling babies are never fondled or caressed. Interruptions are frequent. The mother may rise and walk to another room or may even push the infant away before he has finished. Some babies become so accustomed to being nursed while their mother is standing or walking that they stop suckling and cry if the mother stands motionless for a moment, but will continue suckling as soon as she moves again. During these first weeks, babies are often very sensitive to noises while nursing and will stop and cry if they hear sounds near by. Visual impressions seem to bother them much less, even after they learn to distinguish people at a distance. Quite often a baby will nurse for a minute or two, stop, and be put to bed, but will wake in another few minutes and receive the breast again, only to reject it again after a moment. On several occasions we observed a baby being nursed three times in ten minutes, each time being put to sleep, but being picked up again as soon as it began to cry.

At about two weeks after birth, the baby is given little spoonfuls of sweetened rice water, and tea of dried red rose leaves or of *siempreviva* (*Gomphrena* sp.), sweetened with sugar, is given 'so he will have a healthy color'.

When in the mother's lap, a baby demonstrates his desire to nurse by opening his mouth, and after a few weeks he will push his head rhythmically against the mother's breast. Although such behavior is always interpreted as a sign of hunger, the mother often does not accede immediately, depending upon her activity at the moment, and the baby may begin to cry and to struggle violently. Then she does not wait until the baby has found the breast but thrusts the nipple into his mouth, often almost smothering him. As soon as a baby stops suckling he is 'burped'—i.e., the mother lifts him up on her left arm so that his face lies on her left shoulder, rocks him back and forth, and pats his back to make him belch before putting him to sleep.

During the third month many babies are trained to suckle and to hold up their heads alone, so their mother can weave while caring for them. At the beginning this creates great anxiety on the part of the baby, and he clings frantically with both hands to the mother's breast or her dress, but after a few weeks he learns to acquire positions which enable him to nurse without losing his balance.

At about three months many babies are bottle-fed with fresh but diluted milk, if available. At about four or five months they are given occasional spoonfuls of taro soup, and at six or seven months they are given broth. At eight months most infants eat such solid food as boiled manioc, bananas, or rice, but meat is given only after twelve months. Infants, at about six months, can take solid food with their own hands, and mothers begin handing them morsels instead of putting them into their mouths. Controlled, unilateral movements have generally developed by then and infants begin to make a characteristic gesture expressing desire for food, viz., a repeated closing and opening of the fingers of the right hand.

If the mother becomes pregnant while still nursing an infant, the little one has to be weaned at once and from then on the baby must not sleep next to his mother any more. This is because it is believed that if the unborn child is of different sex from the nursling, the latter would receive serious harm to his health, the principal danger being violent skin eruptions. The milk each woman produces is believed to vary according to the sex of the child and a woman who is nursing a male baby could never nurse a female one or vice versa, as the milk would be 'contrary' (*leche contraria*). For the same reason, a woman who has no milk cannot ask another woman to nurse her child, unless the wet nurse has an infant of the same sex. Should he be of different sex, the 'contrary' milk would cause diarrhea or eruptions, and even the child's mother might fall ill. It might be mentioned here that a wet nurse is called 'mother' by the children she has nursed, sometimes even after they are grown to adulthood. Children of different biological parents who had the same wet nurse consider themselves 'milk brothers' (*hermanos de teta*) and might even continue to call each other brother (or sister) in later life.

If an infant should accidentally sleep with his head upon his pregnant mother's abdomen, it is said to be dangerous to the unborn child who might be hampered in his movements, and so turn himself into a position (*coger cama*) likely to cause a difficult birth.

After nursing a baby, the mother will often carry him to and fro for a while, but without rocking him, until he falls asleep. During the first few months, babies often sleep next to their mothers in the same bed or hammock, but sometimes they are put in a cardboard box close to her. During the daytime the baby is placed in a hammock or on a mat on the floor. Before falling asleep the mother sometimes rocks the hammock or box for a few moments and occasionally sings a lullaby. The rhythmic repetition of a single sound, such as 'ps-ps-ps', is frequently employed to make a baby sleep or to calm his crying. Pacifiers are never used. It is said that in the past it was customary to wrap a piece of raw sugar in a bit of cloth and put it into the baby's mouth, but this is never done today.

An infant is suckled about six to eight times a day, and from three to four times during the night, at least during the first month of life. Lying next to his mother in the hammock or in her lap, the baby is given the breast every time he cries or wakes up. There is no fixed schedule, but occasionally a baby is awakened for feeding if it has not suckled for several hours.

Besides a new pregnancy, there are several other reasons why a baby might be weaned. The mother might feel weak or fall ill; she might be obliged to work harder because she has been abandoned by the child's father; or she just might decide suddenly to wean the child for no apparent reason. Infants are always weaned quite suddenly by rubbing lemon juice or chili peppers on the nipples. They react with violent crying and, depending upon their age, might manifest their displeasure by beating the mother's breasts. Some refuse all other food offered to them, and only hours or even days of fasting and crying will finally make them accept what is given them from a bottle or a spoon. From the moment an infant has been weaned (*despechado, desapartado*), he is never permitted to touch the mother's breast again. Should he try to reach it during the night while sleeping next to her, the mother will separate the infant immediately from her side and put him to sleep in another part of the room. During the days following weaning, infants are told by words and gestures that their mother's breasts are evil-smelling (*son muy hediondos*), but a first taste of lemon or peppers is usually sufficiently effective to wean them at once. Many older children and even adults say that they remember how they were weaned and refer laughingly to their rage and disappointment. Boys often like to brag that they continued to suckle in spite of the lemon juice, but their mothers deny this and declare that they never touched their breasts again after the day they were weaned. Parents are fully aware of some of the undesirable consequences of this practice. For example, they admit that this method of weaning makes the infant 'mad' (*rabioso, bravo*) at his mother, and that hostility between siblings is often initiated by this practice. However, the whole affair is rather taken as a joke and nobody pays any serious attention to the infant's reactions. It may be added here that quite frequently it is the infant's father who insists that the child be weaned as soon as possible so that the mother can resume her full share of work.

Infants are never left in a completely dark room. There is always some light, even during the night. If for some reason or other the light should be taken away so that the baby stays momentarily in darkness, he often begins to cry, but stops as soon as the light is returned, even if the person bringing it should leave again. During the first four or five months most babies are relatively quiet and apparently comfortable in their hammocks or wherever they might have been put to sleep. But from then on they show signs of unrest and are carried a great deal until they begin to crawl. At about seven or eight months, babies sleep considerably less during the daytime and are likely to waken more often during the night.

During these first months the baby is usually dressed in a short sleeveless shirt, open at the back, but some mothers do not bother to make use of even this small garment, leaving the baby naked during the day and only covered with old clothes when he is asleep. A little cotton cap is sometimes put on his head and, in the families of the Plaza barrio, some mothers will put little stockings on his feet when taking him out of the house. The cap always has a tendency to slip down over the eyes, and although babies often cry when this happens, their mothers rarely pay attention. After the first two or three months, dress, if it has been ever used at all, is generally discarded and children are left naked during the daytime. Male children go about nude at least until their third year, but girls are made to wear little shirts or panties at two.

A baby's crying is always interpreted as a desire for food and few women believe that during the first three or four months of life an infant could have other reasons for crying. Cold or pain are hardly ever taken into account and the need for affection and company are never thought of. During the first three months babies cry very little and sleep most of the time, but if they do cry they usually are suckled immediately. Although some mothers show more solicitude than others and are quicker to fulfil the baby's desire to be picked up and fed, many pay attention only after prolonged crying. When the mother is alone in the house, the baby is often left to cry for hours without being given the breast, but as soon as the father arrives, more solicitude is shown and the mother will try to stop the baby's cries by suckling and rocking him. This, however, is rarely done for the infant's sake alone but rather to stop the noise, as many men become irritated when hearing a baby cry insistently. Babies who are about to cry are often immediately given any object that might distract them.

Once an infant begins to crawl, its crying is often interpreted as a desire to be picked up and carried. Often they fall and cry, and some mothers will lift them up and comfort them, but others will pay no attention to the screams. During the last half of the first year, infants often have temper tantrums after falling or knocking against something. After a few minutes of violent screams respiration will almost stop, the face turns purple, and the baby will roll and twist on the floor before starting to breathe and scream again. Sometimes the mother picks up the baby immediately and gives him the breast, which, although the baby does not suckle, smothers the screams. At other times a mother might slap the child and scold him, leaving him to cry without picking him up. Such tantrums are very common in all children, occurring about once a week. The mother's reaction is never one of solicitude but always of anger and ridicule. During temper tantrums babies often urinate and vomit, sometimes moving their heads rhythmically, knocking them against the floor, the wall, or a piece of furniture. An infant who is beginning to crawl often will cling to the mother's dress or try to climb into her lap if she is sitting near by. If the mother is occupied she will discourage him, scolding him or pushing him away, causing screams and, eventually, a prolonged tantrum.

During the first few weeks the baby is often carried. He is handled when taken up to be nursed and put to sleep again, and he is often passed from hand to hand, carried from one room to another, or from the house to the backyard. Sometimes a mother wakes a sleeping baby only to carry him around for a while. After four months, but rarely before that time, a baby may be carried by other children, older siblings, or neighbors, and sometimes even a four-year-old child is allowed to carry him. After six months, all infants are carried straddled on a hip, regardless of sex.

During the first weeks babies often vomit when being carried or rocked, and frequently do so when rocked in a hammock even after they have been accustomed to being rocked or carried. Mothers do not believe that motion itself has anything to do with the vomiting and attribute it rather to suckling in excess. A baby is rarely handled carefully while being carried. Quite often he is dropped through negligence, even by the mother herself. Sometimes a dropped baby is hurt, and in any case it reacts with violent screams, incontinence, and vomiting.

A baby is bathed only about two or three times a week. Mothers claim that they bath the baby every day, but this is the ideal pattern and actually they do not follow it. During the first two weeks or so, the bath water is slightly warmed by putting it in an open vessel in the sunshine and sometimes a few rosemary leaves are added 'to strengthen the flesh' (*para atesar las carnes*). After two weeks, cold water is used and frequently the baby is bathed in the river when his mother goes there to fetch water or to wash clothes. When the water is lukewarm babies seldom cry when being put into the bath or while being washed, but they do so as soon as they are lifted out of it to be dried. Most washing is done with the bare hands, perhaps using a bit of soap and, occasionally, a small rag. The head is washed about every ten days. No effort is made to keep water or soap out of the baby's eyes and mouth, and he is handled rather roughly during the bath. When being bathed in the cold river water, on the other hand, babies cry a great deal, although they are bathed only during the hot hours of the day. They are never put directly into the water but seated on a stone and water is poured over them from a container. During the first few months only the mother or other adult women may bath the baby, as his older siblings or other children are said to be very careless when doing it. About eight days after birth the mother cuts the infant's fingernails and throws them away. No rite whatsoever is connected with this, and from then on the nails are cut occasionally lest they grow too long.

A baby's elimination excites neither loathing nor anger, at least not as far as women are concerned. Men often show open disgust if a baby soils them or if they find the floor dirtied with excrement. From birth on, as soon as an infant begins to urinate or defecate he is lifted up vertically by grasping him under the armpits, until the elimination is complete. Should he soil his mother or any other person while being nursed or carried, he is handled in the same way, being held apart from the body as soon as elimination starts. This gesture is not accompanied by words but is performed with a swift movement, picking him up rapidly and holding him as far as possible from the person's body. Often the infant is held toward the open door or, if time permits, is carried to the backyard or street. At about four months a baby begins to make a characteristic noise before eliminating, thus giving time to lift him up and hold him apart. Some babies make these noises only when preparing to defecate but apparently not before urinating. At about eight months an infant will try to descend from the mother's lap in order to eliminate. This sphincter-training, by holding the infant in the air and apart from the body, is fully recognized as a means of conditioning the baby, and is quite effective if the practice is systematically repeated during the first four months. A mother is blamed should she be inconsistent in following this pattern.

Rarely does a mother clean an infant after he has defecated. Maybe she will rub the baby's buttocks strongly with a towel or with her own skirt, or will wipe the soiled parts of his body with her bare hands. A very common practice is to call a dog and to hold the infant in a position so the animal can lick his buttocks and anus. Dogs are frequently trained to devour all excrements inside the house and are called in should a child soil the floor or a bed. Many infants, when crawling on the floor, eat earth and dust, which often has been moistened by someone's urine. The eating of feces is also quite common and is hardly ever discouraged.

In toilet-training emphasis is placed upon avoidance of elimination in an improper place, but no shame is associated with it and the idea that the child should hide while eliminating is not taught. Cleanliness of the body is not taught in this connection either, and it is believed that contamination with feces could never be responsible for the transmission of disease.

A baby is never cared for by only one person but always by a number of people, such as aunts, grandmothers, older siblings, servants, or neighbors. It is not rare to find an infant whose care is in the hands of six or eight persons, each one taking charge whenever time permits or convenience dictates, but without being assigned certain tasks. During the second month the baby is frequently carried outside of the house and is taken to visit the houses of relatives. The hottest hours of the day are avoided, but in the late afternoon many women carry their babies for a while through the neighbourhood or stand at a fence or street corner while gossiping with relatives or friends. During the third month the mother will take the infant almost daily to the river. While she washes the laundry, the baby sleeps in the shadow of a rock, on a piece of cloth put on the ground. Visiting becomes more frequent after three months, especially visits to the paternal and maternal grandparents. On these occasions, the baby is not always carried by his own mother but by a great many different females of all ages. Men very rarely carry a baby on the street or to a visit.

Many mothers touch the baby only while nursing him or putting him to sleep afterward, while other adults or children are in charge of the other aspects of his care. Therefore, the infant begins to distinguish at about seven months between his mother as a source of food, and other women as sources of attention, affection, and comfort. Mothers are quite aware of this and will often say, 'He only wants me when he feels hungry.' Women frequently talk to babies and sometimes caress them by biting them playfully in cheeks or arms. Some, however, do not talk to them, saying that 'anyway, he won't understand'. Very often a mother will throw the baby into the air and catch him, but otherwise there is little play with infants. The genitals of babies are frequently touched and rubbed in a playful manner by adults or children, not only when nursing but on any other occasion. Male children especially are handled in such a fashion, and often a mother can be seen kissing her infant's penis or fondling it to quiet his crying. Adults make joking remarks about the future virility of the baby, about the size of his penis, and about his reactions to such caresses.

If the baby has an older sibling or lives in the house with any older child, the mother will soon put the older child in charge of the infant. This is frequently done at about four or five months after birth, and from then on the baby is carried a great deal by the older child, being brought back to the mother only for nursing. Older siblings and children in general consider the care for an infant a very unpleasant task and often take out their resentment on the baby, teasing him and handling him roughly. A child nurse, although told to be careful, feels little or no responsibility and often envies the baby for the food and affection he gets, developing strong hostile attitudes against him.

Men as fathers demonstrate not only indifference toward their newborn children, but quite often show a marked loathing for them. 'A baby is so thin and watery' (*aguadito*) one father said with a shudder, while others will complain about their dirty appearance and their foul odor. As sexual intercourse with the mother is resumed a few weeks after delivery, jealousy on this score does not seem to influence men's behavior toward their children. Their crying at night, however, and especially their odor seems to bother men greatly, and they often complain that their mothers do not keep them clean enough. A frequent complaint of the men is that their women do not carry out sphincter-training early enough. Although a mother will sometimes insist that a father pick up his newborn child, he frequently refuses to do so, or will pick him up only for a short moment. There are, however, some exceptions, as some men can be seen carrying their babies, at least inside the house, but they always behave rather clumsily and claim to fear they will drop them. A father who, so far, has had only female offspring, sometimes shows a certain pride in his first son and will occasionally carry him on the street, or even take him on a visit. Fathers rarely play with babies and practically never give them food. If a baby cries, the father may scold him and call the mother, or if a baby falls and has a tantrum he may pick him up and hand him to his mother. Otherwise, there is little physical or other contact between a baby and his father or other men, and although infants do not seem to be afraid of them, they do not associate them with food or affection.

At about three months a baby begins to gabble (*gorgorean*). This is recognized as a new step in his development, an active participation in the world around him, and a mother often points out with pride that her baby has begun to make these noises. At five months an infant is expected to sit up alone, and at six or seven months he is expected to support his head steadily and to begin to crawl. Owing to the demand upon them during nursing, many children are able to keep their heads steady before being able to sit up. At twelve months a child should begin to walk, and at sixteen or eighteen months, to speak. This ideal pattern corresponds fairly well to actual behavior, although there are, of course, many individual variations.

When crawling on the floor, infants cling to the furniture or the walls and so begin to stand. No help is offered during these efforts and should a baby fall, a mother will comment with a shrug of her shoulders that with each fall 'the baby will grow a bit'. At this stage infants will grasp anything they find and carry it immediately to the mouth to suck or chew, as they now begin to cut their teeth. Although an infant is never deliberately taught to walk or even encouraged to do so, the mother is greatly interested in his physical progress and in his learning to walk as soon as possible. The theory is that, once a child can walk, he needs much less attention and can be left alone for hours. A device to train infants to stand and to walk is found in a very few houses. It is said to have been introduced by the first immigrants from the lowlands, and consists of a ring of twigs or vines, about 50 centimeters in diameter and covered with strips of old clothes. This ring (*saltador*) is suspended in a horizontal position from a cross-beam and the infant is placed in it in a sitting position, his seat being two strips of cloth which hang loosely diagonally within the ring. Only by stretching his legs can the baby touch the floor and as the sitting position is quite uncomfortable because of the supporting bands which cut into the buttocks, the baby makes frantic efforts to stand.

Some infants begin to get their teeth at about eight months but many reach twelve months or more before cutting even their first lower teeth. It is said that children are frequently ill *because* of cutting their teeth, but the fact is that at that time they chew and suck many dirty and contaminated objects and thus develop gastrointestinal infections. During this period infants sleep less, cry often, and are generally restless and need more attention.

About two weeks after birth the mother ties to the baby's wrist or neck a cotton string with one or two seeds or beads as a charm against the Evil Eye. Until the third month after birth babies are believed to have very 'weak' blood and any disease suffered during this period is considered to be very dangerous and likely to make the child sickly ever after. Sometimes, when the baby falls ill it is the mother who takes the medicine, believing that she communicates its benefits through her milk. We have known of instances where a nursing mother received daily hypodermic injections in order to cure her baby of diarrhea. As infants rarely are cleaned after elimination, and as they roll and crawl on the dirt floor or in the backyard, they are often covered with dust, soot, and ashes. Skin infections, boils, rashes, and, above all, painful infections of the anal zone, are very frequent and cause much unrest and crying. If a baby hiccups repeatedly it is generally attributed to an 'alteration' of the mother's milk and perhaps he will not be given the breast for several days, being fed meanwhile from a bottle or with a spoon. Some mothers believe that hiccups are symptoms of liver ailments but some others say that a baby hiccups only if he is still hungry, and will give him the breast immediately. Frequent vomiting is attributed also to a 'change' in the mother's milk, but home remedies for this are given only after the eighth month. A few women believe that vomiting is a healthy symptom and that the child will gain weight fast if it vomits frequently.

The death of a baby rarely causes deeply felt sorrow. Most mothers are resigned and fatalistic, even if it is clear that death could have been prevented by better care and food. Carelessness, ignorance, and, at times, open hostility toward the child or his father, may lead a woman to neglect an infant's health to such a point that serious disease and death are the natural consequences. Four recent cases became known to us where small babies had died simply because their mothers were unwilling to make the effort to feed them properly, none of these cases being due to poverty. Public opinion scarcely takes note of such occurrences; for a few days the neighbors will gossip and suspect infanticide but soon everything will be forgotten again. Infanticide as such seems to be rare but it is not unknown. Several cases are told in the village of women who strangled their babies, and others about older women who are said to have killed their daughter's babies at birth.

In all instances, the reason seems to have been fear of poverty, when it became clear that the father of the child had no intention of supporting the woman once she had given birth. Some people assured us that all children who are born with visible physical defects are killed immediately by the midwife, with full consent of the childbearing woman's family. There seems to exist a definite correlation between early weaning and infant mortality from gastrointestinal diseases. Bottle-feeding or feeding from a spoon always carries the danger of contamination, so it is not surprising that the highest incidence of gastroenteritis in infants seems to coincide with the weeks after weaning.

Physical punishment begins practically at birth and consists of light slaps on the hands, arms, legs, or buttocks—but never in the face—if the infant cries incessantly or does not want to sleep. With every month the slaps become harder and at about seven or eight months a baby is sometimes slapped with some force, especially if it begins to eat sand. Long before infants are able to speak, as a matter of fact at about five or six months, their mothers or other adults will threaten them verbally, saying, for example, 'I am going to beat you', or 'The cat (or toad) will come and eat you up'. This is done to silence children who cry in the evening or at night. Putting a finger across the lips, the adult indicates silence and children soon understand this sign. Often a toad is pointed out to the infant while threatening him with it and afterward, whenever they see such an animal, they will be frightened and begin to cry. If a baby handles his genitals he is never punished for it, but thumb-sucking is generally discouraged by slapping his hands and taking his fingers brusquely out of his mouth.

We have referred in the foregoing pages only to the first year of life. During this period of time the infant has been exposed to a series of situations and disciplines which have begun to shape his reactions toward physiological tensions as well as his expectations of other people. The infant has learned that alleviation of hunger is inconsistent and sporadic, that only females—mainly his mother—will provide nourishment, and that its quality and quantity are rarely satisfactory. To this was added the violence of the weaning method, the physical separation from his mother, the frequent gastrointestinal dysfunctions, and the restriction of thumb-sucking. His first exploration of the physical environment were accompanied by the search of food and it was disappointing, and the substitutes found were taken from him and he was punished for chewing or eating sand, stones, or wood. He has learned that his desire for affection and company was always interpreted in terms of desire for food. Sphincter-control was rigidly imposed but otherwise cleanliness was not taught. Sleep and rest were interrupted by others. Many restrictive disciplines were enforced by physical punishment; darkness and animals were frightening; people's hands gave no firm support. Hunger, fear, and the uncertainty of the mother's or other people's reactions to any manifestation of discomfort mark this period of life; no technique has yet been developed that might begin to alleviate these growing tensions, the periodic expression of which takes the form of violent tantrums.

EARLY CHILDHOOD

During the first years of life, even after a child is able to walk and to feed himself, the mother continues to be responsible for seeing that he eats, sleeps, and is tolerably clean. Constant control is exercised over the quantity a child consumes and, should he eat more than his mother thinks is necessary, he is punished by having part of the food taken from him. Individual dislikes for certain foods are always respected and a child is never forced or encouraged to eat something he does not wish to eat. Preferences, however, are sometimes discouraged by pointing out that the preferred food is harmful to health.

Children are rarely offered food in houses they may visit and, as a rule, are taught not to accept food from strangers or from people not belonging to their kin-group. Also, emphasis is placed upon their not accepting food from relatives with whom the family is not on friendly terms. The main reason why children are taught not to accept food outside their homes is the desire to avoid entering a cycle of obligations with another family, but this, of course, is never stated openly; instead, it is tacitly understood that the acceptance of food would be interpreted invariably as a sign of hunger, reflecting upon the status and prestige of the child's family. Never to show hunger outside of one's own home is one of the principal rules of adult social behavior, and by observing this rule the individual can restrict very effectively his obligation to share his food to a small circle of others upon whose reciprocation and co-operation he depends. It is explained to the young child that the food might do harm to his health, and so children begin to develop fear of all foods offered to them by outsiders.

As soon as a child has gained a certain physical independence by being able to walk, he discovers a new resource: theft of food. A definite pattern of food theft can be observed at about two years of age, when a child will steal a morsel in an unobserved moment, eat it at once, and then go to hide somewhere. Severe punishment follows the discovery of these thefts. However, food is never hidden from children but is placed somewhere out of their reach, and adults explain to the child with words and gestures that a certain food must not be touched, for it belongs to another member of the family. Children eat at the same time as their parents, but if these eat at a table, the children sit on the floor or on the doorstep near by. The use of knife, spoon, or fork is not taught. Solid food is eaten with the fingers, while liquid soups are eaten with a crude spoon made from gourd shell.

During the second and third years of life the child is systematically trained to share food with others, especially with members of his kin-group. Morsels are given to him with the words, 'Go ahead. Distribute it. Share it with others.' Obediently the child will break the morsel into pieces and offer every person present a bit, but if he is still too small to do so, the mother will do it for him and return the smallest part to the child. At the beginning children cry when being thus deprived of food they already hold in their hands as their own, but soon they learn the pattern and behave accordingly. Frequently one can see toddlers who, when having their meals, will offer a bit to any person who might pass by.

The common adult practice of refusing food to express anger, is established at an early age, indeed, soon after weaning. After a temper tantrum, a punishment, or any other frustrating experience, small children are likely to reject food. At such times they are never forced to eat. Another habit which begins at about the time of weaning and often continues throughout life is lip-sucking. The newly weaned infant, to simulate the nursing he has been deprived of, sucks his lips, usually the lower one, with a smacking sound. This habit is not discouraged in any way, and soon becomes fixed, so that practically all adults as well as children suck their lips, making the smacking noises of a nursing infant. Children under five years of age, as well as older children, are frequently seen sucking or chewing objects such as pieces of wood, a bit of string, or some fruit kernel. They chew sugar cane and suck the nipples of bottles used in feeding an infant brother or sister, sometimes refusing to return the nipple even when it is needed. These habits are not punished any more after the child has reached about one year of age, nor are they ridiculed.

Geophagy is common in children of four or five years, who eat clay or dry lumps from the mud walls of the house. If this habit continues after five or six years, the mother or some other adult will force the child to eat a lump of earth allegedly brought from the village cemetery, and it is said that this punishment stops the habit quite effectively.

Food soon becomes an imaginary value and most games of small children are concerned with it. They will imitate kitchen scenes, building a little hearth on which pots and pans, simulated by pebbles or fruits, are placed, and will 'cook', or play at 'preparing a meal'. The fascination of the play is often so strong that a child will swallow a large amount of the sand representing 'food', sometimes almost asphyxiating on it.

Food is often the object of fighting between siblings. Any scarce item, especially, may be taken away from a younger child by an older one, either by force or intimidation. This jealousy about food is also obvious in the way older children stare at a nursing baby, often trying to touch or fondle the mother's breast.

Even after a small child can already walk he is carried a great deal, generally by an older sibling. A mother who has a choice will, as a rule, put the infant in charge of an older son so that an older daughter can continue to help her in the household. Sometimes a boy of three or four years will prepare an infant's food and carry the baby inside the house or the yard, and boys of eight or ten years will sometimes be in charge of two infants, a task they fulfil only with utmost reluctance, and with much teasing and mishandling of their younger siblings. Rarely will an older child voluntarily play with a two- or three-year-old, and adults practically never play with their children of any age, although they claim to do so very often.

Children over one year old are bathed occasionally by their mothers or other adults, or even by a child nurse, but such baths are not at fixed intervals, nor are they general in all families. In one family there might be more emphasis upon bathing than in another, and there is variation from daily to weekly baths, while some children are hardly ever bathed at all. From three years on, a child is capable of washing his own hands and face, and sometimes of combing his hair, but little encouragement is given to independence in personal hygiene, and if a child does not wash himself he is not punished for it. Quite on the contrary, it often happens that a child is punished for 'wasting' water if he should wash himself. At four years, children rarely cry when being taken out of a lukewarm bath, or even when being washed in the river.

A child's hair is cut for the first time only after he can speak clearly, as it is believed that he would not learn to do so if it were cut earlier. Toilet-training continues in the manner begun in infancy. At about three years most children will leave the house to eliminate, but in boys complete sphincter-control is achieved only at four or five, and enuresis is frequent until much later. As was mentioned earlier, boys go naked until they reach four or five years of age, but girls wear little shirts or dresses by the end of the first year, and by the end of the second are taught to keep them clean lest people think badly of their mothers.

Younger children always sleep apart from adults, usually in a hammock strung near the bed or hammock of the parents, and often several children will sleep in the same hammock or on a mat on the floor. Sometimes when they feel cold or frightened they will try to climb into their parents' bed. Often they are pushed away and made to sleep alone, but sometimes they are allowed to stay. Women who live alone with their children tell laughingly that, when a man has paid them a night visit, the child has been badly frightened upon realizing that the mother has company in her bed.

Although parents say that sick children are always very well cared for and that no effort or expense is spared in order to restore their health, in the many cases we observed this was not true. Disease is accepted with fatalism and little or nothing is done to cure it. Home remedies are sometimes prepared and a mother might perhaps make a vow to a saint or to the Virgin, promising a candle or a mass should the child recover, but expensive medicines are rarely given to a child, nor is it common that a local specialist is consulted. We know of no case where a sick child was taken to a trained physician in the lowland towns.

The practice of frightening the child by threats is continued systematically at this age level, not just casually, but day by day. As soon as a child who can walk approaches the door, the mother or any other adult calls out, 'If you leave the house, they will get you and take you away.' *They* are the jaguar, the owl, the cat, any of a number of fear-inspiring animals. After the age of three a variety of new threatening apparitions are mentioned, such as witches, the Devil, or certain water demons. Adults will say, 'If you leave, the police will get you', or, 'The Devil will get you and tear your tongue out.' Indians are also represented as evil and dangerous, and a mother will often frighten a child by calling out, 'There comes an Indian!' One woman had a nervous fit in our presence when someone showed her a small turtle, and afterward explained that as a child her parents used to frighten her with such an animal. A male informant said, 'As a child my parents always frightened me, saying that the jaguar was coming for me. Now I am scared even of cats.'

There are several men in the village who, because of their particular physical appearance, are often asked by mothers to come and frighten their disobedient children, and who do so voluntarily. One of them has a face deformed by a rhinoscleroma, while another's is affected by mycodermosis. Called by the mothers, these or other men will put on some disguise and then come to the house and threaten the child with 'carrying it away' or 'eating it up'. Many of our informants told us of these childhood experiences, of how they were threatened with machetes or knives, or made to kiss their mothers as a sign of their obedience. 'That's how our parents domesticated us,' they say (*así nuestros padres nos domesticaron*), and many will add that they became very obedient and well behaved after these punishments. Another informant explained her great fear of darkness saying that her grandmother, with whom she lived alone as a small child, often was afraid at night and woke her to carry her to the house of neighbors to spend the rest of the night there.

Threats of castration are made even before the child has reached the age of twelve months and are repeated ever after. Both men and women will say, 'I am going to castrate you' (*te voy a capar*), and sometimes scissors or knives are displayed with corresponding gestures. Girls are sometimes threatened with animals or objects which might enter their vagina, but it is mostly boys to whom threats of sexual aggression are addressed.

It is understandable then that children at this age are very much afraid of darkness and still never sleep without a light in the room. However, they show little fear of strangers and approach them or talk to them without evident suspicion. Having been taught in babyhood to fear all animals, children are greatly afraid of mules, horses, cows, donkeys, pigs, dogs, or any other large beast which might be met with, until they realize that these animals are generally harmless; then they take pleasure in beating and tormenting them.

At about two years a child owns a small hammock, some clothes, and a bowl or plate. Perhaps his godfather or a relative will make him a gift of a piglet or a chicken 'to see if he is lucky' (*para verle la suerte*), i.e., to test his lucky hand and to see whether these animals will thrive and multiply under his care and ownership. However, a child hardly ever receives such gifts as playthings, it being thought that anything given to a child should have a practical nature.

Respectful behavior toward adults is taught early. At two years of age a child is expected to 'respect' an adult by sitting quietly, never passing in front of him or looking at his face while speaking. This behavior is not explained to the child but is taught by scolding him each time he does one of the forbidden things. As a child is never taught to express gratitude for a favor, there is no repetition of verbal formulas. To say 'please' and 'thank you' would be to express inferiority, and adults do not use these terms either. Obedience, however, is taught daily and insistently, from the time a child is able to walk. Adults will order a child to bring them a certain object, or to deposit it in a certain place. A mother might command a two-year-old child to take a few bananas to the kitchen, or to bring her a piece of wood from the backyard. When several adults are sitting in the presence of children, they will often give them one order after another, naming objects in a monotonous voice and having them brought by one child, taken back by another, handed to a third person, and so on. The objects thus brought are not needed by the person asking for them, and the only reason for these orders is to educate the child to prompt obedience to adults. There is no play involved and all individuals taking part are serious, calling out their orders in the same tone of voice. If a small child has accompanied his parents to the fields, he will always be given something to carry when returning to the village, maybe a fruit or a stick of firewood or a small bag with tubers. Or if nothing else, upon entering the village the father will give the child his hat or his sandals to carry, so the child will not return empty-handed.

At this age, the pattern of food exchange between individuals and families is continuously encouraged by making children share food with others and by sending them to other houses with small gifts. Every time food is brought from a field and almost every time food is prepared, the children will be sent to other homes with which there exist these exchange relations, and it is a very common sight to see small children carrying fruits, tubers, or pots from one house to the other.

The sexual organs, especially of male children, are stimulated frequently in a playful manner although castration threats are often used, too. As children are able to observe the sex life of adults, they soon try to imitate it, and at about four or five years boys and girls imitate coitus in the presence of adults. Such behavior is not punished, as people believe that it is quite natural in children. Masturbation is common at about three years and is always severely punished by slaps and threats of castration, accompanied by the showing of knives and scissors to scare the child. All adults and older children are obliged to denounce masturbatory practices of younger children immediately to the parents. All this in spite of the fact that mothers quite often masturbate their children when putting them to sleep. A certain tendency toward exhibitionism is observed in boys between two and five years. During these ages 'urinating contests'—in which the boys vie to see who can come nearest a target with his stream of urine—are common. Or, in the presence of parents or other people, the boys will try to urinate into a bottle, or will persecute a girl by trying to urinate on her dress. These 'show-offs' are laughed at by the adults, and rather encouraged, but at five years of age the sexes are separated at play, both boys and girls tending to form their own play-groups, without mixing.

Little effort is made to teach children to tell the truth. Sometimes they are scolded for it, but otherwise lying is thought to be a natural tendency which cannot be avoided. Children sometimes boast in the presence of parents or other adults that they are better liars than other children, and adults will laughingly admit such claims. Stealing, however, is severely punished, particularly if a child should steal something belonging to a member of another household. It is not the act of stealing itself which is considered improper, but the possible consequences it might lead to, for example, enmity between two families. All acts of physical aggression a child might commit against his mother are also severely punished, but little attention is paid to verbal aggression and insults. Obscene language is never considered improper for children.

Food is never withheld as a punishment. If a child spoils food or throws it away in a fit of rage, he is obliged to recover it and to eat it, and should he react aggressively, a severe beating is in order. However, should he refuse the food in a quiet manner, there will be no punishment. After eighteen months a child's crying is generally punished with hard slaps; sometimes the father will slap the child for this reason, but more often it is the mother or the child-nurse. The relationships between the child and the sibling (or siblings) in charge of him are frequently extremely hostile. The older children will punish their small charges, take away their food, threaten them with castration and death, drop them intentionally, and frighten them to make them cry.

If a child between one and five years should pass near the barroom, or be seen walking in the general direction of it, adults will exclaim, 'Look at him! He is going for a drink. What a shameless boy!' This is done in a joking manner, but with the serious intention of teaching the child that the barroom is a dangerous and improper place. However, boys of four or five years are often seen watching from across the street the people drinking in the barroom, and play frequently at 'being drunk'. Staggering about with half-closed eyes they will cry, 'I am drunk' ('*toy rascao*'), a play which much amuses adults. Girls of the same age often fashion dolls of odd pieces of clothes and, pretending that 'the doll is hungry', they will play at nursing them or feeding them with a spoon. Even boys will play in this manner and 'suckle' a doll.

Upon numerous occasions we observed that children of four or five years, at being exposed by their parents to a frustrating experience, will project their rage immediately, not upon inanimate objects, but upon any other person present. A child who has been beaten or scolded will make menacing gestures or grimaces at a passer-by or at a casual visitor, or will beat a sibling. This behavior is at times accompanied by slight but definite clonic spasms. On other occasions, a child who has been beaten, scolded, hurried, or ordered to perform some disagreeable task will suddenly shrink away in panic from any adult who might come near, giving the impression that he feels that that person also is responsible for the frustration.

Children of both sexes often intentionally destroy objects, generally something belonging to their mother. They will break a comb or soil a dress and then deny having done it. Sometimes they are punished, but more often they are able to convince their mother of their innocence, by accusing their siblings or other children instead. Much hostility is directed by a child against the straw hat his mother is weaving. This hat is considered as a personal enemy, a rival in the mother's affection, and even toddlers of less than two years of age will furiously tear it from their mother's hands, demanding her attention. Children will hide it, or eliminate upon it, but mothers rarely will punish them for doing so and will say, 'It is their way of punishing me.'

The temper tantrums of the first year continue in more and more violent form, up to the seventh year at least. Children will roll on the floor, beat their heads against the wall, and may even break their teeth while doing so. Very often they beat their fists against their chest and head, tear out their hair, or twist their ears. Sometimes they will bite the floor or a stone, filling their mouths with earth or ashes. As soon as children have learned to speak, they scream threats against their mother, which become increasingly verbose and insulting as the child acquires a wider vocabulary. When touched, they will beat wildly about them. Incontinence often accompanies such tantrums, but vomiting as a sign of protest ceases generally after the first year. Tantrums seem to be considerably more frequent among boys than among girls, who are less exposed to punishment because they are generally more obedient and on better terms with their mothers. These fits of rage (*ataques de rabia*) are hardly commented upon by the adults who witness them. They are neither ridiculed nor punished, but treated with indifference. Night terrors are observed mainly between one and five years. Children wake crying and frightened and have to be calmed, often by being taken into the bed of an adult. It seems possible that some children only pretend to have such frights and nightmares in order to be taken into the bed of the mother.

Even small children of two or three years, after being punished or scolded, will threaten their parents with running away from home. Sometimes they put this into practice, actually leaving the house and spending the day on the street, or in the houses of relatives or friends.

The complete lack of privacy and the indifference with which all bodily functions are treated by adults cause children at a very early age to become acquainted with the intimacies of adult life. Pregnancy and birth, menstruation, coitus, death, violence, and drunkenness all take place before the eyes of children, and little or no effort is made to avoid this. The only exception is in the case of coitus, it being considered improper that a child be aware of it, but adults often do not know that they are being watched and, moreover, they actually care very little if they are seen. Should a couple realize that a child is watching them during intercourse, they simply order him to look the other way. Children demonstrate great curiosity and often simulate sleep in order to observe adults. They also will listen at the walls of other houses, peep through openings into the interior, or follow a couple who walk to the fields.

Scenes of violence often make a deep and lasting impression upon children. Quite often older children, even siblings, after watching how a cow or a pig is butchered, will take a knife and jokingly threaten a smaller child, and we were told of several cases in which the threatened child fainted. Child-nurses say to their charges, 'I will kill you like a pig', thus causing fainting spells and night terrors. Several adults say that they still suffer from nightmares in which they re-experience the fear they felt when, at five or six years, they saw a corpse for the first time. When watching childbirth, children are greatly impressed by the midwife and her activities. When the umbilical cord is cut, they believe that the baby is castrated, and when they see the midwife sucking out the phlegm from the baby's nose, they are under the impression that she drinks the infant's blood. Small children often believe that the midwife intends to kill mother and child, and are horrified at the blood, screams, and acts of violence which invariably accompany birth.

Several adult informants say that when receiving bad news they experience a sensation of numbness and are unable to move or to speak for a while. When asked to explain the causes of this feeling, they declare unanimously that they remember their childhood and their mother telling them to 'be quiet', whenever they began to cry or were in any way emotionally upset. This 'Be quiet! Sit still! Don't move!' of childhood days, repeated daily for years and years, they believe has influenced their reactions to all emotional stimuli in such a way as to make them appear quite apathetic and unable to control muscular movements.

During all these years there is no religious or moral education of a formal nature. That is, children are not taught a special code of behavior the infraction of which might lead to supernatural punishment or guilt feelings. There is, in educational theory and practice, no sin or grace or any certainty that an action—good or evil—will receive reward or punishment in this or another world. All a child is given to understand morally is that he must collaborate in the food production and that he must let others take part in the produce. There is no instruction about honesty or loving one's neighbor or reverencing a supreme being. According to local religious concepts every good or evil action finds its reward or punishment in *this* world, and the child is taught to avoid frictions with society, not because they are inherently 'evil', but because they might endanger his health and food supply. An eventual divine judgment or punishment is never mentioned, but the 'Devil's punishment', i.e., retribution by sorcery practiced by others, is constantly feared and talked about.

The basic techniques of education are fear and bribery. All 'don'ts' are accompanied by threats of physical aggression and danger, while all 'do's' are accompanied by a promise of reward, generally of food. However, such promises are rarely kept, and the threats are carried out inconsistently. Children learn at an early age the fundamental rule of adult behavior, i.e., not to trust in anybody's words or actions, and they develop simultaneously a fatalistic and passive attitude toward the world, always expecting the worst.

It is a generally accepted belief that the children of a 'bad' husband will be well behaved, and vice versa; and that the children of a woman who lives in fairly good relations with her consort, will be very unruly. In the first case it is thought that the father's example will keep the children from being ill-mannered and lazy because their mother will constantly point out that the lack of food or clothes is the father's fault. On the other hand, in a household where there are strong ties between husband and wife, it is suggested that the mother will be too lenient and indulgent with her children and will spoil them.

All during early childhood there is little contact with the father. Whenever a child wants something, he will approach his mother but almost never his father. If the fulfilment of the child's wish depends upon the father's decision, the mother will not ask the child to approach him personally, but will speak to her consort in the child's name.

There is no belief in reincarnation, and it is not customary to give the name of a dead relative to a newborn infant. In one exceptional case we observed that this was done, the child receiving his paternal grandfather's name because the latter had died on the day the child was born. A few months later the child died, and people attributed his death to his having been called by the dead relative's name, declaring that because of it the grandfather's spirit had claimed the child as a servant in the other world.

LATE CHILDHOOD

Children over five years of age eat together with the adults who live under the same roof. Their mother first serves the father and then shares the meal with the children, distributing the food according to the age of all present. Once everyone is served, no food can be exchanged. Sometimes, however, a single large dish or pot is placed before the whole group and everybody helps himself. In the latter case, the children often fight over morsels, each one trying to secure the best for himself at the expense of others. If one does not eat everything allotted to him or taken by him, he is obliged to offer it to someone else, generally a younger sibling. Should a child ask for food shortly after a meal the mother often will prepare some more for him. All individual dislikes are taken into account, as it is thought to be very dangerous for a child's health to oblige him to eat something he does not like. Boys who are late for a meal are punished with slaps unless they have been working, but their share is always kept for them. Not to keep someone's food when he is late to a meal is one of the most unforgivable actions a mother or wife could commit.

Older children are allowed to eat between meals any fruits that might be available. Children between seven and ten years continue to steal food, especially raw sugar, refined sugar, or any other food with a high caloric value. Although they are punished for doing so, such thefts are very common. At this age, should a child refuse food out of rage or anger, he is generally beaten and forced to eat it, but should he refuse for some other reason it is immediately supposed that he is ill. Food ex-

100

change and distribution continue, older children being continuously admonished to share food with their younger siblings. There are a few rare cases of children who do so voluntarily, but most of them are extremely envious of all food a baby or a younger sibling receives.

When a boy reaches ten or twelve years his father will assign to him a small empty plot in his field and allow him to cultivate it. Even a fatherless or illegitimate child may be permitted to cultivate a plot in the fields of a relative, a godfather, or friends. In either case the boy is made responsible from then on for the care of this piece of land. It is always understood that the food produced on such a plot has to be given to the child's mother, and the boy is often quite proud to bring home fruits or tubers planted and harvested by him alone. Boys are eager to be old enough to cultivate a field and speak with pride of their work. Their ready acceptance of agricultural tasks is, of course, partly due to the fact that they thus avoid the boring duty of taking care of infants and younger children, but they also seem truly to enjoy working in the fields.

But even before that age, in fact from six years old on, children represent a most important labor force in the village. They work in the fields, carry burdens, tend the animals, process and prepare food, prepare palm fibers, weave hats, help in house-construction work, run errands, take care of smaller children. There is hardly a task a child of seven or eight is not asked and expected to perform. A more or less strict division of activities between the sexes is observed, boys working mainly outside the house, while girls do the chores inside or near it. Some tasks which later on are assigned to one sex are done by both up to about ten years. For example, boys *and* girls of seven to ten fetch water from the river and also prepare palm fibers, but in later years these become almost exclusively female tasks. Girls and boys are taught to weave hats at about five or six years, carry heavy loads at about seven. Girls sweep the house and the yard at seven or eight, and wash the kitchen utensils; at about ten years they begin to cook.

Respectful behavior toward the father and all adult relatives is stressed during these years. The main emphasis is on obedience, collaboration, not passing in front of a person without asking his pardon, not passing between adults who are engaged in conversation, not making noise or fighting in the presence of adults. Both parents teach the child to use certain words or phrases of courtesy and teach them to address all relatives by formal kinship terms instead of the familiar 'thou' (*vos*). Gift exchange with the maternal grandmother is encouraged, but little sattention is paid to a child's relationships with his or her paternal grandparents.

In spite of the great aggressiveness displayed by children in the intimacy of their homes, they are generally well behaved as soon as a visitor or a stranger appears. If children could be judged only from the impression gained on these occasions, one would conclude that they are very controlled and quiet, polite, respectful, and co-operative. But this is only outward behavior and as soon as the child is alone again within his domestic unit, the rudest behavior is displayed. Although this applies mainly to boys, girls also become increasingly aggressive as they get older and develop strong hostilities against their parents, especially their mother.

Relationships between siblings continue to be markedly hostile. The older ones take away the youngers' food or playthings, beat and push them whenever they can, and try to make them cry. As the mother generally enters in defense of the younger or of the female child, whereas the father favors the son or the older child, such fights lead frequently to frictions between husband and wife. Older children who are obliged to carry a younger sibling will pinch him so he will cry and his mother will carry him for a while, the older brother (or sister) running away in the meantime. At other times they will claim that their charges are hungry and will themselves eat all the food they receive for the younger child. There are, however, some boys and girls who seemingly are willing to take care of a younger sibling, but many do so only in order to escape other kinds of work, such as carrying water or firewood.

Good relations between neighbors depend to a high degree upon the behavior of their children to each other. Parents often forbid their children to visit other houses or to play with neighbors' children for fear they might become involved in fights and thus cause enmity between families. Boys of the Plaza barrio may roam freely in the village but are advised to be careful when going to the Loma, because of the traditional hostility existing between the children of the two barrios. Girls are never allowed to go to the Loma, except in the company of adults, and lomero girls will hardly ever enter the Plaza barrio alone.

Fear, deliberately taught and used, dominates childhood. Children are taught that there is nothing but danger in nature, that the forest, the creeks, and the fields are full of latent enemies. Thunder and lightning, wind and rain, heat and cold, darkness, the rays of the sun, and animals, as well as ancestral spirits, witches and apparitions, the Devil, are all described to children as enemies bent upon causing disease and death. When clouds hang deep over the mountains and darkness comes early in the afternoon, mothers will say to their children: 'The jaguars are coming down to eat us.' Or, when the wind rustles dry leaves at night, they will say they hear witches or the Devil. Any strange noise, the call of a bird, a creaking branch, the flutter of a bat, are interpreted to children as omens, harbingers, or spirits in search of a victim. But the child is not taught any defensive attitude except the passive one of hiding, of being quiet and motionless. A very few mothers teach their children to cross themselves when feeling in danger, and fewer still teach them to say a short prayer, but the only protective measure which is systematically and generally taught is never to leave the house after dark and to sleep always in a lighted room. These teachings have a profound and lasting influence upon children and adolescents. All are extremely afraid to leave their homes after nightfall, be it only to cross the street. If, for some reason or other, it becomes necessary to do so, they will ask an adult to accompany them and will carry torches, sticks, and machetes. Boys and girls even past puberty are afraid when they wake up and find that the light has gone out while they slept. Children do not even dare to leave the house at night in order to eliminate and therefore often soil the living-room. Even adults are very reluctant to go out and so there is a considerable degree of retention caused by this fear of darkness.

Children of both sexes smoke cigars, boys often beginning to do so at about seven or eight. Girls begin generally after puberty. The habit is not discouraged by the adults. As a matter of fact, it is often the mother who introduces the child to it, usually at the age when the permanent teeth are being cut. Children and adults claim that the habit begins suddenly, usually in connection with a certain event which is often recalled throughout life. Many say that they began smoking when they first went coffee-picking; others, that it was during dentition; and others, that they began to smoke when their father died, trying their first cigar during the wake. Alcohol is not permitted to children but occasionally a seven- or eight-year-old boy might drink a sip of rum if it is offered to him.

Masturbation is still punished at this age, but castration threats are not used with older children. All physical contact between boys and girls is forbidden, even during games. Among siblings, however, such contacts are not considered improper. Although ideally a male child should never see his mother or adult sister naked, in the crowded sleeping quarters this cannot always be avoided.

Physical aggressiveness develops rapidly after a child reaches five years. Both boys and girls throw stones at adults, strike them when angry, or insult them with obscene words. Adults with physical handicaps or old people are mocked and insulted; animals are often beaten mercilessly; and smaller siblings are always exposed to slaps and pushes. Seven- or eight-year-old boys often will beat younger children in order to 'teach them respect'. Fights between children and aggressiveness of older children against the younger ones are frequent reasons for frictions between neighbors. Although all adults agree that any child has the right to punish a younger child, they demand retribution if the victim is their own child. An adult will never punish the child of a neighbor or a relative but will always complain first to the child's parents. Perhaps these will authorize the offended person to punish the culprit, but sometimes they will punish him personally, in the presence of the offended party. Should an adult who accuses another person's child of a misdeed be told that the misbehavior was not serious enough to warrant punishment, enmity is likely to develop between the two families. Where enmity already exists, families incite their children to be aggressive against the other's children, in order to annoy them by not giving satisfaction for their complaints. On the other hand, adults will often send a child to spy on matters they are interested in, and much gossip between neighbors is based upon the reports of children who have been told to spy on other people, or who are doing so on their own initiative.

Aggressiveness between children which is limited to words or gestures is hardly ever punished, even if the victim is badly frightened. Food continues to be a frequent motif for fights between children and when the mother serves the meal they will often take away morsels from each other, accuse the mother of favoritism, or try to spoil the other child's food. During the gathering of fruits such as mangoes or avocados, there develop often violent fistfights during which children of both sexes try to take away from each other what they have collected. As a rule, girls are more submissive and respectful to their mothers than boys. At about eight or ten years, boys are often in open rebellion against her authority and might even try to strike her. Quite often they will insult their mothers with the most offensive words and we observed many cases where boys called their mother a whore every time they were punished or ordered to perform a task they did not like.

Lying, although occasionally punished, becomes more and more frequent as children advance in age. Often food is involved, but at other times lying is employed to explain or excuse orders not carried out, thefts of objects, or acts of physical aggressiveness against other children. At the discovery of a theft, children will often accuse innocent younger siblings or even adults. Often a child will go to a neighbor's or relative's house and borrow food, saying that he was sent by his mother. Then he will hide and eat it and, if discovered, will put the blame upon some adult or even on his own mother. Or, as happens frequently, a child who has received a legitimate gift of food for himself will return after a while to the giver and say that it was taken away from him and eaten by the mother, a lie which is very effective in procuring more food from commiserating relatives or neighbors. But there is no shame in being discovered in a lie. Children who are praised by their parents for their honesty will often contradict by pointing out lies and thefts which their elders did not know of up to the moment. This is taken as a sign of cleverness rather than a cause for punishment.

Up until six or seven years corporal punishment is mainly limited to a few slaps but severe beatings are given to children over this age.

A severe beating (*limpia fuerte*) is understood to be a punishment which causes blood to run and which leaves scars, while a lesser beating (*penca*) leaves only a few welts. An angry mother will beat her unruly children with anything at hand, even with a stone or a machete, and some women are said to have nearly killed their children by beating them. Sometimes neighbors interfere if a mother or father is too infuriated and likely to cause serious harm to a child. However, there is much variation. Some adults are permissive, whereas others punish their children almost daily. One woman said, 'If I were to beat them for every misbehavior, my hands would be busy all day long'; another said, 'The more I beat them, the better I like beating them.' A child who is punished by a mother will generally seek protection from the father, and vice versa, and should the other parent not be present, he will look for refuge to an older brother or sister. Sometimes a child will run away from home and hide in the house of a grandmother or an aunt. However, severe physical punishments are not frequent and there is little emphasis upon beating as a disciplinary measure. Attitudes, as a whole, are permissive and resigned, and the education of a child is characterized by continuous naggings, slaps, threats, and admonitions, rather than by beatings.

Night terrors continue through late childhood. Children wake frightened and screaming, saying that they dreamed they were pursued by wild animals. Parents believe that such terrors are mainly due to intestinal parasites, but some say that many children suffer from exaggerated fear of the dark, and that the best remedy is to give them a few hard slaps as soon as they awake in terror.

Parents teach children at an early age to observe class differences. Boys pay little attention to the rules and often placeros and lomeros will play together, but girls are very conscious of social status and a placero girl of eight or ten years will hardly speak to a lomero child. Their mothers tell them: 'Don't mix with them, they are dirt' (*no te juntes, que es mugre*). However, should it happen that a group of girls play a game with a lomero girl, or a child belonging to any lower social stratum, the latter is sure to appear in an inferior role. For example, while playing at preparing a meal, the girls might invite a lomero child to join them but make her carry water, cook the food, and wash the utensils, while the placero girls give orders and expect to be served. This pattern can be observed even among children of the same family unit, the illegitimate or half-siblings being obliged during games to take the inferior part.

As boys and girls are usually strictly separated during games, there is hardly any sex play. Boys of eight or ten years sometimes show a certain tendency to transvestism—i.e., they put on their sister's dresses, have their hair combed like a girl's, and mimic female activities for a few hours—but we never observed cases where girls of that age put on male clothes. Boys up to five or six years often wear their hair long and, at three or four years, even wear ribbons in it.

Because older children take an active part in family economics, they begin to have more contact with their fathers. Although they will hardly ever approach him for food or clothes, they might occasionally ask him for a few coins to buy something from a street vendor or to go to a cockfight. The moment to approach a father for money comes when he is drunk, and a mother will often advise her children to wait for this occasion. So the children will watch to catch the father when he is in the barroom with some friends and will ask him there for money. He then can hardly refuse if he does not wish to appear a miser.

Should a father become annoyed with a child, he seldom punishes him immediately but will rather tell his mother first, and she will tell the child. Should there be further reasons for complaint, the father has the 'right' to punish the child directly. A father is supposed to feel greater affection for his daughters, and a mother for her sons. This is actually true sometimes, especially in the latter case. Mothers have a tendency to give more and better food to their male children 'because males need more food'. But it is also evident that women do this with the calculated purpose of insuring the son's affection and economic help in future years when they themselves might depend on their male offspring's gifts of food.

Some summary remarks on the general quality of parent-child relationships are due at this point. According to ideal standards, parents are obliged to rear their children to become useful members of society. They should provide them with adequate food, clothing, and shelter and should, by the example of their own behavior, teach them to be responsible, hard-working group-members. In their turn, children should love and respect their parents, collaborate actively in the economic life of the family and household unit, and help to support their parents until death. This is the ideal formulation, but in no home were we able to observe even an approximation to this goal. The tensions in the husband-wife relationship influence, as is natural, their relationships with their children, and strong conflicts between generations are the rule. Parents seem to be little aware of this and, while readily recognizing the divergence between ideal and real behavior in their own conjugal relations, they do not seem to believe this is also the case in their relationships with their offspring.

Parent-child relations are largely dominated by the requirement to respect the father and to accept his authority. Obedience is, therefore, stressed but as many children do not live under the same roof with their fathers, this paternal control is often lacking. As the mother's authority over children is little emphasized and as other relatives are rarely interested in exercising a strict control over children not their own, the latter tend soon to disobey all adults and to develop an artificial obedience pattern during the presence of their fathers. In homes based upon Catholic marriage and a nuclear family, relations with children are considerably more harmonious, but as these are rather the exception and not the rule, overall parent-child relationships contain many conflicting aspects.

As a rule, society attributes responsibility of a child's education and behavior to his mother, but where the child lives in the same household with his father, he, too, might be blamed for serious misbehavior of his children. As many women are abandoned by their spouses, or live otherwise under difficult economic conditions, they resent this responsibility and often try to evade it in every way. Nonetheless, whatever education a child receives is due mainly to the mother or to other women such as grandmothers, aunts, or older siblings. The father hardly interferes, except by insisting upon obedience to him and by punishing the child for lack of 'respectful' behavior.

Both parents point out to their children each other's undesirable traits as 'bad example'. Even in the man's presence a woman will tell her children that their father is a lazy and drunken rogue, an utterly irresponsible creature whose habits will only bring misery to his family and should never be imitated. Men are not less articulate in their accusations and tell the children that they should not be as dirty and lazy as their mothers, and that she is to blame for the unappetizing food and the torn clothes. Adultery, physical aggressiveness, and laziness are attributed by each parent to the other as threatening examples of how one should not behave. Even racial prejudices might be used in this context and an annoyed father will tell his children: 'A bunch of Indians, that's what you are, thanks to what you inherited from your mother'. However, illiteracy and ignorance of one of the parents are never referred to on these occasions, as they are not considered to be the personal faults of the individual but of his parents who did not give their children a 'right' education. The wife of an illiterate man will, therefore, never tell her children that this represents a handicap they themselves should avoid. Such discussions and accusations with 'educational' purposes do rarely form a motif for quarrels between spouses, but the accused partner often agrees with the accuser and tells the children that his mother (or father) is quite right in using his person as an example of 'bad' behavior.

The exterior racial characteristics of a child determine to a high degree the manner in which he is reared by his parents or other adults. A father will always prefer a child with a Caucasoid phenotype and will attribute 'bad' personality traits to a child with 'Indian blood'. A mother, however, usually prefers children with alleged 'Indian' traits.

As one woman put it: 'Of an Indian child a mother expects more because he is less pretentious and kinder with her. A white child has higher aspirations because of his father's race. Such a child becomes pretentious, does not help his mother, and often despises her for being an Indian woman.' There is a certain truth in this statement and it is a fact that many children develop contempt for their mothers when these show more 'Indian' traits than they themselves. But favoritism is rare in both parents and they hardly ever show a very marked preference for a certain child. Both change their behavior and affections continuously and the child can never be sure of their reactions to him under any given circumstances. The fear-inspiring father image is obliterated as soon as the child can understand the implications of his mother's accusations against the father. The picture the mother paints for a child of his father is never the one of the hero and of the provider, but of a dangerous brute whose only attribute consists in his physical strength and his 'right' to punish. That the parents have to be respected is rather taught by other relatives the child has contact with, by grandfathers, uncles, or aunts, but as there is no continuity within the family proper, these teachings are rarely followed. In any event, it is the mother who prepares the food and mends the clothes, and who, after all, gives the child a sense of security, and the emotional ties between mother and child are considerably stronger than those that exist in the father-child relationship. A mother is in physical contact with the infants and will occasionally caress and pat an older child, but a father will rarely touch a child and his hands are never a substitute for the mother's.

Children with physical defects that are not directly deforming are generally treated by everyone as if they were completely normal. Often the handicap is considered a blessing, as in the case of the mother of a cross-eyed girl who considered herself lucky because 'she always had wanted a cross-eyed child'. The mother of a child who became blind at ten years when a curer applied a remedy to a slight irritation, proclaimed at once that her boy was a diviner able to see the future.

From early childhood on, boys and girls are expected to work, and most aspects of parent-child relationships are conditioned by this collaboration in the food quest. Laziness or willingness to work are the main criteria according to which parents treat their children, and these criteria distinguish between children as food-consumers and food-producers. To produce food, to give food, means love, affection, protection, obedience, respect. But laziness and gluttony are the daily reproaches parents make to their children. Quite often a child, when ordered to perform a certain task, simply refuses to obey because, having been told so often that he is lazy, he has come to believe it. This continuous pattern of chaffing and reprimanding a child makes him soon quite indifferent to orders and parental authority. Older children and adolescents will do only the urgent work around the house from which they themselves derive a benefit, such as carrying water and firewood or running errands to a store. But tasks such as sweeping and cleaning, mending broken utensils, or taking care of smaller siblings or domestic animals, are done usually only under threats of physical punishment.

As the father is seldom at home, punishment is mostly administered by the mother. Physical punishment begins early, as we have seen, but in the case of small children they are rather punished by the father, who becomes exasperated by their crying, than by the mother. It is generally the rule that a father punishes the male children while the mother will punish the girls and as the latter are almost always near their mothers, they are likely to receive a much greater share of punishments than their brothers do. A father often does not administer the punishment himself but first complains to the mother and asks her to correct the child's behavior. According to ideal patterns this should always be so, but in reality a father sometimes metes out immediate punishment.

As long as children are small and depend upon their parents or at least upon their mothers, they can only develop an attitude of distrustful fear, but once they become adolescents they react differently. Girls, who all have learned to weave straw hats, soon realize their monetary value and begin to weave them, not to contribute to the household budget, but to buy dresses and to save money. Boys learn the monetary value of their work in the fields and begin to earn small sums from occasional employment by adults. This causes renewed reproaches from their parents and now the children begin to protest against harsh treatment. Sometimes there is open rebellion, sometimes a slow retreat paired with expressions of increasing hostility and contempt for their elders.

Children often obtain information that can be used by them for blackmailing one of their parents. They learn of their extramarital affairs, debts, thefts, drunkenness, of money hidden away, or of food concealed from others. Quite often they will readily use this knowledge to intimidate a parent, generally the mother, in order to avoid a punishment or to extort money or food in exchange for their silence. Mistrust is then mutual and parents often suspect their children of spying on them.

An illegitimate child who has been reared by his mother or other adult women often hardly knows his biological father when the latter has abandoned the woman, as frequently happens. Only years later, after the child has reached the age where he can already co-operate effectively in the household, does the father again show interest in his offspring, but this contact a father makes with his illegitimate children is then hardly more than the one that would exist between master and servant.

PUBERTY AND ADOLESCENCE

Puberty comes relatively late, in boys at about fourteen or fifteen years, in girls at about the same period. Adults consider the years of pre-puberty and puberty, i.e., from twelve or thirteen to the onset of full puberty, as a very dangerous period in the individual's life, dangerous in the sense of 'weakness' and 'delicacy' which makes him an easy victim of disease. Although many people claim that mortality is high during these years, we found no evidence for this belief and rather had the impression that youths of this age-group were physically quite healthy and little preoccupied with their health.

The most important social effect of puberty is a change of dress. Boys are now allowed to wear long trousers, and girls wear skirts which reach down over their knees. While the latter seem to show little interest in effecting this change, the boys are greatly preoccupied with it. The long trousers have to be bought with money they earn themselves, and it takes about a year to save enough for this purchase. It is a great moment when the mother or father tells the boy to begin saving money so that he can prepare to buy his first pair of long trousers.

At puberty boys are 'freed' (*quedan libres*), i.e., they are no longer obliged to work exclusively for their parents or guardians. Until a generation ago a boy was 'freed' only at twenty-two, but since then boys have demanded this freedom earlier. Although the duty to help the mother and father with work and food persists for life, once a boy is 'free' he can establish his own home, claim his heritage, establish himself in marriage or concubinage, and live his own life apart from parental tutelage. To reach this liberty is the ambition of all boys. His parents, especially the mother, are often the greatest obstacle. To go without the help and work of a grown boy is often a great loss to his family, and quite frequently adults will do everything in their power to prolong his childhood and to refuse to give 'liberty' to their son. The final separation often comes only after a bitter quarrel between mother and son, the latter accusing the family of exploiting him and the former accusing him of ingratitude and of abandoning his mother to her fate. Mothers who have been abandoned by their husbands, or who expect to be abandoned soon by them, worry a great deal about the approaching moment when their sons or daughters will leave them too. But women sometimes try to smooth the way and suggest that the son leave whenever he wants to, in order to please him. In some cases it happens that a mother wishes her son to establish himself independently as soon as possible, counting upon adopting his first child and rearing the latter to be her servant and companion during later years, when her economic situation may be worse. So the conditions under which a son separates himself from the family vary widely, depending upon the economic situation of the family, upon whether or not his parents can count upon the help of younger siblings who will not reach puberty soon, and upon the strength of emotional ties between parents and sons.

One or two years before being 'freed', a boy will begin to work considerably more, not always for his parents, but rather to gain prestige in the village and to earn some money of his own. A boy who is known to be a hard worker has no difficulty in finding temporary employment in the pay of adults. Such work is not encouraged by the boy's family, who do not profit by it, and often the parents will even forbid a boy to accept such work when offered. Sometimes a boy will sell, without his parent's knowledge, some of the food he harvests on his father's fields. This, if discovered, leads inevitably to serious quarrels within his family. If the youth remains with his parents, he probably is no longer satisfied with receiving only food and shelter in return for his work and may even ask his father or guardian to pay him in money.

Girls, as a rule, are much less anxious to leave the paternal home. Moreover, should a daughter leave and go to live with a man, she and her consort will assist her mother effectively with food and work, and should the man abandon her, the girl will return to her mother. When a girl reaches puberty she tends to become more active in and around the house, and to pay more attention to her personal appearance. A girl who is quick at weaving straw hats and laundering, thrifty in her housework, and clean in her appearance, will soon find various male admirers from among whom she can choose the one who promises to be the best husband. Before reaching nubility, many girls have to be made to work, but, once puberty is attained, a girl works more willingly. As with boys, girls also begin to work for themselves some time before they leave the family. By weaving, laundering, or carrying water they earn small sums which are used to buy new dresses, and although the mother often disapproves, there is little she can do to keep her daughter from acquiring a small wardrobe and a few cosmetics.

A most effective way, however, to make a daughter stay with her mother, is to frighten her with the alleged dangers of childbirth. From earliest youth, girls are told that men are dangerous, evil, aggressive, lazy, and selfish. By the time they reach puberty the problems of pregnancy and childbirth have become very real to them and many a girl will readily postpone courtship and conjugal life out of fear of its consequences. The mother might even accuse her in public of being a thief, or a liar, or of having beaten her, in order to frighten off suitors.

A son who stays on for several years after having reached puberty is called a 'good' son by society. Daughters are hardly ever referred to in these terms, as they usually return eventually to the mother's side after having been abandoned, and they continue throughout life to give their mothers some economic assistance. A girl or a young woman who has been reared by a grandmother, aunt, or some other relative, might refuse to help her mother should she ask for food, saying that, as she did not rear her, she feels no obligation to give her any assistance. Boys and youths who are estranged from their families also may refuse to help their mothers, even though they should ask only for such minor services as carrying water or cutting firewood, saying simply that, as the mother always accused them of laziness, they need not expect anything else from them in the future.

The transition from childhood to puberty and adolescence is always accompanied by marked changes in outlook and behavior, but these can be observed much more readily in boys than in girls. A girl's life changes relatively little; she always preserves her emotional ties with her maternal family, never losing contact with her mother, her grandmother, or her aunts. Even after marriage, she continues to visit them and to help them, and a girl's real home is always the mother's house. This is not the case with boys. Once a son leaves his childhood home, be it his parents', mother's, or grandmother's, he is quite likely to sever all ties, and mutual resentment is often the rule. His hostility, combined with pride, do not allow him to return even in case of failure. Once he leaves he is on his own.

But whether or not he leaves home, all of a sudden, in a matter of a few weeks or at most months, the young man's entire outlook on life, his ambitions, and his values change, and his behavior follows suit. His former mobility of facial expression and gesture is transformed. His face becomes a rigid mask of 'seriousness' which betrays no emotion. The spontaneity of play gives way to silent deliberation. All conversation is dominated by extreme caution so that no word may betray inner feelings. Routine questions as to health, family, or work are answered with monotonous formulas, and any other inquiry is answered with a stereotyped 'I don't know, maybe' (*no sé, quizas*). Tasks which as a 'boy' he did willingly and quickly now become highly problematic, and often are postponed or rejected as impractical. A tremendous mechanism is set into motion completely hiding the individual behind a wall of control and formality. To smile, to laugh, to talk, to ask questions, to joke about people and things, these are now improper. All the former manifestations of aggressiveness are gone; no anger, no fits of sudden rage, no obscene language are now indulged in. In their place are aloofness and apparent indifference. But there is also a certain troubled alertness, seen in the quick furtive glance, in the nervous twitching of the hands, in the halting walk. An exaggerated self-consciousness makes the youth behave as if he were continuously watched, criticized or, worse still, ridiculed. This inner tension which characterizes the adolescent, continues into adulthood, no balance ever being achieved, it seems.

Even within their own age-group there are few themes which are discussed, and all conversation is limited by the great caution in choice of words. Physical appearance is sometimes talked about because adolescents worry a great deal about their hair, their skin color and their stature, as all these influence considerably their class-status. But there is little talk about girls, family affairs, or diseases, and young men in general are rather taciturn and inarticulate.

Boys of fifteen or sixteen years will occasionally spend a night singing, drinking, and playing music in the company of older men who invite them on such sprees. However, the youth rarely seems to enjoy drinking and takes part in such nightly adventures mainly to demonstrate his new manliness. But as soon as the new status is achieved, i.e., when the boy has left his home, such sprees become rare and are marked by increased seriousness. A man might drink and drum all night long without once losing his composure, without becoming aggressive, sentimental, verbose, or amorous.

Sexual experimenting by boys and girls begins at an early age, so that actual sex experience after puberty seems to add little to former knowledge. Boys of sixteen or seventeen generally have sweethearts and visit them whenever possible. Quite often, however, they have their first intercourse with an abandoned woman who has several children to support and who lends her favors in exchange for food the boy brings her. Such relationships are frequently quite public and are little criticized, as it is thought natural for a boy to look for sexual gratification wherever it may be found. No value whatsoever is placed upon a girl's virginity. Although its loss is verbalized as a 'damage' (*perjuicio*) in a moral and physical sense, no one's 'honor' is involved and the man is not blamed or coerced into marriage. First *emissio seminis*, *menarche*, and related matters are freely discussed at puberty between members of the same sex but never in the presence of a person of the opposite sex. After puberty such themes are hardly ever mentioned among men, who consider such talk as very improper, but women continue to speak rather freely among themselves about these matters. Mothers tell their nubile daughters that sexual intercourse is mainly a means of gaining economic advantage from a man. According to them, it is a sacrifice, a favor, which has to be paid for in some way, and to 'give' intercourse without making conditions and obtaining compensation from a man, would be the foolish squandering of the only effective hold women have on men. This idea is deeply rooted and general, and continues to be held throughout life. Men, having been taught the same, accept their obligation for prompt recompense and believe this to be a quite natural advantage women have over them.

During a short period just before adult status is achieved there exists a special joking relationships between adolescents and younger boys. The latter mock and tease the older ones, take away their hats, machetes, or bags, or challenge them to fights. Sometimes a group of four or five boys will playfully attack an adolescent boy, overpower him, and take away his possessions, but all this happens in a playful manner, without blows or offensive words. The older boys accept rather stoically these rough games, but once they tire of them, a few harsh words will restore the 'respect' due to them, and the younger boys will leave laughingly.

After a boy has reached puberty, his parents cannot prohibit his going on drinking sprees and cannot punish him if he returns home in an intoxicated state. Although some parents try to continue their control over the way in which a boy spends his money, there is general agreement that this is also impossible and would only lead to quarrels.

A girl's first menstruation does not seem to be a traumatic experience in any way. A mother does not think it necessary to tell her daughter about menstruation ahead of time as she rightly supposes that all children know about it. The *menarche*, therefore, never comes as a surprise and little importance is attached to it. Women see no reason why they should hide their condition and there is no secrecy or shame involved. On the contrary, details are freely discussed with other female members of the household, often in the presence of small children of both sexes. People say that in times past restrictions during menstruation were numerous and severe, and that there was much reserve and seclusion at the time of the *menarche*. The older women criticize the way in which the younger now quite openly discuss their condition.

Courtship involves considerable anxiety, at least on the part of the young man, who usually is very timid about establishing relations with a girl. As a rule, a youth needs a few strong drinks before he dares to speak to her. Trysts are arranged only at night, in the backyard or on some dark street corner, and lovers are never seen standing or walking together during the daytime, as gossip would probably impede their future meetings. There is no romantic love-making, no letter-writing, no serenading. Physical beauty is of little importance and a man's or woman's attractiveness for the other sex is measured mainly in terms of good health and hard work. The man's principal interest is not in sexual pleasure but in procreation. In order to prove his virility and his status as an adult, he has to beget children. Instead of saying, 'I love you', a young man will say, 'I bet I can get you with child' (*Apuesto que te saco un peláo ; verás que te hago un pichón*). This, in itself, is a declaration of love, a proposal to establish a common household, and a girl is flattered by such words.

Once the girl agrees to live with the man, a date is arranged for her to elope with him. Even if her family has not presented any obstacles to the match, secret elopement at night is the rule for all girls who leave their parents for the first time. At its 'discovery', the girl's mother will break out in tears and accusations of 'ingratitude' against the daughter who has abandoned her and the home where she had been reared and loved. The womenfolk of the neighborhood will join her in these lamentations and soon word will reach the mother as to the whereabouts of the eloped couple. However, this scene is institutionalized and highly stereotyped behavior, as the mother usually knows all details beforehand. Within a few days the episode will not be mentioned any more, although the neighbors may gossip and wonder how long the couple will be living together, prophesying the man will abandon her as soon as the first child is born. The girl's father hardly ever interferes in these matters, and, although suspicion and hostility toward the new son-in-law are also institutionalized attitudes, little or nothing is done to change the course of events.

As soon as the two have established themselves independently, or in the house of relatives, they are considered man and wife, and now a new cycle has begun, married life, the rearing of children, and the daily struggle for existence.

Before going any further in tracing the life of the individual during adulthood, we shall have to return once more to the period of childhood, and to a most important aspect of it: formal schooling. In describing this phase of the individual's education, we shall always keep in mind what has been said so far about the value system and the early disciplines to which the child has been subjected within the framework of the family, because only in this manner shall we be able to understand adult behavior and the values and conflicts that dominate it.

FORMAL SCHOOLING

About 45·2 per cent of all adults in Aritama have attended school (men 38·6 per cent, women 61·4 per cent). The illiteracy rate is 79·44 per cent for men, and 70·56 per cent for women.

Few people in Aritama are able to write more than their names, and fewer still can read a newspaper. Those who *can* read do so very slowly, moving their lips or reading aloud. Adults, when asked to write a few lines, will find all sorts of excuses for not doing so, saying that their eyes hurt, that they forgot their spectacles, or that their hands are trembling from some effort they have just made. However, many illiterates display pencils and fountain-pens clipped to their shirt fronts. One old man who could be seen frequently sitting before his house with a book, admitted candidly that he had never

115

learned to read but that he had acquired considerable prestige by pretending to do so, staring every day for a while at the open pages.

Some twenty villagers, all placeros, received part of their formal education in one of the lowland towns, and at least two went to high school and graduated from universities. However, of these people only a few have returned to their village; the majority have preferred to establish themselves in other towns.

Formal education as offered at the local government schools is a major factor in molding the young individual into the patterns of thought and action that are considered by the community to be desirable. Even one or two years of such education leaves a lasting impression upon him and inevitably influences his life in some important ways. Formal schooling in Aritama is at least one century old. The first schools, which were founded by Catholic missionaries, were taken over by the government in later years and are known at present as 'Rural Schools' (*escuelas rurales*). Administrative officers of these schools are appointed directly by the Secretary of the Municipality who, in turn, is an appointee of the Director of Public Education in the capital of the department. All departmental directors are responsible to the Ministry of Public Education in Bogotá, a special section of which is dedicated to the organization and promotion of rural schools all over the country.

In the Corregimiento of Aritama there exist seven rural schools. Aritama proper has two schools, one for boys and one for girls, both established in the last century. In the satellite hamlets there is no segregation, children of both sexes attending 'mixed' schools (*escuelas mixtas*). The boys' school in Aritama functions in a small one-room hut in the Plaza barrio which has been rented by the government for this purpose. The single room has a dirt floor, two doors, and one window. The furnishings consist of fifteen wooden chairs covered with cowhide, seven wooden desks, a blackboard, and map of Colombia. Color prints of several Colombian national heroes, and an advertisement of a pharmaceutical firm adorn the walls. Behind the teacher's table hangs a picture of the Virgin, on an advertisement of a widely used analgesic. Two books are available for teaching purposes: a catechism and a recent (1950) general teacher's guide published by the Ministry of Public Education. The girls' school has its own building, a wattle-and-daub hut with a thatched roof and a cement floor, right on the main corner of the Plaza. This school building is a single room of some 48 square meters, with two doors and two windows. There are thirty-four chairs, three benches, eight desks, and three blackboards, as well as several color prints of national heroes and Catholic saints. The teacher has no recent government textbooks but owns privately five books on orthography, Church history, Colombian history, a catechism, and a general teacher's guide. In 1952 the government contributed the following items to the girls' school: two boxes of chalk, forty-eight pencils, one hundred pens, eighteen penholders, four erasers, twelve copybooks of forty pages each, sixty-two sketching blocks, and one catechism. Neither of these schools has toilet facilities, bathrooms, or drinking water.

According to law the Colombian school year begins in the first week of February, and lasts through November, interrupted only by a short vacation period between the two national holidays of July 20 (Independence Day) and August 7 (Battle of Boyacá). In Aritama, however, these dates are rarely kept, and school opens or closes whenever local conditions and authorities demand it. Often it happens that the teacher's appointments have not come through or that a newly appointed teacher has not decided yet whether to accept or not, and so opening day is sometimes postponed for months. In 1950 the boys' school opened in April, one month after the girls' school had opened; in 1951 it opened late in February and closed in October; in 1952 school opened in May and closed on November 15. School hours are from 8 A.M. to 11 A.M. and from 1 P.M. to 4 P.M. each day, except Saturday afternoon. In lieu of a school bell, the bell of the near-by church is rung to announce these hours.

Schoolteachers are almost always women, generally natives of the village where they exercise their profession. They are appointed by the departmental authorities and are paid through the municipality. None of the numerous teachers we met had even a high school diploma, the educational background of most consisting of only two or three years of elementary school, followed rarely by a short course at a so-called 'commercial school' (*escuela de comercio*) in one of the lowland towns. To qualify for a teaching post, social status, party politics, kinship, and other personal connections are all-important, completely overshadowing academic qualifications. Gaining and maintaining a teaching position is therefore not easy, and every year at the beginning of the new term there is much fear about reappointments, because of the chance of being replaced by another teacher with better connections. As a matter of fact, teachers *are* changed very frequently, not only because every change in national politics or in the personnel of the departmental government influences their position, but also because there is much jealousy and friction among candidates for any teaching position in every village. Consequently teachers belong to the local elite and occupy a high social status, and Aritama is no exception to this rule. All teachers there, present and past, were members of prominent families from the Plaza, and were very conscious of being 'Spaniards'. This fact causes strong resentments in the village, but it tends to give high prestige value to formal education. Many parents of lower status complain that these teachers mistreat their children or teach them useless things at school, but nevertheless there is the general feeling that getting 'good' schooling depends upon the supervision and guidance of an upper-class señora. Teachers' salaries are fixed at 100 pesos a month, but are actually paid at rather irregular intervals. During our stay in the village the municipal treasury was short of funds to pay the teachers' salaries and the treasurer offered to give to each teacher a corresponding amount of bottles of rum, for resale. As the liquor factory is under state control and provides the principal revenue, similar arrangements are common even in the departmental capital. In Aritama, however, the teachers spurned this offer, because the sale of liquor could hardly be considered worthy of their high social status.

Theoretically, each school in Aritama has a kindergarten and four grades, but in practice there is no such division. The basic distinction is drawn, rather, between 'backward' and 'advanced' pupils, and a child's 'grade' placement depends upon his behavior, his physical appearance, and the class-status of his parents. Furthermore, many children, especially those of placero families, even after having passed their final examinations, do not necessarily move on to the next grade. The teacher, the child, or his parents may decide that he should repeat the same grade in order to learn the lessons in greater detail. This often happens when a teacher is replaced by a new one who is expected to teach the same subjects in a slightly different manner. After finishing school, i.e., after the second grade, many children stay on and repeat the last grade for several years. There are a number of persons who have had up to eight years of schooling by thus repeating the last grade. As a matter of fact, for many placero girls the school is a kind of social circle where 'civilized behavior' is taught and practised, and parents who do not need them at home often let their girls continue year after year.

Detailed records were available only for the girls' school, from 1945 to 1951. During this seven-year period, the total enrolment was 468 girls. Of these, 252 (53·8 per cent) dropped out during or at the end of the first school year; 193 (41·2 per cent) stayed for two years, and eighteen (3·8 per cent) for three years, while only 5 girls (1·06 per cent) stayed for four years. In 1952, a year for which we have records of children of both sexes, 384 children of school age (between five and fourteen years) were in the village, and 133 (34·6 per cent) of them were enrolled (43·6 per cent boys and 56·3 per cent girls). Lomero and placero children were about equal in number at both schools, which means that on the basis of their numbers in the community there is a much higher percentage of the placeros attending than of the lomeros. The average age of first-graders was ten years.

School attendance is sporadic because it depends on many personal factors, on the fiesta season, and on the harvesting season. The records kept by the teachers were so confused that it is impossible to gain a clear picture of attendance, but from observation we judged that the average child misses about one-third of all school days. Attendance at the girls' school is at least twice as regular as at the boys' school for several reasons. In the first place, boys definitely dislike female authoity, and public opinion often agrees with them. At one time when a male teacher happened to be appointed, enrolment of boys rose sharply. In the second place, boys are often needed to work in the fields or around the house, and many parents refuse to send them to school. Girls, on the other hand, are often encouraged or even forced by their parents to attend school, as their elders believe that a few years of formal education may be of great help in their finding a good consort in later years or will enable them to procure some sort of official employment. Should a child not attend school regularly, the teacher may complain to the parents, but if they are of low social status she will not visit them or talk to them on the street. Instead she will complain to the police inspector, who will perhaps impose a fine on the child's family. Teachers know that this is against the law and try to hide the procedure, but the fact that the authorities force school attendance by fining the parents is well known in the village. A frequent excuse for not attending school is that the child's clothes had not been washed and ironed in time, and this excuse is always accepted by the teachers. Should a child be kept from attending because of urgent work in house or field, however, the teachers show considerably less patience and one of them told us: 'The poor don't have any fields, so they don't need their children for work; and the rich don't need them because they have servants.'

Discipline is maintained in school by stringent means. Slaps or thrashings applied with a ruler or a rod are frequent punishments. Occasionally, a child is made to kneel outside the door in the hot sun or is locked into a dark room or is obliged to have a piece of cardboard tied over his face. But ridicule and comparison with the 'Indians' is by far the most common method of punishing a child. Until quite recently disobedient children were pilloried and put in stock or were forced to kneel on potsherds or pebbles while supporting a heavy stone on their heads. Several adults told us that when they were children they were locked into the empty houses of recently deceased persons as punishment for misdemeanors in school.

At the end of the school year the teachers make a short written report to the municipal director of education, stating the number of pupils, with their names, attendance records, age, weight, stature, caries, and final grades. This yearly report, to which is appended an inventory of school equipment, is then signed by the police inspector. This inspector also has to keep in contact with the municipal and departmental authorities who are responsible for the yearly appointment of teachers.

The modern government texts and the curriculum for rural schools in Colombia are well conceived and well adapted to their purpose, viz., that of imparting a basic education. They strongly emphasize practical matters, such as agriculture, reforestation, health, and nutrition. They are well printed and carefully edited in language suited to each grade level. However, the rural teachers use these texts in a very limited way. Not all own them and, of those who do, not all make use of them, either because they prefer to apply their own particular methods or because their own educational background is so insufficient that they are unable to put such textbooks to a fuller use. In Aritama the teachers select from the official curriculum only those subjects which tend to affirm local values. Thus 'citizenship' (*cívica*), 'manners' (*urbanidad*), the care of dress and shoes, needlework, the making of paper flowers, or the tying of ribbons are taught, while all tasks connected with agriculture, housekeeping, hygiene, or any activity which demands collaboration, are ignored. Teachers are very critical of the government program and consider certain subjects quite useless or even offensive. Such government initiatives as reforestation or the establishment of kitchen gardens through rural schools are ridiculed and openly attacked. The teachers say: 'It seems that the government thinks we are a bunch of wild Indians, asking us to make our children plant trees and vegetables.'

The daily subject matter depends very much on the whimsy of the individual teacher, who chooses arithmetic, geography, history, religion, citizenship, 'manners', Spanish, natural history, and a number of ill-defined subjects dealing with a combination of needlework, cosmology, and hygiene. Hardly any teacher in Aritama uses the government textbooks, preferring to employ for teaching purposes a number of their own 'copybooks'. These copybooks have been handed down from one teacher to another, from friends and relatives, such as from aunts and nieces, and contain a more or less complete outline of subject matter arranged as questions and answers. The method of teaching consists of having the children copy, in the course of the year, all the questions and answers and making them memorize both. The teacher reads aloud a question and the children repeat it in unison at the top of their voices for ten, twenty, or fifty times. The answer is read and memorized in the same way, and then some time is spent in copying these same questions and answers into individual notebooks, in exactly the same sequence and wording as is found in the teacher's copybook. The daily routine is about as follows: from 8 A.M. to 9 A.M. the children sit or walk in the schoolyard, memorizing from a copybook a certain number of questions and answers; from 9 A.M. to 10 A.M. they enter the classroom and recite their assignments, and copy them; afterward half an hour is again spent in the yard learning more questions until class is over at 11 A.M. The same pattern is repeated in the afternoon.

To examine a child the teacher recites a question and adds the first two or three words of the answer, whereupon the child continues; a moment before the child finishes the answer, the teacher asks a new question followed by the first words of its answer, and so a monotonous stimulus-response chant is set into operation. There is no need for the child to think, the only requirement being a certain ability at rote memory. If a question is phrased in an unaccustomed manner, the child is totally unable to answer; by the same token, should a child try to phrase an answer in original words, he would be reprimanded for doing so.

The following are excerpts from the notebook of one of the teachers. On citizenship (*instrucción cívica*) it says, for example: 'Monarchy is a form of government which does not exist among civilized nations.' A sample question in citizenship is: 'What has man been created for?' The answer: 'To live in society.' Under natural sciences there are the following problems. Question: 'How does the rabbit reproduce itself?' Answer: 'Directly.' Question: 'How does the bee sleep?' Answer: 'Standing.' Question: 'What are the fins of a fish for?' Answer: 'To descend, ascend, or maintain itself in a vertical position.' There are many dozens of similar questions and answers on cows and pigs and sheep, taught day by day to the second-graders. During the same term Colombian history (*historia patria*) is taught. Sample questions are. 'What kind of people inhabited America before Columbus?' Answer: 'A people which had no knowledge of commodities.' Question: 'How did Bolívar die?' Answer: 'Naked, as he was born.'

As these notebooks have been copied and recopied for years and years, many errors have slipped into the transcriptions, and the children are taught many quite meaningless or contradictory statements, e.g., 'Every action which demonstrates religion is uncivil' (*todo acto que demuestre religión es inurbano*). During a class in geometry the teacher explained several times that a spiral was called a cone. So it said in her copybook and so the children learned it and copied it again. The question came up during final examinations and when the pupil drew a spiral on the blackboard and called it a cone, the teacher was very pleased.

The teachers themselves in their ignorance and lack of perception contribute to this confusion. After explaining that in other countries people speak different languages, such as English, French, or German, one teacher pointed out that the advantage of the Spanish language was that it could be not only spoken but also written. When lecturing on the economic geography of northern Colombia, the same teacher mentioned among the natural resources the existence of orchids (which are of no commercial value) but did not mention petroleum, coffee, or sugar cane. She also pointed out the importance of the pearl trade, although this was discontinued many years ago. When speaking of the economic importance of roads, she said that it was high time a motor road was built between two certain lowland towns, in spite of the fact that such a road had existed for the last twenty years and that she herself had often traveled on it. All this confusion arose only because she was using a copybook which had been written *before* the road had been built, *before* coffee became a major cash crop, and *before* the pearl trade had declined. One teacher who had talked at length about microbes and who had had the children write about this theme, sent an ailing pupil home after diagnosing his trouble as 'suffering from the Evil Eye'. Another teacher whom we asked what she believed exists below the ground, answered that there is 'another world peopled by green dwarfs', but added that her textbook said something else which she did not quite remember.

July 20 is the Colombian national holiday celebrating the country's declaration of independence from Spain, and on this day all schools take part in a special program of parades, recitals, etc., in a nationwide fiesta. In Aritama the best pupil of the boys' school was chosen to recite a poem in public. The poem his teacher had taught him was an inspired eulogy of Spanish military power, describing the glorious victories at Lepanto and Pavia, yet nobody seemed to notice that this recital was rather out of place at this particular date. When we asked one of the teachers for the meaning of Independence Day, she answered that it was the day 'when the slaves were freed all over the world'.

At year's end we assisted at the final examination of fourth-graders, in reality pupils who had attended for five or six years, and we heard the following questions. 'What impelled Columbus' ships?' Answer: 'The wind.' Question: 'How does the hen sleep?' Answer: 'Standing.' Question: 'How does the rabbit defend itself?' Answer: 'By running away.' However, none of the children was able to answer our questions: 'What is the capital of Colombia? Who is the Pope? Where is Venezuela?'

This sort of confusion and misinformation pervades every subject taught at school, and the teachers are certainly not aware of it. To them there are two kinds of knowledge: the empirical knowledge acquired in everyday experience and the 'abstract' knowledge taught at school. These are two sets of viewpoints, two manners of seeing things, and they are not necessarily related or interdependent. The knowledge acquired at school may contradict actual experience (or vice versa), but school learning is 'better' because it is 'civilized' knowledge. On the other hand, as we have said above, only those subjects are selected for teaching which give expression to needs felt, to ambitions cherished, and to goals visualized as desirable. Health education, for example, is mainly oriented toward teaching the child that all physical efforts should be avoided. Great emphasis is placed upon the dangers of overexertion, explaining that movements make the muscles tired, that reading is harmful for the eyes, and that thinking 'heats the head' and is likely to cause dangerous diseases.

All teachers are definitely inclined to consider the local schools as training grounds for the placero minority only, and so give little encouragement to lomero children. Favoritism and racial prejudice and discrimination, as well as social discrimination against children of poor families, are the rule. Teachers insist that children attend classes in new and clean clothes. If a child arrives barefoot or with old and mended clothes, he is scolded and word is sent to the child's family asking the parents to provide new clothes lest the child endanger the school's prestige. Ill-dressed children are ridiculed in public by teachers and by other children alike, and often this is the reason why a child will cease to attend school, or why parents will refuse to enrol their children at all. New and clean clothes are the principal criterion for awarding medals or any other prizes at the end of the school year. A poorly dressed child has no chance to receive such a prize, even if he is an outstanding pupil.

Teachers encourage the girls to carry umbrellas, to use cosmetics, handbags, stockings, and costume jewelry, all of which are expensive items which only the well-to-do can afford, but the girls who do not own such paraphernalia of 'civilization' are likely to be ridiculed. Children of Indian phenotype, when volunteering to answer a question, are often ridiculed by the teacher, and their knowledge is put into doubt. 'You wouldn't know! You better go to the river' (i.e., to fetch water) (*Y tú, qué vas a saber? Véte al río!*), one teacher said to an Indian girl. A woman of marked Indian features told us that when she was a schoolgirl she once produced a particularly well-done piece of needlework which was shown to a visiting school inspector. The inspector called the girl, but upon noticing her physical appearance, he said that it was a pity the teacher had 'wasted her efforts on an Indian who would never be able to take advantage of her education'. Such experiences are not easily forgotten and are likely to produce deep resentments which are shared by entire families or kin-groups. Placero children often molest and even beat children of Indian phenotype, and the teachers not only condone this behavior but actually approve of it with the hope that the 'Indian' child will leave school.

Teachers keep in personal touch with parents of children who belong to their own social class, but will never visit a lomero family to discuss a child's school problems. In general, parents take little interest in their children's attendance or progress and seldom discuss school matters with other parents or with teachers. Many parents believe that by sending their children to school they are doing a personal favor for the government or for the teachers. As school age coincides with the years when a child could begin to take an active part in family earnings, the poorer people consider it a great sacrifice to send their children to school. Many lomero families believe that formal education is not only a loss of valuable time but also constitutes a certain danger, as they fear that their children will be spoiled by the influence of an upper-class placero teacher. On the other hand, many adult lomeros who are illiterates complain bitterly that their own parents did not send them to school and blame them for their present poverty, which they claim is due to their lack of formal education. 'Because they were brutes, they wanted us to be brutes, too,' they say of the older generation.

Our observations of the school system of Aritama revealed two principal problems: one, the composition of the student body, the other, the cultural effects of the teaching methods. As we have pointed out, the teachers, backed by the placeros, consider the school a 'Spanish' institution in which the participation of 'Indian' elements is not considered desirable. There is a strong tendency in the Plaza to monopolize the schools and to make attendance difficult and unpleasant for lomero children. The discriminatory attitude of teachers as well as of placero parents and pupils keeps many lomero families from sending their children to school, either because they cannot afford the high cost of clothes and dresses or because they resent the humiliations to which their children and they themselves will probably be exposed. The school thus increases to a marked degree the already existing intra-village tensions.

For those children who attend school, the methods employed in teaching have a far-reaching influence. In the first place, the child is systematically taught the high prestige value of good clothes and of ceremonial behavior, and is made to abhor and to ridicule all manual labor and co-operative effort. Many children are thus brought into opposition to their parents, who demand collaboration and manual work. In the second place, 'knowledge' is reduced to a set of ready questions and answers, beyond which there is little or nothing added or learned. The same pattern is maintained during adult life, the individual answering standard questions in a perfunctory and stereotyped way and refusing to answer an unaccustomed question because the answer might lower his prestige.

School creates, therefore, a world devoid of all reality. It teaches the children that they are well-dressed, well-fed, God-fearing and hardworking 'Spaniards', who are not only equal but rather superior to all other peoples. They are taught that their village is the 'heart of the world' (*el corazón del mundo*), and that the only forces bent upon destroying this paradise are the despised 'Indians' and the mistrusted 'government'. They are taught that 'work' (*trabajo*) is to be avoided, but that 'employment' (*empleo*) is to be sought, as a sinecure well deserved by anyone who has attended school.

IV

FORMS OF SOCIAL RELATIONSHIPS

THE ancient Tairona culture which in prehistoric and protohistoric times occupied the mountain folds of the Sierra Nevada de Santa Marta was based, as we can infer from archeological evidence, upon a stratified society. In combination with social classes, there seem to have existed totemic clans and several groups with specialized functions, such as priests and warriors. This system came to an end with the Spanish conquest. The Indians were enslaved or fled to the mountain fastnesses, where the old class system soon disintegrated. However, a certain stratification appears to have existed also among different clans, some of which, for reasons of their different mythical origin or specialized ceremonial functions, occupied different levels in the social structure. Some of these clan distinctions continued for some time after the conquest. As a matter of fact, remnants of this stratification can still be observed today among the tribal Indians of the Sierra Nevada.

The great upheaval of the Spanish conquest caused a series of migrations in the course of which entire populations were displaced from one region to another, thereby bringing into contact different ethnic groups which until then had maintained little or no relations with one another. These changes affected not only the Tairona proper but also numerous neighboring groups established in the lowlands, which then sought refuge in the mountains. On the other hand, the Spaniards, as we have pointed out in a previous chapter, founded villages and *encomiendas* to unite in them—for economic, administrative, or religious purposes—all Indians whom they considered to belong to the 'same nation' (*indios de la misma nación*). In this manner they obliged groups that often were quite different to live in the same village and to form a new community. Owing to the incorporation of these foreign elements into independent or refugee groups of Indians, the local aboriginal culture integrated the newcomers as new 'clans', to which a level inferior to the traditional local clans was assigned. The same happened in communities founded by the Spaniards where the local autochthonous clans occupied a higher status, while the newly aggregated groups occupied an inferior position.

129

In Aritama this development probably took place around the middle of the eighteenth century when the inhabitants experienced the first permanent contacts with Spanish culture. At the foundation of the village and while uniting in it all the Indians of the vicinity, many members of neighboring tribes were incorporated into the local tribe, to form since then the indigenous basis of the village population.

Among the ancient Indians of Aritama there existed, according to local traditions, several totemic clans associated with certain animals or plants. One of the most important groups seems to have been the clan *Musíxque*, identified with a small plant of this name (*Cardiospermum punicifolia* DC.), which is found occasionally in the vicinity. Although this clan was probably not the only one in the whole valley, the tribe—now reduced in number and disorganized in many aspects—came to identify itself more and more with this particular group, in such a manner that all Indians of local origin began to refer to themselves as *Musíxque* People (*Gente de Musíxque*), demonstrating in this way their essential unity with the traditional culture. The members of neighbouring tribes, however, who then lived in the village, were designated as *Güiro* People (*Gente de Güiro*), a term which alluded to a clan identified with an edible plant similar to the sweet potato and a certain small quartzite pebble, both called *güiro*, which these Indians used in many of their rituals. Th *Musíxque* People considered themselves superior to the *Güiro* People, the latter forming an intrusive element and an outgroup.

The Spaniards paid little or no attention to these locally recognized distinctions, and referred to all aborigines simply as 'indios'. Within their own Spanish society, however, they recognized a complex system —elaborated mainly during the eighteenth century—according to which there were classificatory terms for different racial mixtures between whites, Indians, and Negroes such as *moreno, pardo, mulato, zambo, mestizo, cuarterón, criollo*, etc. These differences, on the other hand, were not taken into account by the Indians, who referred to their new masters only as 'Spaniards', no matter whether they were whites, Negroes, or Hispanicized Mestizos.

During the early nineteenth century, Aritama was inhabited by Indians and a few 'Spaniards', according to the definition given above, and this situation continued until the second half of the past century. The village was considered by the inhabitants of the neighboring lowland towns to be an Indian village where a few Spaniards lived as administrators, traders, or missionaries. Until approximately the middle of the eighteenth century the inhabitants had practiced exclusively an economy of subsistence and maintenance based upon small cultivated plots and the manufacture of a few utensils for local or family consumption. The first cash crop in the form of sugar cane was introduced in this period, and it appears from contemporary manuscripts that by the late eighteenth century the production of raw sugar had become a major economic activity. To judge, however, from the presence of only three Spaniards in 1803, it seems that this commerce was not yet greatly developed, but was still in the hands of the local Indians, who probably sold their products directly to consumers or retailers in the lowlands.

From the records we have at our disposal it does not seem that this situation underwent substantial changes until approximately the fourth quarter of the past century, when the Colombian Government established the Territorio de Nevada y Motilones as a separate administrative unit. More or less at the same period, probably already beginning in 1860 and culminating in 1890, the ethnic composition of Aritama changed radically, together with its socioeconomic situation. In the second half of the past century a series of civil wars broke out in Colombia, devastating wide regions of the country and affecting heavily the Caribbean coast and the state of Magdalena. The lowlands surrounding the Sierra Nevada suffered considerably under the violence of these events. The general desolation was followed by epidemics and famines. An invasion of locusts ruined many peasants of the lowlands. Large groups of people began to migrate in search of physical security, a more healthful climate, and new land. Beginning in 1860, a few individuals from the smaller towns appeared in Aritama, some also from the larger centers. When the village acquired a certain importance in the newly established Territorio, new immigrants were attracted to it. The majority of the new colonizers who thus invaded Aritama were of triethnic origin but were the carriers of a much more Hispanicized culture than the one then prevalent in the village. Although there were Negroes and descendants of the native lowland tribes among them, once in Aritama they were classified as 'Spaniards', and soon became the dominant element in the village and the entire valley.

Although the new immigrants were all of humble peasant origin and were poor by the standards of the lowland towns, in terms of the traditional economic system of Aritama they had considerable resources. They soon bought practically all the houses around the small village plaza, displacing their former owners to the higher part of the hamlet, where the building of a new barrio was begun. Furthermore, the immigrants bought or claimed the agricultural lands adjacent to their new homes or lying in the river flats, thus taking possession of the most valuable terrain surrounding the village. At the same time they acquired the sugar mills and bought many of the small cane and coffee plantations, as well as pastures that the Indians had established in previous years. The active exploitation of these cash crops, together with their rapid increase, was accompanied by organized commerce and trade, then monopolized by the immigrants. They were the first to open stores where clothes, salt, medicines, and other articles of first necessity were for sale, and at the same time they established themselves as wholesale buyers of all locally produced merchandise, such as raw sugar, coffee, palm fiber products, and cattle. The fiber products included mostly straw hats and had been for many years a local home industry. Their large-scale manufacture and exportation to distant markets of these products, however, began only with the arrival of the newcomers. As the Indians were not accustomed to a monetary economy, a system of barter was introduced by which a person simply paid with his products, evaluated at a fixed price, for any article he wanted to buy at a store. By establishing simultaneously a system of credit and of liquidation of debts by instalments, the new immigrants promptly began to dominate the economy of the village, the aboriginal inhabitants of which soon became indebted to or otherwise dependent upon them. By the end of the past century a fundamental change was thus introduced into the socio-economic structure of the village, a change which naturally affected all other aspects of the local culture as well, setting into motion a series of mechanisms of adaptation which this new situation made necessary.

Among the new immigrants there soon arose a social and economic stratification. Some of them were originally from the larger towns and so felt superior to others who came from small hamlets; some had—or claimed to have—close kinship ties with people of importance who had stayed in the lowlands; others were of Caucasoid phenotype; others had received a certain formal education, and so they began to look down upon the local inhabitants with ill-disguised contempt.

When the new families began to establish themselves in the houses around the plaza, the Indians who had formerly lived there began to form a new nucleus of houses in the upper part of the village. In this manner the two barrios we have mentioned earlier began to be distinguished: the *Plaza*, constituted mainly of houses of the recent immigrants, and the *Loma*, where the Indians now lived. By deriving from the names of these barrios the terms *placero* and *lomero*, two groups of people were distinguished, two 'castes' so to speak: the 'Indians' and the 'Spaniards'. To be sure, certain changes occurred in the course of time among the new immigrants as well. Some of them became successful merchants and acquired a certain capital in land, houses, stores, or cattle; but others lost what little they had brought when they first arrived. Among the latter there were some who, out of sheer necessity, now had to live in the Loma barrio or in the surrounding country, incorporating themselves in this way (very much against their wishes) into the category of 'Indians'. The change of domicile from the Plaza to the Loma, combined with subsistence or maintenance economy, manual labor, and a much lower standard of life, led to their being called 'Indians' also, without taking into account their origin, physical type, or educational level. Some of the local Indians had also been successful economically with the new cash crops and the new opportunities in commerce and trade, but in their case the transition from one group to the other, from Loma to Plaza, was almost impossible. Their physical characteristics, their lineage and kinship ties, and their general mode of behavior were usually powerful obstacles to their being incorporated into the group of 'Spaniards' of the Plaza barrio.

The old clan distinctions and organization, however, have survived to a certain degree, even into the present. The members of about half a dozen families of the Loma are still considered to be *Musíxque* People, while four or five families of the same barrio continue to be associated with the *Güiro* People. Furthermore, each of these families is taken to be the magical 'owner' (*dueño*) of a certain region or valley in the vicinity where there are by tradition the ceremonial sites (*puestos*) of the lineage, although, of course, this concept has nothing to do with actual legal landownership. Each family, too, is still identified with a certain totemic concept such as the *caracolí* tree (*Anarcadium excelsum*), the *macana* tree (*Pyrenoglyphis* sp.), the *laurél* tree (*Aniba perutilis* Hemsl. and *Endlichieria Columbiana*), the *yaréno* tree (indet.), the *casacalá* bird, the cricket, jaguar, mountain lion, owl, and howler monkey. In a manner similar to the custom still prevailing among the tribal Indians of the mountains, these families of Aritama still occasionally exteriorize their clan membership in the colored designs they weave into carrying bags of personal use. There still exist traditional techniques and decorative motives, such as rhomboid patterns, meanders, squares, arrows, etc., which pertain to certain families and which are woven and used only by their members. The older generation is still well aware of these remnants of a clan organization, but the younger people claim ignorance of it or admit its existence only with shame. To be sure, this clan organization long ago lost its functions in regulating marriage and other aspects of social life. At present it is of importance only in connection with certain magico-religious rituals and attitudes which we shall discuss in another chapter.

It is, then, from this historical background that the present social structure arises. While combining elements that go back in their origin to prehistoric times, with concepts of Spanish colonial society, the new regrouping is a complex process which has not yet achieved an integrated equilibrium, but which continues to split the community into segments that often oppose each other without having yet formed a workable framework.

RACE, CLASS, AND STATUS

Three ethnic stocks have met and mixed ever since in Aritama: Indian, Negro, and white, each of them being found occasionally in an almost pure phenotype, but mostly in many different shades of intermixture. Miscegenation, although going back for centuries, has not yet produced a generalized physical type, nor has it led to social attitudes free of racial prejudice and discrimination. On the contrary, the themes of ethnic origin, phenotype, or the alleged heredity of desirable or undesirable personality traits still form a strong emotional problem for the villagers. Their preoccupation with this problem is expressed, among other things, by the many classificatory terms by which individuals or groups are referred to by other individuals or groups that believe themselves to be different.

In a very general way, and not exclusively referring to village conditions, people in Aritama distinguish first of all between 'Indians' (*indios*) and 'civilized people' (*civilizados*), applying the first term to groups of aboriginal culture and language and the second term to the rural and urban Creole population. The younger generation of villagers, mainly the placeros, claim to be *civilizados*, but among the older people of all classes in both barrios one quite often finds the opinion that Aritama is not a 'civilized' village. Frequently a person, when referring to a peasant from the lowlands, will say, 'He is not from Aritama; he is civilized'. Sometimes exactly the same words are used when referring to a placero family the members of which were born in the lowlands, although they have lived all their lives in Aritama. On the other hand, the term *civilizado* is often applied to some of the neighboring tribal communities, and an Indian who speaks some Spanish is called 'very civilizado'. The term 'Indian', however, is employed frequently with reference to Aritama when the speaker wishes to point out the general backwardness and poverty of the villagers, 'We are still very Indian' (*Todavía somos muy indios*) is an often-heard phrase which does not refer to race, but to a social and cultural condition.

The term 'Spaniard' (*español*) is commonly used to designate the placeros or any 'civilized' person from the lowlands, and the expression 'Spaniards of the Plaza' (*los españoles de la Plaza*) refers to the families of recent immigrants who are prominent in the barrio. All Colombians are referred to as 'Spaniards'.

The term *nación* ('nation') is now rarely heard but is still used by the old people when talking about historical events. For example, one might say, 'In other times people of another nation were living in the Plaza barrio', meaning that before the arrival of the immigrants this barrio was occupied by Indians. Or one might say, 'The nation of our time . . .' (*La nación de ahora . . .*), when referring to the Creoles of the lowlands.

In this case the term *nación* is almost equivalent to '*civilizado*'. In a still different sense, the term is employed when referring to a certain personality trait that one believes to be congenital in Indians or Spaniards, and in this case one says, *Eso es de nación*, i.e., 'by birth'.

The term *moro*, literally, 'Moor', is commonly used when referring to the ancient Indians of the valley and the village. A *moro* is a heathen, an unbaptized Indian, and expressions like 'In the time of the Moors' (*en tiempo de los moros; cuando la morisca*) are frequently heard when discussing the history of the region. With the words *reyano, reyana* (from *rey*, i.e. 'king') people refer to Indians who were born in the time of the Spanish Viceregency, and as some of them had acquired fame as curers or shamans, they are still often remembered. The terms *moro* and *reyano* are, of course, quite offensive when used while discussing the genealogy of a local family of high class-status, and to say, of someone: 'His great-grandmother was a *reyana*' is rather an insult.

The term *cimarrón* is synonymous with *moro*, but is also used when speaking of Indians who, although baptized, live without maintaining any contact with the rural Creoles. The placeros will occasionally use this term with reference to certain lomeros who, while owning a house in the village, prefer to spend much of their time living in a hut on their fields. The word *mestizo* is used as an equivalent to Colombian; no biological connotation is implied, but rather a desirable phase of cultural development. Inside the village the term is rarely used except when speaking of a person from the lowlands. A Negro from the coast is usually referred to as *mestizo*, in opposition to an Indian. The term *chino* is roughly equivalent to *indio*. Members of both the Plaza and the Loma sections use this term with reference to the neighboring Indians, and the placeros will use it occasionally when talking about the lomeros. The word *achinado* is derived from it and is used when pointing out physical characteristics that are believed to be typically Indian. Another synonym for *indio* is the term *chula*, which, although somewhat obsolete, can be heard occasionally. It is a rather offensive term if used, for example, in the following way: 'Who does she think she is, being a granddaughter of a chula?' (*Y esa qué se cree qué es, siendo nieta de una chula?*). The term *zambo* is used sometimes when referring to hired laborers of any shade of racial mixture, but it is in no way offensive.

Some other terms of ethnic classification refer to dress. An important difference is made between women who still wear the autochthonous Indian dress called a *manta* (literally, 'blanket') and those who wear European-style dresses (*trajes*). When discussing a family one frequently hears the expression: 'Her (or his) grandmother still wore a manta' (*La abuela era de manta*), in order to make it understood that the person referred to is of Indian extraction. One also hears the expression: 'The mother wore a manta, but the daughters already wear dresses'

(*La máma era de manta, pero las hijas ya son de traje*), and sometimes this is said as a sort of proverb alluding to the rapid change that took place from one generation to the next. The expression *de saco*, literally, 'one who wears a coat', refers to the more Creole-oriented lomeros and to all placeros. In general, few people use coats, but in the Plaza barrio all men own at least one. An offensive expression often used in the Plaza and directed against a lomero is 'That chap believes he owns a coat' (*Ese fulano ya se cree de saco*).

The term *persona de categoría* ('person of standing') is used in the Plaza barrio when referring to an individual who occupies a high social or economic position, but in the Loma barrio the term *persona de manera* ('a person of manners', or 'of means') is used in the same context.

It is obvious that the concept of pertaining to a larger society and to a definite nationality is still lacking in Aritama. The term *colombiano* is rarely heard. Within the small world of the village there are the 'Indians' and the 'Spaniards', but to refer to themselves as 'Colombians' would hardly occur to anyone. Each of these groups considers those of his own category as 'we', and those of the other category as 'they'; when someone in the Plaza speaks of 'them' it is understood that lomeros are meant, and vice versa.

The differing constitution of the two groups associated with the barrios has led to a different stratification in each case, which is based upon varying interpretations of the factors that determine class and status. In the Plaza barrio these criteria are lineage and surname, phenotype, economic activity, social and religious behavior, legitimacy of ascendancy and of one's own marriage, ubication of domicile, degree of formal education, and amount of participation in community affairs. It would be quite impossible to cite these criteria in their order of relative importance, as this depends largely upon the individual case.

These different criteria of class and status have many nuances. Among them a great number of combinations is possible. According to these combinations and often taking into account only a few of the criteria, public opinion assigns status and participation in a certain class. But as many of the attributes can change in the course of time and during an individual's life, his assignation to a certain stratum will also change with the years. Thus an individual may pass through a varying scale. Even within the same nuclear family not all members occupy the same class-status. On the other hand, the particular evaluation of the relative importance of the class and status criteria changes not only with time but varies also with the individual about whom an opinion is expressed. Envy, prestige behavior, traditional attitudes toward certain families, and the marked intrasocial hostility which characterizes all interpersonal relations within the community are all factors which contribute to the interpretation and application of these criteria. Although everyone recognizes and emphasizes that the village has a complex social stratification, the opinions of the individual members of the community contradict one another quite frequently, even on occasions where two people belonging to the same stratum of society express an opinion. This is not surprising if we take into account that the village is passing through a phase of transition during which a change in value orientations is in operation that deeply affects the entire local culture.

The concept of forming a community, of all being *aritameros*, is rarely openly expressed and, when suggested, is not found desirable. Loma and Plaza, the difference between 'we' and 'they', is too strong. Rarely would a person generalize as far as to say, 'we' of 'our village', except when the speaker finds himself outside his valley and in a position in which he feels he must defend himself against an outsider's attacks. An additional factor is the consciousness that each barrio is subdivided into various strata which are not parallel but which are quite different in their formulations. Moreover, there is confusion as to how many such divisions really exist. Some people will mention two, five, or seven classes. It is indeed difficult to bring into agreement the many factors of race, barrio affiliation, social and economic class, and level of ambition. Finally people will say that each individual represents 'a class apart', a unique phenomenon that cannot be grouped with others. However, in spite of the many individual factors, there is a definite 'class-consciousness'. There is agreement that it is possible to define a stratification which, in the case of the Plaza, consists of three social classes across which two economic classes are cutting.

When speaking in very general terms about this theme, many people will say that economic factors are the principal determinants, but as soon as concrete cases are mentioned, one observes invariably that social factors are taken into account when assigning a certain individual to a definite stratum. The three social classes of the Plaza barrio are commonly referred to as *primería*, *segunda*, and *baja* ('first', 'second' and 'lower'). However, the word 'class' is but rarely used and people rather employ the term *sociedad* ('society'), saying, for example, 'So-and-so belongs to my society'.

The *primería* consists exclusively of individuals who immigrated from the larger townships of the lowlands. They, their parents, or grandparents arrived in Aritama during the second half of the past century, or even later, and formed the first nucleus of the Plaza barrio. The origin of the family, lineage, and surname are here of capital importance, but do not always represent determinant factors and have to be combined with one or several others before the individual can be include in this class. If, for example, an individual who belongs to such a family—who has no physical Indian characteristics, is a legitimate child, and has a certain formal education—should live outside the village in free union with a woman and without taking part in the social activities of the village, he would not be accepted into the *primería*. If, however, he should live in the Loma barrio and in relative poverty, but was married in church, should have a good formal education, and should take part in community affairs, he can occupy this position on the highest social level. As a rule, the members of the *primería* claim to have relatives or friends in important positions in the lowland towns and maintain occasional contact with them.

The surname represents a certain problem here. Already during the eighteenth century, the great majority of the Indians of Aritama had adopted Spanish baptismal and surnames, many of which were taken from missionaries, Spanish landowners, or any person of high status living in the vicinity. In this manner, many Indians used the same family names as the immigrants who claimed to be 'Spaniards'. At present about a dozen surnames of placero families are duplicated in the Loma barrio, a fact which causes considerable uneasiness among the placeros concerned. The 'Spanish' family of the Plaza then naturally denies most emphatically any kinship with the 'Indian' family that bears the same surname, while the latter will insinuate (with or without reason) that, after all, they are of 'civilized' origin and more or less closely related to the 'Spanish' family.

Physically, neither the *primería* nor the *segunda* show marked Indian traits. The members of these classes are rather triethnic individuals, with a certain Negroid phenotype predominating. The local interpretation of physical characteristics is, of course, important. Distinctions are made mainly according to the nature of the hair and of the eyes and, to a certain degree, according to stature. Skin color, the shape of the lips or of the nose, or other similar traits are hardly taken into account. In this way, a person with predominantly Negroid features, but with long and wavy hair, is often considered a 'Spaniard'. On the other hand, an individual with predominantly Caucasoid features and a light skin, but with straight black hair, slightly oblique eyes, and of small stature, is considered an 'Indian'. The expressions *pelo maluco* ('bad hair') or *pelo bonito* ('pretty hair') are heard very frequently when discussing the racial characteristics of a person. A marked hypognathism or epicanthic eyefolds, however, are never thought to be racial characteristics. In local terms, then, a person of the *primería* has 'fine blood' (*sangre fina*).

The forms of economic activity the individual might carry on are of considerable importance, at least in the case of men. Cash-cropping, cattle-breeding, and commerce always represent high prestige. Not one member of the *primería* or *segunda* practices a maintenance economy of agriculture or works as a manual laborer. Manual labor, however, is not avoided by them. While their women weave straw hats and do many household chores, the men occasionally work in the fields, fell trees, round up cattle, or themselves take their merchandise to the markets in the lowlands. The ownership of houses, stores, or land is not a necessary condition in order to belong to the *primería*; nor is the relative comfort of the house or the quality and quantity of food consumed of any importance. A member of the *primería* might be poor but does not lose his class-status for this reason. On the contrary, the possession of a large capital, even if accumulated in honorable work, always causes among the members of the *primería* a certain contempt for and suspicion of its owner. If he belongs to a lower social level it is often stated that the mere possession of money would never permit him to rise to the *primería* level.

An important factor is the social behavior of the individual, the 'seriousness of the person' (*la seriedad de la persona*). To say of someone that he is a 'serious person' is equivalent to assigning to him a high status. This seriousness is demonstrated by active participation in village affairs, at least in the life of the Plaza barrio, and by the strict observance of the local moral code. Although extramarital adventures are considered to be the most natural thing for a man, they should never cause public scandal. The seriousness prevents a man from becoming intoxicated frequently in public or in the company of people who occupy a lower social level. It controls his tendency to take part in village gossip and to criticize other people in public; it obliges him to certain patterns of hospitality, of sociability; it implies co-operation in all enterprises oriented toward the 'progress' of the community, and implies participation in some of the religious fiestas. A 'serious' person is at once recognized by his *trato* ('manner', 'approach'), and by his *cultura* ('refinement'). Such a person will readily serve as an adviser and counselor to others, will sponsor public enterprises, direct difficult communal labor projects, or will offer his services and intervention with the municipal authorities or even the departmental offices in order to obtain some benefit for the village or for one of its inhabitants. Activity and readiness to help are characteristic features of such 'seriousness', and the social position of the individual depends to a considerable degree upon this aspect. However, members of the *primería* do not aspire to occupy public office and, in general, do not take part in the official administration of the village. Their influence is indirect but ever present in every aspect of village life.

The majority of the members of the *primería* have received some formal education, be it in a public school in their old hometowns or in a school in Aritama, and almost all of them can write and read. Formal schooling, however, can sometimes be replaced by an untrained but very active intelligence. A person who 'knows much' (*sabe mucho*) and who, perhaps, has a certain specialized knowledge is greatly appreciated. The lack of formal education is never blamed upon the individual but upon his parents, and a person who is intelligent and experienced will not be denied a high class-status if he fulfils some of the other requirements.

The members of the *primería* and *segunda* as a rule live in rather well-built and comfortable houses. Ubication of domicile is important, and status descends usually with increasing distance from the village plaza. Dress is another criterion of importance. Clothes have to be clean and well mended. Women have to have a large wardrobe, although their children may go naked until puberty. Clothing has to be patterned according to the styles used in the lowland towns. Certain items such as umbrellas, handbags, and black shoes are practically diagnostic of membership in the *primería*. Great care is taken to use only somber colors in women's dresses and to distinguish them in small details of cut or workmanship from those that members of other classes might be wearing.

In their relationships with others the *primería* observe a marked ceremonial behavior expressed mainly in forms of greeting, condolence, and hospitality. Other factors are exterior participation in Catholic ritual, friendly and respectful reception of visiting priests, and membership in one of the local lay organizations. Although the members of this local upper class are not always legitimate descendants of a Catholic marriage, they usually marry in church and live in legal marital union with their spouses. The class-status of the wife is always of great importance, and the social position of a man depends to a considerable degree upon his wife's position. To marry a woman from an inferior class would be a serious handicap in maintaining the man's social status and would often force him to descend to a lower level. Many times delay in marrying is explained by the man not having been able to find a suitable match and by his fear of losing his position by marrying a woman from an inferior level. The physical characteristics of the children, together with their home education and formal schooling, also play a certain role in the social position of their parents.

In everyday speech certain differences can be observed. In the *primería* there is emphasis on grammatical purity, but not on adopting a more refined vocabulary, although occasionally rather artificial terms and mannerisms are used. Pronunciation and intonation are quite characteristic, although in the intimacy of the home the speech will be just like that of the lower classes. In conversation with people not of one's kin an artificial tone of voice is employed; the '*d*' in words like *ganado, comido, acabado*, etc., is pronounced with great care, as is the terminal '*s*'. To be able to 'express oneself well' (*expresarse bien*) is an important quality of the *primería*.

Participation in the *primería* depends evidently upon the maintenance of a very fine balance. Any change in the individual's life is likely to affect his class-status, and the latter is confirmed or endangered continuously. This tends to restrict quite considerably the possibilities and the range of activities of a person who often fears to make an important decision simply because the outcome might affect his class-status in an unfavorable way. Members of the *primería*, therefore, rarely show economic initiative because they fear to lose in a transaction.

Similar norms for participation apply for the so-called *segunda*. This is rather a local middle class of merchants, employees, teachers, shopowners, and landholders. It is constituted of individuals who came to the village during the same years as the members of the *primería*, from the lowland towns or the larger villages surrounding them. Once in Aritama many of them lost contact with their relatives who had stayed in the lowlands, but their surnames continued to be known there, and there is still a vague consciousness of kin. Among the members of the *segunda* there are some individuals with certain physical traits that might be interpreted as Indian, but in no case is a definite Indian phenotype present. Economically they are the strongest group in the village. They have acquired the monopoly of palm fiber products, raw sugar, and cattle, and also they own the means of transportation, such as trucks, mules, or teams of oxen. They are not engaged in any direct agricultural work except their cash crops. Their formal educational background is similar to that of the *primería*, but while the latter is somewhat stagnant and very conservative, the members of the *segunda* are intellectually far more active and show much interest in new knowledge, experience, and 'progress'. They occupy the key posts in the local administration, and they receive the travelers or government agents who visit the village. In their social behavior they try to imitate the *primería*. They are not always legitimate descendants of Catholic marriages, but they almost always marry in church. However, economic achievements and assets are not the determinant criteria for class participation but rather 'seriousness', their activity in everything referring to the progress of the village and the well-being of the family. Not all of them live on or near the plaza but many at some distance from it, although always in prominent sites and well-built houses. Additional differences between *primería* and *segunda* can readily be observed on occasions of social gatherings during which people dance. One numerous family, most members of which belong to the *primería*, practically decides the issue of individual status by their willingness to accept or chose partners. At these dances, which are quite frequent in the Plaza barrio, a recurrent occasion for reaffirmation of a person's class-status is offered.

The local lower class (*clase baja*) is constituted mostly of immigrants from small villages and hamlets in the lowlands. They or their parents are often relatives of families belonging to the *segunda*, but who for one reason or another have descended in the social scale and have lost their status, or maybe never possessed one. Although emphatically placeros, among them there are numerous individuals of a markedly Indian phenotype, and there are several whose mothers or grandmothers were Indians or 'Spaniards' who had descended to the 'Indian' level. Some of them own small cash crops or some other minor commercial enterprise, but others sometimes work as hired laborers employed by the two higher classes. Many are illegitimate descendants, and only a few of them marry as Catholics. Their education is very rudimentary, and they never take any decisive part in public or religious matters, although as a rule they are considered as 'serious' and 'cultured' persons.

Cutting across these social classes of the Plaza barrio there exist two economic groups. Although their individual representatives are looked upon with contempt by the members of the *primería* and some of the *segunda*, they are of an ever-increasing importance in the community. The members of the higher economic class are of a very heterogeneous origin, although never of pure Indian stock, and they belong socially to the two highest levels. Their lineage, however, is often difficult to trace and they themselves pay little attention to it. Their physical type is triethnic; their formal schooling is scant, but they are always determined to give their own children a formal education, if possible in an urban medium, outside the village. In many particulars they demonstrate similarities to the urban lower class: in their commercial activity, their political consciousness, their little interest in religious matters. To them the social status of a prospective wife is of little importance as long as the marriage offers sound economic advantages. Their interest in village affairs is much less than, for example, among members of the *segunda*. They are likely to migrate to larger towns, where they are absorbed into the lower classes.

Next to this class, which, without doubt, is of great importance in the changing structure of the village, there exists in the Plaza barrio an inferior economic class formed by impoverished individuals of the lower class who have little or no claim to kinship with other families of higher status. Although considered placeros, they often merge into the general lomero category.

In the Loma barrio there exist no social classes, but only economic levels. Although a few individuals try to identify themselves with the lower class of the Plaza or claim remote kinship with a 'Spanish' family, such claims do not represent a criterion for class-status. The basic distinction is drawn between those who have and those who have not: the owners of small cash crops or maintenance plots, on the one hand, and the owners of mere subsistence plots and the landless, who are mainly a hired labor force. Status is achieved and never inherited, Name, race, language, dress, religious, or social activity is of little importance. The only distinction is made by economic achievement, by hard work, and by the 'seriousness' with which the individual tries to support his family. The lower economic category of the Loma is formed of old Indian families, while the higher one occurs approximately in equal proportion among members of such Indian families and those of 'Spanish' origin that have descended to the 'Indian' level.

Social mobility—both vertical and horizontal—is high in the village but develops rather on the barrio scene without cutting across the entire community. As a matter of fact, marriages or stable free unions between placeros and lomeros are extremely rare, and there is a definite endogamous tendency in each section of the village.

There is considerably more mobility between the *segunda* and the *baja*, than between the *segunda* and the *primería*, the latter being the more exclusive. A male member of the *segunda* who marries a woman of the *primería* will have to fulfil a great many requirements before being fully accepted into her class. It is more likely that the woman will descend in the social scale and become incorporated into her husband's class. For a woman of the *segunda* it is still more difficult to ascend to *primería* status through marriage. Much depends upon domicile, details of dress, phenotype, and her personal attitudes toward other women of the *primería*. Should she not be accepted, her husband does not necessarily descend to her level, but in any event his prestige will be seriously harmed by such a marriage partner. It occurs with some frequency that both male and female members of the *primería* delay marriage for years, stay single, or move to a lowland town for lack of a suitable partner. This contributes to the slow disappearance of the local upper class, which steadily declines in number and influence. This is not due to their economic difficulties but to their ever-increasing conviction that they occupy a level of sophistication which is essentially urban in type and which separates them more and more from the backward peasants of their village. In reality, the *primería* have much in common with the lower urban classes and intermarry occasionally with them in the lowlands, but without returning to their natal village. Although born and raised in Aritama, many of them are ashamed to live there, and they often behave as if they were only casual visitors to the village.

The *segunda* on the other hand intermarry frequently on their own level or with members of the *primería* who are about to lose their class-status, and they—together with the higher economic levels—tend to become the leading force in the village. They find an ample choice of partners and are not likely to migrate to urban centers, their economic interests lying in the village and their class structure being far less impermeable than that of the *primería*. Between the lower class of the Plaza and the lomeros there is occasionally some intermarriage, but mostly in the form of short-term free unions, and the placero partner, even if much poorer than the lomero consort, will insist on maintaining his (or her) status as a 'Spaniard'.

We have not found a single instance where a member of the Loma barrio, male or female, was fully accepted into the Plaza barrio by marriage to one of its members. Of the few cases of such unions on record, the lomero partner was never incorporated into the Plaza, even if economically strong and physically non-Indian. On the contrary, the placero partner lost status and either changed domicile to the Loma, or stayed in the Plaza but stepped down in the social scale and was continuously criticized. Occasionally, of course, a placero family into which a lomero had married will pretend that he occupies placero status, but this is done out of shame and in front of people who are not well acquainted with local conditions. The other villagers know very well that this status is fictitious and that it serves only the purpose of protecting the pride of the placero family. Intermarriage between barrios, i.e., between 'Indians' and 'Spaniards' is definitely not a vehicle for change in the sense that the 'Indian' becomes incorporated into a more general type of Colombian peasant culture. In general, there is a strong tendency toward village endogamy, except for the very few cases of upperclass members who marry in the lowlands and stay there. The people of Aritama will not even marry inhabitants of the satellite villages in the vicinity but prefer to choose their partners from within the closer community. There exist many stereotypes in the village according to which all men from other villages are aggressive and all women lazy or pretentious, and although a man might have concubines and illegitimate children in neighboring hamlets, he will hardly ever bring the woman to live with him in Aritama itself.

FAMILY STRUCTURE AND HOUSEHOLD COMPOSITION

The structure and composition of family and household show significant characteristics and variations in Aritama. Among the Creole-oriented placeros, the basic unit is the biological family composed of parents and their legitimate offspring, all of them living under the same roof; but among the great majority of the villagers there exists a variable and fluctuating system of groupings.

In order to understand the factors that have led to the present situation, we shall have to refer first of all to certain aspects of its historical development. Archeological evidence as well as historical data from sixteenth-century sources, together with ethnographic information on the surviving Indian tribes, demonstrate that aboriginal society in the Sierra Nevada de Santa Marta has been based, for the past five centuries at least, upon the nuclear two-generation family occupying the same home. Polygyny existed among the ancient Tairona and continued for some time after the Spanish conquest, but at present it has almost disappeared among the Indian tribes. We have no information concerning the institutionalized rules that regulated the choice of partners and the marriages between different clans in the valley of Aritama, but it seems certain that, if such rules existed, they had disappeared by the middle of the past century.

At that period, before the arrival of the new immigrants from the lowlands, the Indians of Aritama practiced two forms of marital union: Catholic marriage as the predominant and free monogamous union as an additional and socially recognized alternative form. Only few restrictions in choice of partner existed at that time: a man could not marry his first or second cousin, or his niece, ritual coparent, or godchild. Marriage with a deceased wife's sister was permitted, but a woman was strictly forbidden to marry a dead husband's brother. The bridegroom, after having personally asked the girl's father for her hand, was obliged to build the new home in the close vicinity of his wife's parents and for several years had to assist his father-in-law in agricultural work. The offspring of free unions always used the mother's name and stayed with her until past puberty if the father had abandoned her. However, both Catholic marriage and free unions were quite stable institutions, and separation occurred only rarely.

Already at that time the few Spaniards established in Aritama, or those who lived in the vicinity, kept Indian concubines in the village, a custom strongly criticized by the missionaries but otherwise not only condoned by the inhabitants but actually encouraged by them as they saw economic and prestige advantages in these liaisons. Once the new immigrants and their women arrived, concubinage became generalized, and although the men lived in Catholic marriage with the spouses they had brought from the lowlands, practically all of them kept one or more Indian women. The man simply built or bought a house for his paramour and supported her with occasional gifts, but without living with her under the same roof. The illegitimate offspring of these unions lived in the mother's house and were sometimes incorporated into their biological father's household in the role of domestic servants. Free unions between 'Spaniards' and Indian women could easily and rapidly be dissolved, the woman being allowed to keep the house, in exchange for which the man was absolved from further obligations toward the woman or her children.

For several reasons this form of concubinage with married or unmarried 'Spaniards' was promptly institutionalized and accepted by the Indian population of the village. In the first place, the arrival of the new immigrants had deeply affected the local economic system, bringing misery and hunger to many families. The 'Spaniards' had acquired or usurped the best agricultural lands surrounding the village and had converted most of them into pastures, sugar cane, or coffee plantations, while the Indians had to retreat and found themselves obliged to cultivate their small plots in the steep mountain fields, where the soil was poor and yields low. Concubinage with a 'Spaniard' thus offered to Indian women a certain economic security, as houseownership was connected with it, together with gifts of money, dresses, and the tacit agreement that the woman could use the fruits cultivated on her consort's fields. Hard-pressed parents often encouraged such unions of their daughters. Another incentive, which in many cases seems to have been particularly powerful, consisted in the openly expressed desire of the Indian women to become 'civilized', to wear European-style dresses, to live in better houses, and to occupy a less subordinate position than the one assigned to them by their own local aboriginal culture. Once she lived with a 'Spaniard', a woman could stay at home and avoid hard physical work, while at the same time she acquired a certain prestige and also cherished the hope of having children with a less-pronounced Indian phenotype and, therefore, a brighter future.

Quite often a man would support several concubines simultaneously or change concubines frequently, establishing a series of short-term monogamous unions. The abandoned woman returned to her parents' home, renting or selling the house she had received from her consort; or she procured to find another man. Sometimes a woman would have relations with several men, if a single consort did not appear to her to be a sufficient economic guarantee. Whether in secret or more or less public, such behavior was never thought to border on prostitution but still fell within the framework of concubinage. As a matter of fact, neither the terms nor the concepts of adultery or prostitution were ever applied to these situations. Individual behavior was rather evaluated in terms of a quite natural 'battle of the sexes', during which each one demonstrated cunning and deception.

This system of concubinage and short-term monogamous or polygamous unions, already established in the past century, continues today in the same form and is practiced not only by the placeros but by almost all inhabitants of the village. Even among the upper-class placeros who are married as Catholics, there is not a single man who has not at least one illegitimate child from such an extramarital union. Of course, there are some men with rather monogamous inclinations but they are openly ridiculed by all. Sometimes their economic situation obliges them to be monogamous, but the local prestige system does not permit it and other men would call them cowards and weaklings, and put into doubt their virility. Quite often a man then establishes such extramarital relations only so as not to lose face with his friends and to demonstrate his maleness (*hombría*).

The result of this situation is that in Aritama we find many homes occupied by women and children only, the former living in more or less stable relationships with men who do not live with them but who are members of another household. At first view, this large number of female household heads, together with the high illegitimacy rate, the many children who live with only one of their biological parents, and the continuous change in mating relationships and, therefore, in household composition, induces one to think of disorganization verging on promiscuity, but this overall impression is far from being correct. In reality, there exists a well-patterned system which becomes apparent as soon as numerical analysis is used.

In the first place, it is evident that the social system of Aritama must be analyzed in terms of domestic units, and not of individual families. It is the household—essentially a fluctuating coresident kin-group—that forms the basic functional unit of society, its individual members not being just haphazard constituents but elements that combine under certain conditions. These conditions are subject to a time factor inherent in the developmental cycle through which each household passes in the course of its existence. To a large degree this cycle is determined by physiological stages: relative age, childbearing, menopause, and death; but interrelated social factors also enter, such as jural position of the household member, the sanctioning of the conjugal unit, the differential emphasis on kinship ties, or the economic activity of the individual. As practically each member of the household passes through such stages and their concomitant roles, the configuration of the household group is continuously modified in a way that is logical, both from a biological and sociological point of view. The modification follows certain rules which form a well-defined pattern, the structure and dynamics of which are here of the greatest importance.

But before we try to analyze this system and describe its characteristics, it is necessary first to give certain definitions concerning the nature of mating relationships, and the various forms of relations between the individual member and the head of the household. Catholic marriage represents the only type of conjugal union that is fully recognized by the community as the basic legal, social, and sexual foundation of family life. No matter how frequent other forms of conjugal unions might be, the former is always preferred. Moral or religious concepts are here of little or no importance, the main incentives and decisive factors being considerations of prestige and class-status. Catholic marriage, in terms of the local configuration, means status; it means that the individuals concerned are 'civilized' and Creole-oriented. Even if the marriage breaks up after a few weeks or months, the mere fact of being married according to Catholic ritual represents a permanent social advantage over people who are not married in church and who, therefore, are associated with an 'Indian' level. These ideas, of course, are rarely expressed overtly. On the contrary, free unions and illegitimacy appear to be the accepted rule and are often said to lack all significance in prestige matters. But beneath this apparent indifference or tolerance there is much anxiety and people who live in free union worry a great deal about the ways in which this might affect their social status and the future of their children.

In the following whenever we employ the terms 'marriage', 'husband', 'wife', 'legitimate', we refer to Catholic marriage, its partners, and its offspring. In Aritama the corresponding terms are *matrimonio, esposo, esposa, legítimo*. The next category consists of free unions, of more or less permanent character. This form of conjugal union is not recognized by Colombian law and, of course, not by the Church, but it is very frequent in Aritama. We shall refer then with the term 'free union' to a mating relationship recognized by both members and by the community at large, but which does not necessarily imply coresidence. Those united in a free union—locally called *compromiso*—shall be referred to as 'consorts' (male or female), the equivalent local terms being *compañero, compañera*. The offspring of these unions are referred to as 'illegitimates' and are locally designated as *niños naturales*, i.e., 'natural' children. A third category of conjugal union consists in 'concubinage' and by this term we refer to occasional extramarital (or extra–free union) relationships in which the members are never co-resident. We shall refer to individuals as 'partners' (male or female), the locally used terms being *querido, querida* ('lovers'). The offspring of such unions are locally designated as children procreated 'on the street' (*en la calle*). With the term 'single' we refer to individuals of both sexes and over eighteen years of age who have no children but who probably are consorts or partners in mating relationships with people belonging to other households, but whose relationships are not recognized. The term 'spouse' is used in a general way for members of marriages or free unions. As 'head' of household we designate the person (male or female) who is recognized within and outside the domestic group as the central authority over all vital aspects concerning the household unit. However, this does not imply that this person is also the sole or main provider, nor is land and/or houseownership connected with the concept of headship. In Catholic marriage and in coresident free union, the head is always the male. In a non-coresident free union the head is often the oldest female.

With these definitions in mind, we shall turn now to a detailed analysis of the relationship in which the various household members stand with reference to the head. The data analyzed here cover all households of Aritama, a total of 255, but from the lists given in Tables 18, 19, and 20, twenty-one households, consisting of only one person living alone, have been excluded.

TABLE 18

Relationships with Male Head of Household

Kinship Relation	Number	Per Cent
Wife	51	7·11
Consort	86	11·99
Son of head and wife:		
Under 18	77	10·73
Over 18, single	21	2·92
Son of head and consort:		
Under 18	123	17·15
Over 18, single	19	2·64
In coresident free union, with children	1	0·13
In coresident free union, without children	1	0·13
Daughter of head and wife:		
Under 18	60	8·36
Over 18, single	17	2·37
In free union, not coresident, with children	5	0·69
Daughter of head and consort:		
Under 18	114	15·89
Over 18, single	10	1·39
In coresident free union, with children	1	0·13
In free union, not coresident, with children	3	0·41
Son of head only:		
Under 18	7	0·97
Son of wife only:		
Under 18	2	0·27
Son of consort only:		
Under 18	14	1·95
Over 18, single	1	0·13
Daughter of head only:		
Under 18	2	0·27
Over 18, single	2	0·27
Daughter of wife only:		
Under 18	2	0·27
Daughter of consort only:		
Under 18	14	1·95
Over 18, single	1	0·13
Spouse of son of head and wife:		
Wife	1	0·13
Consort	1	0·13
Spouse of son of head only:		
Consort	1	0·13
Spouse of daughter, coresident	1	0·13
Child of son of head and wife:		
Parents' free union separated and neither co-resident with child	2	0·27

149

TABLE 18 (*continued*)

Kinship Relation	*Number*	*Per Cent*
Parents' free union separated, but father co-resident with child	1	0·13
Child of son of head and consort:		
Parents' free union coresident with child	1	0·13
Parents' free union separated, but father co-resident with child	2	0·27
Parents' free union separated and neither co-resident with child	6	0·83
Child of daughter of head and wife:		
Parents' free union separated, but mother co-resident with child	**8**	1·11
Parents' free union coresident in other house-hold	2	0·27
Child of daughter of head and consort:		
Parents' free union separated, but mother co-resident with child	17	2·37
Sister of head:		
Over 18, single	1	0·13
Brother of head's wife:		
Over 18, single	2	0·27
Sister of head's consort:		
Under 18	3	0·41
Over 18, single	1	0·13
Child of daughter of head's brother:		
Parents not coresident with child	3	0·41
Child of daughter of head's sister:		
Parents not coresident with child	1	0·13
Child of head's sister:		
Over 18, single	1	0·13
Adopted child, no kin, under 18	2	0·27
Servants (no kin):		
Male, under 15	11	1·53
Male, over 15	1	0·13
Female, under 15	4	0·55
Female, over 15, single	5	0·69
Female, over 15, with children	2	0·27
Child of female servant	2	0·27
Total	717	99·00

TABLE 19

RELATIONSHIPS WITH FEMALE HEAD OF HOUSEHOLD

Kinship Relation	Number	Per Cent
Son of head and dead husband:		
Under 18	6	1·78
Over 18, single	1	0·29
Son of head and dead consort:		
Under 18	1	0·29
Son of head and not coresident consort:		
Under 18	64	19·04
Over 18, single	32	9·52
Widower, with children	1	0·29
In coresident free union, with children	2	0·59
In coresident free union, without children	1	0·29
Daughter of head and dead consort:		
Under 18	1	0·29
Daughter of head and not coresident consort:		
Under 18	78	23·21
Over 18, single	28	8·33
In coresident free union, with children	2	0·59
In coresident free union, without children	1	0·29
In free union, not coresident, with children	19	5·65
Spouse of head's son:		
Coresident consorts	3	0·89
Woman only	1	0·29
Spouse of head's daughter:		
Coresident consorts	3	0·89
Child of son of head and not coresident consort:		
Parents' free union coresident with child	2	0·59
Parents' free union not coresident, but mother only coresident with child	2	0·59
Parents' free union not coresident, but father only coresident with child	5	1·48
Parents in free union but not coresident with child	6	1·78
Child of daughter of head and not coresident consort:		
Parents' free union not coresident, but mother only coresident with child	47	13·98
Mother only of head	1	0·29
Sister of head:		
Over 18, single	6	1·78
In free union, not coresident, with children	2	0·59
Brother of head:		
Over 18, single	6	1·78
Child of head's sister, without parents	1	0·29
Child of head's sister, with coresident mother	1	0·29
Child of head's brother, without parents	3	0·89

TABLE 19 (*continued*)

Kinship Relation	*Number*	*Per Cent*
Daughter of head's brother:		
In free union, not coresident, with child	1	0·29
Child of daughter of head's sister:		
Parents' free union not coresident, but mother only with child	2	0·59
Grandchild of head's son:		
Parents' free union not coresident, but mother only with child	1	0·29
Adopted Child:		
Dead husband's child, under 18	1	0·29
No kin	6	1·78
Total	336	99·00

Numerically the composition of the households is as follows:

Number of persons:	1	2	3	4	5	6	7	8	9	10	11	12	13	14
Households:	21	22	34	31	33	33	20	22	7	8	3	8	2	1

The tables can be combined and subdivided as shown in Table 20 (see p. 154).

The data presented in Table 20 allow us to analyze in more detail the composition of the households and the developmental changes that take place within them. We shall refer first of all to those households that have a male head.

Apart from the 12 men who live alone, there are 150 of these households (58·8 per cent), and in all cases the head's wife, or more often his consort, lives with him. The largest category of kin is constituted by the filial generation under eighteen years of age. This category, however, is formed not only by the offspring of the coresident couple, but also by the head's or his spouse's children from previous conjugal unions. It is mainly the head's spouse who thus incorporates her children from former unions into the household, a fact which—in spite of male authority—gives a marked matrifocal character to the group. In only three cases the spouse of an adult son is present, but in only one case is she coresident with her consort, while in the remaining two the latter live apart. In one case the daughter's consort is a member of the household group, but there are eight cases of daughters living in free union or as concubines of men who are members of other households. A relatively large number (41) of adult single sons form part of the unit, while there are slightly fewer adult single daughters. These young and single members of the household groups constitute, of course, the main fluctuating element, and it is between them that new conjugal units are formed which, eventually, establish their own households apart from the parental home. By incorporating, furthermore, the offspring of the filial generation, the household frequently becomes a three-generation group. The largest category of members consists then of children of a daughter who, after having lived in free union or in concubinage with a man, again forms part of the paternal unit. On a much lesser scale this happens also with the offspring of a son, but in these cases it is not usual for the child's father to live within the household, the infant being reared by its grandparents. In only one case a sister of the head is present, but in six cases members of the head's spouse's kin form part of the group. Adopted children are rare, and both they and a fairly large category of servants have no kinship ties with either the head or his spouse.

In households with female heads, of which there exist 84 cases (32·9 per cent), the composition varies significantly. In the first place, the head always lives separated from her spouse, being either past child-bearing age and single, or being the consort or concubine of a man who lives within another household. As in the case of male headship, the largest category of coresident kin is constituted by the head's offspring, and a large number of them (50) are adult daughters, many of whom live or have lived in free union with men who are not coresidents. However, sometimes the spouses of sons or daughters also live within the household. The third generation is formed by the offspring of this filial generation, mainly by children of daughters who are separated or actual consorts or concubines of men who do not live with them. A large number of other kin of the female head, such as siblings or their children, are also present. There are no servants in this type of household, and the only individuals who are not kin are a few adopted children.

We shall turn now to the problem of how these various kinds of household groups come into being. As soon as the individual reaches social maturity, i.e., when young people become 'free', at about seventeen or eighteen years of age, they establish occasional sexual relations with members of the opposite sex. These relations are first carried on in a more or less hidden manner and are, in the beginning, very unstable but become eventually known to the respective parents as soon as a certain permanence is apparent. In the course of such liaisons, which, of course, do not imply coresidence, it is probable that the girl becomes pregnant and bears a child, and, in any event, should the

TABLE 20

Members of Household	Generations	Number of persons composing household													
		1	2	3	4	5	6	7	8	9	10	11	12	13	14
Adult male alone	1	12	—	—	—	—	—	—	—	—	—	—	—	—	—
Adult female alone	1	9	—	—	—	—	—	—	—	—	—	—	—	—	—
Couple without children	1	—	10	—	—	—	—	—	—	—	—	—	—	—	—
Parents with children	2	—	—	18	16	18	19	15	15	3	7	1	5	1	—
Mother alone with children	2	—	10	7	7	9	3	5	2	3	—	—	—	1	—
Father alone with children	2	—	1	5	—	—	—	—	—	—	—	—	—	—	—
Grandmother - grandchildren	2	—	—	1	—	—	—	—	—	—	—	—	—	—	—
Uncle or aunt with nephews and/or nieces	2	—	1	—	1	1	1	—	—	—	—	—	—	—	—
Mother, mother's sibling, and children	2	—	—	—	—	—	1	—	—	—	—	—	—	—	—
Parents, children, and grandchildren	3	—	—	—	—	1	3	1	2	1	—	1	1	—	—
Mother, children, and grandchildren	3	—	—	1	6	3	4	7	—	—	1	1	1	—	1
Mother, mother's sister, children, and grandchildren	3	—	—	1	—	1	1	1	—	—	—	—	—	—	—
Father, children, and grandchildren	3	—	—	—	1	—	—	—	1	—	—	—	—	—	—
Varia		—	—	1	—	—	—	—	1	—	—	—	—	—	—

couple decide to continue these relations, there now exist three possibilities: (1) the mating relationship might continue for years, both partners living in different households and the eventual offspring becoming incorporated into the girl's paternal unit; (2) the girl might leave her natal household and go to live with the man, either within his parental household, or in a newly built, bought, or rented house; (3) the man might join the girl by being incorporated into her household group. Which of these alternatives is taken depends largely upon certain individual conditions. If the male partner is still young, he will be usually too poor to build, buy, or rent a house, but if he has the means to do so, the final decision between neolocal, virilocal, or uxorilocal residence depends upon the particular configuration of the two household groups he and his consort belong to. If the household of one of the partners is dominated by a man—generally the biological father—it rarely happens that a woman will become accepted into it as the consort of a son (or, vice versa, a man as the consort of a daughter), but should the head of the household be a woman, this happens quite frequently, because then the household head is usually interested in adding in this manner to the labor force, the young couple being obliged to contribute actively to the total household economy. The first step, then, depends almost entirely upon the economic conditions of all elements involved. Initial coresidence is either neolocal, in which case a new household unit comes into being, or it begins within the framework of an already existing household group, being usually of a temporary character followed by secession and neolocal residence.

We shall consider now these different types of initial coresidence. In the case of neolocal residence, a two-generation family is formed, which, from then on, might develop into one of several directions. Again, three possibilities are open: (1) the couple might continue to live together, procreating children who, in time, reach nubility, while the household might also begin to incorporate other children or collateral kin of the original couple; (2) the couple might separate again, the woman returning to her natal household; (3) the couple might separate, the woman and her children staying on in the house which has become her property or the rent of which is paid by the man who abandons her. The first is the ideal rule but occurs in only about 60 per cent of all cases. A considerable number of young neolocal households, or virilocal or uxorilocal coresidential unions break up sooner or later, usually because the man establishes relations with other women and ceases to support his family or because his consort's family suggest separation if the man does not contribute economically to his spouse's natal household, an obligation which is especially important in the case of a female-dominated (i.e., mother-in-law-dominated) unit. In any case, neither the two families of orientation nor the community at large expect stability from such early unions but consider this general period of life as one of experimentation, in spite of contrary ideal formulations. The second case is quite frequent, too. There are no obstacles for the reincorporation of woman and child into her parental household. Of 212 cases examined by us, 60·4 per cent were living in neolocal residence, although uxorilocal or virilocal coresidence had preceded this step in many cases; in 17·4 per cent of our cases, the abandoned woman and her children lived within her natal household, either having returned to it when abandoned or never having left it; in 22·1 per cent of all cases, the abandoned woman and her children stayed in the house provided by her first consort. After the dissolution of such an initial union, the woman will usually once more establish relations with a man, and the range of possibilities is then the same as before. Her children from the previous union are incorporated wholly or partly into her second union, and with advancing age and an increasing filial generation, a numerous household group is constituted. The third alternative occurs occasionally and develops in a similar way. The woman might establish a new conjugal union, in this case uxorilocal, or she might be joined by collateral kin, sisters' children, or her own mother, becoming eventually the head of a large household group.

The other alternative of initial coresidence consists in the incorporation of one partner into the household of the other. This occurs frequently, but, in the case of a young couple, it is rarely a permanent arrangement, being rather a transitory stage followed sooner or later by neolocal residence. The couple co-operates with the natal household group of one of the spouses, but as soon as the man has reached a certain economic independence, either by landownership and or houseownership or by wage labor, the couple secedes and establishes its own household. However, this interjacent stage is not necessarily accompanied by stable conjugal relationships. The male partner is likely to have relations with other women or might find it difficult to adapt himself satisfactorily to the various members who constitute the spouse's household, a problem which arises, of course, also in virilocal residence. Harmonious integration thus depends upon the particular configuration of the household unit, and tensions between the in-marrying partner and his spouse's kin will easily precipitate separation or neolocal residence.

The fact that a large number of women have children by more than one man is, therefore, not due to adultery but to the chronological sequence of conjugal unions. Numerically this can be expressed as given in Table 21.

TABLE 21

Number of Women with Children Fathered by

One man	144	Four men	6
Two men	63	Five men	2
Three men	18	Six or more	8

From the foregoing description it has become clear that the variation in size of the different households, which range from one to fourteen members, is due to their being in various stages of development. The coresidential, two-generation nuclear family develops, in time, into a three-generation family composed of several conjugal units, which, in turn, secede and begin to form new households.

During this cycle of continuous fission and fusion, the individual changes his household membership and, together with it, the role associated with status and age. It is, therefore, of interest to describe in greater detail the jural, social, and economic position occupied by the different household members. In the first place, it must be stated that the authority of the household head rarely goes beyond his or her role as father, mother, or main provider. In only a few exceptional cases in the Loma barrio, the stable headship of an older and widely respected man includes also managerial functions in a wider sense and makes him an organizer of the entire household labor effort. But usually the head exercises his authority through the functions and roles as a procreator or child-rearer. This responsibility is derived from the obligations the filial generation has toward the parental generation, viz., the children's or adult son's and daughter's duty to co-operate with their parents and to help support them when in need. However, the full range of a household head's authority depends on the latter's sex. In reality, the *de facto* head is always the woman, even in the newly established nuclear household of a young couple, and there are several factors which affirm her in this position. Through the manufacture of palm fiber products, women occupy a relatively strong economic position, which gives them sufficient independence to manage—temporarily at least—without male support. On the other hand, co-operation within the female line of a kin-group is much stronger than in the male line. A woman can practically always count on the active help of her mother, grandmother, sister, or daughters and finds in this group a kind of security that is almost completely lacking in the situation of the male. When establishing a coresidential conjugal union with a man, a woman enters this relationship under entirely different premises than would a man. While the male depends on her in many aspects of managerial functions, such as food preparation and distribution, child-rearing, water supply, laundering, etc., the woman is not as dependent on him. Her basic needs for survival are guaranteed by her maternal kin and her own productiveness, and her coresidence with a male partner only adds a sort of surplus—usually calculated in terms of dresses, household utensils, and living space—sometimes of houseownership or a rise in social status. A woman always belongs first of all to her family of orientation and so do her children, the family (or families) of procreation she establishes in the course of her life being little more than phases during which an already existing security is being increased, not only for her own benefit but also for her maternal kin. A man, on the other hand, is an isolated individual and finds little or no support in his family of orientation and his kin-group. His economic and social security lies in his work, not in the combined labor effort of a group. And more than that, he often depends economically on the salable products manufactured by his spouse and/or daughters, as agriculture or hired labor do not always provide him with a permanent basis for survival and maintenance of the household. Although he may be the *de jure* head of the household, his authority is not well developed and well defined. Men all over the village form a fluctuating marginal element which gyrates around the stable center formed by the female-dominated complex constituted of child-rearing, hat-weaving, cooking, and laundering. These four activities form the inseparable nucleus around which revolves family and household life, and the man is hardly more than the provider of their raw materials.

Although a young woman when leaving her natal household group changes her jural status insofar as she is now expected to fulfil all duties implied by running her own household, by living in a definite sexual relationship with one male only, and by now forming part of the general category of wives, consorts, and mothers, she never lives entirely under the authority of her male partner, but her maternal kin—especially her mother—continue to exercise authority over her. This is well exteriorized by the manner in which she continues to co-operate with her mother or sisters, either by incorporating their young children into her household or by sharing with her maternal kin the food supply of her neolocal household. A young man, therefore, who lives single or in conjugal union within a household unit has very little authority. When reaching social maturity, his jural status changes from almost complete submission to his parents to independence, insofar as choice of residence or administration of earnings is concerned, but otherwise his family of orientation dominates his activities. The definite change in jural status is achieved only when the youth establishes his own household, and his authority reaches a peak during the early years of his conjugal union, declining steadily as his domestic unit becomes more and more dominated by women.

In the particular social structure of Aritama it is possible and frequent that an individual forms part of more than one household group. This is the case with all women who live outside their parental domestic units but who have not lost claim to membership in them; and also with those men who contribute economically to households other than their natal or conjugal units. A man who lives within his neolocal group but who, at the same time, helps support a concubine or his own mother will be counted as having membership in two households. The authority that gives him this membership is usually proportional to his co-operative effort as a provider, and the community will readily recognize his rights and privileges if he contributes a substantial share to another household's economic efforts.

The basic nature of the household structure and composition is the same for the whole village, and no marked differences can be observed between Loma and Plaza, except that in the latter barrio many individuals marry out and establish themselves neolocally, because their economic situation is generally stronger than that of lomero families. The gradual increase in size of placero households is due mostly to the incorporation of collateral kin.

We shall refer next to another important factor in this system: the legal aspect of the conjugal union itself. Catholic marriage is the rule among the more Creole-oriented placeros, but is infrequent outside this group. It can well be said that this form of conjugal union is a rather unpleasant thought for people of both sexes. A young man who decides to marry according to Church ritual is considered a person of great courage (*de mucho ánimo*) who, in spite of all the experiences of his friends and relatives, risks losing his independence, his peace of mind, and also his money for the sake of the social prestige associated with the approval of the Church and society. If he marries he is considered a fallen hero, a victim of society, and a newly wed man is commiserated and comforted. The cause of his 'disgrace' is the woman whom he married, although to her the idea of marriage is usually just as unpleasant as it is to him. She, also, is considered to be a victim, but not so much of society's rules as a victim of men. At marriage she (supposedly) waives publicly all her rights as an individual, but at the same time she, as well as everybody else, knows that this is only a gesture of the moment and that separation is always possible, male authority being of little importance. But for the rest of their lives the man will think of himself as a victim of women's snares, while the woman will adopt the role of the innocent martyr, abused by her husband and by men in general.

In Catholic marriage local standards demand that each man support his legitimate wife, educate their children, and work sufficiently to maintain the family at least on a subsistence level. In a free union this is not formulated in this manner. The economic conditions or the personal relationships of people who live in free unions are exposed to much less public criticism and gossip than would be the case in Catholic marriage. Those who live in consensual unions do not represent a moral problem to society, but those whose legal marriages are the motives of quarrels and fights are severely criticized. Catholic marriage is considered above all to be a heavy economic responsibility from which almost no escape is possible, as both the law and the Church would punish the individual who did not fulfil his obligations. This is—at least in male terms—the principal argument. Women fear mostly that, once they are married, they will be expected to become entirely subordinate to their husbands; that they will be abandoned and mistreated; and that they would have great difficulties in case of desertion. This is quite true, because a man will hardly ever go to live with a married and abandoned woman, partly out of fear of her legitimate husband, partly because he cannot participate in the woman's property of which she and her husband continue to be the legal owners. On the other hand, men also fear to be exploited and dominated by their wives and often believe that a married woman is more likely to practice sorcery against her spouse than a temporary concubine or a free-union consort, the motive being jealousy or the purpose to inherit the man's property. It is also a fact that women are far more active while living in free union and that they tend to become lazy and negligent once they marry. A free-union consort has to work and has to keep herself reasonably attractive to satisfy her supporter, but a married woman can oblige her husband to support her, while she herself might refuse to work. Under the pretext of ill health, a married woman might limit her contribution to the household economy to a degree which a free-union consort would never dare to practice for fear of being abandoned by the man.

Although both sexes thus accuse each other of not wanting to marry, it seems evident that men offer the most resistance. Together with their fear of being exploited, they know that, once they become married, they will have fewer chances with other women, and as extramarital affairs of men are not only taken for granted but form an important part of their prestige behavior, this consideration is often quite decisive in rejecting Catholic marriage. But there are also other factors at play. At marriage the man is usually obliged to provide the woman with a home of permanent character; in other words, he has to buy or build a house. This house, however, remains his property. In a free union, he often finds it necessary to do the same, but then the house usually becomes the property of the woman, especially after she has borne him several children. In such a free union, this is sometimes the very reason why the woman does not wish to marry in church, because several economic aspects enter the picture. In the first place, her family will advise against legal marriage because the house now forms part not only of the woman's property but to a certain degree, of her whole kin-group. Nominally it is hers but it also belongs to her maternal relatives. The latter fear (and with good reason) that in the case of marriage, the husband would acquire and exercise a certain authority over his wife's possessions, an authority that does not exist in a free union. Marriage is thus often rejected in order to protect the economic interests of the maternal line. On the other hand, once a woman has become the owner of a house or some other property, she might decide to discontinue her relationships with the man and try to find another one. As the new consort also has to give her some property—maybe in the form of furniture, outbuildings, or a sewing machine—in the course of time and of several free unions a woman might acquire a considerable capital, which increases further with the inheritance she receives at her mother's death. The importance of these considerations is evident if we take into account that in Aritama there are no old women who have to work to support themselves; all of them own houses which they can inhabit or rent out and which they have acquired from one or more temporary consorts. It is an important socioeconomic fact to realize that 30·9 per cent of all houses in the village are the property of women.

Men, however, find little or no material advantage in marriage. On establishing themselves in a conjugal union they make a single investment by working sufficiently to buy or build a house and to plant a field. By selling a crop or part of a field they can raise enough capital for a second concubinage or free union, and by hired labor or the sale of livestock they might raise the necessary capital for still another. Catholic marriage would be a disadvantage under these circumstances. Women, although less concerned about the probable restrictions of their former sexual freedom, nevertheless point out frequently that, while their husband's adventures outside of wedlock are condoned by society, their own extramarital experiences would be severely critized by all. Another factor that influences a woman's decision about marriage consists in the high aspirations she has formed while in school. A girl who has a few years of elementary schooling wants to marry an educated, wealthy, and socially prominent person, and will often refuse to marry a local boy, hoping (usually in vain) to find a better match sometime in the future.

The incentives why a young man should wish to marry in church are the following: the acquisition of prestige by the mere fact of Catholic marriage; the possibility of raising his class-status if the woman belongs to a higher social stratum than her husband; the acquisition of property if the woman is the owner or future heir of certain economic assets. A woman's incentives are more of an economic nature, and she might marry most any man who she believes will guarantee her and her children a life free of financial worries. Sometimes a man might decide to marry under the following circumstances: After having lived with several successive free-union consorts, his oldest children begin to represent a high economic value. He then might marry the mother of the most promising child (or children), knowing that once these become independent and secede they can be replaced by other children he has fathered and whom he can incorporate into the household as economic helpers.

It is difficult to oblige a man to marry. In case he has seduced a girl or fathered a child with her, her family—if socially prominent—might threaten the man with complaining to the authorities, but outside the circle of Creole-oriented placeros this practically never happens and even among them positive results are rarely obtained with such threats. If the girl belongs to the lower class of the Plaza or to a lomero family, nothing whatsoever could obligate a man to marry her. Often neither she nor her family would consider such a marriage as desirable, and quite frequently the idea of marriage because an illegitimate child was fathered would never even enter their minds. If the seduced or pregnant girl belongs to a very prominent family and is of legitimate birth herself, the local authorities might fine the man and might perhaps lock him up for a few days, but if she is an illegitimate child, there will be no official pressure at all, even if she is a member of a well-known family. In any event, separation is always possible. Some marriages last only a very short time, and often the couple separates after a few months, each living in a different household. This rarely occurs in the higher strata of the Plaza barrio but is frequent among the rest of the villagers. If the man continues to support his wife and children, but little criticism is leveled at him, and as this is the general rule, such separate households continue to function.

Free union is the most frequent form of conjugal relationship and tends to be a rather stable arrangement. However, even in its more or less permanent form, it is rarely admitted to be a definite situation but is usually rationalized as a phase preceding Catholic marriage. The Spanish term *compromiso* is equivalent to engagement, promise of marriage, and people will often claim that they are about to get married. But marriage as a consequence of long-established free union is exceedingly rare. Public reproval is slight in the cases where a man and a woman live together in free union and take proper care of their children, and the advantages of such unions are, according to them, quite considerable. While in a family based upon Catholic marriage the man is legally the authoritarian and undisputed head of the household, in a permanent free union there is (at least ideally) a certain amount of equality and sharing of duties and privileges, but, of course, the *de facto* head of the household is the woman.

Life is not easy for a young girl as long as she stays within her parental household. She has to help in the kitchen, weave hats, care for younger siblings, carry water, help in the laundering, and sometimes help in the fields. Even in a family of moderate resources such work is hard, and although the girl might be spared the exhausting task of agricultural work, every hour of the day will be filled with some chore which has to be done in house or yard. Many girls of nubile age feel exploited by their elders, humiliated, and disillusioned, and believe that they can free themselves of this condition by becoming the concubines or free-union consorts of men willing to support them. Although a girl will always tell her prospective mate that she lives very comfortably with her parents or relatives and that she sees no reason why she should abandon the security of her home, the words she uses are highly stereotyped and are the institutionalized reaction to a man's invitation to live with him, Gifts and promises are then sufficient to induce her to make a rapid decision, and soon she will tell her lover that she agrees to be 'taken out' by him. In order to 'take out' a girl (*sacarse la muchacha*), it is essential that the man has established good relations with her mother.

It is she, the potential mother-in-law, who decides whether such an arrangement be convenient or not, and the solicitude with which the man treats a girl's mother often gives the impression that he were courting her and not the daughter. When the mother is favorably impressed, she will generally aid the couple to get settled, but when she does not approve of the suitor and his plans, there will be serious difficulties if the girl insists on continuing the affair.

The decisive moment for the stability of a conjugal union comes when the first child is born, and each new child implies—although to a lesser degree—the same basic test of stability. If the father 'takes care of the child' (*atiende el niño*), i.e., pays the midwife, pays for the medicines, and provides more food than usual, then the union can be considered fairly permanent. If he does not, he loses practically every right over the child, and the woman herself is free to leave him or to establish relations with another man. Solicitude, exaggerated preoccupation at the moment of birth, gifts of remedies, clothes, and food are the attitudes expected from a man who lives in stable free union; but if he should fail to call the midwife, or refuse to pay her, and be absent during childbirth, he demonstrates that he is no longer interested in living with the woman, or in claiming the child as his own. A man, on the other hand, profits by his illegitimate offspring if he 'takes care of the children' when they are born. Even though he should abandon the woman, the fact that he paid the expenses of childbirth and contributed to the woman's and child's support with occasional gifts of food and clothing gives him authority over the child, and he is fully entitled to claim his offspring if he sees fit to do so. In this manner, in the course of several short-term free unions, a man forty years of age might command a labor force of numerous children of all ages under twenty who are obliged to work for him.

Little effort is made to conceal the fact that a man has various concubines, and usually everyone knows about it. Public opinion will hardly criticize such behavior. It is condoned if the man offers sufficient economic support to the women and does not mistreat them physically. Sometimes a man's resources are insufficient for this, but if he is a 'serious' person and has gained the esteem of his women's households as a hard worker and good provider, the concubines' mothers, sisters, or aunts are likely to help out and to contribute a share in supporting their kinswoman. If a man who lives in Catholic marriage with a woman establishes a permanent or temporary concubinage with one or more other women, the latter do not participate directly in his food supply but receive instead gifts of money, dresses, shoes, and other personal articles. The legal wife might know of and condone this, but should she ever hear that her husband gave food to one of his concubines, violent reactions are sure to follow. A married man might spend his money on other women, but he should never give them any food with the knowledge of his lawful wife. It is, however, quite common that in such cases the man tacitly allows his concubines and their children to go to his fields and take home whatever fruits they might need for consumption.

While women look to marriage, free union, or concubinage almost exclusively for economic security, men try above all to prove their virility and to procreate as many children as possible, for economic and prestige reasons. A good deal of personal prestige is gained by being able to claim twenty or thirty illegitimate children. A man will state with pride how many children he has fathered in marriage, how many with concubines, and how many 'on the street' (*en la calle*), i.e., during occasional relations which might have lasted for only a few moments. To procreate children is felt to be the only real outlet, the only definite proof of masculinity. It is the only occasion wherein men believe that they are able to affirm themselves. Religion, economy, politics, physical prowess, work or play, dress or education, alcoholism, or physical aggressiveness do not provide the man with the opportunity to demonstrate his maleness and dominance. The procreation of children is believed to be the only proper way of asserting his masculinity. Women will also boast of their illegitimate offspring, even if conceived by several different men. In their terms they have only done their duty; they have repaid the man's investment in the form of children. Not to have done this would be rather a reason for shame. To have been supported by a man for some time without having borne him a child would be a humiliation.

Marriage and free union are essentially economic institutions. Sexual freedom, the fact that neither moral nor religious considerations are of decisive importance, and the always present possibility of separation leave little besides the practical economic foundation of the conjugal union. Except on the highest social and economic levels, the real active part of the population are the women and children. Marriage or free union mark for many men the beginning of the period of life when they can rest, while women and children take care of most chores around the house and the fields. Daily subsistence is assured by the home industry of the women, the sale of some eggs, the food exchange with kinfolk, or the small sums received for occasional hired labor.

One final and important aspect of the general social system of Aritama refers to the position of children. We have already mentioned several times the terms 'father' and 'mother' as those holding authority over their offspring. The authority of biological, coresident parents cannot be questioned, but in the case of a separated parental union or in the case of foster parents, this authority depends on many personal factors. Although a father whose child is being reared in another household does not relinquish his authority over his offspring, his influence is greatly weakened, and in later life such a child is likely to reject all paternal influence. To a certain degree this is also true of children who were not reared by their biological mothers, and although, ideally, such a child should nevertheless accept her authority, this generally does not happen. The emotional tie formed with a substitute mother is often stronger. Then the 'real' mother who holds authority is not always the biological mother but the woman who reared the child; and a grandmother, mother's sister, or other female kin might thus acquire the position of jural mother. That this is a frequent phenomenon can be seen from the many instances in which children are reared by women who are not their biological mothers. Ideally, this mother-child relationship should form the strongest bond in the entire structure of the system, but it is evident that this ideal—as a culturally formulated value—belongs to a chronologically earlier level of historical development, when the two-generation nuclear family was still the principal form of household unit. The three-generation, female-dominated household is a consequence of recent historical events. Within this group the child finds a series of maternal substitutes. The mother-child ties are, therefore, often characterized by ambivalent attitudes.

In view of this situation, it is of interest to observe the residence of children, adolescents, and youths, according to the group within which they are reared and live (Table 22).

TABLE 22

Child lives with	Age Groups									
	0 – 2		3 –5		6 – 10		11 – 15		16 – 18	
	No.	*Per Cent*	*No.*	*Per Cent*	*No.*	*Per Cent*	*No.*	*Per Cent*	*No.*	*Per Cent*
Parents only	66	45·52	62	43·66	94	43·32	51	34·23	12	37·5
Parents and half-siblings	22	15·17	28	19·72	40	18·43	22	14·76	—	—·—
Parents, parents' single siblings	3	2·07	3	2·11	2	0·92	3	2·01	—	—·—
Mother alone	22	15·17	23	16·2	49	22·58	40	26·84	11	34·37
Father alone	—	—·—	—	—·—	—	—·—	2	1·34	2	6·25
Mother, mother's siblings' children	2	1·38	1	0·7	2	0·92	1	0·67	1	3·12
Uncle or aunt	—	—·—	1	0·7	1	0·46	3	2·01	—	—·—
Three-generation household:										
Both parents present	3	2·7	4	2·82	2	0·92	4	2·68	—	—·—
Mother only present	25	17·24	19	13·38	23	10·6	15	10·07	4	12·5
No parent present	2	1·38	1	0·7	4	1·84	8	5·37	2	6·25
Total	143	100·00	142	99·99	217	99·99	149	99·98	32	99·99

As we can see, only 409 (62·6 per cent) of all children under fifteen years of age live with both their biological parents, while the rest live either with their mothers alone or with her within a three-generation household. A small but significant percentage live away from their biological parents (3·06 per cent). During the critical age below two years, 51 (35·1 per cent) children are reared in the absence of their biological fathers, and in at least half these cases no substitute father-figure is present at all. The mother-child bond is consequently a relatively strong one, although the large number of maternal substitutes and the frustrating aspects of the mother image that we have pointed out earlier tend to weaken it. In any event, a child's household membership lies mainly within the range of the female-dominated group, and the father plays an insignificant role in the process of education and socialization of children.

In the foregoing pages we have described the household group in Aritama as a structurally simple but highly effective unit which, in a series of stages, develops according to a definite pattern. The various functions of such a household group include child-rearing, the administration and distribution of resources, and the many other services of daily life, such as cooking, laundering, food preparation, etc., but—above all—a fully developed household unit forms a framework that guarantees security to all members who in the course of their lives find themselves in situations in which they would not be able to survive as isolated individuals. After the dissolution of a conjugal relationship, a woman or a child is never left in helpless misery but can always count upon the backing of a larger unit into which he becomes reincorporated. In illness or childbirth, in economic crises or widowhood, the household group receives and incorporates the afflicted individuals and provides them with all the basic services. In this manner, and also through the ramification of reciprocal services and kinship ties, the developed household is, therefore, of a much greater functional importance than the nuclear family, which, as we have seen, is only a growth stage within a much wider cycle.

KIN AND KINSHIP

Among the primary factors of social structure are the meaning and function of kin and kinship. Although the importance of close kinship ties, uniting large numbers of individuals, is greatly emphasized, in reality the concept and the function of kinship are restricted to a small group of interacting individuals. People talk much about mutual obligations, reciprocity, and the strong emotional ties that should bind the individual to his kin-group, but often add that many people tend to show indifference or even hostility toward their kin. Kinship cohesion evidently depends upon many individual factors: In families where there is a marked vertical social mobility (as, for example, in many Creole-oriented placero families), patterns of envy, shame, and prestige sometimes lead to a loosening of these ties and even to their more or less permanent and total disruption; but in small family groups that belong essentially on the same social and economic level there often exist strong bonds that unite many individuals.

Because of the color and class tensions, people in Aritama are extremely interested in genealogy. Most adults are able to name their great-grandparents, and some will go back even farther into the past. Together with names and dates, they are able to supply detailed information on legitimacy, phenotype, individual status achievements or class participation, economic assets, ubication of domicile, and many personal anecdotes. This genealogical bookkeeping is oriented, above all, in a vertical temporal sense, and its emphasis is placed mainly upon genetic descent and not so much upon an horizontal extension of kinship ties. The tradition of short-term free unions and the great number of illegitimate offspring have, of course, created a very complicated web of relationships that include the entire village and extend over many generations. People who have a detailed knowledge of village genealogy are respected and sometimes rather feared. Both placeros and lomeros alike use this knowledge to slight the prestige of rivaling families or individuals. It is evident that the lomeros have a longer memory and a more complete knowledge of genealogy than the placeros care to admit. The main interest, however, is concentrated on the past, and but little attention is paid to present conditions. As there are no strong bars to marriage or free union with partners of illegitimate descent or with kinfolk such as first cousins, there is little concern with the tracing of horizontal ties.

In Aritama the kin of a person includes the following individuals: In the family of orientation both lines of descent are reckoned, including the spouses of father or mother's siblings and half-siblings. In the second ascending generation only grandparents are included and practically never their siblings. In ego's generation the kin includes siblings and half-siblings, as well as first cousins, and in the first descending generation it includes ego's children, grandchildren, nieces, and nephews. The spouses of ego's siblings are not reckoned as kin nor are the descendants of father's father's siblings nor any members of ego's spouse's family.

The characteristic structural unit consists of short matrilines, usually of three but sometimes of four generations. An individual, therefore, practically always knows his kin. There is little interest in kin members with whom, at some phase of life, there has been no personal acquaintance and interaction. An individual 'belongs' essentially to the maternal line. Relatives on this side, in ascending generations, are known or remembered in much greater detail than those of the paternal line. One's maternal first cousins (although without distinguishing between parallel and cross-cousins) are much closer kin than the paternal ones. Marriage with the former is likely to cause severe criticism. It is condoned with the latter. As we have seen, there is a tendency toward matrilocal residence; inheritance is from mother to daughter but never from mother to son. To a certain degree, class-status is also transmitted from mother to daughter. Law and tradition always favor the maternal line in all cases of inheritance or any kind of economic assistance. It is the girl's mother who accepts or rejects her daughter's suitors, and it is she who receives the abandoned girl and her illegitimate children into her household if a temporary union did not provide her with a home of her own. Illegitimate children bear their mother's name. Even a legitimate child might insist upon using the mother's surname in case a too-close association with the biological father's family is not desirable. If the contrary should happen, i.e., if an illegitimate child should accept the father's surname, this would very likely be interpreted as a serious offense to his mother's kin and as a definite break of all maternal ties. Also, for example, if one should ask a grandmother to name her descendants, she will invariably count only her daughters and their female offspring, without mentioning any male descendant.

The ties structured along the grandmother-daughter-child axis frequently transcend the individual household and then lead to the formation of larger units which resemble matrilineal descent groups. Patterns of reciprocity, such as food exchange, child-rearing, or co-operation in minor productive activities, and also the fact that a definite class cohesion is evident in many instances, indicate that these interdependent units are tied together by bonds which are stronger than those which unite the individual domestic group. The male role is completely marginal in these cases. Such often-heard expressions as *las López* or *las Gómez* ('the López/Gómez women') have no male counterpart. They refer to a group of women and their offspring who are united not only by kinship ties but by many reciprocal services as well. However, such larger units are formed only within the lower socioeconomic strata and then only among families with a great number of active and adult members. In the Plaza barrio such groups are few, but in the Loma there are about eight or ten.

Kinship terminology conforms essentially to Spanish usage, but there is a marked tendency to use classificatory terms, above all in the Loma barrio and in the lower stratum of the Plaza. The following analysis shows these terms and their functioning.

Forms of Social Relationships

I. Consanguinal Relatives

A. Ego's Generation
1. Brothers and half-brothers are grouped together and called 'brother' (*hermano*). In the case of half-brothers, one usually specifies on which side the common parent is, *hermano de padre* or *hermano de madre*. In the lower socioeconomic strata, parallel and cross-cousins are often called 'brothers'. Younger brothers are always called with the diminutive *hermanito*.
2. Sisters and half-sisters are grouped together and called 'sister' (*hermana*). In the case of half-sisters the common parent is specified by saying *hermana de padre* or *hermana de madre*. In the lower strata, parallel or cross-cousins are referred to as 'sisters'. Younger sisters are always referred to with the diminutive *hermanita*.
3. Parallel and cross-cousins are classed together and called 'cousins' (*primos*). First cousins are usually called *primo-hermano*.
4. Parallel and cross-cousins (female) are classed together and called 'cousins' (*primas*). First cousins are usually called *prima-hermana*.

B. First Ascending Generation
1. Father and mother are referred to with isolating terms, *papá*, *máma*.
2. Parallel and cross-uncles of both lines are called 'uncle' (*tío*), optionally 'father' (*papá*).
3. Parallel and cross-aunts of both lines are called 'aunt' (*tía*), optionally 'mother' (*máma*).

C. Second Ascending Generation
1. Grandfathers of both lines are called 'grandfather' (*abuelo*), optionally with the diminutive *abuelito*. Occasionally the Indian term *táita* is used.
2. Grandmothers of both lines are called 'grandmother' (*abuela*), with the diminutive *abuelita*. Occasionally the Indian terms *súcui* ('paternal grandmother') and *ánsi* ('maternal grandmother') are used.
3. Grandparents' siblings of both lines are called *tío-abuelo*, *tía-abuela*: optionally the terms *abuelo*, *abuela* are employed.

D. Third Ascending Generation
1. Great-grandparents of both lines are called *bisabuelo de padre*, *bisabuelo de madre*, *bisabuela de padre*, *bisabuela de madre*. Optionally the terms *abuelo*, *abuela* are used.

E. First Descending Generation
1. Sons and daughters are called *hijo*, *hija*. The youngest son is called *vejé*. Occasionally a daughter is called by the Indian term *dúga*.
2. Sons and daughters of ego's siblings or half-siblings are called *sobrino*, *sobrina*; the feminine term is almost always used in its diminutive form *sobrinita*. It is common usage to call them 'sons' or 'daughters'.

F. Second Descending Generation
1. Grandchildren are classed together with ego's sibling's grandchildren and are called *nieto*, *nieta*. The endearing term *nietecita* is common.

II. Classificatory Relatives

A. Ego's Generation
  1. Every person of the same sex, age-group, and class-status is called—at least inside the village—*primo, prima,* i.e., 'cousin'. The term for 'brother' (*hermano*) or an abbreviated diminutive derived therefrom (*mano, manito*) is used occasionally in a joking sense, but only when referring to males.

B. First Ascending Generation
  1. Godfathers or foster fathers are usually called 'father' (*papá*).
  2. Godmothers or stepmothers are usually called 'mother' (*máma*).
  3. Any person of the older generation may be called—within the village—'uncle' or 'aunt' (*tío, tía*), but outside the village such a person would be called 'cousin' (*primo, prima*). The first two terms are used only on the same social level; the last two terms are used without taking into account social or economic criteria, although sometimes marked class differences might impede their use.
  4. Women who have nubile daughters of the same age-group as ego or somewhat younger, are jokingly called 'mother-in-law' (*suegra*).

C. Second Ascending Generation
  1. Any person of the same generation as ego's grandparents may be called—within the village—'uncle' or 'aunt' (*tío, tía*), but will be called 'grandfather', 'grandmother' (*abuelo, abuela*) outside the village.

D. First Descending Generation
  1. Male and female godchildren are classed with ego's grandchildren and with sons and daughters of ritual coparents and may be called 'son' or 'daughter' (*hijo, hija*).

III. In-laws

A. Spouses' siblings and siblings' spouses are called by the same term, *cuñado, cuñada.*

B. Spouses' parents are called 'father-in-law', 'mother-in-law' (*suegro, suegra*).

The use of classificatory terms outside of kin proper, implies familiarity, affection and, above all, respect. This pattern often includes entire families that—although no recognized kinship exists between them—consider themselves as 'cousins'. In many cases—mostly in the Loma barrio—only parallel and cross-cousins of the maternal line are included among the kin. The cousins of the paternal line are sometimes not considered kin and are not referred to by a kinship term. Between old women and children of both sexes who are not related the exchange of kinship terms used between aunt and nephews/nieces is common and denotes respect-behavior toward the woman.

The extension of kinship ties in the form of ritual coparenthood (*compadrazgo*) is practiced but is of little functional importance. Four main types are distinguished locally: the *compadrazgo de agua*, for which the chosen godfather personally baptizes *sub conditione* the newborn but sickly child when no Catholic priest is available, so the infant will not die a *moro* ('heathen'); the *compadrazgo de oleo*, which refers to the regular ceremony of Catholic baptism celebrated by the priest; and the *compadrazgo de confirmación*, which takes place when the child reaches the age of confirmation. The *compadrazgo de matrimonio* is established at the Catholic marriage of a couple.

Ideally, a strong spiritual bond is established between the child (*ahijado, ahijada*), the ritual coparent (*padrino, madrina*), and the biological parents (*compadre, comadre*), a bond which is supposed to find its expression in spiritual guidance of the child, mutual assistance between all partners concerned, and a strict pattern of respect-behavior. As a matter of fact, this bond includes an incest taboo, for the three interacting persons are considered to form a close-knit union. At their deaths the godparents are expected to leave a substantial share of their property to the child. When meeting on the street or inside a house, the child is supposed to greet his *padrino* respectfully and to ask for his blessing, pronouncing a short prayer, *el alabado sea Dios*. On Christmas Day the *padrino* or *madrina* should make a small gift (*agüinaldo*) to the child, and during the rest of the year should make some occasional gifts, such as food, medicines, or perhaps clothes. If the child should die, the *padrino* is obliged to pay for the coffin and any expenses caused by the wake and burial. The principal occasions when mutual help should be given spontaneously between *compadres*, or between coparents and godchildren, arise during sickness, communal labor efforts, intervillage frictions, or difficulties with the law. Being sanctioned and strongly recommended by the Church, the institution of ritual coparenthood should also tend to provide orphaned children with a home and with moral guidance given by the godparents.

The most common type of ritual kinship is the *compadrazgo de oleo*. *Compadres de agua* are relatively rare, the same as *compadres de confirmación*, and practically no value at all is attributed to the latter form. Frequently the *compadre de agua* is also the *compadre de oleo*. For each child only one or two coparents of each sex are chosen, but in the case of a marriage there might be a great number of *padrinos* and *madrinos*. It is understood that then there exists hardly any obligation beyond the presentation of a small gift to the newly wed couple.

Any adult person, relative or friend—even a non-Catholic, can be a coparent, but usually people will choose an individual of established status, experience, and economic position. A prospective *padrino* is never approached directly by the interested party, but the proposal is made through an intermediary, maybe a close relative or a mutual friend. To refuse such a proposal is considered to be a great offense, and no instances were known where a person had declined to accept this honor. The *padrino de oleo* will first pay the priest's small fee and buy a little dress for the infant, returning then to the house of the parents, where he will hand both the dress and the receipt of the parish to the child's mother. After the rite of baptism is over, the party returns to the parents' house and the new *compadre* will buy a round of drinks for all present and perhaps give a few coins to other children, so they can buy some sweets. The new *compadres* exchange a few stereotyped phrases, assuring their willingness to be of mutual assistance.

Practically all placeros are in some kind of *compadre* relationship among themselves, but they will never propose that a lomero be a coparent. The latter, however, almost always chose their *compadres* from among the residents of the Plaza barrio.

A child calls his or her godparents *padrino* or *madrina*; these in turn call the child *ahijado* or *ahijada*. Among themselves the coparents of a child—unless they are man and wife—call each other *compadre* and *comadre*, but only if one of them is the biological parent of the child. When they are *padrinos* of a child who is not related biologically to either of them, they do not use these terms and are not considered to be ritually related to each other. Among *padrinos de matrimonio* these terms are never used. Quite frequently the terms *padrino* and *madrina* become practically hereditary for at least two generations or are transferable to persons between whom there are no ritual ties at all. The following cases are typical: Two men were *compadres* and used this term when addressing each other. When one of them died, his son began to address the other as *compadre*, although no ritual kinship had ever existed between them. Our informants interpreted this transference as a sign of respect and assured us that beyond that it did not imply any kind of mutual obligations. In another case, a girl had a *madrina de oleo*, and, therefore, the girl's mother and the coparent were *comadres*. When the girl's mother died, the girl's sister began to call the same woman *madrina*, although there were no ceremonial kinship ties between them, the sister's real *madrina* being a different woman. On the other hand, the term *compadre* does frequently replace kinship terms such as 'son' or 'father'. When a child's *padrino* is his father's brother, the two brothers will refer to each other as *compadres*, and the same might happen with father and son if they are *compadres* and prefer this form of address to the use of kinship terms or proper names. A woman might call her son *compadre* if he happens to be the godfather of her child from a later conjugal union.

Quite contrary to ideal rules for ritual coparenthood, the main incentive is immediate economic gain. Many people are only interested in obtaining small gifts and afterward maintain no relations whatsoever with their coparents, although they expect them to be of assistance to the child in case there should be need. For the same reason there is no tendency to keep ritual coparenthood restricted to the village or the wider region, and any temporary resident or traveler might be asked to become a *padrino*, although he might never return to the village again. Sometimes a woman will ask a man to be the *padrino* of her child, without first consulting the child's father, and the latter might learn only afterward that he has a new *compadre*.

Ceremonial coparenthood is always interpreted in terms of the *padrino* acquiring a certain jural authority over the child. Once the child reaches an age when it constitutes a labor force, the *padrino* might ask the parents to let their child live in his household to help with the daily chores, without receiving any recompense other than food and shelter. Among the poorer people this often represents a great help and such an arrangement is usually thought to be very desirable, it being understood that all persons involved will profit greatly. A *padrino* has the right to punish and to reward and may also return the child to his parents in case he does not need or want his services any more. It is quite clear that the importance of the *compadrazgo* institution does not lie in its significance as a system of social control on the level of *compadres* but rather in the *padrino-ahijado* (or *madrina-ahijada*) relationship, the basic function of which consists in supplying the *compadres* (or *comadres*) with a free labour force, while at the same time freeing the parents of the child of any obligation to their offspring. A *compadre* and *padrino* can always 'cede the right' (*ceder el derecho*) over a child to the child's parents, simply by returning the baptismal fee he paid, to the mother or father of the godchild. This done, he ceases to be a *compadre* and *padrino*, and the parents can give the money to another person, who then automatically assumes the functions of the former godparent. It is also common to establish a *compadrazgo* with a person to whom one owes a favor. In this way all previous claims must be forgotten by the new *compadre*, and his continued insistence on fulfilling them would be taken as a gross insult to his new coparents.

Ceremonial coparenthood is rarely discussed in Aritama and the bonds established by it are so weak as to be of little real importance. Enmities, or sexual relations among coparents, or between coparent and godchild are quite common, and although public opinion might sometimes denounce and condemn such behavior, there are no effective means to control it. One has the impression that this institution, which is so important in other parts of Colombia, has lost (or perhaps never developed) its force as a system of social control, and that it is maintained at present only as a feeble and futile effort to curb the prevailing intrasocial tensions.

ILLEGITIMACY AND ADOPTION

As we have mentioned before, among all the placeros married as Catholics there is not a single man who has only legitimate children, but that without exception each one has at least one illegitimate child. This situation represents by no means a covert feature of the local culture; on the contrary, it is often mentioned with pride. The men often brag about their illegitimate offspring, and even a lawful wife will sometimes recognize, with ill-disguised satisfaction, that her husband has proved his virility by procreating numerous and varied descendants. Men will boast about their children, bet on how many women they might get with child, and keep detailed count in order to know whether a pregnancy is due to their fatherhood or to that of a rival.

Quite apart from the psychological aspects underlying such behavior patterns, there are economic considerations that are openly discussed. Any illegitimate child that 'has been taken care of' (*ha sido atentido*) by his biological father is considered practically his servant. This, at least, is the local theory among the poorer classes and mainly in the Loma barrio. Although in reality there exists little factual evidence, the theme of exploitation of children is much discussed and we shall first of all state the public attitudes held outside the Plaza nucleus. According to our informants, the father claims (*reclama*) such a child from its mother during infancy and takes it to his home, where it is incorporated into his household. The child lives with its legitimate half-siblings but is never fully accepted by them or by the father's legitimate wife, being simply a future servant of inferior position. This dependency lasts for both sexes until they have reached seventeen or eighteen years of age. Only then are they set 'free' (*libres*) and may leave the household and lead their own lives, but in any event they are obliged to help their father economically at any time should he ask for it. In reality, however, such cases are certainly not so frequent as people say they are. Illegitimate children do represent an important labor force for a man— but only occasionally, not for years on end. They might feel obliged to volunteer or they might be asked to help in a harvest, in a communal labor project, in times of illness or crop failure, and probably will not receive wages but only food and shelter for their work. This co-operation, however, is not permanent. The lomeros tend to interpret this arrangement as an abuse committed by the 'Spaniards' and are likely to exaggerate greatly the quite imaginary hardships such children are said to suffer at the hands of their parents. For many men of the Plaza section this occasional help is an incentive to procreate illegitimate offspring, but also they tend to exaggerate its effectiveness and frequency.

At some time during adolescence the illegitimate child begins to realize that his surname sometimes represents an obstacle in achieving status and in being incorporated into a higher social level. As all illegitimate children bear their mother's name and as this is often associated with the 'Indian' families, there arise the following possibilities: The child might live in the Loma barrio and accept the status of 'Indian'; or the child might try to influence his father to recognize him legally and let him use his surname; or the child might 'steal' the father's name (*robarse el apellido*), sign with it, and use it in every occasion, public or private. The first case is quite frequent and contributes, of course, to the formation of a group of strongly resentful individuals; the second alternative occurs at times, but the outcome depends on whether the illegitimate child has 'made good', is a hard worker, and has shown some affection and loyalty toward his biological father. The result also depends upon the attitude of the legitimate children, who, perhaps, do not wish to receive the half-brother or half-sister as an individual with equal rights. The 'stealing' of a name occurs rarely, but when it does, it becomes notorious. When a name is 'stolen' it is because an adolescent has acquired a certain economic status and does not show any marked Indian traits in his physical appearance. The lomeros, however, are likely to consider the child or youth as still belonging to them, whereas the placeros never forget his origin and never accept him into their barrio structure. But outside the village and with strangers, the youth might appear to be a legitimate son or daughter of a placero, i.e., might acquire a high class-status. Here, however, we repeat that the lomeros consider it as shocking for an individual to renounce his mother's name, because this is equivalent to severing all ties with the maternal kin.

According to Colombian law, any child, whether legitimate or not, and whether recognized by his father or not, has the same right to inherit. This law, however, is little known in Aritama. It so happens that, as a rule, an illegitimate child does not always inherit from his father, although occasionally the authorities will intervene and consider it convenient that such a child should participate. In this case, the police inspector will call the mother or the illegitimate children and communicate to them that they are included among the heirs. It then occurs quite frequently that a child or a mother refuses to accept such an inheritance or any part of it, sometimes saying that they would accept it if it were offered by the legitimate children but not under pressure exercised by the law. The reason is evidently that the illegitimate children and their mothers fear the legitimate heirs, who would be likely to become their bitter enemies if they should accept a share of the inheritance.

Catholic marriage with a free-union consort legitimizes all children born before it, but mere recognition before the proper authorities, although valid before the law, is not always thought to be valid by the local society. It diminishes the stigma of illegitimate birth, but the child continues to be in the status of one born out of wedlock. Other ways of diminishing the social stigma consist in his father 'making a present' of his name (*regalar el apellido*) to the child, i.e., authorizing him to use his surname, or in continuing to support the child's mother for the rest of her life. It must be added here that we know of no instance where a man had refused to admit his fatherhood of a child, but this, of course, does not mean that he would recognize the child publicly as his heir.

In Aritama, just as in many other communities in the Colombian lowlands, an infant or child, whether legitimate or not, is sometimes adopted by another family, not always of the kin. This custom is quite general in the rural Creole population and also in the lower urban classes. In Aritama, adoption is occasionally practised with the first children of economically hard-pressed parents who live in free union, but it occurs also in Catholic marriage, in the event that the child represents a heavy economic burden to its biological parents. In all of these cases it is frequent that the couple promises, before the child is born, to give it to the mother of the man or woman, or perhaps to the female consort's sister. Although it is said that the child's mother is absolutely free to decide whether she wants to separate herself from the child or not, the child's father and other relatives often exercise definite pressure on her. Quite frequently a child is taken away from its mother entirely against her will. If, for example, the woman should reject the proposal of her spouse's mother to adopt the child, this would be taken as an offense against the man's family and might even lead to the dissolution of the conjugal union. On the other hand, it is quite often the child's father who insists upon having the infant adopted, and the child's mother agrees only out of fear of losing her consort and of displeasing his family.

Public opinion always advises that illegitimate children or children of very poor Catholic marriages be raised by their maternal or paternal grandmothers, who are then obliged at their deaths to include these grandchildren among their heirs. The children's grandmothers verbalize adoption in terms of 'education' and economic help for the young couple, but paternal grandmothers state sometimes quite openly that they adopted a child for 'convenience' (*por conveniencia*), to have a domestic servant in later years. Maternal grandmothers say rather that they did so 'out of pity' (*por condolencia*) for the infant, but they, too, obviously have an economic interest in adoption. It can be observed that, while paternal grandmothers will adopt grandchildren of both sexes, maternal grandmothers prefer male infants, apparently because they intend to have them work in the fields and contribute to the maintenance of the maternal line's property. In such an adoption, as soon as the child is weaned the grandmother takes the infant home with her, where he is reared from then on by her, her coresident daughters, or other relatives who might live under the same roof. There are more than twenty such adopted children in the village, called *entenados*, who occupy the position of servants or future servants. Not only grandmothers, however, adopt children. In the event a man has fathered a child with a woman whose family is very poor and numerically small, the father's sister or some other paternal relative might adopt the infant. In any case, it appears that such children are adopted not so much out of pity or to help their parents, but rather with a definite economic purpose in view. Quite often a man who has fathered a child with a concubine insists that, once the infant has been weaned, his own mother, i.e., the child's paternal grandmother, take charge of it because he interprets this as a compensation for the diminished economic help he now gives to his own mother as a result of having established himself in concubinage or free union. A second child borne by the same woman would then stay with her, this being interpreted as an economic backing for the future. It also happens that a girl's mother agrees to the daughter's concubinage only under the condition that the first child be given to her, to be reared as a future servant. In all these circumstances, the fact that children become the objects of economic transactions is never criticized, and public attitudes are quite different from those demonstrated should the father take economic advantage of his illegitimate offspring. As a matter of fact, the adoption complex is, according to local tradition, an old and important institution. On the other hand, obligatory child labor for a father is said to be a recent development which began only after the immigrants from the lowlands had arrived in the valley.

Adoption does not imply any rite or formal statement, nor is it a matter that is ever brought before the local authorities. It is a private arrangement in which it is understood by all persons that the individual who feeds the child automatically acquires the right to use the child's services, once he has reached the age where he is economically productive. The adoptive parents can at any moment return the child to his biological parents and in this case—which occurs very rarely—the parents are obliged to compensate the adoptive parents in some way for the expenses they have had while the child was under their care.

In some extreme situations it happens at times that a mother has her child adopted by someone 'for punishment' (*por castigo*) or because she was 'weary' (*aburrida*) of it. Only few of these people believe that children need certain foods or hygienic conditions according to their age; and few of them realize the need for affection that a child feels. The majority believe that any adult or servant or older child is an adequate parent-substitute. Children are sometimes kept as one would keep some rather valueless animal, such as a dog or a pet, which should forage for itself and which is to blame in the event it becomes under-nourished and sick. As for the mother, separation from her child apparently means little, as many women are greatly relieved to have their children taken care of by others, even if they should not see them again for a long time.

PERSONAL NAMES

It is the general custom in all Latin America for a person's name to be formed of three parts: the baptismal name (or names), the father's surname, and the mother's surname. For example, a man called Pedro Gómez López is the son Pedro of a man surnamed Gómez and a woman surnamed López. If Pedro Gómez López or Pedro Gómez L., as he might choose to abbreviate it, marries a woman named María Rodríguez Martinez, she will then call herself María Rodríguez de Gómez, joining her father's surname to her husband's by adding the preposition, *de* ('of') but dropping her mother's surname, Martínez. A son or a daughter of this marriage would use the surnames Gómez Rodríguez. In the event Pedro should die, his wife would insert the word *viuda* ('widow'), abbreviated *vda.*, before the *de*. People of illegitimate birth who have not been recognized legally by their biological fathers use the mother's surname. Occasionally a compound name can be inherited as a whole, and in this manner a tripart compound surname is formed. However, many people use only one surname, the father's, for reasons that pertain to certain prestige considerations. A person's surnames are often indicative of social class, and an individual whose father's surname belongs to a well-known and old family, while his mother's is rather common, will sometimes drop the latter. But if the opposite is true and the mother's surname is indicative of higher class-status, he will, of course, insist upon using it. On the other hand, there are many people whose parents' surnames are both common and do not denote any particular status who will either use both or only the father's surname.

Although this is the common rule all over Colombia, including, of course, the lowland towns and villages of the Caribbean coast, in Aritama it is not always observed. Here there is considerable confusion in names, which is noticeable not only to the outsider but which causes much comment among the villagers as well. In the first place, almost all these people use only one surname, very often the mother's, dropping the father's completely. In the second place, in the course of time and according to changing factors of personal prestige and public opinion, they will sometimes change this surname, being known for some years and to some people by their mother's name, while at other periods of their lives they use their father's surname, or occasionally even the surname of a grandparent.

When we first established contact with the individual villagers, who introduced themselves or were introduced to us by others, we learned many names which, after a few days or weeks, turned out to be not the usual names under which those persons were known within their own community. During the process of getting acquainted, some people tried to impress us by introducing themselves, if illegitimate, with their father's name, or they were reduced to a lower class-status for personal reasons by those who introduced them to us with their mother's names, although they were of legitimate birth. Since many surnames are associated with the 'Indian' section of the village, while others are taken to be indicative of 'Spanish' origin, an additional problem was created.

On the other hand, in the course of his life an individual is likely to rise and descend occasionally in the social scale. The many ups and downs that mark the careers of those whose social mobility is great are often expressed in their use of surnames. As long as a person of illegitimate birth is of low status, he might be known only by his mother's name, but as soon as he begins to rise to higher levels, he might adopt his father's name, especially if it is a surname associated with higher economic or social status. This individual initiative is then subjected to the scrutiny of the community, which will decide whether or not such a change is justified. The father might protest and declare publicly that his illegitimate son has no right to use his name; or he might legally recognize his child and thus give him this right. Sometimes the father will 'make him a gift of his name', simply by agreeing that his son use it, but without legal recognition, being then able to withdraw his 'gift' if he should become displeased with the son's behavior. But no matter what the father's attitude may be in such cases, it is the community that agrees or does not agree to the use of a person's name. It is the subtle weighing of the many factors that form a person's status and prestige that determines in the last analysis by what name he shall be known. If no general agreement is reached, such a person might be known under different names all his life.

At the time of our census there were forty-three different family names in Aritama. Of these about ten were associated with the 'Indians', the remaining thirty-three being considered 'Spanish' names. It must be pointed out here that the number of different family names is in no way indicative of the number of people bearing them. Certain 'Indian' family names are used by more than a hundred individuals, while certain 'Spanish' names are limited to only one or two individuals. Seven family names occur in the 'Indian' barrio as well as in the 'Spanish' barrio. The latter bearers of these names go to great pains in trying to explain that they are no kin of the 'Indian' family. This may be true in some cases, but in others it is doubtful. It seems more probable that both families had a common origin but became socially separated in later times. There is also much emphasis on the 'proper' spelling of certain surnames. The Florez family, for example, which is of high class-status, insists on having the name written with a *z*, in order to avoid any possible confusion with the Flores family of the Loma barrio, which is considered to be of 'Indian' origin. The latter, however, are eager to explain that both families had a common ancestor who immigrated some eighty years ago but whose descendants split into 'rich' and 'poor' branches.

As to the ethnic origins of local family names, the following can be said: Of the forty-three surnames, the majority are Castillian; four are Basque; two are Portuguese or western Iberian; two Andalusian-Arabic; one Galician; one Catalan; and two French. Not one name is of American Indian origin. In the census of the 'Indians of Aritama', taken by the Spanish authorities in 1803, distinction is made between Indians, of whom sixty-nine men are mentioned by name, and the three Spaniards married to Indian women. While the Spaniards are referred to by only one surname, one of which survives in the Plaza barrio, thirty-two Indians are mentioned only by their Spanish baptismal names. Of their surnames, six survive in the Loma barrio. Another six are associated now with 'Spanish' families of the Plaza barrio. Four Indian surnames, now extinct, preceded by Spanish baptismal names are given, while the remaining surnames are now unknown in the village and its vicinity. Many of the family names now in use in the village were introduced by the immigrants of the second half of the past century, but it is also evident that some of the 'old' names that are considered 'Indian' now were adopted during the nineteenth century, shortly after the War of Independence, from Spanish or Creole landholders or officials, from missionaries, encomenderos, or godfathers, and thus became established in the village, replacing entirely the old aboriginal names. The existence of two French surnames suggests that they were introduced during the past century by several French colonists who came to the lowlands and who were promptly absorbed into the rural and urban Creole culture.

While the problem of surnames and their use is of outstanding importance to the villagers, expressing many tensions in regard to status and prestige, the baptismal names are also a matter of interest and a focus of certain anxieties. The majority of the older generation and many of the people over fifteen years of age have baptismal names characteristic of much of rural Latin America. These names are derived from those of the Holy Family, the saints and angels, from ritual aspects of the Catholic Church, from biblical personages, or from ancient mythology.

Among male names we find Jesús, José, and Joaquín (the father of the Virgin Mary), the first being frequently combined with the one of a saint as, for example, in José de Jesús, or with the name of the Virgin, as in Jesús María. The following names of saints are found: Adalberto, Adolfo, Aguedo, Augustín, Alfonso, Alejandro, Andrés, Apolinar, Atanasio, Bartolo, Beltrán (San Luís Beltrán), Benedicto, Benigno, Benito, Bernabé, Bernardo, Bienvenido, Blás, Calixto, Camilo, Carlos, Casimiro, Cipriano, Cirilo, Ciro, Clemente, Cornelio, Cristóbal, Damián, Daniél, Darío, Demetrio, Desiderio, Dimas, Diómedes, Edilberto, Eduardo, Elías, Eliseo, Eloy, Emilio, Enrique, Erasmo, Estanislao, Eugenio, Ernesto, Evarista, Feliciano, Félix, Fermín, Fernando, Fidél, Francisco, Genaro, Gerardo, Germán, Gonzaga, Gregorio, Guillermo, Hermenegildo, Hernando, Hilario, Hipólito, Ignacio, Isidoro (Isidro), Jacinto, Jacobo, Jaime, Juan (Bautista), Julián, Julio, Justo, Laureano, Leandro, León, Leonardo, Liborio, Lucas, Luís, Marcelino, Marcelo, Marcos, Martín, Matías, Mauricio, Modesto, Narciso, Nazario, Néstor, Nicanor, Nicolás, Nolasco, Octavio, Osvaldo, Pablo, Pantaleón, Pascual, Pedro, Porfirio, Ramiro, Régulo, Ricardo, Roberto, Samuel, Sebastián, Segundo, Senén, Silvestre, Simón, Sixto, Tomás, Urbano, Vicente, Víctor, Victoriano.

Other names are those of biblical personages, such as Abrahán, Adán, Davíd, Efraín, Eliécer, Isaias, Ismael, Moisés, Nehemías, Neftalí, Rubén. Others are derived from the archangels or angels: Angel, Gabriel, Miguel, Rafael, Serafín. Some men use names connected with the Virgin Mary, such as Mercedes and Encarnación, although these are usually female names. Roman and Greek mythology and history supply the names Alcides, Aníbal, Cercio (from Cercion?), César, Diógenes, Elio (from Elion?), Eulíses (from Ulíses), Hermes, Héctor, Juvenal, Leonídas, Marco Aurelio, Marco Tulio, Milcíades, Néstor, Numa, Plinio, Tácito, Tiberio. The surnames of Colombian national heroes are also used as baptismal names: Bolívar, Santander, Ricaurte, and so are Napoleón and Nelson.

Other names are Abelardo, Abelino, Adaúlfo (from Adolfo), Adicto, Adulfo, Algemiro, Alisandro, Alonso, Armando, Arnoldo, Antolín, Antolino, Brígido, Brigilio, Custodio, Danilo, Delfilio, Delfio, Delfín, Delio, Domingo, Donaldo, Eduvino, Emiliano, Enemías, Etelio, Eudoxio, Eures, Evangelista, Generoso, Gilberto, Ginaldo, Gonzalo, Gustavo, Haroldo, Higinio, Hugues, Jesualdo, Julis, Laudelino, Leonel, Lino, Ludovino, Manuel, Margario, Maximiliano, Medardo, Mélido, Mérilo, Mirto, Moroso, Nicomedes, Obdulio, Orlando, Otoniél, Paulino, Raúl, Reginaldo, Reinaldo, René, Rigoberto, Rodrigo, Román, Romélo, Sordio, Teodoro, Tibaldo, Uberto, Ulpiano, Wilson, Yesíd.

Among women the different manifestations of the Virgin are expressed in the following names: María (Mary), Carmen (Our Lady of

Mount Carmel), Pilar (a shrine in Zaragoza), Rosario (Rosary), Mercedes (Mercies), Amparo (Protection), Dolores (Sorrows), Luz (Light)-Candelaria (Candlemas, Purification), Natividad (Nativity), Concepción (Immaculate Conception), Guadalupe (the patroness of Latin America), Remedios (Remedies), Soledad (a shrine in México), Lourdes (a shrine in France). Among female names the following are of saints: Adelaida, Amalia, Ana, Aurelia, Aurora, Beatríz, Benita, Blanca, Brígida, Casilda, Cecilia, Clara, Cornelia, Crescencia, Cristina, Eduvigis, Efigenia, Elena, Elisabet, Eufemia, Fausta, Felicitas, Felipa, Filomena, Florencia, Florentina, Gala, Genoveva, Gertrudis, Irene, Inés, Isabél, Juana, Julia, Justa, Lucía, Lucila, Marcelina, Margarita, Matilde, Máxima, Mónica, Paula, Paulina, Petronila, Praxedes, Rosa, Roselina, Rosalía, Silvia, Sofía, Susana, Teodora, Teófila, Teresa, Virginia. The following names are adapted from the names of male saints: Andrea, Antonia, Bautista, Benigna, Emilia, Estefanía, Ernestina, Francisca, Feliza, Georgina, Gregoria, Inocencia, Jacinta, Jacoba-Joaquina, Josefa, Josefina, Lorenza, Luisa, Manuela, Martina, Nicolasa, Pascuala, Petra, Rafaela, Ramona, Sebastiana, Simona, Sixta-Names derived from the angels, Church holidays, etc., are Angela. Angélica, Asunción, Ceferina, Cruz Santa, Dominga, Encarnación, Gloria, Pastora, Reyes, Salvadora, Santa, Trinidad, Victoria, Victoriana. Biblical names are Abigaíl, Betsabé, Ester, Edith, Judith, Neftalina, Noemí, Rebeca, Ruth, Sara.

Other female baptismal names are Abdulia, Abelina, Adalia, Aída, Alba, Alejandrina, Alicia, Altagracia, Altamira, Aminta, Andreana, Anelina, Arcilia, Arsenia, Aura, Baldomera, Basílida, Benilda, Bercelia, Berta, Betsy, Betulia, Bolivia, Brunilda, Carlina, Carlota, Carmelina, Carolina, Celia, Celina, Cesárea, Cesarina, Cibelia, Clarelina, Clemencia, Corina, Covarita, Delfina, Denis, Digna, Dilia, Dioselina, Dora, Ecilda, Edilsa, Edelmira, Edilma, Edita, Edudina, Elbia, Eleuteria, Elfa, Eligia, Eliodora, Elodia, Elodina, Eloisa, Elsi, Elvira, Emelina, Emma, Ena, Eneida, Euria, Ercilia, Erlinda, Eroina, Estrella, Eterlina, Etilbia, Eustorjia, Fani, Felicia, Fidelina, Flor, Florinda, Francia, Geneca, Gladys, Graciela, Heladia, Hilda, Himelda, Hipólita, Iberia, Ilsa, Emelda, Irma, Irmia, Isaura, Isolina, Jacobina, Lastenia, Laudelina, Laura, Leonilde, Leonor, Leonora, Leticia, Lía, Lucadia, Lucinda, Malvina, Mariana, Marina, Mary, Mausolina, Melba, Mélida, Mira, Mireya, Mirta, Mirza, Nancy, Nerit, Nibia, Nicasia, Nícida, Nora, Obdulia, Odilia, Olga, Olimpia, Olivia, Oristela, Oscarea, Perfecta, Policarpa, Presenta, Priscila, Raimunda, Remigia, Rita, Silveria, Sonia, Telecila, Teolinda, Teonice, Tirsa, Tovarita, Urbencia, Ventura, Vercelia, Yolanda, Zaída, Zenaída, Zenít, Zenobia, Zoila, Zoraída.

A remarkable thing is that in a village of hardly more than 1,300, inhabitants, more than five hundred different baptismal names should be in use. Obviously there is no family tradition of certain names, no family devotion to certain saints, but rather an obsessive search for new and highly individualized names. The reasons for this are once more problems of prestige. People worry a great deal about their names and those of their yet unbaptized children, believing that some names are definitely associated with the 'Indians' whereas others are 'civilized' and 'Spanish'. To have a 'pretty' name is considered to be a very definite social asset, and people who happen to have 'ugly' names feel ashamed of them and are often mocked by others. All 'old' names are thought to be ugly, such as Baldomero, Laudelino, Marcelino, Benedicto, etc., whereas 'new' (i.e. 'modern') names are Numa, Mirto, Eduvino, Alcides, or Dagoberto. Among female names the following are considered particularly 'ugly': Amparo, Bernabela, Cruz Santa, Ercilia, Eloisa, Guadalupe, Teófila, Tránsito; whereas the following are mentioned as very 'pretty': Adaní, Berta, Denis, Génis, Hilda, Judith, Ligia, Marqueza, Miriam, Mirza, Nancy. As is evident from the different lists of names given above, there are many that seem to be local variations or even inventions. This is, of course, due in part to the fact that most people only hear their names but hardly ever read or write them.

A great many people are known mainly by their nicknames (*sobrenombres*) and these are very standardized in the village. People become so accustomed to them that they often forget their proper names and have to ask their parents or relatives. Many nicknames are simply abbreviations of the baptismal name or diminutives of it, but others are said to be derived from the child's first efforts to pronounce his name. Table 23 contains the most commonly used nicknames of these types.

TABLE 23

MEN		WOMEN	
Nickname	*Name*	*Nickname*	*Name*
Baldo	Baldeomero	Aleja	Alejandrina
Berna	Bernabé	Anga	Angela
Cáli	Calixto	Came	Carmen
Chelo	Marcelo	Cata	Catalina
Chema	José María	Cova	Covarita
Chepa	Marcelino	Cru	Cruz Santa
Chico	Francisco	Cola	Nicolasa
Chuchu	Jesús	Cande	Candelaria
Dáni	Daniél	Conce	Concepción
Fíde	Fidel	Derma	Edelmira
Gina	Reginaldo	Chela	Marcela
Goyo	Gregorio	Chcya	Bercella
Jito	Benedicto	Chiche	Patricia

TABLE 23 (*continued*)

MEN		WOMEN	
Nickname	*Name*	*Nickname*	*Name*
Juancho	Juan	Dole	Dolores
Mani	Manuel	Fefa	Josefa
Laude	Laudelino	Fina	Delfina
Mando	Armando	Fetíca	Perfecta
Mígue	Miguel	Goya	Gregoria
Mingo	Domingo	Guarda	Guadalupe
Meche	Mercedes	Icha	Felicitas
Nei, Nel	Manuel	Ina	Eroina
Nido	Bienvenido	Leona	Pantaleona
Nino	Benigno	Lola	Dolores
Naza	Nazario	Mati	Matilde
Noño	Antonio	Mári	María
Ono	Diógenes	Méma	Emma
Páu	Paul	Macú	María de la Cruz
Pita	Rafita	Macha	Máxima
Polo	Apolinar	Minga	Dominga
Poncho	Alfonso	Mona	Ramona
Rafa, Rafita	Rafael	Petra	Petronila
Robayo	Román	Pola	Hipólita
Santa	Santander	Senta	Presenta
Silva	Silverio	Tibe	Natividad
Ton	Antonio	Tita	Bautista
Yeyo	Aurelio	Trini	Trinidad

Frequently such a nickname is combined with a kinship term or with the terms used between ritual coparents, resulting in the following forms: Pa Mígue (compadre Miguel), Compa Ono (compadre Dió-genes), or Mano Yeyo (hermano Aurelio). In order to distinguish during conversation between individuals who have the same baptismal name, one of them is changed somehow, generally by saying it in the diminutive or augmentative form, such as Miguelito–Miguelón. Nicknames are rarely descriptive, such as La Bronca (i.e., *ronca*, 'hoarse'), but many refer to phenotype and ethnic descent: El Negro ('Negro'), La Morena ('the dark-skinned one'), La Mona ('the fair one'), La Blanca ('the white one'), El Turco ('the Turk', i.e. of siro-lebanese origin).

INTERPERSONAL RELATIONS WITHIN THE FAMILY

All women envy men and all of them, young or old, say that they wish they had been born men and not women. Men are thought to be superior to women in almost every respect, and not even a woman who has suffered greatly and has been abandoned and mistreated, would doubt the male's superiority and 'right' to do as he pleases. Sexual promiscuity, laziness, and aggressiveness are, in the opinion of women, his 'birthright' (*su privilegio de nacimiento*). Men 'have the authority to do whatever they please' (*tienen el poder de hacer lo que quieren*), whereas women do not have it. The most miserable creature, it is said, is worth more than any woman. A few young women quote the saying: 'After God, man; after man, the dog; after the dog, the woman' (*Después de Dios, el hombre; después del hombre, el perro; después del perro, la mujer*), but older women will not agree with this and will justify men's behavior by pointing out that also among animals the male of the species is more powerful and valuable than the female and that such is the nature of life.

If one would judge from what the majority of adult women say, one might think that male authority is well established and unquestioned, but this is certainly not the fact. Women in Aritama have—for evident economic reasons—an institutionalized tendency to overplay outwardly the male's importance in the family, to flatter him, and to adopt a submissive air, but underneath and within the intimacy of the home the situation is quite different. Although within the framework of his family the man pretends to be the undisputed head, he seldom is more than a tolerated guest, and except during the period of early conjugal life, his authority is not so readily accepted as he is likely to proclaim. Women are well aware that men like to play a dominant and authoritarian role and adapt their behavior to it in a shrewd way that satisfies both partners. Outwardly submissive and obedient, women's tactics consist in recognizing demurely the male's 'rights' and 'privileges', while at the same time they actually do not let them interfere too much in the administration of the household. A man's orders are humbly accepted but not always carried out; whatever is done because he demands it is rather a concession to his vanity made for the sake of peace than obedience to the family head. As women do not depend entirely upon male support but can count upon their maternal kin and their own productiveness as weavers or palm-fiber goods, they can—within certain limits—afford to ignore their spouses' authority and simply lend them a deaf ear.

Men, however, play their role of dignified husbands and fathers whose superiority must be demonstrated in every detail. The man's hammock occupies the best spot in the house; the best of the food is for him; his shirt has to be carefully washed, starched, and ironed, and his trousers neatly mended. As a bachelor he may have been a pleasant fellow, on friendly terms with other men and women, but once established in a conjugal union and surrounded by children and a household of his own, all this has had to change, and now the serious and preoccupied face has to exteriorize the responsibilities he claims to feel for his family. But to his wife he is not much more than a rascal, an irresponsible rogue who has to be dealt with carefully lest he cause serious damage. As long as he does a minimum of work, as long as he contributes with some agricultural labor or the earnings as a hired hand, his presence is necessary and he has to be humored and made to believe that he is the respected center of the household. Men have to be tolerated and have to be 'pleased' (*complacer*) because, as women say with a shrug, in a home there have to be order and a man's authority (*debe haber orden y respeto de hombre*).

The ideal husband is above all a provider of food. This obligation is so primordial that many people were at a loss when asked to state other desirable traits in a prospective marriage partner and declared that this was the one and only condition his family and society expected him to fulfil. However, after some thought people added that a married man should not be too 'scandalous' (*escandaloso*) with other women, giving to understand that, while extramarital relations were taken for granted, they should not become a public scandal. Some others added that a man should provide clothing for the family. From the ideal wife, however, men and society ask a great deal more. In the first place she should be submissive and obedient to her husband, whom she should 'attend to' (*atender*) in every possible way, above all in preparing his food, laundering his clothes, and keeping the house tidy. She should rear his children with care and should co-operate actively in making a living for the family. Emphasis is placed upon fidelity, thriftiness, and cleanliness in her person. She should always know how to maintain friendly relations with the kin-group and the neighbors; she should avoid all gossip; and, most important, she should never practice any kind of sorcery against her husband or anyone else.

The ideal formulation and the actual behavior are so divergent that no one ever tries to cover up the harsh facts of tension, hostility, and aggressiveness. These form one of the few characteristics of the local culture that is openly discussed by all. As a matter of fact, in all homes, whether they are sanctioned by a Catholic marriage or based upon a temporary or more permanent free union, the dominant impression is one of open hostility. This hostile atmosphere is by no means covert. Society clearly recognizes its existence and regards it as a lamentable, slightly amusing, but otherwise inalterable fact. Its causes, forms, and consequences are freely discussed and constitute one of the main topics of daily village gossip. That they also constitute a focal point of individual anxieties is only too evident.

The main accusation formulated by the women against their husbands is that the latter do not provide them with sufficient food or money to maintain their families and that they are lazy and thriftless in their work. It is true that quite frequently a man will spend all his daily or weekly earnings outside his home and leave the woman alone to worry about food and clothing. But when returning home from the street, the husband will impetuously demand to be served, and if there is no food ready or available, or it does not suit his tastes, he is likely to become infuriated. The woman is thus forced to contribute very actively in supporting the household. When the man works and provides food from his fields or money from wage labor, the woman can limit her activities to her house, the kitchen, and the backyard; but when he is lazy or ill, or simply does not find work, the whole burden of supporting the family falls upon her shoulders and she is expected to carry the responsibility for the household. The latter is often the case and the critical moment arrives when the woman is forced to do a man's work in the fields. It can be said that this situation is very much the rule in the Loma barrio and that many households are supported almost exclusively through the labor of women and children.

Although women's work is hard, even such tasks as would fall normally within the range of most female activities are deeply resented by them. Women do not like to wash their husband's clothes, to prepare their food, or to rear their children. Above all the last, the so-called 'struggle with the children' (*la lidia de los hijos*), is considered to be a most unpleasant task, and women complain continuously about the efforts made by them in raising their infants. Laundering, food preparation, and child-rearing are the three activities women believe to have been allotted to them unjustly by men. In carrying out these tasks they are convinced that they are doing a great favour to their husbands, a favour which is never fully repaid. In their minds, child-rearing does not form part of a normal husband-wife relationship, but that progeny are conceived and reared mostly in order to satisfy the man's prestige and economic ambitions. Few women will admit that they love their children or that childbearing is a natural function of the female sex. They might find a child to be *curioso*, a word which denotes but little affection. Only as soon as the child begins to collaborate in the food quest it is qualified as 'good' or 'bad', in other words, as useful or useless. These, at least, are the manifest attitudes, which, of course, are conditioned by the quality of relations with men.

Men rarely feel obliged to feed and clothe their families and to provide an adequate shelter for them, and whenever they do so they never fail to point out how generous they are. To be prodded into activity, to be asked for food or money, is always taken as an insult and what a man does not give spontaneously is rarely obtained from him by admonition. This situation would, of course, be untenable if women were entirely dependent upon male support, but as they all have their home industry of weaving straw hats, they and their children can survive the critical periods when there is no male support. The money a woman earns through her sale of the articles she manufactures is always considered to be her own and no man would dare to ask his wife or consort even for a small sum obtained by the sale of these products.

The motives for friction within the family, and above all in the husband-wife relationship, are relatively standardized but repeat themselves with periodic persistence. One occasion for trouble is when the man asks for his laundry and the woman says that she has not yet washed and ironed his shirts and trousers. On his return from the field or from any kind of work in or around the village, first of all the man wants to eat and to change his clothes. In the event these are not ready, there is likely to be a scene. The offense is still worse if the man intended to visit a friend or go to a fiesta and finds that his wife has not prepared his clothes. She will try to find excuses, saying that she was occupied with the children or with some other urgent chore, but it is quite evident that often a woman will be intentionally negligent in this matter in order to 'punish' (*castigar*) her husband or to precipitate a separation.

Another cause for the continuous tensions are the man's extramarital adventures. Trouble starts as soon as the man leaves the house in anger, because his wife suspects that he will go to see another woman. Although women insist that they are not jealous at all, they are so in a high degree and are constantly spying on their husbands. They will ask third persons if they have seen the man, in whose company, where, and when. On his return home, his spouse will try to check on the truthfulness of his account of how he spent the day, asking malicious questions, and finally accusing him openly of having been with another woman. Men resent any interference in their activities outside their homes and interpret it as a sign of criticism and mistrust. While men say that they resent the spying of their women, these say that they will not stand for any infidelity of their husbands. Men are very much afraid that their womenfolk will 'do something to them' in case they learn that they have a concubine—i.e., they fear sorcery. As a matter of fact, the most feared person because of her potential magical aggressiveness is always the woman with whom a man lives. Only a few of the placero women are possibly excluded here, but all other women are suspected of practicing Black Magic against men, especially against a consort who they know is supporting another woman. Men, as a general rule, are not so jealous and would not employ sorcery in order to punish a wayward woman. Even if a man learns that his concubine has established relations with another man, this would not be a reason for enmity or bad feelings. On the other hand, married women or women who live in a permanent free union are greatly afraid of magical aggression practiced by the man's concubines. When a man begins to court another woman who is suspected of having done magical harm to other people, his wife is sometimes brought to the point where she abandons her husband to save herself and her children from the rival's wrath.

From mistrust and offensive words to physical aggression there is only one step. Open aggressiveness in the man usually begins directed against some inanimate object. With a sweeping movement of the arm he will send plates, dishes, and cups in a clattering mass to the floor, turn over the table and proceed then to the methodical destruction of any furniture that might come within his reach. These outbursts are not necessarily accompanied by words but can occur without the man uttering a sound. Once the destruction becomes aimed more specifically at the woman, the man will grasp her personal belongings, dresses, shoes, or weaving utensils, and throw them through the open door into the street. This process, called 'to throw the stuff out' (*sacar los chismes*), is accompanied by screams and vituperations. Blows and kicks may follow, and if a good stick is available the woman will receive a sound thrashing, against which she hardly ever tries to defend herself. Many times the children also receive their share of violence, although they do not intervene in the affair at all. A highly typical aggressive action consists in the man taking the straw hat his woman has been weaving and hacking it viciously into pieces with his machete. All this is, of course, quite reminiscent of the pattern of temper tantrums in children and of the infant's attitude toward the straw hat which is a rival in occupying the mother's attention.

Although in the course of this struggle each partner loudly voices the intention to kill the other, we have never heard of a serious intent to put this into action. The worst offense a woman can commit against a man is to call his mother a whore. She will do so almost only in the presence of others, because the man's rage will then be dangerous and she might have to depend upon the help of others. This sort of insult usually precipitates a separation and words to this effect are sometimes intentionally used when a woman wants to leave her consort. A man will scream, 'Your people are no good; you are no good either, you are a slut!' (*Tu gente no sirve, y tu tampoco; eres una vagabunda*), or he might say, 'You are just like your own folks: whores, all of them!' (*Eres igualita que tus gentes: unas putas todas!*). Women sometimes faint or have fits (*ataques*) during such scenes. Only then might the neighbors interfere and try to calm the man.

During such domestic quarrels the man accuses his wife of the following faults: not preparing his food on time, not having his shirts washed and ironed, not seeing to it that the children and she herself are clean. Adultery in women is rarely a cause for physical aggression against a wife or consort, but the man rather 'throws out her stuff' or leaves the house not to return, a reaction which is generally found to be justified by society. Although such scenes are violent and noisy, hardly ever any serious damage is done to one of the contestants. Never a more dangerous weapon than a stick is employed, and most fighting is done with words and violent gestures. Blows and kicks also occur, and the man might pull the woman's hair and slap her face. The neighbors are eager spectators but rarely interfere.

At last the man leaves the house and spends the rest of the day wandering about in the streets or maybe visiting a friend. Sometimes he will visit another woman or go to drink, but the latter is rather unlikely and very rarely does a man take to drink after a domestic quarrel. If the man should not return and goes to live in another household, his mother's or his concubine's, eventually the woman will send a child to him every day to take him his food and laundry. These are symbols of peace and submission, and often the man will return to his old home after having spent a few days away from it.

Women often complain about the mistreatment they receive at the hands of their menfolk, but they are likely to add that they have become well accustomed to it. This does not seem to be exaggerated, since people in Aritama consider it as utterly unbelievable that in other places or countries there should be couples who do not fight frequently in the same way and for the very same reasons. In the history of the past hundred years, only two cases of marriages are remembered in which the partners lived harmoniously and without quarrelling. Such cases, however, are thought to be very suspect. As a matter of fact, a couple who do not fight frequently are thought to be 'tied together' (*amarrados*) by magic exercised by one of the partners. It is generally believed to be the woman who 'ties' the husband to her by the use of magic potions, making him submissive and resigned. Such couples are ridiculed openly, and neighbors or friends try in every way to disturb the apparent harmony by gossip, false accusations, and open insinuations of sorcery. Since men fear that a woman is able to bewitch a man so that he becomes a drunkard, a thief, or a person who never finds work, gossip about alleged sorcery in the family is a major disorganizing force.

Peace returns to the home as soon as the husband and father leaves it. Women are much more content and happy during their husband's absences, and although they suspect that these take advantage of their absences to visit other women, they often prefer to have them leave the home for awhile. If a man does not leave his house and stays at home for several days or weeks, as may happen, the woman might eventually employ some sort of magic remedy to make him leave. Frequently she will pay a specialist to buy some candles for a saint and to recite certain prayers so that something occurs that would oblige her consort to leave.

It is quite remarkable to see how her spirits change as soon as he steps out of his home and how the hostile mood returns the very moment he enters it again.

There is little or no mutual confidence and trust between husband and wife or between free-union consorts, and there is hardly a topic they can discuss quite frankly. Little mention is made of the behavior and education of their children; financial matters are hardly ever discussed, except for what each partner believes to be 'convenient' (*conveniente*) for the other to know, and misleading statements or open lies are frequent. The only topics of conversation that can be treated are disease and the general village gossip of the moment, but otherwise there is very little to be spoken of.

A wife often borrows money or food, or buys dresses, without the knowledge of her husband, and frequently a woman will also sell dresses or household utensils behind the husband's back. Generally she is the only person within the family who profits by such transactions, and she makes loans or purchases for her own benefit and not in order to give better food or clothing to the children.

There is no doubt that the first years of conjugal life are the most difficult for women, and that quarrels tend to subside after a woman has reached about thirty years of age. This is due not to a lessening of the man's aggressiveness but rather to the stronger economic position women acquire in time, which gives them a certain security of action, joined with indifference to the man's complaints. Women over forty-five rarely have domestic troubles with their husbands or consorts.

Men say that women are extremely timid in establishing sexual relations and that they never demonstrate sexual desire. According to them, women have to be aroused, seduced, and taken by force. Women fully agree with this statement and declare that they never experience the slightest desire for sexual gratification and that they submit to such contacts only to please their men. Coitus is verbalized on the part of women as an 'abuse' (*abuso*), a humiliating and disagreeable act during which only pains are felt. In other words, men revel in their alleged role as powerful seducers, while women claim to be their unwilling victims. Although women insist on never feeling desire and gratification, they are quick to add that—even if they felt them—they could never admit it because immediately the whole village would know about it. Society would criticize them severely and all men would despise them. Men do admit desire and gratification but claim to feel, in the intimacy of intercourse itself, an enervating pain during ejaculation. Younger women apparently believe this to be true, but the older ones have their doubts and occasionally make fun of men who pretend to feel such 'pains'.

Once a man has shown his intents by insinuating words and caresses, the woman usually refuses his advances, claiming illness and fatigue, and demonstrating indifference. A woman might say, 'I cannot eat your kisses' (*Yo no voy a comer besos*), suggesting thereby that, if the man wishes her to submit, he will have to give or at least to promise her more money for food or clothes. Women of experience might ask the man to pay in advance or to first bring them a certain amount of food. Even in long-established marriage or free union, a woman rarely submits without plaintively asking for some gift, some favor, without which she would feel utterly shameless and irresponsible. The first refusal is institutionalized behavior, meant to arouse the man's desire, but it all too often seems to dampen a man's intentions to a degree where he loses all interest and becomes inhibited to a point where the woman has to take the initiative. Coitus itself is then an act of violence, which, as a rule, leaves the woman unsatisfied. During the act she has to remain motionless and completely passive, never demonstrating any pleasure, but should rather try to resist, however feebly, the man's actions. Coitus often takes place under conditions that make haste necessary and that are uncomfortable for both partners. Because of the crowded sleeping quarters, where other adults or children are always present, some couples leave the house at night and go to the backyard, but others stay inside, risking being seen or heard by others. The fear of darkness, of interruptions, of discovery, make cohabitation an anxiety-charged experience. Clothes are hardly removed nor is the act accompanied by kissing or caresses. These frustrating aspects of intercourse are well recognized by both sexes and are expressed in mutual accusations. Men claim that the female sexual organ is too large, while women say that men's penises are too short. Older women, who are likely to talk freely about these matters, say that men usually ejaculate long before the woman has reached orgasm and that this continuous frustration is often the motive for adultery in women. As a matter of fact, to cause a woman's orgasm (*sacarle la piedra*) is considered by men to be a special feat which only few can perform. Impotence in men—for physical or psychological reasons—seems to be frequent, even among the young and relatively healthy people, and many men admit quite frankly that, apart from the difficulty in satisfying various concubines, they suffer from inhibitions they cannot explain and are often incapable of performing the sexual act. Venereal disease seems to play a certain role in this problem, but the principal causes are probably of a psychological nature.

Relations between concubines of the same man, or between a legitimate wife and her husband's concubines, are generally dominated by fear of sorcery. Among these women there is little food exchange, evidently for fear of poison, and they spy upon one another to see whether the man gives one of them more food or money than to another. On the street they will avoid one another and they will also be very careful in expressing any criticism in public, in order not to cause the ill-will of a rival. In case an illegitimate child is born to one of the concubines, the legitimate wife will eventually visit her and bring a small gift, exchanging upon this occasion a few words with the women. However, beneath this apparent indifference displayed by rivaling women, there is much hatred and jealousy. Each fears becoming a victim of the other's magical aggression. As long as the women concerned keep up this appearance of indifference there are no quarrels, but should one of them begin to brag about the preferential treatment she receives from a man or should she openly criticize her rivals, jealous rage dominates over fear. Open insults easily turn into physical violence. Women will beat one another, pull their rivals by the hair, tear their clothes, and threaten them with death and sorcery.

Among men who contend for the favor of the same woman there is considerably less tension. They will not try to avoid one another, and even if they are certain of the concubine's infidelity, they will maintain friendly relations. In their case there is no fear of sorcery, and they will never become aggressive against a rival. A woman's infidelity is never blamed upon the seducer but on her, and men see no reason why they should become enemies over so paltry a matter.

When a couple lives under the same roof with other men or women, a certain amount of promiscuity is almost taken for granted, and as long as such relations do not become too public and notorious, little fuss is made about them. Sometimes two sisters, or mother and daughter, will have relations with the same man. Father and son might court the same woman. An elderly woman might try to seduce her daughter's consort, or a daughter might attempt to elope with her mother's temporary companion. Such relationships, the developments they take, and the tensions they cause are the common gossip of the village.

The more Creole-oriented placeros say that practically all women of the Loma barrio, and of the lower stratum of the Plaza, are little better than prostitutes. This statement is exaggerated, but sometimes it is difficult to distinguish between short-term concubinage and prostitution, especially if one takes into account the pattern according to which sexual favors have to be compensated. A woman who has been abandoned by her consort and who has to support several small children might occasionally take money for sexual intercourse, until she finds a man who is willing to live with her in a more or less stable union. Such fleeting relationships are kept secret as long as a woman depends upon them, but as soon as she quarrels with such an occasional visitor or finds a new consort, she might admit and even publicize what happened in order to shame the men who 'took advantage of her misery', notwithstanding the fact that it was generally she who offered herself to them in the first place. On the other hand, it is quite frequent that a girl not only of the lower class but also of considerably higher class-status proposes to a well-to-do visitor to the village that she become his concubine under the condition that the man take her away from the village and establish her in one of the lowland towns, even if she knows that she will soon be abandoned by him.

In all forms of conjugal unions, the influence of the family of procreation is much stronger than that of the family of orientation, at least with reference to the man's position. A man's principal obligations are always to his wife and her parents, but a woman has practically no obligations whatsoever to the man's family. For this reason men are very reluctant to co-operate with their wives' families and try to limit it to a minimum. A marriage or free union, therefore, almost always causes strong tensions between the families of the two conjugal partners. As soon as the couple make clear their intentions to live together, the two families practically declare war, by criticizing, suspecting, and slandering each other. Once the couple lives independently, this struggle ceases to a certain point but continues covertly, the in-laws watching now with critical eyes to see whether or not the man fulfils his obligations to them. The man is obliged to work for his father-in-law in the latter's fields, to help him out with money, and to give him food whenever possible. He should lend effective help if the father-in-law organizes a communal labor project and should solidarize with him if he should have difficulties with the law or become involved in quarrels with his neighbors. To the mother-in-law he should make regular gifts of food, the same as to his wife's sisters and brothers. In reality, in any conjugal union its stability depends to a large degree upon the attitude the girl's mother assumes. Since she, the mother, takes an eminently selfish interest in her daughter's marriage or free union, she will try to break up the union as soon as she thinks that she does not derive a personal benefit from it and will attempt to find a more promising suitor for her daughter. Toward his family of orientation a son owes only occasional help, especially if they are poor, but a daughter is strictly obliged to assist her mother during all her life. The man's mother, on the other hand, is, even in the case of a Catholic marriage, quite often a bitter enemy of her new daughter-in-law. As soon as the man takes one or more concubines, his mother is likely to form an alliance with them to show thus her contempt for the girl and to demonstrate that she, the daughter-in-law, has hardly any right over her husband. To the man's mother, the daughter-in-law is only one of the many women her son might have, but one whom she accuses of taking advantage of her by using her status as legal wife to 'exploit' her husband.

As we have mentioned already, during quarrels between spouses the man often insults his wife's family. The latter, of course, soon learn about this and if they feel that they are not receiving the economic help they expected when agreeing to the marriage or free union, they will insist on separation, accusing the man of mistreating their daughter. Such quarrels between a son-in-law and his wife's family often take on the character of personal vengeance. Everything is done to break up the union, not because the man mistreated his wife, but because he insulted her family.

Relationships with other in-laws are rather tenuous and occasional. Brothers-in-law should be friends and should co-operate, and ideally they should be more closely united than cousins, but more often the tensions described above affect this relationship and they are rarely on friendly terms with one another. Ideally, a woman should co-operate with her husband's sisters while avoiding his brothers, but in reality, in the first relationship there is often enmity, and in the second, adultery is not infrequent.

RECREATIONAL ACTIVITIES

Aritama is a very quiet village and its people are not given to play, music, or entertainment. They try to avoid close personal relationships and all public occasions in which friendly interaction is demanded. Self-conscious and controlled, they find no enjoyment in gatherings or games, and on the few occasions when such contacts are institution-alized, as, for example, during the yearly fiestas, there is always a certain amount of tension because of the ever-present envy and gossip of prestige behavior.

The only sport that attracts people and, even this, only a small frac-tion of the village population, is cockfighting. Cockfighting is a common popular amusement all over the lowlands and was introduced in Aritama by the immigrants of the past century. Ever since, it has continued to be a placero sport, and only very few people of the Loma barrio take any part in it. Cockfighting is limited to the dry season when people can travel easily between villages. In Aritama the cocking season begins the day of the Immaculate Conception, December 8, but frequently a few trial fights (*riñas de tope*) precede it in late November. From then on, almost every Sunday there are cocking-mains (*peleas de gallo, riñas de gallo*) in the large cockpit (*gallera*) belonging to one of the placeros, until some time in April. Each month, on a certain day, a large cocking-main is held at a different lowland town and cockfighters from all over the countryside congregate there. About half a dozen placeros own game fowl, some thirty or forty birds in all, and they organize the mains in Aritama. The training of the gamecocks for the pit begins about a month before the main is fought, when the birds are brought to the village from the farms where they have been bred. Five or six different breeds are distinguished by the local specialists and the individual birds are given meticulous care by their owners. Wing and tail feathers are cut and rump feathers are trimmed every four or five months, but the real training (*cuido*) begins approximately two weeks before the first main. The feathers are trimmed once more and the birds are frequently rubbed with orange halves, rum, dry tobacco leaves, and rosemary. Six days before the fight they are given a daily ration of exactly half an ounce of maize and twelve tumblerfuls of water. Before an important match, the owners take their gamecocks to one of the Indian shamans, who then performs a special rite over the birds in order to insure their victory. The last days before the main the birds are kept in a dark room, and all noise is prohibited near them. Before the fight the cocks are 'heeled' (*calzado*) with large sharply pointed spurs taken from a common cock and fastened on with beeswax and thread. On entering the pit three tumblers of water are given to the bird to drink.

A cockfight generally consists of four or five mains, in each of which two cocks are matched by their owners, who hold them in position, beak to beak, as the main begins (*picar los gallos*). After the first furtive strokes (*tiros blancos*), the real fight (*riña*) starts, and now each stroke with beak or spur—all having their specific traditional names—is closely watched and loudly acclaimed, until one of the two cocks is defeated. The wounds of a victorious cock are immediately attended to by sucking the blood out of them with the mouth, followed by a renewed rubdown with orange halves or an injection with antibiotics. Attendance at cockfights is all male, but children are admitted and are generally eager onlookers. There is often heavy betting at the pitside and competing owners will frequently bet as much as the worth of a cow or a bull. The cocking-mains are perhaps the only occasion when we have seen people behave quite spontaneously, losing their usual emotional control and becoming extremely excited. The sweating, blood-smeared faces of the cock-owners who try to cure the wounds of their birds, the bills being thrown into the pit by the betters, and the wildly cheering crowd—all stand in stark contrast to the rigid composure observed on other occasions.

The people of Aritama are, according to the lowland Creoles, heavy drinkers, but this is definitely not true. The fact is, however, that when they travel outside their village they usually embark upon the trip in a somewhat intoxicated state and try to overcome their insecurity in front of the lowlanders by drinking heavily while among them. But back in their own village alcohol consumption is very low. Occasionally a few people who work a still will go on a spree, but otherwise there is very little drinking. The boisterous drunks who infest the village streets and taverns of the lowlands, especially during the weekends, are never seen in Aritama. Even during the fiesta season, at marriages, baptisms, or wakes, one hardly ever sees an intoxicated person, and those who can be seen are unobtrusive and silent. The only exception are the gravediggers, whose very activity is an institutionalized occasion for drinking, but even they look at drunkenness rather as an occupational hazard and find no enjoyment in it.

Near the village plaza there is a small canteen room with a billiard table, a few chairs and empty crates, where beer and rum are sold by one of the placero merchants. It is patronized almost exclusively by placeros who will drink an occasional bottle of beer or a glass of rum, but it is a quiet place and there is little conversation. Sometimes in the evening a few of the younger people will play a game of billiards for a while, observed from the door by some passers-by or a few children, but the canteen is certainly not a place for merry reunions where village affairs or politics would be discussed. Naturally, to go to the canteen carries a certain prestige and this is the reason why the lomeros who are too poor to go are very critical of this establishment. One time, when the owner could not find a suitable place to rent and considered moving the canteen to the Loma barrio, there was open resistance and he was forced to stay near the plaza.

The function of alcohol is still very limited in Aritama, but under the increasing influence of Creole culture, of prestige behavior, and the desire to overcome social insecurity, it is slowly becoming stronger. Sometimes a passer-by who sees a few placeros drinking beer in the canteen will step in and ask for a bottle, only to show that he, too, can afford it. A person when asked to join a group of people who are drinking feels obliged to pay several rounds and to 'catch up' with the others. People are surprisingly frank about it and admit afterwards quite openly that they did not want to drink, that it made them feel sick and fear for their health, and that the expense seriously affected their meager budget, but they will add that there was no other way out and that they would have lost face had they refused.

The various stages of intoxication are quite characteristic. After the first euphoria accompanied by small talk and a few jokes there may be some singing, and someone may go and bring a drum and play it for a while, but soon all conversation stops and gloominess sets in. There is never open physical aggressiveness of serious proportions, nor is there merry socializing, romantic serenading, obscene talk, or political discussion of any kind. One man will sing, perhaps, another play the drum or rattle, while the others sit and listen, drinking in silence and only rarely making physical contacts or attempts at conversation.

People who are about to ask for a loan, who want to propose to a girl, or who have to speak to a person of authority on some important matter are likely to take a few drinks before facing such situations, but weekends, religious fiestas, domestic quarrels, economic failure, or loneliness are never occasions for drinking and the very idea appears strange to the people. Even the Creole-oriented placeros are not likely to consume any considerable amount of alcohol at such times.

In Aritama almost only cigars are smoked, and these are made by the women from locally grown tobacco. Cigarettes, although available at some stores, are rarely consumed, and their use is limited almost entirely to a few inhabitants of the Plaza. There are no heavy smokers among the placeros, and some people will carry a pack of cigarettes rather for prestige reasons than for personal use. It is quite remarkable that most cigar-smoking is done by persons of both sexes of the Loma barrio, while only a few placeros will be seen smoking cigars. This may be due partly to the fact that cigars are smoked mainly when people are doing some physical work outside their homes and not when they are at leisure. Cigars are quite definitely associated with labourers, and there is a social stigma attached to their use. Many women of the Loma have the habit—common in the Colombian tropics—of smoking with the burning end inside the mouth and occasionally removing the cigar to shake off the ashes. People claim that this way of smoking is particularly pleasurable.

The blaring loudspeakers and phonographs so dear to the lowland Creoles have not arrived yet in Aritama, and all music is still played by individuals who have their own instruments. The principal and typical musical instrument is a vertical flute (*gaita*) of cane, which is played in pairs ('male' and 'female') to the accompaniment of a gourd rattle. The music (*son*) played on these flutes is strongly reminiscent of that played on ceremonial occasions and on similar instruments by the tribal Indians. Lately people in Aritama have become aware of the fact that this form of musical entertainment is essentially Indian, and an increasing resistance to it can be observed among the placeros and many of the younger lomeros who criticize it as 'uncivilized' music. Lately the accordion, the mouth harp, and the guitar have begun to replace the old instruments, and Creole music of the African type is becoming more and more common.

However, the most frequent and typical expression of music is singing. People in Aritama pride themselves on having many good singers of short couplets (*coplas*), generally improvised on the spur of the moment and making sarcastic reference to village affairs or to the behavior of certain individuals. These singers, most of them lomeros of all ages, will meet occasionally for a *parranda*, a revel, and sing for hours, sometimes accompanied by flutes, rattles, or drums. If two or three good singers meet there will be a sort of contest, the participants alternating rapidly in singing in a high-pitched falsetto voice and trying to compose new couplets filled with witty allusions, which gradually become more and more aggressive.

Social dancing is very rare and when it occurs the accompanying music is played by an accordion or by flutes only. Some prominent members of the Plaza barrio arrange a dance party (*sopa*, literally, 'a soup') once in a while where a few girls and boys shuffle around in a rhythm imitating Creole dances, but these entertainments are not very common. However, a dance is always an important status-defining occasion, and much gossip goes on afterwards as to who was invited, who were dancing partners, and who did not attend and why.

All visiting is restricted to a very small circle of kinfolk and, perhaps, to neighbors or a few friends who are ill. A woman may visit a sister or aunt to help her for a while in her household chores, or a man may talk over the fence with his neighbor, but otherwise the visiting pattern of the Creoles is wholly absent. If people meet at someone's house, they hardly ever carry on conversations but just sit or help in some useful task. Whereas in the lowlands people will put a few chairs on the street and sit in front of their houses passing the early evening hours talking and visiting, in Aritama this is not the custom, except in a very few placero homes. In the lowlands these groups of people, sitting or walking back and forth on the street, offer an important occasion for social contact, but in Aritama they are avoided. Should a few placeros be seen sitting before their houses, others are likely to avoid passing by so as not to have to greet them or be exposed to possible criticism.

Except for the cockfights, there are no sports or games in which adults might take part. A lonely pair of elderly placeros can be seen once in a while playing checkers in the evening, but there are no card games, and the few people who play billiards have not mastered the rudiments of the game.

Even children's games are limited and very simple. Small children play with marbles or dolls made by their mothers from a piece of cloth, and boys will play with wooden tops or make a kite from a small piece of paper. Sometimes a group of older boys will meet in a backyard or on the outskirts of the village to play 'Revenue Agents and Moon-shiners' or similar games, but adults frown upon such diversions. Girls will sometimes dance in a circle, holding hands and singing little songs of Spanish folklore with much reference to kings, princes, and the beautiful streets of Madrid. There is but little aggressiveness in children's games, co-operation is not demanded, and leadership is rarely seen. A half-forgotten rhyme is sung, someone is acclaimed to be 'it', the others will run and hide, and soon the group disperses again and the game is over. This is in striking contrast to the Creole villages, where the early evening hours are usually filled with the screams and laughter of groups at play.

In recent years there has been a growing tendency for older boys to form small gangs (*pandillas*). There were four of them in the village when we were there: the 'Eagles' (*Aguilas*), a group of placero boys; the 'Troublemakers' (*Buscaruidos*), a group of boys living in the western section of the Loma; the 'Indians', who live in the poorest section of the Loma; and the 'Lazy Ones' (*Los Flojos*), of the northern outskirts of the Loma barrio. Each gang has two 'chiefs' (*jefes*), who are not elected but are simple recognized for their leadership and the intelligence they display in organizing games and excursions or in establishing diplomatic relations with other gangs. If the two leaders do not agree upon a point, it is the majority that decides the course of action to be taken. Membership is open only to boys of an immediate neighborhood who are introduced by others who are already members, but there is no initiation nor are they especially pledged to observe definite rules. Age varies from six to fifteen.

The stated purpose of these gangs is to organize games, bathing excursions, the gathering of wild-growing fruits, or visits to distant fields owned by the families of the members. Otherwise, each gang limits its activities to the barrio neighborhood. Enmity between gangs is frequent and should they meet the boys will throw stones and exchange insults. But alliances are also frequent, above all when the three Loma gangs mean to attack the placero 'Eagles'. Any invasion into lomero territory is taken as an insult, and sometimes furious battles are fought between these groups. Within the Loma barrio the 'Lazy Ones' are feared for their aggressiveness and shrewd tactics. However, in case of conflict all barrio differences are forgotten, and aggressiveness alone becomes the criterion for alliances, the 'Eagles' joining the 'Lazy Ones' against the 'Troublemakers' and 'Indians'. Within each gang there is much emphasis upon discipline, co-operation and food-sharing, and a system of fines is established to control all members, generally consisting of small sums of money, a belt, a handkerchief, or some other object of little value. A frequent punishment for misbehavior consists in making the culprit kneel while balancing a heavy stone upon his head. The other boys crouch close to him so that if he moves and throws off the stone it will touch and probably hurt one of them. This is then considered an intentional aggression and the boy is beaten by the whole group. But there is no aggressiveness against adults, no 'ganging up' on girls, and these gangs rarely do any damage to public or private property. However, they are very loosely organized, and although there is little quarreling about who is to be leader, personal enmities between gang members whose families are not on friendly terms often lead to the disruption of the whole group. The adults pay little attention to the activities of these gangs, and even for the boys themselves they are not of great importance. Loyalties change easily and membership fluctuates greatly.

In concluding we might add that it is interesting to note that all aesthetic expression in Aritama is limited to the occasional singing. There are no storytellers, no wood-carvers, potters, or basket-makers. The few goods woven of fibers or made of wood are strictly utilitarian and devoid of all adornments. There is no love for flowers, for colors, or for form. There is no creativeness.

V

FORMS OF PRODUCTION AND PROPERTY

LAND AND LAND USE

THE slopes of the neighboring mountains are exposed, in part, to the seasonal tradewinds, and the foothills form part of the dry, arid belt that stretches over a wide area of the Caribbean coast of Colombia. As the rainfalls are concentrated into two months of the year (May and October), their torrential impact carries away the dry, parched soil wherever it is devoid of a protective plant cover. The steep mountain folds, often reaching inclinations of 45°, are thus swept clean of soil soon after such cover has been removed, and only grass covers the mountain sides between patches of exposed bedrock. However, all slopes and ravines protected against the winds are still forested —at least in regions where there is no human occupation—but it is apparent that the deforestation of other slopes is due partly to biological pressure.

From the history of human occupation of this general region, it is obvious that profound ecological changes have taken place in it. Man's tools—the ax, the bushknife and, especially, man-set fire—have modified the plant cover and the composition of the soil, leading new forms of plant and animal life to occupy the land thus used. Man's domestic animals, left to roam freely, have exercised an additional and heavy pressure. In an area characterized by a long dry season and by slow vegetation growth, it is but natural that human occupation should lead to the complete transformation of the landscape.

Erosion and the consequent need for soil conservation seem to have been problems recognized during prehistoric times. The local aboriginal population during the centuries preceding the Spanish conquest built agricultural terraces of long rows of stones in order to conserve the surface soil, and such terraces and retention walls, together with small irrigation systems, can be observed in many parts of the valley. But the main pressure seems to have been exercised by man during the last five hundred years. The Spanish conquest introduced three new elements which, if not controlled intelligently, had to contribute enormously to the transformation, if not devastation, of the land: iron tools, livestock,

202

and sugar cane. Axes and machetes made it possible to clear large areas in a short time. Cattle, horses, mules, burros, and goats were left to graze and multiply freely. The manufacture of raw sugar depended upon large amounts of firewood. While the few Indian huts had walls woven of cane, the construction of larger and more numerous houses of wattle and daub consumed a great amount of sturdy wood. Tremendous quantities of trees had to be cut to provide fence posts. All this, combined with the continuous slash-and-burn technique of shifting agriculture, has evidently led to extensive deforestation and desiccation of the land.

The population increase produced during the second half of the past century by the lowland immigrants put new demands upon the land resources. The introduction of coffee plantations, of more cattle, and of more sugar mills led, necessarily, to the utilization of hitherto unexploited regions and also to the establishment of satellite hamlets which became centers of new pioneer areas. At the same time the social structure changed. From the interaction of all these factors new forms of adaptation emerged. Because of the new goals and new means of achieving them, new conflicts and new ways of avoiding them, a new balance between man and the land had to be achieved. In the following pages we shall describe briefly this relationship as it can be observed at present.

The land that surrounds the village and that constitutes the Corregimiento de Aritama consists mainly of steep mountain folds which form the main valley and several small neighboring valleys. In the valley bottoms, near the rivers or creeks, there are sometimes stretches of more or less flat land, and in some regions toward the lowlands there are slightly undulated plains. The different types of land lying between the tropical lowlands and the cool uplands are locally classified into four categories: (1) *cerros* ('peaks'), (2) *lomas* ('hills'), (3) *rastrojos* ('underbrush'), and (4) *sabanas* ('grassy plains'). The *cerros* are the large mountain peaks and ridges that surround and enclose the valley. Their highest parts and most of their southwestern slopes, which are protected against the trade winds, are usually covered with humid virgin forest that begins at approximately 2,000 meters, but small patches of forest can sometimes be found farther down, following the principal streams.

The *lomas* are the foothills and folds of these *cerros*, covered with grass but devoid of large trees or shrubs. In large part, this seems to be a region deforested and degraded by long periods of cultivation, burning, and erosion; it is now invaded by grasses and unable to support any other type of vegetation. As *rastrojos* are designated the regions covered with secondary growth, where the forest has been felled and where the soil has been left to recuperate after having been under cultivation for some time. These *rastrojos* are located, usually, on the lower limit of the humid forest—i.e., they represent a pioneer advance—but small patches can be found in the folds, at lower altitudes. What is called here savannas or grassy plains are the flat or gently rolling regions, mainly toward the lowlands, covered with grass and some isolated trees and shrubs. In the direction of the cool uplands there exist a few savannas near the trails, and it seems probable that most of these grasslands are the result of soil degradation over the centuries.

The proportional distribution of these land types is as follows: *cerros*, 30 per cent, *lomas*, 60 per cent, *rastrojos*, 8 per cent, and *sabanas*, 2 per cent. These percentages are, of course, based only upon observation, local information, and a set of incomplete sketch maps. According to these data, of the total land resources available about 70 per cent are completely sterile and of no value to agriculture. The remaining 30 per cent are distributed thus: On the lower parts of the *cerros* as well as in the *rastrojos*, mainly in the small valleys that dissect the folds, there are limited areas which are profitable for agriculture. The *sabanas* and *lomas*, on the other hand, cannot be used for cultivation and have value only as pastures, except for a few small extensions. These pastures, however, are also of poor quality and only the few pastures, on river flats are adequate. In the forest of the *cerros*, above 2,000 meters altitude and at more than a day's journey from the village, there are a few small coffee plantations and fields, but the poor quality of the soil, the difficult topography of the terrain, and its distance from the village make this a region of little immediate value. Land appropriate for agricultural purposes is, therefore, restricted to a few mountain folds and river flats where, thanks to small courses of water and the accumulation of alluvial soil, there exist a few areas where small crops can be planted. It is principally from these plots that the people derive their daily food supply.

Potential agricultural lands are classified into five categories, according to their quality and location: (1) *de primera* ('first grade'), more or less flat forested terrain, covered with only few stones or boulders (2) *de segunda* ('second grade'), forested mountain folds, with stones and boulders; (3) *de tercera* ('third grade'), *rastrojo*, i.e., secondary growth; (4) *de cuarta* ('fourth grade'), savanna country; and (5) *de quinta* ('fifth grade'), *lomas* or grass-covered mountainsides. As the two last categories can be used almost only for grazing, and the two first categories are very scarce, the principal agricultural activity develops in the underbrush of secondary growth. Within these categories the quality of the soil itself varies. Locally four classes of soil are distinguished, all suitable for agricultural purposes: (1) *Tierra negra* ('black soil')—this is the best, but it is found only in a few places in the *rastrojo* and in the so-called first-grade land. Practically all food plants can be cultivated in this soil, the color of which is not black but dark brown or yellowish. (2) *Tierra colorada* ('red soil')—this is the most common type of soil and most fields consist of this kind; it contains a considerable amount of reddish clay. (3) *Tierra arenosa* ('sandy soil')—this soil is similar to the red soil but contains a high percentage of sand and gravel, and only certain food plants can be cultivated in it. (4) *Tierra arcillosa* ('clayey soil')—this type is also similiar to the second class, but has a yellowish color owing to its clay content.

Chemical analysis made of samples of the two principal categories, black and red, by the Chemical Laboratory of the Colombian Ministry of Mining, gave the results shown in Table 24. It must be pointed out here that our sample of black soil was obtained from a field cleared in secondary growth of the so-called third grade, and not from a first-grade plot cleared in the forest. However, as most agricultural lands lie within third-grade land and red soil, the two samples seem to be fairly representative of the soil properties in general.

TABLE 24

Element	Black soil (kg/pa)	Red soil (kg/pa)
Assimilable phosphorus (P)	300, very rich	30, very poor
Assimilable potassium (K)	350, very rich	180, rich
Assimilable calcium (C)	10,000, very rich	1,000, very poor
Nitrogen and organic matter	very poor	very poor

The average depth of the agricultural soil is shallow, rarely reaching 30 or 40 centimeters and most usually about 25 centimeters. The substratum consists generally of gravel or *caliche*, a limestone rock, sometimes with a second stratum of *cascajo*, a light-colored sandstone. Bedrock is sometimes found immediately beneath the top soil. As any cultivable soil is called *barro* ('clay'), terms like *barro calichoso* or *barro arenoso* are frequently used. Distinction is also made between *tierra suelta* ('loose soil', i.e., 'sandy soil') and *tierra apretada* ('compact soil', i.e., clay-containing). The term *barníl* is used for clay deposits, often in different colors. Sterile rocky soils are called *pedregales*. Referring to the amount of humidity, soils are classified into *pantanosa* ('swampy'), *tierra fresca* ('somewhat humid'), *tierra de reguío* ('irrigated soil'), and *tierra seca* or *peladero*, i.e., any dry and sterile soil.

Crops vary according to the quality of the soil. In black soil all food plants can be cultivated with good results. Red soil is used especially for manioc, yams, and sweet potatoes, but maize and plantains do not thrive well in it. The sandy soil is used primarily for yams, but manioc and sweet potatoes can also be cultivated in it, as can pumpkins, calabashes, watermelons, and tobacco. It is not adequate for maize, and plantains or bananas thrive in it only for a short time. Sugar cane can also be planted in sandy soil. Almost all food plants can be cultivated in clayey soil, but yields are said to be of poor quality.

No lands arc held in communal ownership, all holdings being

privately owned. However, only about a dozen people, almost all of them placeros, have legal titles to their land. Five types of landholdings are distinguished. A *finca* consists of a house surrounded by coffee or sugar-cane plantations adjoining a plot where the basic staple foods are cultivated. The owner does not live there permanently, but he visits the land occasionally, maybe once a week, and sometimes spends a day or two there. A *roza* is a small field where root crops and plantains are cultivated. There may be a hut where the owner might pass the night occasionally, but more often than not there is no permanent construction of any kind. A *posesión* is a large *roza*, generally with adjoining pastures and some livestock. There is a house and the owner occupies it almost permanently. A *terreno* is an empty, unplanted field, not yet cultivated or, perhaps, left to recuperate after having been cultivated for some time. A *potrero*, finally, is a pasture for livestock. An additional type of holding is a *solar*, which is a house lot; but this term is used only for property lying within the immediate village boundaries.

These types of landholdings can be acquired in different ways. They can be bought, inherited, received as gifts, or claimed as *baldío*, i.e., as ownerless virgin land. The purchase of land is never a mere private affair between two people but always concerns the entire community. Both parties will consult a number of appraisers and will discuss with them size, quality of soil, boundaries, and price, and usually the whole village will know of such a transaction, no matter how small. Once the price has been agreed upon, the deal is made verbally in the presence of witnesses, but legal registration or the presence of a member of the local authorities is not thought to be necessary. Almost all purchases of land are paid for in instalments over several months or years. These instalments are usually paid for with the produce of the land purchased, and in case of crop failure the creditor has no right to urge payment. About fifteen or twenty such deals are made every year in the village, almost all of them involving sums far below 1,000 pesos. Death, illness, or poverty are the principal reasons for selling land, and as agricultural plots are scarce, prospective buyers will approach the owner of a field as soon as it has become known that he is in a precarious economic situation. When land is inherited by several people, as often happens, the matter is almost always brought before the local authorities, for quarrels over distribution are practically certain to result. As a rule, every heir will claim the coffee plantation, while none will accept the pastures of poor quality. The affair is generally settled by adjudging the coffee to one heir, who is then obliged to pay a certain sum each year to those who received the rest of the land. The unwritten law favors the person who is known to have taken an active interest in agriculture, and the local authorities are guided in their final decisions by this tradition. Occasionally ownership is transferred by gift. A godfather might give a small plot to his godchild, or an old man might give part of his land to a trusted person in exchange for the promise to defray his burial expenses. Such gifts are legalized by witnesses, but are hardly ever made before the village authorities. Unoccupied, ownerless virgin land can be claimed by anyone who clears and cultivates it. Under such circumstances ownership is established by witnesses, and eventually the interested party will communicate his claims to the local authorities in order to avoid later intruders on his new property.

Land prices in 1954 were as follows: One hectare of first-grade new land with legal titles sold for about 20 pesos, and for half this price if there was no title to it. One hectare of secondary growth was worth from 25 to 30 pesos, and only half this sum if no title existed. Pastures sold at 100 to 150 pesos a hectare, depending upon the quality of the grass. A coffee plantation or a *roza* of one hectare sold for about 200 pesos. In the course of the year prices hardly varied but were determined, of course, by the quality of the soil, the existence and kind of fruit trees and fences, the amount of care that had been given to the land, and its walking distance from the village.

Government taxes are paid yearly on land and houses, the amount of these taxes being determined by what the person declares. These declarations are, of course, rather dubious, as the precise extension of land-ownership is always a closely guarded family secret. Some people declare less than they really own in order to evade the taxes; others declare more than they own in order to gain social prestige and economic credit. As few people have legal titles to their land, wherein the exact extension would be stated, there is hardly any way to ascertain the total amount of privately owned land and the uses to which it is put. From tax declarations made by the 402 individual owners who filled out the forms, of all the taxable property in the entire Corregimiento we have compiled the following data: The total extent of private land-holdings amounted to 3,055 hectares, valued at 368,000 pesos, and the total amount of taxes paid on this land was 687,26 pesos. On 457 houses, valued 97,820 pesos, a total of 197.14 pesos in taxes was paid. For every 500 pesos worth of land a tax of one peso was collected, and for a house an average yearly tax of 40 centavos was paid.

Government property within the limits of the Corregimiento amounts to very little. The municipality owns four houses used as schools, valued at 850 pesos all together; one house where the police inspector has his office, valued at 600 pesos; and a small house valued at 350 pesos and used as the slaughterhouse. The Church owns the house of the parish priest, valued at 3,000 pesos, and the church building itself, valued at 4,000 pesos.

Any privately owned land is jealousy guarded by its owner. Even if only underbrush grows on it, the proprietor expects to be asked for his permission if someone wants to cut a stick or to gather wild fruits. Even the stones on one's land are considered valuable property, since they can be used in the construction of fences.

Of the nearly 3,000 hectares privately owned in the Corregimiento, only about half are in actual use, i.e., 1,500 hectares, more or less. Of these, 700 hectares are pastures, while the remaining 800 hectares are distributed thus: 300 hectares for coffee, 150 hectares for sugar cane, and 350 hectares for fields with food plants. In other words, only 11·66 per cent of the privately owned land is used to produce food for daily consumption, while 23·33 per cent is used for pastures, and 15 per cent for cash crops. The remaining 50 per cent, although made up of private properties, is not utilized at all, either because it consists of sterile and valueless land or because exploitation represents too high a cost. The owner whose household labor force is too small and who cannot afford hired labor lets his land lie fallow.

Of the 171 landowning households in the village we have the following information on how this property was acquired: seventy-three fields (42·6 per cent) are new land cleared by the present owner; seventy-three fields (42·6 per cent) were purchased as already productive land; twenty fields (11·6 per cent) were acquired by inheritance; and five fields (3 per cent) were received as gifts. These data show several facts that are highly significant. In the first place, it is evident that land-ownership is seldom acquired by inheritance and if so, we know of no case where it was held for more than two generations. In nineteen cases the fields were inherited by the present owner from his father, the father having cleared or bought it, and in one single instance a field was willed by grandfather to grandson. In the second place, it is obvious that many people have bought their land. The incidence of land purchase and the clearing of new land is given in Table 25 by five-year periods, including all landholdings owned at present by the villagers.

TABLE 25

Acquired Between	Acquired by Clearing	Purchase
1948–52	14	26
1943–47	17	19
1938–42	17	19
1933–37	5	1
1928–32	10	3
1923–27	1	—
1918–22	3	2
1913–17	—	—
1908–12	5	2
1903–07	1	1
Total	73	73

To clear new land is difficult and calls for co-operation, which is not always to be found. Besides, many people feel degraded or humilated by this kind of work, because it is regarded as an 'Indian' activity; so they prefer to buy a field already cleared by others that still promises fair yields. On the other hand, coffee-growing received its main impulse with rising prices during the first years of World War II, and this (together with the increased availability of cash for land) explains the increase of newly opened fields in recent years. This cash crop has had a profound influence upon the system of agriculture and land tenure in the valley of Aritama, an influence which, in many ways, has been harmful to the community. We shall consider this problem further below, but we must return first to the basic techniques of agriculture as it is practiced in the valley at present.

Actual cultivation of fields is carried out by brand-tillage. The principal phases, from the first clearing of a plot to its final abandonment and reversion to secondary growth, are as follows: During the first months of the dry season, usually in December or January, the men and the older children of a household group will begin the *rebusque* ('gleaning') i.e., they will cut down the underbrush that surrounds the larger trees of the forest in order to make space for using an ax. During this work only bushknives are used and a short hooked stick that is used with the left hand to bend branches, tear off vines, or gather the cut-wood together. The trees are then felled, leaving only short stumps, and the smaller branches are cut with a machete and left to dry. This phase is by all accounts the most difficult and energy-consuming, especially if the owner of the plot is alone or has only a small labor force at his disposal. During the last weeks of February or early in March, the *quema*, i.e., the 'firing' begins. As there is practically no rainfall during these months, the wood is by now well dried and the men, using torches of bark and straw, set fire at several points in the field. This might take only a day or two; then begins the next step, called *repique* ('chopping'), during which the larger charred trunks are cut into pieces with an ax and burned again, together with all branches and sticks that might have escaped the first firing. This is slow and heavy work, men and children laboring with soot-covered faces and clothes, carrying stones and trunks toward the periphery of the plot, and cleaning the field as well as circumstances will permit. The field is now ready for planting, but usually people wait for the first slight shower to remove some of the ashes before they actually begin to plant.

Planting is done by men and women, with the use of a dibbling-stick. The seeds are buried superficially and earth is stamped over them. Once this has been done, the family will return only sporadically to the field, for weeding. There are two planting seasons: the *siembra de primera* ('first sowing'), which begins with the first rains, usually after March 20, and the *siembra de segunda* ('second sowing'), which takes place during the month of August. The second season until recently was traditionally divided into six *coas* ('dibbling-sticks'), i.e., days dedicated to a saint of the Catholic Church on which the planting should be done. They are: first *coa*, on August 10, *San Lorenzo*; second *coa*, on August 15, *Virgen del Transito*; third *coa*, on August 24, *San Bartolomé*; fourth *coa*, on August 28, *San Agustín*; fifth *coa*, on August 30, *Santa Rosa*; and sixth *coa*, on September 8, *Virgen de Chiquinquirá*. This division, however, has now ceased to influence the planting cycle; although people remember these days occasionally, they seldom adapt their activities to them any more.

Almost no food plant has a vegetative cycle of less than twelve months, and so the harvesting and planting seasons can be said to coincide. Although planting is limited to a certain time of the year, depending on the rains, there is no definite ripening season that would require certain fruits to be always gathered at a certain moment. This is because the soil varies in quality and the fields in altitudinal range and because certain varieties of the same crop ripen sooner than others, making it necessary for harvesting to be done all year round, as is characteristic of the root-crop complex. In reality, these fields are nothing more than kitchen gardens, where the daily food supply, consisting mainly of starchy roots and some plantains, is grown. Such a plot is usually referred to as a *roza de pan coger*, an expression which can be translated freely as 'field of daily subsistence'.

An average field of these food plants produces for about five years, after which the soil is likely to be exhausted and the owner abandons it to clear and plant a new field, if he can find labor and funds and a suitable tract of land not too far from the village. Since this is often impossible, many people practice rotation on the same plot, planting only a small part of it, while the rest is left to recuperate under brush fallow. The cycle of this rotation depends somewhat on the cultigen. For maize, for example, the land is cropped for only one year. Certain varieties of manioc and, sometimes, plantains yield fruit for five years, but the great majority of the other plants do not produce after two or three years. A field is, therefore, divided into small parcels, some under cultivation and some vacant and left to recuperate. But the length of productivity depends also upon the intensity of yearly burning, upon extent of erosion, upon the particular topography of the field, and, of course, upon the amount of care given to the land. Thus a few fields might be productive for twenty or thirty years, but many others, which lie on steep hillsides, have to be abandoned after five or six years. Vegetation is of slow growth and only after a five-year interval does second growth produce, under favorable conditions, trees of more than 10 centimeters in diameter. More often than not, adequate regeneration does not take place, and grass invades the abandoned fields, which soon become part of the sterile savannas.

The average area of a *roza* owned by a household is about two hectares, even the wealthiest placeros hardly ever owning more than this. Of this tract of land only approximately one third (about one *cabulla*, i.e., an area of 80 by 80 meters) is under cultivation, while the rest is covered by brush fallow or is already eroded or invaded by grass. There is often a small house, or rather a temporary shed, on these fields, constructed as a shelter against a sudden rain shower, for cooking a meal, or for passing an occasional night or two. Such huts are often found deserted in the second growth of abandoned fields, or their former sites can be recognized by a calabash or lemon tree or by some pepper plants growing nearby, the hut itself having disappeared.

During agricultural work each household group operates as an independent unit. Small co-operative groups, consisting of three or four men and based on the principle of reciprocity, are sometimes formed for clearing new land in uninhabited virgin forest, but usually these individual smallholdings are worked only by the members of a household unit. Women, however, rarely work in the fields, occupying themselves, rather, with the weaving of hats. The amount of time actually spent on fields is not increased by this lack of labor force, since a plot, once it is under production, requires relatively little care. A man or the children might go once or twice a week for a few hours to do some weeding or to gather a few tubers and fruits, but a larger group of people will hardly ever be seen engaged in agricultural tasks. Sometimes, if the owners can afford it, hired labor is used, usually young, newly married men who have no land of their own. But this happens only in cases where the owner is a well-to-do placero or where cash crops must be harvested in a limited time.

There are only two forms of shared exploitation of landholdings. In the first, the owner plants the field with coffee trees and permits another person to sow food plants between the trees during three or four years. In this manner the coffee-grower avoids the expense of weeding or of planting shade trees, such as plantains. There is, however, in this form of sharing a certain risk involved for the owner. Should the tenant, without the owner's knowledge, plant a few additional coffee trees, he can eventually claim ownership to the land or part of it if the original owner has not legalized his right to the land. In the second form, a landless person is simply permitted to plant a small *roza* on an owner's land, without any payment or participation in the produce. There are in Aritama five cases of landless households that work borrowed land (*tierra prestada*); in each case the land belongs to a member of the landless person's kin.

In the immediate vicinity of the village agricultural lands are very scarce. In those regions where the soils are best, fields are crowded closely together, a veritable jigsaw puzzle of tiny, irregularly shaped plots. Until relatively recent times, boundaries were marked merely by rows of trees or stones, but during the last fifteen years barbed-wire fences have become common. This scarcity of land, the increase of livestock, and the fear that others might try to appropriate one's land by force or ruse have led to a craze for fencing in one's plot, even at a high cost. Expropriation and counterclaims are frequent. Cases are reported of people who, in the lowland towns, took out legal titles to land that was already occupied by others but that had not yet been adjudged to them by the authorities, thus expropriating such titleless original owners. It would be difficult to tell how much of this is exaggeration and how much is the truth, but it is evident that in some instances certain people appropriated land in this manner.

Colonization of new land proceeds very slowly. The fear of isolation, of disease, of long and tiresome trails, and the deep-set fear of nature in general, keep most people as close as possible to the village, so that although there are regions farther back in the mountains where profitable fields could be established, very few are developed. Any pioneering of new territory that does occur is always unplanned and casual. Accessibility is always an important factor, and under present conditions most potentially profitable areas are too far removed from the village to be worked systematically. Of fifty fields cleared during the twenty years between 1932 and 1952, nineteen lie at more than 10 kilometers distance from the village, while twenty-two lie at more than 15 kilometers from it. In mountainous country, with steep slopes, ravines, and rivers to cross, such distances are serious obstacles to exploitation. So clearing and cultivation are limited to the felling of secondary growth in the surroundings, tasks in which women and children can help if necessary. But the monetary cost of clearing new land is not high. Table 26 shows the average expense for one hectare situated at two hours' walking distance from the village and located in heavy secondary growth.

TABLE 26

Activity	Laborers	Days	Cost Pesos	Man-Days
Clearing	2	8	30	16
Burning	2	1	5	2
Chopping	2	3	15	6
Total	—	—	50	—

This amount, of course, rises considerably if the work is carried out in virgin forest where large trees have to be felled and where the laborers have to bring a large amount of food with them.

A valid appraisal of the problem of shifting cultivation and brand-tillage is impossible, because the precise effect that burning has upon the soil is not known, as far as chemical and physical changes of the soil properties are concerned. The particular topographical nature of the field that is fired determines the amount of damage done by the firing. In relatively flat terrain, there seems to be no clear evidence that the land is degraded by burning, and as long as such a field is reasonably cared for afterward, no harmful flora or fauna seem to result. The problem is entirely different in hillside cultivation. Here, fire is more difficult to control. Frequently it ascends the slopes and destroys the vegetation on soils not intended for cultivation. Then erosion is bound to set in, and before long a large amount of good soil will have been washed down the slope. But slope cultivation is easier than clearing flat land. Trunks or stones can be removed much more easily, simply by rolling them down the decline, and trees felled on steep slopes fall downward by their own weight. This relative ease of clearing slopes leads, of course, to a preference for fields located in such a position. In flat or slightly undulating terrain, trees have to be cut into pieces, and the charred trunks have to be dug up and burned anew. Brand-tillage in itself is a labor-saving technique. To clear a field without burning it would be a task much too heavy, costly, and time-consuming, even if several men worked together. By burning, however, a single person can clear large areas in a few days, without having to hire labor. Agricultural techniques and land-use are closely related to the prevailing social structure, and no matter how wasteful they may appear, have to be judged from this point of view.

But there are also other factors involved. In Aritama people burn their fields and pastures not only during the dry season but at any time of the year, after a few days of sunshine have dried the leaves and grass. There is always smoke rising up somewhere in the mountains, and all too-often the fires spread uncontrollably for days and even weeks, covering hundreds of hectares and even entire valleys up to the headwaters of the streams. To set fire to dry grass or underbrush is a temptation no villager can resist. When walking to their fields they are likely to ignite any patch of dry grass. Some say they do so in order to clear the trail; others, to kill the snakes; others, with the express intention of causing damage to an enemy's property. At the end of the dry season, when people are waiting for the first rains to fall, a certain element of sympathetic magic is apparent in the burning. The heavy billowing clouds of smoke are said to 'call the rain' (*llaman la lluvia*), and people anxiously watch the horizon for the first rain clouds to build up. Furthermore, in Aritama as among other Colombian peasants, there is a tendency to cut down or to burn any tree whatsoever. Trees are often considered to be 'dirty' and dangerous because of the leaves and branches that drop from them. Obscene names are given to large trees, and many trees along the trails show the marks of the machetes of passers-by who slashed at them wilfully. A man whom we asked to explain why he was cutting down a tree near the village entrance, answered: 'So that progress may enter' (*para que entre el progreso*). The local authorities and public opinion often agree with this point of view, and the desolate aspect of the streets and plazas of many Colombian villages is due to the opinion that trees are not 'civilized', and that decent people should not live 'in the bush'.

The relationship between deforestation and erosion is recognized by only a few people in the village, and they do nothing about it. Although the government discourages burning, an effective control has not yet been established. Occasionally a visiting government agent will try to explain how damage could be avoided, but people shrug off his advice. The lack of co-operation on the family or community level, the lack of better tools and better techniques, the lack of money for hired labor—all make it impossible to clear fields without the help of fire. Besides, the majority never admit that fire, deforestation, erosion, and crop failure are connected, preferring to put the blame for the poverty of their land upon the cattle-owners, the so-called rich, the politicians, the government. 'The government wants to starve us to death', people said when being told that burning was to be outlawed. But the fact that there have been changes for the worse in the quality and quantity of agricultural soils is well recognized, although not understood. All people over fifty years of age assured us that in their youth there was more rainfall and that the soil layer was thicker and more fertile than it is now. They can point out creeks or small lagoons they once knew as brimful, but which today are completely dry, even during the rainy season, and they mention forest and heavy underbrush where now there are desolate savannas. Deep barrancos and ravines, old streambeds now dry, and dried-up swamps—all indicate that precipitation and soil humidity were higher in the past. On many of the savannas or in the sandy sterile regions of the valley, there lie large granite boulders. They are blackened by fire and on their lower parts horizontal stripes of different shades of black and gray indicate successive burnings of the surrounding land. Many, lying now on sterile soil devoid of any plant cover, show the last marks of fire at 30 or 40 centimeters above the present ground, indicating the amount of erosion that has taken place since the rock lay in grassy or forested soil. A similar phenomenon can be observed on many houses in the village. Houses built on level ground about fifty or sixty years ago, now stand on square bases often more than one meter high, the surrounding ground having been eroded away and the street level lowered.

A final word must be said about the landless. Of the 261 households that form the village and its immediate surroundings, 90 (34·4 per cent) do not own land. In most cases (43·5 per cent) such households consist of women who live alone with their small children, having been abandoned by their consorts or now living in concubinage with a man who lives in another house. Another large group (29·4 per cent) is formed by the nuclear families of young couples the men of which work as hired laborers, often outside the Corregimiento. Thirteen (15·2 per cent) women, all of them past childbearing age, live alone in their houses, as do four (4·7 per cent) old men. There are also four (4·7 per cent) households made up of grandmothers, their daughters, and their small grandchildren, and two (2·4 per cent) households where the grandfather lives with his sons and grandchildren. All these people earn their living by weaving hats, and in exchange for minor services receive food from relatives who own fields.

As we have seen in the foregoing pages, the system of land tenure and usage reflects in detail the different aspects of social structure, together with the historical changes that have led to its present form. The restriction of agricultural activity and, consequently, of the potential food supply depend, obviously, not so much upon the available land resources as upon such factors as the lack of co-operative enterprise, the handicap of primitive techniques, of prestige behavior, and, last but not least, the limitations to all physical efforts imposed by malnutrition.

GARDEN CROPS AND TREES

The starchy roots cultivated by the villagers in their fields are *yuca* ('sweet manioc'), *ñame* ('yams'), *batata* ('sweet potato'), and *arracacha* (*Arracacia xanthorrhiza*). Among the many varieties of sweet manioc, a positive distinction is made between 'Indian' and 'Spanish' kinds, people claiming that the latter are of recent introduction and that the so-called Indian varieties do not thrive well in the lower reaches of the valley. Preferred varieties are the *yuca india* and the 'Spanish' *yuca Mampollona*, both of which reproduce abundantly for several years in the same field and which are said to be particularly well acclimatized. Manioc is planted in stems, each about 25 centimeters long, which are stuck vertically into the slightly loosened soil, at about one meter apart. Planting is done in April and the first tubers can be harvested a year later, except the variety called *yuca Cartagena*, which ripens in ten months. Sweet potatoes are planted in April or May and usually can be harvested after eight months. As with manioc, 'Indian' and 'Spanish' varieties of sweet potatoes are distinguished, the principal kinds being *Montañera Blanca*, *Montañera Amarilla*, *Sananguera*, *Curera*, *Batatica de Dios*, and *Batatica Chepe*. Sometimes sweet potatoes are planted by burying a few tubercles superficially, at distances of 8 or 10 meters

215

apart, but generally they are allowed simply to reproduce from a few fruits left in the ground during harvest. Yams are planted in April, in the same way as sweet potatoes, and are harvested after eleven or twelve months. Arracacha is planted only at altitudes above 1,200 meters, but few people like this tuber, and it is very little cultivated.

The common plantain or cooking banana, together with the sweet banana, are important food plants for all regions lying below 1,200 meters above sea level and are found in all fields and also in many backyards. The principal varieties distinguished are *guinéo verde*, *guinéo maduro*, *guinéo criollo*, and *dominico*. Several varieties of beans are planted in April, but although they are greatly valued as food, little care is taken in their cultivation. Most of them can be harvested after two or three months. Pigeon peas, another highly valued food, are also little cultivated. When planted in April, they can be gathered at the beginning of the dry season.

Most food plants are said to have a specific 'temperature' and to be either 'hot' or 'cold'. This quality does not necessarily apply to the fruit it bears, but is said to be inherent in the plant and has to be taken into account when establishing a field, as certain plants might receive harm when planted too close to others which have a different 'temperature'. 'Cold' plants, when sown close to 'hot' plants, are said to whither and to develop poorly. So a certain distance and order has to be maintained when distributing a field or garden. 'Cold' plants are the following: plantain, banana, yams, arracacha, sweet potato, payaya, pineapple, hog plum, guanábana, and all citrus fruits. The variety of banana called *guinéo criollo* is regarded as particularly 'cold'. 'Hot' plants are manioc, kidney beans, avocado, mango, and coconut; maize, pigeon peas, and sugar cane are considered to be 'very hot'. The common *lata* (*Bactris minor*), a wild-growing cane widely used in the construction of houses or fences, and the common mountain grass that grows on the hillsides are also 'hot'. Tobacco and chili peppers are the 'hottest' of all. A field, therefore, may be planted in the following manner: Pigeon peas are planted on the periphery and are never mixed with any other plant. 'Hot' plants may be mixed, i.e., maize, manioc, and beans, but care is taken to sow 'very hot' plants such as chili peppers and tobacco at some distance from the others. 'Cold' plants can also be mixed but have to be separated by some distance from the 'hot' plants. It must be pointed out here that the concepts of 'hot' and 'cold' refer to the plant alone and not to the fruit it bears. Although the manioc plant is 'hot', the tuber is considered to be 'cold'; the batata plant is 'cold' but its fruit is 'hot'; and the mango tree, although 'hot', bears 'cold' fruit.

Some minor crops remain to be mentioned. An important garden crop is the *ahuyama* (*Cucurbita moschata*), a giant squash which is commonly found in fields and backyards. They grow without needing any care, and are frequently planted near the house. Peppers (*Capsicum* spp.) of two varieties are also grown, and some *achiote* (*Bixa orellana*) is found occasionally, the seeds being used for coloring soups or boiled rice. Shallots are planted at altitudes over 1,200 meters, at any time of the year, and can be cut in six months. They are highly esteemed as a condiment and as a green leaf in stews and soups. Cacao was planted widely during the past century, but at present only a few people have cacao trees under cultivation.

In 1946, the Colombian Ministry of National Economy began a nationwide campaign through which it tried to encourage the establishment of kitchen gardens, in order to supplement the diet of the rural population. A booklet called *The Kitchen Garden* (*La Huerta Casera*) was published and widely distributed, and at the same time the government sent agents to visit the villages and distribute free vegetable seeds (carrots, red beets, cabbages, tomatoes, etc.) and to teach the people how to plant them. These agents also visited Aritama, and at the time of our study we found some of the booklets still in the hands of a few placero families. The kitchen gardens, however, had been abandoned as soon as the government agents had left. There were several reasons for their non-acceptance. In the first place, local food habits and tastes are deeply rooted and could not be modified so suddenly. A detailed previous study of prevailing attitudes and habits would have been necessary. In the second place, the booklet, although it stated that it was meant to be read by 'humble peasants', was written in a rather complex style, incomprehensible even to the most sophisticated villager. It contained expressions like 'predatory economy', and 'the multiplication of species'; it defined agriculture in highly poetic terms, made reference to the aborigines of Tasmania, and was illustrated with a number of drawings depicting people and situations that did not represent peasant life as it really is in the Colombian tropics. In the third place, there were many prestige factors involved that made the project undesirable. That the government should ask them to till the soil, to irrigate, and carefully tend a crop that produced only a 'few leaves and tiny roots', was interpreted as an attack upon the dignity of the villagers, who, by their refusal to comply, meant to demonstrate that they 'were not wild Indians as the government seemed to think'. In addition, people were not used to handling small seeds (except perhaps tobacco) and did not know how to keep them, plant them, or collect them, and when the agency, after some time, stopped free distribution, expecting the people to have already gathered a sufficient supply from their gardens, it was accused of 'abandonment', 'abuse', etc. So the campaign failed and the general feeling was one of righteous indignation whenever the topic was mentioned.

Maize is a crop of very little importance in Aritama. Yields are poor, partly because of the inferior quality of the dry and eroded soil, partly because of inadequate seed grain. Not all people plant maize, and those who do hardly ever plant more than a few square meters. A quarter of an hectare was about the largest maize field we saw in the entire Corregimiento. The principal types of maize are *maiz amarillo* ('yellow') and *maize blanco* ('white'), but in comparison with that planted in the lowlands these varieties are poorly developed; ears are small and irregular, with small kernels of a flattened shape. Maize is planted in late April, as soon as the rains begin. At distances of about 2 meters small holes 10 centimeters deep are made in the soil with a dibbling-stick, and three or four grains are dropped into each, the earth then being stamped over them with the foot. About 25 pounds of seed are needed to plant one hectare, and to give a yield of about 300 pounds. Maize patches have to be weeded as soon as the plants are about 25 centimeters high (*a cola de gallo*, i.e., 'like a cock's tail'). This weeding, called *desahogue* (literally, 'un-drowning'), is sometimes repeated after a few months. Some time before the harvest, the ears are bent (*doblada*), and all during the growth of the plant great care has to be taken to protect the crop against birds, ants, rats, and squirrels. Usually a person, often a child, is employed for the *pajareo*, i.e., to scare away all animals. Maize generally yields only one crop a year, and after that the soil is said to be exhausted.

Production costs for one hectare of maize are given in Table 27.

TABLE 27

Activity	Laborers	Days	Cost Pesos	Man-Days
Planting	1	2	5	2
"Pajareo"	1	20	10	20
"Doblada"	2	8	40	16
Harvest	2	5	25	10
Transport	2	$2\frac{1}{2}$	12	5

An average of 20 *quintales*, i.e., 2,000 pounds per hectare, at the current price of 5 pesos per *quintal* would not even pay costs if hired labor were employed.

The two principal fruit-bearing trees are avocado and mango, both of which produce fruits of good quality. There are about 1,000 avocado trees in the Corregimiento, about equally divided between placeros and lomeros. All these trees are privately owned among some twenty individuals. No special care is taken of the trees, which are visited only during the harvest, from May to September. The ripe fruit is collected by throwing sticks and stones at it or by having boys climb up to shake the branches. Much of the fruit is thus damaged and lost, but as the harvest is plentiful, only the best fruit is used and the rest is thrown to the pigs. Frequently an avocado tree is simply felled in order that its fruit may be harvested more easily, and we never heard of people planting new trees for the ones they destroyed. Occasionally a merchant from the lowland towns will come and buy large quantities of avocados, but otherwise most of the fruit is consumed locally. It is of small commercial value, a dozen selling for a few centavos. Two classes of avocados are distinguished: a 'long' and a 'round' kind, the former being said to have the better flavor. Several kinds of mango are distinguished: *Mango Largo, Hilachudo, Rosa, Mango de Teta, Canime, No-se-te-vé, Chancleta, Número Seis*. The first kind is said to be very old in the region, whereas the others are said to have been introduced about eighty years ago, from the vicinity of the lowland towns. There are some 500 mango trees in the surroundings of Aritama, all of them privately owned.

Some 30 coconut palms grow in and around the village, their ownership being divided among fifteen individuals, most of them lomeros. They bear little fruit, which is rarely sold but is consumed by their owners. Ownership of avocado, mango, and coconut trees often does not coincide with the ownership of the land upon which they grow— that is, a person may own trees growing on someone else's land, a circumstance which leads to quarrels between tree- and landowners.

Lagenaria (*calabazo*) and Crescentia gourd trees (*totumo*) are found here and there, usually near houses or in old fields. They are used exclusively for manufacturing containers from their shells, and some of these trees are privately owned. Some citrus fruit trees, hog-plum trees, and papaya trees grow in the backyards, as do many kinds of native fruit-bearing trees, the fruits of which are gathered occasionally.

Tobacco is grown on a small scale by some of the poorer people. The following local varieties are distinguished: *Cola de Caballo* ('horse tail'), *Lengua de Vaca* ('cow's tongue'), *Lengua de Venado* ('deer's tongue') *Frente de Toro* ('bull's forehead'), *Pegadito* (literally, 'close-growing'), *Cañuela* ('little cane'), and *Virginia*. The last two are considered to be the best varieties. Kept first in seedbeds, the seedlings are transplanted and spaced at 2 meters distance when about 10 centimeters high, and from then on they demand little care except occasional weeding and loosening of the soil near the stem of the plant. The first leaves can be picked about three months after planting, but the plants are rarely productive for more than one year. The first harvest, during which only the lower leaves are taken, is called *tierrero*, while the last is named *La Copa* (literally, 'treetop'), the others not having any special names. The leaves are strung on fiber threads with the help of a long, flat, wooden needle and are then hung to dry in a shadowy but ventilated place, generally outside the house. Once their color is a dark brown, they are slightly moistened and then pressed between horizontally placed flat stones. The dried leaves are sold at 50 centavos a pound in the local stores or at a slightly higher price in the lowlands. As 300 tobacco plants will yield approximately 100 pounds of dry leaves, the gain is considerable, but many people find the care of the plants bothersome.

CASH CROPS

The first coffee plantations were established in the valley of Aritama about 1870, but very few people dedicated themselves to this new cash crop, and during the following fifty years these plantations had little or no economic importance for the village. Around 1920, with the rise of coffee prices, new plantations were established by some people, only to be abandoned again when prices dropped a few years later. Beginning in 1940, however, coffee-growing once more became important, and since then it has developed slowly but steadily into a major cash crop.

In other parts of Colombia the best climate for coffee lies between approximately 1,200 and 1,800 meters above sea level, with temperatures between 17° and 24° C., but in the valley of Aritama conditions suitable for coffee are found as low as 700 meters altitude, the upper limit reaching to about 1,400 meters. According to the government agents in charge of the maintenance and development of local coffee plantations, the available soil is not adequate for extensive coffee-growing, partly because of its poor chemical composition, and partly because of the difficult topography. Technically, there should be about 1,650 coffee trees to a hectare, but the villagers of Aritama believe that it would be a waste of land to plant the trees at more than 2 meters distance from each other, and will sometimes plant up to 3,000 or 3,500 trees on a hectare. Furthermore, little care is taken of the individual trees, which are hardly ever pruned and are left to reproduce freely. Because of this general lack of systematic cultivation and the poor quality of the thin soil cover, yields are relatively low. While in the interior provinces of Colombia one hectare might yield about one ton a year (twenty *quintales*), in the region of Aritama five or six quintales (i.e., one-quarter ton) a year are the average harvest. However, this coffee is of very good quality (Type Excelso) and brings good market prices.

There are about sixty coffee plantations in the surroundings, with a total of 300 hectares planted with more than half a million coffee trees. The total yearly produce approaches about 7,000 *arrobas*, i.e., more than 87 tons of coffee. According to the experts, this yield could be

220

doubled if the individual coffee-growers would adopt even the basic rules of planting and pruning, but few people believe that they can learn anything from the government agents; and so, although this crop is developing, it makes only slow progress. One major obstacle is the ants, which if not controlled, can destroy one hectare in three or four days; but as insecticides are expensive, the control of this pest is neglected and remains a constant danger to the crops.

In Colombia practically all coffee is grown under shade trees. In Aritama, guamo trees, avocado trees, and plantains are preferred for this purpose. The coffee-picking season begins, on the lower limit of the plantations, around the middle of September and lasts in the higher regions through January and sometimes the beginning of February. The principal harvest-time is October and November, months with frequent and torrential rainfall, which not only endanger the crop but also the health of the people engaged in harvesting. Small plantations can be picked rather easily by a family, women and children taking active part in it, but larger crops always represent a major problem, as it is often difficult to recruit sufficient pickers. A coffee-picker is paid 'by the tin' (*por lata*), i.e., he receives a standard price of 30 to 45 centavos for each 5-gallon tin can of berries. A good worker can fill from eight to ten tins a day, a child about half as many, and a good daily average is seven tins.

The berries are first dried and then put into a hand-operated depulping machine (*despulpadora*) or are simply pounded with a pestle in a wooden mortar to remove the green outside skin and pulp from the berry. The beans are then washed and again dried in the sun, often on large wooden frames covered with wire-mesh. The parchment coffee (*café de patio*) is then packed for transport in large fiber sacks, each weighing 110 pounds. Sometimes the parchment hull is removed before packing by pounding the dry beans in a mortar, and in that case each sack is made to weigh 100 pounds. About ten sacks can be pulped in a day. The dry beans are separated into two qualities, a work that is usually done by children and, on an average, 100 pounds can be sorted thus in a day. Transportation is usually by mule, burro, or oxen, and such beasts of burden can carry approximately 200 pounds on each trip, i.e., two sacks. But much of the coffee is carried to market by the harvesters themselves, a man or woman being able to carry up to 75 pounds on his back. Among the poorer people it is customary to lend the few primitive pulping machines free of charge and also the available mules or burros; but any well-to-do coffee-grower has to pay for these services if he does not own machinery or pack animals.

Marketing the coffee is the next problem. In the village there are more than a dozen buyers, all of them belonging to the Plaza section.' In 1953, a 100-pound sack of high-quality coffee cost a buyer 100 pesos, while the lower quality cost him about 80 pesos. The buyers, after having paid 2 pesos for each loaded mule from the village to the nearest road, and 1 peso per sack for freight on the truck, then sold a 100-pound sack for 105·65 pesos to the agency of the local Federación Nacional de Cafeteros, the semiofficial coffee-grower's association, making a profit of about 3·65 pesos for each sack. Theoretically, at least, this was and still is the process.

But in reality, marketing the coffee is rather different in most cases. In the first place, it is very common for a grower to sell a coffee harvest, or part of it, in advance. Many are forced to do so by lack of money to pay for hired labor during May, when men are needed to clean the plantations of the rapidly growing weeds that spring up with the first heavy rains. Instead of risking loss of their entire crop, they sell a few hundred pounds of their next harvest to a local buyer at a low price, in order to pay for help in the weeding. Or cash might suddenly be needed for some other reason, maybe an illness, an urgent trip, or a marriage; thus many of the small owners will receive money in the course of the year in anticipation of future harvests. It is only natural that in these cases the local buyers dictate the prices. So in May or June a grower might receive from 15 to 20 pesos for 100 pounds of coffee deliverable during the next picking season (and should he happen to be of Indian stock, he might get as little as 12 pesos per 100 pounds), at which time it would otherwise have brought him 100 pesos.

In the second place, many of the owners of the larger coffee plantations borrow from the Caja Agraria, the government-sponsored institution that makes small loans to individuals in order to encourage certain crops. This loan is then used to pay for the labor employed in cleaning and picking. Loans are usually about 500 pesos, which have to be returned in nine or twelve months. But here another problem arises. The laborers, whenever they need money, approach the owners of the plantations and ask them to advance small sums to be repaid by work during the picking season. These sums vary from 10 to 50 pesos, and to refuse to make such a loan would be practically impossible, as the owner of the plantation cannot afford to antagonize any worker and thus lose a single man during the rush of the picking season, when his whole capital depends upon the effective co-operation of his laborers. So during the whole year such loans are made, until finally the harvest-time arrives. Then the true difficulty appears. Some of the borrowers present themselves, but work only long enough to repay the debt they had contracted and then leave. Others claim to be ill and refuse to work; still others simply disappear from the village and go to live in their fields, in order to avoid the work. Others may go as hired laborers to distant valleys where coffee is also grown and harvested and where, perhaps, higher prices are paid than by the local plantation-owners and where they are not in debt. The plantation-owner of Aritama has no effective way to make these people fulfil their obligations—i.e., to repay their debts by working for him. Should he complain to the law, people will call him a miser and a 'persecutor of the poor', as they would have had he refused to give loans. He would make himself hated, and nobody would want to work for him during future harvests. Thus, the owner of the plantation is often left without sufficient laborers, and has to hire new ones, whom, of course, he has to pay immediately. Therefore, many people are unable to repay the Caja Agraria or, if they repay, are left with practically no money at all.

Greed, combined with this unhealthy credit system as practiced by the owners of the plantations and the local buyers, seriously handicaps the development of coffee-growing. However, more and more people are establishing small plantations, usually of a size that can be harvested by the owner's household group, without depending upon hired labor or loans.

Prestige is a strong incentive for these small landowners. Cash-cropping is regarded as a 'Spanish' activity, a 'civilized' kind of work, in contrast to subsistence or maintenance agriculture. Many people turn their fields into coffee plantations, thus seriously limiting their food supply but gaining prestige in the village. Coffee means ready cash; it means new clothes, money for travel and recreation, money to be spent during the fiesta season in May and June, when the harvest is over. That at the same time the individual food supply diminishes is a fact that few people seem to correlate with cash-cropping.

Sugar cane is another important cash crop. It is planted in the first two categories of soil, and the lower limit for its culvitation is in the vicinity of the village, the best crops being obtained at about 1,000 or 1,200 meters altitude. Most sugar-cane plantations occupy river flats, but some are also found on steep hillsides, but always near a creek. Locally the following varieties are distinguished: *Caña Blanca*, a short cane with rather weak roots; *Caña Blanca Rayada*, a cane with blueish stripes; *Caña Blanca Criolla*, *Caña Morada Rayada*, *Caña Morada Obscura*, *Caña Zamba Blanca*, *Caña Zamba Morada*, *Caña Cubana*, and *Caña Piojota*. The last two varieties were introduced only about ten years ago, and as they thrive particularly well and are apparently resistant to leaf-mosaic, they have replaced most other varieties. Sugar cane was planted in the region during the eighteenth century. It is said that the variety *Morada Obscura* was the first one to be introduced by the Spaniards. Today only the neighboring Indian tribes cultivate the two *Morada* varieties, the villagers having almost completely abandoned them.

For planting sugar cane either ratoons or 30-centimeterlong cuttings are used. The former are planted in an oblique position, whereas the latter are used vertically. Generally, these are planted in groups of four, leaving a distance of one meter between groups. Although under ideal conditions more than 30,000 canes could be planted on one hectare, in reality there are only about 2,500 or 3,000 to the hectare. A newly established plantation of cane yields its first crop after one year, but from then on the canes can be cut every six months for several years. About two or three times a year the field has to be weeded and cleaned, a task which takes one man about eight days each time. When cutting the cane, two men work together. One cuts the stems with a heavy machete, striking obliquely at the base of them, while the other cuts off the upper part, tears off a few leaves, and throws the stalks on a heap. One hectare of cane can be cut by two men in four days. All canes have to be processed on the day they are cut, as otherwise the juice would dry out and ferment, and so they have to be transported immediately to the mill by burrow or mule.

There are some seventy sugar mills (*trapiches*) in the valley, all of them powered by oxen. Until about thirty years ago all mills were made locally of wood, but then iron mills were introduced and after 1940 these began to replace almost completely the primitive wooden mills, of which today only fifteen are still operating. Basically, a sugar mill consists of three vertical cogged cylinders between which the cane is crushed so that the juice can be gathered in a container. One of these cylinders is connected on its top to a long, horizontal bar, which, in turn, is drawn in a circle by a pair of oxen driven slowly around the mill. There must always be two or three teams of oxen available, as they have to be changed frequently. Near the mill there is a large open-walled structure with a thatched roof under which a heavy hemispherical iron cauldron (*fondo*), imbedded in a low hearth of stones and clay, is heated to boil the cane juice until it crystallizes. When an iron mill is used, each cane is passed only once between the rotating cylinders, and only one man is needed to attend to this part of the work, but in a mill with wooden cylinders the cane is passed twice through them before the juice is thoroughly squeezed out, and therefore a second person is needed to return the cane. In general, an iron mill is about 30 per cent more effective than a wooden one and saves much labor and repair. The cauldrons have a capacity of 80 or a 100 gallons, and each cauldronful (*fondada*) is sufficient syrup to make 36 or 40 cakes of crystallized raw sugar (*panela*). The thick mass, which is constantly stirred with a wooden paddle, is placed, after cooling a little, into adjustable wooden frames and molded into square, brick-shaped pieces (*panelones*), which are then left to harden. Each of these cakes weighs between 3 and 4 pounds, and eight of them, wrapped and tied in plantain leaves, make a 'package' (*paquete*). These packages are then transported to the village, a burro carrying four of them, while a good mule may carry eight. In the village each individual cake is sold for 60 centavos, while a package of eight cakes sells for 4 pesos. In the neighboring lowland towns prices are about 25 per cent higher.

One hectare of good cane such as *Piojota* yields about 300 packages of cakes, while an inferior variety such as *Morada* may yield about 200 packages. Although this appears to be a fairly good profit, production costs are high and a number of circumstances tend to reduce the gains. The milling process requires at least five laborers—one to lead the oxen, one to drive them on, one to feed the canes to the mill, another to stir and skim the boiling juice and to mold it into cakes, and still another to carry water. Packing and transportation to the village are additional expenses in labor. A major problem is firewood, which is scarce everywhere in the vicinity of the valley. To boil the juice of one hectare of cane, four *burros* (i.e., the quantity of wood one man can cut in two days) are needed, and as the surroundings of the sugar mills are generally devoid of forest or underbrush, firewood often has to be brought from far away. People who do not own a mill or have oxen usually make the following arrangement: the owner of the mill furnishes the oxen, their drivers, and the firewood and receives in exchange half of the produce.

Production costs for one hectare of cane are given in Table 28. In this example it is supposed that the owner of the cane also owns the mill and the oxen.

TABLE 28

Activity	Laborers	Days	Cost pesos	Man-Days
Planting	2	5	25·00	10
Three weedings	1	20	50·00	20
Cutting cane	2	4	20·00	8
Transport to mill	2	2	10·00	4
Cutting wood	1	8	20·00	8
Transport to mill	1	2	5·00	2
Milling	5	15	187·50	75
Transport to village	2	10	50·00	20
Total	—	—	367·50	—

If we take an average of 250 packages per hectare, this would give a net gain of 632·50 pesos. But we have to take into account the following consideration: hardly ever does a person have available one entire hectare with ripe cane ready to be processed. The general rule is to cut a quarter or half a hectare, or even less, and to process the cane according to the availability of firewood, oxen, transportation, and labor. A man might thus earn about 100 or 200 pesos by several days of hard work, but most of this money he will use to pay old debts to stores, to the people who buy the raw sugar and who advanced him some money, or to the laborers who helped him. But even if he should harvest one or more hectares, the gain, distributed over six months, is a relatively small one.

Cane-growing is principally an activity of the lomeros, who own fifty of the seventy mills. However, there is a steady decline of this crop, owing in part to the increasing scarcity of firewood and partly to the tendency to convert cane fields into coffee plantations. It would be impossible to calculate the total raw sugar production of the valley, as the sale is not monopolized. Individual buyers from the neighboring towns or villages frequently travel to the sugar mills, and the owners of the latter often travel to other villages to sell their produce.

DOMESTIC ANIMALS

There are about 1,000 head of cattle in the Corregimiento, practically all owned by placeros. When speaking with the owners, one gets the impression that there is a thriving livestock industry in the valley, as there is much talk about pastures, cattle ranches (*hatos*), imported grasses, and cattle prices, but in reality most of this display is merely to impress the listener, to gain prestige for the owner. The very mixed-breed *criollo* cattle are of inferior quality, undernourished and lean, poor milkers, and have tough meat, but they are frugal and relatively parasite-resistant. The poor pastures over which the cows are left to roam are quite inadequate for developing healthy and productive herds. Cows have to wander daily about 10 kilometers to find sufficient fodder. If people see these cattle wandering far distances in search of food, they will say that the cows 'like to walk' (*les gusta caminar*). There are no cattle dips, and salt is given only rarely. Although there are no warble flies, ticks are abundant, and the cattle seem to suffer greatly from them. Very little care is taken of herds or individual animals. The owner might have a look at his cattle a few times a month, but otherwise the cows are left to graze and wander about, with neither corral nor stable. Apart from their prestige value, cattle are bred mainly for beef for local consumption. No cheese or butter is made, and milk is rarely available. Hides are staked and sun-dried, and are sold for 4 or 5 pesos each to a local storekeeper, who resells them at a good profit in the lowlands, where they are tanned. The following cattle prices were given for 1953.

cows	150 to 200 pesos
calves 1 year	45 to 50
bullocks, 2 years	75 to 80

heifers, 1 years	120 to 130 pesos
oxen	150 to 200
pack oxen	200 to 250
breeding bulls	over 500

About six months in good pasture are necessary to fatten a cow, but all pastures in the Corregimiento are of very poor quality. The coarse, short native grasses, such as *pasto de cerro, Guayacana,* and *Cortadora,* which cover the slopes, are inadequate for cattle and only the *Granadillo* grass, which grows during the rainy season in some parts, is of a slightly better quality. New forage crops are still rare but are being introduced gradually. *Pará (Panicum barbinode), Guinéa* or *India (Panicum maximum),* and *Yaraguá* or *Faraguá,* the African molasses grass (*Melinos minutiflora*) are now grown by some of the cattle-owners, and the latter, which is prolific, may eventually put a check to erosion. However, as rotational grazing is not practiced, these newly introduced grasses do not yet thrive well. Furthermore, the *Yaraguá* has one serious disadvantage: its long trailing culms form a thick carpet that burns easily when dry and makes the destructive grass fires of the dry season practically uncontrollable.

Sometimes the owner of cattle will give his entire output of milk in exchange for the right to graze another person's pastures. A frequent arrangement is the following: The owner of one or more cows turns them over to another person, who sees to it that they are well-fed and who receives in exchange for his care half of the offspring born during the next two years, or a third of the offspring and all the milk.

Veterinary knowledge is very limited. *Carbón,* a disease characterized by fever and diarrhea, killed many cattle some ten years ago. Hoof-and-mouth disease (*aftosa*) does not seem to have reached the village, but *huequera,* an endemic disease which destroys the horns, is common. To cure it the points are cut off, the interior is filled with salt, and wooden pegs are driven into the holes.

Oxen are of great importance as pack animals. On the steep slippery mountain trails they are much more sure-footed than mules, and, being cloven-footed, they are more steady when walking through deep mud. Much of the raw sugar and heavy root crops are transported by oxen.

The small *roza* owners are deeply worried about the increase of loose livestock. There exists a government decree according to which only the grassy plains below the village are to be used as grazing lands, while the hillsides are reserved for agriculture; but as the placeros, who are the cattle-owners, hold all the key posts in the local administration, this decree is ignored, and cattle are allowed to roam anywhere in the entire valley. Loose cattle cause considerable damage to cultivated fields, but the small landholders are helpless. At the same time, the molasses grass planted by the cattlemen is invading the agricultural plots, stifling the growth of all food plants. Many of the poorer people believe quite seriously that the cattle-owners, backed secretly by the government, are preparing a kind of plot 'to kill the poor', and to displace them from their land, which then would be used exclusively for livestock. There can be no doubt that cattle-raising and the increase of pasture-land represent a serious menace to the small *rozas*, but aspects of prestige behavior also play an important part in this development. Cattle-breeding, like coffee-growing, is considered to be 'Spanish' and 'civilized', as opposed to farming, which is 'Indian'. There is clearly a tendency toward an increasing development of cattle-raising and cash crops, not so much for the immediate benefit of the owner as for prestige reasons—i.e., to earn 'respect' by demonstrating one's 'progressiveness' and 'civilization'.

Some thirty mules and horses, most of them owned by placeros, are used for riding and for transporting loads. High-backed Spanish saddles and long, metal, shoe-shaped stirrups are the rule. Occasionally a horse has to be 'broken in', and in the lowlands there are several well-known *amansadores* (tamers) who will 'break' a horse for a small fee, in five to ten days. When not in use, horses and mules are left to graze with the cattle.

The most important domestic animal for the average villager is the burro; some two hundred are owned in Aritama. Their upkeep and care do not represent any cost, but at the same time they are the most efficient carriers of heavy burdens. Provided with a wooden pack saddle, they carry their owner to the fields and return heavily loaded to the village. Even well-to-do placeros will ride a burro.

There are some three hundred pigs in the village, most families owning one or two. Four breeds are distinguished: *puerco largo* ('long pig'), a large gray animal with excellent meat; *polanchino*, a big, heavy animal with large ears; *choncho*, a short, thick-set breed; and *guango*, a breed with a thick, turned-up snout. The first two are considered to be the best breeds. The *puerco largo* is said to be the original breed brought by the Spaniards, whereas the others are said to be of recent introduction. They all produce litters of eight to ten piglets a year. As a rule, practically no food is given to them; instead they live on garbage. But sometimes a pig is fattened 'on the halves' (*al partir*), i.e., the owner turns it over to another person who fattens it and receives in return half of the yearly litter. Boars are sometimes castrated. The following prices were quoted for 1953: piglets, 10 pesos; hogs, according to size, 80 to 100 pesos. An average pig yields about 50 pounds of meat and bones, which are sold together, and 25 gallons of fat, one gallon selling at 3·60 pesos. Hog cholera, which appears occasionally, is cured with sulfa tablets. Men never take care of pigs; they are usually looked after by children. Pigs are fattened during the avocado harvest and slaughtered when it is over in September. However, all during the year pigs are butchered occasionally.

There are a few goats, sheep, chickens, and ducks in the village, but they are considered to be 'poor man's livestock' (*cría de pobres*), and a person who does not also own some cattle and mules will not keep such small animals lest he be identified with the poorest class of people. Eggs are hardly ever eaten by those who own the chickens but are sold to the stores, where the placero families buy them. Few people of the village eat fowl, but hens or chickens are sold during fiesta times, when visitors to the village may buy them. There are no henhouses or chicken-coops, the birds roosting on trees in the backyards.

Small native bees (*avispas*) are kept by some people, in hives made of large Lagenaria gourds, provided with a small, square, lateral opening that is covered with a piece of gourd shell stuck on with wax. To start a hive, the bees' nests are dug out of the ground or cut out of a tree trunk, and an *hijo*, i.e., a piece of honeycomb, is placed in the gourd. Several varieties of bees are distinguished: *Angelita*, *Negrita*, *Rongói*, and *Míngana* (or *Carga-Barro*). All except the *Negrita* are stingless. *Rongói* and *Míngana* bees live underground, although the latter sometimes make their nests in hollow trees. The best honey is produced by *Negrita* bees. When the weight of the gourd indicates that honey is plentiful, the honeycombs are taken out through the lateral opening and the honey is squeezed out by hand. The black wax is pounded between stones, washed, and used to impermeabilize ropes. Honey is used mainly as a medicine. During the last decades of the nineteenth century, honey was used to prepare a certain ceremonial food of sweetened black beans, but because new immigrants mocked the people for it, saying that this was an Indian superstition, the custom was discontinued.

Lean and frightened mongrel dogs are numerous. Most are kept as watchdogs and as such are of considerable value, but they are beaten and mistreated every hour of the day. It is curious to note that there are practically no cats in the village. The two or three cats we saw had no owners and, should they be caught, they would be stoned to death. People hate and fear cats in Aritama.

HUNTING AND FISHING

There is very little game in the valley and few people hunt it. As most shotguns were confiscated long ago by the authorities, hunting is done mostly with dogs, and once the game is brought to bay it is killed with a machete or a stone. Sometimes deer are hunted, and paca, a little rodent which is smoked out of its cave.

Iguanas, large, fierce-looking lizards, are hunted during the dry season and every year many hundreds of them are brought to the village for sale. These animals are hunted along the larger streams of the lowlands, and small groups of men and boys will spend three or four days on such excursions, bringing back the catch on their burros. In order to bring back the animals alive, which preserves them fresh for selling, their hindlegs are broken and a steel pin is inserted in the brain, between the eyes. The mouth is sewed up with needle and thread, for these animals will bite. In this defenseless state they can be kept for days. The catch is divided into equal parts and each man sells his iguanas from his house, at some 50 centavos apiece. The local authorities and the people of the Plaza barrio in general are very sensitive on the subject of the villagers eating iguanas, considering it a shame that such 'Indian' customs should still prevail. Occasionally the police inspector has even outlawed this food and has fined any hunter or consumer caught, but, yearly, many hundreds of these animals are eaten during the dry season, when food is scarce, and even fear of loss of prestige has not been able to suppress this habit.

There is a small group of people, all of them lomeros, who organize occasional fishing excursions to the lowlands during the dry season. As the rivers carry little water then, the fish gather in pools, where they can be caught easily. Such expeditions, made up of ten or fifteen men accompanied by their women and children, carry with them food for several days and establish temporary camps on the riverbanks wherever they find a pool with fish. Some people own small casting nets (*atarrayas*), but most fishing is done with plant piscicides. The roots of the *barbasco* plant (*Tephrosia toxicaria*) are pounded on a flat rock with a wooden beetle, and the crushed mass is put into several wide-meshed fiber bags, which are then dipped by a rope into the water and moved up and down. A few hundred meters below the pool a weir (*troja*) is constructed of stones, or a wooden fencelike structure is built across the river, and the stunned or dead fish are collected from there into bags. The milky sap of the *ceiba* tree (*Ceiba pentandra*) is often used in the same way. Dynamite, whenever available, is preferred to anything else. Some men shoot fish with a bow and arrow, usually makeshift weapons manufactured on the spot, but some own good fishing arrows and harpoons acquired from the Indians. At night fish are occasionally killed with a machete. While one man holds a torch close to the water to attract the fish, another crouches on the riverbank, a hand with a machete submerged, and strikes horizontally as the fish pass. The catch is divided by the *cacique*, a man chosen by the others because of his experience and authority. The *cacique* himself does receive a larger share, and the distribution often causes quarrels between the members of the group, and few people care to be chosen *cacique de pesca* ('chief of the fishing'), as they are often abused and insulted for not distributing the catch in a manner satisfactory to all. Most of the fish are consumed immediately, but some are sun-dried and taken back to the village where they can be sold. It is of interest to note that only in cases of fishing expeditions are co-operative groups formed which go beyond kinship lines.

Occasionally the honey and wax of wild bees are collected, and the following varieties are mentioned: The *Mulata* bee is stingless and produces a whitish wax which is sold to cobblers in the lowlands, who use it to prepare their thread; the *Candelita*, the sting of which causes only slight swelling, also produces a valuable wax, but its honey is said to have an unpleasant odor. The *Mosca Real* is a large bee which stings fiercely, but is highly esteemed for its honey; while the *Comején* bee, a small, yellow insect which is also feared because of its sting, produces little honey.

HOME INDUSTRIES

Palm fibers provide the basis for an important home industry, that of hat-weaving. The raw material is found all over the countryside and is easily and rapidly processed and woven into bands, which are then sewed together with needle and thread. One hat per day is the average production of one person, generally a woman or child; but some people, by working more than five hours a day, can make one and a half or even two hats a day. Few men weave hats, but about 250 women and older children of all classes weave every day throughout the year. The total monthly output is about 6,000 hats, or 500 dozen. The local stores buy these hats any time they are offered for sale, at 50 centavos apiece, and sell them by the thousands in the lowland towns, from whence they are resold over wide areas. Hats are woven in many villages and hamlets in the vicinity, and Aritama is an important center of production.

It can well be said that the home manufacture of hats is the one stable basis of family economics. Coffee, sugar cane, cattle, or other crops or activities bring occasional income, but the humble straw hat, which represents a regular 50 centavos a day, is the foundation of life for the majority of the villagers. During the coffee-picking season, when women could earn considerably more money, as they would receive 1·60 pesos for every 4-gallon tin of berries—the average amount of one day's picking—most prefer to stay at home and earn less by weaving hats. Dresses are always paid for with hats and not in cash, the shopkeepers themselves insisting on this form of payment.

Until approximately twenty years ago most men also were actively engaged in weaving hats, but at present only the very poor will do so and even they will often try to hide their activity from strangers or from villagers of higher status. Men ceased to weave as the direct result of the establishment of a network of roads that connected the lowland

231

towns with each other and eventually brought Aritama into closer contact with urban life. Motor transportation, radio, and cinema rapidly transformed the attitudes of the lowland townsmen, and they began to ridicule the inhabitants of isolated rural villages like Aritama, referring to them as 'hat-weaving Indians'. This caused the men of Aritama to abandon, quite suddenly, the weaving of hats, an activity which from then on became a woman's task. Characteristically, when asked directly why they quit weaving, the men will answer that they had to work in their fields, or that because of the low prices 'it was not worthwhile' to weave; but sooner or later all will admit that they became ashamed to be seen weaving 'like any old Indian woman'.

ILLEGAL DISTILLING

There are some thirty or forty primitive distilleries (*alhambiques*) in the Corregimiento, and the rum (*chirrinche*) they produce is famous far beyond the limits of the valley for its quality. Although these stills are outlawed by the government, the home manufacture of rum is flourishing and the villagers take a quiet pride in their ability not only to produce a good quality of liquor but also to evade successfully the control of the government agents.

The process consists in boiling fermented raw sugar in a clay vessel on top of which another vessel has been placed in an inverted position, the latter being provided with a thin tube through which the distilled liquid flows into an additional container. Often the owner of a still is also the owner of a sugar-cane plantation, but sometimes the cane or the raw sugar are bought for the purpose. The so-called 'white cane' (*Caña Blanca*) is preferred as it is said that its juice will ferment in five or six days, whereas the other varieties of cane, especially all those cultivated in the lower portions of the valley, take up to fifteen or twenty days to ferment. One package of raw sugar weighing 25 pounds will produce from 3 to 4 gallons of liquor. About 250 pounds are used in each operation, making some 40 gallons, worth 120 pesos, gross, and bringing a net return of about 80 pesos. In theory, this would be a very profitable affair, but in practice there arise a great many problems. In the first place, the distilling of rum demands the co-operation of several people, quite often of two or three households. Firewood has to be cut and transported; the cane has to be processed; the raw sugar has to be boiled; and the whole process of distilling has to be carefully controlled. Sentinels have to be placed all around the spot, and a number of people have to be bribed lest they betray the operators. In the second place, once the liquor has begun to flow, the temptation to drink it is usually stronger than the need to sell it. Each time rum is distilled all the participants are likely to be intoxicated for days, and by the time every-

232

one is sober again there is little left for commercial purposes. However, there can be no doubt that, occasionally, a man who operates his still in secrecy and with the help of only a few people, can earn a tidy sum from the sale of rum to ready customers, especially in the lowland towns. A common accusation leveled by the lomeros at certain placero families is that they made their fortunes in this manner.

HOUSE CONSTRUCTION

There are a number of vacant lots (*solares*) in the village, where houses can be built, and on the periphery of the settlement there are still many more. The average price of a lot measuring 20 by 20 meters is about 100 pesos, but frequently the person who wants to build a house prefers to buy an old house and its site at some 200 pesos and tear it down, as he thus saves the labor of leveling the ground and is able to use the beams and posts of the old construction for the new one.

The problem of obtaining wood suitable for house construction has become very pressing in recent years. The increase in population, together with the desire to build larger houses, makes it actually very difficult to find good timber at reasonable prices. Enormous amounts of good wood have gone into fences or have been burned as fuel for boiling raw sugar, and, as no reforestation has been practiced, adequate building materials have become very scarce. Hardwood which will not rot or become infested by insects is found only at distances that make transportation of large timber quite impossible; so houses are often constructed of soft wood which rots easily. Long beams or posts are practically unobtainable today and any recent construction can be readily recognized by the many joints with which the larger beams are fitted together.

The size of houses is measured in *varas*, a measure equivalent to 80 centimeters, an average-size house being about 10 varas long. The cost of construction is about as follows:

Materials	25 main posts (*horcones*)	125·00 pesos
	7 tie- and cross-beams (*vigas*)	70·00
	40 rafters (*varas*)	80·00
	500 canes (*latas*)	50·00
	straw for thatching	130·00
	12 pounds of wire	7·20
	Total	462·20 pesos

Labor:	3 men, 4 days, to build the framework (*armar*)	12 man-days
	3 men, 2 days, to tie canes to rods (*enjaular*)	6
	3 men, 2 days, to tie canes to walls (*enjaular*)	6

3 men, 2 days, to thatch roof (*empajar*)	6
3 men, 4 days, to make mud walls (*embarrar*)	12
Total	42 man-days

At a daily wage of 2 pesos a man, plus food worth 1 peso for each laborer, the total cost is as follows:

Materials	462·20 pesos
Labor	123·00
Total	585·20 pesos

The same house with a roof of corrugated iron would cost about 100 pesos more. Instead of the horizontal roof rods, the forty-eight tiles, costing 384 pesos, are nailed to lath (twenty-four at 1 peso each), the total price going up to 675 pesos. Whitewashing, flooring, and the manufacture of doors and windows are, of course, additional expenses in both types of construction.

However, few people would build a house under these conditions. As a rule, the owner acquires the necessary materials in the course of months, or even of years, cutting a beam here and a post there, slowly assembling all the wood he might need. The cost of building materials is, therefore, rather to be measured in terms of time. The construction of the framework, the putting on of the roof, and the plastering of the mudwalls are carried out by communal labor, during which the owner of the house provides only food and drink. Some people who cannot afford an invitation to communal labor divide the process of construction over several weeks or months, building up the framework first and thatching the roof or building the walls whenever there is money and labor force available. In this manner the construction of a house might be a matter of years.

VI

FORMS OF DISTRIBUTION AND LABOR

COMMERCE AND CREDIT

THERE are seven general stores (*tiendas*) in the village, and in addition to these, a few people keep a small stock of articles of primary necessity in their homes for sale to neighbors. However, the stores, most of which are located in the Plaza barrio, are the main centers of all local commerce, and it is there that people buy and sell the manifold articles that are needed or produced day by day.

All stores are owned by placeros and occupy a room in the house where the owner's family lives. There is a wooden counter, behind which there are large shelves with merchandise, and some objects such as brooms, a basket with eggs, or a few ready-made children's clothes are suspended from the cross-beams. All *tiendas* are managed by their owners personally, assisted by their wives, children, or occasionally a trusted relative. They are open all day long, even on Sundays, and although after dark the door leading to the street will be locked, customers are served until the owner himself retires for the night.

All stores operate on a credit basis. All accept straw hats in payment, for the storekeepers are also the monopolists of all locally manufactured products. Credit is given only to 'free people' (*gente libre*), i.e., not to children or youths who still work for parents or relatives. Feeble-minded persons, epileptics, and non-residents are equally excluded from credit, but the latter might find a well-known resident to vouch for them. As a general rule, every client is responsible for payment of what he buys, and even a husband and wife are kept on two different accounts and cannot be held mutually responsible. Even if a couple should open credit at a store and declare their willingness to accept such mutual responsibility, the account will be kept under the woman's name and in this case it is she who will be held responsible by the store-owner for the payment of the purchases both make. The reason for this is that women, by weaving hats, are economically more stable than men, who depend on crops, trade, or hired labor. People often open accounts at several stores and do not show a marked preference for a certain establishment.

Only articles worth less than 45 centavos, such as a bottle of kerosene, a pound of rice, or a box of matches, are paid for in cash at most stores. Practically everything above the sum mentioned is paid in kind, be it in straw hats, coffee, or raw sugar. Occasionally, however, a store might insist on payment being made in cash, while other stores might accept maize, tobacco, or even livestock at fixed prices. Seasonal variations or the store-owner's recent personal experiences might influence this choice. The prices of all articles sold at the stores vary according to the form of payment: the lowest price is obtained by paying in cash, while a 10 to 20 per cent increase is the rule when paying in kind or buying on credit. When asked for the price of an article, the shopowner will always quote the credit price first, but will reduce it as soon as the customer states that he is willing to pay cash.

The following articles are never sold on credit: rice, fat, bread, refined sugar, kerosene, laxatives, and cigarettes. As a general rule food is not sold on credit except to a few close friends of the Plaza. Credit, however, is freely given for ready-made shirts and trousers, for women's and children's dresses, fabrics, shoes, machetes, kitchen utensils, medicines, cheap jewelry, and cosmetics. Practically everyone buys these articles on credit, and the shopowner will hardly ever fix a day for payment, it being understood that the debt will be paid approximately in a year's time, be it in small instalments or by full payment in cash or kind. To fix a certain term would be taken as a gross insult by the client, and a shopowner would dare to do so only with a person who is known by everyone to be a poor risk. Many debts are settled just before the fiesta season begins, because then the coffee harvest makes ready cash available, and people want to buy new clothes on newly opened credit. But there is no fixed rule. People pay whenever they can, and as the shopowners know in great detail the economic situation of every individual customer, they can always limit or extend their credit. Since all shopowners are placeros of high economic and social status, many of them occupying leading positions in the village, it is not difficult for them to oblige a reluctant debtor to pay up. If a person cannot pay in cash or kind, there are two other ways in which he can repay his debts: by offering to work for the shopowner or by turning over to him a child who, as the creditor's servant, pays with his work for the father's debts. These two forms of payment are frequently imposed by the local authorities, who condemn a child or an adult debtor to this kind of bondage, which is then well taken advantage of by the creditor. For example, when a man works for a shopowner in order to pay his debts, the daily wages are fixed at 10 or 20 per cent less than he would receive as a hired laborer. Non-fulfilment of the promise to pay a debt is a serious matter which is almost always brought before the police inspector (usually a shopowner himself), who then decides in which way the debtor will have to pay. Difficulties arise if the debtor is a placero of high status, but this is seldom known to happen. Should a person owe several stores and have difficulties in paying, the creditors never combine their actions against him, but each one separately presents the matter to the authorities, asking for fulfilment of obligations.

The credit system causes much anxiety and hostility in the village, for practically all lomeros are in debt to the shopowners, usually on account of new clothes. When accepting payment of debts in straw hats, the creditors will always find fault with the article, criticizing its size or workmanship in order to fix the lowest possible price for it. However, they will not accept a customer's complaint about their own merchandise, even if it should be found faulty or damaged. To ask for a rebate when purchasing something is common practice and all commercial transactions take this into account, but prices are reduced only if the shopowner has a personal interest in satisfying a client, whereas he is likely to reply rather rudely to such a suggestion if made by someone he does not value particularly. The poorer people and the lomeros in general are, therefore, very timid when making a purchase and hardly ever ask for a rebate, for fear of being rebuked.

A detailed inventory shows that the total value of the merchandise owned by an average village store is about 4,000 pesos. Approximately 70 per cent of this value consists of articles of clothing: drill or cotton fabrics, silk, ready-made shirts and trousers, women's underwear, children's clothes, shoes, belts, hats, etc. About 5 per cent consists of medicines. The remaining 25 per cent includes the many articles of daily consumption such as oil, fat, salt, rice, matches, cheese, cutlery, soap, yarn, and miscellaneous items like flashlight batteries and aluminum vessels. With the exception of machetes and flashlights, which are all made in the United States, all other articles are of Colombian manufacture. Several times a year the shopowners travel to the lowland towns, where they buy their goods and also sell the products they have received in payment at their stores.

A survey of the stores made in the month of October, i.e., just before the principal coffee harvest, showed that each store opened credit accounts for about 1,000 to 3,000 pesos, apart from what the debtors had already paid in the course of the year. This sum, or at least a large fraction of it, was expected by the shopowners to be paid in November and December with the cash earned by hired labor during the picking season, or by the owners of small plantations by the sale of their coffee. However, certain differences between individual stores could also be observed with reference to the credit system. Tables 29 and 30 show two extreme cases, each covering thirty days in October.

TABLE 29

STORE A

Sales Paid in			Debts Paid in				
Cash	*Hats*	*Credit*	*Cash*	*Hats*	*Coffee*	*Sugar*	*Labor*
254·80	649·30	907·70	843·30	529·00	126·00	90·00	176·50
Total sales: 1,811·80			Total debts paid: 1,764·80 Unpaid: 885·00				

TABLE 30

STORE B

Sales Paid in			Debts Paid in				
Cash	*Hats*	*Credit*	*Cash*	*Hats*	*Coffee*	*Sugar*	*Labor*
691·00	10·90	0·35	13·00	—	—	20·00	24·50
Total sales: 702.25			Total debts paid: 57.50 Unpaid: 2,995·75				

Store A had given ample credit to his customers and had accepted a large number of straw hats in payment. The store, being known to buy these as well as coffee and raw sugar at any time of the year and at good prices, was patronized by many people from the Loma who paid a large part of their current debts in cash they earned as hired laborers. They were interested in conserving their credit and in being able to sell their own goods at any convenient time. Store B, on the other hand, had been catering mainly to the people of the Plaza and opened credit for them. However, after its customers had accumulated a large amount of debts, mainly for clothes, it stopped all credit again and during the month of October accepted only cash. Although the customers still owed almost 3,000 pesos, a relatively large sum, the shopowner trusted that he would be repaid by the end of the year from the produce of the coffee harvest, as it eventually happened.

Seen within the social context of the village, the function of the stores is, strictly, an economic one. They never are places where people might gather for an exchange of gossip and information. There are no benches or seats for the customers, and clients are not encouraged to stay for a chat. The owner's personal friends or a distinguished visitor to the village might be invited to an adjoining room, but otherwise the shopowner is neither interested in carrying on conversations with his clients nor in spending more time than necessary in serving them. Men rarely go to a store except to sell their coffee or raw sugar. Most shopping is done by women and children, who are more interested in chat-

1. Scattered houses huddle in deep, boulder-strewn mountainfolds.

2. Silent and empty streets climb over the rocky hills. The people of the Loma barrio prefer to live behind closed doors.

3. A village street; in the right foreground the house of a prominent landowner of the Plaza.

4. In the Loma barrio many women live alone
with their children, separated from their husbands.

5. This dancer carrying a bird-mask and a palm-
leaf dress impersonates one of the eagles of
St. John the Baptist during the *Corpus* fiesta.

6. When the weather is fair a rickety truck provides a doubtful means of transportation between the village and the neighboring towns.

7. A house lot is cleared by communal labor. Huge boulders have to be moved with levers.

8. A long wooden fence divides the two barrios of the village. It separates two ways of life as well: the "Spaniards" and the "Indians."

9. A fresh grave is being covered with heavy stones so the dangerous spirit may not rise again.

10. Schoolchildren carry an image of the Virgin in solemn procession led

11. Old women of native Indian stock still wear the aboriginal garment of rough white cotton cloth. They are a thorn in the eye of the more progressive-minded villagers.

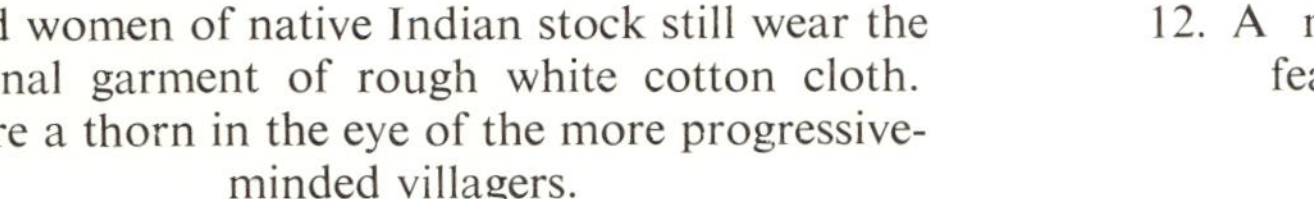

12. A man from the Loma barrio. His Indian features mirror distrust and resignation.

13. Baseball cap and T-shirt form the Sunday
best of youngsters in the Plaza barrio.

14. Young ladies from the Plaza barrio still
wear the Spanish mantilla.

ting with people they meet on their way than in exposing themselves to the critical eye of the store-owners, who outside of his small circle of well-to do placeros, is generally avoided because many people fear that he might make some unpleasant remark about their credit.

Behind the shopowner's back there is, of course, a great deal of gossip and criticism, which frequently takes the form of magical aggression. As a matter of fact, the store-owners are disliked by all lomeros, and any form of dishonesty and greed is readily attributed to them. As a number of shopowners occupy official positions in the local administration, many lomeros believe that the stores are somehow connected with the government, and that the merchants are really government agents trying to 'exploit the poor'. 'We are all slaves of the government's stores' is an expression often heard when people discuss their debts. There is, of course, no connection whatsoever between the authorities and the stores, which are all private enterprises, but many people tend to identify the two.

Some of the lomeros who produce coffee, raw sugar or livestock occasionally sell their products in the neighboring villages, where they can obtain better prices, but only those who have no or few debts at stores can do this. Besides, the problem of transportation has to be taken into account. As the trucks and mule teams are also owned by placeros, the latter can always exercise a certain control over these sales outside of the village. The credit system and the ensuing continuous indebtedness thus form a vicious cycle from which it is difficult to escape. Most debts are incurred for clothes, especially for those that are acquired for prestige reasons. This factor, however, is so powerful in the local culture that the individual often prefers to be in debt as long as he can keep up the appearance of being 'civilized'.

HOUSEHOLD BUDGETS

Standards of wealth and the difference between 'rich' and 'poor' are mainly dependent upon the ownership of assets that produce money. A man who owns a shop or who has cattle, sugar mills, or coffee plantations is considered rich, whereas the poor have hardly more than their *roza*, some coffee trees, and some sugar cane. Land- or house-ownership in themselves are not criteria of wealth; it depends on what grows on the land and to what use the house is put. Even a man with large and fertile fields will be considered as much 'poorer' than one who owns a few hectares of coffee or cane, or one who has ten head of cattle. It is the cash crop Fond the livestock, and the prestige associated with them, that determine the difference between wealth and poverty, not the steady and bountiful supply a large subsistence plot might provide for its owner.

Average individual landownership and use, according to barrio, can be represented as in Table 31.

TABLE 31

Use	*Lomeros*	*Placeros*
Roza	2·0 hectares	2·0 hectares
Coffee	2·0	5·0
Sugar cane	1·5	2·0
Various crops	1·0	1·5
Pastures	1·5	24·0
Total average	8·0 hectares	34·5 hectares

As can be seen readily, the average placero owns more than twice as many coffee trees as the average lomero. Practically all pastures are in the hands of the members of the Plaza barrio. As a matter of fact, 80 per cent of all the cattle in the Corregimiento is owned by placeros. It is necessary to keep this in mind when speaking of individual household budgets.

The following data are given here as representative samples of income and expenditures of two families: A, a lomero family, and B, a family of the Plaza barrio.

The average weekly expenditures of Family A, which consists of the father, mother, an eighteen-year-old son, and four children between five and eight years of age, are as follows:

	Pesos
raw sugar	0·35
coffee	0·75
manioc	0·50
meat or cheese	1·80
salt	0·10
kerosene	0·10
soap	0·15
matches	0·05
yarn	0·25
palm fibers	0·80
Total	4·85

All these articles had to be paid for in cash that was obtained by the sale of straw hats the family was weaving. The mother and the children produced eleven hats weekly. At 0·45 centavos a hat, the total sum obtained was 4·95 pesos a week. The father owns a small *roza* where he grows the basic staple foods, and in his backyard he also has some kitchen crops and a small plot planted with tobacco. In this way, survival is insured at a minimum cost of about 20 pesos a month for the entire family. All other expenditures were paid for with money gained in wage labor, the sale of tobacco leaves, laundering, and occasional small sums that were obtained at irregular intervals.

The yearly expenditures of the father were as follows:

	Pesos
1 pair of trousers	12·00
1 shirt	6·50
2 pairs of sandals	3·00
1 straw hat	1·20
6 haircuts	1·80
Total	24·50

These expenses were paid by him by the sale, for 15 pesos, of a small plot in the backyard and the rest by selling his tobacco crop.

The mother's expenses during the same year were:

	Pesos
2 dresses	25·00
1 pair of sandals	1·50
1 pair of slippers	2·00
1 kerosene lamp	4·00
2 spoons	1·00
2 small wooden seats	3·50
church contribution	2·00
pulling of tooth	0·80
medicines	2·50
Total	42·30

To this sum must be added the expenditures for the children, for which the mother was also responsible:

	Pesos
4 dresses for the girls	30·00
2 suits for the boy	9·00
2 pairs of sandals	2·40
Total	41·40

Part of the total amount of 83·70 pesos was paid by for the mother with the money she learned laundering, at about 6 pesos a month. At year's end she still owed some 20 pesos to the store.

The eighteen-year-old son's expenditures for clothes during the same year were:

	Pesos
1 pair of trousers	15·00
1 shirt	12·00
1 undershirt	1·40
1 pair of socks	2·00
1 pair of shoes	23·00
1 straw hat	1·20
Total	54·60

Of this sum he paid 15 pesos in cash he had saved, and 22 pesos in cash that he had earned as a laborer at a sugar mill, still owing 17 pesos at year's end to the store. Additional household expenses were the following:

	Pesos
200 pounds of barbed wire to fence father's yard	54·00
1½ pounds of iron clamps for same	1·20
1 long machete for personal use	11·00
1 short machete for personal use	5·00
2 pounds insecticide for father's yard	4·00
gift for little brother (suit)	4·50
trip to the next town to buy clothes	2·00
8 haircuts	4·00
10 packs of cigarettes	3·50
alchohol, entertainments, etc	20·00
Total	109·00

This sum he paid with the sale of some raw sugar he had received in exchange for his work at his paternal uncle's sugar mill.

Total expenditures for the entire family (three adults and four children) were about 500 pesos a year, a sum which represents about forty days of wage labor, at 2·50 pesos a day. Although both father and son were offered work on several occasions during the year, at times when they had nothing to do, both declined and contented themselves with earning just enough money to pay for the expenditures listed above.

Family B consists of the father, mother, and three children between two and ten years of age. The father is a small merchant but owns a *roza* where he grows several garden crops and some coffee. Weekly expenditures of the family were:

	Pesos
bread	1·20
eggs	2·60
fowl	3·00
meat or cheese	12·20
spaghetti	0·30

	Pesos
milk	3·80
potatoes	0·40
maize	1·50
rice	1·25
fat	1·65
cabbage	0·10
tomatoes	0·45
onions	0·80
raw sugar	0·50
sugar	0·53
salt	0·10
condiments	0·30
sweets	0·65
Total	31·83

The monthly expenses of some 125 pesos for food alone were paid for in cash obtained through the sale of coffee and the profit made on the store. There was an additional expense of 1·80 pesos for kerosene, 2 pesos for firewood, and 0·50 centavo for soap, each week.

The father's expenditure for clothes, during the whole year, were:

	Pesos
1 suit of white khaki	60·00
1 pair of trousers	8·00
3 shirts	22·00
1 pair of shoes	25·00
1 hat	15·00
Total	130·000

Besides, there were the following expenses, in the course of the year:

	Pesos
trips to the next town	120·00
church contribution	5·00
beer and rum	235·00
newspapers	3·00
musicians and dances	40·00
cigarettes	25·00
haircuts	12·00
taxes paid on store	24·00
taxes paid on land	10·80
postage	5·00
agricultural tools	15·00
concrete	45·00
whitewashing house	10·00

	Pesos
400 pounds barbed wire	108·00
putting up fence	50·00
cleaning pastures	150·00
harvesting coffee	15·00
purchase of livestock	240·00
fodder for cattle	45·00
medicines	30·00
Total	1,187·80

The mother's yearly expenses were as follows, including expenditures for children and servants:

	Pesos
1 servant girl	180·00
3 silk dresses	76·00
4 cotton dresses	52·00
1 pair of shoes	12·00
1 pair of slippers	6·00
6 children's dresses	50·00
4 pairs of sandals	4·80
kitchenware	30·00
medicines for children	50·00
pulling of tooth	1·00
cosmetics	4·00
toilet articles	5·00
soap for kitchen	3·00
gifts to friends	10·00
extras	5·00
Total	488·80

The total yearly budget of this family reaches over 3,000 pesos, i.e., about six times the amount needed by Family A.

CORREGIMIENTO AND CHURCH FINANCES

The small expenses caused by the local administration are paid for with funds obtained from a variety of taxes and contributions. The employees and their respective salaries are the following: the Corregidor (or police inspector), 150 pesos monthly; the secretary (*Secretario*), 70 pesos; and the treasurer (*Sub-Tesorero*), 50 pesos monthly. These salaries are paid with funds raised by taxing, and any excess income is to be sent to the treasury of the municipality. This, however, happens only rarely and the few pesos that occasionally remain after all salaries are paid are rather spent on office equipment or on any repairs the inspector's office might need. The schoolteachers are paid by the municipality, the same as the policemen, and thus do not represent any expense to the local administration.

The principal income is represented by fines (*multas*). These are imposed by the police inspector in cases of physical aggression such as a drunken fight or wife-beating. Each participant is fined about 10 pesos or maybe 15, and if a larger group was engaged in a fistfight, as much as 100 pesos might be collected. The doings of one small neighboring hamlet, the inhabitants of which are rather hot-tempered, are watched hopefully every time cash is low, and eventually a policeman is sent there to see if he can fine someone. Very often people are not fined immediately for an aggressive act but are made to pay a security (*fianza*) if they promise to abstain from further trouble. These securities, however, are not returned to the person should he restrain his behavior from then on.

The slaughter of cattle is subject to two taxes. A permit has to be obtained, and after payment of 12·50 pesos for each animal, a receipt is given, without which the owner could not sell the hide. For pigs only 3 pesos are charged. The price paid for butchering cattle includes 10 pesos for the right to use the slaughterhouse and its small corral-like inclosure (*coso*), and represents the 'slaughterhouse fee' (*derecho de matadero*). The additional 2·50 pesos are for the permit to kill the cattle (*derecho de desgüelle*). Large stores (*pulperías*) pay a tax of 10 to 15 pesos each a month. On small-scale domestic sales of miscellaneous merchandise (*tiendas*) from 2 to 5 pesos are paid. Licenses (*patentes*) and permits (*placas*) are minor categories of sales taxes on occasional sales and are about 2 pesos a month each. One who charges for cutting hair is classified as a specialist barber and has to pay a fee (*derecho de peluquería*). Although there are only two such 'specialists' in the village for some complicated administrative reason they are grouped into three categories (*primera, segunda, tercera clase*) and pay 2·20, 1·50, or 1 peso, respectively, every month, one of them alternating between second and third class. Traveling salesmen (*cacharreros*) have to pay a tax of 1 or 2 pesos a day for the right to display and sell their wares from house to house. They come mainly during the fiesta season, but even then there are few.

All public dances or entertainments, for which the organizers charge small entrance fees, are assessed a tax. Distinction is made between a *cumbia* and a *gaita*, the former being a dance accompanied with an accordion or string instruments, while the latter's accompaniment is played on two flutes. The tax is about 2 pesos. The same sum is charged for organizing a cockfight (*derecho de gallera*). Another category of entertainment tax is called simply 'games' (*juegos*) and includes all sorts of games which are brought to the village during fiestas. Generally they consist of a roulette-like device, a pin-and-ring game, or similar entertainments. The tax is 2 pesos a day. Some rarely occurring items are the 1·50-peso charged on a charity bazaar, the 1·60-peso tax on the slaughter of a goat, or the security asked of a person to guarantee the fulfilment of a labor contract.

An average month (July) gave the following balance:

	Pesos
fines (10)	89·00
slaughterhouse (13)	25·00
securities (7)	16·00
dance music (3)	6·00
Total	136·00

A detailed study of the financial situation of the Corregimiento over the last twenty years did not reveal any significant changes, except that since 1950 the number and amounts of fines have been greatly increased. In 1952, of a total income of 2,007 pesos for one year, 65·50 pesos were sent to the municipal treasury, while the remainder was spent on salaries and occasional expenses.

Although many people in both sections of the village claim that the Church is 'abusing' the generosity of the poor and is charging too much in contributions and for fees, the reality is quite different. During the month of January, when there was a priest in the village, the parish had the following income:

	Pesos
baptismal fees (7)	2·10
marriages (3)	1·50
fees for copies of documents	2·55
Total	6·15

As there were no other funds, the priest paid 18 pesos for oil and candles out of his own pocket. In May, i.e., during the main fiesta season, the income of the parish was as follows:

	Pesos
alms collected at Mass	3·15
alms collected during Procession	3·20
salves sung during Procession	14·00
two Masses	8·00
baptismal fees	13·20
Total	41·55

The priest had to work his own little vegetable garden to make ends meet, and often enough had only one meal a day.

PATTERNS OF FOOD EXCHANGE

Because food is valued so highly in Aritama, it represents the ideal gift. As such it represents a sacrifice, a very effective way of appeasing people and supernatural beings. To withhold food is a serious offense, whereas to offer food is a way of showing that the giver is well-meaning and harmless. Food exchange becomes, therefore, a major means of social control.

Food of one's own is never deliberately destroyed unless an individual wishes to express hostility within the household, and in this case the destruction is considered to be justified. To destroy other people's food, directly or through sorcery, is always a serious crime. Aggressiveness against the food supply of others is emphatically condemned, but it is practiced secretly, usually through magic. However, this form of aggression occurs only outside a certain circle of individuals united by kinship ties, while within the kin there exists the institution of gift exchange, which expresses cohesion and co-operation.

Every member of the community is obliged to make gifts of food at certain intervals to certain other members, who are obliged to make similar gifts in return. This mutual obligation is claimed to be purely a matter of friendship and well-meaning toward one's fellow men and is not said to have any economic motivation, but it is quite evident that this is a very important economic institution. The frequency with which these gifts are made varies between daily and monthly exchanges, but as a general rule they are made every second or third day. The quality of the foodstuffs depends upon their availability, but all foods are considered equally desirable and acceptable. The quantity of the gift has to correspond to the economic position of the giver, i.e., a poor man may return a small amount in acknowledgment of a larger amount received, without being criticized for doing so.

We have detailed data on this pattern of food exchange in a section of the Loma barrio composed of sixteen households. These data, taken during a thirty-day period, are shown in Table 32. Each individual gives to certain persons and receives gifts from them in turn. The gifts consist either of raw fruits or cooked dishes.

From this tabulation it can be seen, in the first place, that the number of recipients varies considerably, the highest being 13 and 3 the lowest. Only one individual does not receive any food. In the second place it is evident that the number of individual recipients does not always correspond to the number of distributions received. There are only four cases in which the individual gives to the same number of people as give to him. In six cases the individual receives from more persons than he gives to, and in another six cases the contrary is true. Overall, the

TABLE 32

Giver	Gives to	Receives from	Distribu-tions made	Distribu-tions re-ceived	Distributions of			
					Raw		Cooked	
					Made	Rec.	Made	Rec.
1. F–40	5	10	73	93	—	58	73	35
2. F–35	4	5	128	53	30	33	98	20
3. F–24	6	6	130	104	40	36	90	68
4. M–56	4	1	52	4	36	4	16	—
5. F–19	—	2	—	34	—	—	—	34
6. M–65	5	4	44	120	44	—	—	120
7. F–50	13	13	264	185	38	23	226	162
8. M–25	12	2	30	20	30	—	—	20
9. F–17	6	6	144	110	4	23	140	90
10. F–30	9	6	62	86	28	26	34	60
11. F–30	4	6	40	35	2	31	38	4
12. M–28	4	3	48	84	18	24	30	60
13. F–35	7	7	156	138	16	18	140	120
14. F–55	7	9	212	194	32	92	180	102
15. F–25	3	2	54	60	24	—	30	60
16. F–30	5	9	128	150	8	48	120	102
Total	94	91	1,563	1,470	350	413	1,215	1,057

NOTE: M = male; F = female; the numbers to the right indicate the age.

number of distributors almost equals the number of recipients, there existing only a deficit of three individuals who did not reciprocate.

In the third and fourth columns, which show the number of gifts made and received monthly, we observe that the number of gifts made varies from 30 to 264. In seven cases people gave more than 100 gifts a month, and in another seven cases more than 100 were received, while in six cases mentioned above the numbers are equal. In all these cases we deal with individuals whose exchange was reciprocated in total, in that they received from exactly as many people as they themselves gave to. In the total numbers a difference of 93 gifts that were not returned is observed, corresponding to three individuals who did not return gifts they had received.

In columns five and six, which list the number of raw foods given or received, in eight cases a greater number of people who gave raw food, and in another eight cases a smaller number of people who received raw food, is observed. As to the total number of monthly distributions made by each individual, it varies from 2 to 44, while receipt of gifts varies from 4 to 92. This is the only case in which the number of receipts is higher than the number of gifts (in spite of three individuals not having taken part), there being an excess of 63 monthly receipts for each of the sixteen individuals in every month.

Finally, we see in columns seven and eight that the largest numerical disproportion exists between the number of distributions and receptions of cooked food. The total difference of 158 cases corresponds approximately to an individual loss of ten distributions a month. There are ten cases in which more gifts of cooked food are given than received.

This seems to indicate that the patterns of food distribution and exchange have in many details an individual character and do not function as a rigid set of patterns but rather tend to be adapted to personal situations. It can only be stated that, as a general rule, the individual has to give away monthly a larger amount of cooked food than he receives but that in turn he receives a larger amount of raw food than he gives away to others. It must be pointed out here that a gift of raw food is generally more substantial than one of cooked food, the latter being usually a single portion, whereas the former often represents several portions.

Some additional details of the distribution of raw and cooked foods are given in Table 33. In the first column we observe the frequency of these distributions and in the following the number of cases of each type.

TABLE 33

Distributions	Raw	Cooked
Daily	3	36
Thrice a week	6	6
Twice a week	10	5
Weekly	23	5
Twice a month	4	1
Monthly	8	1

We can see quite clearly that raw food is distributed on a weekly basis, whereas cooked food is distributed daily. Here it has to be pointed out that gifts of raw food, although larger than gifts of cooked food, are not stored by the recipient but are partly consumed immediately, and partly redistributed to others. Raw food is also often distributed twice a week.

The pattern of distribution, from the point of view of gifts received in exchange for distributions made, is given in Table 34.

TABLE 34

Receipts	Raw	Cooked
Daily	4	32
Thrice a week	7	4
Twice a week	14	3
Weekly	20	6
Twice a month	6	—
Monthly	5	1

This seems to indicate that the daily distribution of cooked food, and the weekly distribution of raw food, are compensated in the same manner, although in both cases a small deficit for the givers can be observed, who, however, make a certain gain in the distribution of raw food. As a matter of fact, this gain represents an incentive because it is a utility even if one takes into account the expense of labor, firewood, etc., in converting the raw food a into cooked dish.

It must be pointed out here that we do not try to find a balance or an individual economic disequilibrium. We have recorded only the number of actual transactions and their frequency, but not the weight of the exchanged food or its commercial value. And even if we knew that a certain individual gave three green plantains and received for them one cooked manioc tuber, this would not give us a precise scale, because the real value depends upon the size of the tuber or fruit, its variety, and its commercial cost, which varies according to season and availability.

We have, furthermore, compared givers and recipients in their social relationships. In order to do this we have established categories for all individuals who take part in the institution of food exchange described in Table 32.

A = exchange between mother and sons and/or daughters
B = exchange between father and sons and/or daughters
C = exchange between siblings
D = exchange between cousins (cross and parallel, maternal or paternal)
E = exchange between nephews and nieces, maternal or paternal uncles and aunts, and their collateral relatives
F = exchange between Ego and sons and daughters of brothers and sisters, or of parallel or cross-cousins (maternal or paternal)
G = exchange between Ego and in-laws
H = exchange between Ego and ceremonial kin
I = exchange between Ego and non-kin neighbors

TABLE 35

Relationship	Number of Exchanges	Per Cent
A	11	17·44
B	4	6·45
C	10	16·00
D	5	8·00
E	6	9·63
F	6	9·63
G	12	19·36
H	4	6·45
I	4	6·45

As we can see, the most important exchange seems to exist between a person and his in-laws, followed by exchange between mother and children and by exchange between siblings. All other relationships are considerably less important. However, it must be kept in mind that this tabulation refers to the *existence* of a food exchange in certain combinations of individuals and does not show individual reciprocity in the exchange pattern. For example, in relationship A mothers and sons (or daughters) receive food in 20 cases and return food, within the same relationship, in 25 cases, while in relationship G food is given to only seven in-laws, being received from ten in-laws. Accordingly, the food exchange between mother and children is more frequent than the one between a person and his in-laws. On the other hand, food exchange between siblings is very frequent too, 27 gifts being made and 24 being received.

We shall now examine briefly this exchange pattern within its cultural context. All families represented by the sixteen individuals who exchange food own fields, but these are distant from the village. People tend to go to these plots as rarely as possible in order to save work, and when they do go they bring back the maximum amount of food they or their burros can carry. These fruits, however, are not stored, and there are no storage facilities or granaries in the houses, a fact which is due to the general opinion that the storing of food is an antisocial practice. The mere fact of a person's having more food in the house than the family can possibly consume at the moment would be interpreted as a hostile attitude, and the individual would see himself obliged to give away the surplus to people who possibly would not return the gifts. In order to avoid such 'loss' of gifts, all surplus raw food is distributed as soon as it is brought from the fields, before the obligation arises to make gifts to visitors who do not form part of the exchange cycle. In this manner it proves to be very economic to give away all the surplus at once, because the giver knows that in turn he will receive his share of the surplus of others. This means that the giver can stay at home without returning to his field for several days, just as if he had kept for himself all he brought back to the village.

The individual agricultural food supply is never very stable. Droughts or rains, insects, cattle, fire—any might destroy a field. But if a crop fails, the individuals to whom food was usually returned continue to bring their gifts and will even make them more plentiful and varied, although the recipient cannot return them at the moment. Of course, once he harvests a fairly good crop again, he is expected to reciprocate generously the help received during his own spell of ill luck.

Few individuals plant all food plants, and those planted do not always yield equal crops. Therefore, during food exchange there exists the possibility of receiving some foods that are not to be found in the recipient's fields, and thus he has a chance to change his monotonous diet.

The exchange of food is also a deposit that the individual makes in the form of good care of others, expecting them to return it in times of need. In this way two persons might exchange food for years, but at the moment one of them loses his field or crop, the other party is obliged to continue giving him food, even for the rest of his life. In the same way a person might give regularly to another individual without ever receiving anything in exchange, the repayment being postponed for the occasion when the giver cannot maintain his family any more. The recipient is then obliged to give food to the former giver's wife, mother, or children. If an old person gives away food without receiving any in immediate exchange, the return gifts are expected to be made as soon as the person dies, the beneficiaries being the orphaned children or the widow. Frequently a person distributes gifts without receiving return gifts because he is paying for past favors or services received by his parents, who were unable to return them during their lifetimes. In some cases an individual will distribute food to a large number of others, receiving payment in kind from only a few of them. This is due to the fact that the return gifts are not meant for the person who made the many distributions, but for his relatives (mother, siblings, children), who, in their turn, transfer the benefit to the person who motivated it.

We have mentioned earlier that the patterns of food exchange are established early in childhood. At about ten years of age a child begins to take part in agriculture, planting a diminutive plot in a corner of his father's field. Adults and older siblings help the boy to weed and maintain this little plantation, but the distribution of the crop is the child's own affair. Such a child distributes the fruits to his mother and siblings, having been taught to do so since early childhood. The first solid food an infant is made to eat is taken from his mother's dish. Small morsels are taken from the food of his siblings and are given to the infant, who is thus continuously given an example of food distribution within his family. To eat alone is one of the worst faults an individual could have. We have observed cases of food exchange between children of six years and oldsters of eighty.

Love, friendship, and kin cohesion are expressed through food exchange. When a man begins to court a girl, the most important thing is to give food to her mother in order to win her confidence and make her favorably inclined. The basis of courtship is always food. It is distributed in increasing quantities as relations become firmer. Once the couple has procreated children, the principal business of the man is to keep his mother-in-law satisfied by regular gifts of food, because on this depends the quality of his relations with his wife. If a man wishes to break off his relationship with a girl, he only needs to cease giving food to her mother, because at once the latter will influence the girl to leave the man. A married man's first obligation is to provide food for his wife, but a married woman's duty is to let her mother share the food supplied by the women's husband.

On the wider barrio and village scene most social ties are expressed in terms of food exchange. When asked if he considered his paternal aunt as belonging to his family, a man answered. 'No, she does not exchange food with me.' Sibling relationships, which are generally hostile as long as they live under the same roof, tend to become considerably more friendly as soon as each establishes his own household and takes part in the cycle of food exchange.

Marital stability is weak, and women are frequently abandoned by their consorts. Among the sixteen cases we have cited in Table 32, four are men, but of the twelve women none is married by the Church; six are abandoned by their male companions; two have husbands but these live at the moment with other women. Only four women live under the same roof with their men. The difficult situation of the abandoned wife is greatly alleviated by the food exchange system, because her mother, sisters, and other relatives or neighbors continue making her gifts of food, expecting them to be returned as soon as the woman finds a new consort.

In the whole section of the village where we have studied the pattern of food exchange, there is only one household the members of which do not give or receive any food, although they own fields and crops. This household is disliked by all, its members are not visited, and a very low social status is assigned to them. Every time their names were mentioned, the comments were: 'They are like that. They don't distribute food; they are backwooders' (*montunos*). The person of highest status is No. 7 (Table 32). A grandmother and a very active woman, she enjoys the benefit of food exchange with her mother, aunts, nieces, sons, daughters, and neighbors. Her son (No. 8), who works in the fields inherited from his father and who lives with his mother, is obliged to make many gifts of food to relatives who do not return them to him, but to his mother. This, however, he does in order to gain prestige, and also because indirectly, by living in his mother's house, he receives a benefit. Another individual of high status is No. 1, owing to her being descended from one of the first families of the Plaza barrio. Although a very poor woman who was abandoned by her husband, she nevertheless receives food from ten individuals, being obliged to return to only five of them part of the gifts received.

The institution of food exchange represents an important factor in the stabilization of the individual's régime of security. The food supply of a person is endangered by (*a*) magical factors, i.e., envy of others transformed into magical aggression which might cause illness, death, crop failure, abandonment by the spouse, loss of status and prestige; (*b*) factors rationalized as 'natural' and avoidable, such as erosion, soil degradation, climatic changes, fire, insects, etc. On the other hand, the individual's food supply is insured by the following factors: (*a*) food exchange between father, mother, sons, daughters, siblings, in-laws, neighbors, etc.; (*b*) the individual's own magical practices oriented toward the defense of his crops and other sources of food, against hostile forces; (*c*) the institutionalized rule not to store food. In the societal sphere, the endangering factors are overcome through the institutionalization of food exchange. They represent a control system that tends to hinder the individual from achieving a higher status level from which recrimination might be directed against those who remained on a lower level. This conflict is overcome by acceptance of and participation in the food exchange. In this way the individual makes manifest his desire not to be attacked and demonstrates his intention not to be aggressive against his fellow men. In the ensuing conflict, the most notable element is the anxiety that dominates everything concerning the individual food supply.

LABOR DIVISION AND SPECIALIZATION

The division of economic activities according to sex is taught from early childhood. In the section dealing with child-training and the general educational process, the formation of this pattern is described in some chronological detail; in the following discussion we shall limit our observations to some of the more marked aspects observed during adult life.

It might be said that the basic division is drawn between indoor and outdoor activities, associated with producing and processing, respectively. A woman's tasks are limited mainly to the home and the back-yard, while a man's work is conceived of as lying outside of his house. In practice, however, this is not always true. Often enough, women have to work in the fields, and their participation in outdoor work is becoming more and more frequent through the increasing cash-crop orientation, which depends upon a numerous labor force during the harvesting months. On the other hand, men pass a good deal of their time indoors, often in idleness but sometimes occupied with repairs, the raw processing of palm leaves, or similar small chores. Although, ideally, the man should be the food-provider and producer while the woman is the food-processor, many families—especially in the Loma barrio—live entirely on the income provided by the manufacture of palm fiber products, a female home industry. The menfolk of such households like to underplay the importance of this income and often speak of quite imaginary activities in the fields, business transactions, or other projects through which they pretend to contribute to the household budget. It is evident that the fact that many women—and children as well—carry a heavy

254

share of the economic responsibility is well recognized by the men, and that they feel degraded by it.

Class and status differences establish, of course, additional subdivisions in male and female activities. While in the Loma barrio of the village the men do not believe that their women are working too much, in the Plaza barrio they are keenly conscious that a woman's activities should be limited to chores which befit her class-status. To work as a seamstress, a schoolteacher, or as a clerk in a store are all activities that carry high prestige, but manual labor in the fields, at harvest, or even the washing of one's own clothes, are definitely associated with a low class-status. However, cooking, the mending of clothes, or the cleaning of household utensils are not damaging to one's prestige.

But all these are matters that depend to a very high degree upon the individual. Some people simply cannot 'afford' to do certain things because of the particular obligations imposed by prestige patterns, whereas others feel safe enough to risk a slight loss of prestige. In general terms, it can be said that with increasing lowland influence the division of labor between the sexes becomes less and less marked. Among the more lowland-oriented placero families there is considerably more collaboration within the family—as far as interchangeable activities are concerned—than in the Loma barrio. A man from the Loma would rather go without a hot meal than to cook one himself should his wife be ill or absent, whereas a placero will readily do so if circumstances deprive him momentarily of female help. In the same manner, placero women will occasionally do a man's work, whereas a woman from the Loma would avoid it at any cost, fearing to lose prestige.

A few words should be said here about specialists. Labor specialization is still very little developed; not a single individual makes a living exclusively by a certain specialized activity. The shopkeepers are also coffee-growers and cattle-breeders; the two or three carpenters are also masons, own fields, and work as hired laborers at odd jobs. The tailor owns a small store and a coffee plantation and also runs a kind of boardinghouse for transients, while the cobbler owns several small fields and works at times as a carpenter. Everyone derives his daily sustenance from a variety of activities, among which his special trade or skill provides only a fraction.

A general outline of labor division is given in Table 36.

TABLE 36

Activities	Men	Women	Male children	Female children
Productive occupations				
Farming	x	x	x	x
Hired labor	x	–	x	–
Gardening	x	x	x	x

TABLE 36 (*continued*)

Activities	Men	Women	Male children	Female children
Productive occupations				
House-building	x	x	x	x
Twining thread	–	x	x	x
Carpentry	x	–	–	–
Tailoring	x	x	–	–
Broom-making	x	–	x	–
Shoemaking	x	x	–	–
Hat-making	x	–	–	–
Beekeeping	x	–	x	–
Baking bread	–	x	–	x
Distributive occupations:				
Storekeeping	x	x	x	x
Domestic Service	–	x	x	x
Trading	x	x	–	–
Butchering	x	–	–	–
Local food-selling	x	x	x	x
Transport	x	x	x	x
Service occupations:				
Raw sugar processing	x	x	x	x
Schoolteachers	x	x	–	–
Barbers	x	–	–	–
Water-selling	–	x	–	x
Firewood-selling	x	x	x	–
Barroom	x	–	–	–
Political offices	x	x	–	–
Musicians	x	–	x	–
Prayer-makers	–	x	–	–
Midwifery	–	x	–	–
Domestic service	–	x	x	x
Healers, 'curiosos'	x	–	–	–
Gravediggers	x	–	–	–
Ritual dancers	x	–	x	–

NOTE: x = active; – = not active.

A few explanatory notes may be appended here. As hired labor, women take part during the coffee-picking season but not otherwise, and their participation at that time is a recent development owing to the lack of labor force. Women's footwear is always made by women.

The changing pattern of economic activity, especially the cash-crop orientation and to a certain degree mere physical necessity, have deeply affected the old rigid system of labor division. Although the old pattern is still being taught to children, in adult economic behavior it is no longer followed in detail. Fewer and fewer distinctions are drawn, and there are more and more activities that are carried out by both sexes simply because survival or maintenance of a given economic level demands it.

CO-OPERATIVE LABOR

The principal example of co-operative labor is house construction. As a rule, the person who wishes to build a house tells one of the leading lomeros of his plans and asks him 'to represent him' (*que lo represente*) in the construction work. The latter, after having ascertained the general conditions of the work, organizes the working party by sending word to a large group of neighbors. A date is set and the work is generally finished in a day's time. Before agreeing to organize such a building gang the supervisor always takes detailed stock of the available materials and of the food the owner of the house is obliged to give to the workers. For the construction of an average-size two-room house, the following elements are required:

> 30 pounds of yams and plantains
> 15 pounds of meat (three pigs if beef is not available)
> 10 pounds of coffee
> 25 pounds of raw sugar
> 10 pounds of tobacco (in cigars)
> 10 gallons of rum
> 1 pound of salt

House construction by co-operative labor is always an undertaking of a festive and social nature, and there is much merrymaking and joking, but without singing or instrumental music. It is also an important occasion for the settling of old feuds. A personal enemy of the houseowner might take part—although uninvited—in the work and thus demonstrate his willingness to forget old grievances, a gesture which is always gladly accepted. Or, on the other hand, a person might refuse to co-operate, thus making it publicly known that he is on bad terms with the owner. The latter always watches anxiously the arrival of the participants, because their number and cheerfulness are indicative of the owner's status and general relationships with the neighborhood.

But not all houses are built by communal labor. Although until about twenty or thirty years ago practically all houses in and around the village were built by such voluntary working parties, the custom has been abandoned in the Plaza barrio. The placeros today are obliged to hire laborers, and only in exceptional cases will people agree to organize a working party for an individual of this section of the village.

Some public works, such as road- or bridge-building, are also accomplished by communal labor, but on such projects the general atmosphere is much less cheerful. Many people shirk this kind of obligation, pretending to be ill or to be occupied with some more important task. Others send their children or offer to lend tools but will not participate in the work personally. The placeros hardly ever take part in such undertakings, except as supervisors or organizers, but will contribute small sums toward a fund for buying food for the workers.

On the family and kinship level, co-operative labor is a serious problem because of the hostile quality of most interpersonal relations. There can be no doubt that many of the difficulties created by dwindling land resources and hired labor could be solved by co-operative groups, but the same forces that have upset the former man-land balance have also disturbed the social equilibrium of co-operation and reciprocity. There are minor exceptions: the clearing of new land in virgin forest, house and road construction, a fishing excursion, maybe; but otherwise co-operation in terms of effective reciprocal manual labor that cannot be accomplished profitably by the individual is very limited indeed and is often restricted to an almost symbolic level. Co-operativeness is a value, but by withholding it it becomes a powerful factor in social controls. The virtue of co-operation is extolled emphatically, but on the level of individual economic thinking it is used as a tool to control others who might profit by it more than the individual thinks safe.

It is not unusual to see a casual passer-by join any working group and help for a few minutes. A few stones are carried or some sticks are cut or a pack saddle is adjusted by the person who happens to pass. Or a visitor to other people's houses might pull out a few weeds in the backyard or pick up some object from the floor and put it in its proper place. Such little gestures seem to be automatic, but they are studied and purposely performed and critically watched. Not only do they express the casual friendliness of the neighbor, but also reflect a group attitude and as such are of great importance to all concerned. However, there is always the feeling that such co-operativeness is in many cases a danger and a nuisance because it gives the donor a right to expect free help in return. Most people are extremely wary of establishing such cycles of obligation. The motives of any favor done for a person are always analyzed with suspicion, the idea of disinterested help or friendliness being quite incomprehensible. The smallest gift is interpreted as probably being but a bait used to establish a chain of mutual obligation, in which the one who did the first favor will invariably benefit most and put the other party in an unfavorable position. This applies from the offer of a cigarette to the free administration of a vaccine through a government agency. As a matter of fact, the services provided by these agencies would be more readily accepted if people had to pay a small sum for them, as then they would feel no further obligation and would lose their fear of having to return the service.

ATTITUDES AND PATTERNS OF WORK

In Aritama 'work' (*trabajo*) is always interpreted in terms of suffering, of pain and humiliation; as a matter of fact, it is often referred to as 'God's punishment'. There is no pride in work, no dignity in effort.

However, the term 'work' has a special definition in this village. Only physical effort—especially that connected with agricultural pursuits— is considered to be 'work'. Handicrafts or intellectual or administrative activities are not included under this term. 'Work' and 'labor' are always associated in the public mind with the poor people, with those who must toil in order not to starve. In this sense it has come to have a wider connotation. For example, poor people *always* work. Even when walking, resting, eating, or sleeping they are 'working'. It is 'work' just to carry the burden of poverty. Thus 'work' is not only an activity but also a state or condition of mind and body.

By this same token, a merchant or the owner of a large tract of land does not 'work', even though he may put forth considerable physical effort in carrying out his obligations and forwarding the interests of his property. His efforts cannot be called 'work' because he is 'well-off'. Business (*negocio*) and trade (*comercio*) and employment (*empleo*) are all quite different and distinct concepts, and are not considered to be even related to 'work'. 'Employment' especially connotes any position carrying prestige but almost or wholly devoid of personal responsibility (i.e., a sinecure) and is highly desirable, in fact is regarded as a privilege. Even members of the political administration, schoolteachers, or truck-drivers do not 'work'—and indeed do not feel obligated to maintain a continuous effort.

The villager's fatalistic outlook on life results in failure to see a relationship between work and one's economic condition. Having enough is thought to be almost entirely due to 'luck' (*suerte*) and is never believed to be brought about or furthered by personal effort and initiative. This 'lucky' accumulation of wealth is suspected of being the result of shrewd, if not immoral, practices in business transactions, but work, in the sense of persistent individual effort, is never recognized as the reason back of success. Those whose lot it is to toil in order to survive were simply born without luck and even if it should cross their path they would not recognize it and would no doubt throw it away because they are 'brutes' (*brutos*).

Although there are always opportunities for earning money, very few people in the village take full advantage of them. The first question a person asks himself before making a business deal or a labor contract is 'What obligation do I incur? What shall I lose if I agree to work?' Although the laborer knows that he can earn money by his work, he does not offer his services; he waits until he is called, and then quite

259

often he refuses to accept because he 'does not like' (*no le gusta*) his temporary employer or the wages offered or the kind of work asked of him. Every day there arise such opportunities for earning a living beyond the narrow limits of mere subsistence, either by wage labor, domestic service, repair jobs, or transportation service or by the home manufacture of salable goods. But those who might profit by such work are often more than reluctant to accept what might be to them an unpleasant and even dangerous position.

There are two principal reasons for this attitude. In the first place, the prospective worker feels himself in an inferior position as soon as he agrees to work for someone else. His self-esteem (*amor propio*) is affected, and he feels humiliated and slighted because by working for others he admits publicly his needy situation (*su situación de necesidad*). To be in need is humiliating. A self-respecting person who wants to be respected by others takes pride in saying, 'I have no need' (*no tengo la necesidad*). In the second place, to work for more than subsistence or a given maintenance level is almost always interpreted as social ambitiousness, and the individual is thus exposed to the envy of others who might try to curb this ambition by gossip or magic. It is, therefore, not only the employer-employee relationship that is avoided as far as possible, but even independent work for one's own benefit, because it is likely to produce a notable surplus.

All this, of course, does not mean that hired labor, or labor of any other kind, is nonexistent or that all people live on a mere subsistence level. Physical necessity and prestige factors are powerful incentives to work, but the scope and intensity of this work are severely limited by the considerations mentioned above. The continuity and range of the effort made in making a living, in raising one's standard of living, or in exploiting to the fullest all potential resources do not depend so much upon the individual's intentions, ambitions, or capacities but rather upon his recognition of certain limits which his society imposes upon him. Every individual has to know just how far he can go in his efforts; just how much prestige he can afford to lose in one sphere if he is to acquire it in another. Each man must judge for himself how much of his labor effort will be accepted as adequate and normal by society and how much might be interpreted as aggressive behavior and ambitiousness unbecoming his particular class-status. What the casual observer would simply call laziness, inertia, or lack of responsibility must then be viewed rather as evidence of a very fine social balance which has to be maintained by a conscious effort to restrict one's personal ambitions and potential resources. People do not shirk labor; they have developed their own patterns of work according to their particular socioeconomic structure, their value system, and the physiological conditions inherent in the climate and their health status. To speak, then, of the 'duty to work' or of the 'dignity of work' is quite meaningless, as such concepts presuppose an entirely different cultural tradition and orientation. It seems that the nagging insistence with which members of one culture call those of others 'lazy' is partly due to incomprehension of this highly complex balance.

In Aritama the principal incentive to work—next to the fulfilment of basic physiological needs—is prestige. To a very high degree prestige is gained through the acquisition of clothes, and the most common reason for working and earning money is to buy new clothes. The acquisition of land, of more or better food, of ready cash for unforeseen events such as illness or the purchase of livestock, furniture, or tools are practically never incentives to work. Only a very few individuals, generally of high-class status and belonging to the urban-oriented placeros, sometimes work for the special purpose of buying a house, a lot, or a piece of furniture.

Apart from this type of activity which is oriented toward the acquisition of a surplus, there are two basic work patterns: the day-by-day economic activity and the activity that follows cycles of necessity. The first type is found almost only among the members of the twenty or so leading families of the Plaza, whose work is patterned by daily gains and expenditures and the accumulation of a capital. They are the shop-owners, the employees, the cattle-breeders, the people who manufacture raw sugar in large quantities, and the few part-time specialists. They represent, by all standards, the most sophisticated group, the one most similar to the general rural culture of the lowlands. But the rest of the villagers—about 80 per cent—work mainly by cycles, the only continuous activity being the manufacture of palm fiber products by the women. These cycles are many. Some are parallel, while others tend to overlap. The smallest cycle is established by the weaving industry, a woman exchanging or selling her products every two or three days, or once a week. Another cycle is the man's agricultural labor; according to season and crop, the harvests are brought from the fields every so often. Other cycles are yearly and involve the planting or harvesting season— above all of coffee. The coffee-picking season is the most important event of the economic year, and most of the cash spent on clothes and fiesta participation is earned during this time. There are also small individual cycles of work. A man might work for a few days as a hired hand only to buy a shirt; another might work for a few weeks just before the fiesta season to buy a new suit of clothes. A very common practice is to work hard during the coffee-picking season to earn enough money to pay all or most of one's debts and then to live the rest of the year, or at least a large part of it, on credit. While the womenfolk continue their daily weaving of straw hats, the men visit their fields once or twice a week to bring back some tubers or bananas, but otherwise people who have worked as coffee-pickers do no productive work until the next coffee season. If such a person were offered work of any kind he would decline it. He has credit and a few pesos cash, so why should he work? The pattern is to earn money rapidly, in a few hours or days or weeks of hard work, and then to retire and spend it leisurely, doing no work at all.

That under these conditions hired labor presents many problems is to be expected. The first difficulty arises as soon as the employer begins to look for laborers. Very rarely, practically never, can a person be approached directly and asked to work for a certain time and wage. This would be embarrassing for both parties and most humiliating for the one who is offered the work. The latter is likely to refuse, to feel offended, or even to answer haughtily, 'I myself am looking for hired help.' Such arrangements, therefore, must be made through an intermediary—a relative, a friend, or a compadre who, with the necessary diplomacy and caution, suggests that the one accept the work and conditions offered by the other.

In all labor relations absolute equality of 'dignity' and 'respect' is called for, and it must always be understood that by agreeing to work for another person no position of inferiority is implied. Once the work has been explained in detail, it is common that the laborer asks for some time to 'think it over'. This is done even though a man may be in urgent need of cash or may have already decided to accept the work, because in this way he can show that he is not pressed and in no way eager to work for others. Days or even weeks may pass before the employer is notified of the final decision, and meanwhile the laborer, in his daily conversations, makes occasional sly allusions to his popularity as a hard worker, his willingness to 'help out others who are pressed for workers', or his reluctance to accept the work, he being a busy man himself. In this manner the laborer affirms his independent position and rationalizes the humiliating aspect of the work.

These attitudes continue when the employer and employee finally meet face to face. It is the laborer who speaks now in a loud, angry, and demanding voice, who criticizes and disobeys, who complains constantly about the work, the food, and the wages. The employer, on the other hand, speaking in a low and casual tone, is as polite as possible and tries to persuade the laborer to perform his work in a certain way. Apparently simple tasks become now problematic: the felling of a tree, the mending of a fence, the harvest of an acre of coffee. The laborer's standard reply is that 'it can't be done' (*no se puede*), and he will produce a great many reasons why the work is impracticable under the given circumstances: because it is too late or too soon; because the wood or the burro or the tools are useless; because it is a loss of time and effort; and so forth. However, meanwhile the work proceeds. If it does not turn out to the entire satisfaction of the employer, the laborer certainly will not accept the blame for it, but will put it upon a great many other circumstances. All this is, of course, a standard pattern of behavior, well known to the employer, who has to accept it if he wants the work done at all.

Many laborers when starting work will bring along a helper (*ayudante*). This is always a person of lower status than the laborer himself, maybe a woman, a child, or a younger sibling, who receives a small (10 to 20 per cent) share of the wages. It is quite common that this helper does most of the actual work, while the hired laborer himself only directs it or perhaps even takes no part in it at all. As a woman or child may be unable to accomplish certain tasks that demand physical strength, the work is often done in a very inefficient manner, but the employer is quite helpless on such occasions. Should he insist that the laborer he hired perform the work himself, the latter is likely to feel offended, and both he and his helper might leave.

Even if a labor contract—all by oral agreement—asks for the accomplishment of a certain task within a certain time-span, say one week or one month, the laborer always feels free to stop at any moment he might choose and to leave the work unfinished. After having worked for a few hours or days a man might say to his employer, 'I have pleased you already' (*ya le complací*), abandoning the work. Hired labor is always regarded as a 'favor' the laborer does for the employer, and the time limit is, therefore, not imposed by the latter but by the laborer himself, who at any moment might call a halt and abandon the work. By the same token, hired labor is interpreted by the laborer as a 'loss of time'. In fact, wage labor is quite often referred to with precisely these words. A man, when asked whether he has worked lately for wages, is likely to answer, 'Yes, I lost four days working for so and so' (*Perdí cuatro días trabajando para fulano*).

This concept of 'time' and its 'loss' in connection with work is of considerable importance in all labor relations. Time is plentiful and nobody is pressed for it, but as soon as work—especially hired labor—is concerned, the time-span it involves becomes of utmost importance to people. Quite apart from the loss of prestige, or the idea of 'doing a favor', a man who works for another or for his own benefit feels that he gives two things of his own: physical effort and time. In a certain way it is felt that there should be separate payment for both and that the 'rich' take advantage of the 'poor' by paying them only for their work. Some examples may illustrate this point: A man who owned a large tobacco plantation spent months on end sitting in his hammock and complaining of his poverty, while living on the returns of the straw hats his women-folk were weaving. When asked why he did not cut, process, and sell his tobacco, he answered, 'How could I do that? Sure, I could sell the tobacco, but who would pay me for the time I lose in cutting it? Nobody I tell you. I would be a fool if I worked in that way for others, free of charge.' Another man hired a laborer to work in a field that was at an hour's distance from the village. The laborer considered these daily two-hour walks as part of his eight-hour day and stayed at his job only six hours, while asking to be paid for eight.

This confusion of 'paid work' and 'paid time' obviously arises from the fact that concepts such as the eight-hour day, overtime, time off for lunch, etc., have reached the village only in recent years, and many people are as yet unable to incorporate them into their private economic system and work-patterns. People traditionally worked intermittently, at no fixed hours, and at no fixed daily wages. Hired labor was conceived of in terms of a round-figure price for the performance of a certain task such as clearing a hectare of underbrush, boiling a caldronful of raw sugar, or cutting a donkey load of firewood. This type of work did not involve a time concept but depended rather upon the laborer's skill, the availability and efficiency of his helpers, and the general pace a person set when he started out on his work. But the idea that a man should work precisely eight hours a day, from 8 A.M. to 6 P.M., with time out for lunch and extra pay for overtime (but no pay at all for the time spent in walking from or to work), was and still is difficult to understand. As soon as a man was contracted he expected to be paid for every hour of every day, even if he did not begin his work yet, because now he was 'on So-and-so's account' (*por cuenta de fulano*). So a laborer who has been contracted for a week finishes his work hurriedly in three days but demands to be paid for seven days; others do not take time off for lunch, preferring to leave early in the afternoon, a practice that disturbs the rhythm of any co-operative work, such as the felling of a tree or the rounding up of cattle.

Although a hired laborer is supposed to work eight hours a day, in reality he hardly ever works more than three or four. There are continuous interruptions which are not due to a real need for rest or 'catching one's breath', but are simply devices to pass the time without effort or to prolong the task in a manner that makes it necessary for the employer to pay for additional working days. If a man works for his own benefit, he does so in a fairly continuous manner, resting only if need be; but a hired hand will always try to win time by cleaning his tools, scratching, eliminating, drinking water, or laboriously sharpening his machete. There are a great number of ways by which a laborer can protract his work, and they are taught by father to son and by the older people to the younger. 'One would be a fool to work hard for a person who can afford to hire laborers' is an often-heard statement. On the other hand, there are, of course, physiological limits to work at tropical temperatures, and if, besides, a person is physically and psychologically handicapped, being undernourished and anxiety-ridden, what seems to be loitering and indolence is often simply a necessary economy of effort.

An additional problem is caused by the food a hired laborer consumes. Until recently it was the general custom for the employer of agricultural laborers to provide their food. These then took along their women and children, the whole family subsisting on the ration given to the hired hand. Today, however, many employers prefer to pay higher wages and let the laborer bring his own food. Many people are utterly unable to understand this system of work and recompense. They have come to believe that the employer should really pay them fourfold: work, time, food, *and* subsistence of their family. If the employer tries to explain that the higher wages he pays are meant to cover all 'four' items, the laborer feels he has been taken advantage of by the 'rich', or by the 'government' which introduced the working-day schedule and the minimum salary for hired labor. Mutual resentment and accusations are the rule in such situations, and the position of the employer becomes increasingly difficult if his capital depends upon a readily available labor force, such as would be the case with coffee-growers or the owners of large sugar-cane fields.

Let us now return once more to the problems of prestige behavior with reference to work and hired labor. A difficult moment arises when the laborer receives his wages. He never asks for them in person but sends some other individual—a woman or a child—who reminds the employer that the laborer expects to be paid. Should the employer pay his workers personally, or as soon as the day or the work is over, this might be interpreted as an offense or, at least, as a very embarrassing situation. Quite often a laborer will let several days, or even weeks, pass before sending for his money, meanwhile building up his hurt pride by telling others: 'So-and-so owes me money, but I can wait; I don't need it.'

Another difficult situation is created when a laborer has to ask for a loan, a raise in pay, or a small sum in advance. Sometimes he will do so personally, fortified by a few drinks of rum, but more often he will send a friend or a child as an intermediary. In any case, a child is sent first to ascertain that the employer is alone, because to ask him for money in the presence of others would be impossible. Once together with the employer, the laborer is often too timid to carry out the purpose of his visit and will postpone his plans until he has an opportunity to approach a relative of his employer and ask him to intervene for him.

A large percentage of wage-earners in Aritama prefer to work outside the valley, in the lowland towns or in villages where they are not known personally. When questioned for their reasons people will reply that the pay is better, and that the employers are 'more respectful'. This, however, is quite untrue, for, on the contrary, wages are often considerably lower for migrant workers, and employers are far more demanding and strict. The real reason why work outside the valley is preferred is that the individual thus escapes from the narrow patterns of his local prestige system. In the lowlands or in other valleys no one cares who his family may be, no one criticizes his name, his skin color, his illegitimate birth. The foreman, the landowner, the employer, are all people who are unaware of and not interested in the class and barrio distinctions drawn in Aritama, and they judge the migrant laborer only by his performance as a worker. While in his own valley and village, the laborer of Aritama is sullen, slow, undependable, and always in opposition to his employer, outside his local cultural restrictions he is known to be a hard-working, dependable, and uncomplaining individual.

The fact that many people prefer to work outside their valley has very serious consequences on economic life in the village. In the neighboring valleys where the average temperature is slightly higher, the coffee-picking season begins in November, and many families of the Loma barrio leave the village to work there as hired laborers. By early December they have earned enough cash to last them through the fiesta season, so upon their return to the village they do not want to help in the coffee harvest of the local plantations, which then is only beginning. They have enough money to pay their most urgent debts, to buy some clothes, and to live for a few months without having to work. Why, then, should they bother to work more? But the local coffee-growers who depend on hired labor do need them, and this 'need' puts them in an inferior position. Now they, the 'rich', can be called wretched (*miserables*) because they want to save their harvest. But if one of them should hire laborers from some other valley, not natives of the village, he would be sure to be bitterly attacked for doing so and to be accused of 'robbing the poor'.

THE DAILY RHYTHM OF WORK

Table 37 represents a sample of individual work executed by twelve men during one month.

Number 1 is fifty years old and lives with a woman and several small children. He worked for five days in his field and during another five days helped his cousin to put a new thatched roof on a house, without receiving any pay for this work. For another five days he worked clearing a field, at 1·80 pesos a day, but he spent more than two weeks in his hammock feeling sick and unable to work. Although he had earned only 9 pesos during the entire month, the hats his wife was weaving every day provided sufficient food for the family and even enabled him to buy some medicines.

Number 2 spent only two days in his field but did no physical work himself, limiting his activities to an inspection tour. As his properties are distant from the village, three days were spent traveling. A married

TABLE 37

One Month's Activity of Twelve Men (In Days)

Activity	1	2	3	4	5	6	7	8	9	10	11	12
Working in own field	5	2	—	2	—	15	7	—	10	2	—	—
Working in own house	—	—	—	2	—	—	—	—	6	—	7	—
Helping out others	5	—	1	2	—	2	—	2	—	—	1	1
Wage labor	5	—	8	3	15	4	15	10	—	14	9	—
Traveling	—	3	2	—	—	—	—	—	4	—	—	—
Sick and not working	15	25	—	2	2	3	—	4	—	14	2	6
Not working	15	28	21	21	15	9	8	18	14	14	13	29

man of forty with a numerous family, he lived on money earned during the last coffee harvest. He spent three weeks hardly leaving his house, claiming that he felt seriously ill.

Number 3 is a twenty-year-old bachelor. For eight days he worked in the field of a relative, who gave him food and a share of the fruits they harvested. Two days were spent traveling to the field and one day in helping a neighbor to weed a backyard. The rest of the month was spent in his house or on the street.

Number 4 is forty years old and has a large family. After having spent two days in his field, he spent another two days weaving hats and two days helping a neighbor to pick coffee. During three days he worked at the slaughterhouse and received 3 pesos worth of meat for his work. For two days he had a bad cold, and the rest of the month he spent in his house or sitting in the backyard.

Number 5 is twenty years old and lives with a woman who has two small children by him. He spent two weeks picking coffee at 1·50 pesos a day. Upon his return he felt sick and did not work any more for the rest of the month.

Number 6 is twenty-five years old and lives with a woman and three children. For two weeks he worked at picking coffee, making 1·50 pesos a day, and afterward he worked in the village at several odd jobs for four days. During two days he helped a relative in his backyard, and for three days he felt sick.

Number 7 is twenty-four, married, and has two children. For one week he picked coffee on his own plantation, and then he worked as a coffee-picker during two weeks for others. One week he spent at home without working.

Number 8 is twenty-five, married, and has six children. For ten days he worked as a coffee-picker for 1·50 pesos a day, and for two days he helped a neighbor to pick his crop without receiving pay. The rest of the month he spent at home without doing any work.

Number 9 is twenty-eight, also married, and has three children. For ten days he cleaned his fields and picked some of his own coffee, and six days he spent sorting and pounding the beans. Four days were spent in travel to a village where he sold his coffee, and two weeks were spent without any work.

Number 10 is twenty-five, married, and has two children. For two days he worked in his field, and two weeks were spent in wage labor working off and on in other fields. The rest of the month he felt too sick to work and stayed at home.

Number 11 is forty-four years old and lives with a woman and several grown children. For one week he stayed at home weaving and for nine days he worked in the field of his father, who gave him a share in the harvest of tubers. The rest of the month he spent at home, except for one day when he helped to carry materials for house construction.

Number 12 is a forty-year-old bachelor who lives with relatives and who suffers recurrent epileptoid fits. He spent one day helping a neighbor to clean a backyard, but the rest of the month he stayed at home without doing any work.

According to our knowledge, these twelve men, who are all neighbors and lomeros, form a representative sample. As the data were taken during a month of maximum activity during the coffee harvest, it may be supposed that during the rest of the year the pace of individual work was considerably slower.

The data in Table 38 give a synchronic record of daily activities of a lomero family during three days in September, a month of average activity.

TABLE 38
September 23

Time	Father	Mother	Elder Daughter	Younger Daughter	Boy
6–6:30 A.M.	Sleeps	Rises, washes, makes fire	Sleeps	Sleeps	Sleeps
6:30–7 A.M.	„	Prepares coffee	Rises, washes, drinks coffee	Rises, washes, drinks coffee	„
7–7:30 A.M.	„	Washes pots, heats water, prepares dye, dyes thread	Fetches water	Sweeps floor	Rises
7:30–8 A.M.	„	Weaves hat	Sits on door-step	Fetches water	Goes on errand
8–8:30 A.M.	Rises, drinks coffee	Fetches water	Weaves hat	Peels plantains, boils water	Leaves to ask for sick relative

Time	Father	Mother	Elder Daughter	Younger Daughter	Boy
8:30–9 A.M.	Goes to plot to see if ants did damage	Spins thread	Helps mother	Helps mother	Visits a neighbor
9–9:30 A.M.	Returns and eats plantains	Eats plantains and splits wood	Eats plantains and prepares tobacco leaves	Eats plantains and helps sister	Eats and helps sisters
9:30–10 A.M.	Picks tobacco leaves	Visits neighbor	Threads leaves	Helps sister	Helps sisters
10–10:30 A.M.	Ties leaves	Visiting	,,	,,	Plays
10:30–11 A.M.	,,	,,	,,	,,	Sits on doorstep
11–11:30	,,	,,	Weaves hat	Weaves hat	,,
11:30–12 A.M.	Rests	,,	Makes fire	Peels plantains, boils water	,,
12:30–1 P.M.	Lies in hammock	,,	Prepares thread	Goes for firewood	Goes with sister
1–1:30 P.M.	Sits and rests	Weaves hat	Weaves hat	Prepares thread	Plays
1:30–2 P.M.	In hammock	,,	Brings water	Weaves hat	Rests
2–2:30 P.M.	Threads leaves	,,	Spins thread	Helps sister	Goes on errand
2:30–3 P.M.	,,	,,	,,	,,	,,
3–3:30 P.M.	Eats lunch	Eats lunch	Eats lunch	Eats lunch	Eats lunch
3:30–4 P.M.	Threads leaves	Washes pots	Feeds pig	Rests	Rests
4–4:30 P.M.	,,	Weaves hat	Weaves hat	Weaves hat	Plays
4:30–5 P.M.	,,	Mends clothes	Mends clothes	Mends clothes	,,
5–5:30 P.M.	Rests	Twines thread	Twines thread	Feeds pig	,,
5:30–6 P.M.	In hammock	,,	,,	Twines thread	,,
6–6:30 P.M.	Sits and rests	Finishes hat	Weaves hat	Weaves hat	Rests
6:30–7 P.M.	Goes to sleep	Talks	Talks	Talks	Talks
7–7:30 P.M.	Sleeps	Arranges kitchen	Goes to sleep	Goes to sleep	Goes to sleep

Time	Father	Mother	Elder Daughter	Younger Daughter	Boy
6–6:30 A.M.	Sleeps	Rises, washes, makes fire	Sleeps	Sleeps	Sleeps
6:30–7 A.M.	,,	Prepares and drinks coffee	Rises and drinks coffee	Rises and drinks coffee	,,
7–7:30 A.M.	Rises	Goes for water	Goes for water	Goes for water	Rises
7:30–8 A.M.	Walks in yard	Boils water	Helps mother	Sweeps floor	Takes peelings to neighbor's pig
8–8:30 A.M.	Breakfasts	Visiting	Breakfasts	Breakfasts	Breakfasts
8:30–9 A.M.	In hammock	,,	Twines thread	Twines thread	Plays
9–9:30 A.M.	,,	Breakfasts	Washes pots	Feeds pig	,,
9:30–10 A.M.	Dries tobacco	Helps father	Rests	Rests	Rests
10–10:30 A.M.	,,	,,	Talks	Talks	Sits on doorstep
10:30–11 A.M.	Rests	Heats iron	Stirs fire	Cleans up leaves	Talks to mother
11–11:30 A.M.	,,	Irons	Weaves hat	Weaves hat	Goes on errand
11:30–12 A.M.	In hammock	,,	,,	,,	On errand
12–12:30 P.M.	,,	,,	Stirs fire	,,	Sits in backyard
12:30–1 P.M.	,,	Weaves hat	Weaves hat	,,	Rests
1–1:30 P.M.	,,	Rests	Rests	Rests	Visiting
1:30–2 P.M.	Weaves hat	Goes to wash	Helps mother	Weaves hat	Goes with mother
2–2:30 P.M.	,,	Laundering	Laundering	,,	Bathes
2:30–3 P.M.	In hammock	,,	,,	,,	,,
3–3:30 P.M.	,,	,,	,,	Prepares food	,,
3:30–4 P.M.	,,	,,	,,	Cooking	,,
4–4:30 P.M.	Eats lunch	Eats lunch	Eats lunch	Eats lunch	Eats lunch
4:30–5 P.M.	Weaves hat	Spins thread	Spins thread	Spins thread	Feeds pig
5–5:30 P.M.	Rests	Washes pots	Twines thread	Twines thread	Visiting
5:30–6 P.M.	In hammock	Weaves hat	Weaves hat	Weaves hat	Plays
6–6:30 P.M.	,,	,,	,,	,,	Sleeps
6:30–7 P.M.	Sleeps	Sleeps	Sleeps	Sleeps	,,

Time	Father	Mother	Elder Daughter	Younger Daughter	Boy
6–6:30 A.M.	Sleeps	Rises and washes	Sleeps	Sleeps	Sleeps
6:30–7 A.M.	Rises, drinks coffee	Prepares coffee	Drinks coffee	Drinks coffee	Drinks coffee
7–7:30 A.M.	Rests	Goes for water	Twines thread	Twines thread	Sits on doorstep
7:30–8 A.M.	Walks in yard	Fetching water	,,	,,	,,
8–8:30 A.M.	Sits in yard	Goes to sell hats	Goes for water	Goes for water	,,
8:30–9 A.M.	,,	Selling hats	Prepares food	Prepares food	Plays
9–9:30 A.M.	In hammock	Returns	,,	,,	,,
9:30–10 A.M.	,,	Goes to wash	Cooks	Cooks	Goes with mother
10–10:30 A.M.	,,	Laundering	,,	,,	Bathes
10:30–11 A.M.	Weaves hat	,,	Walks in yard	Walks in yard	,,
11–11:30 A.M.	Walks in yard	,,	Weaves hat	Weaves hat	On street
11:30–12 A.M.	Weaves hat	,,	,,	,,	,,
12–12:30 P.M.	,,	Returns with laundry	,,	,,	,,
12:30–1 P.M.	In hammock	Weaves hat	,,	Twines thread	Sits inside
1–1:30 P.M.	Eats lunch	Eats lunch	Eats lunch	Eats lunch	Eats lunch
1:30–2 P.M.	In hammock	Washes pots	Helps mother	Helps mother	Sits inside
2–2:30 P.M.	,,	,,	Goes to river	Weaves hat	Feeds pig
2:30–3 P.M.	Weaves hat	Goes to river	Laundering	,,	Plays
3–3:30 P.M.	Prepares tobacco	Laundering	,,	,,	On errand
3:30–4 P.M.	In hammock	,,	,,	,,	,,
4–4:30 P.M.	Cuts grass for burro	,,	,,	Prepares food	,,
4:30–5 P.M.	Cleans yard	,,	,,	Cooks	,,
5–5:30 P.M.	Eats	Eats	Eats	Eats	Eats
5:30–6 P.M.	In hammock	Weaves hat	Washes pots	Rests	Plays
6–6:30 P.M.	Sleeps	,,	Weaves hat	Sick, resting	,,
6:30–7 P.M.	,,	Sleeps	Sleeps	Sleeps	Sleeps

PART III

Cultural Configurations of Reality

VII

DIMENSIONS OF THE NATURAL

EVERY individual human being is thought to consist of four different parts: the 'person' (*persona*), the 'spirit' (*espíritu*), the 'soul' (*alma*), and the 'body' (*cuerpo*). The person is represented by the individual's congenital traits and culturally conditioned characteristics. It is his 'personality' (*personalidad, carácter*), his unique way of feeling, thinking, and acting. Man is thought to be born evil, and it is this innate part of his person which contains evilness, whereas the acquired part, his 'education', tends to suppress this inclination and to steer the person toward the good. To do good or evil is thought to depend exclusively upon the 'person' which does so quite consciously.

The spirit controls the person. It tries to lead it and orient it and is like 'another person' but in essence a good one. It never inclines the individual toward evil but, on the contrary, struggles against the 'person's' innate tendency to evil and tries to affirm the acquired good traits. It inclines the person toward what it ought to do. However, as people are imagined as essentially evil, the spirit often fails and then becomes evil itself.

The soul holds no relationship whatsoever to the other components. It is neither good nor evil. It represents a factor of vitality; it is that part of the being that has the capacity for giving or receiving love. Whereas the person and the spirit are individualized entities, the soul is thought to be very similar to all other souls. Only souls that are 'identical', or nearly so, feel love for each other, and only if this is true can the soul make itself felt as an active power, even though the person or the spirit resists this power. The spirit and the soul of an individual never change of themselves but only when the spirit becomes dominated by the person. However, the person changes greatly. The soul has its seat in the heart and therefore in the blood, whereas the person and the spirit inhabit the entire body. Listlessness affects the entire organism and then a person feels 'disspirited'.

There is but little detailed knowledge of human anatomy and physiology, and most references to body parts and their functioning are very vague. Although both children and adults have frequent occasion to watch the butchering of game or domestic animals, few people draw comparisons with the anatomy of man. Human skeletons occasionally found in the ground are never touched, because it is feared they are contaminated with evil magical powers. Even the people who specialize in the curing of disease or in assisting at childbirth show a very scanty understanding of anatomical detail and physiological functioning and are often unable to identify or localize the larger bones or internal organs of the human body.

The following list contains the local names of those human bones which are known: Cranium (*hueso de la cabeza*), Os frontale (*frente*), Os sphenoidale (*el sentido*), Fontanella (*mollera*), Arcus zygomaticus (*cachete*), Mandibula (*quijada*), Clavicula (*candelero*), Scapula (*espaldila*), Costae (*costillal*), Corpus sterni (*paletica del pecho*), Vertebra prominens cervicalis VII (*cogote*), Os coxae (*hueso de la viuda*), Os sacrum (*rabadilla*), Os coccygis (*rabito del culo*), Femur (*muzlo*), Humerus (*brazo*), Ulna and Radius (*antebrazo*), Patella (*chocosuela*), Os calcaneum (*garrete*), Tibia (*canilla*), Ossa carpalia (*muñeca*), Ossa metacarpalia (*vaquitas*), Ossa metatarsalia (*cañitas*). Individual muscles, tendons, ligaments, or nerves are not distinguished and all tendons are called 'strings' (*cuerdas*), and when speaking of muscles, only leg and arm muscles are meant. The internal organs are: frontal part of the brain (*sesos*), occipital part of the brain (*cerebro*), heart (*corazón*), lungs (*pulmones*), liver (*higado*), gall bladder (*vesicula*), stomach (*estómago*), intestines (*tripas*), kidneys (*riñones*), spleen (*bazo*), bladder (*vejiga*), and uterus (*matriz*).

The blood is thought to represent the essential life-force and is, therefore, believed to be the most important single component of the human body. The fact of its circulation, however, is recognized only in women while the blood of the male is said to be 'quiet'. The basis for this belief is the menstrual cycle, during which the woman is thought to eliminate periodically a surplus of 'bad' blood. In healthy persons the blood is said to be constantly renewed by the food and beverages consumed, a process which slows down or stops entirely if the person is exposed to illness.

The principal respiratory organ is believed to be the heart, which is imagined as a birdlike body, the wings of which are the lungs. These 'wings fan the heart' and in case they should stop and fold over it, the person would die. The nervous system as such is not recognized, but the heart is also thought of as the seat of all emotional feelings, over which a certain control is exercised by a close connection between the heart and the brain. The frontal lobes, however, are said to have no function at all, and the processes of 'thinking' and 'feeling' are said to develop in the heart and in the occipital regions of the brain. In women the uterus is thought to be an organ closely connected with emotional states; it is believed to be 'like an animal', having a life of its own and occasionally wandering about in the abdominal cavity. Although digestion and elimination are recognized as very important functions, little is known about the processes involved.

Conception and the first stages in the development of a new life are imagined in the following manner: the semen is a kind of 'saliva' excreted by the kidneys and accumulated in the testes. Occasionally the semen contains a drop of blood which proceeds from the kidneys and which is discharged during ejaculation, causing great pain to the male. From this drop of blood which penetrates into the uterus the embryo develops. The female embryo is formed from a heart-shaped drop of blood and its sex is determined only after four or five months of pregnancy, but a male embryo develops from an irregularly shaped drop, his sex being determined within two weeks after conception. The life-giving principle is in the man's semen while the woman is only a sort of incubator. The embryo, and later on the fetus, receives nourishment through the umbilical cord and absorbs through it the liquid food the mother consumes. Birth is said to take place eight months and eight days after conception.

Puberty, fertility, sterility, menopause, abortions, the processes of growth and aging, and to a certain extent, even death—are all interpreted in terms of 'weak' or 'strong' blood.

Disease (its cause, symptoms, and treatment) is the focus of many strong anxieties in the village. It is the recurrent theme of daily conversation and intimate worry and affects all other aspects of life, being closely interrelated with social and economic conditions, with magico-religious beliefs, and with all aspects of food, sex, and aggression. The fear of disease and the fight against disease dominate the village life to a point where no one is free of its oppressive presence at any instant of existence.

Disease itself is thought to exist as a neutral part of nature, representing a permanent potential danger to mankind, but one which can affect the individual only under certain conditions. These conditions are two-fold: the aggressive intention of another person and the individual's susceptibility to disease. A disease can strike only if these two factors coincide. An individual who is not subject to the malevolence of others can expose himself to situations that would ordinarily make him susceptible to illness without running any risk; but as soon as this exposure coincides with someone's malevolent wishes toward him, it is certain that disease will strike. In the same manner, if an individual is the subject of another's malevolence but carefully avoids all occasions that might make him susceptible to disease, he can avoid disease itself. The coincidence of the two factors, deliberate malevolence of others and individual susceptibility, is expressed in the terms 'it coincided on him' (*le convino*).

It is believed that disease is not really of supernatural origin but is an element of nature which can be handled in a supernatural way. The fact of falling ill is always interpreted as the result of sorcery, as a vengeance, or as a punishment meted out by God but more often by ancestral spirits which use human agency. Disease is, therefore, an instrument that is used by others to vex or to destroy a chosen victim. Even the slightest indisposition is thought to be caused in this manner, and disease or death are always attributed to the malevolence of others. The common saying is: 'no one dies without having been made to' (*nadie muere sin que le echen algo*). In an extreme case a person might even cause his own illness, either as a self-punishment or as a kind of suicide or as an attitude of defiance or to humiliate others or to gain a privileged position exempt of social responsibilities. However, none of these different beliefs about disease changes its essentially 'natural' character. It is regarded as a latent force which can be used and directed toward a certain objective.

In order to utilize this force, i.e., to do harm to another person by making him fall ill, it is not necessary to exercise magic through a complex ritual. Sometimes the firm desire that an enemy might fall ill is thought to be sufficient to achieve this end. The envy felt at seeing the success, the prestige, or the good health of others is in itself an attitude of aggressiveness sufficiently strong to cause the disease of the envied in case he is susceptible to it. A mere glance, a gesture, a prayer, or a slight physical contact with the enemy can be the immediate cause of his disease. In some cases this hostility might take more complex forms and might use specially prepared objects, prayers, or certain potions, but often the simple fact of existing hostility is believed to be sufficient to harm the victim who is susceptible to it.

We have said above that blood is thought to be the most vital single component of the human organism. Accordingly, the susceptibility to disease depends to a high degree upon certain characteristics associated with the person's blood. The blood can either be 'strong' or 'weak', and only a 'weakness of the blood' (*debilidad de la sangre*) makes a person susceptible to disease. All diseases are thought to enter the blood stream and to affect the organism through it, causing local symptoms or a general condition of ill-health. Pathogenic factors can be manifold and of different intensities or consequences, but their harmful action depends entirely upon the state of the blood.

The condition of the blood is thought to vary according to sex and age, according to the time of the day and the season of the year, to physical or mental activity, and to the psychological state of the individual. The blood, therefore, 'changes' continuously and with it changes the natural resistance and defenses of the person. In the first place, there are certain supposedly innate differences: some people are born with 'strong' blood and some with 'weak' blood; children born before full term or those who have been fathered by old men are said to have 'weak' blood. Occasionally a hereditary tendency toward one or the other of these qualities is pointed out, but otherwise these conditions are explained by the food habits of the mother or the particular circumstances at birth. A man and a woman who both have 'strong' blood are likely to transmit this quality to their offspring, while a woman who had insufficient nourishment during pregnancy or who had gynecological difficulties during birth is likely to transmit 'weak' blood to her child. In the second place there are sexual differences: a man's blood is always 'stronger' than a woman's because a man's blood is thought to be 'quiet'. In women, however, the blood circulates and in doing so acquires unexplained impurities that are eliminated every month by menstruation, which is considered to take place in order to 'purify' the blood. Differences of 'temperature' are also said to be significant. The blood of a woman is said to be 'hotter' than that of men, making women more susceptible to certain diseases such as infections and digestive dysfunctions. 'Heat' and 'weakness' are associated here, both making women an easier prey to disease than men.

Apart from these supposedly innate properties, there are said to be certain occasions and situations during which a person's blood is 'weak'. During the pubertal stage of boys and girls their blood is 'weak', as is manifest in pimples, acne, pallor, and occasional inappetence. An attractive woman or a handsome man has 'weak' blood in comparison with people who are considered unattractive and plain looking. People who are stout, jovial, popular, smiling, and extraverted have 'weaker' blood than their opposites. After sundown everyone's blood becomes 'weak', recovering its previous level of strength only after dawn each day. If a person does not sleep sufficiently, for example, while attending to a sick child, a wake, or some urgent work, his blood will 'weaken'. Physical fatigue, sexual relations, menstruation, menopause, drunkenness, fear, rage, jealousy, exposure to the sun or the rain, fasting, or any physical or mental stress—all are occasions that temporarily 'weaken' the blood. In special danger of an onset of 'weakness' are women in childbirth, travelers, persons who have witnessed or taken part in physical aggression, persons who have recently had a supernatural vision. Also musicians, gravediggers, or people who have been dancing are likely to 'weaken' their blood during their activities. Menstruating and pregnant women are said to have very 'weak' blood, and, as 'all the pores are open', they easily fall victim to diseases. They must never visit other sick people nor assist at wakes. Abortions or difficulties during delivery are always attributed to 'weak' blood.

As we can see from this list, the eventual 'weakness' of the blood cannot always be controlled or avoided by the individual, because certain factors governing it are innate, or inherent in a number of unavoidable situations, i.e., situations that are beyond the direct control of the person. Such factors are heredity, sex, age, time, climate, atmospheric phenomena, physical appearance, wakes, burials, hallucinations, and the care of the sick. On the other hand, it is obvious that many of the factors claimed to cause 'weak' blood are contained in controllable occasions or situations, for example, sociableness, gaiety, alcoholic euphoria, sexual excitement, travel, participation in music and dancing, abundant food, physical aggressiveness, rage, fear, and all other states of violent emotions.

It is notable that these factors coincide with situations that are not approved of by the local culture. Consequently, the danger of 'weakening' one's blood acts as a control system: that is, the individual is made to conform to the local code of behavior by fear of punishment in the form of 'weak blood'. Thus even envy and malice toward one's neighbor are to a certain extent expressions of a social code. The local culture condemns sociableness, drunkenness, music, dancing, etc. etc., not for 'hygienic' reasons, i.e., not because they might cause disease, but in order to avoid stress caused by the struggle for prestige. In the same manner, physical handsomeness, a harmonious family life, good health, and any tendency toward accelerated change, represent asocial forms of behavior because they all deviate from the norm. Such qualities or behavior necessarily cause envy, and so the individual in question is considered as having 'weak' blood and as being an easy prey to disease. On the other hand, the belief in ghostly apparitions can, in part, be interpreted in terms of a prohibition to leave the home after nightfall, so that the individual cannot take part in entertainments, commit theft, or look for extramarital adventures. The controllable situations are thus the attitudes that are reprovable, and their interpretation in terms of danger to one's health forms a very efficient system of social control.

That such a system should have been adopted is probably due mainly to the lack of other control systems formulated on higher levels. The concept of punishment and reward in an extraterrestrial existence practically does not exist, and the belief that every evil deed will find its just punishment in this world is general. The real problem of disease, therefore, has its origin not in the sphere of supernatural controls, but in the sphere of society and family. It is in this configuration that the individual really feels profound gratifications and anxieties, and it is in this sphere that he must adapt his behavior to the institutionalized norms if he does not wish to be punished by society.

God, the saints, and the ancestral spirits, in their capacities as judges or executors of punishment, play a minor role in these concepts. The ancestors are essentially evil, and immortality is desirable only insofar as it offers the opportunity for the spirit to take revenge that he was unable to take during his lifetime. Besides, it is evident that disease is hardly ever interpreted as a punishment for infractions of a religious code but principally as a penalty paid for inadequate social behavior.

This general concept of disease reflects marked intrasocial hostility and a high degree of individual insecurity. The person who feels attacked at every instant turns into an aggressor. This explains to some extent why certain emotional states acquire such importance in the theory of diseases, especially if we take into account the patterns of envy behavior which represent one of the principal control systems. As a matter of fact, it is envy (basically envy of food but, consciously envy of prestige, status, health, phenotype, lineage, education) which is the real driving force of this mechanism. All individual differences are best leveled by disease, through which the victim is reduced to a level equal or inferior to the one of his aggressor. The magical handling of disease becomes, therefore, a most efficient weapon in this struggle. A sick person cannot work, will lose his physical attractions, will have heavy expenses, and will thereby be reduced to a subordinate level.

POPULAR ETIOLOGY AND CLASSIFICATION OF DISEASES

It is generally believed in Aritama that diseases are carried by the air and that they have the substance of a fine invisible dust which enters the human body through the respiratory organs, the ears, or the pores of the skin. Among the old people there still exists the belief that each of the 'four winds' carries certain diseases and that the 'powder' (*polvo*) each one brings has a different color: blue (digestive diseases) for North, black (fever) for West, red (respiratory diseases) for South, and white (pneumonia) for East. The great majority, however, have abandoned this concept but insist that it is mainly the wind coming up from the lowlands which brings all diseases.

Diseases can be grouped into two general categories according to their manifestations. A basic division that is generally recognized is between those which have clearly defined symptoms and which may or may not have been caused by the magic of an enemy, and those which present a polymorphous syndrome of progressive ailment and which are always thought to be caused by sorcery. The first category is generally considered as curable, as it is supposed that the diseases will affect the organism only in a superficial physical sense; the second category, however, affects a vital principle, a part of the being that is beyond mere medication as applied commonly in everyday life. In this case the symptoms are depressive states, the rejection of food, insomnia and a general apathy, lassitude, and melancholy which often last for months or even years before they finally lead to death. In these cases the intervention of specialists becomes a matter of utmost urgency, but more often the patient 'dies' (in a psychological sense) while still alive physically. This phenomenon is expressed by the words 'He does not belong to this life any more, but to the other' (*Ya no es de esta vida sino de la otra*).

Some diseases such as advanced forms of mental illness (*locura, loquera*), idiocy, alalias, glandular disturbances, etc., are almost always believed to be caused by a personal enemy and only rarely by other agents. Bad falls, colds, headaches, or toothaches, on the other hand, are thought to be caused by dissatisfied ancestors or by other spirits, such as the ones associated with streams, mountains, or rocks.

A disease sent by an ancestor is rarely thought to be very serious, because it represents only a memento, a warning that the person should remember the dead relative and make an occasional offering to his spirit. Only in extraordinary cases, for example, an openly sacrilegious act such as cutting down a sacred tree, might the disease prove to be fatal. Much the same can be said about diseases supposed to have been sent by God, i.e., a supreme being that might be either Christ, the Virgin Mary, a saint, or the sun. Nor are these diseases likely to be very serious, although they might be painful and take a long time to cure. God does not warn but punishes, and such punishment is occasionally strong and lasting. The most dangerous and feared diseases, therefore, are the ones that are believed to have been caused by an enemy who wishes to destroy his opponent out of envy. This enemy will first use personal charms and practices but eventually will also be able to influence God and/or the ancestral spirits, thus eliminating the victim by a combination of diverse powers. As these diseases are difficult to diagnose, not having any easily identifiable special symptoms but affecting deeply the psychological sphere, they represent the most anxiety-charged form of disease. The details of its early manifestations indicate the direction from which the attack was made and will determine to a large extent the treatment adopted.

A further, and more precise classification of disease also generally recognized by all, is made on the basis of 'temperature', and in this manner 'hot' and 'cold' diseases are distinguished. In general terms, it can be said that the lower portion of the human body, approximately from the diaphragm downward is affected by 'hot' diseases, while the regions above this point are affected by 'cold' diseases. The facial part of the head including the ears, eyes, and teeth, are affected by 'cold' diseases, but the occipital part, the mouth and the throat are likely to suffer from 'hot' diseases. To a certain degree the difference between 'hot' and 'cold' seems to correlate with diseases of the respiratory and digestive organs, respectively. All other diseases are brought into this relationship according to their proximity or apparent connection with these general zones of the body.

Among the more frequent 'hot' or 'cold' diseases are those caused by 'bad air' (*mal aire*) and the 'bad wind' (*mal viento*). Bad airs are a potential danger at any time of the year and are often related to fetid odors or to sudden gusts or currents of air. Bad winds are generally limited to the dry season and are related to the strong, cool trade winds.

An 'air' enters the organism and 'walks through the blood' (*camina por la sangre*), causing ill-defined symptoms such as low fever, pains in the whole body, and sometimes chills. If the 'air' is furthermore 'humid', it might produce swellings, chilblains, and *mazamorra* (a skin disease). The 'damp wind' (*viento de agua*) and the 'dry wind' (*viento seco*) are also 'airs', not 'winds', and appear in sudden gusts of hot air currents. An 'air' can enter the blood directly through an open wound or sore and, however small, such a lesion should never be exposed to the daylight. People who have a slight fever should not leave their houses because the 'fever might catch the air' (*la fiebre se aira*) and might rise. All odors coming from carrion, garbage, privies, swamps, caves, sickrooms, or anthills are 'hot airs' and cause such symptoms as headache, fever, inappetence, and a general malaise, which although rarely causing death, are nevertheless considered as serious signs of illness. The stench of pigstys, chickencoops, or other places where domestic animals are kept is not believed to be harmful.

The 'bad winds' which are frequent during the dry season are said to produce well-defined symptoms of 'cold' diseases. Included here are fever, measles, smallpox, pneumonia, grippe, and bronchitis. 'Winds' are always associated with 'cold', and often the two terms are interchangeable. A 'wind' or a 'cold' is said to 'walk through the bones' (*caminan por los huesos*) and to cause an acute localized pain after a while. Sometimes a slight luxation or a torn muscle is interpreted as 'winds'.

Certain other diseases are associated with psychological states. One of them is 'fright' (*espanto, susto*). A person 'catches fright' (*coge susto*) at witnessing an accident or a scene of physical violence or at meeting with a snake, an angry bull, or any other fierce or dangerous animal. The sight of a corpse is frequently cited as a cause of such fright. Fright is, moreover, always associated with 'cold'; the 'blood is frightened' (*se espanta la sangre*), the person turns pale and is taken by a slight chill (*calentura chica*) as a first symptom. A prolonged chill (*calentura grande*) demonstrates the intensity of the fright suffered; if the chill is not accompanied by fever, it is called a 'dog's cold' (*frío de perro*). The symptoms of such a prolonged feverish condition are strong headaches and a general malaise followed by cutaneous eruptions, irritation of the eyes which sometimes leads to conjunctivitis (*ceguera*) or even to momentary or prolonged blindness, alalia, and a strong sensation of cold. A frightened person 'grows cold' (*se queda fría*), and it is precisely this cold that is the most dangerous symptom. The worst form of fright is the one experienced at the sight of a supernatural vision, and it is said that the beholder dies soon afterward, at times almost immediately. Often he loses consciousness for several hours or days but recovers the faculty of speech shortly before death and describes in detail the vision he had. We shall refer to these phenomena in more detail in another chapter.

Apretamiento, literally 'anguish', also called 'sorrow' (*pena, sentimiento*) or simply 'pain' (*dolor*, in a psychological sense), is another dangerous disease. The causes can be many, but usually they are the grief experienced at the death of a beloved or the shame felt after an economic failure, a public humiliation, or a physical punishment inflicted by a parent or a spouse. In these cases 'the heart tightens' (*el corazón se aprieta*), 'the wings of the heart drop' (*se le caen las alas del corazón*), and the patient rejects food, suffers from insomnia, is listless and depressed, and spends day and night in a state of melancholia, which sometimes lasts for years.

Sorrow, shame, or rage are all occasions when the 'blood is weak' and serious diseases are likely to strike as a consequence. Common causes for 'sorrow' (*tristeza*) arise when a child is taken away from the mother or when a grown son leaves the family to work in another village. Shame (*vergüenza*) is frequently said to lead to disease and death, above all in cases where a person has been caught stealing out of necessity or has been ridiculed in public for wearing old and torn clothes. Rage (*ira, soberbia*) is thought to be a substance that is formed in the blood at certain occasions and that has to be eliminated by violent action, lest it 'poison the blood' (*envenena la sangre*). If an individual is allowed to express fully his fury in word and deed, he probably will not suffer any ill consequences as far as his health is concerned, but death might occur easily should someone try to keep him from too-violent actions. It is said that enraged persons often faint (i.e., escape) before being able to do any serious harm.

Another disease is *el Mal de Ojo*, attributed to the Evil Eye (*Mal Ojo*) and caused by a person who has a 'strong glance' (*la vista fuerte*). Often the person who has this power is not responsible or even conscious of it, but on occasions such a person will use this alleged force with the express intention of doing harm. Above all, children are exposed to this disease, but adults may also fall victims to it. In children, the Evil Eye is said to be always fatal. 'The bile is ruptured' (*se les revienta la hiel*); the patient dies after having fallen into a comatose state accompanied by high fever, alalia, occasionally vomiting of greenish matter and being covered with dark spots all over the body.

A more benign variety of the former is the 'evil affection' (*mal de cariño*). It is not caused by the glance but by the fondling, the affection, the fancy an adult person might take to a child not his own, to an animal, a tree, or any inanimate object. It is mainly a disease that befalls children and is said to be easily distinguishable from the Evil Eye because the victim develops a few small purplish spots behind the left ear or on the sole of one foot. Continuous weeping and moaning are said to be characteristic symptoms, and a child suffering from this disease will lose his hair, and his features will be greatly changed.

A greatly feared disease is said to be caused by enemies who by sorcery introduce an animal into the stomach of a person. Snakes, frogs, toads, lizards, spiders, or scorpions are said to be used by such individuals and to cause a painful death if not cured rapidly by powerful countermagic. During our stay in Aritama a woman died because, it was said, an enemy had introduced a monkey into her body. Relatives who took care of her until death told us that the groaning and kicking of the animal could be clearly heard, seen, and felt. Also, inanimate matter such as stones, lumps of clay, or large pieces of wood can be introduced by sorcery into a person's body, it is believed.

A few diseases of minor importance but of some frequency are *mala mojada* ('bad drenching', 'wetting'), *mala agachada* ('bad stoop'), and *mala fuerza* ('bad stress', 'force'). In the first case rheumatic (?) pains are felt in the hands and arms, generally by women who have been laundering for hours in the cold river water or who have had to put their hands alternately into hot and cold water while cooking or washing. The other two diseases are attributed by us to muscular strain caused by a sudden movement or by lifting a heavy weight. The symptoms of all three are often confused with *aires*, and it is said that a *mala mojada* can be the cause of an *aire* entering the organism.

Some diseases are believed to be transmitted by direct contact with or by seeing a diseased person, but the possibility of contagion in such a case is thought to be controlled by the diseased, who can intentionally transmit his illness to another person. To visit an enemy who is sick is, therefore, thought to be quite dangerous, as he probably will 'stick the diseases on to' the visitor (*le pega la enfermedad*), simply by wishing him to fall ill. Syphilis (*sangre descompuesta*) is believed to be transmitted only by direct sexual contact, not by contact with open sores. Other venereal diseases are thought to be transmitted by sitting on a chair that is still warm with the body heat of a diseased person or by eating fruits that are still warm from having been exposed to the sun. Smallpox (*viruela*) is thought to be transmitted by contact with the corpse or bones of a person who died of this disease. Tuberculosis (*tisis*) is thought to be hereditary, as are individual cases of hysteroid or epileptoid fits (*ataques*). Body heat of other people and an invisible pathogenic effluvium (*vaho*), often controlled by the person, are also greatly feared as disease-causing forces.

Food is thought to be one of the main causes of all diseases, and people are constantly wondering whether or not a certain food they have eaten will agree with them. The use of salt as a condiment is believed to be a very harmful practice; some people in the poorer sections of the village use almost none or very little, and it is said that they are healthier than others, suffering only occasionally from headaches, slight fevers, or colds, but never from any serious disease.

Other diseases named by the villagers are measels (*sarampión*) believed to be associated with 'viento'; colds (*resfriado, catarro*), believed to be caused by sudden changes in temperature; a feverish condition called *tabardillo*, which is attributed to physical exercise in the sun and is accompanied by strong headaches and nose-bleeding; secondary syphilitic lesions (*cáncer*), not believed to be of venereal origin but thought to be a disease caused by infected insect bites; mycodermosis (*pinta, ahumado, carate*), attributed to the bites of simulia flies and to the 'decomposition of the blood'; gonorrhea (*mal de orina, chancro*), attributed to eating of sun-warm watermelons or papayas; malaria (*paludismo*), attributed to insect bites; melanosis (*paño*), attributed to liver ailments. Other diseases and afflictions named are chronic malaria (*calenturas viejas*), pyorrhea and stomatitis (*corrimiento*), meningitis (*fiebre cerebral*), itch or mange (*La Sabrocita*, i.e., 'the delicious one'), arthritis (*picada de tuétano*), arthritis deformans (*goma*), papiloma (*ojo de pescado*), zona herpes (*culebrilla, culebrina*), enterocolitis or acute appendicitis (?) (*colerín*), colitis, gastroenteritis, and diarrhea (*daño*), intestinal parasites (*gusanos*), pneumonia (*pulmonía*), asthma (*asma*), colic (*torzones*), pimples, boils, acne (*granos*), styes (*orzuelos*), glaucoma (*nube*), conjunctivitis or ophthalmia neonatorum (*ceguera*), menstrual pains (*pasmo*, i.e., '*espasmo*'), spastic tremor (*parál*). The following conditions can also be mentioned here: headache, toothache, stomach-ache, liver ailments, throat and ear infections, infected wounds, heartburn, torticolis. Toothache is believed to be caused by tiny worms which drill the tooth, and two kinds are recognized: 'little white-headed worms' (*gusano cabecita mona*) and 'little black-headed worms' (*gusano cabecita negra*).

The dry season, i.e., the months from December to March, is greatly feared, and it is said that the incidence of diseases is particularly high then. There are several facts that appear to corroborate and justify this belief. In the first place, during these months the common houseflies are very abundant. In the second place, the sun-dried refuse is converted into dust which is then blown by the wind in every direction. There is also a marked change in the dietary patterns, as much dried fish is imported at this time, and a great number of wild-growing fruits are gathered. As the roads are then suitable for motor transportation, there is much more travel and consequent contagion from the lowland villages. At night the temperature drops markedly and many people do not have blankets to cover themselves against the cold night air. As the dry season is also the coffee-picking season, there is more money in the village, more alcohol, dances, fights, and a general increase in emotionally charged situations. A higher incidence of disease during these months is, therefore, quite probable.

PROPHYLAXIS, DIAGNOSIS, AND THERAPY

Although considerable efforts are made to prevent disease, only few collective or individual measures are scientificially sound. Personal hygiene, cleanliness, and the avoidance of contaminated food or water are not considered to be related to the incidence of disease; on the other hand, dietary restrictions, changes in the temperature, and certain activities are thought to be closely related to it. Foods that are expensive are, as a rule, thought to be harmful to one's health, and children are taught at an early age to avoid them. Meat and fats are believed to cause intestinal parasites; tomatoes are said to cause tumors; lemons to 'weaken' the blood and to cause the growth of white hair; raw sugar to produce bile trouble. The consumption of pork, fowl, or goat meat is believed to provoke the inflammation of any small sore a person might have.

Menstruation and pregnancy are always considered to be diseases, and a great many precautions are taken during these periods. A menstruating woman should never eat lemons because this would interrupt the menses at once, besides causing her to have spots all over the body. No sweet or acid food should be eaten at all; she should not use perfumes or soap, and should not wash her body or comb her hair. All these proscriptions apply also to pregnant women during the last three months of gestation. A menstruating woman should not go to see a newborn infant because the umbilicus would become infected; only after the child has eaten food seasoned with salt has this danger passed. A woman who is nursing a baby should not walk in the sun because the heat would 'dry up the milk' and alter its quality in a manner very harmful to the infant. For the same reason, she should avoid quarrels with her husband.

Sudden changes in temperature are thought to be extremely harmful, and this is one of the reasons why contact with water is to be avoided. After cooking, ironing, or toasting coffee, one should not put one's hands into cool water or stand in a draft or give the breast to an infant. After one has walked in the sun, cool shade is to be avoided, and, similarly, heat may be harmful to a person who has spent some time in

287

a cool place. People who have danced, assisted at a wake, suffered from insomnia, or who have in any way run the risk of 'weakening' their blood, should by all means avoid contact with cool water. Warm water, however, is also feared, as it might cause fever and contribute to 'weaken' the blood. Even a few drops of rain are thought to be harmful, and to be thoroughly drenched by a shower is thought to lead to serious illness. The temperature of water and contact with water are always blamed for all sorts of ailments, and the fact that such contact can hardly be avoided is the cause for much complaining about man's fate in this world.

Perfumes, especially a cheap commercial product called *Agua de Florida*, are thought to have strong prophylactic value in certain cases of exposure. When visiting a sick person or while attending at a wake, people often sprinkle such perfumes on their faces, hair, hands, and clothes, or press a scented handkerchief to their noses or mouths.

We have mentioned already that the body heat of other people is thought to be a danger to one's health. For this reason, close bodily contacts should be avoided if possible. Church attendance, travel in crowded trucks, participation in dances, the purchase of meat in the crowded slaughterhouse, are occasions when such contact is likely and to be feared. The sun as a source of heat is greatly feared, much more so than the heat from an open fire. To sit upon a hot stone or log is said to cause venereal diseases, and to touch sun-warmed objects is often believed to produce arthritis.

Several government agencies have visited the village on different missions connected with public health campaigns. It is told in the village that upon one occasion the agents tried to extort money from the inhabitants by charging a fee for individual vaccinations which according to law were to be given free of charge. Others are said to have confiscated large amounts of medicines in the local stores, only to sell them in the next village. Drunkenness, abuse, and theft are attributed to these missions, and there is a general mistrust and dislike of any government-sponsored campaign. When, during our stay, the arrival of a group connected with the DDT campaign was announced, there were strong feelings of hostility against them. People feared they would steal their chickens, violate the women, charge high prices for fumigation, and commit all sorts of abuses. A considerable number of people simply locked their houses and went to live in their fields; others left the village in order to visit friends or relatives in the vicinity. When the group arrived, even the highest local authorities refused to have their houses fumigated, under the pretext that it was too much bother to move the furniture, and nobody wanted to rent mules or horses for transportation of the health team and their equipment. Some people of high neighborhood status, however, had their houses fumigated, and others did not wish to lag behind and so also agreed to have their homes sprayed with DDT. For some weeks afterward people were full of praise for the effective extermination of many insect pests, but when after a while the pests returned, the government was blamed for having sent people who 'did not know their jobs'. Furthermore, that this campaign had anything to do with the prevention of disease was not recognized at all, and people thought that the government just wasted money in killing off some bothersome but otherwise quite harmless insects.

Although, as we have pointed out, people are very cautious and much concerned about their health, there is a general agreement that disease is unavoidable and forms an essential part of life. Sorcery and the 'weakness' of the blood are ever present, and the individual lives constantly under the threat of illness, anxiously watching out for the first symptoms to develop.

A specialist is almost always called in to make a diagnosis. After a few searching questions concerning the patient's enemies who might have caused the disease, the practitioner goes to great length in asking in detail about the food consumed during recent days or weeks, about any hallucinations, heavy physical efforts, or exposure to sun, rain, wind, or water. The pulse is taken and if it beats rapidly then a 'hot' disease is diagnosed or, vice versa, a 'cold' disease. Facial expression is studied carefully, but the body is not examined except in the case of fractures, pregnancy, or accidents. Some specialists examine the urine. A strong yellow color is thought to indicate liver trouble; a reddish color, kidney trouble, and a cloudy appearance, 'cold bladder' (*vejiga fría*). The pupils of the eyes are examined because they are said to show whether the disease is due to a very potent witchcraft. Fecal matter, sputum, and vomit are occasionally examined and intestinal diseases are diagnosed from them. Some specialists among the neighboring Indian tribes will prick the patient's finger with a needle and look at the blood for signs of 'weakness'. Small pimples, boils, itching sores, and all other cutaneous infections are considered to be very important in diagnosing diseases correctly, especially those caused by emotional stress, hallucinations, and magic; and their location, size, and color are observed in detail.

As a general rule, a disease is diagnosed and prognosed as dangerous and caused by witchcraft if the patient feels worse during the night, but if discomfort is greater during the daytime its cure is considered easy. If a sick person hiccups frequently this is taken to be a very serious symptom.

Practically all children, as well as many adults, wear an archeological necklace bead or some *musíxke* seeds, often tied around the wrist. This is supposed to be effective in warding off the Evil Eye, as it is said that if someone casts it on the wearer, the bead or seeds will break in two.

Physical efforts in general are said to damage the lungs (*dañan los pulmones*); above all, rhythmic movements of the arms and hands such as in cutting, sawing, pushing loads, or weaving are considered to be dangerous. Girls during the prepubertal years are believed to be very exposed to this danger when making twine for the manufacture of fiber bags. As a matter of fact, any kind of work is a potential danger to one's health, and on this point people are very emphatic. Work is 'bad' for the back and the ribs; it 'ruins the body'; all internal organs are 'broken' (*se revientan*); the 'bones are bent'; and the pain associated with all this 'weakens the blood' and leads to all kinds of serious diseases. To knead bread is considered to be very hard work, and a woman who dares run the risk is openly admired for her courage. Any intellectual activity is, if possible, still more dangerous because it is believed to affect the brain in a most damaging way, leading to 'madness' (*locura*). Reading, writing, counting, or the effort expended in learning something new for example, a song, a recipe, or a new technique in weaving, are thought to be very exhausting activities, causing a 'hot head' (*se calienta la cabeza*) and leading eventually to mental diseases. Parents often take their children out of school for fear they will be made 'mad' by learning 'too much'. Intelligence and 'madness' are always thought to be closely related.

The classification of diseases into 'hot' and 'cold' types serves as an index to their treatment, which is based primarily upon the use of 'hot' and 'cold' foods, and 'hot' and 'cold' medicines. All foods are classified in this manner, the 'hot' or 'cold' quality of any food being partly derived from the influence it has upon a certain type of ailment. 'Hot' foods are beef, fowl, rabbit, goat, cheese, fat, oil, sweet potatoes, bread, coffee, watermelons, honey, ice cream, onions, pepper, salt, alcoholic beverages, guava, sapota, mamey, guanabana. Of prepared foods in which different elements are combined, the common stew (*sancocho*) is considered to be 'hot'. 'Cold' foods are pork, fish, milk, manioc, plantains, bananas, rice, taro, potatoes, maize, cabbage, tortillas, beans, pigeon peas, pumpkins, papayas, mangoes, coconuts, tomatoes, avocados, and all citric fruits. The daily diet of the individual should be balanced between 'hot' and 'cold', containing an equal amount of both elements, because a lack of equilibrium might cause the 'weakness' of the blood. Predominantly 'hot' foods would cause 'hot' diseases, and 'cold' foods 'cold' diseases.

In everyday life, since everyone knows to which category each food pertains, he balances his diet almost automatically, but at the moment a person falls ill, this differentiation assumes paramount importance. An individual suffering from a 'hot' disease must eat 'cold' foods, and if suffering from a 'cold' disease he must consume only 'hot' foods. Equilibrium has been lost and has now to be re-established. However, the quality of 'hot' and 'cold' of certain foods can be balanced by the addition of other foods or condiments of opposed quality, so that the diet is made less monotonous. For example, a person suffering from bronchitis (a 'cold' disease) can eat fish ('cold') if it is prepared with plenty of salt ('hot'), and in the same way he can eat pork ('cold') if it is prepared with plenty of chili peppers ('hot'). If, however, there is fever, no 'hot' foods at all must be consumed, as any amount of them would contribute to the 'heat' and make the fever rise. Therefore, the diet has to be balanced in a most careful way in order not to harm the patient seriously. Fever in itself does not always mean that the disease is 'hot', but represents only part of a total syndrome which acquires great importance only insofar as the patient's diet is concerned.

The many medicinal herbs used in the village also fall into these two categories. For example, viravira (*Achyrocline* sp.), verbena (*Heliotropium indicum* L.), romero (*Rosmarinus officinalis*) are 'hot' plants, while matarratón (*Gliricidia sepium*) and manzanilla (*Matricaria chamomilla* L.) are 'cold'. Commercial medicines bought at the local stores or in the lowland towns are also classified 'hot' or 'cold' according to the effect they have (or are supposed to have) upon different diseases. Antibiotics and aspirin are thus 'hot', while a laxative or a mentholated salve would be 'cold'.

While all this is common knowledge, some finer distinctions are drawn by the specialists. These point out that the manioc plant is 'hot', but its tuber is 'cold', while the avocado tree is 'hot' and its fruit is 'cold'. The fruit of the avocado, moreover, is 'cold' only for diseases of the chest ('cold'), while it is 'hot' for diseases of the liver ('hot').

The strict observation of the rules imposed by the two categories of 'hot' and 'cold' is imperative in the treatment of all diseases. Other fundamental rules are that the patient must not wash his body for three days after treatment has begun and that all medicines must be taken at four-day intervals. Each kind of disease, moreover, needs an additional specific therapy, the form and orientation of which depend upon many individual factors related to the patient, the specialist, and the disease itself. Apart from dietary restrictions, we find the following basic methods of treatment used: poultices, infusions, massages, magical 'extraction' of the disease, prayers, sprinkling with liquids, offerings, contact with magical objects, minor surgical practices, intramuscular injections, commercial medicines, taken either orally or applied externally, and scientific therapy under the supervision of a trained physician.

Poultices are used mainly to treat local infections, skin diseases, and localized internal or muscular pains. Practically all poultices are prepared by boiling the leaves of certain herbs and applying the warm water to the affected part of the body. Usually a cloth is dipped into the liquid and then tied to the body, but sometimes the water is sprinkled or brushed over the affected part with a feather. Often an entire fresh leaf is applied directly to the body. Medicines other than herbs are rarely used in these preparations, but occasionally we find salt, sugar, rum, milk, etc., added to the liquid prepared from herbs.

Infusions in the form of herb teas, sometimes mixed with other specific matter, are used mainly in the treatment of internal diseases of a more serious character than the ones mentioned above. They are prescribed in diseases of the respiratory or digestive organs, venereal disease, snake or insect bites, cardiac conditions, and all complications that might arise during or after childbirth.

Massages are rarely used. Midwives employ them during the last few months before birth and during birth itself, and occasionally they are used for arthritic pains or in cases of sprained ankle or torticulis. The belief that a disease can be extracted from the organism as if it were a concrete body is found occasionally and a form of massage is employed in such cases. For example, warts and styes are treated with certain movements of the hands and fingers which imitate grasping and tearing them off. Once they have been 'torn away' from the body, the healer imitates the act of 'throwing away'. Often a small hole is dug in the corner of a room and the wart is 'buried' in it. In massaging, all movements have to go from the trunk toward the limbs and to their extremities, the fingers or the toes. Only in this way can an 'air', wind' or 'cold' be extracted from the body. In such cases, massage begins with very soft movements, increasing in strength and pressure. Starting from the point where the pain is localized, the 'air' is 'pushed' toward the next extremity, eventually to the tip of the nose or even the penis, and is thus 'extracted' from the organism. However, the essence of the disease may now cling to the hands of the healer; so he now massages his own hands in order to 'push the air' toward the fingertips, from where it can be 'shaken off'. A special form of massage is sometimes employed in cases of muscular pains in the back. The patient lies naked, face down, and a child walks barefoot up and down his back. A male patient has to be massaged thus by a female child and vice versa, and the name of the child must be Juana or Juan, as the case may be, to make the cure really effective.

Prayers are often used in combination with herb medicine as a treatment. It is never the patient who prays but always a paid *rezandera*. Most of the prayers are of common Catholic usage, but some are considered to be very secret. The exact word-by-word rendering of the prayer or formula is of greatest importance, and the slightest mistake might make the procedure a failure. While the common prayers are pronounced in a more or less normal voice, all secret formulas are spoken almost inaudibly.

Offerings to the ancestors are a common part of any treatment of disease. Every important organ of the body is associated with a certain small stone, generally an archeological necklace bead of polished quarzite. Many people own a number of these stones, but others buy them in the village or from the neighboring Indians, once the necessity arises. Some of the beads have to be carried on the body, around the neck or the wrist, in order to effect the cure, but others have to be ground to powder, which is then wrapped in leaves and offered to the ancestral spirits. These small bundles are generally made by the patient himself, but sometimes a relative or a specialist makes them for him. They are deposited at a sacred site, while at the same time a short prayer is said asking the ancestors to 'take away' the disease.

If the person is seriously ill and is believed to be close to death, a little seashell is procured and is ritually buried 'in his stead'. Long, pointed Turitella shells represent men, and small, rose-colored Venus shells women. Some people keep such shells on hand, but otherwise they have to be bought, or brought from the sea. The shell is wrapped in leaves and with the bundle circles are described around the patient. Then it is carried at once to a sacred site where a mock-burial is performed, during which the shell is referred to by the name of the patient.

Sometimes mere contact with a certain object said to possess magical qualities is said to cure a disease. The cold feet of a dead child applied to a goiter are said to reduce it rapidly. If a child does not walk after having reached twelve or fourteen months, his mother might take him to the slaughterhouse and wrap him for a while in the still warm rumen of a cow that has just been killed. A few hairs from the head of a Negro from San Basilio de Palenque, a small village in the Department of Bolívar, are said to cure fever. A necklace of *musíxke* seeds is a powerful protection against some diseases. Many curers who cannot, or wish not to, visit the patient personally send a handkerchief over which they have pronounced a secret formula, and this cloth is then tied over the affected part of the body. Snakebites are often treated in this manner. To women in difficult childbirth, such a curer will send his hat, which she puts on while in labor. A necklace of onions is said to cure intestinal worms in children. A stye can be cured by rubbing a finger rapidly in the palm of the other hand, touching the sore spot with it and then cocking the eye three times at a flying hawk. If a child is suffering from the consequences of the Evil Eye and the parents know the culprit, they will approach him and ask for a small piece of cloth from his skirt or trousers. The cloth is then burned and the child inhales the smoke. Although this is considered to be a very effective remedy, few people remember having seen it practiced, and the disease is, rather, thought to be incurable. A child who is suffering from *Mal de Cariño* is taken to a place where a black cow is lying and is put for a while on the same spot, after the animal has been chased away.

To sprinkle the patient with certain liquids, such as perfume or rum, is also a common practice, and it is said to be of great benefit if the disease was caused by the sorcery of a dangerous enemy. Most Indian curers will ask for a bottle of rum, drink half of it, and sprinkle the other half over the patient. However, under no circumstances do they do this when treating another Indian from their own tribe.

Direct surgical intervention is very rare. Boils are sometimes slashed with a flamed knife, and cuts are sewed up with standard surgical needles and catgut by one or two of the more educated curers. Fractures are set by several specialists, who use long wooden splinters or boards to immobilize the limb. Many patients are treated with intramuscular injections of commercial drugs, and a number of people own syringes and will make injections for a small fee. The syringe and needles are boiled meticulously, this being only a sort of ritual, after which both can be touched again with unsterilized fingers or clothes before use. Some curers practice bloodletting. The painful part is cut crosswise with a sharp knife, and a small glass in which a bit of alcohol-drenched cotton has been burned is cupped over the wound. The flow of blood is of no importance in this case, as it is believed that the hot cup 'extracts the cold'.

Many modern drugs can be bought at local stores where penicillin, sulfas, and antihistamines occupy the same shelves as patent medicines, perfumes, and cheap ointments. As is common throughout Colombia, there is no effective control over the sale of potentially dangerous drugs. All are sold freely to any client, even to children. Patent medicines claimed to 'fortify the blood' are in great demand, as are also sweet, syrupy cough medicines, mentholated ointments, and various strong-smelling salves or potions.

Few people ever consult the trained physicians in the nearby town, and fewer still go to the government hospital there, although treatment is free of charge, even for major operations. During two years (1950–52) only four women from the village went there for childbirth, and all of them belonged to educated placero families. One of the reasons for the avoidance of this excellent service is that in Aritama it is believed that the soul of a deceased person wanders for nine nights over a long dark trail that leads to the Beyond, a trail which is lighted only by the candles that burn at his wake during these nine days and nights. In the town, however, this belief is not held, and a wake there lasts only three nights. It is quite natural, therefore, that a person from Aritama prefers to die in his own village and not in the town hospital, because his spirit might lose the way if left without light after only three nights of wandering.

The Indian curers and shamans of the mountains are famous throughout the surrounding territory for their treatments of mental disorders and are often consulted by both the rural and the urban inhabitants, there being no one in Aritama who claims to be a specialist in such cases. Treatment is always preceded by lengthy diagnosis which takes many different forms. Sometimes the curer will place a glass of water between himself and the patient, and it is said that the water suddenly 'turns into blood', which is then examined. Detailed questions as to food habits, sexual relations, participation in physical aggressions, situation of domicile, and location of sleeping quarters are common. Often diagnosis is made rapidly, based upon what the patient or his relatives might tell about the development of the disease, and sometimes the curer never sees the patient, relying entirely upon such information or upon divining. The confession of 'sins'—of deed or, above all, of intent—is considered to be part of the treatment and is often said to be sufficient to effect a permanent cure. In some types of treatment, symbolic objects are used: sticks have to be broken by the patient, stones carried to faraway places where they have to be buried or thrown away. For each 'sin' committed the curer will make a knot in a piece of string, which the patient then takes home with him with the instruction to open these knots at certain time-intervals. On other occasions the patient is asked to return to certain places that are associated with the first manifestations of his illness and to perform there certain rites, such as walking around in a clockwise or counterclockwise direction, or burying special offerings. The curer often asks the patient to concentrate on certain events in the past or on people he knows who might have caused the disease. While concentrating thus, the patient has to throw away certain objects, eliminating thereby the cause of the illness. Many stories are told about successful cures, but it is also pointed out that the Indians will not treat patients whose disease they suspect is due to syphilitic lesions, brain lesions received during difficult birth, or to epileptoid phenomena.

A few words must be said about the medicinal herbs commonly employed in curing. Some of the more common of such plants are often grown in the backyards, and the womenfolk see to it that they are watered and kept from being spoiled by animals. Also, while walking or working in the surroundings of the village, people always keep a sharp eye out for wild medicinal herbs and, once the necessity arises, know at once where a certain herb can be found. The average individual will collect such herbs from any place at any time of the year or of the day, but the specialists insist that the effectiveness of a medicine depends to a high degree upon many details which have to be observed while gathering and preparing it. These detailed procedures are often considered to be professional secrets, and the fame a curer may acquire by his effective treatments is often attributed to his personal knowledge of where, when, and how to collect the herbs he employs. Another theory held by specialists is that the development of a disease depends entirely upon whether the patient lives in the same place where he contracted it, or whether he went to live afterward in another place. A serious disease might be made of minor importance by changing the domicile, and, vice versa, a disease of little importance in one place might develop into a major ailment if the patient moves into another environment. Furthermore, the remedy has to be prepared under the same conditions that were prevalent in the place where the disease was originally contracted. A disease contracted in a neighboring town cannot be cured with herbs gathered near Aritama, for instance, nor can a medicine brought from another town cure a disease contracted in Aritama. As living up to these concepts entails much travel and expense, one of the local specialists has developed a new theory, according to which all diseases wherever contracted can be cured with local medicines if the herbs are collected at certain spots. For example, a disease contracted in the lowlands has to be cured with herbs picked on a very stony soil, whereas a disease contracted in the highlands can be cured only by herbs gathered at a very clean spot where there are no scrubs or stones.

As a general rule it is said that herbs that grow near a creek are 'weak' and little effective as medicines, while 'strong' herbs grow near large rivers or at great distances from the village. Medicinal herbs should be gathered on Thursdays or on Good Friday, exactly at noon, because then 'they are very strong and won't get spoiled'. The herbs are dried and then boiled in water, each one apart or in certain combinations. Every time a new herb is added to the water, a corresponding spell has to be pronounced, and as soon the liquid has boiled thoroughly it is poured into individual bottles. Some specialists pronounce the spell only when pouring the finished concoction into the container, but this is thought to be harmful by other curers, who insist that the spell has to be said individually for each herb as it is thrown into the cooking vessel. The hot liquid often makes the bottles burst and this is invariably interpreted as a sign of the 'force' of the medicine. The curer always tells the patient whether the medicine he prepared for him is 'weak' or 'strong'. Some curers consider the color of the bottle glass to be of great importance, using different colors for different diseases: blue for gastrointestinal diseases, red for respiratory diseases, and transparent glass for diseases of the urogenital system. This belief in the importance of the color of the container was introduced in Aritama only some twenty years ago but by now has been adopted even by the Indian curers. The colorful presentation of commercial medicines, which are often packed in bottles of differently colored glass, has probably contributed to this belief, but it is also evident that there is a similarity between this concept and the old belief in different-colored disease-carrying winds. It is also a rule that the patient must not use a spoon, but must drink the medicine directly from the bottle, lest its effectiveness be impaired.

It is commonly believed that small infants who have not yet been weaned must not take any medicines. Instead, their mother should take them and their healing qualities will be transmitted to the baby through the milk. Some medicines, especially vermifuges or laxatives, should be taken only when the moon is waning, as it is believed that during the crescent all intestinal parasites are immune to such remedies. A person who wishes to be successful in curing snakebite must never kill a snake, because if he does so his 'secret' in preparing the medicine will be lost. If, however, he is forced to kill a snake in self-defense, he should at once call upon San Benito and ask the snake for pardon, using a certain magical formula. It may be mentioned here parenthetically that, in accordance with the general Hippocratic theories underlying many of these beliefs, a medicine is always referred to by the name of *contra*.

THE SPECIALISTS

The word *curandero* is little known in Aritama and people who specialize in curing diseases are rather called *curiosos*, literally 'curious ones', though both words are derived from *curar*—meaning to take care, to heal, to cure. There are different kinds of *curiosos*, most of them more or less specialized in certain diseases: 'hot', or 'cold' ones, snakebite, fractures, venereal diseases, children's diseases, or mental diseases. Midwives are also *curiosas*, as pregnancy and birth are always treated as if they were essentially pathological states of the organism. Within the village there live only a few specialists, but in the vicinity there are about twenty people known as *curiosos*. As all local shops sell commercial medicines, shopowners are often asked to recommend a treatment and are only too pleased to oblige a customer in order to sell their wares. Occasionally a traveling *curioso* comes to Aritama and stays there for a few days or weeks, being recommended from house to house, and living free of charge in the homes of people he might be treating. Self-styled 'dentists' also appear once in a while, or people selling patent medicines.

With one exception, all curiosos are taken to be essentially well-meaning and harmless, i.e., to be interested only in curing disease, not in doing harm to the patient. The exception is an old man who, although a curer of some renown, is suspected of practicing sorcery occasionally for an attractive fee. But usually a patient approaches a curioso without fear of being harmed intentionally, although perhaps with little confidence in the specialist's abilities. There is no curioso of real fame in the neighborhood, and the ones who lay claim to this title often commit blunders which lessen their prestige. This lack of trustworthy specialists is recognized by the people and is often discussed as being one of the principal reasons for the frequency of serious disease and sudden death. In olden times, it is claimed, the curiosos not only cured their individual patients but also took active measures to protect the community against all illness, for example, making offerings, pronouncing spells, or exorcizing evil influences; in other words, by assuming priestly functions. Today, however, only a few people do such things and when they do the ritual is, in the eyes of the villagers, an ineffective one. The curers are said to have lost their power and their ancient esoteric knowledge. The names of famous curers of the past century are pronounced with awe, but when speaking of the curiosos living now, people shrug their shoulders. Sometimes, they say, they achieve a cure, but more often they fail in it.

Quite a contrary opinion is held of the Indian shamans. The native priests of the neighboring tribes are famed for their knowledge of magic potions, ancient chants and rites, and their ability to diagnose and treat efficiently all diseases caused by sorcery imposed by an enemy. All old Indians, even women, are supposed to be potential curers, and their services are held in very high esteem by all inhabitants of Aritama. However, the Indian curers, unlike the village specialists, are often feared by their patients. They are frequently accused of taking bribes from enemies of the patient and even of killing the latter occasionally. At other times they are said to protract the cure in order to charge fees for weeks and months on end. Their fees are always high and they are very shrewd in all their dealings with their 'civilized' patient.

Then there are the trained physicians in the neighboring lowland towns. Only the most creole-oriented call upon them, and even they hardly ever follow the treatment prescribed by them. As many physicians will tell the patient the result of his diagnosis, the latter often fails to return for treatment, preferring to try to cure the disease in his own way. Others, when receiving a prescription, buy only the least expensive medicines or take them only for a few days without going through the whole treatment. If, then, the disease is not cured, the physician is blamed. Even surgical interventions which result in spectacular recovery are seldom appreciated as really life-saving performances of the physician. More likely than not, he is blamed for having cut off or cut out something of essential value to the patient, of having caused pain, or of having charged an excessive fee for 'only one hour's work'. All in all, there is no trust in the trained physician either.

As a general rule, it can be said that people combine the services of two kinds cf the available specialists: i.e., the lomeros call upon the curioso and the Indian, while the placeros call upon the Indian and the trained physician. Sometimes all three are consulted, and each of the treatments prescribed is followed in part, the patient meanwhile carefully comparing the results to see which seems the most effective. In the last resort, it is most often the Indian curer who is preferred and to whom credit is given for the cure.

A specialist is never approached in public or visited openly. A meeting is arranged by a third person, often a relative or a close friend, and the curioso or Indian is visited (or visits the patient) in a manner that will not attract the attention of neighbors. Such visits are made in the evening or at night, using backdoors or lonely trails, and information is exchanged in a whisper. This secrecy is due to the patient's fear that his enemies might find out and influence the curer to do him harm, and the curer himself prefers to stay in the background in order not to get involved in the patient's enmities. Even when consulting a trained physician in a large lowland town, people are not likely to tell his name openly. The Indian curers rarely visit patients in the village, preferring that they come to their houses, which are often at a considerable distance in the mountains. Often they diagnose the disease without ever seeing the patient, relying entirely upon information obtained from relatives or by divination, and they send their medicines or instructions by carriers who hurry back and forth. The curiosos also prefer to be consulted in their own homes. Bystanders, even close relatives, are rarely permitted to be present during the visit, and it is understood that the patient should not divulge the details of his treatment, lest his enemies be enabled to use a more powerful magic against him.

The specialists in bone fractures and open wounds or the midwives generally are willing to go to see their patients, even at night and at long distances. They never consider themselves to be mere technicians, but are always imbued with the air and manner of magicians, accompanying their treatments with spells, mumbled prayers, or magic gestures. The setting of a broken bone or the sewing up of a cut is quite often a public performance, with a curious crowd gathering around. The patient is neither encouraged nor mocked nor pitied, but there is rather an awe-struck curiosity, a fearful interest in the proceedings. No help is offered or demanded, and the practitioner goes about his work in silence and with great seriousness. As fractures, bruises, or cuts are generally not thought to have magical causes, no secrecy is required in these cases.

There are about four or five midwives in Aritama and no child is born without the assistance of one. All are elderly or old women. They never act as curers of disease, but some of them know a few Catholic prayers and are also in demand as *rezanderas*. Their intervention begins several months before parturition, with massages of the pregnant woman and the prescribing of herb teas. There is, as we shall see later, a definite correlation between midwife and witch, and midwives are often suspected of killing a mother or her child intentionally and of enjoying the suffering of both. Their visits are not kept secret but are, rather, publicized and much talked about.

The specialists in Aritama have few problems in collecting their fees, as it is generally believed that these have to be paid promptly, lest the disease return or a new one strike. This belief is an expression of the fear that people have of some of their own curers and shows the basic distrust with which they regard their treatments.

In case of very serious disease, many curers refuse to treat a patient, declaring that 'he does not belong to this world any more'. In a case where the prognosis holds little hope for the patient's recovery, the curer never hesitates to tell him so, and some people then abandon all hope and return to their homes expecting death, without trying to cure their ailment. The general tendency of the curers, however, is one of optimism, although not exactly of cheerfulness. The fight against disease and death is essentially a fight against the magic power of the patient's enemies, and to win in this struggle means more than merely conquering a disease. The curer's pride and ability are involved, and even if the patient dies, his family will rarely bear a grudge against the unsuccessful specialist.

The fame of the Indian curers has traveled far, and people often come from distant places to consult them. Although the Indian or Mestizo curers in the region of Aritama are not particularly famous, they were visited during our stay in the village by an odd assortment of strangers. Some had come from the large coastal cities; others from Venezuela; and at least one was a registered nurse from the capital of the republic. Most of these people come to obtain charms which will bring back a lost love, cure a husband or brother of alcoholism, or insure its owner against disease and bad fortune. The Indians are well aware of the credulity of their Colombian customers and exploit them in every way. They know very well what sort of ritual or treatment will impress their clients. For example, they receive them in the darkest corner of their huts or on a lonely spot near the river; they make them carry stones to and fro, tie and untie knots, repeat certain actions a certain number of times, such as walking around a house or a hut, or sipping water at a certain place in the river. Finally, they will sell them a few dry coca leaves or a small necklace bead of glass or plastic as a charm to be worn on the body. This sort of treatment is strictly for the 'tourist trade', but with the local inhabitants they try to be sincere, although they themselves often do not believe in the effectiveness of their cures. The fact that nature cures many patients is in the curer's favor, since he is often given the credit by patients who believe blindly in his supernatural power.

One of the Indian curers who visited the village while we were there greatly impressed the villagers by suddenly producing a small magnet and with it picking up a few nails he had thrown on the floor. To people who had never seen anything like it, this performance was proof enough of his powers. While hardly looking at his patient, the Indian diagnosed his trouble as 'liver', and charged 20 pesos, which were paid immediately.

MIDWIFERY

Conception and pregnancy are not shrouded in mystery or prudery, and both sexes from early youth are well acquainted with the basic physiological facts. Observation and discussion dispel any doubt or ignorance a child might harbor, and a girl of twelve or thirteen years of age, when having her first sexual experience, knows full well that intercourse will, sooner or later, lead to pregnancy. There are no inhibitions and neither the loss of virginity nor premarital pregnancy is interpreted as 'dishonoring' the girl or her family.

Commercial contraceptives are unknown but intercourse in a standing position is said to prevent conception. Childless women, or women who have had no children for several years, are often ridiculed by others who openly accuse them of practicing intercourse in this position in order to avoid pregnancy. Female attitudes are quite inconsistent, in that all women, without exception, are eager to learn about contraceptives and birth control for themselves, but at the same time they will ridicule and criticize any woman who seems to have avoided conception.

Deliberate abortion of a girl's first or even second pregnancy is seldom attempted, but the use of abortives is frequent once a woman has borne several children and doubts her ability to support more. Quite often it is really fear of childbirth rather than her poverty which induces a woman to take an abortive. Men do not believe in the efficacy of such home remedies as are used by the women to produce abortions and are probably right in attributing little or no value to them.

Public reaction to pregnancy is one of cheerful ridicule. Both men and women, when meeting a pregnant woman anywhere, are likely to make joking remarks. No woman tries ever to hide her condition but will appear in public until the last moment. However, as has been pointed out already, pregnancy is always thought to be a disease. As soon as menstruation stops a woman considers herself seriously sick. If she has to continue her daily chores in spite of her state, as is usually the case, she complains of her husband's indifference toward her 'illness'. In addition to the use of home remedies such as herbal infusions and massages, a number of taboos have to be observed. If she should pass near a field where pumpkins or calabashes are growing these fruits will shrivel and die; if a man who has been bitten by a snake should see her, his condition is likely to get worse. A pregnant woman is said to be invulnerable to snakes, but if a snake that has been near such a woman should afterward bite a man the poison will be mortal. A morsel of meat that has been touched by a pregnant woman should never be given to a hunting dog, lest the animal be spoiled (*dañado*) and lose the ability to scent game. Although, ideally, intercourse should stop about four months before birth, it is often continued until a few days before delivery and is resumed shortly after it. However, some men show a marked loathing for pregnant women and often establish sexual relations with another woman during the pregnancy of their own consorts. During pregnancy women often develop definite cravings (*antojos*) for certain foods, often for cheese or slightly fermented sugar-cane juice. Sometimes, however, these foods produce nausea and vomiting, and the woman may then develop a loathing for her former preferences. Many pregnant women eat clay and often carry a piece of it hidden in their blouses. Frequently they are small pieces of mud taken from the walls. As this is an *antojo*, there is no reproval and it is considered as quite natural.

The occasion upon which conception takes place or concomitant events are said to have a certain significance. For example, children conceived during the crescent of the moon are said to suffer in later life from seizures (*ataques*) or are likely to stutter. A bowlegged child we knew was said to have been conceived while his mother was looking at a chair that had curved legs. There is also a general belief in prenatal experiences of the child. Physical constitution or character traits are often attributed to emotional or sensorial experiences of the mother during pregnancy, and a number of people claim to 'remember' events that happened while they were still *in utero*. Most of all, sudden movements and shocks are thus 'remembered', and some people say that they 'felt the blow' when their mother slipped on the trail, while others claim to have felt the fear their mothers experienced at the sight of a supernatural vision or a scene of violence or a dangerous animal. One informant claimed to have 'seen' from his mother's womb how two policemen arrested his father and led him away, an event which happened several months before his birth. Many others refer to the 'dark of night' (*la obscuridad de la noche*) they felt while still in the womb, and some claim to have heard voices, music, or people fighting. One woman whose children were particularly dirty explained that she had never bathed or washed while pregnant and that this had obviously influenced her unborn children. The mother of an epileptic child said that during pregnancy she had seen a misshapen tree trunk in the twilight and had been shaken by fright, thus causing the unborn child's future illness.

Experiences during the third month of pregnancy, especially, are said to influence the child strongly and to be perceived by the fetus. There seems to be no doubt that during pregnancy the fetus is exposed to a series of experiences, both physical and emotional, which might influence certain aspects of behavior and constitution after birth. During the second month, the mother's abdomen is massaged in order to 'turn the child' (*voltear el niño*), a practice that is believed to be necessary lest it 'settle down' (*coge cama*) and cease to develop normally. The mother of the pregnant woman, an aunt, sister, or a midwife performs the massages, which, as pregnancy advances, becomes more and more violent. During the eighth month the massage is particularly strong, and premature birth is sometimes the result. We shall refer to this practice in more detail below.

All movements of the fetus are thought to be caused by its search for food (*buscando comida*), and it is believed that the fetus tries to reach the breasts by pushing upward. Every time the fetus 'jumps', the mother has to eat something quickly in order to satisfy its hunger. During the first month of pregnancy the embryo is believed to be located near the heart—just below it—and during this period women can often be observed making a protective gesture by pressing the right hand over this part of the body while walking or standing.

As patterns of behavior during childbirth seem to have changed quite considerably during the last generations, it might be helpful to present here a short outline of what we have learned of the ancient practices as compared to the more recent developments. Until the beginning of this century, it is claimed, childbirth had been a rather simple matter, patterned essentially after traditional Indian usages and characterized by a minimum of external interference. The expectant mother continued her domestic tasks until labor began, after which she was confined to her hammock or mat, giving birth in a reclining position. During the last moments preceding actual birth, the husband firmly embraced her abdomen and executed rhythmic pressure downward, but nobody ever tried to extract the child or the afterbirth. Medication consisted of simple infusions of herbs, and once the child was born the mother was carefully washed with lukewarm water. Complications arose only rarely and once in awhile a woman died of puerperal fever or for other reasons, but, according to our information, this happened in few cases. As a general rule, the mother was able to return to her housework after some three or four days, suffering no ill consequences even after several births.

Professional midwifery did not exist at that time and everything concerning parturition was left to the older female relatives of the child-bearing woman, generally to her mother. Childbirth was considered neither a moment of physical danger, nor an important social event.

Except for a few simple offerings to the ancestors, no special preparations were made by the family and only its immediate members took part in it, neighbors or friends hardly taking any notice of the event.

The changes that were introduced by the lowland immigrants in the second half of the past century, modified many aspects of the economic and social structure. The fact that from then on a great many women found themselves early abandoned with illegitimate children to support caused an entirely new situation to arise. Also, since the concubinage system gave young women a far better chance of finding economic support (i.e., a man) than older women, a severe tension between age-groups developed. Middle-aged women began to show marked hostility toward the girls and younger women who easily obtained economic help and who sometimes acquired considerable property in the course of several short-term conjugal unions. This rivalry between young and old women has continued ever since and is today a characteristic aspect of interpersonal relations in the village.

It was in the first decade of this century that a far-reaching change was introduced into the attitudes toward childbirth. Its immediate promoter was a woman named Carmen, who had recently arrived from one of the villages in the lowlands and who settled down in Aritama, where she proclaimed herself to be a midwife. To be attended by a midwife in those days, especially by a 'Spanish' one from the lowlands, was a matter of prestige to most villagers, and to call for Carmen's services was soon the proper thing to do in order to show one's progressiveness. Carmen acted with great energy. Condemning the prevailing pattern as 'Indian' and dangerous, she introduced an entirely new way of assisting at childbirth, consisting partly of lowland practices and partly of her own ways of dealing with this problem.

In the first place, Carmen insisted upon violent abdominal massage, beginning as early as the first two or three months of pregnancy. Next, she explained that birth was due eight months and eight days after the beginning of the last menstrual period. Therefore, if an expectant mother felt some slight pains during the eighth month of pregnancy, Carmen decided that birth was imminent and proceeded at once to produce it artificially. The expectant mother was given strong doses of laxatives, enemas, and vaginal douches, and was made to walk up and down for hours at a time. Carmen massaged her violently, scolding, and insulting her at the same time, and sometimes beating her when she protested against this treatment. Frequently, the midwife asked for male help and had two men take hold of the woman's arms and shake her as violently as possible. A strong rope was tied to a crossbeam, and the woman, sitting on the floor or bed, was told to cling to it each time she felt pain. A strip of strong cloth or a rope was wound tightly around her body below the breasts ('so the child won't ascend'), often causing great difficulty in breathing. Meanwhile herbal infusions were administered, as well as wine or beaten eggs with sugar and pepper. The abdomen was sprinkled with oil and violently rubbed. The absence of uterine contractions the midwife attributed simply to the 'weakness' or 'cowardice' of her patients, attitudes of which she used to make a great point. If birth still did not occur, Carmen intervened more directly. By introducing her hand into the vagina and opening and breaking the walls of the placenta, she caused the amniotic fluid to emerge, trying at the same time to grasp the child and extract it. Frequently, she introduced the other hand into the rectum while doing this. The last step in this procedure was to 'cut' the woman. For this she generally used her long thumbnails, but on occasion she used a pair of scissors or a strip of strong cotton cloth which she employed as a saw. Thus she opened the vagina, then introducing her hand and extracting the child. As many women thus handled did not eject the afterbirth, this meant a new intervention. The result of such treatment was that birth was often delayed for hours or days, during which the patient, if not unconscious, was screaming from pain. It is hardly necessary to add that during all these procedures no aseptic measures at all were taken. We had the opportunity of watching Carmen exercising her profession, and we also witnessed births attended by other midwives. In all cases the procedure was similar. Some of the births were undoubtedly artificially produced by massage, beatings, violent exercise, and the direct intervention of the midwife, but others were allowed to develop to full term, the real ordeal beginning only after the woman was in labor.

The consequences of Carmen's methods were soon felt in the village. Of thirty-four cases with fatal results of which we have detailed information, half were attended by Carmen, while the other half were assisted by women who had been 'trained' by her and followed her methods. Of these thirty-four cases, twenty-three ended in the death of mother and child, the latter generally *in utero*; six ended in the death of the child only, and five in the death of the mother only.

But the most remarkable point of the matter was that, in spite of the dire results, Carmen's method of assisting at childbirth became accepted as very sound and effective. As a matter of fact, the expectant mother's female relatives supported her treatment enthusiastically and helped her in every step of it, and other women who copied her methods began to establish themselves as midwives. This development began to influence all attitudes toward childbearing, pregnancy, and birth. In the first place, pregnancy came to be considered a particularly dangerous 'disease', and birth itself a torture which probably would end in death. Carmen had also introduced a fixed set of objects which had to be prepared for a birth: a new starched bedcloth, a chamberpot for the disposal of the placenta, a pair of scissors, candles, cigars, and liquor.

As we may remember, practically all these objects are now accepted as essential items in all cases of death, and many of them are stereotyped equipment of witches.

While the new method of assisting at birth had been very favorably received by many villagers, this, of course, was not true of the child-bearing women themselves. The ordeal of giving birth became a horrifying prospect. But here we must add another and most important point: according to Carmen, only the first and maybe the second child were born after eight months and eight days, while successive children were born after nine months. Therefore, the violent treatment was given only to young women and girls, not to older women who had already borne several children. In the latter cases the midwife often refused to assist at all, or, when assisting, limited her intervention to slight massages. In this may lie the explanation of acceptance of the new pattern. Carmen's methods had provided the community with a new control system, an effective means of keeping the younger generation of women from having affairs with men. At present it is relatively difficult for a man to find a young girl for a concubine, and more frequently than not he will establish relations with an older woman. The new pattern, therefore, serves several purposes: the older generation of women has been given a strong argument for teaching their daughters that men are dangerous, that pregnancy is a 'disease', and that childbirth means almost certain death. At the same time it obliges the men to look for older female companions, and thus gives economic security to many women who, before, had considerable difficulty in finding male support. The fact that these violent practices were accepted so widely is clearly due to approval by the older generation of women, who, of course, exercise a strong influence upon everything related to pregnancy, childbirth, and domestic medical practices in general. That strong hostility toward children in general, marked by frankly infanticidal tendencies, also developed is not surprising.

We shall return once more to the act of childbirth. Once the child is born, the midwife shouts 'male' or 'female', as the case may be, and communicates in this manner to everyone that birth has taken place. At once she cuts the umbilical cord without sterilizing the scissors she uses and without waiting for an additional flow of blood. The piece attached to the infant—about five centimeters in length—is cauterized with a burning candle. Applying her mouth to the infant's nose the midwife sucks out the phlegm, massaging the body and shaking it vehemently to make it breathe. Placing a finger under the infant's palate she presses upward in order to prevent a 'fallen palate' (*paladar caído*), which would make the child stutter. Oil or grease is applied to the skin and the infant's nose is pinched and 'shaped'. At once a mild laxative is administered, a treatment which is thought to be very important as the infant must eliminate as soon as possible 'all the dirt it has inside'. A tight cap made from an old stocking is placed upon the infant's head, where it stays for the next few days in order 'to shape it well'. At last the baby is wrapped in an old shirt and placed near the mother, but separated from her body by some old clothes.

The midwife now buries the afterbirth in the backyard, but the site where this has been done has no importance in the future. The umbilical cord, however, is kept by the mother and is preserved so the child will be lucky during his life. In the case of a stillbirth, the body is dressed in a little shirt and adorned with a crown of paper flowers, both being prepared rapidly by those present. After having been placed for a short time upon a table or a box for everyone to see, the corpse is buried in the backyard by the father or a neighbor. Should the child be born alive but in imminent danger of dying, a godfather is chosen and the rite of baptism is hastily performed before death. In this case the infant is buried by relatives or gravediggers in the village cemetery.

Unlike the treatment of other diseases, viewing the ministrations of a midwife during childbirth is not limited to close relatives or specialists, but practically anyone can be present. Only during the last moments, some of the crowd may be asked to leave the room. But otherwise, men, women, and children of all ages, dogs and chickens are in the same room, the adults talking, smoking, and giving advice. There is an atmosphere of anxiety and impending doom. The older women insult publicly the father of the yet unborn child, accusing him for being responsible for all the pains, dangers, and expenses. The childbearing woman is the object of condolence and pity. Her mother, sisters, and other female relatives gather weeping at her side and tell her that the hour of death is approaching. Once birth takes place, screams of pain intermingled with insults against the father of the child are the rule, and men keep rather in the background, the scene being dominated by the women, above all the midwife. No prayers are said, but the midwife usually brings a candle, which she lights for San Ramón, the patron saint of women in labor. Sometimes a person who knows a secret prayer for acceleration of childbirth pronounces it over one of the woman's handkerchiefs, which is then placed for a while upon her abdomen.

The supposed dangers of pregnancy and birth are taught to children at an early age, and the cases wherein death actually occurred are kept constantly before the eyes of the nubile girls. Mothers take pride in scaring their daughters with the most lurid accounts of births they claim to have witnessed, and girls are often threatened with the words: 'If you go on like this you will die in childbirth, just like X'. One mother whose daughter was expecting her first child, told us, 'I have scared her so much that after giving birth to her child she will have a taller story to tell than I myself who have given birth to twelve children.'

Public attitudes toward the practices of the midwives at childbirth vary according to sex and generation. Young women who expect their first or second child are terrified at the prospect and only during the last hours before actual birth show a passive attitude, due mainly to utter exhaustion from the preceding treatment. The older generation of women stoutly defend the violent practices, claiming that the younger women are 'too weak' to give birth without direct intervention. However, some of them secretly admit that the whole procedure is partly or mainly meant to impress and to be a dramatic warning to young women. The later, being largely dependent upon their elders and having been taught since infancy that childbirth means torture, hardly ever protest. Men are more articulate, but their opinion is little heeded in these matters. They denounce openly the violent practices and declare that the midwives and other old women take a sadistic pleasure in deliberately exposing the women to needless torture. Some say, however, that the child-bearing women themselves are responsible, asking the midwife to produce birth during the eighth month in order to kill the infant. The midwives also claim that some women practically oblige them to do so, even when it is clear that normal parturition is still days or weeks off.

But the important point is that the mortality of women during or due to childbirth is apparently very low, reaching, according to our data, hardly 2 per cent of all births. The thirty-four cases with fatal results were spread over thirty years, i.e., there has been about one such case every year. To this single case a normative value is attributed, generalizing for all birth, only to control thereby the younger generation of women. When discussing mortality at childbirth with the villagers, one is likely to gain the erroneous impression that the rate is high. Considering the nutritional deficiencies, the lack of antiseptic measures, and, above all, the violent methods employed at birth, a relatively high rate would not be surprising, but quantitative data and a detailed study of case histories show that, in spite of everything, death at birth is a rare phenomenon.

It is evident that the violent pattern of assistance at childbirth was introduced by a single individual, and that its full acceptance and approval was achieved only because the new technique filled a definite need of the community, or of a significant segment of it. This seems to indicate that in Aritama, even behavior patterns as traditional as the ones observed during pregnancy and birth, can change abruptly if an important sector of the community deems it necessary. The fact that thereby the welfare of the older generation is put high above that of the younger and future generations is rationalized in terms of the 'weakness' of the younger.

It is probable that the real damage done by these practices is not limited to the fact that some women die in childbirth. Very possibly it affects the surviving children. We have already mentioned the many cases of epileptoid and other symptoms which might have been caused by brain lesions contracted during birth. The high anxiety level of the childbearing women themselves might also lead to emotional disturbances in the child's later life.

THE SOCIAL INTERPRETATION OF DISEASE

The interpretation of disease as due to one's neighbor's hostility, i.e., in terms of an ever-present danger which might strike at a moment's notice simply because one man has become the object of another man's envy, is probably the main reason for the anxiety-charged atmosphere which pervades the entire village. By attributing disease-producing power to the tensions created by prestige behavior and envy, an inescapable cycle is formed, giving rise to aggression. As a matter of fact, it is not so much disease itself that is feared as what it stands for, i.e. the neighbor's ill-will. And in these circumstances the 'neighbor' is one's wife, one's sibling, one's relatives, or friends.

Although diseases are attributed to the 'winds' and the 'airs', to fright, the Evil Eye, etc., etc., their real cause is always believed to be in sorcery. At the moment a person falls ill, the first question that is formulated in everybody's mind is 'Who caused the disease?' All the details of diagnosis and therapy are dependent on the answer to this prime question. Once the identity of the culprit is known, the seriousness of the disease can be appreciated, the possibilities of its cure can be prognosticated, and the kind of treatment it requires can be determined. To establish the identity of the offender is usually not difficult. An individual knows his overt enemies and suspects at once which of them might be interested in doing him harm at any given moment. Or relatives and friends will readily volunteer their opinions. By far the best way of discovering one's hitherto unsuspected enemies is in a simple analysis of one's own feelings and actions or reactions toward other people. Such soul-searching, however, is rarely done consciously. Some people admit that, in the last analysis, they themselves might be responsible for their own diseases by having intentionally caused another person's animosity, and so they come to believe that the disease was 'God's punishment' (*castigo de Dios*) for their own evil deed. These people are among the few practicing Catholics who interpret disease and health in terms of punishment and reward. But the great majority do not think in that pattern. To them, envy and hostility are very real dangers to their bodies and souls, dangers to which they may fall an innocent victim simply because they enjoyed good health, raised a good crop, and were appreciated by a few other people. Counterattack in the form of injurious gossip and deliberate Black Magic seems to them the only way out, the only means by which they might avoid this danger. Thus an endless cycle is established by which everyone becomes his neighbor's enemy.

Sometimes, however, the identification of the enemy who sent the disease is not easy, and a specialist has to be consulted, a curioso or an Indian shaman. Weeks and months may pass before the patient knows who caused the illness, and in the meantime he is paying high fees to the curers, diviners, and/or Indians, not yet for treatment, but only for their search for the culprit. These expenses grow when treatment is begun and increase further when the patient decides to take revenge. Magical objects such as stones or necklace beads have to be bought, some to be offered to the ancestral spirits, some to be thrown into the enemy's backyard or upon the roof of his house. Some specialists ask for payment in the form of cattle or land, and many a patient has lost his property trying to counteract sorcery and to cure a disease he believed had been caused by it.

Accumulated and verified experience, in other words, the 'science' of the local culture, has developed certain concepts, and certain forms of treatment are advocated which, according to modern scientific medicine, are often ineffective or even harmful. Some of the traditional remedies, however, are recognized as having, occasionally, a certain therapeutic value. Among the latter there are some (for example, medicinal herbs or dietary prescriptions and restrictions) that form an integral part of the traditional culture, while others, such as commercial drugs, have found their way to the village only recently. Although people here distinguish quite clearly between traditional concepts or practices and others of recent introduction, the individual does not distinguish in a strict sense between magical and empirical elements. The recognized efficiency of an antibiotic or the acceptance of a vaccine or of a surgical intervention does not alter the general conviction that the disease, which has been caused by magic, requires a magical treatment. No one believes that scientific medication (in the sense of our culture) can really cure such a disease unless it is combined with the necessary magical remedies and practices. The scientific and 'modern' medicine may relieve and soothe and certainly gives prestige to the individual using it, but no one believes that it ever can eradicate the disease as efficiently as a proper traditional practice. A modern scientific medicine, it is believed, cures only a certain part or a certain dimension of the body, but it is of no avail in the case of an ailment that affects the essential balance of the individual's regime of security, which is, after all, the real vital principle involved.

Of course, modern science is also interpreted in terms of magic. Pills and tablets have different colors and shapes. So do their containers.

They have to be taken at certain 'magic' intervals and in certain quantities and combinations. There is a 'magical' correlation between medicine and diet dictating that certain remedies be taken on an empty stomach, others before meals, and still others after meals. Antiseptic practices, laboratory tests, or hypodermic injections are always seen in terms of magical procedures. Thus there is no difficulty in incorporating all these concepts into the traditional conceptual framework. They do not form a foreign body in local beliefs and practices, but only a *new* body which can be rationalized and explained and which acquires significance and function as it is integrated with the local pattern. To do this the new treatment must be 'useful' (*que sirva*). This 'usefulness', however, is not determined by its empirical adequacy but rather corresponds to local functions assigned to it and to quite personal interpretations. A treatment or particular medicine may be adopted, not because it is known to be effective in preventing or in curing disease, but because its possession and use gratify social, economic, or magicoreligious needs, or relieves tensions that are not necessarily related to the phenomenon of the disease itself.

Regardless of what kind of treatment is employed, if the patient dies it does not follow that the treatment was inadequate, but rather that the enemy who produced the disease 'knew more', and was 'stronger'. The curing of a disease has always the character of a struggle, a competition between the individual and his counselors on one side, and his aggressor on the other. The struggle is not against the disease, but against the evil power that produced it. One does not try to cure symptoms, but to eliminate a basic magical cause of the symptoms. For this very reason, the mere mechanical or physical application of a modern scientific treatment is not believed to be sufficient; it must be combined, reinterpreted, and manipulated in a manner that tends to cure not only the disease but also the patient. The inner balance, which the individual loses as soon as he falls ill, depends only to a small degree upon biological and physiological factors. To the people of Aritama there is a dimension to disease entirely beyond the influence of medical treatment, a dimension which appertains only to the individual himself and to his will and which no other agent can ever hope to touch. In this sphere, there are specific components that manifest themselves in the case of any ailment, even a very minor one, and the mere recovery of the body, however brought about (i.e., by traditional or scientific treatment), is not thought to be conclusive unless it stimulates, simultaneously, a certain vitality, a certain desire to overcome the evil, a desire the force of which depends entirely and exclusively upon the individual himself. This positive and saving factor is in force as soon as the patient begins to believe that 'his time has not yet come'; that in spite of disease and aggression there is his 'luck', his 'destiny', which make him able to carry on. At this moment his enemy's magic has been conquered, i.e., the patient has conquered his own anxieties and guilt feelings and has, momentarily at least, come to terms with life.Recovery is then inevitable and will be 'complete'.

That these concepts can play such an important role is not astonishing if we take into account the part played by psychological factors, by emotional states, in popular etiology of disease. In a purely organic sense, many of these people are not sickly. But their emotional unbalance makes them 'feel sick'.

There are two fundamental social uses to which disease may be put, viz., to demonstrate one's harmlessness and to gain prestige. Generally they are combined and the individual takes advantage of both aspects. By being sick a person demonstrates that he has been victimized by others, or by society at large, and that, in his present state, he has ceased to be a potential danger to others, except to the person whom he suspects of having sent the illness. Therefore he will exaggerate his ailments and point out his helplessness, his defeat. To say about someone, 'He is always ill' (*él vive enfermo*), means that he is harmless, i.e., a 'good' person. A sick person occupies a privileged position which allows him to neglect obligations, to reconcile himself with former enemies, to receive favors without having to return them. He is socially irresponsible and, by the mere words 'I am sick' escapes immediately from all the tedium and trials and obligations of everyday life. To doubt such a person's sincerity would be not only a serious breach of manners but an unforgivable insult to his self-esteem and dignity. A sick individual is never impure or evil, but is almost 'sacred', sacred because world-controlling forces are involved—forces which have made him an instrument and a victim in order to demonstrate their power. No one would dare doubt the reality of a disease, even if all symptoms are lacking, and the individual's claim to illness places him in a special category of people, on another level of of experience, action, and cognition.

As most treatments of diseases include all kinds of 'medicine'—i.e., offerings to the ancestors, home remedies, prayers to the saints, modern scientific medicine, commercial patent drugs, and magical procedures performed by curiosos or Indians—the sick person has ample opportunity to acquire prestige. To pray to the Catholic saints or to take a commercial medicine is to be 'civilized', and although there is little faith in their efficacy, these practices prevent one's being taken for a backward *Indio*. The more costly the medicine, the better; and the more publicly the purchase is made, the higher the prestige. We have often seen a person on the streets carrying a bottle of medicine as if it were the Holy Grail.

Even people who are quite healthy often take medicine, any medicine. Near the large water jar in the living-room or on a table next to the door, there are often a few bottles and boxes of pills, ostentatiously placed there so that every visitor can see them. Sometimes they are only for display, but more often than not the members of the household actually take these medicines, although they will declare at the same time that they are not ill. The attitude is one of, 'We can afford it so we'll do it!' High prestige is gained by taking hypodermic injections of any kind. To be able to say: 'I am getting some injections' (*Me están inyectando*) gives a great deal of superiority. Medicines, like food, are also the ideal gift. A husband's or a father's love and solicitude are always measured by his willingness to buy medicines for his family. But even if there is no need for them at all, a bottle of cough medicine, a few sulfa tablets, or a syrup to 'strengthen the blood' are always welcome presents.

In Aritama, the healthy individual, the individual who is fit physically and mentally, is considered dangerous and is therefore an asocial element. His health and vitality make people suspect that he is 'on his way up' (*que va para arriba*), i.e., on his way to new and superior levels of Creole orientation. But society does not approve of this and tries to reduce him to a 'normal', neutral state. To admit openly that one is healthy is to challenge the social order. The usual and more acceptable attitude is one of complaints, of exaggerating the importance of any boil, any cough, any sneeze. To live 'suffering' (*sufriendo, padeciendo, aguantando*) is perhaps not a Christian virtue, but in Aritama it is the best way to demonstrate that one is a well-meaning and harmless member of the community.

THE PSYCHOCULTURAL INTERPRETATION OF FOOD

The kind of food people eat in Aritama does not depend only upon the availability of the potential foodstuffs, upon what the soil produces, or upon what the individual can afford to buy, but is determined to a large degree by psychological, physiological, and cultural factors. Some foods are consumed because the metabolic need for them expresses itself in definite cravings; others because they gratify psychological necessities; others simply because it is customary to eat them. There are sociological and magico-religious factors, environmental conditions, and traumatic situations involved. As in any other field (and perhaps more than in others) cultural selectivity operates in the choice of what, why, when, and how people eat, formulating the concepts of 'good' and 'bad' food, 'healthful' or 'unhealthful', 'agreeable' or 'disagreeable' foods. Although there are, of course, differences as to group or individual taste, there is an overall pattern of permanent attitudes which is characteristic for the community. In the following pages we shall describe this pattern, as far as psychocultural factors are concerned, and we shall point out some of the attitudes that people express toward their diet and some of the ideas they connect with it.

By the great majority of the people food is considered to be the principal necessity for survival, and its acquisition is the main object of all activities. It has a highly emotional value, both for the individual and for his group, a value much elaborated in everyday conversation and in intimate thought, in socioeconomic and magico-religious life, in dreams and hallucinations, in folklore and myth. Food, of course, is closely related to health, and an adequate food supply means security and well-being, status and function. However, food is to be obtained through work, and work, it is said in Aritama, is 'God's punishment'. The acquisition of food by agriculture is considered a humiliating activity, an exhausting physical labor, and an almost rewardless task. There is no love for the land, no dignity in work, no satisfaction in planting and harvesting. People feel condemned to toil forever for their food, condemned by irresponsible and unjust powers which rule life.

This may be one of the reasons why food procurement is limited to the bare essentials. Most people recognize that they could eat more or better if they wanted to, but the additional labor this would involve is thought to be a waste of energy. That more or better food would also mean more energy is no incentive. A workable balance has been found, and the general aim is to produce and consume only enough food to survive and to be able to work physically for two or three hours a day. Beyond that, all efforts are considered as unnecessary and even damaging to one's health and prestige, and so to one's self-esteem.

Such attitudes are shared by all except a few sophisticated placero families who recognize food not only as a biological necessity, but also as a means to acquire energies which can be transformed into activities concerned with other things than mere physical survival. Family life, the education of the children, the acquisition of a better house, commerce, physical fitness, better clothing, travel, and entertainment are all incentives to the acquisition of food adequate in quantity and quality. As a group and as individuals, these families have acquired and developed tastes and preferences that spur them to increased effort. Although to them the *quality* of food has little importance except, maybe, as a prestige factor, the possession of a permanent and adequate food *supply* is associated with social and economic status.

In Aritama, every individual is obliged to produce food, beginning in early childhood. Male children at five years of age already sow maize, and at seven or eight years are expected to plant such fruits as bananas, plantains, or manioc. Girls of the same age are not expected to be really active in planting or harvesting, but are put to weaving straw hats which are sold, or exchanged at the local stores. Although the household members will insist to a questioner that this early training in food production is made necessary by the need for nourishment, in reality the incentive for work is the acquisition of clothes. Children are not taught that it is necessary to produce food so they or others may eat, but that it is necessary to produce *salable* foods, or salable straw hats which can be converted into cash for clothes and dresses to be worn during fiestas. This pattern is continued throughout adolescence and plays an important part during the whole life of the individual. Although, in the last resort, food is the ultimate value, the 'humiliating' effort in procuring it is raised to the level of prestige behavior. Only when a man reaches eighty or ninety years of age is his physical work limited to production of food for his direct personal consumption. Women are not expected to work steadily in the fields, but rather to dedicate themselves to food preparation and the weaving of straw hats. However, depending upon circumstances, a woman will work during the planting or harvesting season in much the same way as a man.

The only exceptions considered justifiable are people who are sick or who suffer from a permanent physical handicap, such as blindness or loss of a limb. Pregnant women are expected to work until the moment of childbirth and to continue to work while suckling their babies. Persons suffering from mental disorders, epileptics, spastics, etc., also work, and are excused only from certain physically dangerous tasks or during serious spells of their afflictions. Several categories of people are suspected of not producing food, and a certain hostility is expressed toward them. Among these are numbered the shopowners, the permanent or temporary employees of the government, agricultural experts, and even priests. In the case of the priests it is clear that they would not work in order to gain prestige through acquisition of new clothes; and so resentment is directed against them as 'not even' being food producers. Ideally, it is felt that class or status considerations should not interfere with the obligation to produce food, but in reality the members of the higher social and economic segments do not work in the fields.

It is assumed by the villagers that individual food intake varies according to age, sex, and activity. Infants and younger children are thought to need only small amounts of a liquid dietary, but by age three or four this is supposed to contain more and more solid foods, especially starchy tubers. The quality of this diet then does not change throughout life, except that old people are thought to need much less food than younger or middle-aged persons. Also women are supposed to need less than men of the same age-group, and men who do hard physical work are thought to eat more than others who are only moderately active. That pregnant women might have higher requirements is not recognized. Quantitative or qualitative variations in the individual food consumption are taken for granted during sickness, childbirth, in all situations of emotional stress, and on a few ceremonial occasions. In these cases specific diets are prescribed, or food intake is limited or increased.

These assumptions, however, are largely belied by actual behavior. As a matter of fact, infants are given solid food already before they reach two years of age. Women eat, on the average, at least as much as men, and the latter are likely to criticize this and to accuse them of 'wasting' food in this manner. Furthermore, old people tend to eat more or less the same amounts as younger people and, besides, they very often develop definite cravings and preferences for certain foods, such as meat or cheese. By the younger generation this is considered as irresponsibility, spitefulness, and criticism, and they in turn insist that old people keep active as food-producers until their deaths. Tensions within the family are frequently caused by the attitude of the young or middle-aged males who resent the food consumption of their spouses or elders. Women are less likely to complain about their husbands and the older generation.

TABLE 39

Food	Loma	Plaza	Food	Loma	Plaza
Beef	High	High	Garlic	Medium	High
Pork	High	High	Shallots	Medium	High
Fowl	High	Low	Cabbage	Medium	Medium
Fish (dry)	High	High	Raw sugar	High	High
Fish (fresh)	Medium	High	Bread	High	Low
Game	Medium	High	Tortillas	High	Medium
Eggs	Low	High	Spaghetti	Medium	High
Cheese	High	High	Sweets	High	Low
Fat	High	Low	Ice-cream	Medium	None
Rice	High	High	Avocado	High	High
Plantains	Low	Medium	Mango	High	High
Bananas	Low	Medium	Pineapple	High	High
Manioc	High	Low	Citrus	Medium	High
Taro	High	Low	Papaya	High	High
Sweet potato	Medium	Low	Black coffee	None	Medium
Yams	Medium	Low	Milk	Medium	High
Maize	Medium	High	Water	Medium	Medium
Potato	Medium	High	Beer	High	Medium
Beans	Medium	Medium	Chocolate	Medium	Medium
Pigeon peas	Medium	Low	Rum	Medium	Medium
Pumpkin	None	High	Soda pop	Low	Medium
Tomato	Medium	Low	Wood	Medium	Low
Lettuce	Medium	Low	Clay	Low	None
Onion	Medium	High	Tobacco	Low	None

According to local belief the nutritive value of a food lies in its 'substance' (*substancia*), an inherent quality, invisible and weightless. The nutritive value of the principal foods is commonly rated as given in Table 39.

It is obvious that both groups attribute lower values to the easily available foods. While the lomeros recognize the importance of proteins and fats, and the value of tubers such as manioc and taro, they underestimate the value of eggs, milk, plantains, bananas, and pumpkins. The prestige factor which makes the lomeros attribute high values to bread, sweets, and beer is lacking among the placeros, who show far better judgment as to the real nutritive values than do the lomeros.

In spite of the foregoing ratings, prestige foods are almost always thought to have a high nutritive value. They are mainly the following items: lean meat, chicken, eggs, spaghetti, potatoes, bread, crackers, oats, sweets, powdered milk, wine, condiments. All fried foods and all foods prepared with fat or oil carry high prestige, the same as baked foods, the use of aniline dyes in sweets, or combinations of different condiments. Certain combinations of foods or dishes are of high prestige, such as rice and meat, rice and eggs, potatoes and eggs, milk with coffee and bread, meat broth and bread, wine and crackers. As a general rule, all store-bought foods have prestige, except perhaps rice, which is too common an item. On the other hand, there are a number of socially scorned foods. To eat game, iguanas, small fish, or ants means that the consumer occupies a very low class-status. Any food preparation that does not contain fat or oil is considered to be 'poor man's food' (*comida de pobre*), the same as a stew that does not contain meat.

Certain foods are associated with the sex of the consumer. 'Men's food' (*comida de hombre*) are game, fried pork ribs, fried eggs, sour milk, and bull's testicles. The typical male fiesta food is chicken stew (*sancocho de gallina*). The meat of the ocelot (*tigrillo*) is greatly esteemed by men but is never consumed by women. Female foods (*comida de mujer*) are cow udder, milk, all foods of baked dough and, in general, most sweets.

Foods are classified first of all into 'soft' (*suaves*) and 'heavy' (*pesados*) foods. This refers principally to digestibility, and the two concepts are also related to the consistency of the feces. Starchy foods, green plantains, fish, pork, eggs, beans, pigeon peas, mangoes, and coconuts are said to be 'heavy', while 'soft' foods are broth, very tender meat, fowl, boiled bananas, yams, pumpkins, sweet potatoes, avocados, beef, maize, pineapples, papayas, and tomatoes. All these 'soft' foods are said to be easily digested and never to cause sickness. The 'heavy' foods are thought to be difficult to digest and generally harmful to one's health.

We have already mentioned in another chapter the difference between 'hot' and 'cold' foods, and the theory that the ideal diet should be balanced between 'hot' and 'cold'. The fact that 'cold' foods predominate in the actual dietary is well recognized by the lomeros and causes considerable worry, but little can be done about it because many of the 'hot' foods have to be bought and are often unavailable to the individual consumer. Some people tend to associate 'hot' with 'heavy', in opposition to 'cold' and 'soft', thus making the diet of the lomeros better balanced than that of the Creole-oriented placeros, since soft foods are regarded as healthful.

Dietary choice and food acceptance depend to a high degree upon the physical properties of food. A hedonic scale of palatability is always based upon the factors of appearance, odor, temperature, texture, taste, and flavor. The exterior appearance of a food item is generally of little importance to the consumer, except in the case of meat or fish, in which traces of blood are considered very repulsive. Such foods must be always prepared in a manner that eliminates the 'raw' (*crudo*) aspect. There exists an ideal color preference for brownish-yellow foods, which are thought to be more nourishing than others, but the usual and accustomed color of most foods of the basic daily fare is gray. Some people feel repelled by dirty or fly-infested foods, but this is by no means a general attitude. The smell of a food, however, is of great importance in determining palatability. Some foods are eaten with relish because they 'look like' other desirable but unavailable foods, but in these cases it is almost always said that 'this tastes like . . . because it smells like . . .'. This form of substitution refers generally to meat, cheese, or potatoes. People who would not eat monkeys, marsupials, cats, fish, larvae, or some of the sweetish-acid wild-growing fruits explained their aversions in terms of nauseating and loathsome odors, but did not refer to the appearance or taste of these foods.

The temperature of prepared foods is also of a certain importance. Most meals are served lukewarm or almost cold, and only in the case of broth or black coffee is it insisted that they be served hot. The meal of a household member who is momentarily absent is never reheated but is consumed cold as soon as he returns to the house. Any warmed-over food is thought to be very dangerous to health and a person who consumes such food is likely to 'poison' himself (*se envenena, se revienta*). Part of the food prepared for lunch is often kept for dinner, but it is never served hot. To eat sun-warmed fruits is also considered to be very unhealthful. As far as texture is concerned, the preferred quality depends on the food in which it is found. Dryness or mushiness are disliked in all foods, whereas softness or moistness are preferred in the daily starchy diet. Meat, however, should never be soft but should be rendered tough, elastic, even crisp, by frying or roasting it in excess. Hardness is also preferred in cheese, eggs, and sweets. Expensive foods and highly nutritious foods should offer resistance to chewing and sucking, and should never be soft and easily swallowed. A piece of tough and stringy meat is thought to be much more nourishing than tender meat. The daily normative diet of tubers, plantains, bananas, and rice has a soft texture, but to make the meal really satisfying it should contain at least a small piece of something tough and elastic which can be chewed for a while.

Meat should be salty. Black coffee should be sweet. Otherwise salt and sugar are used very sparingly. Salty, bitter, or sour tastes are always thought to be somewhat harmful to health. Highly seasoned foods are also feared, and except for chili peppers, few condiments are used. It is believed that strongly flavored foods augment their palatability, but leave the consumer dissatisfied, as they are never prepared in such quantities as to produce the sensation of being 'full'.

The sensation of hunger is said to be felt as an unpleasant itching of the whole body, accompanied by a feeling of physical weakness. Yawning and more or less audible sighs are taken to be sure signs of hunger. It is said that hunger is a passing sensation which is easily and rapidly satisfied by any food, even in small amounts, but that appetite is a permanent condition which never finds satisfaction. However, as soon as a person is hungry and begins to eat, the sensation of appetite is said to disappear and to return only after hunger has been appeased. This is thought to be very harmful to health, and people complain often that their food, although appeasing the sensation of hunger, does not delay sufficiently the recurrent sensation of 'appetite'. Hunger is often defined as 'necessity to eat' (*la necesidad de comer*), whereas appetite is 'desire to eat' (*deseo de comer*). It is evident then that satiety is not reached and that it does not determine when one should stop eating. A person stops rather because there is no more food or because he reaches a limit beyond which his eating would be considered as deliberate aggression. A certain point of satiety is reached when the person feels 'full' (*harto*), but this does not mean that his 'desire' for more or different food is satisfied. It is generally recognized the foods containing proteins or fats delay the recurrent sensation of hunger, whereas starchy foods appease it only for a few hours. The consumption of such starchy foods, however, is believed to be essential because the physical sensation of 'fullness' (*hartedad*) is thought to be very necessary for health.

It is generally believed that the amount of fecal matter excreted corresponds exactly to the amount of food consumed. During digestion the 'substance' of the food is assimilated by the body, and during this process gases are formed which have to be eliminated as soon as possible lest they cause serious harm to the body. Physical exercise after meals is recommended as a sure way to 'eliminate the gases', but for people more than forty years of age a short nap is said to be essential after eating a meal. To take a bath or even to wash one's face shortly after eating is thought to be very dangerous. The chewing of the food and the state of one's teeth is not thought to have any influence upon digestion, and it is believed that swallowing without chewing can bring no harm. Even people with good teeth show a marked tendency to eat large pieces of solid food with a minimum of chewing, eating rapidly and trying anxiously to swallow as fast as possible their portion of the daily meal. Characteristically, this behavior is described with the following words: 'One always eats with despair, and in a hurry' (*uno siempre come desesperado y con afán*). The individual process of digestion is a daily topic of conversation. Both adults and children will discuss how many bowel movements they have had, mentioning the color and texture of the feces, and relating them to the food consumed previously. Constipation is more feared than diarrhea, and laxatives are probably the most frequently consumed remedies of all. Their different trademarks, prices, and effects are discussed in detail, and the day's conversation with neighbors or friends often begins with an account of projected or effected purges.

The pattern of meals is highly irregular. Prepared food is hardly ever served at a certain hour of the day, but there is often a variation of one or two hours on successive days. Nor is there much emphasis on all household members eating simultaneously. There is no conversation during the meal, everyone eating rapidly and with ill-humored faces, sometimes with a tendency to hide while eating by turning the back to the others. The social atmosphere during meals is always one of subdued hostility. The different menu items are not discussed and personal preferences are not openly shown. Complaints about the monotony of the daily fare are almost never heard except from old people. On the contrary, the repetitive element is valued and believed to be healthful. When sitting down to eat most people know beforehand what the meal will be. No one ever expects a new item or a new form of preparation.

It is very doubtful whether people can regulate their diet by selecting foods that satisfy bodily needs. In Aritama, the lack of animal proteins is probably expressed by the frequent and sudden cravings for meat, fish, or cheese, but, as we have pointed out above, the craving could also be due partly to the desire to chew and suck foods that offer resistance. There is certainly no deficiency of ascorbic acid, but still many people develop sudden cravings for citric fruits. Hyperphagia of certain foods is practiced occasionally in the Loma barrio, especially during the avocado harvest or when wild fruits are available. Such fruits are often eaten in such a quantity as to cause acute gastric distress. Game, also, is often overeaten, as there exist no techniques to preserve the excess meat by salting or smoking it. Individual predilections or sudden cravings for certain foods are always for items not easily available at the moment but not impossible to acquire by an outlay of money or work. Such sudden cravings for meat or cheese are frequent among women of all ages, while men tend to develop them only late in life.

In individual predilections the factor of nutritive value and of health is of secondary importance, and the taste of the food concerned is of still less significance, However, as a rule there is a positive correlation between what people 'like' and what they believe is beneficial for their health, whereas, on the other hand, foods that are considered to 'taste' disagreeable are never liked, although the convenience of eating them is fully recognized. These correlations are never consciously formulated but are easily established by checking individual reactions to predilected foods. Such foods are often items with a high protein content but in this case the convenience of eating them is not stated, but rather their pleasant taste is referred to. In food predilections that refer to tubers and fruits, the taste is of little or no importance, but their relation to health is always pointed out.

Food and health are closely related in everyday life and thought. However, it is not recognized that the quality of the daily dietary might be a direct cause of sickness, but rather it is accepted that certain individual items and certain preparations or combinations of them will cause disease. A knowledge of deficiency diseases being completely lacking, food is mainly thought of in relation to its digestibility or to the classic differentiation between 'hot' and 'cold' foods.

Most individual aversions are explained in terms of health attitudes. The fact is, however, that it is generally the fear of poison which determines these reactions, a fear which is freely admitted. Neither prestige factors nor the lack of nutrition, even to the point of starvation, will persuade a person to accept a certain food which he has decided, arbitrarily, is deleterious to his health. Even though he knows that others eat this food without suffering any ill effects, he is still convinced that it would be harmful to him individually, and cannot bring himself to eat it. If it is urged upon him, he becomes angry, and manifests nausea (without, however, vomiting) and then complains of loss of appetite for *any* food. This revulsion might last for several days or even longer.

Intrinsically loathsome are all putrified and fetid foods. Acid, bitter, or astringent foods cause less repugnance. The repulsiveness of putrefaction and fetidity, however, applies only to meat, fish, and eggs, but never to fruits or cheese. In the latter cases the rotten parts are simply cut off and the rest is eaten. The limit of what is meant by putrefaction in meat or fish, however, is very relative. What to a Westerner would appear to be a very unpleasant *haut goût* is apparently not noticed at all, and even a marked smell, color, or texture indicating advanced putrefaction does not make meat inedible. It is rubbed thoroughly with vinegar, garlic, and peppers and then fried until its texture is crisp or even tough. But there is a limit to the stage of putrefaction and once this has been reached, the meat is discarded. Acid foods are considered to be very disagreeable but essentially healthful and are accepted by adults almost only for that reason. Children, however, seem to enjoy them, without being aware, of course, of their nutrient content.

We have already mentioned that the consumption of meat has a high prestige value, probably the highest of any foodstuff. Both palatability and prestige are greatly increased by certain preparations, such as fried meat or its combination with other highly desirable foods like cheese or rice. As many people are unable to buy meat regularly, this lack is often made easier to bear by attributing to meat a harmful influence on health and children are taught that it causes intestinal worms. The belief of desirable foods being harmful to health can be illustrated by the following two examples: A fairly well-educated placero had read a leaflet published by the Colombian Ministry of Agriculture in which the nutritive value of tomatoes was extolled. Unable to buy tomatoes, he planted a few seeds but had to give up when ants destroyed the growing plants. Shortly afterward he went to visit a friend at a hospital in one of the lowland towns. There he was told of a woman who had an uterine tumor removed, which, according to the story, 'looked just like a tomato'. Upon his return to the village he spread the news that tomato seeds were likely to cause uterine tumors, a theory which was accepted by all who found tomatoes difficult to obtain and which made people who had until then eaten them abstain from future use. In another case a boy selling ice-cream cones entered a room where several adults and a four-year-old child were gathered. When the child insisted upon having a cone, the adults said flatly, 'The cones are bad', each adult saying the same words with hypnotic intensity. The child began to cry until one of the men said, 'You can have one some other day when they bring them in hot. Today all the cones are cold.' There was no joke involved, but these words were said with all seriousness and were repeated by the others until the child stopped crying.

Meat, sweets, and citric fruits are foods that should not be eaten at certain times. There are definite restrictions on them during illness, pregnancy, or the postpartum days. Certain food combinations that are said to be extremely harmful to health are the following: pork and raw sugar, fried eggs and sugar-cane juice, bitter fruits and milk, watermelons and milk, alcoholic beverages and commercial medicines. Beans, coconuts, mangoes, and avocados are considered as very harmful to the liver, while sugar cane is said to be dangerous to people who suffer from colds. This means, again, that foods that have to be bought, or that are desirable but scarce, are harmful to health, frequently because they are said to 'weaken' the blood. These concepts are sometimes empirically established but more often are based on purely psychological reactions to the greater or lesser difficulty of satisfying a specific hunger. Some foods are rejected by the individual because they remind him consciously or subconsciously of previous traumatic experiences, of fecal matter, or of poisonous foods. The sight of a blood-stained piece of meat disturbs some people, who claim not to be able to eat meat for days afterward. One informant who had an aversion to fish told us that once he had seen a blood-stained fish which reminded him at once of an abortion. Another informant who never ate papayas explained that as a three-year-old boy he had felt very hungry and had cried at the sight of a papaya, whereupon his mother became angry and forced him to eat the entire fruit at once. Indigestion and vomiting followed, and he never again wanted to touch this fruit.

Certain foods are highly emotion-charged, and among them we must mention first of all milk. Milk is generally regarded as a female food and a food for infants, but in reality both sexes show a marked aversion to it, although women tend to be less articulate in verbalizing it. To a great many people milk is disgusting and loathsome. This aversion is not rationalized in terms of endangering health, but is a purely affective response which is simply explained as disgust, without taking into account nutritional convenience, temperature, taste, or flavor. People who do not drink milk hardly ever say so in few and sober words, but are likely to become verbose, pointing out with a mixture of pride and disgust that they would never consume such a thing. However, this aversion refers only to milk in its natural state. Transformed into cheese, sour milk, butter, or mixed with dough or soups it is readily accepted. It is the white liquid which is abhorred. It seems possible that this type of food aversion has its origin in the weaning situation and the individual's attitude toward the mother image. We observed that many people who do drink milk in its natural form had been bottle-fed or were weaned late.

Meat is another food with a high emotional charge, but in this case acceptance or rejection is rationalized in terms of health, convenience, and other factors. Meat, principally beef, is thought to form an essential part of a healthful diet, and its scarcity or cost is the object of much concern. The importance of meat is so high that rarely will a woman, much less a child, be entrusted with its purchase. It is the men who go to the slaughterhouse to buy it. Should meat not be available for several days or should the prospective buyer, in spite of having the money, not be able to obtain a palatable portion, his reactions are likely to be quite violent. The lack of meat is not met with a shrug of the shoulders, but with anger and recriminations against those who were able to obtain some. Children up to six years can be seen crying at the news that no cattle have been slaughtered that day, and adults will heatedly discuss the matter. The gift of a piece of meat, however small, is a sign of love, of friendship. The theft of meat is a very serious offense.

There are few definite food taboos in Aritama. Those that do exist are not clearly formulated but are strictly observed by common consent. For example, dogs, burros, mules, horses, vampire bats, and large felines are completely prohibited as food. Snakes, rats, ants, larvae, iguanas, and ocelots, however, are eaten by many people, in spite of the fact that some of these foods—notably iguanas and certain small river fish—are socially scorned as being 'Indian food' (*comida de indio*). Special additional prohibitions are observed during sickness, pregnancy, and childbirth for reasons of health. On a very few ceremonial occasions, prohibitions such as the abstention from meat on Good Friday, are also observed. In the latter case, individual supernatural punishment by ancestral spirits is feared, but the other tabooed foods are rejected mainly for the underlying fear of poison. Many informants stated that the prohibited foods probably were insipid, but that they might actually be unpleasant in taste was never mentioned.

Many attitudes toward food develop in an imaginary sphere. As will be seen, in regard to the general availability and distribution of foods there exist many elaborated beliefs which possess absolutely no basis in reality. Meat and cheese, for example, are said to be available all year round, the people being very ready to state that there is always a plentiful supply. This is definitely not the case, as weeks, or even months, may pass without any of these items being available in the village. Individual reactions to this fact invariably express strong intergroup hostilities, the placeros being blamed by the lomeros for not wanting to sell their cattle or their cheese, waiting, instead, for the price to go up. The availability of eggs, fowl, peas, bread, and potatoes is also highly exaggerated, everyone insisting that these items are abundant. In reality, they are quite scarce and at times unavailable. The foods mentioned are all of a highly desirable character but are unavailable to many because of their high price. It is obvious, therefore, that the insistence upon their abundance is the result of strong anxieties caused by their scarcity. A constant elaboration of such themes forms one of the main topics of daily conversation. During the early morning hours most village talk is concerned with whether or not cattle have been slaughtered, and the news, whether true or not, is called from house to house, across streets and fences, from hill to hill. This problem of meat is discussed even by many persons who have no intention or possibility of buying any but who go to great length in talking about prices, the desirability of certain cuts, or the palatability of certain preparations.

Similar behavior patterns can be observed in connection with many other highly desirable foods. The arrival at a local store of a load of potatoes, of cheese, dried fish, or peas is news that spreads rapidly.

The available amounts are exaggerated, as is the individual's intention or capacity of buying. Also, for example, preparations for the baking of bread are discussed widely. Would-be buyers spend much time in speculations as to when the product will be ready for sale. Often such food rumors start without any factual basis and spread for hours or days over the village until it has become clear to everyone that the desired food simply is not available.

Any discussion of ceremonial occasions, such as the yearly fiesta cycle of Holy Week, San Rafael, and Corpus, always leads to detailed descriptions of the abundant and delicious dishes to be prepared by even the most humble people. In reality, there is never any such preparation, as only a few of the well-to-do placero families will actually eat some special dish on those days. Perhaps some old woman will prepare a few aniline-dyed sweets and send her little niece to sell them on the street, or another might bake two dozen small buns, but otherwise the much-talked-about fiesta foods belong to the realm of the imagination.

Parallel with imaginary abundance, run imaginary want and even famine. Notwithstanding the obvious availability of certain foods such as tubers, plantains, or bananas, people often are likely to belittle their importance and will declare that the land is sterile, that the crops failed, or that an imagined lack of labor caused their loss. Certain months of the year, quite contrary to actual experience, are said to be times of hardship, and the time-lapse since certain foods were eaten last is often grossly exaggerated. Utterly unfounded political rumors frequently contribute to a pessimistic outlook on the future food situation.

In reality, only the following foods are not available all year: dried fish, avocados, mangoes, potatoes, and some of the wild-growing fruits. All other foods are either grown or manufactured, or can be bought. Even if no cattle were slaughtered at the moment, meat can be bought in neighboring villages, or any man can buy an animal and slaughter it for sale. The fact, however, that these foods *can* be bought is never mentioned, even by the most sophisticated. There is a sharp contrast between ideal self-sufficiency by growing one's own food, and actual cash-cropping which provides money to buy food with.

The basic year-round food supply of starchy roots and tubers has to be supplemented with certain other items such as rice, fat, cheese, or meat, all of which have to be bought with cash or the equivalent in hand-woven straw hats. Cash is available to most people only during the months when crops are gathered and sold. It is during these months, that the food situation becomes slightly better, not during the months when people depend entirely upon the yield of their own fields and upon their women's output of straw hats. The coffee harvest generally begins in December, and people earn cash either as owners of the crop or as relatively well-paid harvesters. In February, after the coffee harvest is over, many men work as paid laborers preparing the year's first planting. The money earned is spent during the months of unemployment that follow, until after Corpus Christi in June, but in July the avocado harvest begins and lasts until the next coffee harvest. Much of the money earned is spent for things other than food, but a considerable amount *is* spent on food. The generally accepted idea that the food situation is most alarming during the dry season is not borne out by facts, but is the outgrowth of the conflict between the old-established agricultural pattern of subsistence and the recent introduction of cash crops. This is definitely a limiting factor on the individual's awareness of food possibilities.

In reality, of course, no one is entirely self-sufficient. All depend to some degree upon the productiveness of others. Even the poorest have to buy salt, fat, matches, clothing, or cooking-pots. Nonetheless, self-sufficiency is extolled. The general opinion is that everyone produces as much or more than he consumes. When it is pointed out that this is not the case, attitudes change abruptly into self-commiseration, and ultimately the local or central government is blamed for neglect. In spite of wanting always to give an impression of independence, self-sufficiency, and personal initiative, as soon as limiting factors are pointed out, everyone is loud in his blame of his elders and of all persons or institutions that represent authority. Supernatural reasons are rarely given as excuse or explanation for this state of things, but part of the responsibility for manifest failure is attributed to the climate, the lack of rains, and the progressive desiccation of the agricultural lands.

All people believe that the community produces a considerable surplus of food which is sold or given away. 'We have always food to spare,' people will say; 'we never feel the want of anything.' When asked for details of this alleged surplus, it is answered that the people of a certain neighboring hamlet sell plantains to a lowland town; that the inhabitants of another hamlet gave several loads of manioc to relatives living in a third hamlet; that one Indian tribe sells raw sugar in the lowlands, while another sells potatoes to some neighboring village. All this is true enough but, of course, has nothing to do with the situation in Aritama itself, where there is obviously no surplus, except perhaps in the commercially sold cash crops of coffee and sugar cane. The fact is that much food has to be imported to Aritama, not only such commercial foods as rice, fat, and cheese, but also such supposedly abundant home-grown products as maize, manioc, plantains, and bananas are frequently brought from the lowlands because the local supply of these foods is insufficient. Every time a certain locally produced food is unavailable for a few days, the shopkeepers, authorities, or other individuals are suspected and accused of speculating in prices or of having secretly sold huge quantities of these foods to other villages which were supposedly at the point of starvation and were willing to pay high prices. All this is entirely imaginary, the fact being that the food production simply does not keep pace with local demand.

The different attitudes toward food described in the foregoing pages are acquired by the individual at an early age. By training, experience, and imitation the child learns that the food supply is insecure, that its permanency depends to a high degree upon a proper balance in inter-personal relations, and that the lack of food means disease and ulti-mately death. The infant soon learns that the mother, as a source of food supply, is not fully satisfying and that she is likely to change the quan-tity and quality of the desirable intake. The experience of weaning, followed by the nursing of a sibling, introduces the problem of rivalry on the same age-level, a problem which soon becomes more acute in the infant–child-nurse situation. Crawling and walking lead to a new dimension in the food search, and now food theft and its ensuing punishment and guilt are added to the conflict. The child is made to realize that the possession of food obliges the owner to share what he has with certain other individuals, who in turn requite a share, leaving the original owner not with a surplus but with the bare essential. At the same time the child learns to use food to express emotions by rejecting or by offering it and that it can be used as an instrument of power by depriving or rewarding others. All this the child is taught quite con-sistently until it has developed a set of patterns that interrelate his own production and consumption to that of his group. Simultaneously, with reference to the child's own security system, he is taught to avoid or to prefer certain foods, certain quantities, or certain preparations—some rationalized in terms of health, others in terms of prestige. The first relationship of children to the supernatural, to saints, and to the Virgin are almost always limited to prayers for food. Children up to ten or twelve years will carry on long conversations with images, asking them to be given a bit of food (*que les boten una miga*). A seven-year-old boy adorned a calendar picture of a saint with flowers, prayed for food, and ended by threatening to take the flowers away if his prayer was not granted. Boys of twelve to fifteen will begin to make vows with the same end. The preoccupation with food continues in an imaginary sphere, in children's games, in riddles and folktales, dreams and night-mares.

Next to the mother, there are certain persons who have a specific influence on food attitudes. Curers, midwives, men with more or less recognized priestly functions, Indian shamans, and trained physicians—they all will speak of food in connection with disease, child-birth, or any other crisis, reaffirming in many instances the beliefs and patterns es-tablished by early childhood disciplines. In no other area of individual behavior can one observe such continuity and consistency in method or theory than in food behavior.

With regard to the common foods that form the basic daily diet, we can distinguish certain changes in the gustatory response of certain age-groups, a phenomenon which is of interest in the learning process. Children of three to five years of age already react with open disgust and anger to evil-smelling, dirty, or slightly putrid foods. They do not cry or vomit, but show rage and try to destroy the food or throw it away. Between six and eight years there is a marked aversion to foods prepared with garlic, onions, or shallots, verbalized often in terms of unpleasant body odors. If pieces of these condiments are in any food, they are taken out and thrown away with rage, but the food itself is eaten. Tears, nausea, and verbal expressions of disgust seem to be absent at this age. Around nine or ten years children frequently develop temporary aversions to the starchy staple foods—rice included—and to meat and chili peppers. Although they usually eat their meals, they do so with disgust and loathing, explaining this reaction as their being weary (*aburridos*) of eating every day the same insipid fare. This attitude often persists for several years and disappears definitely only after the individual is obliged to produce most of the food he consumes. During late middle age, and above all during old age, a similar attitude appears again, this time much more sharply defined and expressed in violently aggressive reactions. At this period of life people often suddenly refuse to eat a meal which does not contain meat, fish, or cheese and express this rage in harsh accusations against their wives, husbands, children, or grandchildren. These attitudes are frequently found among all classes, in varying intensity but forming a definite pattern. Usually beginning with a depressive state which sets in shortly before the meal and developing into violent rages with physical aggressiveness, this type of behavior often leads to the destruction of furniture and other inanimate objects.

Individual negative reactions toward foods commonly consumed are usually determined by their availability or by previous experience. People who are in no position to choose what they eat rarely reject the basic diet, except children or old persons. Minor items are sometimes refused as being unhealthful, as mentioned above. Childhood experiences connected with blood, feces, rotten eggs, or abortions were given by some people as individual reasons for not eating or not liking to eat certain foods, but these cases were relatively rare, and no definite pattern was observed in them.

Two types of marked autoprivations are, however, of importance. In Aritama, as elsewhere in Colombia, to offer a visitor a cup of black coffee and to accept it is basic courtesy. It was, therefore, surprising to observe that many people never accepted this offer when made by other villagers. Some would claim ill health; others would say that they had had a cup just before they arrived; and still others had evidently given up coffee altogether. Investigations into the underlying causes of these refusals revealed the following reasons, cited here in their order of relative importance, as stated by the informants: (1) fear of contagious diseases (2) fear of poison (3) shyness. The first reason is obviously untrue, as in Aritama the recognition of contamination and contagion hardly can be said to exist at all. The third reason is also quite fictitious; people are timid but never so much so as to refuse a cup of coffee offered by a person they have known all their lives. Evidently the fear of being poisoned is responsible for this pattern, which thus expresses, once more, the strong hostilities and anxieties that dominate the village scene.

Another type of autoprivation has its roots in prestige behavior. People deprive themselves of food in order to save money for clothes to be worn in public, especially during fiestas. Everyone is willing to sacrifice food, even to the point of acute physical discomfort, to buy new clothes. In no field other than that of individual food consumption is such sacrifice thought to be practicable, but in this department this behavior is considered by all to be quite normal. As a matter of fact, an individual who would eat well while wearing old clothes would be considered as an abnormal and miserly person.

To reject food during meals in one's own home is a very common practice in Aritama. The family will gather around the cooking-pot or the table, but one member will, with a wordless gesture, refuse to eat, while sitting and staring at the others. Eventually the person might get up and leave the room or the house. As one informant put it: 'One rejects food in order to show that one is disgusted and annoyed.' This does not always mean that the person is disgusted with the food itself, but it is a common expression of the male's hostility toward his women-folk, especially his wife. As practiced by men, the pattern varies, the aggression being directed against the wife, but not against the mother, the exact behavior depending upon the intensity of the hostile feelings toward the former. If a man violently throws the food away, his rage is probably directed against the quality of the food and not against the person who prepared it. But if a man refuses to eat, and leaves his home, and accepts food in another household, this is always interpreted as a very grave offense against his wife. Among women, this pattern is found only during late middle and old age, and is more often than not directed against the food itself, although they may also demonstrate in this way their hostility toward other members of the household.

It is also common for both sexes and all ages to refuse food during highly emotional states, for example, at and after the death of a family member, during the sickness of a close relative, or during a difficult economic situation. Fear of poison, as mentioned earlier, is another frequent reason why people, especially men, refuse food. This pattern is observed in their own houses, where men fear to be poisoned by their wives. The wives, in turn, often refuse food offered to them by women of other households whom they believe to be potential rivals or enemies. Another frequent reason given for refusing food is bad health. In this case patterns vary widely according to the individual's interpretation of his state of health and the supposed influence foods of a certain type might have upon it. That reasons of health are often used as mere pretexts, the real cause being fear of poison, is also quite frequent, but sometimes the underlying real reason consists in the individual's not wanting to enter a cycle of mutual obligations. In other words, acceptance of food would mean that the person or family who offered it would acquire a right to ask a favor in return, and this is avoided by not accepting the offer in the first place. Such a cycle of mutual food exchange is kept restricted to a close group of people united by kinship, but is rarely widened to include other members of the community.

The disparity between food production and food consumption is seen by all inhabitants, but in quite unrealistic terms. The fact that food is scarce and hunger prevalent is always attributed to the land, the climate, the government, the 'rich', to individual laziness, ignorance, or bad luck, but never to general social and economic factors such as population increase, mismanagement of the land resources, and prestige cash-cropping. Out of this attitude grows a series of opinions which refer to individual and collective productiveness and self-sufficiency, but none of which corresponds to the real state of things.

No one in Aritama raises potatoes. All potatoes consumed locally are bought from the Indians. When asked why people do not grow their own potatoes in the highlands of the valley, the following reasons were given: (1) too much work and trouble (2) the highlands are the legitimate property of the Indians (3) no seed potatoes can be obtained (4) the soil is inadequate. In reality, the work of growing potatoes is not any harder than many other generally practiced agricultural activities; the landownership of the Indians is not recognized or respected by anyone in the village; seed potatoes can be had from the Indians for nothing or very little; suitable land is available in many parts.

When it was asked why people do not hunt or fish with more frequency, the following reasons were given: (1) the surrounding country is too dangerous and wild (2) snakes might bite the hunter or fisherman (3) the lowlands where fish can be caught are unhealthful (4) too much valuable time is lost in hunting and fishing. It is quite obvious that none of these reasons is valid. The real reasons for this negative attitude of self-limitation of a potential food supply are manifold. In part, it is due to the evident unwillingness of these people to co-operate, which would be essential in activities like potato-growing, hunting, and fishing. In part, physiological factors are responsible, the listlessness produced by undernourishment obliging people to live with a minimum of physical effort. Fear of new surroundings and new situations also plays a certain part. A further real reason of importance is the fact that potato-growing, hunting, and fishing are associated with Indian tribal life, and constitute, therefore, despicable and humiliating activities.

It is one of the prime laws of behavior never to admit to hunger outside one's own home. Our survey of the individual food situation was, therefore, an extremely embarrassing matter, and most people tried to avoid the theme. To insist on discussing it was highly offensive, and as a rule all questions were answered in a perfunctory and stereotyped manner, the questioner being assured that the food situation could hardly be better and that it was satisfying from every point of view. However, when this barrier was broken down, an altogether different picture was revealed, one dominated by hunger and fear of hunger. Excepting always the few placero families, it can be said that no one considers his daily food intake to be nearly sufficient and really satisfying.

Food is never a matter of indifference but always one fraught with strong emotions. So our questioning brought first emphatic claims of abundance, but sooner or later the admission that one is always hungry. Once the individual informant recognizes the many contradictions he has indulged in while depicting the general food situation in the most optimistic terms, he will admit that 'other' people are suffering from want but that he himself and his family always manage to eat well, if not abundantly. At this point the informants tend to show signs of increasing uneasiness and excitement expressed in accusations of 'laziness' of the 'others' who, they claim, could eat more and better if they only would work more. Further discussion of the individual's personal daily food intake, and the gratification and satiety derived from it, leads often to self-accusations, such as 'ignorance', and 'lack of civilization', and culminates finally in the admission that his own food intake is insufficient both in quantity and quality. The constant envy and mischievousness of one's neighbors is pointed out, their lack of co-operation, and the selfishness of the members of one's family, who always ask for more food than the head of the household can provide.

Hunger is then a recurrent theme, and the entire process from production to consumption develops in a hostile atmosphere, where every individual is resentful for having to share his supply with others and for depending upon others for help once his own contribution should be too meager for survival. There is a limit to the possibilities of adaptation to malnutrition, a point where acute disease and open aggression set in, but while this limit has not yet been reached, the systems of social control that try to maintain a balance are proving to be less and less effective.

THE SICK COMMUNITY

We shall return once more to the problem of ill health and to the broader question of how it affects sociocultural behavior. Sickness, as we have seen, is a steady companion of life in Aritama. Already during the first weeks after birth most infants begin to suffer from cutaneous irritations which eventually develop into painful infections. At the time when children begin to crawl and to cut their first teeth, contamination from the chewing and sucking of dirty objects leads frequently to diarrhea, and acute gastrointestinal diseases are practically the rule at the time of weaning. Severe irritations of the anal zone are common, as are painful staphylococcal pyodermas. From this age on, more or less periodic spells of diarrhea caused by enteric diseases continue throughout life, the same as respiratory ailments—bronchitis, colds, or throat infections. Quite apart from the many serious diseases such as pneumonia, amoebic dysentery, or hepatic dysfunctions, the incidence of which seems to be high, but which, of course, do not affect all inhabitants, the average individual suffers from infancy to death from the toxic effects of a series of minor ailments—mostly gastrointestinal and respiratory—the phasic recurrence of which marks every year of life. The respiratory diseases are perhaps easier to bear because they rarely last longer than a few days or, at most, weeks, but intestinal parasites and anemia are conditions that may last for many years. If we add to this the poor quality and meager quantity of the individual food intake, we come to the necessary conclusion that Aritama is a sick community.

The high incidence of disease is, of course, not due only to inadequate sanitary and hygienic conditions and to a bodily constitution weakened by lifelong undernourishment. There are other factors at play as well. Partial maternal deprivation and the consequent anxiety-charged experiences of infancy and childhood are most likely to lead to functional disorders, in this case neurotic disturbances, and it is these and their manifestations and consequences that are, naturally, of the highest importance to the quality of the sociocultural expressions of the group. The problem of mental ill health leads us, then, to consider the concept of 'normalcy'. Although it seems obvious that what is normal or abnormal depends on the cultural context of the particular manifestation, one might establish a limit beyond which certain individual or collective expressions of a psychogenic nature must be designated as pathological. This 'ceiling', it seems, is reached as soon as the emotional responses become frankly destructive to the functioning of the individual as a group-member. As to neurotic disorders of this type, we have

332

mentioned already in the foregoing chapters the relative frequency of hysterical or hysteroid manifestations, the hallucinatory imagery (cf. chap. IX), somnambulism, certain phobias, and, above all, the strong anxieties connected with most interpersonal relations, the spirit world, magical aggression, the food situation, the threat of disease and death, and so forth. It is apparently here, in this free-floating anxiety, where a borderline is reached beyond which the individual's social functioning is seriously impaired. The patterns and attitudes we have described when speaking of magical aggression suggest occasionally a psychoneurotic level that borders on paranoid schizophrenia. When speaking of Aritama as a sick community, we must, then, include in this concept also certain aspects of the state of mental health of the inhabitants.

The point that is of interest is the sociocultural significance of health and disease, the ways in which ill health becomes a tool in social relationships and in which it tends to shape individual behavior and general local culture content. Since infancy the individual has been taught that illness forms an essential part of life. To a large degree the daily 'dos' and 'don'ts' of child-training refer to the avoidance of illness, and every child is used to seeing ill people, hearing their ailments discussed by others, and listening to their own descriptions of symptoms and treatments. The education *by* fear and *to* fear makes constant use of the specter of disease as a controlling force which may strike at any moment. In reality, the controlling power of society is illness and all moral law enforcement is accomplished through the menace of disease. But the child is not only given to understand that such exterior influences as a rain shower, a drought, or a certain food might cause ill health; he is also taught, explicitly or implicitly, that rage, joy, sudden fear, or prolonged sorrow might lead to organic dysfunctions.

The question, then, is 'What do people do with their disease? How do they "use" it?'

One cannot speak of hypochondriasis in Aritama. Ill health is too much of a real problem for everyone. People do not exaggerate if they worry constantly about trifling symptoms, because they know by daily experience that there exists the likelihood that such symptoms might develop eventually into ailments of serious proportions. Practically in every household there is always someone ill with a cold, a spell of dysentery, a rheumatic pain, or an infected boil. The fear of falling ill or of an illness becoming worse dominates daily life, and all people are constantly preoccupied with the effects their food might produce, with abrupt changes in temperature, undue physical efforts, or certain emotional states. Now, as an ill person changes status, becoming the center of attention and acquiring privileges insofar as social interaction, co-operation, labor, food, and rest are concerned, the more or less conscious flight into disease becomes, even in childhood, a means by which reality is avoided and gratifications are sought. At the same time, illness becomes an aggressive, accusatory attitude by which the parents—and later on society as large—are blamed for one's disease.

This 'social use' of disease, as we might call it, is readily seen in daily relationships. In the first place, no one, under any circumstances, will publicly or privately admit to good health. On the contrary, everyone is ready to complain of ailments, of some illness passed through recently or prognosticated by some slight symptom; of the inefficiency of a certain treatment, or the cost and length of time it involved. The common formula of greeting 'How did you pass the night?' (*Cómo ha pasado la noche?*) expresses genuine concern over the health of the person thus greeted. This concern is also continuously shown by commenting on any symptoms that might suggest ill health in other people: if someone coughs it is concluded that a bad cold is approaching; if someone rests for a while in a hammock, visitors will ask at once if he feels ill. During or after a rain shower people will ask the passers-by whether they got wet, advise them to return home, or else suggest they walk faster or slower. There are continuous comments about this person looking pale, and that one thin, and a third one trying to hide a serious illness. By the same token, one's own slightest discomfort is given much importance. People will plaintively speak of the 'bad night' (*mala noche*) they have just passed, of their 'raging' (*rabiando*) from pain, or their utter inappetence which keeps them from eating 'anything'. When talking about past diseases—real or imaginary—people will frequently use expressions like 'I was about to die . . .' (*Estuve de muerte*) or 'I was seriously ill' (*Estuve grave*), finishing their account with 'If it hadn't been for . . .' at which point the benefit of a certain medicine is extolled or the treatment of a certain curer is praised. But underneath these overt attitudes one can, of course, easily discern the subjacent hostilities and consequent guilt feelings. The true situation may be formulated in terms of 'Don't hurt me; I am a poor, harmless, defenseless, sick person'.

The high incidence of disease and the constant fear of it are, of course, factors that tend to shape the individual's entire outlook on life, especially if the person has been exposed to such ailments ever since infancy. Chronic parasitosis and undernourishment are the most common impairments of people's health, and many more or less acute derangements certainly contribute to the formation of an interrelated range of specific personality types in which fatalism, materialism, aggressiveness, and envy are common traits. At the same time, it is obvious that a disease affects not only its victim but also his whole household group, his kin, and his entire community. The incapacitation or death of the main provider, or the sudden break of affective bonds between mother and child or husband and wife influence not only the socioeconomic structure but the surviving members' expectancies, ambitions, and hopes as well. It is natural, then, that the concept and fact of disease play an important role in all dimensions of behavior. Disease controls all physical and mental efforts; its threat becomes an instrument of magical aggression or the manifestation of God's wrath. Health is a precious state to be envied and, therefore, becomes a danger.

Practically all material needs of the people are fulfilled very inadequately. There is no need to repeat here what we have said already about housing and nourishment, birth and child-rearing, sanitary and hygienic conditions, all aspects which contain elements that endanger health. But emphasis must be given to the fact that in this manner all choice of action with regard to food, work, sleep, recreation, and social intercourse in general is greatly limited and determined mainly by this ever-present fear of illness.

One might wonder what differences exist between a culture in which the average lifespan of the individual member is, say, fifty years, and another culture in which it is fifteen or twenty years less. In Aritama, only 29 per cent of the entire adult male population reach an age above forty-five years, and only 12·6 per cent reach more than sixty years. In other words, only a small percentage of people reach that phase of emotional development during which the mature mind preoccupies itself with problems other than the mere fulfilment of material needs, the foundation of a family, the achievement of economic security and status. The phase of creativeness, of the conservation and interpretation of a cultural heritage is missing. Life ends at a time when the individual has barely reached a mature phase of social, intellectual, and psychological development which would allow him full participation, recognition, and satisfaction within his community. In the short period of maybe fifteen years, between the gaining of independence from the family of orientation and the final decline of health, there is hardly time enough for founding a new household unit or for acquiring status and a definite function in society. There is no time at all for a mature mind to come to terms with life itself and life in society. There is no time for a fuller appreciation of cultural values, for insight and sublimation. This later phase, then, is missing and one might speculate upon the possibility that in a culture where death during early middle age is the rule the value system and the institutions based upon it would differ in certain significant aspects from those that exist in a culture where the average lifespan is longer.

In Aritama the concept of what we call 'old age' is transferred to the period of the forties, and those individuals who reach the fifties or sixties simply go beyond the cultural expectations and, somehow, fall outside the range of individual function. There is no room and no use for them. Old people are not respected, feared, or loved. Their advice is not sought by the younger generation, nor are they believed to possess any special knowledge which might be useful. Their occasional esoteric knowledge is but little appreciated and they are only consulted on genealogical matters, their information then being used as a weapon in the struggle for prestige. The old have no function as educators, counselors, curers, or storytellers, nor is their criticism feared by the younger people. They are never thought to be the keepers of a valuable tradition, but rather the representatives of a shameful 'Indian' past. This attitude toward the old is rather unusual and, certainly, significant within the context of culture change. It expresses the general rejection of anything that might be tradition-oriented in the community and of the entire local cultural heritage. By rejecting the old, the old values and goals are repudiated, and with them, as we shall see further on, a certain personality type. But at the same time, old people represent in a certain way disease, infirmity, long-suffering; and by rejecting them the younger generations demonstrate also their fear of these conditions. To reach a ripe old age is not a goal for the villagers but rather a threat, as it would only mean additional years of increased physical suffering.

VIII

DIMENSIONS OF THE SUPERNATURAL

HISTORICALLY, many different religious influences have met and mingled in Aritama—the ancient Indian religions of the highland and lowland tribes, Catholicism as taught during four centuries, early European pagan beliefs introduced by the Spanish colonizers and, finally, Protestantism. From all these varied sources, sifted through the screen of fear and hope, people have selected those elements that have seemed to be the most satisfying for their needs and have formed of them their own system of beliefs in the Supernatural, the Sacred, the Absolute, and man's relationship to it. It would be meaningless to separate religious attitudes and practices in Aritama into Christian or pagan, Spanish or Indian categories, and it would be misleading to think in terms of a breakdown of aboriginal traditions under the impact of a new religious system or in terms of stubborn survivals and retentions in the midst of growing exterior pressure. For there has been no such breakdown. There have been only slow change and reinterpretation, slow development and painfully slow replacement, but there is above all the single enduring mold of local tradition into which every new influence is pressed and shaped until it has become a meaningful part of the whole. Religious attitudes in Aritama form an integrated system, not only with respect to the wider context of the culture, but in itself, as a conceptual framework for man's relationship to the supernatural.

Within this framework, individual attitudes or practices develop on the series of levels to which a man is bound by race, class, or status. The details of religious expression, therefore, might receive different emphases with different individuals, although the basic structure and content remain the same. Some people—for reasons based on personal preference, experience or prestige—might put their faith in Christ, in a saint, or in the spirit of a long-dead ancestor; some, for similar reasons, might be active in a lay brotherhood, in a ceremonial dance-group, or as grave-diggers. Some might go to Confession, but some might prefer to whisper their sins into a bundle of leaves and throw them into the river; some might burn a candle before the image of the Virgin, but some might burn it in the shade of a boulder where a rain spirit is said to dwell. But the fundamental beliefs are the same in each case.

Among the modern Indian tribes of the Sierra Nevada the core of all religious concepts is the 'Mother', a benevolent female creator and law-giver whose sons and daughters were the first priestly culture heroes and founders of the first patri- and matrilineages. This mother divinity is a symbol of fertility and, as such, is related to the yearly cycle of planting and harvesting, of solstices and equinoxes, which marks the principal collective ceremonials. These are the benign powers which have to be inclined favorably toward man by offerings, prayers, and a number of other ritual practices. On the other hand, the destructive powers of the universe are personified in the spirits of the dead. These also have to be appeased by offerings which are meant to be 'food'. These concepts go back to the early sixteenth century and there is considerable archeological evidence for their existence in prehistoric times. We have every reason to believe that the ancient Indians of Aritama had an identical or very similar religious system, which as a functioning complex, lasted well into the Spanish colonial period.

Change as brought about by internal development and external stimuli has transformed, in the course of time, many aspects of the old religious system. There is no starting point from which to measure this change because it is perpetual, but in our case we might take the general period of the Spanish conquest as a convenient base line against which some of the more marked transformations might be evaluated. The aboriginal religion of the Indians of Aritama can be supposed to have been strongly influenced by the activity of early missionaries who, off and on during the first centuries after the conquest, visited the valley. However, in spite of the fact that the Indians of the late seventeenth century agreed to have their idols and temples destroyed, important remnants, not only of the aboriginal belief system but also of its formal organization, survived at least until the end of the nineteenth century. At the time of the arrival of the lowland immigrants, there still existed an Indian sacerdotal class and a temple-centered religion. However, the concept of the superior female divinity, the great Mother god-dess, had practically disappeared by this time. It does not seem to have been reinterpreted and transformed into a Virgin cult, but simply to have ceased to form part of the religious system, of which the core now became the fertility cult connected with the sun, with solstices and equinoxes. Parallel to this, the aboriginal concepts pertaining to the spirits of the dead continued, and, associated with both, there continued the major or minor ritual practices which accompanied these concepts. It seems to have been a well-integrated system organized by a special priesthood, but already by that time, about a century ago, exterior influences had become incorporated into it. Christ as a sun god, the Corpus Christi fiesta as a solstice ritual, San Rafael as an equinoctial rain ceremony, the ancestral spirits as 'Souls of Purgatory', were all identifications easy to establish, and even the life of Christ became the story of a miracle-working local shaman. There was, then, continuity of concepts and a ready adaptation of new ideas into an old and meaningful framework.

This continuity depended to a large degree upon the permanent presence of an organized priesthood. Traditionally, the Indian shamans had a strong influence over all civil affairs of their communities, and their authority often overshadowed that of the local chieftains. At the same time they were economically inactive, inasmuch as they lived from gifts and tributes given to them by the people. Once the village came under Spanish administration, the entire position of this priesthood was changed. The shaman became a mere spiritual leader subordinated to a civil administrator, and, with a permanent Catholic priest in the village, he became a magician. Forced to provide for its own needs, accused of sorcery, deprived of its former status and of many of its functions, local shamanism as an organized entity, as a 'church' so to speak, declined rapidly. Some of the shamans died without leaving descendants or apprentices; others fled and went to live with neighboring tribes which were still beyond the reach of direct external influence; others stayed, but now they were poor and powerless. This decline of the local priesthood, which occurred late in the past century marked the end of formalized Indian religion. However, it was not replaced suddenly by Catholicism. Although missionary influence was strong in the early years of the present century, it was not permanent enough to introduce a stable belief system. Instead, it provided only a superficial set of reference points, which were related by the people to the traditionally recognized religious concepts. Sin, grace, and redemption, Heaven and Hell, the Trinity, the saints, the Sacraments—all were interpreted in local terms, according to old-established ways of dealing with the supernatural. Because of the sporadic character of mission work, there was never time enough to educate whole generations in a Christian way of life.

It it not surprising that in the course of this development there should have arisen many tensions for the individual. Quite apart from the immediate contact situation, with all its socioeconomic consequences, the entire equilibrium of personal security was disturbed. The old religious organization was gone and the new one was still insufficiently understood or assimilated to provide more than a few isolated points of reference. All that remained of the old were the basic concepts of a fertility cult and ancestor worship, but both the old and the new ideas were now left to the individual to handle, without priestly guidance, without the fixed form of a collective manifestation. There followed, then, renewed reinterpretation and secularization, and many elements that formerly had belonged to the sphere of collective priest-organized ritual now became highly personalized procedures, performed for individual ends, and eventually transformed sacred elements into magical lore.

At present, man's sinfulness, man's suffering, and man's certainty of death form the great common foundation of the religious system. There is, first of all, the belief that man is born evil and that this evilness expresses itself in his capacity for making others suffer. The whole concept of sin is built around man's inharmonious relations with his fellow-men rather than the inadequacy of his relations with the supernatural. Religion, therefore, is mainly a system by which supernatural powers are invoked to control interpersonal human relations. This control is exercised on different levels: God, be it Christ or any other power, is a supreme judge who punishes on this earth the misdeeds of man against his fellows. There is hardly any punishment or reward in the afterlife, but men suffer for their actions or enjoy their recompense during their earthly existence. But this is a remote level, one on which God's powers are recognized but rarely implored because they are too impersonal, too far removed from the daily give-and-take of social intercourse to be of practical value to the individual. Often an evil deed might remain unpunished by God, perhaps because those who accused the sinner did not know how to approach him, being sinners themselves.

Then there is another level, one which is more closely connected with the affairs of each individual, one which forms the really effective control of his actions and attitudes—the level of the ancestral spirits. Life does not end at death, but the expressions of the afterlife are patterned after life on earth. The spirits of the dead continue to need food and shelter, company and affection. In fact, they are not even immortal, because they are eventually replaced by new spirit-generations and thereby pushed back into oblivion and annihilation. With the exception of a few oustanding cases—outstanding because of their extraordinary earthly accomplishments—only two or three generations of ancestors form the spirit world. These ancestral spirits are powerful because they continue to participate in the lives of their surviving families, demanding all the privileges received or denied to them during their own lives, and in any case due them according to custom. To gain fulfilment of their claims on the living, and to command their respect and help, the dead use their power to cause disease and death, famine and drought. All the aggressiveness, all the Black Magic they had used while on this earth, they can now use in a far more potent form, while, at the same time, they cannot be attacked by the living. They can only be appeased, satisfied, fed, respected, but no one can escape from their continuous control.

The belief in the spirits of the dead must also be understood in terms of a series of levels onto which the individual projects his concepts. On the tradition-oriented aboriginal level, the individual establishes the concept of the *sixquinyáni*, which include the twelve ancestral figures: grandparents and great-grandparents. Beyond them—i.e., referring to the further ascending generations—he designates the ancestors as 'devils', as evil spirits which are largely beyond control. The more Creole-oriented individual who is under the influence of Spanish colonial concepts of medieval type, establishes the concept of 'souls' (*ánimas*), and then from it, with increasing Creole influence, he develops the concept of 'poor souls', 'souls of Purgatory', and the Christian concept of the soul in an ultraterrestrial existence. There is then no contradiction, no difference, between a grandmother's spirit, a 'devil', a spiritual 'owner', a 'soul in penance'.

The core of all supernatural beliefs in Aritama, therefore, is formed by this complex body of attitudes toward the spirits of the dead. In comparison with these beliefs, neither the existing formalized Christian concepts nor any other belief-system has a marked importance as a nucleus of religious thought and practice. The recognized controlling power of the universe is held by the ancestral spirits, the *sixquinyáni*. But to the people of Aritama this belief in the spirits of the deceased is not in any way opposed to the teachings of the Church. Far from recognizing that their concept of the relationship between the living and the dead actually forms a foreign body within the framework of Christianity—even as Christianity is understood in rural Colombia—they believe it to be an elaboration of the precepts laid down by Catholicism.

But before going into any further details of this belief-system, we shall outline the character of the current local concepts of Christianity, together with some aspects of their historical development.

The Catholic religion was introduced in the Sierra Nevada of Santa Marta early in the sixteenth century, when the first Spanish missionaries penetrated to the Indian villages and began to teach and baptize the inhabitants. During the century of military conquest, i.e., approximately between 1520 and 1620, mission influence was strong and continuous in the surroundings of the principal Spanish settlements, but was considerably weaker in the more remote villages, which received only sporadic visits from friars stationed in the lowland towns. However, the general dispersal of the tribes after their final defeat in 1599, when the survivors fled toward the less accessible parts of the mountains, contributed to the spread of the religion of the conquerors among the more isolated Indians, as many of the refugees had lived in or near the mission centers and had been exposed to the teachings of the priests. As we have pointed out already in a previous chapter, there was but little organized missional activity during the seventeenth century, and it seems that many Indian groups that had become missionized during earlier contacts reverted again to their old tribal religion. Active missionary work was carried on again during the eighteenth century, and Aritama seems to have become a parish some time after 1750. In 1803 a Spanish priest resided in the village, but it is doubtful whether there was a permanent mission there during the War of Independence or in the turbulent years following it. The years between 1870 and 1880 seem again to have seen much missionary activity, and at the turn of the century there were, occasionally, two resident priests in the village. During the first decades of the twentieth century, however, there were apparently no permanent missionaries stationed at Aritama, but after the re-establishment of the old mission center at San Sebastián de Rábago, the village was again frequently visited by Catholic priests who operated from their bases at Santa Marta, Ríohacha, Valledupar, or San Sebastián. These priests, from the middle of the eighteenth century, belonged to the Capuchin order of Valencia, which had been put in charge of the mission territory of the Sierra Nevada, and most of them were Spaniards, but occasionally priests not belonging to any specific order were put in charge of the parish of Aritama.

Church records preserved in Aritama go back to the middle of the past century and show that throughout the last hundred years or so the village was visited almost yearly by a Catholic priest who baptized the newborn and married the adults. However, these records do not provide exact information, as many parents had their children baptized in other villages or lowland towns and because the records do not distinguish between the inhabitants of Aritama and the members of the neighboring Indian tribes. As the latter frequently use the same patronyms as the people of Aritama, it is impossible to make good use of the church records.

The first mention of San Rafael, the patron saint of the village, goes back to 1803, but the statue of this saint which is kept in the church appears to be considerably older. In any case, it seems certain that the cult of this saint was established, at the latest, during the second half of the eighteenth century. However, neither in Aritama nor in the surrounding villages is there any other saint whose worship seems to go back for any considerable time.

The exterior manifestations of the Catholic tradition are centered in the little church, a fairly large barnlike structure of brick and stone combined with adobe, covered with a roof of corrugated metal. Architecturally, it has no definite style, having been rebuilt and readapted many times in the past. There is a small belfry with a little bell, which is tolled by a rope hanging down on the outside wall. With the exception of the patron saint's statue, the interior of the church is quite modern. There is a statue of San Antonio and one of the Immaculata, besides a few framed oil prints, some flower-pots, and candles. A few wooden benches and a font complete the furnishings.

In addition to the church, there is the cemetery with its few wooden crosses, and at the entrance to the village, as is so characteristic of Colombian Creole settlements, there is a concrete statue of the Virgin, standing on a high pedestal on top of a little hill. Otherwise, exterior signs of Christianity are few. Nowhere are there roadside crosses, shrines, or images. No house is adorned with any Christian symbol on its outside, no place is named after a saint. Most families of the Plaza barrio own a few cheap color prints of saints or perhaps a framed picture of the Sacred Heart of Jesus, but in most houses there are hardly any such pictures or prints to be found. People do not wear crosses, religious medals, or rosaries. No man lifts his hat when passing in front of the church or of the statue of the Virgin, and, except during Mass, we never saw a person making the sign of the cross.

There are several lay organizations, all of quite recent introduction: the Daughters of Mary (*Hijas de María*) are a group of unmarried girls, while the Brethren of the Sacred Heart (*Hermanos del Sagrado Corazón*) are married or unmarried men. Membership is scanty and practically all are placeros of the higher social strata. These organizations do not hold meetings or any organized worship, their main function consisting in carrying images during processions. The Daughters of Mary will occasionally collect alms for some charitable purpose organized by a visiting priest.

The following holidays of the Catholic Church are celebrated in Aritama: Holy Week, San Rafael, Corpus Christi, All Soul's Day, and Christmas. Occasionally the day of the Virgin of Fatima (May 13) or of the Immaculata (December 8) is celebrated, but not as a general rule. Some people include San Antonio in the religious calendar. The principal fiesta days are San Rafael and Corpus Christi, all other occasions being of little importance and often not being visibly celebrated at all.

There is some confusion about the status of Catholic priests, and many people in the village seem to believe that all priests except Capuchins and Franciscans are allowed to marry. For this reason members of these orders are preferred, and other priests are looked upon with certain suspicions. The lack of a permanent parish priest is a frequent theme of conversation in the Plaza barrio, but this is in strong contrast to the behavior observed once a priest arrives. He is closely watched, criticized, suspected, and even abused, the general attitude being one of hostility or, at the best, of indifference.

The attitude toward the Catholic Church, its teachings and its ministers, differs somewhat from the Loma to the Plaza barrios. Although the inhabitants of both sections vary little in their ignorance and resistance to the Catholic faith, their traditional backgrounds have led to different interpretations. On the one hand, the aboriginal tradition is stronger in the Loma barrio and Christian concepts are more often reinterpreted in terms of the old Indian religion. On the other hand, the lomeros have retained certain details of Catholic ritual that have become obsolete elsewhere. The placeros accuse the lomeros of not being 'good Christians' and condemn some of their beliefs and practices as pagan superstitions when actually they are merely medieval Catholic. This criticism leads eventually to the suppression of these rites as the lomeros begin to consider them as 'Indian' and, therefore, as shameful. In the Plaza barrio, there is little moral preoccupation; the outlook is essentially materialistic, and emphasis is placed upon exterior rites, the participation in organized ceremonial, in the brotherhoods, and the cult of the saints. In the Loma there is, exteriorly at least, a stronger insistence upon fundamental morals in terms of 'justice' and 'charity'. Although devoid of ritual, the religious outlook of the lomeros often bespeaks a higher moral level than the one of most placeros. However, as a whole, both in the Loma and the Plaza, Catholicism seems to have been in a steady decline during the last fifty years. As far as can be judged from the attitudes and conduct of the older generation, Christian teachings were more fully understood and practiced before the new immigrants had made themselves the dominant group in the village, even if Indian influence was stronger then. As one of the old men put it: 'We were brutes then, but we believed in God'.

At present, the little people know of the teachings of the Catholic Church consists of a body of disconnected ideas and pictures, vague memories of grandmother tales, snatches of conversation overheard in the lowlands, or a few words or gestures observed at Mass. According to most people, the Holy Trinity consists of Christ, the Virgin, and the Devil. Many believe that Christ and the Virgin Mary are a heavenly couple and that the saints, or at least some of them, are their offspring. The concepts of God, Father, and the Holy Ghost are practically unknown. We did not find a single person who knew the Ten Commandments, who knew more than three of the sacraments, or who could explain, even in the simplest words, the meaning of Holy Mass. The life of Christ is thought to be mere myth or he is incorporated into local traditions as a healer and miracle-working visitor. Some people identify Christ with the sun; others consider him a sort of superior saint, but one with no special functions or powers. His moral teachings are unknown and rarely are prayers addressed to him. By some he is thought to have been an Indian shaman, a *mochilero*, i.e., a sorcerer who carried his magical equipment in a woven fiber bag (*mochila*). He is said to have lived for many years near Aritama, performing miracles by spreading the dust of certain pulverized minerals in the four directions and by blowing upon people or objects in order to cure or transform them. It is from him that the Indian shamans are said to have learned most of their secrets and inherited their present power. This is one basis for the belief that the magico-religious practices of the neighboring Indian tribes are quite in keeping with the Catholic faith. The Virgin Mary is thought to be a saint, and women take her to be a special protectress of their sex. She is asked to provide good-looking husbands, money, or healthy children, but she is never actively worshiped. In her identity as Our Lady of Mount Carmel (*Virgen del Carmen*), she is said to be the protectress of men. Some people address the Virgin of the Rosary (*Virgen del Rosario*) to ask for rain or to make a vow, but these are rare and individual cases. Other representations such as Our Lady of Fatima or the Immaculata are little known and have no followers.

The saints of the Catholic Church are considerably better understood and therefore are more important. Saints can be handled, Christ not. Christ is somehow too far removed from people's daily affairs to take any specific interest in them, but saints are 'almost people', they are more human, more specialized, they are close to this world. To Christ 'only the saints can speak', but men cannot pray to him. This, however, does not mean that the saints are thought to be intermediaries between Christ and mankind; they can 'speak to him' on their own behalf, but they can work miracles or help mankind in other ways by using their own power, which is not derived from Christ and which is generally specialized in a certain field. San Rafael, as the patron saint of the village, is venerated as the bringer of rain and the protector of the crops. San Antonio is called upon in order to retrieve stolen or lost property; he is also the protector of domestic fowl, and candles should be burned before his image to insure healthy chickens. San Martín de Loba is addressed in cases of disease. San Bartolo (or Bartolomé) and San Ramón are called upon during difficult childbirth, and the former is the defender against evil apparitions. San Cirenéo and San Joaquín appear only in a few secret formulas used in curing. All these saints as well as the Virgin have to be cajoled, coached, or threatened into action because, it is said, they are lazy and forgetful. They are respected for their powers but, as they have to be treated like difficult children, there is something exasperating about them. If candles, prayers, and vows are to no avail, people will therefore resort to direct coercion. The saint has to be 'punished' then. If San Rafael should neglect to produce rain, people will enter the church and take away his staff until he obliges. The Christ Child is taken from the arms of Our Lady of the Rosary in order to obtain favors. Certain saints are associated with Colombian political parties and accordingly 'punishment' can be inflicted by strangling the image with a thin ribbon, the color of which is representative of the opposition. The Virgin, San Rafael, and San

Antonio are said to be Conservatives, associated with the color blue, while the Sacred Heart of Jesus and San Martín de Loba are Liberals and therefore 'reds'. The ribbon is bound around the neck of the statue and is tightened each day for several days until the desired results have been obtained or hope abandoned. Another form of 'punishment' consists in exposing the images to the full rays of the sun at noontime, preferably on top or a roof. Harsh words and open insults are used in addressing the images upon these occasions.

The few images of saints found in individual homes are all of wood. Only a wooden image can 'hear'; one made of laurel-wood has extra keen ears. The wood an image is made of should be that of the tree associated with one's family because then 'the saint knows one, he belongs to one's family'. As the majority of modern images of saints are of materials other than wood, the few wooden ones are in great demand and are borrowed frequently from house to house. The images of stone, concrete, plaster, or clay, which 'cannot hear', are scorned and ridiculed, including the statue of the Virgin at the village entrance. People openly say, 'They are not real saints at all; they cannot hear.'

The images found in private homes are mostly of San Antonio, San Martín de Loba, and San Rafael, and besides these, as already stated, there are a few cheap color prints with representations of Christ or of the Virgin. The owners of these images generally know a few prayers, and if a person wants to obtain a favor from a saint, the owner of the images may be asked to burn a candle and to pray in that person's name. The supplicant has to bring the candle and pays a small fee, maybe 5 or 10 centavos, for having the prayer said. If San Antonio is asked to help retrieve lost or stolen property, the fee is paid only after the objects have been recovered. Sometimes a vigil (*velorio*) is kept for a certain saint to celebrate his day. The image is placed upon a table surrounded by other images, flowers, and a few fruits; and candles are burned in front of it. Such vigils are kept in three houses for San Antonio, in one for San Martín de Loba, and in another house for San Rafael, but they are not public occasions for worship and no prayers are organized at them. Some neighbors may come by to see the arrangements, to bring a banana or a pineapple, or to leave a few coins for a new candle, but otherwise there is no general participation in the saint's cult. Sometimes, if a drought threatens a crop, an image will be carried by one or two men to the field and put up there for a while, surrounded by a few flowers and fruits, until rain begins to fall. The fruits offered to an image can be consumed by the owner of the saint, but the person who made the offering is not allowed to eat any part of it. However, if the owner of the image eats the fruit, he has to make a vow to burn a whole package of candles during the next year's vigil.

A few words should be said here about the Devil. According to local beliefs the Devil is essentially the personification of the spirits of the dead and is, therefore, generally referred to in the plural (*los diablos*). The ancestral spirits, as we have shown, play an all-important role in the religious system and form a powerful controlling force which is essentially malignant in character. These spirits are then 'the devils', but when one is accused of 'working with the Devil', people mean to say that he practices Black Magic in order to harm others, and in this case the Devil is imagined as a specific personification of evil.

As all afterlife is conceived of as lying in the realm of 'the devils', the Catholic concepts relating to the Hereafter have little or no function. The terms *Limbo*, *Purgatorio*, *Gloria*, and *Inferno* are sometimes mentioned, but there is no elaboration of them and they do not form a part of the belief system.

Catholicism in Aritama is, then, not a living and controlling force or guide. In its few exterior aspects the Church is not essential, and processions or burials are carried out even if there is no priest present. It is obvious that the Church is far from being the center of village affairs, which contrasts sharply with the pride and faith in a Catholic heritage found in the lowland villages. In our house-to-house census the question about the religious denomination of the individuals was seldom answered. Many people just laughed and said, 'We have no religion. We don't believe in anything; we don't go to church.' Others said, 'You might as well write: none.' In the Loma barrio a number of people answered, 'We believe what the placeros believe', but hardly anybody answered that he was a Catholic. When the question was asked directly: 'Are you a Catholic?' most people answered in the negative However, there are few people in Aritama who would openly deny the existence of God and even the ones who claim to have no religion at all will state that they believe in a supreme power. But what this god's or this power's identity or attributes are hardly anyone could answer. To many it was the sun, to many others it was Christ, but there was confusion as to whether or not the sun was Christ. Others said that God was the Virgin Mary; others believed that he was personified in the snow peaks; some added that the Virgin lived in the snow peaks, but that God lived in Heaven. All agreed that God, whatever he be, was above all a vengeful judge, not a benevolent father.

About half a dozen years before this study was undertaken, a Protestant missionary had settled down in Aritama, and the manner in which this new religion was received in view of the conditions described above is of a certain interest. The missionary bought a small house on the outskirts of the village and began to build a chapel Living in very humble conditions himself and doing charitable work among the poor, he soon won the confidence of a group of people, principally in the Loma barrio, and a few of them eventually became converts. This Protestant missionary activity in Aritama coincided with a period of political upheaval in Colombia. In the bitter struggle between the two traditional political parties, the Liberals and the Conservatives, the former lost their position of power, and during many years, guerrilla warfare devastated part of the country. The severe pressure exercised by the Conservative government on its political enemies caused considerable unrest even in the small villages of the coast, where the majority of the people were Liberals and resented deeply the often harsh measures taken against them. In Aritama, where political power was exercised by placeros who belonged to the Conservative party, the new Protestant movement soon became identified with the oppressed Liberal party. Liberalism, anticlerical in general, believed it had found in Protestantism, if not a weapon, at least a temporary refuge where its people could feel secure, united, and among friends.

This movement began in the Loma barrio and its influence, whatever it amounted to, stayed mainly limited to this section of the village. Since the leading families of the Plaza barrio were Conservatives and the Liberals of the Plaza depended heavily upon these families for economic or prestige reasons, they dared not oppose their views concerning Protestantism; so Protestantism became identified with the poorest Indian level. Although this situation led to certain tensions or reinforced old ones, there soon developed a remarkable tolerance on both sides, a united front in the face of outside criticism. Whenever the civil authorities, the police, or the Catholic clergy attacked the Protestant leader, the whole village rose in his defense and openly denounced the aggression as unjust and undesirable. This attitude was the expression of one of the basic tenets of the local value system: "Respect, in order to be respected" (*Respetar para que respeten*). Quite particularly in matters of religion and magic the people of all levels and groupings, regardless of status, had always been very sensitive to criticism and ridicule, leveled at them by the lowland people. Each man felt himself to have the right to worship in his own way, to solve these very private problems in the manner he saw fit, and, therefore, any interference with the Protestants was resented by everybody.

This solidarity in the face of exterior pressure, however, did not eliminate or even alleviate the intra-village tensions caused by Protestantism, and these were now added to an already very precarious situation. To a people who, because of their isolation, had passed centuries without going beyond the barest rudiments of the Catholic faith, this sudden introduction of Protestantism—associated in their thinking with political partisanship—was very confusing. There was always the great ambition to be 'civilized', to become a Colombian, and there was the bitter fact that the acceptance of Protestantism formed an additional and very serious obstacle on the difficult road to this goal. A person from Aritama, even a so-called Indian, could eventually be accepted into the social and cultural structure of the lowlands if he adopted a few exterior traits of the rural Creole culture predominant in those parts, but if he proclaimed himself to be a Protestant, he limited his chances of acceptance, because he thus demonstrated himself to be definitely at variance with Creole customs and values. This was all the more true because the teachings of the missionary were not so much concerned with the positive values of a new ethos, as with a campaign against Catholicism. To be a Protestant meant above all to be a fervent anti-Catholic.

So only a small number of people accepted Protestantism and became open converts, but to a great many more the issue involved came to be of a wider importance. The opposition between Protestantism and Catholicism was, of course, not formulated by them on a theological level, but on the level of party politics, race, caste, or wealth. Nobody knew or cared about religious differences or political ideologies, but Protestant versus Catholic meant Loma versus Plaza, Indians versus Spaniards, poor against rich. Even among the ones who had been converted and who had been formally rebaptized as Protestants, there were those who admitted that they had been attracted mainly by political considerations, i.e., by the old Loma-Plaza identifications, or by the prayer meetings, the singing, and, to a certain degree, by gifts they had received from the missionary. That religious convictions did not play *any* role among them was clearly shown by their continued participation in Catholic rituals, such as the burning of candles to the saints or taking part in processions. Of course, such participation did not signify Catholic conviction so much as service to customary magical or prestige patterns. Many of the converts insisted that they were thus merely practicing the tolerance the Protestant missionary had asked for and had received, and accused him of being intolerant himself when he asked them to stop going to Mass or addressing the saints. Others used Protestantism for still other ends, such as accepting conversion as a penance or as a sacrifice to save the life of a sick child, after having made a vow to this effect to the Virgin Mary.

The main problem was the lack of priests in the village, the lack of men with esoteric knowledge and priestly functions, no matter whether Catholic, Protestant, or pagan—men who, in these difficult times, could have been guides to the people and acted as intermediaries between society and the remote supernatural powers. The local Indian priests had died and the tribal shamans lived far away and spoke little or no Spanish. The Catholic priests came and went. They said Mass and led processions; they baptized children and collected alms, but they did no teaching or counseling. Their contacts were limited to the Plaza barrio, to a small group of wealthy 'Spaniards', and they maintained hardly any relations with the people of the Loma. They took it for granted that the people knew the essentials of the Catholic faith. What was ignorance and shame of ignorance they took for indifference. But Catholicism or Protestantism, even today, are to most people little else than labels a person might choose for any number of reasons except religious conviction. Most people have their children baptized in church mainly because it is 'civilized' to do so; of those who go to Mass, most do so because of its aspect as a prestige-carrying social gathering; prestige factors make people take part in processions, join lay organizations, or get married in church; political or economic reasons make them become Protestants, but not faith in the Christian religion. Twenty per cent of all children under five years of age are unbaptized; 40 per cent of all adults over twenty have received only the Sacrament of Baptism without even having been confirmed, having gone to confession, or having partaken of Communion.

In a vague way Catholicism is confused with the remnants of an ancient sun cult. To the large majority of the villagers, except the more sophisticated placeros and a few isolated individuals from both barrios, the supreme divine being is the sun, called *kâke* ('father') or *Dios Kâke*. However, its supreme power is thought to be very remote, so remote in fact that, like God or Christ, it plays only a minor role in determining individual actions and attitudes. Indeed, the sun is God, is Christ, a supreme judge of human affairs, but it is not a power that is likely to interfere in daily individual problems of good and evil, of punishment and reward. It is a power half-forgotten, suddenly recalled, never clearly stated. Some people worship it, some do not and the latter do not believe that any harm could befall them because of that. When speaking of religious personifications, people rarely mention the sun, but when their attention is called to this omission they assure one apologetically that its power is supreme and that 'the sun is God'. But there is very little elaboration of detail as to its nature, functions, or worship. There is a vague concept that the sun is in all essence a benevolent power; but since it has above all the character of a supreme judge, it is also thought that it might punish and eventually kill a culprit.

Although the sun is often identified with Christ, it is more often imagined as an old Indian shaman who walks slowly over the sky. At noon he sits down to rest and chews coca leaves. The moon is his wife and the stars are their children. The sun is associated with fire, and fire is regarded as sacred. Today food is offered to the sun, but in times past fire made of special sacred woods was burned on the same sites.

These ideas are obviously of Indian origin, but it would be difficult to decide to what degree they represent a retention of ancient local beliefs and to what degree they reflect the religious system of the neighboring tribes. The identification of Christ with the sun is quite evident during the Corpus Christi fiesta, which is here essentially a solstice ceremonial in which the golden monstrance is thought to represent the sun with its rays. Solstice as well as equinox ceremonies are important in the religion of the neighboring tribes. But, although the moon is said to be the sun's spouse, she is never identified with the Virgin. And so it seems more probable that the entire complex of the sun cult in Aritama is based upon local aboriginal traditions, reinforced somewhat by the religious practices of the neighboring Indians, but easily confused or reinterpreted in Catholic terms.

As a supreme judge the sun is often called upon in prayers. These prayers have to be said at the moment when the sun appears on the horizon. The person kneels facing the East, extending both arms horizontally, and then kisses the earth in front of him, supporting the body on both palms put flat on the ground. While praying, he kneels upright again, with open arms bent in a right angle at the elbows, the forearms vertical and both palms facing the sun. Often the prayers are said in the ancient Indian language, but people who do not know it may say them in Spanish. The formulas most frequently used are 'Oh, great sun, thou who givest us light, as thou givest light to the whole world, grant to me that . . .' or 'Oh, my father, oh sun, as I cannot do justice, to thee I put my plight, so justice will be thine and punishment will come to . . .' Frequently people pray in this manner on the trail between the village and the river, as they go to bathe or to fetch water early in the morning. Women especially pray to the sun to 'do justice' (*pedir justicia*). Rarely the sun is asked to cure a disease, to protect a harvest, or to help in obtaining economic profit, but generally only 'justice' is asked of the sun. Sometimes a person will take the *corpus delicti* and show it to the sun—a dead animal, a broken object, or a piece of merchandize bought at great expense and found to be of inferior quality. The meat bought before dawn at the slaughterhouse and taken to the river to be washed is often shown to the sun, which is asked to punish the owners of the cattle who sell it at high prices. At times death is asked as the only punishment thought to be 'just' for a person. When we first heard of people who had been 'killed by the sun' we naïvely thought they had died of sun-stroke but soon found out that their sudden deaths had been attributed to the sun's 'justice'. In practically all cases when the sun is asked to 'do justice', the accusations are leveled against the 'Spaniards' of the Plaza. Often they are accused of having 'stolen' the land of a lomero, of having appropriated it in a criminal way by forcing its owner to sell out or by applying some sort of pressure on him. The eventual death of such a person is reported gleefully as a proof that the sun, at long last, has heard the prayers, and even if a person died a natural death years after having appropriated the land, it is generally thought to be the punishment meted out by the sun.

The morning star (*Molendero*) is sometimes addressed in prayers, as are the Pleiades (*Cabrillas*) and the three stars forming Orion's Belt (*Los Tres Reyes*). Their position is associated with the time of the year when different crops have to be planted, and the prayers are said to insure their growth. However, this is now rather obsolete and people who pray to these stars formulate their prayers as if they were addressed to the sun. We knew of no instance of prayers being said to the moon.

We shall return once more to the ancestral spirits and see how this belief-system affects and conditions individual behavior. The word *sixquinyáni* means literally 'dead people'. The terms *moros* (i.e., 'Moors'), *abuelos* ('grandparents'), or *antiguos* ('ancient ones') are used sometimes as synonyms and occasionally the spirits are referred to as *diablos* ('devils'), as we have mentioned already. These spirits include all the dead ancestors but in a very specific sense the grandparents—above all the two grandmothers—of the individual. They are the real owners of the land, of the houses, of plants and animals. At their death they did not forfeit their rights but only leased the land to their descendants to enjoy the usufruct of it as long as they are willing to pay the rental in form of offerings. The living generation are thus only guests on this land, temporary tenants whose life and well-being depend upon their recognizing this condition and upon their acting according to the rules it implies. The dead are bent upon destroying men because they are envious of their being alive; they are envious of their food and shelter, their spouses and children, their health and property. They do not want to be forgotten and excluded, and they do not want the living to forget the old ways, the old customs. They send them disease and disgrace, so they will constantly remember that the land is not theirs but belongs to their forefathers and that they have to appease and pay tribute to them if they wish to live on it.

The offerings are made in the form of food, the most cherished possession here and in the afterworld. The *sixquinyáni* need food and water, and firewood; at times they need a servant and then they claim a child and cause his death, so his spirit will come to serve them. Or at times they feel lonely and then they claim an adult, a relative perhaps, to keep them company.

But the living individual is controlled most effectively through the power of the dead to send disease. Should a descendant be forgetful of his offerings, the spirits will remind him by sending him some kind of illness, but once the offering has been made they will cure him again. On the other hand, they are envious of the prosperity of their descendants, of all the things they themselves did not have and enjoy while they were alive. So, if the living should boast of their health or luck or property, the spirits are likely to destroy it and take revenge by making its possessor poor and ill. Anything that might rise above the average will call their envious attention—a beautiful woman, a healthy child, a strong man, a tree laden with fruit, a new dress, a plentiful harvest. Sometimes the living even deem it necessary to destroy such obvious prosperity in order not to awaken the spirit's envy.

The individual lives, therefore, in constant fear of annoying the spirits, either by failing to make sufficient offerings or by awakening their envy. At no time does there exist the certainty that the spirits are appeased. And there are many contradictory beliefs. At night the *sixquinyáni* go dancing, singing, and talking through the streets. When they pass the house of a relative who makes them frequent offerings, they are likely to say, 'Let us go in and see him. He always pays us.' And then they enter and the person dies. But if they pass a house of someone who makes but few offerings, they might most likely say, 'He is a miser. We won't visit him'; and so pass by. Therefore, some people say that it is better to make few offerings, so one will be forgotten by the spirits, whereas others claim that this might cause their wrath and lead to certain destruction. There seems to be no way out.

The individual alone cannot master all the complexities of ritual, of offerings, divining, and prayer. There are too many spirits, too many sites where offerings can or should be made, too many different reasons why they must be made. Ill health or economic failure might be caused by any one or by many different factors, and each particular case needs special attention, its own ritual. In past times the local Indian shamans took care of these matters. They made collective offerings or advised the individual in the details of time, place, and nature of his personal ritual. But now there are no shamans any more in the village, and the few old men who claim to have esoteric knowledge are not trusted by everyone. The shamans of the neighboring Indian tribes speak little Spanish and charge high fees for their services; besides, they live at great distances from the village and are not at hand when needed most. To many people this lack of priestly guidance constitutes a very serious problem. They feel helpless, unable to cope with their fate, unable to accept it. One old woman said, 'When I feel pain, whenever I am ill, whenever I need something—to whom shall I turn? There is no one left. All the old priests have died.' Above all, the fear of disease gives rise to this despair; the mysterious and sudden appearance of illness, which, according to local belief, is the work of the ancestors or of Black Magic.

To know how to appease the ancestral spirits is a matter of bare self-defense and does not involve moral considerations. The spirits do not exercise any control over the moral life of the living and do not in any way enforce social order. They will not punish a man for being a thief or a murderer, or for abandoning his family. They are not so much concerned with what people do as with what people might have to share with them. They are parasites, they are selfish, interested only in their own food. They will punish only if they feel neglected or insulted. They will mete out punishment to a man who plants a field without making the prescribed offering, or to one who desecrates a site of offerings or defiles a grave; but they will not interfere if he attacks his neighbor or beats his wife or steals a cow. They simply are not concerned with the moral order of things. They are not intermediaries between man and God, between the living and a supreme judge. They have nothing to do with the sun, the saints, the Virgin, Christ, or any other supernatural power. Still, they are the center of all individual religion, because they control the land, the food supply of the living, and, above all, their health.

There is no love for the ancestors, no real worship. They are essentially evil and dangerous, and so they are feared; but they cannot be avoided. Their awful presence is felt at every step—in the tree that was planted by them, in the field they owned and cleared, in the trail they used to walk. They appear in dreams and nightmares; they manifest themselves in ghostly apparitions. They can be heard at night singing and talking in the dark, whistling in the air or moaning in the forest. They are a heavy burden each human being carries along on the road of life. Old people, remembering the hard times they have seen, often speak of the revenge they can take upon their enemies. With ill-disguised bitterness they point out that their descendants, who at present pay scant attention to their needs, will after their death depend entirely upon their benevolence and will regret their misdeeds. So the only law of moral significance derived from the relationship with the ancestors concerns the way children should behave toward their elders. They are obliged to help them and feed them in old age, lest they turn into vengeful spirits.

These ideas are widespread and deeply rooted in Aritama, and very few individuals would dare to defy the tradition and openly hold different views. The belief in the ancestral spirits is in no way limited to the people of the Loma or to the families of Indian origin, but is common to placero and lomero alike. Even among the most sophisticated placeros any discussion of these beliefs and practices causes uneasiness and contradictions. They will condemn one belief as sheer nonsense and superstition but defend another one because there is 'proof'. And isn't there? Did not the boy who threw a stone into the pool develop a high fever a few hours later? Did not the neighbor die three days after his grandmother appeared in his dream? Did not this friend's luck change to disgrace the day he cut down the old tree sacred to his kin? It is easy to speak of stupid Indian superstitions and of old wives' tales as long as there is a bottle of rum, while the hot noonday sun penetrates the darkest corners of the crooked streets, while one hears and sees familiar things all around. But once night has fallen and silence descends over the village and the valley, these very same things begin to look different and there will not be a man, woman, or child who would not admit that the *sixquinyáni* are lurking in the darkness, asking for food and threatening all and sundry with disease.

SACRED SITES AND OFFERINGS

Contact with the supernatural is established principally through offerings. These offerings are in the form of food, and the ritual of depositing such an offering at a sacred place is interpreted as feeding the spirits of the ancestors.

As we have pointed out already, the ancestors are the owners of the physical universe, and, therefore, mankind has to obtain from them a permit, a sort of lease to the land, before they can make use of the soil, the plants, the animals, or the diverse products derived from them, and for this permit they have to pay tribute to the spirit-owner of the property. Besides, each species or each circumscribed group of objects, such as rocks, springs, or trails, has a specific ancestral owner (*dueño*), who is often referred to as the 'father' or 'mother' of those certain animals, plants, or objects. Offerings to these special spirits have to be made at certain spots.

In general, it can be said that all topographical features such as mountain peaks, hilltops, caves, large boulders, springs, cascades, lakes, swamps, and deep pools in the river are sacred places. Any bizarre rock formation, strangely formed hills, or narrow gorges are thought to have a hidden significance. So do dangerous spots on the trails, such as river crossings, or any place where an accident has happened, where a horse or dog might have been observed to shy repeatedly, or which animals seem to avoid. None of these sites is thought to be associated with the saints of the Catholic Church or with any other aspect of Christianity; none of them is marked with a cross. They belong to the *sixquinyáni* and are their dwelling places. Inside the village and surrounding it all over the valley there are many of these sites, sacred, tabooed, or in some way or another connected with a supernatural being and its power. Some of them are known to only a few people, and of some traditions have become lost; no trail passes near them, and only vague memories exist of their former importance. But others are known to everybody. Some of these are avoided by everyone or approached only with great fear; others continue to be the center of frequent rites and offerings; at some, instead of fear, people feel the presence of a friendly power, but this is rare.

All known sacred sites can be grouped into a number of categories, according to their nature. First of all, there are the sites where a mythical or historical personnage is said to be buried, generally a famous Indian shaman (*mama*) of old times. There are five or six such places. The most important of them until a few years ago was a huge flat boulder right in the middle of the village, called *La Piedra Yesío*. Although any huge sacred stone is designated by the Indian term *yesío*, the use of the full expression 'La Piedra Yesío' always refers to this particular site. It is said that below this boulder there is buried the legendary shaman *Taita Munsu*; but others say that a woman was burired there, an old Indian with great supernatural powers who once upon a time was the female chief of the village. Until recently people deposited offerings there, and during the Corpus Christi fiesta the men used to dance around the stone, which was said to be the 'Center of the Earth'. As a matter of fact, during the Corpus festivities this stone was the real center of worship, and not the church, a circumstance that seems to have disturbed some of the local authorities. In order to put an end to this ritual, which every year brought upon the village the ridicule of visitors from the lowlands, a newly appointed government agent ordered the stone buried. The police organized a labor force, and although many people protested and refused to take part in the digging, the stone was finally buried. It is said that shortly afterward the authority concerned was forced to resign and leave the village and that several of the laborers, including the police sergeant who directed the work, died sudden deaths.

A few kilometers to the north of the village, on the trail which leads to a grassy expanse, or savanna, there is said to be the burial place of the mythical shaman *Teraca*, the owner of rain and fertility. The spot is marked by a large heap of stones (*pila de piedras*) piled up by passers-by. According to tradition, Teraca said that he would grant a wish to anyone who contributed toward covering his remains with stones and who brought him food, and he is still called upon to fulfil this promise by most people who use this trail. For tribute to him stones should be taken, not from nearby, but from outside the territory lying between the two creeks that bound the savanna. Food offerings are still made also, people depositing some fruits or tubers, but sometimes the offerings are only a few leaves symbolizing coca, or twigs as firewood for Teraca's hearth. Floral offerings are also made occasionally. When depositing the offering, the person says in a loud voice, 'So I may have a good journey' or 'So I may be well received where I go!' or any similar wish. Sometimes, in case Teraca did not grant a wish made at an earlier occasion, the offended person curses him and threatens not to bring him food any more. A similar *pila de piedras*, as these sites are called, can be seen on the trail to the lowlands. There two legendary brothers, the shamans *Mancanica* and *Dugenica* are said to be buried, and offerings are made there. There are six or seven such burial sites in the valley. They are not feared and people do not try to avoid them. When passing them in the dark the possibility of seeing an apparition of the dead shaman's spirit is considered likely, and this, like any other apparition, might cause disease and death; but otherwise no marked anxiety is connected with these sites, which are supposed to shelter rather benign powers.

Another type of sacred site consists of spots where there is said to dwell the spirit of a dead shaman but without his body being buried there. Such a site is called *compuesto,* a word which can be translated as 'bewitched', 'enchanted', or even 'poisoned'. Often these sites are supposed to contain treasures accumulated by the shaman and now watched over by the spirit. Such places are always thought to be the abode of evil powers and should be avoided as far as possible. No offerings are made there, and by approaching them one exposes oneself to disease and death. Sometimes such sites are in caves, at other times in deep pools in the river. Several people are said to have drowned there while bathing, fishing, or while searching for a stray animal, but their bodies were never recovered. The pool is said to have turned red with blood, and it is supposed that at the bottom of it there lies the shaman's spirit in the shape of a huge man-eating snake. Such pools or caves harboring evil spirits are very numerous throughout the valley and its surroundings.

There are also many sites which are not associated with the spirits of human beings, legendary or historical, but which are said to be the abodes of monsters, such as horned snakes, black dogs, or mermaids. All of them are bodies of water, pools, swampy depressions, or glacier lakes in the highlands. When passing one of these spots, the traveler should refrain from speaking, whistling, or making any noise. By no means should he throw stones into the water, and, in case of mountain lakes, he should not even look at them. Some lakes are supposed to contain treasures in the form of frogs and lizards of pure gold, and in order to tempt the traveler, the spirit or monster might put some of these objects on his trail. Many of these places are said to 'thunder' or to 'sing' (*truenan, cantan*). As one approaches, a thundering sound can be heard, and often rain or lightning will fall quite unexpectedly. These places are said to have different degrees of magical power (*fuerza*), and a certain lake high up in the mountains is said to be the 'captain' of all others. These 'thundering' pools are rarely the dwelling places of monstrous snakes, which are said to prefer quiet waters, but are inhabited by nameless evil forces that may appear in many different shapes. Of one pool not far from the village it is said that from it the first horses emerged, and to this day in order to improve their breed people will make occasional offerings there. At some boulders near the river pregnant women make offerings in order to insure an easy birth; at other boulders near the water women with children make offerings in order to protect the life and health of their offspring. At a boulder called *Piedra Lisa* ('Smooth stone'), which lies near a spring, collective or individual offerings try to insure a steady water supply. Near the present cemetery there used to be a small lagoon where people made offerings to appease a monster that 'threw stones' at passers-by. Lately the lagoon has dried up and the monster is said to have abandoned it, but the spot is still thought to be dangerous. At every point where a trail crosses the periphery of the village there is a sacred site, generally a boulder, where people leaving the village in the morning will deposit a small offering in order to insure success in their day's work. Often they will do the same at their return to the village, as a sign of gratitude for favors received during their absence.

In the region of Aritama, near the many small streams and creeks there grows the *caracolí* (*Anarcadium excelsum*), one of the most imposing trees of the Colombian tropics. This tree is sacred to all people, but most specifically to certain families which have a totemic relationship with it. As long as these trees are small, no special attention is paid to them, but when they are old and gnarled and have attained great size, they must be treated as respectfully as would be a venerated ancestor. A tree that is very old is called a *murundúa* and becomes a place for offerings. There are four such old trees near the village, and a number of lesser ones are found at several spots in the valley. These old trees are said to have been planted by the ancient shamans and 'Moors', the spirits of whom still dwell in them. Nobody should cut or burn these trees lest illness and death befall him, and many stories are told of the dire consequences of such sacrilegious actions, some of which have occurred quite recently. Passers-by address these trees with respectful words, sometimes using kinship terms, and will deposit stones, food, or other offerings at their bases. Such trees are more sacred than any *piedra yesío*; at the same time, they are danger spots where the spirit of the tree's owner might appear at night to the passer-by and claim his life and soul.

Another type of sacred site are the so-called *talanqueras* ('gates'). These are certain spots on the trails leading to Aritama where a magical limit is drawn through which only desirable things may pass. By depositing offerings at these places, the entrance of unwelcome strangers, diseases, or any other evil can be blocked. This ritual is called 'to lock the door' (*cerrar la puerta*). Most of these spots are marked by boulders, and most of them are located on the trails descending to the lowlands, whence most evil influences are supposed to come.

Sites where mythical or historical personages endowed with magical powers used to live are feared and respected. Among them are all the places where, according to tradition or memory, there once stood a ceremonial house. People who in ignorance or defiance build a house at such a spot or clear a field there are likely to fall ill and to die if they do not leave immediately upon discovering the nature of the place. Accidents are likely to happen on those spots, lightning might strike a house, insects may cause the failure of crops, and, above all, the apparition of the spirit might appear there, with all its consequences of disease and death. The same dangers are to be reckoned with at places where some important historical event took place, such as the site where the Spaniards are said to have caught up with a fleeing shaman, forcing him to accept baptism.

Some sites are evil because they are associated with the wandering souls of the recently dead doing penance. Near the northern entrance of the village is a spot that is said to be visited by the souls of people shortly before their actual physical death, while they are in agony retracing their earthly steps. Principally the souls of the *carriceros*, men who liked to play the flute (*carrizo*), are gathered there, and at night one might hear the lashing of a whip as the Devil drives them together. At another spot nearby, the souls are said to gather in preparation for their lonely march to the other world.

Certain sites are used for divinatory practices without being necessarily associated with a spirit-owner or with offerings. One of them is *La Piedra que habla* ('The stone that speaks'), on the mule trail to the lowlands. The passer-by hears voices there informing him of the sudden death of a friend he is about to visit or of approaching disease. Near the river there are two strangely shaped boulders called *La Mesa del Diablo* ('The Devil's Table') because one is similar to a table while the other resembles a chair. There the Devil sits and writes the death dates of all passers-by into his book.

Some cleft boulders are called *piedras para botar culebras* ('stones to throw snakes away to'). Any snake killed in the surroundings should be thrown at once into the slit, 'so people won't step upon their poisonous bones'. The area surrounding such stones, of which there are three quite near the village, is strictly tabooed for sexual intercourse, and persons of different sex should not even approach them together.

Any archeological site—such as a burial place, an old house site or midden site, ancient architectural features, surface sherds or petroglyphs—is sacred and is considered to be very dangerous. No one should touch an archeological object, lest his hand and arm should wither and dry up, or a severe skin eruption affect him. All kinds of diseases are likely to attack a person who unwittingly touches such an object, and women are said to become prone to excruciating toothaches after they have come into contact with one. Monolithic stone slabs stuck vertically in the earth are called *disígua* and can be found at several spots in the surroundings. They are said to mark sites where evil 'Moors' had their dwellings, and sexual intercourse on or near these sites is prohibited. Should a man and a woman pass near them, the man should go far ahead and should take care that his shadow does not touch the woman's. It is also prohibited to expectorate on or near these sites.

Besides the categories mentioned above, there are a great many sites which lack any specific tradition but which nevertheless are considered as sacred or dangerous. Sexual taboos are associated with all sites where there are large boulders (*piedras lisas*) or where a coca plantation is said to have existed in old times. Any person with Indian ancestry is said to fall ill at the mere sight of the *Piedra Blanca* ('White stone'), a strange looking rock formation near the valley entrance. Nobody should touch the *Piedra Caliente* ('Hot stone'), a rock at the confluence of two nearby streams and no one should bathe in the pool nearby because it is said to be enchanted, and the bather will feel so well in its water that he will spend hours there, falling seriously ill after leaving it. Dozens of similar places surround the village and the satellite hamlets, and cover the entire valley. All places where a trail crosses a stream are sacred spots where offerings should be made. Children should always be carried across a stream because if they should wade even a shallow creek the spirit-owner of the place might afflict them with a disease.

We shall turn now to how offerings are performed, to the ritual they require, and to the individual's participation in this phase of religious practice. To make an offering is called 'to pay' (*pagar*), and an offering is called a 'payment' (*pagamiento*). At the sacred boulders called *piedras lisas* are deposited offerings to the ancestral spirits in general, often without asking for any personal benefit but rather in the name of the community. At Corpus Christi these offerings are collective and are deposited at the site by a group of men especially intrusted with the performance of the rite. Other such offerings are made by individuals, either at a boulder or at the foot of a *murundúa* tree. Far more frequent are offerings made to insure personal prosperity. They are deposited at a *piedra lisa*, sometimes at a boulder near a stream or near the house of the individual, sometimes in his fields. These offerings represent the 'rental' (*alquiler*) of the land and are thought to insure plentiful harvests. Every time an archeological object is found during agricultural labors, an offering is made immediately in order to appease its ancient owner and maker. Rainfall is insured by offerings at Teraca's grave. At similar spots offerings are made to insure healthy and plentiful domestic animals. Barren women deposit offerings at certain boulders by the water in order to bear offspring. Before one goes on a journey, offerings are made at the boulders situated at the periphery of the village. When cutting wood or straw for house construction, one makes offerings to the ancestral owners of these plants, and the same practice is observed when building a road, a bridge, or a new sugar mill. At the spot where individual families obtain their daily water supply, occasional offerings are also indicated. In the same manner, offerings are made to stabilize or raise the prices of certain products such as straw hats, raw sugar, coffee, or cattle. The performance of offerings to the ancestors in order to obtain their help against a threatening epidemic used to be made until recently by the whole village, but lately has become rather a family rite or even an individual rite.

The material objects used as offerings vary greatly according to the surviving clan traditions, to the purpose of the offering, and to the esoteric knowledge of the person performing it. When speaking of sacred sites in general, we have already mentioned that stones are deposited at some of them. These stones are of different sizes—from a small pebble to a heavy rock—but no importance is attached to their shape, color, or mineral composition. We have also mentioned fruits, twigs, or leaves deposited as offerings. In the following we shall list objects according to their local names, physical characteristics, magical properties, and other aspects.

Stones, irregularly shaped, or archeological necklace beads:

Bixtan-cuítsi, bright red, symbolizes a plantain fruit. Offered to insure wealth.
Bun-cuítsi, gray quartzite; symbolizes a manioc tuber. Offered to bring prosperity; also used as a defense against disease and for curing.
Mamayére, orange-colored limestone; symbolizes the sun (?). Offered to insure wealth; also protects against and cures disease.
Hayu-cuítsi (or *Mucudjorna*), greenish-gray. Offered to insure prosperity, to protect and cure.
Teban-cuítsi, light rose-colored. Protects against and cures disease.
Due-name, dark gray; offering made to propitiate the spirit of a dead enemy.
Gúmu-gaca, purple-colored; offering for curing disease.
Chingamoco (or *Chengamoco*), grayish; as an offering it is used for many different purposes and is by far the most important single stone offering. Stones with a necklike protuberance are considered to be the replica of their owner or of a certain person.
Man-yíssí (or *Man-cuítsi*), yellow; details unknown.
Síncue, greenish-gray; offering to insure rainfall.

Vegetable matter, unmodified or modified:

Giiíro, seed of an edible plant similar to sweet potatoes; used as an offering only by persons who belong to this clan.
Musíxkc, seed of *Cardiospermum halicacabum*, a round black seed with a white, heart-shaped spot; used as an offering only by persons who belong to this clan.

Chéca, grayish-white seeds strung like a small necklace; to cure diseases of cattle.

Beans (local name unknown), small, white-and-black; used by only one Indian family, as offering to ancestors.

Palo Brasil (*Hematoxylon Brasiletto* Karst.), *morito*, a tree (undetermined), *Ciruelo Jobo*, a tree (undetermined); small zoomorphic figures made of the wood of these trees are used as offerings to insure healthy domestic animals.

Algarrobo (*Hymenaea Courbaril* L.), the resin of this tree is used as an offering to cure disease.

Algódon (*Gossypium*, various species), the seeds of the different kinds are used as offerings to insure health. Occasionally short threads of twisted cotton are also used to insure luck on voyages.

Yarinchímana, the seed of *Paeonia* sp., of a bright red color; used in many different kinds of offerings, and also in Black Magic.

Mollusk shells, unmodified:

Tax-cuítsi, fragment of *Strombus* sp. symbolizing a banana; is used generally in combination with *Bixtan-cuítsi* (cf. above) to insure economic gain.

Dundjurica (Hispaniolized *tundurito*), small bivalves (*Venus*) sp. or elongated gastropods (*Turritella* sp.); the first symbolize the female sex, the second the male. Used as protective offerings.

Necklace beads of European type:

Red glass with white center; offered to insure wealth.

Silver-colored glass; offered to insure economic gain.

Red glass; offered to insure health.

Yellow glass; offered to insure health.

Red coral imitation, combined with red glass bead with white center; offered to insure health.

Bottle glass splinters:

Thick brownish; offered to insure good sales of illegal rum and to protect distillery from discovery.

Thick transparent; to insure public appreciation.

Discoid transparent; to insure public appreciation and good friends.

Black or dark-colored; offered to make an enemy 'tame' (*manso*) and harmless.

Other objects:

Cerruchero (*Buprestis*), a large bright-colored beetle. A diminutive pack-saddle of wood is tied on its back and loaded with offerings, after which the animal is killed with a needle or knife and deposited as an offering to insure healthy cattle, oxen, mules, and donkeys. The beetle's wings are sometimes used as separate offerings, generally to cure disease.

Pubic hair nail clippings, human seminal fluid, and saliva are used occasionally, wrapped in a bit of cotton; mainly to cure disease.

Before the offering is made the object has to be prepared in a special way. As a general rule, the *Musíxke* people pulverize all stones or other materials except the *chingamoco*, while the *Güìro* people offer the whole object without modifying it. To 'pulverize' (*pangar*)—a word which is a common term for preparing an offering—two stones are used, any stones that might be at hand. While rubbing and crushing the object between these stones, the person doing so tries to be alone and concentrates upon the purpose of the offering, formulating in his mind words to that effect, such as: 'So you will cure my son and won't let him fall ill again' or 'So my field might produce plenty of food'. At this point no individual spirit is invoked, but an indefinite impersonal power referred to with terms like 'you' or 'they'.

Now the powder, or the entire object, whichever form is used, is wrapped into three small pieces torn from the dry, smooth interior leaf of an ear of corn. These pieces, which measure about 2 centimeters in length, have to be arranged in such a manner that they overlap while being folded, forming a small compact package which is called by the Indian word *ambúro* or, in Spanish, a *bohote*. An offering generally consists of some fifteen or twenty of these little packages, some containing one certain material, while others might contain a combination of several. Two *ambúros* containing four *Musíxke* seeds each are called a *bollo*, and here it will be recalled that this word is the name for a common food preparation of maize in which the dough is boiled while wrapped in leaves. It must always be kept in mind that all offerings, no matter what they contain, symbolize food for the ancestral spirits; so the tiny *ambúro* packages are really diminutive reproductions of maize *bollos*. This little package is now tightly closed with a piece of string, often of red thread, or with a thin fiber torn from a dry maize leaf. Sometimes diminutive carrying bags, woven of cotton thread and about 3 centimeters long, are used as containers for the tiny packages. It should also be added here that under special circumstances, for example, in an emergency where no adequate materials are available, a person might concentrate and wrap only the 'spirit' of the objects into the maize leaves.

The person now takes each package successively in his right hand and describes a circular movement around his head six times. The first three times he starts from the forehead and moves horizontally in a clockwise direction around his head; then he repeats the same movement counterclockwise. By this action, which is called *amburear*, the offering becomes identified with the individual and his spirit enters it. If an offering is made to cure an ill person, the patient should make the packages himself, but occasionally a close relative might do him this service. If an offering is made to insure a higher price for some salable object or to protect a house or a field, the six movements are made by encircling the merchandize or by carrying the offering around the place or object.

Once all this has been done, the offering is ready to be deposited at a sacred site. This is done either by the individual himself or by a person especially intrusted or authorized to do so, perhaps an old man or an Indian shaman. While going to the sacred spot the person should wear his oldest clothes in order not to arouse the envy of the ancestors. Upon leaving the house or the spot where the offerings were prepared, the donor has to sing *anchayámo*, a certain ceremonial song, which upon arrival at the site is replaced by the singing of *cuncháma*. Both are a nasal chant, hardly audible, and composed of long-drawn and often repeated words in the ancient local Indian language. Few people understand the words they are singing, and most of them only hum a singsong without any words at all. There are many different chants of *anchayámo* and *cuncháma*, but to the uninitiated they all sound very much alike. Certain songs are associated with the cardinal points and with certain geographical regions within the valley, and so the song a donor has to sing depends on the location of the site where the offerings are to be deposited.

Upon arrival at the sacred site, the supplicant stops and begins to untie the little packages he has been carrying in his bag. While doing so, he concentrates again and then calls in a low voice to his ancestors, individually, each by his or her name. In general only twelve ancestors are called upon: the four grandparents and the eight great-grandparents, the paternal grandmother being called with special insistence and respect. The invocation should be pronounced in the old native tongue, but few people now know more of it than the mere kinship terms and so use Spanish instead. Sometimes the spirits of the ancestors will manifest themselves and the person believes he sees them, not only as vague shadows but with recognizable features; but at other times he will only feel their presence in the wind, in the movement of the grass and the leaves of the trees. This invocation is likely to attract the spirits of other dead relatives besides the twelve ancestors mentioned, or even of dead enemies, and the person feels surrounded by them, all awaiting their share of food. Now addressing each spirit by name, the supplicant blows upon the stone powder and disperses the dust into the air or, if offering whole objects, makes a small hole in the ground and empties the contents of the packages into it. The offerings can also be deposited into the cracks of the boulder or of the bark of a tree, or in any natural depression or hole of the surface. While doing this the person says, 'Here, take this! This is food for you, and for you, and for you, too!' or similar words to that effect.

One man who made an offering in our presence suddenly stared at a certain spot and said in a surprised and troubled voice, 'Well, so you, too, have come! You, too, want food! Take, then. There is something for you, too!' One informant said that he had been making an offering to cure a sick relative and that when he started to unwrap the first package it had slipped from his fingers and fallen on the ground. He knew then that his relative was going to die, and so it happened the same evening. The fact that the offering fell to the ground was interpreted as the refusal of the spirit, who slapped his fingers because he did not wish to accept the offering.

Once an offering has been deposited, the person returns to his daily chores and changes again into his everyday clothes. Offerings made by other people are never disturbed, not even touched, as the ancestors to whom they were made would take vengeance by sending a disease to the meddlesome one. On certain boulders or trees near the trail one may find, therefore, hundreds of small offerings of different kinds, put there by the people who passed by and who had asked the spirits for a successful day's work.

Offerings made in a field, upon clearing a new piece of land, or upon planting a new crop are not made to individual ancestors but to the spirits of the dead in general and to a number of other spirits which are thought to be the specific owners of certain food plants. Also, the sun and the moon are invoked in these cases, and the offerings are deposited at the periphery of the field, in the direction where the sun and the moon rise at this time of the year. Other offerings are buried at the oriental and occidental limits of the plot, always in equal numbers. The *Musixke* people almost invariably deposite ten *bollos* in each field.

Once a year, at no fixed date but usually in January, collective offerings, consisting mainly of *chingamoco*, are made to the spirits of the ancestors. A certain individual, often the leader of one of the ceremonial groups, collects the offerings from house to house and will receive at the same time money, food, or any merchandize that people might be able to spare. These objects, together with the offerings, are then taken to one of the neighboring Indian shamans, who then performs the rituals and receives the collected goods in payment for his services.

Offerings to the sun are rare. They are the only offerings that do not depend on a certain sacred spot. They can be performed at any isolated flat and dry place where there are neither stones nor plants and where full sunlight falls during much of the day. Toward the west of the village there is a rock with a deeply engraved prehistoric petroglyph showing a 'sun-face', and at this spot sun offerings are made occasionally. Similar offerings are made at a boulder to the west of the village, although it does not bear a petroglyph. Although most people say that the sun can only be implored for 'justice', others state that women who do not want to have more children or who, being sterile, do want them, make occasional offerings there. All offerings to the sun must consist of whole stones, not of pulverized matter. The rare offerings that are made to the moon and to Venus should always be deposited at dawn.

At two places offerings are made to insure rainfall. One of them is Teraca's grave, and the other is a boulder near a small creek toward the western entrance of the village. In 1945, when a strong drought threatened to destroy the crops, the villagers invited a large group of neighboring Indians, together with their shaman, to dance and sing at Teraca's grave.

Sometimes it is difficult to obtain the various materials used in making offerings. Modern necklace beads are for sale at the local stores, and most vegetable or animal matter or bottle glass are easily found, but archeological beads, shells, or certain stones are often difficult to find. The *Mamayére* is found only in the highlands; the *Bun-cuítsi* only at a hilltop in the lowlands; and the *Hayu-cuítsi* comes from a certain creek at several hours' distance from the village. While these stones are collected, *cuncháma* has to be sung, a different song for each different stone. Shells are brought from the coast of Santa Marta or Ríohacha, and sometimes a person is sent there specifically to gather shells on the beaches. All Indian tribes of the highlands readily buy all such shells and stones that a person might bring back from one of these trips. The places where stones or shells can be gathered abundantly are thought to be enchanted or to be caches of legendary shamans who left these objects to posterity in order to receive plentiful offerings. Archeological necklace beads, however, can be gathered only by an Indian shaman.

Only adults of either sex can make an offering. None should be made on Sundays. Usually a propitious day can be determined by divination, sometimes with the help of an Indian shaman. In the past, most of the offerings to the ancestors were made not by the individual himself but by one of the *mámas*, the native shamans residing in Aritama, although a few were made without this priestly intervention. During the last decades, however, a serious problem has arisen with the death of the last local native priests. Today there is no *máma* in Aritama, at least none who would be recognized as such by all people. There are a few old men with varying degrees of esoteric knowledge, but not all people trust them, and the fact that many offerings fail to bring the expected results is not blamed upon the unwillingness of the spirit world but upon the incompetence and ignorance of the men pretending to carry out these priestly functions.

This situation has led to a new development in the whole sphere of relationships with the supernatural powers. In the first place, all offerings or other contacts with the forces controlling the universe have tended to become more and more individualized, being expressed in highly personal terms and modified according to the needs or knowledge of the person. The details of the rituals, therefore, are changing with individual interpretation. Some people dare not modify the traditional procedures; others believe themselves to have discovered or rediscovered 'empirically' more effective ways; others still are completely ignorant and depend entirely upon what other people tell them to do. But the ones who believe they know are likely to keep to themselves what they consider to be a precious secret, an individual power given to them and to them alone. This confusion has given rise to envy and hostility, to suspicions and accusations. All individual rituals are filled with anxiety because of the absence of fixed rules. The overwhelming need to perform the rites is deeply felt, but the doubts concerning the 'correctness' of the performance, its ultimate acceptability to the supernatural powers, cause a profound feeling of helplessness.

In the second place, this situation has led many people to put their trust in the shamans of the neighboring Indian tribes. But here, also, difficulties are encountered. Few of the shamans speak Spanish; most of them live at a considerable distance from the village and are not easy to contact in an emergency. Besides, all of them charge high prices for any service they are asked to perform, and many people cannot afford to consult them. Or they fear that a shaman might be annoyed and take revenge if offered an unsatisfactory payment. As there is much rivalry among shamans, each claiming to have more knowledge and power than the other, people also fear to become involved in their private enmities and to fall victim to their 'professional' hostilities. However, the general attitude toward the Indian shamans is one of trust and respect, and in many matters, either private or communal, their services are becoming more and more indispensable.

THE FIESTA CYCLE

San Rafael is the patron saint of the village and his day is celebrated every year. He is associated with rain and fertility, being the patron of the crops, and his fiesta marks the beginning of the rainy season. This fiesta is an important social event. In spring the dry, yellow mountain folds and the barren hills and plains are suddenly transformed into luxuriant green; every tree and shrub sprouts and blossoms; and just as nature changes its dress at this time of the year so does San Rafael, and so do the people. Months before the fiesta somebody weaves with meticulous care a tiny straw hat for the saint's image to wear on this day and during the rest of the year. Shortly before the fiesta, the wooden statue is taken down from its accustomed place in the church to be cleaned and scrubbed and to receive a new coat of paint. The color of the saint's garb is changed every year, and there is much discussion in the village as to the possible political color symbolism or the general appearance of the statue.

People, too, change their dress on this day. About two months before the fiesta, the stores sell great quantities of home products or cash crops to the lowland merchants and buy instead a stock of multicolored garments. Suits, dresses, shirts and shoes, underwear, belts, handkerchiefs, and whatever else might be considered necessary for a well-dressed person are carried up to the village. It is a social obligation to buy a new dress for the fiesta of San Rafael. People save all year long for this occasion and the local tailor is busy for months beforehand with the many orders he receives. To appear with new clothes on San Rafael's day is a matter of prestige and is the only occasion of the year when each individual can demonstrate openly that he is a 'civilized' and 'serious' person.

There is money in the village in May. The coffee harvest which ended early in March leaves good cash, and the first general harvest of the year, beginning in April, offers additional income. San Rafael marks the end and the beginning of the economic year. Old debts are paid up and new accounts are opened. This is the day for spending freely, for giving away one's last peso for clothes, food, or drink.

The fiesta is organized by the *Mayordomo*, who has held this office for many years, having accepted it as a vow. He is assisted by several *Oficiales* who volunteer their services for each different day of the fiesta and who might hold the office for this day only or for several years. The Oficiales have to carry the burden of the expenses incurred during the fiesta. The Mayordomo determines the approximate amount necessary, generally about 300 or 400 pesos, including the hiring of an orchestra, the purchase of fireworks, and the priest's fees. Several of the girls of the Daughters of Mary, a lay organization, have made arrangements with a priest in the next lowland town and have obtained his promise to officiate at Mass and to lead the procession.

During the years when we stayed in Aritama the worship of Our Lady of Fatima was introduced into the lowland towns. The priest who came to the village for San Rafael brought the new image of Our Lady in order to introduce it to the inhabitants and to establish her cult from that day on. The two fiestas were, therefore, combined, and extended over four days.

The orchestra arrived in the afternoon preceding the first fiesta day, though it was not to begin to play until the following morning. In the same evening the church bell was tolled, a few firecrackers were shot off, and then half a dozen women, all of them of the Plaza, assisted at the Rosary. Most people had been working all day, and soon everybody retired. The next day, the first day of fiesta for Our Lady of Fatima, there was a Mass and Communion at 7 A.M. However, only the Daughters of

Mary and a few other women attended, a lonely man from the Loma barrio keeping well in the background. A few of the women communed. During the sermon the orchestra began playing on the plaza and soon the few churchgoers left to join the crowd listening to the music. On our way home we asked a number of people why they had not gone to Mass; a typical answer was 'They say that this Virgin is a *goda* [a "goth", i.e., a member of the Conservative party] and goes robbing the Liberals. We don't like her.' One of the leading members of a lay brotherhood told us: 'Men don't go to worship the Virgin; that's why only the Daughters of Mary went; it's their day. We shall go when San Rafael is celebrated.' Another religious leader said that he did not want to inaugurate his new suit because he wanted to show off in it at San Rafael's procession.

In the afternoon the image of Our Lady of Fatima was carried in procession through the village. Upon leaving the church, there were not sufficient men available to carry the statue and so the Daughters of Mary had to lend a hand, instead of walking behind. Almost only women and children went along, but when the band began to play and the little group started to walk up the plaza, some men who had not been at Mass left their houses and joined the procession. The priest stopped several times to give his blessing to a house and to sing a Salve, while the Daughters of Mary sang the chorus. All through the village the owners of only ten houses asked for this blessing, and a little boy collected 1 peso for each Salve sung. While the procession proceeded, the band played the same hymn over and over. One of the drummers had to be carried by two serious-faced companions because he had had one drink too many, but that did not keep him frc n beating the drum. At its return to the plaza the procession consisted oɩ almost 200 persons, most of them placero women and children. The image was placed on an altar inside the church, and soon the crowd dispersed. In the evening of the following day there was again a Rosary, but once more only a few women were present. There was no festive atmosphere during these days, no dances or reunions.

The next day was San Rafael. At 8 A.M. Mass started while the band played dance tunes at the church door and firecrackers were shot off. After the sermon the priest blessed a newly adapted altar and then once more addressed his flock, going into a detailed account of church finances. As it was already past 10 A.M. before he finished and the sun was very hot, he decided to have the procession in the afternoon. This caused considerable discontent. According to tradition the procession should take place in the morning and the image be returned to its shrine in church before noon. The priest did not know this custom, and as nobody wanted to tell him there was nothing done about his decision.

At 3 P.M. people gathered for the procession. The band began to play and eight men carried the image. Advancing slowly, the procession stopped at the usual sites, and, in between, many stops were made where the priest sang a Laudate. For each a boy collected 50 centavos. Two policemen joined the procession, walking ahead of it and firing their carbines and revolvers into the air, stopping sometimes to reload and fire again. The men who carried the image took turns with other men who wanted to demonstrate thus their devotion to the saint. Although many women went along, none of them carried the image. The procession again consisted of considerably more women than men, and a great number of children. All wore new clothes and some of them carried umbrellas. A good number of people seemed to be little accustomed to all this finery. Some stumbled along painfully, having put their new shoes on the wrong feet; others sported new ties hanging from their necks without having been knotted. Several women had their new dresses put on the wrong way, with the front part in the back. Very self-consciously they walked along, trying to keep in step with the music and looking uneasily at the ground. Most people carried in their hands bundles of from three to eight burning candles. They scraped off the molten wax and put it in their mouths, chewing the lumps as they went along. The whole procession seemed to be chewing, masticating open-mouthed the wax that dripped from their candles. There were no prayers, no songs, only the long walk up to the Loma, the sharp turn, the return to the Plaza and the church. It was nearly 6 P.M. when the procession returned, and the image was placed again in its accustomed place. Some 250 people, all in all, had taken part. According to tradition two flute-players walk backward in front of the image, their faces turned up to it as they play their flutes. But this year they refused to appear, saying that they did not wish to be punished by the saint, who undoubtedly was annoyed by the breach of tradition committed by holding his procession in the afternoon. People agreed with them. As a matter of fact, at the image's return to the church a rain shower is supposed to fall, but this year nothing of the sort happened. This proved that the saint felt slighted.

The entire village considers the saint a miracle-worker, a protector to whom veneration is due, but the attitudes differ widely in degree between lomeros and placeros. Although they consider him to be the patron saint of the whole village, the lomeros do not pay exterior homage to him. In their opinion, the saint exists and functions with or without a cult. They believe in the saint's magical power, but no exterior expression of this faith is thought to be necessary. Therefore, they do not go to Mass or join the procession. To the placeros, on the other hand, the most important part of the cult is the procession, the Mass, and the prayers. But they do not believe in the saint's powers. They do not feel certain that the saint is a real force; they doubt that he has the personal, particular attributes which the lomeros see in him. They do not identify the village and its life with this image. For the placeros the saint is logically associated with Catholicism, but this is not necessarily so in the Loma barrio, where San Rafael is rather taken to be the personification of an impartial benign power, the power of rain and of plant growth. To the placeros San Rafael is but one of many saints, and at that a rather ugly and primitive one, whereas to the lomeros he represents an important protective force. Of course, most of the placeros are not agriculturalists, and although they deal with the products of agriculture, they are not in close contact with the peasant's continuous preoccupation with rain or drought. So the lomeros consider San Rafael to be 'their' saint, but do not feel that the procession is 'theirs'. This is clearly expressed in the attendance. The upper class, the *primería*, did not attend, but were represented by their children. From the Loma only people who depended economically upon the placeros attended, such as servants and laborers and some people who wanted to demonstrate their solidarity with the Plaza.

Participation in the procession is largely a prestige test. Only people with a brand-new dress take part in it, and only people who wish to demonstrate in public that they are not 'Indians' but God-fearing 'civilizados'. For weeks and months after the fiesta the villagers will discuss who took part and who did not; what clothes were worn and by whom, if the people who wore them paid for them in cash or bought them on credit, how they fitted, how they looked, how they impressed others. In the final analysis public opinion decides whether the participant has been trying in vain to ascend in status or whether he has already achieved it. It is a bitter test, and to many people the day of San Rafael is a day of humiliation, defeat, and ridicule.

The next fiesta in the year would be Holy Week (*Semana Santa*). As a Catholic ritual, Holy Week has little or no importance in Aritama. Few people associate it clearly with the Passion, Death, and Resurrection of Christ, and the whole period is thought of only as the time when 'Our Lord is dead'. If a priest is in the village a Mass will be said and perhaps a procession will be held, but rarely is there one available at this occasion.

In popular belief, however, Holy Week has importance as a period of restrictions and taboos. Most, if not all of them, symbolize sexual abstinence, and it is thought that thus the fertility of the fields will be furthered. All instruments with points or with a cutting edge should be hidden away in a corner of the house, and guns should be put with the muzzle downward. No one should cut wood or straw or peel any fruit by cutting or scraping. No brooms should be used for sweeping. On Good Friday no cooking should be done, although the hearthfire may be kept burning. No one should take a bath and by no means should music be made. There is much talk about certain foods which are to be eaten during Holy Week, and people will talk for weeks in advance about the many fine dishes they are going to prepare for this occasion. Food for Holy Week should consist mainly of sweets, beans, rice boiled in milk, cheese, and fish, and no salt whatever should be used in preparing these dishes. However, in reality there is hardly any change in the daily diet. But few families would actually change their daily pattern, except maybe by abstaining from meat on Good Friday. It is said that on Easter Day all old cooking vessels should be broken and thrown away, but in practice this is not done either, partly because aluminum or iron cauldrons have replaced the earthenware containers of earlier days. Life goes on much the same with hardly an interruption in the daily routine except that most people stay at home, having brought the necessary food from their fields during the previous days. There is no music and no entertainment.

Good Friday is the special day of the year for certain magical practices. This is the only day when one can learn the secret prayers to cure headache, toothache, hemorrhages, to make cattle throw off worms, or to induce rain. These prayers can be learned only at midnight, and there is much anticipatory village talk on this topic. However, little of all this is actually done. The only practice we saw performed on this day was that several women and children went at noon to look for some small, hard sprouts called *higüitos* ('little figs'), which appear at the trunks of certain trees such as the *matarratón* (*Gliricidia sepium*), *quebracho* (*Astronium graveolens* Jacq.), and *piñón* (*Jatropha Curcas* L.). They perforated those they found with a needle and tied them to the wrists or necks of several newborn babies to protect them against the Evil Eye. We were also told that in times past the wealthier villagers invited their servants and laborers during Holy Week for three days of eating and drinking, but few people remember having witnessed this custom. There is a general belief that during the days and nights of Holy Week the spirits of the dead are more likely to visit their families and to roam about more freely than during other times of the year. This seems to account for the fact that most people stay at home and hardly leave their houses, much less stroll in the village.

The fiesta of Corpus Christi is considered by all to be the most important religious ceremony of the year. However, little importance is attached to its traditional Catholic ritual, for nobody in the village knows the real meaning of this feast. Being celebrated at no fixed date but shortly after Trinity Sunday, it always falls on a June day, close to the solstice, and is by the majority of people taken to be a ceremony in honor of the sun. Having reached its greatest declination, the sun has to be 'turned back' (*dar la vuelta*), and this day really marks the end of the year and the beginning of a new ceremonial cycle. Although all classes consider Corpus Christi to be a very important event, it is essentially a fiesta of the Loma and of the poorer classes of the Plaza, the 'Spaniards' looking upon it with a certain contempt and refusing to take part in it unless there is a Catholic priest present—in which case we were told the celebration takes on a few more 'civilized' characteristics.

There was no priest in Aritama when Corpus Christi was celebrated during our stay. Early in April traditional ceremonial dance groups were organized and spent the interim practicing dances and songs. Every Saturday evening and throughout each Sunday, they gathered at some house for rehearsals. In the absence of the priest, these dances are the most important part of the ritual. There are three groups of dancers: the *Diablos* ('Devils'), the *Negros* ('Negroes'), and the *Cucambas* (the eagles of St. John the Baptist). The Diablos wear horned masks with protruding tongues and long fangs. A wig of hair made from tinted fibers covers the head, and strings of seed rattles are tied below the knees, around the ankles, and held in the hands. Huge iron spurs are worn on the naked feet, and some wear sheepskins thrown over their backs, studded with small pieces of mirror. Multicolored ribbons and rosettes are worn by all and some of the dancers have castanets. The Negros paint their faces with charcoal and wear long necklaces of dried seeds, shells, or bottle tops. Slung over their shoulders they carry several bags full of broken bottles or old tin containers. Their straw hats are covered with flowers, and each man carries a wooden swordlike club painted with diagonal stripes. Some dancers, too, appear in female dress disguised as *Negritas* (little Negro girls). The Cucambas wear a wide skirt of palm leaves tied around the waist and another similar one tied around the neck, so that the whole body is covered from head to foot with the rustling leaves. They wear a wooden mask representing a bird with a long straight beak. Ribbons and flowers cover the back part of the head. All these dancers have made a solemn vow to dance thus disguised each year at the Corpus Christi feast for the rest of their lives. Some of them who had been seriously ill while still small infants had had the vow made for them by their mothers. Others had made the vow in later years, often as adults, but for the very same reason. Having been spared miraculously from imminent death, the dancers consider themselves as '*prestados*', i.e., living on borrowed time. They 'do not quite belong to this world'.

The actual celebration begins before dawn on Corpus Christi day, when a group of men, among them some of the dancers, meet at a sacred boulder near the village. Standing on its flat top, they silently watch the horizon to the east. At sunrise they watch the clouds, their shapes and colors, and the passing birds, and from what they see they foretell what fortune will befall the village during the next twelve months. It is said that the clouds take the shape of a large crowd of people dancing and that among them each inhabitant of the village can be recognized. The ones who do not appear will die before the year is over. It is also believed that, should any of the dancers slip and fall during their performance that day, he will die shortly afterward. After descending from the boulder, one man buries at its foot the collective offerings to the sun which the others give him.

A short time later, at about 7 A.M., the three groups of dancers, about thirty persons in all, meet before the church. The two Cucambas ascend slowly, heads reverently bowed, and stand inside the door facing the main altar; behind them come the Diablos, and last the Negros. While the leader of the Cucamba dancers beats a heavy drum which hangs from his left shoulder and sings toward the altar, the Cucambas dance on the doorstep, accompanying their dance with a gourd rattle. After about half an hour, the Cucambas step back and the Diablos and Negros begin to dance, but without entering the church. Gesticulating threateningly toward the altar, they hurl screams at it and behave as if in defiance of the Cucamba's reverent dance. Their accompaniment is also drums and rattles. The dancers then leave the space immediately before the church and turn toward the plaza and the village. Traditionally, there are seven sites (*puestos*) where they repeat their dances, four of them located at the main entrances to the village, which correspond to the cardinal points, and three inside the village—the house of the Corregidor, the church, and the middle of the plaza. Having finished their first dance at the church door, the groups dance at each site in succession, moving counterclockwise through the village and finally returning to the church. Here, while the Diablos and Negros stand in silence at the foot of the steps leading up to the door, the Cucambas mount, deeply bowed, and dance sedately and reverently, again accompanied by the drumbeat and singing verses toward the main altar. The other dancers then follow and form a circle around the Cucambas, but without dancing themselves. Shortly before the Cucambas finish their performance one of the Negro dancers kneels down in the middle of the staircase and says a silent prayer. The words of this prayer, though inaudible, are in the old Indian language, and the text is very secret, the wording being changed from year to year. During this prayer all descend the staircase again and dance once more before the church, each group apart and accompanied by its own instruments. At the moment when the man who has been offering the prayer rises to his feet, the dance finishes and the groups disperse. With this act all the ritual and ceremony are over. The rest of the day and the night are dedicated strictly to merrymaking and drinking.

When a Catholic priest is present, some of the details of this ritual are changed, and certain Catholic features added, but the beliefs and motives of the participants remain the same. The priest conducts an early Mass, to which many of the placeros come, and then he leads a procession carrying the Host on a golden monstrance through the village. This procession, which stops at temporary altars erected at the seven traditional dance sites, is made up of the three dance groups in full regalia and of miscellaneous followers, but only the Cucambas perform. They accompany the Host, walking and dancing continuously around it and lifting their rattles up to it. The colorful performances at the church are omitted in favor of the priest's sermon, but it is poorly attended.

One week after Corpus Christi the *Octava* is celebrated and the dances are repeated. In past times the dances were performed for five consecutive weeks celebrating the *Octava, Octavita, Contra-Octava, Bírria,* and *El Día,* until, after the last performance, the Cucambas sang a special song of departure. But nowadays only Corpus Christi and the Octava are celebrated.

During the next four months the ceremonial calendar is blank, until early in November, when All Soul's Day is celebrated. Shortly after noon on November 2, one of the principal members of the dance groups goes from house to house with a few children to begin celebration of this date, the *Día de los Angelitos* ('Day of the Little Angels'). He carries a wooden cross, about 40 centimeters high, covered with freshly cut flowers, mostly yellow ones, and behind him runs a boy tinkling a bell. Soon a crowd of about 100 children has assembled, all of them screaming and jostling. As they follow their leader from door to door, the children call:

Casa de teja,	(House with a tile roof,
Donde vive una vieja;	Where an old woman lives;
Casa de rosa	House of roses,
Donde vive la hermosa;	Where a pretty girl lives;
Casa de pino,	House of pinewood,
Donde vive un mezquino.	Where a miser lives!)

At each house they repeat this little song:

Angelitos somos;	(We are little angels;
Del cielo venimos;	We come from Heaven;
Pidiendo limosnas	Asking for alms
Para nosotros mismos.	For ourselves.)

The leader sings the first stanza, the children sing the second, he the third, and they the fourth. In response, from every house people throw some fruit into the air above the crowd, and the children try to catch them, putting these gifts into the bags they are carrying. Pieces of sugar cane, plantains, bananas, and all kinds of other fruit are thus collected, and after a few hours they have gathered a considerable amount of food. In times past the children took this food into the church, where they built a fire and cooked it. All night was spent in cooking and eating and tolling the church bell, because it was thought that the poor souls of Purgatory were taking part in the feast. Sometimes, when a priest was in the village, the food was given to him, and only the smallest children were allowed to keep some sugar cane. But for several years now no nightwatch has been kept, and the children carry the food home, where they eat it with their families.

Later in the afternoon the children meet on the plaza. Many adults arrive at the same time and the fathers of some of the boys between six and ten years of age begin to pair them off according to similar physical strength. All wear their oldest clothes and most of them are half-naked. Surrounded by a yelling crowd, two of the boys are 'launched' (*echados*) by their elders and begin to fight. While they hit at each other clumsily, the spectators encourage them with screams and insults. After a few minutes of half-hearted blows, one of the boys usually begins to cry and runs away, leaving a winner who is also close to tears. Another pair is then pushed into the circle and start to fight. Some of the boys whose fathers have not come ask other men to 'launch' them. There are about ten or twelve such fights, and after they are over the crowd disperses, laughing. The winners do not receive any award, but the losers are ridiculed and scolded by other boys. During the fight the spectators use terms employed in cockfighting. It is evident that most of the boys are afraid to fight and have to be prodded on by their parents, who try to shame them into fighting. Some people told us that only boys born on the same day and year should fight; others said that they should be born on November 2; others insisted that only equal fitness counted. No explanation for this practice was given. All Soul's Day had always been celebrated in this way, people said.

November 2 is the only day in the year when women may go to the cemetery to visit the graves of relatives, and then only in the company of a Catholic priest. The year we were there no priest was in the village. No one went to the church or to the cemetery, and there were no flowers or prayers for the dead.

Christmas is not celebrated in Aritama. It is a simple 'holy day', like any other. We spent two Christmas Eves in the village and on the first a priest was present and a midnight Mass (*Misa de Gallo*) was said, but very few people attended and hardly more were present at Mass on December 25. No priest was present the second year. There were no special foods, no music, no festive mood at all, and these days passed like any other both years. Few people know the meaning of this date. Most think it is a feast marking the beginning of the cockfight season.

When someone suggested that it is the day 'when the Christ Child went asking for alms' the others laughed and said that Christ had nothing to do with it. All they knew was that in other villages it was a day to drink and to dance. However, the old people remember a time when Christmas was still a festive occasion, although even they do not know what it stood for. They say there were dances and gatherings, street vendors sold special dishes, and music was played at many homes. The midnight Mass was a merry gathering and people played all sorts of flutes, pipes, and whistles before the altar. But not so today.

Carnival is celebrated only in the Loma barrio and is mainly an entertainment for children and a few young people. It is organized every year by the same individual, a well-known dancer whose father had been the organizer in past times. The principal preparations consist in practicing a dance called *Baile de las Chinitas* ('Dance of the Little Indian Girls'), which is clearly inspired by the *chichamaya* dance of the Guajiro Indians. Beginning early in January a group of boys and girls meet at different houses where they play the drum and rehearse the dance. During the Carnival, this group walks singing and playing through the village, some of them disguised, some wearing only crowns of paper flowers. A huge wooden mortar and its heavy pestle are carried along, and wherever there are a few onlookers it is put down, two girls begin to pound it, and the group dances around them. The leader is disguised as *La Mano Larga* ('The Long Hand') and wears a long white gown. Two enormously long arms—broomsticks held in each hand— are covered by the flowing gown and terminate in huge claws of cut tin. A white cardboard mask with red eyes and mouth covers the face. With his long arms he makes menacing gestures and tries to catch the small children who crowd around. Another man is disguised as a jaguar and is followed by a hunter and his dogs. Several girls are dressed as 'soldiers', and chase a group of 'Indians' who 'came trading'. Another man carries a large casting net which he suddenly throws over the crowd, and whoever gets caught by it has to buy himself free by paying a few small coins. However, there is very little elaboration and only token participation. In a few hours everything is over. There are no dances in the evening or any other form of social gathering. The placeros consider the Carnival an 'Indian' tradition and take no part in it.

DEATH AND THE BEYOND

According to local belief, about nine days before death occurs the spirit (*espíritu*) of a doomed person begins to 'retrace its steps' (*recoger los pasos*), visiting all places where the individual has been in his lifetime. The spirit appears there as a shadow in the shape of the person, and some people can see it and recognize it, as can dogs or horses. The spirit is then suffering (*penando*) for the evil deeds the individual committed. Driven by the Devil, who carries a large whip and uses it mercilessly, the spirit is taken over the trails he used to walk, and at night, it is said, one can hear the lashing of the whip, the clanking of chains, and the screams of pain. In the meantime, the individual is still alive and may not even feel ill at all. But if his spirit has been seen or heard and identified by someone, people will say, *Ya no es de este mundo sino del otro; ya lo entregaron* ('He does not belong to this world any more but to the other; they [the ancestral spirits] have turned him in already').

As soon as a sick person falls into a coma, the furniture and all other household utensils are removed from the house and taken to the home of a relative, if possible at a considerable distance, and only the most necessary objects used in the care of the dying person are left in the house. Although in the daytime most family members, relatives, and friends will stay in or near the house, they will sleep in other homes, and only the principal members of the family will stay on, taking turns in the care of the dying. Only the latter's food can be prepared here. All other food is cooked in the houses of relatives and eaten there. To approach an agonizing person is thought to be dangerous not so much because of fear of contagion but because people believe that a dying man's wish to live is so strong that he might 'take along' some of the living. Because of this many people die alone, their deaths being discovered only some time after its occurrence.

As soon as death has occurred (or sometimes even while the person is still in a comatose state), a number of preparations are made. One member of the family, generally its male head, in order to 'speed the soul on its way' burns a dry leaf of *pune* (*Espeletia* sp.), carrying the smoking leaf around the room. Immediately afterward the healthiest member of the family dips his fingers into a small container of holy water and makes four crosses on the corpse: forehead, chest, hands, and feet. At the same time another relative closes the eyes of the dead person by pressing two fingers upon the eyelids for a few minutes. Should they stay open, the dead might want to 'take along' someone to keep him company. However, in the case of children the eyes are intentionally kept wide open by spreading the eyelids with little wooden splinters or with straws. While all this is done, three Masses should be said for the poor soul, because if this is not done right away the soul will have to suffer in Purgatory, being unable to proceed on the way to the Beyond. When there is a Catholic priest in the village, it sometimes happens that he is asked to say Death Mass for the soul of a person who is still in coma.

For the wake which follows, all relatives, friends, and neighbors change into their best clothes and meet at the house of the mourning family. The men wear clean white trousers and shirts, new straw hats, and often new sandals, and every man brings a chair or two. The women wear black dresses. The undertakers and gravediggers, a group of men supervised by the oldest of them, are called in by a member of the dead person's family, and the first thing they do upon entering the house is to ask loudly for the clothes to dress the corpse in. This request has important implications. Every adult of either sex is supposed to own a new dress or suit which is carefully put away in a chest to be used only at his death. To die without leaving this set of clothes means shame to one's family, and such irresponsibility would be remembered in the village for many decades. There are instances told of people who were too unthrifty or too poor to buy these clothes in time and whose family had to borrow or buy them, being thus exposed to shame and ridicule. So, when the undertakers ask for the clothes they do so loudly and publicly as one of the final tests of the dead person's status, and when they receive them they carry the bundle ostentatiously to the darkened room to dress the body. Men are dressed in white drill trousers, a white long-sleeved shirt, and white socks. A coat is rarely put on, and they never receive underwear. Women are dressed in a dark dress, and their feet are covered with sandals or shoes, the undertakers leaving the room while some of the older women of the household arrange the body. Children are dressed in white, and some paper flowers are put on their heads. The hair of all corpses is carefully combed and heavily perfumed; the chin is held up with a ribbon of black cloth and a similar ribbon is used to tie the feet together at the ankles. The hands are folded over the chest and tied together, and, if available, a small cross is placed between the fingers. Flowers are placed near the body of a dead child but not that of an adult. Some women who have lost a child earlier will place a few flowers in the hands of his deceased playmate, with the hope that the more recently dead will take this gift to the one they had lost. Until recently it was the general custom to place beneath each armpit and parallel to the body a long wing feather of the red macaw, and these feathers were kept in each house for this purpose. This was to enable the spirit to fly to the Beyond in the shape of the bird. Now, however, this custom is rarely observed except by some of the lomero families.

When the corpse is dressed, a new white bedsheet is hung over one of the walls of the room, and a cross of black cloth is affixed to it in the middle. Then a table is put in front of the wall and pushed close to it. A wooden cross or an image of Christ, four burning candles, and a glass of water are placed upon the table, the image or cross being flanked by pairs of candles with the glass standing in front of it, but no flowers are allowed. The water is meant to quench the thirst of the spirit on the way to the Beyond, and, once the wake is over, the glass cannot be used for drinking any more but is kept to serve at another wake. In front of the table, resting upon two chairs or boxes, the coffin is set, the corpse lying in it upon a thick layer of *matarratón* leaves. Otherwise the house is empty. At death's approach everything had been removed and even the hearthfire had been extinguished, not to be lit again for nine days and nine nights.

While the women are busy with these arrangements, the men are bringing in the chairs and placing them along the walls, all around the room, and the people begin to assemble for the wake (*velorio*). In past times—about one generation ago—each person attending a wake first took a piece of burning *pune* and walked around the house with it, and two little heaps of dry leaves were prepared in the backyard, one for men and another for women. But this custom is obsolete now. Some women pray, others weep; children, dogs, pigs, and chickens are chased away. In the meantime the *rezandera* has arrived, and now she raises her voice, beginning the Rosary. While these prayers are said, some of the women retire to the kitchen of a neighboring house, and after a while black coffee will be served to all. The women stay with the corpse, but the men sit in the adjoining room or gather in the patio, and the long wake is under way.

A wake lasts for nine days and nights. It is believed that during all this time the dead man's spirit is wandering over the great Zigzag Trail (*Camino Culebreado*) toward a distant mountain peak, illuminated on the way by the candles which burn day and night and guided by the prayers which are being continuously said. On this trail the spirit is attacked by the little bird *sipipire*, but the red macaw feathers turn into wings and help it to escape the danger. Three rivers have to be crossed: the River of Tears, swollen with the tears of the mourners; the River of Milk; and the River of Blood. At each river a dog is waiting —black, white, or red, in that order—and if the person has not mistreated dogs during his life, the animal will help him across the water, the spirit grasping its tail. But if the person has ever mistreated a dog, it will not help him now, and the spirit has to wait until the river falls enough to be waded, meanwhile being punished by the sipipíre birds. But after the three rivers are safely crossed the spirit enters the Beyond, the land of the snow peaks. This final refuge is reached during the ninth night of the wake.

During these nine days and nights the mourners are faithful and the rezandera diligently recites her prayers, being joined in them occasionally by a few other women who know the words. The candles are carefully watched, but only during the night before the burial and later during the ninth night are all four of them lighted. During the other nights only two are kept burning and during the daytime only one. During the first night the dead person's female relatives take turns addressing the corpse, praising his generosity, fidelity, thriftiness, and altruism. Favors or gifts received from him are enumerated in detail, such as furniture, chests, clothes, or kitchenware. The parties the dead organized are described, his skill as a musician or dancer is praised, and his hard life as a laborer discussed. Almost always allusions are made to the dead man's or woman's unfailing generosity to the family, and often the plea 'remember me once you have arrived' is added after praising this trait. As death is almost always taken to be the result of Black Magic, suspicions are voiced concerning the dead person's enemies, but a name is never mentioned. A daughter will scream, 'O mother! You, who always did the best for me; you, who gave me my education; you, who fulfilled every wish of mine!' A widow might say, 'My husband; all he owned we spent freely and he never complained.' The most frequently heard exclamations are 'Ay, what shall we eat tomorrow? How shall I give food to my children, now that you are dead?' Men are considerably less articulate, but once in a while they might be heard to say, 'Right! Very true! That's the way it is!' in answer to the women's praise of the deceased's character. Sometimes a mourner's—especially a woman's—grief will be so deep and resentful that she will challenge all recognized supreme powers, insulting Christ, the Virgin, or the ancestral spirits in word and gesture. Such violent reactions are not frequent but they do occur occasionally, and people are then greatly afraid that some supernatural punishment may befall the blasphemer. However, there is no hysterical screaming or weeping on these occasions, but rather a deep and bitter resentment against the injustice of human fate.

During the first and ninth nights all mourners stay awake until dawn, but during the remaining nights only the family members stay up, while the other mourners take leave before midnight. The women usually talk of death and disease and praise the dead person's memory, but the men gather apart to tell jokes and stories, mostly of ghosts and apparitions. There is one man in the village who is in charge of supervising all wakes, and he sees that respectful order is kept during the gathering. However, sometimes there is much noise and merrymaking, and some men or boys may have to be told to leave if they do not behave more respectfully. On the last night of the wake each person takes a piece of burning *pune*, divides it into two fragments, and carries one in each hand. If the one in the left hand, the 'female' hand, burns out faster, then a woman of one's family will die soon; if it is the one in the right hand, then it will be a male member.

Coffee is served freely during the wake, and the supervisor distributes cigars to men and women. During the last night one of the women of the family brings a tray with bread and cheese, offering it first to the older women, then to the others according to age, and last to the men. Cigars, food, and coffee, frequently rum also, a few leaves of tobacco, or a bit of raw sugar may be contributed by relatives or friends who for some reason or other are unable to attend the wake.

During the last night of the wake each relative of the deceased makes a small package of maize leaves containing chingamoco. With this offering in the right hand, he walks clockwise around the exact spot where death took place, and it is said that at this exact moment the spirit has arrived in the Beyond. The magic circle thus drawn around the spot prevents the spirit's return to it. The next day these offerings are deposited at one of the sacred sites.

Many stories are told of strange happenings at deaths or wakes. The soul or spirit of an evil person is said to take the shape of a black and ugly bird, but in the case of a good person it appears as a white bird 'like an angel'. Many people say that the spirit escapes in human shape, as a small replica of the individual, and some say that it appears in the shape of a green fly. These different manifestations are said to have been seen or heard during the wake, causing those present to panic. Once, it is told, all the mourners fell asleep during a wake, and the wind blew out the candles. In the dark the dead man's voice called out, 'Make light! I cannot see the trail!' Another time, when an evil old woman died, her spirit departed as a huge black bird, extinguishing with its fluttering wings all the lights and leaving the mourners in darkness. The soul-birds sometimes return to earth in the shape of certain birds like the *guacaó* or the *biusúri*, which may appear to an individual or may be heard by many, announcing death and disease. A bird that appears to a person is always identified with the grandmother, and shortly after a wake is over people watch out anxiously for these harbingers of death.

Burial takes place the day after the first night of the wake. Many people buy or make a coffin during their lifetime and keep it ready for the event of their death, but otherwise the nearest relatives have to buy one. To have a coffin ready is not considered a duty, and its importance is small in comparison with the significance attached to the set of new clothes. Until about thirty years ago a special coffin, called the *Cajón de las Animas* ('poor soul's coffin'), was kept in church to be used for carrying the dead from their houses to the cemetery, after which it was returned to the church. At that time it was the custom to wrap the corpse in a hammock, but at present the general custom is to wrap it in a new white bedsheet. Before the coffin is closed, the dead person's belongings—clothes, covers, hats, bags, chamber pot, and eating utensils—are put into it. Should there not be room enough, a male relative may carry these objects behind the coffin and bury them at its foot. The dying sometimes make special requests in this connection. One dying man's desire to be buried with a bottle of rum was granted, as was another's wish to be buried with a diminutive machete of wood. When the lid is nailed down, the mourners rise and say, 'Pray for me and for your family.' At the same time the church bell tolls once, and the men get ready to carry the coffin to the cemetery. The coffin is taken through the main door head first, and at this moment the bell tolls twice. It tolls thrice and for the last time when the funeral procession passes the church. Only men accompany the coffin. If when they first lift it up the burden seems to be heavy, they are satisfied because this means that they themselves still have many years to live, but should the coffin seem light to one of them he will most probably die soon.

Women never enter the cemetery except on All Soul's Day and then, as we have pointed out, in the company of a priest, but there are many women in the village who have never set foot in it because the 'cold of the dead' (*el frío de los muertos*) is likely to cause abortions, sterility, interruption of the menstrual cycle, or other abnormalities. Even a man does not enter the cemetery in his sober mind. They are, as a rule, in a more or less advanced state of intoxication, as are the gravediggers who have been at work since they received the rum and the cigars which are the customary payment for digging a grave. They work and drink in silence with tense, harassed faces, digging, carrying stones, drinking again and again until they fall to the ground. Some lie in a stupor in the grass covering the graves of strangers or close relatives; others stumble between the mounds offering their bottles to each other. But there is no joking or storytelling. Only once in a while a man will say, 'So we are digging a grave! Doing a good job at it, too. Working hard, drinking hard. Now we are drunk and the job is done.'

At the time when the Cajón de las Animas was still in use, people were buried directly in the soil, being lifted from the coffin by ropes previously tied around the waist. Once the body had been lowered into the shallow oblong pit, it was covered by alternating layers of sand and stone. At the beginning of this century, however, immigrants from the lowlands introduced new practices. The coffin was buried with the body, and graves were dug much deeper, reaching about 2 meters, and at the bottom a side-chamber was added, into which the coffin, or part of it, could be pushed. This is the prevailing custom today. There are three different types of side-chambers: 'headwise' (*de cabeza*), 'sidewise' (*de lado*) and 'head-and-sidewise' (*de cabeza y de lado*). The position depends only upon the vicinity of other graves, the contents of which should not be disturbed. As the cemetery is small and occupied to the limits of its capacity, the gravediggers have to make test pits and have to use considerable skill in order not to disturb a neighboring grave and its own side-chamber. After the coffin has been lowered, two men jump after it and untie the ropes, which are then pulled up again. Then they push the coffin into the lateral opening, always head first. Sometimes the coffin disappears completely and then the opening is closed with a few wooden boards. The main object is to prevent the earth's touching the body, any contact between the corpse and the soil having come to be considered as 'disrespectful'. A few people now throw a handful of earth upon the coffin, and the gravediggers then fill the shaft while the mourners leave. Heavy round stones are sometimes brought from the river and placed around the mouth of the grave, upon which a small mound of earth is piled. Until very recent times it was the custom for each mourner to carry a heavy stone from the nearby creek to the grave, filling the shaft with more stones than earth. This was done 'so the dead won't come back'. Once the shaft was filled each mourner took a small pebble or a lump of clay, kissed it, and then deposited it upon the grave, but at present this custom is considered as too dangerous because it is thought that diseases can be contracted this way. Lately the custom of carrying heavy stones is disappearing, too; only occasionally do the mourners bring a few stones to be placed around the mound.

Not all people are buried in the village cemetery. At some distance from the houses, at a lonely spot on the mountain slope, there is another small cemetery reserved for people who die of contagious diseases, such as measles, smallpox, or tuberculosis. Also suicides and the excommunicated are buried there, and on top of each grave a *matarratón* tree has been planted so that everybody will be able to recognize the place and its supposed dangers. Unbaptized children are buried in the backyards or almost anywhere near the houses.

Of all the many graves in the village cemetery only four are marked with crosses. The rest are grass-covered mounds, marked sometimes with a green-leaved plant but otherwise unidentified. There are no flowers, no prayers, and no one ever clears the weeds or cleans the paths.

As soon as the mourners return to the village and the house, two of the candles are extinguished and food is prepared in a neighboring home for the gravediggers. This custom, however, is disappearing rapidly because most of the men are usually too drunk to find their way or to be able to eat. After the ninth night's wake, the family sometimes kill a cow or a steer that belonged to the deceased and invite all the people who attended for the entire wake for a day of eating and drinking. The candles are kept to be used as medicine, to be burned to a saint, or to be employed in Black Magic.

Until some fifty years ago, a native shaman led the gravediggers, after they had finished the burial, to one of the sacred sites, generally a *piedra lisa*. There they deposited their tools, and the shaman went through the ceremonial of *minchá púne*, translated as 'encircling with incense'. Two small bundles of dry *fraylejón* (*Espeletia* sp.) were set on fire, one to the east and the other to the west of the heap of tools. Crouching down over the smoke each man was purified. At present, those who have touched the corpse or helped dig the grave wash their hands and arms with rum.

During wakes or burials hardly any status distinctions are made. Wealthy people might get a 'major burial' (*entierro mayor*), at which several stops (*pozos, paradas*) are made on the way from the house to the cemetery. At the same places where the small altars at Corpus Christi are erected, a table covered with a black cloth is placed, and at each of these spots the coffin rests for a while.

As a rule a family will abandon a house where someone has died. During the last century it was abandoned completely, and the whole site was considered to be contaminated, even to the wood and stones used in its construction. But today, although this custom is still observed, most people abandon the house for only a few months, after which they return to it. If any merchandize, food, or other goods were for sale at the house, people generally stop buying there for several months, because the 'disease' is thought to contaminate everything in it. Above all, no raw sugar will be bought at such a house.

Formal periods of mourning, in the Catholic sense, are not observed Mourning is rarely expressed in clothes or in a marked change of behavior during the time following the death of a relative. Women may dress in black or gray for a few days or weeks, but few do so. A widow or a widower, or the mother of a dead child, will take part in fiestas, traveling, or social gatherings as soon as the wake is over.

SOME ASPECTS OF RITUAL IN EVERYDAY LIFE

In the following pages we shall describe a series of ritual practices and concepts which are customary upon certain occasions during the life of the individual. We shall refer mainly to divination, vows, prayers, magico-religious practices connected with economic activities, and miscellaneous ritualistic expressions.

Divinatory practices play an important role in everyday life and also upon certain specific occasions. Most, if not all, diviners are men, and many of them are also curers of diseases. Diviners are never thought to be evil or dangerous people and are not feared. All divining powers are said to be innate, bestowed upon the individual by the ancestral spirits. Sometimes it is held that they are hereditary and that the supernatural faculty can be traced to an ancestor who was a native shaman or a person with extraordinary esoteric knowledge. There are several different methods of divination, some of them exercised only by certain people but some are of common knowledge and practiced by all adults. One important method is called *cuíni* and the person who practices it is called a *cuíno*. In this form of divination the sudden twitching of muscles is interpreted in different ways. The diviner sits on a low stool, with both legs stretched out in front of him and crossed at the ankles, the right above the left. The hands are kept folded on the lap. After a short moment of mental concentration a question is asked, to be answered 'yes' or 'no', 'true' or 'false'. If the muscles of the great toe of the right foot twitch rapidly, the answer is in the affirmative; if no twitching occurs it is negative. This method is used only by certain individuals, but other types of muscle twitching can be interpreted by anybody. If, for example, the external oblique muscles of the trunk begin to twitch, someone, maybe the diviner himself, is to die soon, because it is there that the undertakers grasp the corpse when they are about to dress it. If arm muscles (*Brachio-radialis, flexor carpi ulnaris*) or leg muscles (*gastrocnemius, tibilalis anterior*) should twitch, one will be imprisoned and tied with ropes. If the muscles of the mouth twitch, the wild boars are destroying one's fields. If the right eye twitches, one will weep soon, but if it is the left eye, someone else will weep. Divining through *cuíni* is not a secret matter and is used widely to ask for return of lost objects, the usefulness of a certain medicine, or the arrival of news or strangers.

Some people are said to possess what is called *sohorí*, the faculty of seeing into the past or the future simply by concentration. The term is derived from the Arabic *zahorí*, originally meaning 'geomancer', but it is used here to identify people who are said to be able to locate lost objects, a stray domestic animal, or a long-lost relative by mental concentration. Children who are born blind, crippled, or in a caul are said to have this power. Sometimes a pregnant woman will believe she has heard her unborn child cry in the womb, and—if she does not tell anyone about it—the child will become a seer, a *sohorí*.

Divination with the *buncuéca* is practiced by the Indian shamans and also by a few old villagers who claim knowledge of it. The *buncuéca* is a small cotton bag containing archeological necklace beads, little pebbles used as offerings, pieces of glass and thread, and other materials used in curing, offerings, or witchcraft. The bag is lifted up by its handle and is set down slowly upon the ground. Then, without touching it, questions are asked, and the bag is watched closely for any sound coming from it. The slight noise produced by the settling of its contents constitutes the answer. This method is used mainly for curing diseases, i.e., to ascertain the adequacy of a treatment or to foretell whether a patient will live or die. Sometimes a diviner will conjure up the spirit of a dead child into a tiny bundle of dry maize-husk leaves. This is called a *chéndo*. The bundle is then placed in the *buncuéca*, which is treated as described, and the answers are thought to be of particular value because 'the chéndo never lies'. It is thought that the child's spirit questions directly the spirits of the ancestors and communicates their decision to the *buncuéca*. This type of divination can be performed only at a certain sacred site on the trail toward the mountains. Until recently, when a child died his mother prepared several bundles with offerings of food and one bundle representing the child itself. Upon arrival at the site, which consists of a circle of stones, the shaman took the bundles and placed the one identified with the dead child in the middle and the offerings to the left, i.e., south of it. The shaman then consulted the *buncuéca*, asking how long each member of the child's family had still to live.

Other forms of divination, such as by burning of *pune* leaves, the lifting of a coffin, or the interpretation of clouds at Corpus Christi, have been mentioned already.

Several methods of divining can be performed by any individual for his own purposes. For example, a small twig of the *albahaca* plant (*Ocimum micranthum* Willd.) is placed for the night at the extreme end of one's hammock. The next morning the name one hears pronounced first by another person will be the name of a future lover. Or a small piece of wood the size of a match stick is rolled into a bit of paper and placed behind the ear while walking through the village. Upon returning home the position of the paper in relation to the stick is observed and interpreted as significant of one's popularity. Girls looking for a husband break, on June 24 at noon, a raw egg into a glass of water, without looking at it and while reciting the verse:

Juan de los Juanes;	(John of all Johns;
Juan del Paraiso:	John of Paradise;
Dadme salud primero	First give me health
Y un buen esposo.	And then a good husband.)

After twenty-four hours the contents of the glass are 'read'. If the 'bridal veil' (the yolk casing) is broken, the girl will die soon. If not, she will soon find a husband.

Some people practice fortunetelling with cards or coffee grounds, but both these methods are quite recent and not yet fully accepted. In the villages and towns of the lowlands there are several famous diviners who are occasionally consulted by people from Aritama. Some of them use a mirror to identify a thief or to recover some lost or stolen property. The diviner asks the client to identify the culprit 'appearing' in the mirror, escaping thereby the responsibility of making the accusation himself. Also, bottles of transparent glass, filled with water or rum, or small pieces of broken glass or mirrors are used for crystal-gazing and divining. By the same method people try to find out whether a disease has a natural or magical origin. The identity of a murderer can be established as follows: The forehead of the victim is crossed with a silver coin, which is then placed upon his chest while the corpse is carried to the grave. There the body is buried face down, and watch is kept for nine nights nearby, because the murderer is supposed to come to the grave in a dazed and helpless state. This custom also has been introduced only recently from the lowlands, where it is quite common.

On the evening of December 25 twelve little piles of salt are placed upon a wooden board. The next morning they are examined to see which are damp and which dry, this being an indication of the weather that will prevail during each month of the coming year. This custom is called *coger las Cabañuelas*.

Divining is practiced as a preventive as well as a curative art. Most impending disgraces, if foretold in time, can be averted by immediate offerings, and only in case of repeated indications of imminent death is fate accepted as unavoidable. To a very large extent divination is employed to identify personal enemies who are thought to have caused diseases, death, or other evil through Black Magic. A good deal of money is spent by persons eager to know their enemies, and once they believe they do know them, more money is spent for Black Magic to harm them. Because of this constant preoccupation, the slow divinatory practices of the Indian shamans are falling into disuse, many people preferring the more rapid method of a pack of cards or a glance at a mirror, as practiced by the people of the lowlands.

Vows (*promesas*) are made almost exclusively during serious illness. A person when very ill will make a vow to a saint, to the Virgin, to the sun or to an ancestral spirit to perform a certain task or to avoid a certain action if his life should be spared. In the case of a sick child the parents make this vow in the child's name and not in their own. Most vows, if taken seriously, as they are in general, last for a lifetime.

Many ceremonial functions are fulfilled because of such vows. The Mayordomo and the Oficiales of the fiestas have made the vow to hold these offices, and all members of the three dance groups of Corpus Christi have made vows to the same effect. People who were saved from death after making a vow form, in a certain way, a group apart. They believe themselves to be living on borrowed time (*son prestados*), and so they have to watch their steps lest death should take what is already overdue it. They are closer to death than to life.

Simple individual vows consist of promising a candle, a Mass, or a prayer to a saint. A girl had made a vow to wear only white dresses until her former lover should return to the village. Other people might make a vow to offer the best fruits of their field to a saint for a favor received. A vow that is disappearing lately is that of *pedir la alerta* ('to call the alert') on All Soul's Day (November 2). Having made this vow, a man goes at midnight, alone and sober, to the cemetery and walks for a while among the graves calling the poor souls (*ánimas*) by name to follow him. He then returns to the village without ever looking back, leading the ghostly crowd, and walks with a little bell from door to door, awakening the people and asking them to pray for the dead souls. Knocking on the door he says:

Alerta, alerta;	(Alert, alert;
La Muerte está en la puerta!	Death stands at the door!
Hermano si la quereis ver	Brother, if thou wantest to see it,
Asomáte y la vereis!	Approach and behold!)

He then adds, *Vengo a que me receis un par de Ave Marías y las Animas del Purgatorio!* ('I come to have you pray two Hail Mary's and the Souls of Purgatory!'). From inside the house the occupants pray and having finished call out, *Ya está despachado!* ('You are ready!'); the *promesero* answers, *Dios se lo pague y las ánimas se lo pagarán!* ('May God and the poor souls repay you for it!'). Before dawn he returns to the cemetery and with him the souls that had accompanied him. About ten years ago was the last time that this vow was taken in the village.

While the Catholic type of *promesa* is but little practiced, there are other types of vows which are rather frequent. One of them is called *pedir para malo*, an expression that can be translated freely as 'to ask that something turn into evil'. This vow is made before an Indian shaman and is as follows: If an adult member of the family is seriously ill, the father or the mother or any other person who might be the head of the family may ask the supernatural powers to spare the life of the sick person but to turn, instead, the smallest child of the family into an 'evil' person. If the sick recovers, the child thus condemned is henceforth considered to be a potential criminal, and his entire education within the family is changed. No further control is exercised over his actions; he is not reprimanded for anything he might do, as any asocial behavior on his part is taken to be the natural consequence of this sacrificial offering. While they are alive the child's parents may keep performing yearly offerings to the ancestors and thus keep them from destroying him completely by making him commit serious crimes for which he would be punished by society. But once the child is old enough to understand the meaning of his situation, he is told that should his parents die he would be completely lost to the evil powers. We knew of several cases where this sacrificial vow was taken, and most people in the village who had a criminal record or who were otherwise asocial explained to us that their actions were due to their having been *pedidos para malo* by their parents when they were still small children. Variations of this practice are those called *pedir para flojo* and *pedir para ladrón* (to ask that someone be lazy, or a thief). In these cases an expectant mother who fears she might have a stillbirth begs the ancestors to spare the unborn child's life, even though they cause him, as an adult, to be lazy, thievish, or crippled. The fear of a stillbirth is often produced by divination shortly before birth, and so such vows are quite frequent. A recent development in this pattern is shown in the following vows: A mother or father of a sick child promises the Virgin that he will become a Protestant if the life of the child should be spared. As Protestantism is said to have no relations with the ancestor or sun worship, to accept conversion to this sect is a very serious crime, and the adult thereby invites many supernatural punishments. Among the Protestants of the village there are several who accepted conversion for this very reason, i.e., as a sacrifice to save another person's life.

Some people, especially women, take a vow to appear as ghosts. Disguised with a white bedsheet they will walk about at night, having to master their own fear while frightening other people. Some of the ghostly apparitions that were reported were probably these *promeseras*. However, no humorous element is involved at all, these matters being taken very seriously.

Divinatory practices, vows, and, of course, offerings and sacrifices are often combined with prayers. Not many people know the common Catholic prayers, and the few who do know several of them are considered privileged because they possess, it is believed, a defense against certain magical aggressions as well as a curative power in the event of disease. Prayers are, therefore, largely a private matter and are rarely organized and collective. Even during organized occasions only few people will actually join in the prayer. The occasions when prayers are considered to be not only appropriate but necessary are (1) at a wake and (2) after the appearance of a spirit that is thought to have manifested itself in order to ask a relative to pray for him. Although it is said that there is no punishment in afterlife, inconsistency is common, and some people insist that the ancestral spirits derive a benefit from prayers said by their surviving relatives. Others, though, say that such prayers represent a 'kind of nourishment'. As some informants put it: 'Here we pay the *sixquinyáni* thus: the people who believe in stones as food pay with stones, and those who believe in prayers, pay in prayers.' Among the more sophisticated placeros the offerings at sacred sites are usually replaced by prayers, and they will pay a rezandera to pray for their dead relatives. But such people constitute a small minority, and even they sometimes make offerings at sacred sites, just like the rest of the villagers.

Prayers are sometimes said during illness or to ask for the help of a saint in some project or during processions. Great emphasis is always put upon the correct working, the slightest change affecting the value of the prayer. This does not apply with ancestral spirits, which are rather addressed in an informal conversational tone. More formalized prayers are used when addressing the sun or other heavenly bodies. When addressing the ancestors it has to be kept in mind that 'to the dead, one day is one year', and therefore one asks, for example, for 'thirty days of life'. Only petitionary prayers are used; always something specific is asked for—health, money, punishment for others, or some economic advantage for oneself. Prayers that are said by a specialist, be it a *rezandera* or a Catholic priest, on behalf of another person always have to be paid for lest they have no value at all. Often a priest will refuse to accept money from a very poor person, and this causes a considerable dilemma because one cannot tell him that payment is necessary to make the prayer effective. The most important prayers are secret ones which are said in connection with curing or sorcery, *La Magnífica* is such a secret prayer and is taught by a master to his pupil upon completion of his apprenticeship in the magic arts. *La Oración del Santísimo* is known only to the participants of the Corpus Christi dances and is addressed to the sun, either in Spanish or in the old Indian language. There is also a category of 'evil prayers' (*oraciones malas*), which are used in Black Magic and which consist usually in saying the words of a prayer backward.

Praying does not form an essential part of individual religious behavior. Except at school, children are not taught to pray and the Catholic concept of daily prayers is not found in the village. Only adults pray and then only under certain circumstances, such as during illness, when feeling in danger, when wishing to harm someone else, or when in need of food.

We shall refer now to certain magico-religious practices of the individual in connection with his economic activities. All agricultural activities call for the observation of many ritual patterns. In the first place, as the land itself is thought to be owned by the ancestral spirits, these spirit-owners have to be favorably influenced by offerings made as 'payments' for the use of the soil. In the second place, upon making a new clearing not only the individual spirit-owners of all trees to be felled must be given offerings but also the spirits that are associated with the rocks, the creeks, the rain, and the different food plants. Before burning a new field for the first time, one should not drink water from the midnight preceding setting the fire until after the fire has been extinguished. When planting a newly cleared field, the first food plant to be sown must be the *guineo criollo* or *camburo* (*Musa sapientum*), which is said to be the 'mother' of all other plants or the 'government' (*gobierno*) of the new field. Next, a manioc seedling is planted in each corner of the field at the cardinal points to 'protect' the other plants. Only then can the rest of the field be planted. After having planted the remaining manioc, the man should return to his home and keep the legs of his youngest male child crossed for a while so the manioc tubers will grow strong and thick. The first fruits of the harvest of a new field, especially the first ears from a new field of corn, should always be given to an Indian shaman, lest the owner fall seriously ill. The first cluster of ripe bananas should be cut and hung on a nearby tree for the soul-birds of the ancestors.

It is believed that some people are born with a 'bad hand' (*mala mano*) and some with a 'good hand' (*buena mano*) for planting certain plants or raising certain domestic animals. This quality cannot be changed in any way throughout life, not even by magic. Women generally have a 'good hand' for planting manioc, beans, and flowers, while men have a 'good hand' for plantains and bananas. If a person with a 'bad hand' cuts a banana it will spoil in a few hours, and if he tears out a manioc tuber it will be rotten the next day. Certain plants if sown by such a person might grow but will not bear fruit. Some people cannot even prepare meat because it will spoil at their touch. As a general rule, nothing should be planted with the left hand because the seed would spoil. However, some people who have traveled recently to Barranquilla, one of the large coastal towns, were told there that the papaya should be planted with the left hand, and others were told in the lowland towns that the same hand should be used for manioc. While planting manioc, one should not smoke lest the tubers have a bitter taste, and while planting pineapple one should eat a piece of raw sugar so the fruits will be sweet. Beans should always be planted with a digging stick of *guamo* wood (*Inga* sp.) so the bean pods will grow as large as those the guamo tree bears; for planting sugar cane one should use a stick of *cardoncillo* wood (indet.), and then the canes will be as straight and strong as the stick. An expecting or menstruating woman should never sow anything because the fruits would spoil. She should never even approach a field because her presence will make the plants wither. People who have attended a wake or a burial should not plant during the next twenty-four hours.

As a general rule, a field should be planted only during the decrease of the moon, and corn or beans should be harvested during the same phase. Only taro should be planted during the crescent. Slight earthquakes are said to affect the fertility of fields and of trees. If a fruit-bearing tree suddenly loses all its blossoms, it is said that an earthquake has caused this.

Very few beliefs of magical character are connected with the breeding of domestic animals. A brooding hen that leaves the nest before hatching the eggs has tobacco smoke blown on its head; a bitch in heat receives a necklace of cylindrical sections of a cornhusk, each to represent a puppy. As there is very little hunting or fishing around the village, there are relatively few magical practices connected with these activities. Each group of animals is said to have its 'chief' (*jefe*), which one should never kill. If one by mistake or through ignorance should do so, the hunter is bound to die soon. Some animals of each species are said to have a magical 'stone' somewhere in their body—birds, mammals, and fish in their heads, and reptiles or amphibians in their stomach. According to the species, these 'stones' (probably gastroliths) are said to have different colors, and should a hunter obtain one of them, his luck in hunting that particular species will be greatly increased. Of a man who obtained the *piedra de los pescados* ('stone of fishes') it was said that besides becoming a very resourceful fisherman, his luck with the ladies also became quite remarkable. Before one goes on a hunt, offerings should be made to the ancestors and permission solicited to kill their animal wards. Sometimes these offerings are given to an Indian shaman who afterward receives part of the kill. Fishermen make offerings at the sacred site where the two shaman brothers are said to be buried, asking for their protection. Each hunting or fishing party chooses its 'cacique', who being the most proficient member, is the leader for the day and is responsible for the offerings. In recompense he receives about a third of the catch. A hunter or fisherman may eat any part of his kill or catch. The bones are thrown away or burned, but the skulls of peccaris are kept and hung from a rafter to insure future luck in hunting these animals. The night before a hunting or fishing trip all men should abstain from sexual intercourse, and men whose women are pregnant should not go fishing, as they would only waste their time. All hunting and fishing accessories, such as guns, traps, fishing tackle, casting nets, or even dogs, are said to be very exposed to Black Magic and can be easily spoiled (*trastornar*) by an enemy.

During the late nineteenth century it was still the general custom for all people except the lowland immigrants to have their children 'baptized' by a local native shaman, a ceremony for which the hybrid verb *doaquichar* was used. The ritual took place near the river, on top or at the foot of a large boulder. Ceremonially prepared food, consisting mainly of beans cooked without salt, was brought by the parents to the shaman. The latter took a small cross formed of two cotton threads knotted together in the middle and passed this object three times before the mouth of the infant. Then taking small morsels of each different kind of food, the shaman smeared some of it over the child's mouth and finally took a tiny gourd vessel from which he poured water on the infant's head. The child received an Indian name which was to be kept secret and was to be used only as his identification in his relationships to the supernatural forces. At present only the tradition-oriented lomeros have their children baptized in this way. No individual names are given any more, but each male child receives the name *búnco*, while each female child is called *búncua*. This rite takes place before or after the Catholic baptism. The boulder at which a child has been thus baptized is considered to be an important sacred site where the individual must go at times if he wants to establish an especially close contact with the ancestral spirits. Mothers and grandmothers generally show their children or grandchildren these boulders so they can make offerings there after their elders' deaths.

Male initiation rites seem to be unknown. Ritual defloration of girls reaching puberty was commonly practiced until the late nineteenth century but seems to have disappeared now, although it may still occur in some isolated cases. The girl was taken by her parents to one of the native shamans, who in a specially constructed beehive-like hut near the river, himself deflowered her. The ritual seems to have been very similar to one still in use among the neighboring Indians.

During the last century the Indian custom of 'confession' was commonly practiced in Aritama. During reunions in a ceremonial house, confession was often collective and public, each individual telling in detail his evil actions, thoughts, or intentions, being given 'counsel' (*consejo*) afterward by the shaman. At variance with the present Indian custom, this counsel was always given in private and in the shaman's own house. A form of confession still in practice in Aritama consists of making a small bundle of maize leaves, just like the ones used for offerings, holding it close to the lips and 'confessing' to it, after which it is deposited at a sacred site, thrown into a creek, or given to an Indian shaman. This is done especially in cases of illness. However, the Catholic concept of repentance has no function in this ritual, but it is believed that a disease can be cured more easily once the 'sins' have been confessed and 'thrown away'.

Among many people of the Loma barrio it is still customary to 'baptize' a new house (*componer la casa*). This ritual is always celebrated by an Indian shaman who has been asked to come to the village for this purpose. The owner of the house designates a man and his wife as *padrino* and *madrina* of the building, and while the former brings the firewood, the latter brings food, generally manioc, plantains, and a certain kind of beans. At midnight the food is cooked, but the fire must not be prepared inside the house, and glowing embers for starting it have to be brought by the padrino from his own hearth. No salt whatever is added to the food, and the beans are prepared as a separate dish. The shaman eats first, then giving to each person present a small morsel. Now he proceeds to 'feed' each principal beam or rafter of the house, smearing bits of cooked food on them with the padrino assisting him. After this has been done, incense (*pune*) is burned inside the house, and the burning leaves are carried around it. Leaf bundles with offerings of whole archeological quartzite beads are buried at the four corners and under the doorstep, and diminutive cotton bags (*buncuéca*) made by the owner of the house and filled with pulverized offerings are hung at different places from the inside of the roof. The shaman then calls together the owner, his family, and the padrinos to 'give counsel', explaining that they now owe each other mutual respect. Sugar mills or outbuildings are baptized in the same manner, as well as bridges. Some of the store-owners of the Plaza have their establishments thus 'baptized' in order to insure them good sales and prevent theft.

Rites of purification are now rather obsolete and are practiced only occasionally. We have already referred to some of those that are customary during a wake or a burial. A house or any spot where evil powers are thought to dwell can be purified by the burning of *pune* incense over all objects that are thought to be contaminated. Pieces of the smoking leaves are carried around in the right or the left hand, in a clockwise or counterclockwise direction, while the ancestors are invoked and *cuncháma* is sung. While we were in Aritama a stranger had taken lodgings for a few days with a local placero family and had been charged an outrageous price for them. Before leaving the village the man gave free flow to his anger and asked publicly that a supernatural punishment might befall the house. The next day the owners organized a *fiesta infantil* ('children's party'), inviting to it a great number of girls who had not reached puberty yet. The children were treated to soft drinks and cookies and were told to dance. All afternoon and late into the night the girls danced to the rhythm of a drum accompanied by their own children's songs, while the adults stood gravely around seeing to it that at no time should the dance lag. The owner of the house explained that the dancing of the 'innocent little angels' would exorcise all evil powers. On similar occasions holy water is sprinkled into the corners of a house or a room to keep out evil spirits. The same is done if fire or an oncoming storm should threaten a house.

If a girl should be lazy or slow in weaving hats, her parents will take her to an Indian shaman who prepares magically the needle she is using, so she will work faster. This ritual is called 'to blow upon the needle' (*soplar la aguja*) or *anguriar la aguja*, an Indian-Spanish hybrid expression meaning 'to enchant the needle'.

Some ritual practices are connected with totemic concepts. When one enters the forest, certain ritual attitudes have to be observed, as several trees are believed to be related to one's family (*son de la famlia de uno*). Passing one of these trees might cause a skin disease if this ritual is not observed. Above all, the *yaréno* tree (indet.) is supposed to cause severe inflammation, a rashlike eruption, and other symptoms. In order to avoid this, people will say, *Mis-cau co náno, yaréno naro* ('Don't harm me, yareno; I belong to your family as your brother'). Often people will add, 'Rather do some harm to the X family!' If for some reason or other one has to fell a yaréno tree or cuts it accidently, one has to say, *Yaréno cunáro* ('Yaréno, I am your brother'). However, a person can break his relationship with a tree without being punished for it but forfeiting forever any protection the tree might give him. In this case one takes a stick from another wood and beats the tree until parts of the bark come off. To urinate at the trunk of the tree is also a way to make this relationship cease. If, in a bundle of firewood gathered by another person, one should see a piece of wood belonging to the tree of one's family, one should not only close one's eyes but should also cover them with both hands. The *higuerón* (*Ficus* sp.), *caracolí* (*Anarcadium excelsum*), and *macana* (*Pyrenoglyphis* sp.) are all trees which are associated with certain families of the village. Another tree called *laurél* (*Aniba perutilis* Hemsl. and *Endlichieria Columbiana*) should never be cut because this wood is used to make statues of saints. The *pionío* (*Paeonia* sp.) should not be cut either.

MAGICAL AGGRESSION

The individual performance of magical practices intended to be harmful to other people is one of the most dominant aspects of supernatural beliefs in Aritama. Every individual lives in constant fear of the magical aggression of others, and the general social atmosphere in the village is one of mutual suspicion, of latent danger, and hidden hostility, which pervade every aspect of life. The most immediate reason for magical aggression is envy. Anything that might be interpreted as a personal advantage over others is envied: good health, economic assets, good physical appearance, popularity, a harmonious family life, a new dress. All these and other aspects imply prestige and, with it, power and authority over others. Aggressive magic is, therefore, intended to prevent or to destroy this power and to act as a leveling force. As a system of social control, Black Magic is of tremendous importance, because it governs all interpersonal relationships.

Among the Indians of the Sierra Nevada forms of aggressive magic are rare. As a matter of fact, it probably exists only among rival shamans; it is not practiced by the people. Whatever traits of aboriginal culture have survived or have been adopted in Aritama have thus been reinterpreted, and the aggressive elements they contain are evidently a recent development. As a complex, Black Magic of Mediterranean type is also of recent introduction in Aritama, dating mainly from the later part of the past century, when it was introduced by the new immigrants from the lowlands. In those days, when an Indian shaman was approached by an inhabitant of Aritama and asked to perform some magical practice harmful to another person, the shaman scolded the man for his evil intentions and generally refused to comply. But under the increasing influence of the contact situation, with changing economic patterns, the insecurity of the food supply, and the uncertainties of a new prestige system, magical aggression became an accepted part of the

396

general social atmosphere. It is probable that magical practices of aboriginal type developed during the same period, as a defensive pattern and in order to counteract the apparent dangers of a foreign body of esoteric knowledge. The shamans became more obliging, often in view of the high fees offered for their services, and finally became quite specialized in the particular quality of hostile interpersonal relations common in Aritama. Without ever applying the same methods inside their own tribe, they began to adapt traditional procedures of dealing magically with nature or with the dead to the situation of the contact village. It seems evident that most shamans, past or present, never believed in the efficacy of the aggressive magic they were asked to perform. Such practices did not form part of their own culture, but they saw that the Mestizos could be greatly impressed by any simple Indian ritual, attributing to it a mysterious power which could be used in settling their own affairs. So the Indians produced, eventually, an artificial Black Magic—for exportation, so to speak—while the local inhabitants of Indian tradition also modified such religious aspects as offerings, prayers, or divination into instruments of aggression against the living. From this blending of traditional Indian religious concepts, general Southern European magic, and new elements developed only now under the stress of the contact situation, the complex of Black Magic which dominates the village scene of Aritama at present seems to have arisen. It was the contact situation which led, if not to the origin, at least to the intensification of magical practices of an aggressive nature.

During the forty years between 1860 and 1900, the village acquired fame as a center of witchcraft, and during these years there lived a number of magicians whose names are still well remembered. Even today, although most of the famous practitioners have died long since, the people of Aritama still have a wide reputation in the lowlands for their magical practices. They are feared and distrusted, or ridiculed and insulted, but nevertheless the lowland people feel a deep respect for the villagers' magic. The villagers know this well enough, and their reaction is one of guilty pride. They will deny the stories of witchcraft which the outsiders tell about the village, but when feeling offended they will readily threaten their enemy with Black Magic.

Any visitor to Aritama who stays for some time will soon become involved in this atmosphere of magical aggression. During our first night in the village we heard a shrill whistling sound at midnight, probably from a flight of birds passing over the houses. When we inquired casually the next morning if others, too, had heard the strange noise, we met with sullen stares and uneasy answers. It was an evil omen, we were told; someone wanted us to leave soon; to someone we were unwelcome guests and the whistling was a warning to us. A spell of dysentery, a cold, an open sore which took months to heal, all were interpreted readily as 'someone's' aggressive magic, to make us leave the village. When ants destroyed our little vegetable garden people smiled knowingly. We decided to let it be known that we had knowledge of some powerful countermagic and that we were not defenseless when attacked. This settled the situation and from then on, with the exception of occasional minor insinuations, the villagers excepted us from the threat of their own magical persecutions.

Practically any adult person is suspected of being a potential enemy and a practitioner of Black Magic. Some have been observed, others boast of it, some claim innocence and ignorance concerning all these matters, but there is no doubt that in one way or the other the whole community is involved in a continuous cycle of magical aggressions. Some people are thought to be especially dangerous and endowed with magical powers. Those who were never baptized according to Catholic ritual are said to have special malignant qualities and we knew several children and adolescents who had not received this sacrament because their parents wanted them to possess these faculties as a defense in the future.

People in Aritama do not believe in the possibility of natural death. All diseases are supposed to attack an individual only through the more or less direct agency of an enemy. Economic loss, crop failure, the disease or death of domestic animals, are all attributed to sorcery, as are the sudden manifestations of undesirable personality traits, of drunkenness, physical violence, impotence, thievishness, laziness, or marital instability. All forms of mental disorder are thought to be caused by magic. An individual's sudden decision to leave the village, temporarily or permanently, is always thought to be motivated by the magic of an interested party. A family or an individual who has to sell a house, a field, or a domestic animal is likely to practice magic against the new owner, and when involving houses, this practice may take the form of a lifelong vengeance, above all by people who used to own houses in the Plaza barrio but were forced to sell them and to move to the Loma. A debtor will often practice Black Magic against a creditor, or a laborer against his employer.

In all these situations the injured party immediately concentrates on finding out the identity of the enemy, because only then can measures be taken to avoid utter ruin or death. The causes have to be treated, not the symptoms. Here, divining practices play an important role, and no expense is spared in the attempt to identify the culprit. As the range of potential enemies is very wide, a person rarely knows offhand which one of them could be responsible for his disgrace or discomfort and, therefore, has to have recourse to divination. If personal divinatory practices should not seem to be sufficient, a specialist is consulted, often an Indian shaman. Once it is established that the ill effect was not caused by annoyed ancestors but by a living person of known identity, defensive and curative measures are taken which tend not only to re-establish health and well-being but also to destroy the enemy.

A common technique in the practice of aggressive magic makes use of a small bundle of corn leaves which is deposited at the victim's house. Wrapped into the tiny bundle, which measures one inch square or less, are certain materials the nature of which depends on the desired results. For example, in order to kill a person, a bit of dust is gathered from underneath the doorstep of the prospective victim's house, or, better still, some of the very fine dust that accumulates in the eye of the door hinge. Also, a bit of earth upon which the person has stepped recently can be used. Once this powder has been wrapped in the leaves, the bundle is taken in the right hand and afterward in the left, each time describing with it a clockwise or counterclockwise motion over the spot from which the dust was taken. The package is then taken again in the right hand, and keeping it close to the lips, a spell is pronounced over it. This act is called 'baptizing', and the formula runs: 'I want X to die!' or anything to that effect. Then at nighttime this bundle is thrown upon the roof of the house of the victim or is buried in the backyard or is just thrown over the fence into the patio. In another version, instead of dust, some *musíxke* seeds or three whole chingamoco stones are used, but in this case the victim will not necessarily die but will fall ill or lose his property. Often an incision is filed around one end of an oblong chingamoco stone, and onto this 'neck' (*cuello*) two *musíxke* seeds are tied or, instead of them, two tiny pebbles, one round and another flat. This object is then wrapped in maize leaves, the invocation is performed, and the package is tied onto a hidden spot on the house post from which the intended victim usually hangs his hammock. The use of chingamoco stones in this type of magic is so frequent that the word has become synonymous with Black Magic in general and is also used to designate any bundle of corn leaves, even though it contains other materials. In all cases, the magical bundles are carried in a circular motion around the head, exactly as in making an offering. The result of the aggression depends mainly upon the words which the enchanter mutters into the package and with which he asks for a certain disgrace or other dire consequence to befall his enemy.

Another technique by which a curse can be inflicted upon a person is to bind him with invisible threads. This is done by walking around the victim while holding the chingamoco or any other kind of magic package in the hand inside the pocket. Either on the street or inside a house during a casual visit, a person may walk three times in a counter-clockwise direction around his victim. This idea of 'binding' or 'tying up' a person with invisible threads is expressed in the word *amarrar* ('to fetter'). If an Indian shaman is consulted beforehand he will generally give detailed instructions as to the hand in which the magical bundle is to be held, how many times and in what direction the victim is to be bound, and on what occasion this should be done.

If the intended victim of a magical aggression should discover what has happened before it takes effect—for example, if he should find a bundle on his roof or in his backyard—the evil curse can be reversed so it will strike the one who cast it. 'Reversing the evil' (*voltear el mal*) is practiced whenever possible and is considered to be far more effective than any other form of magical aggression. The object of such a re-directed spell has no defense whatsoever and receives a fatal punishment. In order to 'reverse the spell' the person who has been attacked takes the bundle he has found, or makes another one just like it, and says, holding it to his lips, 'X, I accuse you!' (*Fulano, te acuso*). Then he goes to a creek with running water, again lifts the bundle to his lips, and says, 'The evil you have intended to befall me I shall not accept. May it befall you who sent it!' After these words the bundle is thrown into the running water and the curse has been 'turned back' (*volteado*). Some people prefer to give such a package to a shaman or a magician of renown to throw into the water. To 'accuse' (*acusar*) a person in this manner is a very serious action because the curse is said to be almost always fatal. A slightly different technique is used to counter serious magically induced disease. For example, should a family member fall ill because of a curse put upon him by an unknown enemy, another member consults a shaman and asks him to transfer the curse to another. The shaman names another member of the family, generally a child, and, if the sick person agrees, transfers the spell to this innocent and healthy person. This procedure, called 'to reverse the accusation' (*voltear el acuso*), is quite usual if the first victim is an important food-provider. But the new victim must be of the same sex and belong to his close kin. Sometimes it is possible to transfer the spell to a highly cherished domestic animal, such as bull or a sow, and in this case also it must be of the same sex as the original victim.

Disease and damage-causing charms containing chingamoco, cotton seeds, or other materials are also thrown into the fields, the cattle corral, pigpen, garden, or kitchen, or any other place where harm is intended. If someone wants a woman to die in childbirth or to have a stillbirth, the bundle is buried or deposited just outside her door. Chingamoco bundles are also used against any undesirable person whom one wants to leave the village, such as foreigners, policemen, missionaries, traders, or any person considered dangerous. In many of these cases collective action is taken, and the bundles are prepared by a large number of people who are especially interested in getting rid of the unwanted visitor. This is called 'to throw someone out of the village' (*botar del pueblo*) and is quite a common practice.

Another way of causing harm is to administer to the victim some kind of magic concoction or potion. The bones of toads, lizards, and small land turtles are ground into a fine powder and put into a cup of black coffee or, preferably, into a glass of milk, to be offered to the unsuspecting victim. One or several of these animals are said to come to life again inside the person, causing a slow and very painful death. The ground bones of a black donkey are said to be a very potent poison if mixed with a drink. Other ingredients of such potions (*tomas, bebidas compuestas*) are toad's blood, menstrual blood, and ground human bones from the cemetery. The powder can also be put into cigars or cigarettes, which are then offered to the intended victim; or a bit of toad's blood can be dripped into the huge water jar that stands in the corner of his house.

Strong smells play an important part in aggressive magic. A person who smells of garlic, onions, vanilla, ginger root, lemon, or perfume, or a house or any other object that might have such a smell are thought to be particularly exposed to magical aggression, and friends who notice the scent will warn the person of this danger. However, about 1940 a cheap commercial product called *Agua de Alhucema* ('lavender water') became known to be a strong prophylactic if used on the chest, arms, and legs of an endangered person.

Another means of making an enemy fall ill or even killing him is to simulate his wake. A table is covered with a white bedsheet, and a cross is placed in the center. A lighted candle is put on each corner of the table and then the prayers usually said at a wake are pronounced, mentioning in them the name of the enemy as though he had died already. In these cases, the candles are always burned upside down, i.e., they are lighted on the wrong end and placed with the pointed end downward.

Candles are burned thus for other purposes, too. A thief can be made to return stolen property or can be made seriously ill by burning a single candle upside down on the spot where the theft was committed. A thin strip studded with thorns is torn from the side of a long sisal leaf and is bent in a circle surrounding the candle, with the thorns upward. Often the victim is directly identified with a candle, and needles or thorns are thrust into it one by one, each time calling the enemy's name. The candle stands, in such cases, on a table covered with a black cloth. This method can be practiced only on Friday or Saturday nights.

Another magical device consists of taking a large ripe plantain of the *serrano* variety and pricking it with a poisoned thorn, after which it is put under a new cooking vessel. Three days later it is said that both the plantain and the victims have 'burst' (*se revientan*). Or, if an enemy has been bitten by a snake his certain death can be produced by throwing a bit of yellow chicken excrement wrapped in a small piece of cloth through the window of his room. Or if among a group of laborers one of them distinguishes himself by rapid and hard work, some of the others will try to curb his ambition in the following way: Early in the morning before the others have arrived, one man will mark a cross on the spot where the intended victim works and then will say the Lord's Prayer and the Hail Mary three times. It is claimed that after this the good laborer will be slow in his work; he will become tired and thirsty, unable to keep up his former pace. Or if in such a party there should be one who eats more than the others of the food supplied by the employer, the cook will take a mouthful of water and spit it upon the floor in cross-shape. From then on there will be no one eating at the expense of his fellow laborers.

Agricultural utensils, like machetes, are very exposed to damage by magic, as are all hunting and fishing accessories, traps, guns, fishhooks, nets, and the like. The scent of a good hunting dog can be spoiled forever by an enemy who envies its owner for this possession.

To have another person comb one's hair is thought to be very dangerous. Perfumes and strongly scented oils or pomades should never be accepted from a stranger or a potential enemy because they are likely to enchant their user. Without knowing what has caused it, he will fall under a spell which might eventually kill him.

Wayward husbands or lovers, drunkards, or other people who are feared because of their violent behavior or bad temper, can be 'tamed' (*amansar*) by magical means, whereupon they become listless and weak. Women in love with a reluctant male will 'tie him up' (*amarrar*); he will then become a faithful lover and husband, and accept all mistreatments and abuses from his wife without ever complaining. A number of specific love charms are used. They contain an aggressive element, as they are meant not only to awaken love but to put the lover into an inferior and dependent position. A love potion called *maranguángo* will make a man abandon his wife and home in order to follow the woman who cast the spell over him, and he might even become a criminal under its influence. Women use as love magic the pulverized bones of a certain white hummingbird which were first cleaned in an anthill. They are administered in a cup of black coffee or mixed with food. Men put pubic hair or a bit of borax into a cigarette, which they then offer to their prospective loves. To walk three times around a woman while handling in one's pocket seven small strands of thread, each of a different color, is also said to be a potent love charm.

An important form of aggressive magic is practiced by people who cast the Evil Eye (*Mal Ojo*). These people are said to have a 'strong glance' (*vista fuerte*), which is caused by an 'electric force' and which destroys anything they might look at with envy or curiosity. Although it is said that not all of them do so intentionally and that some are hardly aware of having this power, the general belief is that a number of people in the village exercise this force daily and with the worst intentions. A person, especially a child or a woman, will fall ill when struck by the Evil Eye; a crop will be spoiled, a plant will wither, wood will rot, a glass will break. In Aritama, economic assets such as houses, crops, domestic animals, or fruit trees are said to be much more exposed to the Evil Eye than people themselves. The reason: envy. It is significant that in the Plaza barrio people believe that the eye color of such a person is always dark, while the lomeros say that only light-eyed people possess the Evil Eye. The general symptoms of a person struck by this glance, the remedies, and the apotropaic measures used against it will be discussed in another chapter. Here we only want to point out that this belief is one aspect of aggressive magic.

Black Magic is also applied to political affairs. Within the village the Corregidor, the police, and the leaders of the political factions are likely to be attacked with magic by their opponents. Occasionally this magic will also be applied to the wider political scene. Presidential candidates, senators, and political leaders of whom newspaper photographs can be obtained are subjected to enchantment—i.e., they are pricked with needles or otherwise bewitched—and we knew of several cases where the authorities themselves took active part in these procedures in an attempt to influence the political developments of the nation. Quite often the Indian shamans are asked to perform these rites, and sometimes, when political tensions are high, groups of villagers will visit them and discuss at length the curses to be put upon the political leaders.

So we see that aggressive magic pervades every aspect of village life. In the eyes of the inhabitants there is, of course, ample proof that their magical practices are successful. The incidence of disease is high; crop failure is frequent; the instability of marital life, of government employment, of the prices of cash crops is marked; and all provide 'proof' that malicious envy and sorcery exercise a permanent control over the individual. In this suspicion-ridden atmosphere any calamity is immediately attributed to the magic of an enemy who, through ill will and envy, caused the trouble. The best prophylactic measure an individual can take, in all cases, therefore, consists in not appearing enviable in the first place and in pretending to be poor, ill, and already in trouble. One should, therefore, never boast of one's health and property, never make an ostentatious display of one's belongings or qualities, never let it be known that one possesses some advantage over others. Only a very small circle of close relatives are excluded from magical aggression. No sorcery is practiced between father and son, or between mother and daughter; although strong tensions might arise between them, the practice of magic is ruled out in these cases. However, between husband and wife, between siblings, and in any other kin relationship, aggressive magic is frequent, and beyond the elementary family anybody is suspect. It is characteristic that when speaking of an apparently harmless person no one would say positively, 'He does not practice sorcery,' but rather 'He is not known yet to practice it' (*Todavía no se le ha sabido*).

It is not always quite clear exactly what supernatural power is invoked to cause the desired effects in Black Magic. Many people will say that it is the 'Devil' (*el Maligno*) and to practice aggressive magic is often called 'to work with the Devil' (*trabajar con el Maligno*). Others say that the power comes from a specific ancestral spirit, from a grandmother, the spirit-owner of a tree, a rock, or a spring. Others believe that it emanates from the sun itself. There is no agreement on the source of this power, but everything seems to point to the ancestral spirits as the real disease- and disgrace-causing agents, because by propitiatory offerings they can be made to turn their wrath upon their descendants' enemies. From there it is only a step to ask the saints of the Catholic Church to make their powers felt by punishing another person.

A few words may be added here on suicide as a form of aggressive magic. A routine inquiry concerning the occurrence of suicides in Aritama did not produce any information, and people assured us that no one had ever committed suicide by hanging, drowning, or other violent means. We left the matter at this point but soon discovered that the lack of information was due to the inadequate phrasing of our initial questions. As a matter of fact, suicide does exist, but in a form that, at first, passed unnoticed by us. A person who wants to commit suicide prepares a small offering for his ancestors, including in the bundle a *musíxke* seed or a *güiro*, according to the group with which the person is associated. While wrapping up this offering in the thin inner leaves of an ear of corn, the person invokes the ancestor, usually the maternal grandmother, telling her spirit that soon her help will be required. This small package is then deposited at a sacred spot—at a boulder, in a cave, near a waterfall, a pool in the river, or at the cemetery. If the person's mother has been baptized according to the traditional Indian ritual, the offering will be deposited at the boulder where this had taken place, or it will be thrown into the water where there is a strong current. At the same time the individual weeps and cries out the grandmother's name, asking her spirit to 'take him away'. The words used upon these occasions are 'Take this, so you will take me away, as I don't want to live any more; take me away, grandmother, so I can be with you!' (*Toma, para que me lleveis con vos, que ya no quiero vivir más; llevame, para estar allá con vos!*) or 'Grandmother, I don't want to live any more; come for me!' (*Abuela, no quiero vivir más; venga por mí!*). The person then returns to the village and is said to fall ill almost immediately, dying shortly afterward.

This form of suicide is called 'to accuse oneself' or 'to make an accusation' (*acusarse, hacer un acuso*). As soon as the offering has been made and the words have been spoken, the person is said to be 'condemned' (*condenada*), and there is practically no way to save him from death. No curioso or Indian shaman will lend his services in such a case, to which the saying is applied that 'the plantain, once it is yellow cannot be made green again'.

The motivations for which a person might commit suicide are family conflicts, jealousy, death of a beloved relative, physical aggression suffered at the hands of a husband, or humiliations and insults suffered innocently from neighbors or family members. Economic difficulties or incurable diseases were never mentioned as reasons for suicide. Suicide never takes the form of self-punishment but is always a spiteful attitude directed against an individual, the family, or society at large, and the person will make the most of it in order to blame others for his death. Suicide threats are never used, neither by adults nor by children, and the person's intentions are not revealed beforehand. Only when the offering has been made, i.e., when the person is already 'condemned to death', will he tell everybody concerned of what he has done and will thus find satisfaction in observing the feelings of the ones he is blaming for his imminent death. The spirit of a person who has died by suicide and who has put the blame for it upon others is, of course, particularly dangerous and feared, and suicide is, therefore, a supreme form of magical vengeance and not only an empty accusatory demonstration.

The following recent cases of suicide involved three women, and we were told that men rarely commit suicide, although some examples were given. One woman who lived in the same household with her mother-in-law had several fights with her and finally exclaimed, 'You are not my mother and yet you insult me! Now you will see what happens!' She threw the offering into the river calling her grandmother's spirit and returned home. After a few days she developed a high fever, of which she died soon afterward. Another woman had a fight with her husband, after which she went to the cemetery, where she buried her offering in one of the graves of her mother's family. When she told her husband about it he promised to mend his ways and showed every sign of repentance, and so the woman returned to the cemetery and tried to recover the offering. Eventually, after some digging she found it, but when she was about to grasp it the bundle slipped from her fingers and 'vanished into the ground as if pulled by the hands of the dead'. She died several days later without having been able to recover the offering. The third woman buried her offering at a swampy spot, after a fight with her husband, and died a few weeks afterward.

INDIVIDUAL POWERS

The formal organization of magico-religious activities, including curing, has always been in the hands of specialists who were recognized as possessing an esoteric knowledge not shared by others. This knowledge was said to be acquired either congenitally or by oral transmission from father to son or by experience and the occasional teachings of others. There is an obvious correlation between the attributes of a shaman, or magician, and any physical handicap he may have. People who are born blind, are lame or deformed, have lost a limb in an accident, are sterile, dwarfish, or in some other way abnormal are said to possess special knowledge and power. This is the rule today, and it seems to have been the same in the past, as far back as people can remember.

Of the Indian priests who have lived during the past 150 years, most have belonged to families still living in the village, but some of them were members of the neighboring Indian tribes, and their descendants now live in the tribal territories. Their training, attributes, and functions were practically the same as the ones still observed among the modern tribes, where they combine sacerdotal functions with magical practices and curing, representing, at the same time, the recognized civil authority of their respective villages. Traditionally, there were from three to four shamans in the village, one of them occupying the leading position, while others lived in the surrounding country.

As we have mentioned already, the power and quality of the native priesthood declined rapidly after the arrival of the lowland immigrants. At the beginning of this century there still lived several old shamans, but the last of them died some twenty years ago. From then on, no local native priest lived in the village, and so the shamans of other villages were called upon by the people of Aritama. Many people also began to call on the neighboring Indian shamans, and at the present there live two or three men with priestly functions at some two or three hour's distance, and several Indian priests live at about half a day's distance from the village. As these specialists are, therefore, not readily accessible and are often reluctant to travel to the village for fear of being ridiculed by the Creole-oriented placeros, several old men of the Loma barrio, or of the more immediate surroundings of the village, have gained a certain influence. Although not having recognized sacerdotal status, their esoteric knowledge has given them a certain amount of prestige, and they are frequently consulted. Often they will establish contact with the Indian shamans, serving thus as intermediaries; but sometimes they offer their own services, as far as their knowledge permits them. This situation, however, has proved to be far from satisfactory. Many people distrust the ability of the local specialists, but, on the other hand, they are unable to engage the services of an Indian shaman. The latter, as we have mentioned, have become increasingly aware of the commercial value of their services to people anxious to be cured, to identify an enemy, or to protect themselves or their kin and possessions against aggressive magic. They are likely to charge high fees, and so a number of people cannot afford to appeal to them. The linguistic problem also forms an obstacle. The Indians speak hardly any Spanish, so that detailed explanations of individual rituals and performances cannot be given by them. Few people in Aritama speak any language other than Spanish and conversations often have to be carried on through bilingual Indian interpreters, a fact which is very disturbing in these private matters. The lack of widely recognized and trusted spiritual leaders is thus a very real problem in Aritama.

Specialists of traditional Spanish type are the *rezanderas*. All are women, generally old ones, and they have been taught by their parents or in a mission school, but they do not combine other functions with their prayers. They are called to pray at wakes and occasionally they are paid to pray for some person who wants a prayer said in his name. Besides this, a rezandera is asked to pray for certain specific favors: to win at a cockfight, to retrieve lost or stolen property, to make the husband leave the house and work, or to make the husband give money to his wife. On the other hand, she is never asked to pray in order to acquire wealth, to bring back a wayward husband, or to procure a mate. Her functions are, therefore, quite specialized and do not overlap with the functions of other practitioners or with the private ritual of the individual.

Several activities are organized and led by individuals who have made a vow, and these also might be called specialists. They are the undertakers and gravediggers, the leaders of the ceremonial dance groups, and the men in charge of the supervision of wakes or the organization of collective offerings to the ancestors. We have referred already to the nature of these vows and the activities of those who take them. All these people have taken upon them the dangers of being closely associated with death and the dead, and it is not by coincidence that we find among them all those villagers who have a criminal record.

Medical practitioners (*curiosos, curanderos*) form another category. Many of them specialized in fractures, snakebite, or certain diseases, and all of them use a great many magical procedures in combination with herb medicines or even modern scientific practices. Among them there are a few who are feared because they are suspected of practicing Black Magic. The real magicians (*brujos*), however, are generally very specialized and are not common curers. They all have acquired their esoteric knowledge from elder relatives, during travel to faraway villages, or while living among the Indians. Although feared, they are often consulted by people who wish to identify and harm an enemy. These sorcerers are said to die a most horrible death. During their prolonged agony they are said first to shrink into tiny batlike beings, then in the next instant to assume formidable size, filling the entire room. Ghostly horsemen are seen riding through their bedrooms, unknown black birds extinguish the lights with their wings, and strange noises are heard everywhere. People who claim to have witnessed such phenomena are deeply convinced of their actual existence, and many cases, some of them quite recent, are cited.

Inside the village, a person who wishes to become a curer or a magician can learn the common lore of magic and perhaps a few secret formulas or recipes only from the few old men who claim to possess such knowledge; but, if he wishes to specialize, he has to turn to other masters living at some distance from the village. There are several small hamlets in the lowlands that are famous for their specialists, and an apprentice may go there to learn his trade. This apprenticeship lasts several years, during which the novice lives with or near his master, helping him in his daily work in exchange for food and board; or he will live nearby as a laborer. Once the master considers that his pupil has learned enough to return to his home, he arranges for a final examination, the result of which is considered to be decisive. The details of this experience will be described in another chapter.

Witches must be included in the discussion of 'specialists', because they are real people of flesh and bone, supposed to be endowed with certain supernatural powers. In Aritama many of them are known by name and are avoided; others are suspected and are watched for any sign that might give them away. On several occasions alleged witches have been caught and given a sound beating by the assembled populace, but they are never seriously harmed or exiled. Some of them even occupy a relatively high status as midwives, rezanderas, or curers.

Witches are regarded as confirmed thieves. In order to escape quickly they learn to fly—by drinking the blood of a newborn infant. When about to take off, a witch crosses her legs behind her neck and says the Lord's Prayer and a Hail Mary backward, adding as a final spell, 'Without God, nor Law, nor Holy Mary!' (*Sin Dios, ni Ley, ni Santa María*). Some are said to be able to change themselves into jaguars or pigs, but most of them take the shape of ugly black birds or huge black moths. They are often covered with a long white bedsheet while flying, and its fluttering sound in the air is a sure sign that a witch is passing by. However, it is only their spirit that flies, although in a visible form; meanwhile, the body rests in a deep trance. Several children, it is said, have discovered their mothers to be witches by finding them so sound asleep that they believed they were ill or had fainted, because they were unable to awaken them. While roaming at night about the village the witches, it is claimed, gather upon a roof and, making a small opening in it, lower their long noses, which are like a thin tubular feeler, to explore the room below. If they find a chest where money is kept, they lift its contents up through the roof. If they find a newborn child, they will suck its blood at the umbilicus. The child will usually die after a few such nightly visits, but several people are said to have been able to save the child by cutting the thin tube with a pair of scissors. Sometimes the witches gather in the open country and dance and play music, and at other times they are said to meet at the cemetery, where they open a fresh grave and devour morsels of putrid flesh. In the course of their nightly forays they acquire great wealth and so they are able to offer a high ransom should they be caught.

There are several ways to catch a witch. If a person hears one settling upon the roof he might call out, 'Why don't you come tomorrow for some salt?' If the next day a woman comes and asks to borrow salt, one knows who the witch was. Two rather secret methods of catching a witch are the following: While the witch is on the roof, one should leave the house silently and throw a handful of mustard seeds at her. Witches are said to have an irresistible compulsion to count them, and while doing so will be unaware of anything else and so can be easily caught. The other method consists in leaving the house and turning a man's shirt inside out, the witch being paralyzed at seeing this done. Once caught and identified, a witch is likely to offer her captor a great amount of money so he won't give away her identity, and several wealthy men in the village are said to have acquired their properties in this manner. To fetter a witch one should never use ropes, because she will break even the strongest, but one should tie her with a very fine thread called *trenza chía*, from which she is unable to escape.

Witches are also likely to play pranks on lonely travelers at night. They will tie their donkeys or mules to a tree or will dance around a drunken man, leading him into the forest until he loses the way. They also may appear as old women and try to lead little girls to far-off places, where they are found after days of searching, in a half-crazed state, with their clothes torn and their bodies covered with bruises. Sometimes they will place a coffin with four lighted candles on top on a lonely spot on the trail, in order to scare a traveler. If the person has the courage to draw a cross on the lid and to sit on it until dawn by that time the witch must return to her body, and he might catch her and ask for ransom money. Often a group of witches, it is said, surround a person they meet at night and chain him with thin threads which he is unable to break. They are also likely to poison food they find in a house, and sometimes they will put ground human bones into a dish to kill an enemy. To protect a house against witches, lights are kept burning all night long and a pair of scissors is opened so it will form a cross and is placed upon a table or beneath one's pillow. When a witch dies, it is said that all candles go out suddenly, with thunder and lightning filling the sky.

Witches are entirely different from spirits and ghostly apparitions. They are people, 'evil' people, of course, but they live like any other villager, except that they have acquired the power to fly and to send their spirit on nightly excursions while they themselves are asleep at home. Of several girls in the village who were being raised by grandmothers suspected of being witches it is said that they were not baptized, because to do so would make it impossible for them to acquire their grandmother's powers. They liked to scare their playmates with threats, and were avoided by many children and people in general who feared to incur their wrath.

OMENS, HARBINGERS, AND TABOOS

There are a great many phenomena that prognosticate good or ill fate. The latter are far more frequent and are often associated with the sight or sound of certain animals, generally birds, which are said to be the soul-birds of the ancestors. The concept of ill omen is called *urúmo*, an Indian term which is used in expressions like '*hacer urúmo*' ('to prognosticate evil') or '*ser urúmo*' ('to be an evil omen').

The following omens prognosticate death, sometimes of the beholder but more often of his relatives: a gray or black butterfly entering the house, a gray or black butterfly sitting on the door (owner's death), a flock of egrets, a woodpecker pecking (nailing down of coffin lid), *chiscuáque* or *biusúri* birds singing, a *guacaó* bird singing near or south of the village, the same bird singing near the cemetery (death of an important person), a hen crowing like a cock, a bull digging up the soil in the backyard, cockroaches rustling in the roof at night, a green fly entering a house, hiccuping after drinking coffee ('next coffee during a wake'), choking while eating, traveling on Sunday the seventh, harvesting a plentiful crop.

Bad luck in general is prognosticated by a cock crowing without other cocks answering, a skunk seen while hunting, a double rainbow, a lunar eclipse, travel on Tuesday or any holiday. The visit of evil spirits is heralded by a chirping bat following a traveler at night, the crackling of the hearthfire at night. Bloodshed and violence are presaged by the song of the *chiscuáque* bird, a rainbow encircling a house, sun or moon encircled by wide halos. Hunger is foreshown by many red macaws or green parrots.

Good news is prognosticated by a colorful butterfly entering the room; money, by a weaverbird singing near the house, a bed being carried across the street, or the casual finding of a button. If black

410

coffee spills into the hearthfire, a gift will be received soon. Meat will be available soon if a woodpecker, a *bungáca*, or a *guatapára* bird is heard singing or if a black fly enters a house, while a chirping bat presages the arrival of fish in the village. A colorful butterfly resting on the body of a person promises a new dress; letters containing good news are foretold by hummingbirds or black bumblebees entering a room. Visitors are announced by a cock crowing while sitting on a fence or on a pole (visiting horseman), by a *paraguanáta* bird resting on the roof, or by the hearth fire crackling in the daytime. In the last case, to make the visitor bring a gift of food some paper or straw should be thrown into the fire. By beating upon the embers with a stick the visitor (even a spirit) can be made to stay away.

When at daybreak the sky is gray and rainy, it is bad luck to say, 'What a sad day!' and to step out of one's hammock in the morning with the left foot first spoils the whole day's work. If one has something to sell and the first prospective buyer is a woman, the sale will yield no profit. Should one use aniline colors instead of vegetable colors for dyeing, all palm trees will die, and after having finished weaving a hat, one should gather up all bits of straw lying on the floor lest one step on them and become lazy and listless. As soon as a woman has finished weaving a hat and cuts off the last thread, she should use it at once to weave the beginning of a new hat lest her fingers become stiff.

One should never throw peels or husks of fruits or tubers into the backyard at night, 'because they will get scared'. However, one may throw a bit of ashes on them to make them 'less afraid'. One should not bring firewood directly from the forest into the house lest the 'Mother of Firewood' enter too and cause some disease; one should leave the wood in the backyard and bring it in only after dark. Above all, one should never sweep the backyard at night lest one lose all one's property.

If a person lights a candle, lamp, or hearthfire and it starts immediately to burn brightly, this is a lucky sign. One should never extinguish a fire with water, nor should one ever urinate into the hearthfire, as this would bring bad luck. When seeing the new moon for the first time, one should show it a silver coin for good luck, but when seeing a lunar eclipse one should go to bed at once lest he fall ill. When seeing a dog defecating, one should make gestures as if gathering money into one's pocket. If while eating one drops a bit of food, an absent family member is hungry, and it is bad luck not to inquire about him.

A man should never approach a river or creek without carrying a machete; and a woman should carry a carrying bag, lest all 'fish will laugh at one'. Near the water women should be careful not to lose a hair while combing themselves, because in the afterworld they will have to account for every hair, and should some be missing they will have to return to find them. When an infant's hair is cut for the first time, the clippings are put away in the thatch of the roof so the child will soon learn to speak. A pregnant woman should not eat of an animal her husband has killed lest he lose his skill in hunting, but she can eat the fish he caught. A menstruating woman should not step over an infant lying on the floor, because this would cause serious disease. Should she do so unintentionally, she should step over it again twice in a crosswise fashion.

IX

DIMENSIONS OF CONSCIOUSNESS

THE CHARACTER OF HALLUCINATORY EXPERIENCE

IN a previous chapter we have already mentioned briefly the belief in ghosts, many of which are said to roam at night in the village and its surroundings. The emotional importance of this belief is such that it seems necessary to investigate this aspect of the local culture in greater detail, as a fuller understanding of it might shed some light upon certain psychological problems.

The belief in ghosts, revenants and other similar apparitions is very common throughout rural and urban Colombia, but the intensity of these beliefs and the interpretation of details vary considerably from place to place. Furthermore, such beliefs are limited mainly to a lower rural level and tend to disappear with increasing urban influence. In Aritama, however, the entire village lives under the permanent fear of apparitions, and even the most sophisticated inhabitants are firmly convinced of their existence. Everyone is terrified by the thought of seeing or hearing a ghost. After nightfall only a very courageous person will dare to leave the house, even if only to cross the backyard or street in order to visit a neighbor, or to go to the cooking houses, which are usually a little distance from the living quarters. This fear is not so much concerned with the actual perception of a ghost as with the consequences such an experience is said to have. It is believed that a person who claims to have seen a ghost will fall seriously ill and perhaps die after a few days. That this is a very real problem is demonstrated by the fact, observed by us, that people actually did fall ill after claiming to have had such an experience, an eventuality which seems to indicate that their emotional imbalance leads occasionally to grave psychosomatic disturbances. It would appear, therefore, to be of interest to study in more detail the recurrent patterns involved in this complex of beliefs.

We shall first of all describe the peculiarities of these ghostly phenomena. They fall into particular categories, the principal one being made up of certain male or female phantoms or personifications. The male ones are *El Caballero* ('The Horseman'), *El Silborcito* ('The Little

Whistler'), and *El Salvaje* ('The Savage'); the female ones are *La Montuna* ('The Forest Dweller'), *La Llorona* ('The Weeping Woman'), *La Lavandera* ('The Washerwoman'), *La Ligerita* ('The Nimble Woman'), *La Tejedora* ('The Spinning Woman'), *La Máma del Monte* ('The Mother of the Forest'), *La Sirena* ('The Siren'), *La Viejita* ('The Little Old Woman'). Malignant theriomorphic apparitions are *El Burrucoco* ('pigmy owl'), *El Perro Negro* ('black dog'), *El Berraco* ('boar'), *El Sapo* ('toad'), *La Sierpe* ('serpent'), *La Tuqueca* ('gecko'), and *El Murciélago* ('bat'). Another category is comprised of the *sixquinyani*, the spirits of the dead; another of apparitions of the Devil (*El Maligno, Diablo, Ño Mano*) in person; another of *brujas* ('witches'). The last category consists of several ill-defined apparitions called *bultos* (literally, 'bulks'), or *pantamas* ('phantoms', from the Spanish *fantasma*). *La Petaca* ('The Leather Trunk') is also an uncanny manifestation, but one which is never seen, only heard.

The individual characteristics of these apparitions are the following: *El Caballero* is seen as a tall man on horseback, sometimes stark naked, sometimes wearing a white suit, a broad-rimmed hat, and smoking a cigar. His mount is lame or three-legged. When he rides through the narrow streets and between the houses, his horse brushes against the walls and fences, and his presence can be recognized by the clanking of the stirrups, the noise of spurs and chains, and the rhythmical squeaking of the saddle. *El Silborcito* is said to look like a dwarf wearing a large peaked hat. He passes rapidly through the air or near the ground, making a penetrating whistling sound which can be heard from far away. *El Salvaje* is a mountain spirit, a being shaped like a man, but with the legs twisted so that the heels point forward when he walks. His body is covered with long, coarse hair, and he is said to carry off women and to rape them. Late in the evening his melancholy cry can be heard in the mountains.

Of the female apparitions *La Montuna* is foremost. She is described as a dwarflike woman but with beautiful features, her long hair falling down her back, while her large breasts are bare. She is an Indian woman, wearing only a short skirt and carrying a woven bag slung over one shoulder. Some say she has only one breast, in the middle of the chest, and some that she wears flowers in her hair. All agree that she is a chthonian being, living under the ground near swamps or pools, but digging her way more rapidly than a man can walk, and her burrowing makes the earth tremble. When appearing above ground, she lies flat on the earth making a groaning, rhythmical noise, with her mouth close to the ground. If observed, she will attack the onlooker, encircle him and squeeze milk from her breast into his eyes, blinding him or causing a severe skin eruption. She is also said to carry off unbaptized children, to eat them or to abandon them somewhere far away in a thicket, where they are found half-dead after days of searching. *La Llorona* is a woman who cries and sighs convulsively at night in the streets, wandering between the houses, brushing against the walls and weeping desolately while stumbling along with tear-blinded eyes. She, also, is said to steal children and to carry them off. *La Lavandera* is seen at night near the river. With her beetle she steadily beats the bundle of clothes she is washing, as washerwomen will do, and by this noise she can be recognized from afar. The rustle of freshly starched linen and the splashing sound of wet laundry are signs that she is near. *La Ligerita* is a gaily dancing woman who carries a huge hat which she tries to put on people she encounters on the dark streets. *La Tejedora* is a woman who walks or stands spinning thread with her spindle, deep in the night, and the whirring sound of the flywheel, when everybody is asleep, betrays her presence. *La Máma del Monte* seduces the lonely wanderer in the forest and kills him with her clawlike fingers while embracing him with her four arms. She is a beautiful woman who wears a flowing white robe, and she lures the stranger farther and farther into the mountain fastnesses until he is lost. *La Sirena* is a beautiful naked maiden seen in daytime sitting on the boulders near the river, combing her hair with a golden comb. When she notices that someone is watching her, she punishes him by throwing stones and sticks. *La Viejita* also lives near the river and is an ugly old woman who can be seen washing human intestines in the water. It is said that 'she buys the bellies of the dead' when the spirit wanders by on the way to the Beyond.

All these uncanny apparitions display a typical behavior. They are said to appear suddenly out of nowhere, surrounded by a faint glow of light which makes them hardly visible. They do not speak but gesture, often dancing around their victim so fast that he stumbles when trying to escape. They silently block his way or force him to go in another direction until he loses the trail. Quite often they do not notice an approaching person, but their rage knows no bounds when they realize that they themselves have been watched. Their anger is also aroused by anyone's trying mockingly to imitate their actions or sounds, and many people feel somehow compelled to do just this.

The animal apparitions are no less dangerous. *El Burrucoco* tears out people's eyes and carries off small children. *El Perro Negro* is a fierce black dog with red-glowing eyes, which, night after night, steals into the houses of lonely women and appears in their nightmares as an insatiable incubus. Near the cemetery or on lonely trails the dog will suddenly appear to people who return late to their homes and chases them while they flee headlong. The grunting of the spirit-boar or sow and the noise of its nursing piglets, or of the heavy movements it makes when turning in its wallow, can be heard in places where it is known that no pigs are kept. The toad and the gecko are also recognized by their smacking noises and by their enormous size in comparison with their normal prototypes. The gecko, too, is a dangerous incubus, as is also the serpent. The bat is the Devil's harbinger and follows the wanderer, announcing his master's approach.

We have mentioned already the *sixquinyáni*, the Devil, and the witches in another chapter and need not repeat their description here. The so-called bulks and phantoms are shapeless apparitions which seem to hover motionless over a spot, disappearing and reappearing suddenly, changing their size from tiny glowing specks to enormous cloud-like shapes. *La Petaca* is recognized by the dry rattling clatter an old leather trunk would make when being rapidly pulled over an uneven floor.

In all these apparitions it is possible to discern certain patterns repeated frequently. For example, a vaguely glowing light that makes for difficult vision is associated with all personifications except *El Salvaje*, *La Sirena*, and *La Máma del Monte*, which are apparitions said to be observed during the daytime. Another characteristic common to all is a certain evil smell, often compared with a strong female body odor. Much emphasis is placed by the informants upon this particular odor, which accompanies all apparitions. Another recurrent note is of rhythmic movements and sounds, such as found in the description of *El Caballero*, *La Montuna*, *La Llorona*, *La Ligerita*, and *La Tejedora*. The Siren also is described as 'combing and combing and combing', and of the gecko it is said that it pats a sleeping woman's body rhythmically with its toes, which are furnished with adhesive disks. There is also in all cases a strong emphasis on vision, i.e., on watching, on being blinded, and on punishment if a stealthy watcher is found out. It is also evident that many of these personifications are interpreted in terms of sexual aggression: *La Máma del Monte*, *El Salvaje*, *El Gecko*, *El Perro Negro*, *La Sierpe*. Sexual interest is also manifest in the personifications of *La Sirena* and *La Montuna*.

Leaving the description of the various manifestations for the moment, let us now turn to the individual who has the preternatural experience, to his reactions, or the consequences of the encounter.

Practically every adult inhabitant of the village, and many adolescents, claim to have had preternatural experiences with personifications such as the ones described above. In the course of our stay in Aritama, at least twenty apparitions were recorded by the people, i.e., about every three weeks some member of the community claimed to have seen or heard one of the preternatural beings. These apparitions were observed in the following order of frequency: *Silborcito*, *Montuna*, *Llorona*, *Lavandera*, *Caballero*, *Perro Negro*, *Tejedora*, *Berraco*. Uncanny toads, owls, bats, and geckos were seen and heard so frequently that we kept no record of their appearance.

Most apparitions occur at night, generally to people who for some reason or other are still out of doors. This reason, however, is quite often one that is not socially approved: a man might be on his way to a rendezvous with a concubine, a woman might slip away to meet a lover, someone might have been drinking with companions and returns home late, or another might have been trying to steal some wood from a fence or a chicken from the Padre's henhouse. In any case, the reason *why* the person should have been out that late at night is often rather embarrassing, as we could well notice when questioning our informants. People who are out that late are, of course, likely to be somewhat upset emotionally, to feel euphorious, to feel guilt, to fear being seen or punished. Furthermore, all over the village and its periphery there are certain spots with which there are associated legends, accidents, offerings, apparitions, and the like. The *locus classicus* is the cemetery—but then there is the church; the huge boulders where offerings and divinations take place at the Corpus fiesta; the house sites where legendary Indian shamans have lived; the spot where a man was killed by unknown hands, where a child died under a falling rock, or where a witch is said to have strangled a babe. To pass in the dark near such a spot is likely to cause an uncanny feeling even in the stoutest heart, and in spite of a few drinks of rum.

To this atmosphere there are added strange noises and evil smells. The clop-clop of a donkey wandering through the empty streets, a flight of nightbirds sweeping over the village, a sleeper calling out in his dream, the muffled weeping of a sick child—all this is likely to sound different at night. The dogs burrowing in the trash heaps, the chamber pots emptied into the street, the general habit of defecating mainly after nightfall in the backyard, saturate the air with odors which are less pronounced in the daytime. Sometimes a person might be alone in a house at night and might be awakened by an uncanny noise, a fleeting shadow sweeping over the walls, or a sudden draught of cold air. Or someone might enter his lonely sleeping quarters at night and feel there the presence of something unknown and dangerous, of something that pervades the room and has not been there before. It is on just such occasions that people believe themselves likely suddenly to face some apparition, and in judging that person's account, one must see it within the whole atmosphere and circumstance in which this apparition is thought to appear.

However, no apparition is ever described by the frightened ones as a nameless, unrecognizable, indefinite being. Instead it is immediately identified as a certain kind of thing. A projective process is at work by which a predetermined image in the observer's mind is transferred to and identified with some certain natural occurrence which cannot be rationalized at the given moment. The image exists in the observer's mind as a traditional, culturally defined phenomenon such as the *Montuna*, the *Caballero*, or any other of the many personifications, but the fact that the observer never has any doubt about what he heard or saw, identifying it immediately as this or that apparition, means that there is also a selective process involved by which the observer chooses, unconsciously, from a wide range of ready images.

It seems evident that different people have a particular tendency toward certain hallucinations. In general, it can be said that men are more susceptible to any such experience than are women; that while some people have only acoustical experiences, others have a tendency toward visual experiences; some 'hear' or 'smell', whereas others 'see' or 'feel'. There is, then, an individual difference. The importance of certain images is conditioned by the emotional dimensions and experiential ranges of the individual person.

Reactions to such an experience follow a definite pattern. To begin with, after observing and identifying the apparition, the person tries to flee. An intense cold is felt, and numbness of the limbs is often mentioned. Invariably the person is absolutely unable to utter a sound and often feels paralyzed, unable to move. In the latter state, he often faints on the spot, or when flight is possible, he faints as soon as he arrives at his house or a friend's, or as soon as other people arrive. Inability to speak continues for several hours, during which the victim remains in a catatonic stupor, often accompanied by fever. The next morning speech is regained and the person relates in detail the previous night's experience, but the fever persists and further complications are likely to develop. After a particularly fearful experience some people are said to die after a few, generally 'three', days. Others recover but their health is impaired forever (at least in their own opinion). Others regain their usual state of health and are not any worse for having had the hallucination.

So for our informants. Of many people who had died in previous years we were told that their death had been due to having been victims of an apparition, and some people who obviously were suffering from some disease believed that their ill health had been caused by a preternatural experience they had had in the past.

The symptoms of people who had suffered such a magic fright and been made ill by it were in all cases very similar. There is a general depressive state, a listlessness accompanied by strong pains in the back of the head, a slight fever mainly in the evening hours, pallor, difficulty in co-ordinating movements, lack of appetite, insomnia, and a general apathy. This polymorphous syndrome can then develop in any number of directions: the individual might begin to suffer from gastrointestinal or respiratory diseases of asthmatic type, severe skin eruptions, hysteroid pains, or a number of ill-defined and difficult-to-locate ailments.

There can be no doubt that the pathological condition, either physical or psychical, was in many cases already present in a more or less latent form *before* the supernatural experience occurred. In other cases, the physiological consequences are of a psychosomatic order. It seems, then, that the preternatural experience only served to 'trigger off' the dysfunction, but it is also apparent that the patient himself unconsciously 'chose' the moment of the apparition, conditioned to it by the atmosphere of the setting.

However, not always do these circumstances combine in a manner to create a preternatural experience. Many people can be out of doors at night without having such an experience, even though they are fearful of it and feel guilty for being out late. The specialized constellation arises only at times when some unconscious element suddenly falls into place and establishes a circuit that connects significant isolated factors of time and place, past experience, and present situation. In other words, it seems that an apparition is seen only when the psychologically predisposed individual is suddenly able to associate a physical stimulus of smell, color, movement, or sound with an unconsciously known but temporarily repressed situation, which is then transformed into the culturally identifiable personification. The apparitions seem, therefore, to have essentially the character of cover images for past traumatic experiences.

If this interpretation of the phenomena under discussion is correct, it follows that there exist in the culture of the village conditions that produce strong traumatic experiences which the individual is unable to rationalize or sublimate, and which, remaining unsuccessfully repressed, cause a high level of anxiety. It is our suggestion that the traumatic nucleus in question is the child's witnessing of parental coitus. In this connection we shall try to present some observations that we believe to be relevant to this inquiry.

All children sleep in the same room with their parents or other adults, and generally share their beds or hammocks during the first years of life. As many houses consist of only one single room, this situation is unavoidable, but even in cases where two or more rooms are available, it is usual for all those who live under the same roof to share the same sleeping quarters. Furthermore, as we have already pointed out, the people show great fear of sleeping in complete darkness and always keep a light, however feeble, burning all night in a corner of the room. Under these circumstances it is natural that children would sooner or later have occasion to witness parental intercourse, as this usually takes place in the sleeping quarters. Even if the couple should retire to the next room, the frequent lack of doors and the presence of light would make observation possible. Women who live alone in a house with their children are often visited at night by their temporary consorts, who though they knock softly at the door or the walls or whistle or imitate the cry of a nightbird, as signal to be let in, seldom arrive unseen or unheard by the children.

Comparison of some of the elements of the hallucinatory images with those of the primal scene is evident, and a series of parallels between them might be established.

General setting of the hallucination—The visitation occurs at night, in semidarkness or illuminated by a faint glow. The place is the bed, the house, the cemetery, or some other spot with a high emotional content.

Auditory phenomena—The observers hears strange noises, a 'tumult', the voices of animals, or whistling sounds. Furtive steps and subdued voices are heard, such as the sound of freshly starched linen, of bed-sheets being moved, of 'wings'. Scraping and rattling sounds along the wall or fence are noticed. There is the rhythmic noise and trembling, of a squeaking saddle, of something rocking, someone 'beating laundry', of rhythmic groaning or weeping. There are noises 'as if a person was being strangled', 'as if someone jumped into water', 'as if a horseman was passing by'. A woman's voice is heard to groan, to complain, to laugh, or to weep.

Visual phenomena—The observer sees a 'white, shapeless bulk', a naked or half-naked man or woman, a woman who dances or flies, or a woman who hides in order to 'eat bones' (a motif that appears in the account of the *Máma del Monte*). A woman with four arms and a being with the heels pointing forward are obviously interpretations of coital postures. The 'black dog' that attacks a reclining woman in her hammock is described in the folktales as an incubus. A woman moving rhythmically or lying on the ground is seen in *La Montuna*, *La Lavandera*, and *La Sirena*. The image of a 'dancing woman' could be derived from the sight of sexual intercourse being performed in a standing position, as this is taken to be a contraceptive precaution. Associated images are a horseman (*Caballero*), a woman lying face down and groaning (*Montuna*), and women with mysterious 'flowers' or gifts.

Haptic phenomena—The observer feels a sudden draught of cold air while lying in bed, as if someone had taken away his covers or as if someone had opened the door. The walls and the ground itself seem to tremble as if a strong wind or a subterranean animal were shaking them.

Mephitic phenomena—A strong odor or stench is perceived, compared frequently with female body odor, the odor of feces, or of putrefaction.

Observer's attitude—The observer's reaction is one of curiosity paired with fear. A strong scoptophilic element is always present and eventually he hides in order to see better, but in any case he experiences a tremendous anxiety, vertigo, intense 'cold', and finally 'faints', i.e., escapes from the vision. Only the next morning can he tell what he has seen or heard. The dangers, i.e., punishments, that follow the experience are disease and death, blindness, an eye disease, and during the apparition the observer is in danger of being 'swallowed', and feels 'petrified', being unable to move.

All of these impressions and reactions have their parallels in childhood situations. Infantile fantasies about women with large breasts, like *La Montuna*, are quite common, and many children, when asked to describe a woman of their acquaintance, will refer to her as 'very large breasted' (*muy tetona*). Nubile girls with swelling breasts are often mocked with the words 'You are bigger-breasted than *La Montuna*' (*Eres más tetona que La Montuna*). The idea that *La Montuna* has only one single breast can also be explained as an infantile fantasy based upon the nursing situation and the frustrating aspect of being allowed only one breast at a time. The daily activities of women are all carried out in the presence of small children and in collaboration with older ones, and in *La Tejedora* or *La Lavandera* we recognize thus the two principal activities of the mother. That the spirit-sow is also an infantile maternal image is quite probable. All children live in close contact with pigs and show a marked interest in their habits. A sow's pregnancy or its suckling piglets are closely watched and are often discussed by children. The close association of this scene with odors, pregnancy, birth, and nursing is probably early established in the child's imagination. Furthermore, 'pig' is a frequently used word in scolding children for their misbehavior, and they often use it themselves when insulting their mothers in a fit of rage. Childish insults directed against the mother include also the words 'whore' and 'witch', a constellation of concepts which, when reinterpreted later, are seen to encompass much of the emotional world of the adult.

The olfactory aspect of the hallucinatory experiences we have mentioned above also has its childhood parallels. In the unventilated sleeping quarters the air is saturated with strong body odors and gases, and children seem to be very aware of this fact and mention it quite often in conversation. The lack of bodily cleanliness in women is remarkable and forms the object of frequent complaints by men. As a matter of fact, husbands often quarrel with their womenfolk for this reason, and in daily conversation there are frequent allusions to unpleasant or pleasant odors. The association between ghostly apparitions and strong odors would, therefore, be explained by a subconscious association of such bad odors with the sleeping quarters or the mother image, i.e., with the scene of the original traumatic situation. Perfumes are often used as love charms, and unknown perfumes or soaps are greatly feared because they are believed to enchant a person and to influence him in a mysterious way, bringing the individual who accepted the perfume wholly under the spell of the one who gave it. There exists, thus, a strong emotional attitude toward olfactory sensations in connection with sexual anxieties.

These obvious parallels incline us to attribute most, if not all, hallucinations consisting of ghostly apparitions to the primal-scene trauma. The effect of this trauma upon the child varies greatly, of course, according to specific content, its degree of emotion, the age of the observer, and many individual factors in the child's previous experience. The variety of hallucinatory images seems to correspond essentially to different degrees of experience and to various types of mental connections that are established by them. The frequency of non-optical stimuli, such as haptic, kinesthetic, and mephitic phenomena, indicates that there is a wide range of traumatic experience of which, according to age and mastery, different visual interpretations have been made. It is also obvious that the frequency of their occurrence and the emotional importance given these ghostly apparitions represent a subsconscious desire for repetition of the traumatic events, i.e., a periodic evocation of the repressed scene as a kind of hallucinatory wish-fulfilment. This scoptophilic tendency is, of course, punishable and the apotropaic throwing of a hat, a cigar, a firebrand, or a strong-smelling fruit toward the threatening image, seems to represent the self-castration of the observer. The intensive sexual fears which originate from witnessing the primal scene as a child are apparently never fully overcome or integrated during adult life and lead finally to this highly patterned type of schizophrenic hallucination.

We shall now examine another aspect of beliefs that is correlated with yet another childhood experience. The widespread belief in and fear of witches, as opposed to hallucinations, seems to be related primarily to the second aspect of the traumatic nucleus: the child's witnessing of childbirth in all its details, as supervised by local midwives.

In another chapter we have already mentioned that witches are almost invariably pictured as old women who wear kerchiefs tied around their heads and who fly at night through the air in search of newborn babes they might steal and/or kill. They are dressed in flowing white robes which flutter wildly while they fly, and by this noise their presence can be recognized. Once the witch has located a house, she will settle down on the roof and drop a thin fleshy tube (*chimbusto*) through the thatch, searching with it for the child and then sucking his blood by attaching the end of the tube to the umbilicus. In the same way a witch will steal money or other valuables kept in a chest or in any other hiding place. Some people are said to have surprised witches during their activities and to have punished them by cutting the tube with a pair of scissors. It is also said that an open pair of scissors, if left lying on the table, will scare away witches. Witches are said to steal infants, strangle them to suck their blood, and bury them in the backyards. As a matter of fact, it is said they live on the blood of small babes, drinking it vampire-like by sucking their umbilici or their noses. Sometimes the witches are said to place a coffin topped with lighted candles on the trail in order to frighten late travelers. They are also said to acquire great riches but to suffer from severe headaches because of their nightly excursions. Witches like to smoke cigars and are often referred to in connection with food: they eat children, dig up corpses in order to devour them, and can be recognized when eating rice, because a witch always eats grain by grain and never by the spoonful. Witches are said not to be spirits but living people imbued with evil powers that they use for acquiring wealth and doing mischief to others. The best defense against them is the Catholic prayers. At the sight of a cross or a rosary they flee. Witches are said to be seen frequently flying over the village, or to appear suddenly on lonely trails or in dark corners. Often they are said to rest on the roof of a house, which trembles under their weight, and the rustling of the leaves and of their robes frighten the occupants.

Although the observer feels fear in the presence of a witch, he often assumes a challenging attitude, insulting her and trying to catch her. This attitude, however, can only be adopted if the person knows some apotropaic means by which he can overcome or avert the danger. He might pronounce a prayer, call out the holy name of Mary, or banish the witch with a magically fortified machete. Sometimes, however, the witch overpowers the person, leads him astray, or makes him fall and lie unconscious for hours. Seeing a witch has no ill consequences for the health of the observer, but it is greatly feared because of her physical aggressiveness and the revenge she might take by killing children and/or stealing property.

The correlation of these beliefs with the effects of the childbirth scene on the mind of an infant or child seems to be obvious. In Aritama, all children are allowed to be present when their mother or any other woman gives birth, and as long as a child is not in the way, he can watch every phase of the process. It is usual in Aritama that all births are attended by a midwife who is called in as soon as labors begin and who, generally, has already massaged the woman frequently during the last months of pregnancy. Every midwife is an old woman who, as soon as labor begins, assumes the principal role in the household and displays a very authoritative behavior. A number of specific preparations are made for the birth. A large cauldron is put on the fire to heat water; all windows, doors, and other openings of the house are carefully closed so that the woman in labor will not be exposed to evil 'winds' or 'airs', and the sleeping quarters where birth takes place are lit only by several candles, which have to be furnished by the household for this occasion. A new, freshly starched bedcloth is another prerequisite, as is also a pair of scissors with which to cut the umbilical cord. Cigars must be provided and the midwife goes about her tasks with a kerchief tied around her head and smoking a cigar.

The parallelism between witch and midwife is thus quite evident. In infantile imagination the midwife commits an act of violence in an atmosphere of general anguish, screams, and excitement. There is blood and the steaming cauldron, the rustle of white linen, the candles and the prayers. Picking up the crying newborn she cuts the umbilical cord with her scissors, cauterizes the end with a burning candle or her cigar, and then, by putting her mouth to his nose, she sucks out the phlegm to make the child breathe more freely. Shortly afterward she can be seen burying the placenta in the backyard, her hands and dress still bloodstained. Or else she can be observed crouching near the fire and concocting an herbal infusion. Exactly the same images that are associated with witches can thus be seen associated with midwifery: cauldron, candles, cigars, bedsheets, scissors, prayers, the cutting of a mysterious 'tube', and the burying of something in the backyard. All this, seen by the uncertain light of swaying candles and under pressure of the excitement present, is bound to make a deep impression upon the child who watches the events from some dark corner. It is a scene of aggression during which a newborn child is 'stolen', 'eaten', 'castrated', 'killed', 'buried', or 'cooked'. Sometimes the mother dies in childbirth, and the scene of violence ends with a wake, with a coffin topped with candles standing in the middle of the room.

Midwives receive their meals in the house where they lend their services, and they insist upon plentiful and good food, a fact which also might impress a hungry child who watches the strange woman eat rice and meat. As they also charge high fees which are frequently talked about by the family, midwives are often accused of taking advantage of and extorting money from poor people, and such conversations would contribute to making a child imagine that midwives, i.e., witches, acquire great wealth. The hallucinatory image of *La Viejita*, who 'buys dead people's bellies' and eats them, is probably based in part upon the observation of the midwife handling the afterbirth.

It is quite probable that in infantile fantasies the two traumatic experiences, i.e., witnessing parental coitus and childbirth, become confused, and that there is some overlapping of images, which then are projected outward and create the horrifying hallucinations of ghosts, spirits, witches, and vampires. In any case, the two correlations we have suggested so far between childhood traumata and popular demonology should be significant insofar as they tend to shed some light upon the mechanisms of the projective system and the origin of local folk fantasies concerning ghosts and other preternatural apparitions. It is also interesting to note that the two traumatic situations affect the individual in very different dimensions and intensities. While the primal-scene trauma causes anxieties of a deep and lasting type which lead eventually to neurotic attitudes, the childbirth trauma is projected on a quite different level and creates images that are far less anxiety-charged and that apparently are not conducive to any form of overt neurotic behavior.

THE ELABORATION OF TRAUMATIC EXPERIENCE

We shall return once more to the individual and his early childhood and shall try to follow from the very beginning the sequence of primary experiences and their subsequent elaboration and integration, as observed in the child's growing apprehension of the preternatural.

In the course of our conversations with children and adolescents we noticed that during early and late childhood the supernatural personifications were interpreted as 'natural' phenomena, while adolescents already referred this kind of experience to a 'preternatural' level. In between these ages, i.e., during the prepubertal stage and puberty itself, there was a complete blocking of all spontaneous interpretation or intellectual elaboration, and there was no response whatsoever to the stimulus of the preternatural. A child in the first ten years or so of life would talk volubly about spirits, witches, or theriomorphic apparitions, just as if they formed an essential part of everyday tangible experiences. A phase characterized by negativism followed, and after that, in the postpubertal and adolescent ages, the same themes were referred to as belonging to a dangerous preternatural sphere of anxiety-charged experience. In order to test this casual observation, we compiled a list of thirty themes and had individuals of different age-groups tell us what they knew and thought about them. This list included eleven anthropomorphic apparitions, six theriomorphic apparitions, the *sixquinyáni*, the Witches, the Devil, five natural phenomena (rainbow, storm, earthquake, thunder, sun), and five references to common supernatural themes: the Netherworld, the End of the World, the Beyond, the Dead, and the Evil Pools.

Children between five and seven years described the anthropomorphic apparitions in terms of everyday people, men or women, who 'lived somewhere' in the village and who were 'bad'. They were pictured as 'stealing' or 'eating' disobedient children, as throwing them into pools to drown, or as carrying them off into the forest. Some children said that they had seen or heard them, but associated them with neighbors and even identified some by name. No emphasis was placed on the scene occurring at night, but strange noises were associated with the personification. The 'dangerous' animals were elaborated far more, being described as 'piglike', 'large-bellied', 'dripping milk' (gecko, toad), and poisonous. They were described as common animals which could be eaten, stoned, and killed, and many children elaborated upon the latter possibilities. Fluttering, squeaking, or groaning noises were often associated, as was also the fear of being devoured or at least bitten by these animals. All other themes were treated in a similar, quite 'natural' fashion. The dead were 'eaten by worms' and 'went to hell', while the sun was a small tortilla, and the Devil was but a man who beat other men.

Between seven and ten years there was more elaboration of anthropomorphic personifications, but they were not identified any more with the villagers but were thought instead to live somewhere apart, under the ground, in caves, in pools, or in other dark and hidden places. They were said now to frighten and attack not only disobedient children but any child and also adults, and there was some elaboration of fantasies of how certain people of their acquaintance had had to fight them off. Smells and noises were mentioned, and now the scene was set at nighttime. The danger of being devoured was rarely referred to. Direct descriptive statements which were frequent in younger children were now avoided and most descriptions were preceded by expressions like 'people say', 'I am told that . . .', etc. The animals were also described in greater detail, and aggressive fantasies of beating and killing them were also frequent. Nowhere was reference made to the ghostly and preternatural character of anthropomorphic or theriomorphic personifications, and all dangers were described in terms of physical harm and aggression, never in terms of fright or eventual disease.

During the prepubertal stage and the time of puberty, the attitude of children of both sexes changed completely. Most questions were met with blank faces or were answered in the negative by saying that they 'never had heard' of such and such a thing. 'I don't know', 'I have not heard of it', 'I never saw anything like it' were the answers to practically all questions. Rarely a short, perfunctory affirmative answer was given, for example, that *La Montuna* was 'some animal' or that *El Caballero* was 'a dead man'.

After puberty and in an adolescent stage there again occurred a change. Now, all of a sudden, the reactions were verbose and highly emotional. All personifications were seen on a preternatural level, imbued with mysterious powers and bent upon causing death and disease. From hearsay and from personal experience there was much descriptive elaboration and a constant emphasis upon the imminent danger to one's health. Physical aggressiveness was not mentioned any more, but details of illness were told and retold, and many individual cases were cited of people who had died after having seen an apparition.

APOTROPAIC ATTITUDES AND HALLUCINATORY IMAGES

It is generally believed by the villagers that the evil influences and consequences of preternatural apparitions can be effectively counteracted and neutralized if the individual possesses some knowledge of defensive means. These would consist of certain prayers, names, or other magical utterings; of certain gestures or postures; or of certain magical objects which could protect their owner. However, only very few people in the village actually have this esoteric knowledge, and this lack of magical defenses is recognized as constituting an additional focus of anxiety.

Among the rural population of Colombia people know a great many defensive measures, such as prayers or magic formulas, and any kind of apotropaion can be bought in the town market, at cheap jewelry stores or from traveling peddlers. In Aritama, however, there is a quite notable lack of such objects and practices, and although people know that there exist formulas, gestures, and material objects which might protect their user, they do not generally employ them—at least not with a frequency in proportion to their fear of the preternatural. Amulets or other material objects are not sold in the village, nor are they bought in the lowland towns, as the villagers believe that such imported objects would not offer an effective defense against local dangers, having been intended as protection against evil influences that exist in other regions. Prayers or magic words and formulas are known to some people but are jealously kept secret from others and are not taught to children. Hardly anybody wears an amulet, except perhaps small children who might have a few beads or fruit kernels tied to their wrists in order to ward off the Evil Eye.

The following are some apotropaic methods which are said to be effective in warding off the dangers of the preternatural, but which are, as we have pointed out, actually seldom used. In the first place, as soon as an individual sees or hears an apparition or has a definite foreboding of preternatural danger, he should not walk straight ahead but should proceed sideways in a crablike fashion. In this way a face-to-face situation is avoided, as most ghosts are said to appear in the middle of the trail, either in front or behind their victims. Any challenging attitudes, such as talking, singing, or whistling should likewise be avoided, and the person should advance silently, closing the eyes as soon as he catches a glimpse of the apparition. Any object the person might carry that has a strong smell, such as onions or lemons, should be thrown away immediately, as they might attract attention to him. If the person is smoking a cigar he should throw it in the direction of the apparition, and should the encounter take place in a house, a bit of glowing charcoal can be used. A man might throw his hat in the direction of the vision.

Any Catholic prayer is said to be an efficient means of checking evil preternatural forces, and the words *Ave María Purísima* (or *Ave María Santísima*) are said to have a particular power, except over *La Montuna*. Invocations of S. Bartholomew (*San Bartolo*) are also said to have great power, and if the person cannot say a whole prayer, he might at least call out, *San Bartolomé, llévatelo lejos!* ('S. Bartholomew, take it away!'). It is interesting to observe that this same saint is considered to be the special protector of women in labor, being invoked during cases of difficult childbirth. The untranslated Indian word *niacué* is also said to have magic power against apparitions when called out aloud.

The sign of the cross, holy water, rosaries, or small amulets of Catholic tradition are not used, but some people say that certain small stones which have been specially prepared by an Indian shaman can be carried in a pocket or in a carrying bag for protection. There is much talk about the effectiveness of machetes that have had the point magically prepared (*compuesto*). Such machetes (*hojas de cruz*) are never used for work but are kept only to be taken along on nightly excursions or travel to far-off places, and the blade should be carried pointing over the right shoulder, to ward off dangers from behind.

Attitudes toward witches are rather different. Aggressiveness is said to be the best defense against them, and the person should insult the witch with the vilest and obscenest terms that might come to his mind, while attacking her with a machete.

But all this, as we have said above, is only the theory of defense against apparitions. In reality people who believe themselves to be in danger do not pray or walk sideways or invoke a saint, but instead stand dumbfounded or flee headlong. Only very few of our informants said that they had been able to mutter *Ave María Purísima*, and all others assured us that they were unable to speak or call out, and that they could flee only by making a great effort, their limbs feeling paralyzed and heavy as lead.

The lack of apotropaic practices in a people who live under the constant fear of seeing apparitions which are believed to be extremely harmful is not difficult to explain if we take into account that there exists a subconscious desire of having such hallucinations, of 'watching' them, i.e., the parents. The fact that the scoptophilic interests are sometimes punished by death and disease, and sometimes left unpunished, the watcher being allowed to recover from his initial shock, is due probably to the ambivalent attitude the individual is likely to develop with reference to the parental image.

COMATOSE, HYPNAGOGIC, AND OTHER HALLUCINATIONS

As far as we can judge from twenty-six cases we have recorded, there is quite a definite pattern to the content of hallucinations experienced during comatose states or high fever. Almost invariably people imagine that they have died already and that they are on their way to, or just arriving at, the Beyond. There they see beautiful houses, all white-washed, with tables laden with food, and many people eating and drinking merrily. In some cases the person awakes from his trance for no obvious reason, but more often he is confronted by an old woman who chases him from this paradise by saying that his time has not yet come to enter it. The fact that a patient recovers from his disease is often attributed to the food he imagines himself to have eaten during his hallucinations, and patients who are offered food after awakening from a comatose state will often refuse it by claiming that they had just had a plentiful meal in the Beyond.

There are, however, some cases that deviate in certain respects from this pattern. One female informant reported the following hallucination: After losing consciousness during a high (typhoid?) fever, she imagined herself to be walking along the banks of a river lined by trees. She noticed that no stones were in the riverbed and that the water was flowing very smoothly. After a while she arrived at a house. Feeling hungry, she wanted to ask for food (an unthinkable action in conscious behavior) and so knocked on the door, but when nobody answered she entered the house (again a reprovable action) and saw a bearded man sitting in the single room. He made a sign with his hand, asking her to leave, whereupon she awoke. Another informant, an old man, told that during a spell of high fever he saw his long-dead sister enter the room and offer him a bundle of food, saying that this would cure him. Suspecting a ruse, he unwrapped the food and found that it consisted of sand enveloped in thick strands of hair. This hallucination is probably related to the common belief that the inhabitants of the Netherworld eat sand. A young woman told that when severely ill and in a comatose state, she had a vision of two men offering her money so she would not 'sell her soul to the Devil' in exchange for curing her.

Hypnagogic hallucinations often follow a very similar pattern, people vividly imagining that they see or smell food, that they find trees bearing ripe fruit, that they are offered food, or that they prepare food and eat abundantly. This type of hallucination seems to be remarkably devoid of sexual content and, as in the case of comatose visions, centers upon food.

Some other forms of hallucinatory experience may be mentioned here. One of our informants had a ten-year-old boy, an adopted child, who was sent one day to cut firewood. While thus occupied the boy saw an unknown horseman approaching, followed by two men on foot. The child became afraid and hid in the bushes, but from his hiding place he saw with horror that his double had stayed behind, on the trail. He watched as the three men took his double and led it away with tied hands. The child returned home and told the vision. Several days later he died of 'fever'.

Another theme concerns the wraith. A person is simultaneously seen or heard at two places, at a great distance from each other, but is conscious of having been only at one place. If this should happen to someone it means that he is going to live for a long time yet, but it spells imminent doom for the ones who saw or heard the wraith. This belief seems to be related to the one concerning the wandering soul of a dying person.

An important hallucinatory element is related to a theme that we might call the 'magician's trial'. This is a recurrent theme in all conversations dealing with the preternatural and contains the following elements: A young man who is a magician's or *curioso*'s apprentice has to pass a final test before being told the fundamental secret of Black Magic by his master. Master and pupil go to an isolated place, and the former leaves the pupil alone, promising to return soon. During his absence the pupil is attacked by animals or natural forces. When the master returns he is told what happened and evaluates the pupil's merits according to his behavior during the trial. The following are three 'eyewitness accounts' of such trials, given to us by people who claim to have been the protagonists: In the first case the magician invited the pupil for a walk to show him a tree he claimed to have felled. At a lonely spot the magician told the pupil to wait and went on alone. After a short while a great storm broke and lightning struck nearby, but the frightened pupil stood his ground until the storm was over and his master returned. When told about the storm, the master agreed that the pupil had passed the test. In the second case the magician told the pupil to cut several vines at a lonely spot in the forest. While alone the pupil was attacked by a wild boar. He defended himself with his machete but finally fled. On the trail he met his master and told him what had happened. The master said, 'Didn't you recognize me? I had turned into a boar. As long as you are afraid of me you won't be able to learn anything.' The pupil did not pass the test. In the third case, a man asked one of the principal members of a dance group of the Corpus fiesta to teach him the secret prayer of the dancers so that he might form part of their group. The man refused at first but finally agreed to meet the other at night, near the river. The pupil arrived first and was attacked by a wild boar. After some struggle the boar fled, and shortly afterward the man arrived. When told of the successful fight with the boar, he agreed immediately to teach the pupil the secret prayer.

Other stories about similar trials contain the same elements, with slight variations. The animal is always a wild boar, except in one case where it is told that the pupil was swallowed by a huge snake, in the belly of which he remained for nine days. When the pupil told this experience to his master the latter said, 'Very good; now you have learned everything.'

To have had a hallucination, be it a ghostly apparition or a comatose vision, carries with it considerable prestige. Practically all people claim to have met some kind of ghost, but the prestige depends upon the particular combination of circumstances, the degree of danger, the attitude of the observer, and the consequences of the event. Almost everybody has *heard* the whistling of *El Silborcito* or the moaning of *La Montuna*, or has listened to the witches settling on the roof at night, but such experiences are far too common to have any special meaning. To acquire prestige, a person has to *see*. To be persecuted by a ghost, to find one's way blocked by it, or to be in danger of being devoured are the factors that make for prestige. The victim of such an apparition will admit his fright, his efforts to run away, and his ultimate reaction of fainting, without ever associating such behavior with cowardice. Fear, flight, and unconsciousness are under these circumstances considered to be quite normal reactions, and nobody blames a person for having acted this way. A phantom tale does not contain the elements of heroic exploit but rather those of the Magic Flight motif. But the real prestige-bearing factor consists in the eventual absence of fatal or near-fatal consequences of such an apparition. To fall ill for a while is part of normal behavior, but prestige depends upon the 'miraculous' way in which the victim recovered. Recovery from high fever is more 'miraculous' than recovery from pains or from a general malaise, and the person who survives a serious disease believed to have been caused by an apparition is certain to gain life-long prestige by this experience. Finally, it is necessary to point out that in Aritama, the consequences of ghostly apparitions are never verbalized in terms of soul-loss or spirit-possession.

DREAMS AND THEIR INTERPRETATION

Most people claim to dream frequently and to have occasional nightmares, and there is a considerable interest in dream interpretation. Dreams are discussed with relatives and friends, but there are no specialists in the village who might be called upon in doubtful cases, and dreams that do not contain generally known symbols are interpreted in a highly personal manner. Practically every adult individual knows some fifteen or twenty dream symbols and will interpret his own dreams if they have made a strong impression upon him or happened to occur on the eve of some important event. Many lucky or unfortunate occurrences in a person's life will be attributed to dreams by retrospective interpretation, even if the dream occurred months or years before the happening.

Besides the two general categories of 'good' and 'evil' dreams, most of them are interpreted in the usual terms of misfortune, disease, death, money, and luck. In Table 40 we have collected the meanings together with their symbols, which are all of common knowledge in the village.

TABLE 40

Significance	*Symbol*
Health and happiness	Dead people, death of mother, illness of others, grass-covered hills (tombs), flowers, eggs, bread, to be devoured by the sea, to be saved from drowning in a river, to travel to an Indian village
Wealth	Snake, fish, black dog, witch, naked man, armadillo, lice, the sea, death of others, counting money, receiving gifts
Food	Snake in field, to kill livestock, to be bitten by snake
Misfortune and misery	Marriage ceremony, cockfight, horseback riding, dancing, money, gold, silver, jewelry, egg shells, blood, ripe plantains
Aggression, theft, enemies, gossip, etc.	Bulls, fish, snakes, soap, beans, ripe bananas, rainbow, river, swollen river, to bathe, to be carried off by river, to defecate
Disease of dreamer	Bulls, fire, fresh fish, vulture on roof, black cattle, attack by cattle, to bathe, to fish, to travel to lowland town
Tears, sadness, fright	Pearls, salt, bananas, butterfly, fish, swollen river, to fly, to comb one's hair near river
Death of relatives	Procession, priest outside of church, bride without groom, dead woman offering meat, house breaking down, house construction, mud wall construction, falling walls, loss of tooth, pulling of tooth, crossing a river, to drown, to dance, to do household chores, to butcher, to butcher pig, blood, bulls, gold
Sudden travel	Horseback riding
Baptism	Priest inside church
Meeting with friend	Bananas

As is apparent from this list, the largest number of symbols refer to the death of relatives. If one accepts the view that dreams are frequently a form of wish fulfilment, the emphasis on dreams that predict the death of relatives would tend to reflect the high level of hostility which prevails in most, if not all, interpersonal relations. It is then also significant that to dream of the death of one's mother, or of dead or ill people, tombs, and flowers, is interpreted as predicting happiness and that to dream of other people's deaths is said to predict wealth. Quite characteristically, it is said in the village that nobody ever has a dream announcing the dreamer's own death, but always other people's deaths.

A number of dreams, however, are interpreted in terms of the dreamer's misfortune, and it is interesting to observe what kind of symbols are thus interpreted. It seems that there are two sets involved that represent anxiety-charged situations: one set concerns Creole-oriented tendencies, and another set has a sexual significance. As we have pointed out already, any individual who shows overt Creole orientation is likely to be victimized through gossip or other forms of collective or individual aggressiveness. A number of symbols which are related to this orientation and which are in daily conversation associated with 'Spanish' attitudes are marriage ceremony, cockfight, horseback riding, cattle, money, silver, gold, jewelry. It would seem, therefore, that the things for which these symbols stand are rejected and are transformed into dangers for the individual's health, life, and happiness. On the other hand, some of these symbols, as well as the ones of bulls, fish, snakes, ripe bananas, pearls, salt, dancing, flying, and combing, can probably be interpreted as sexual symbols, and the fact that they predict evil would suggest once more the strong anxieties with respect to all sexual activity.

FOLKTALES AND THEIR SIGNIFICANCE

There exists a considerable body of folktales in the village. Although there are no institutionalized occasions when such tales are told, most people know a number of them. There are no specialized storytellers, but some people, generally old men, are known to have a wide repertoire of tales and, occasionally, might be asked to tell a story or two.

In general, most tales are of European-Mediterranean type. However, there are also a few tales that were clearly taken over from the Indians, and sporadic Indian elements have been incorporated into a European framework. Stylistically, these tales are tightly structured, and although there occurs some clustering of motifs, the principal theme is generally quite clearly developed. There is little tiresome detail and no interest in individual motivation of the actors. The emphasis is on action, and each tale points out a specific moral.

Under the category of legends and traditions there exist the usual tales

433

referring to the first foundation of the village, to famous Indian shamans and healers, to buried treasures, hidden caves, or semihistorical personages who are said to have performed strange and wonderful deeds or whose burial places are still pointed out. There are several legends telling of how Christ visited the valley and went to live with the Indians, how he taught them the art of divination and healing, and how he performed miracles. With many of the major landmarks of the region there are connected legends of magicians, strange accidents, miracles, or dangers, and a great many tales are told about evil water-spirits which are said to live in the deep pools in the river and to enchant or kill the unwary passer-by.

Animal tales of the Reynard the Fox cycle are frequent, the trickster being usually a rabbit or some other small and insignificant animal, which plays its tricks on larger ones. However, the trickster is generally caught in the end and is punished for his pranks. Very frequently the animal stories develop in a kinship or friendship constellation, the trickster being a married man or being with friends and companions. There are a few stories of vampires and revenants, of the man who married a witch, of succubi and incubi, jaguar demons, and deals with the Devil. Stories about bets won and riddles solved by ruse are also frequent.

Anecdotes and jests constitute another type of story frequently heard. There are the well-known tales of foolishness and cleverness, of contests won by deception, of bargains and cheats, of parsons and rogues, of Indians, Negroes, or wandering strangers. Another very characteristic cycle of stories concerns two *compadres*, one of them rich, active, greedy, and foolish, and the other poor, lazy, generous, and clever. During their travels, adventures, or daily doings, the rich *compadre* always loses, while the poor and lazy one is rewarded by luck or assisted by supernatural helpers.

A more complex type of tale develops in a setting of Good and Bad Family Relations. This type is quite elaborate and represents the core of local folktales. A very frequent motif is the one of the youngest son, often an illegitimate or unwanted child, who leaves home and performs clever deeds, outwitting his envious brothers, enemies, or ogres with the assistance of supernatural helpers, the story often ending with the Prodigal's Return motif. This type of story very frequently contains such elements as the Visit to an Enchanted Place, the Magic Flight, the Rescue, the King's Tasks, or the Quest for a Lost Wife or Lover. Helpful animals, often horses, play an important part in these stories, as do also kindly old men or women who give the hero helpful counsel, a magic wand, or some other marvelous object in gratitude for food the youth shared with them. Seduction, abduction, elopement, and adultery are frequent minor motifs of these tales.

Other complex tales, also developed in a setting of intrafamily relations, contain the following leading motifs: The Swan Maiden, The Maiden in the Tower, The Twins, The Sleeping Beauty, The Louse Skin, The Tar Baby, The Forbidden Chamber, The Monster as Bridegroom, Red Ridinghood, Snow White, Cinderella, Hansel and Gretel, the Circe motif, the kind and unkind motif. These tales contain many of the elements mentioned above, together with others like the shoe test, knowledge of animal speech, the magic ring, substitute of bride, extraordinary strength, magic remedies for blindness. The central figure is sometimes a youth, sometimes a girl, who is made unjustly to suffer by evil kings, ogres, stepmothers, or witches but who overcomes all obstacles and is finally rewarded.

In the particular elaboration and relative frequency of specific motifs, cultural selectiveness evidently plays an important part. Every society tends to make its own creative selection of motifs and their accompanying morals, which are then patterned in a unique manner to express the desires or fears that are prevalent in that society. There is no random acceptance of motifs but, like any other facet of culture, they are chosen for their specific function, and they are combined into a coherent whole, the popularity of which depends on the degree to which the components continue to satisfy felt needs. The motifs are adapted to local situations and are elaborated in a manner that is easily understood by all. They mirror local conditions, and their motivations and morals are explained in terms of locally accepted values. A body of folktales would, therefore, reflect the social and psychological problems of a given society and thus offer an insight into the ambitions and anxieties of the people. Furthermore, the specific details of the selected motifs express a symbolism which is locally understood and which fits into a traditional pattern of subconscious mythological thought and symbolic equivalence. This does not mean that the underlying concrete meanings are fully grasped, but that they form a satisfactory expression of individual, but widely shared, hidden feelings. With this theory in mind we shall now try to analyze some of the principal components of the local folktales in order to see if they can contribute to our understanding of the people of Aritama.

We have already pointed out that the main body of folktales is made up of stories that develop in a framework of interpersonal relations within the household. Father and mother, or foster parents, are generally pictured as cruel and demanding, while brothers and sisters appear as mischievous enemies, and the central figure of the tale—a boy or a girl—abandons the home or is expelled from it. This general theme is, of course, well known in the village and corresponds to a very real situation. Although the child in reality does not leave the village, there is a rather definite break with the parental home. Sibling rivalry as depicted in tales is also a fact in real life, as is the man's difficult quest of a woman, the tasks that have to be accomplished to win her, and her frequent infidelity or desertion. In the stories, just as in reality, the heroine is often married to an 'ogre', is mistreated, elopes with a lover, and is perhaps punished or makes good her escape. So far, then, there is little difference between fact and fiction.

In the picture of the youth's adventures away from his (or her) family, there also appear several recurrent themes which are significant, in view of real-life situations. In the first place, help is often given to the wanderer by old people, either men or women, who live alone and who help the hero to overcome his obstacles out of gratitude for his having willingly shared his food with them. This theme seems to reflect the fact that a large number of children are brought up by their grandparents or other relatives of their generation, with whom mutual relationships are often much more intimate than between child and biological parent. That the sharing of food with the older generation brings benefits stands as a general moral precept. On the other hand, the demanding father figure, be it the biological father, stepfather, king, ogre, or magician, is paralleled by a cruel mother image, a stepmother or witch. These are seen as determined to destroy the youth, to send him away from them, to sell him for a handsome profit, or even to kill him. But in the end he always is victorious. In a number of stories the child is on good terms with one parent but is persecuted by the other, or contends with his siblings for the father's (rarely the mother's) favor, though sometimes a grown boy kills his father in order to avenge his mother's misery. In other tales, father and son are rivals for the love of the same woman, and the Oedipus theme is sometimes very elaborate.

If we compare these mythical configurations with the actual conditions prevailing in village family life we see at once a strong parallelism in the basic quality of mutual feelings and subconscious drives. Judging by the contents of tales of this type, it would seem that the principal tensions in family relationships come from unsolved Oedipal situations, from sibling rivalry, from the continuous quest of female, i.e., mother-wife approval. It also seems evident that the youngest, the unwanted, or the illegitimate child is subconsciously the cause of marked guilt-feelings on the part of adults, since the stories always depict his long struggle and final reward, while the parental figures are always punished or eliminated from his experience.

Many tales emphasize the plight of the affection-seeking, honest man who falls under the spell of an evil woman and who is unable to escape or extricate himself from her charm. Like Circe, she changes her lovers into beasts, and the spell can only be broken through the interference of a child or youth who, with the help of magic, overcomes the power of the sorceress. The faithful husband is a more frequent figure in stories than the faithful wife, a fact which hardly corresponds to reality but which is significant in that it seems to point to the man's desire to be the object of permanent affection of one single mother-wife image. The recurrent theme of the substitute bride might be a reflection of the practice of successive short-term conjugal unions, as well as of a mother-wife substitution complex. The frequency of this theme, together with its complications, suggests that this is a source of male anxieties. It must be pointed out, moreover, that the unconscious elaboration of tales and the social transmission of them are essentially a male activity. These are not 'grandmother tales'. Men tell them and enlarge upon them, and all have a definite masculine orientation. Consequently, they are likely to reflect only a partial picture of the deeper problems, as they do not express clearly or so fully female desires or fears.

The stories of the two *compadres* are of a somewhat different category, expressing the hostility between economic levels. The belief that luck, not work, is the only means by which a poor man may change his condition is reflected here. The poor man's generosity is pointed out, his 'innocence' and willingness to help and to share, whereas the greedy partner is always punished by fate. Honesty and hard work are not found to be qualities of the poor *compadre*, but rather shrewdness and his faith in a 'good star'. Although God is not mentioned by name in these stories, they often tend to point out a kind of divine justice which, in the end, rewards the suffering and punishes the greedy.

Jests, anecdotes, realistic stories, and animal tales, although frequently heard, are almost always short and simple, but reflections of family relations and of wider social relationships are often found in them. In these tales women are frequently ridiculed, blamed for a man's ill luck, or punished for their faithlessness. The moral is drawn from the hero's shrewdness and quick wit, or from the ignorant's credulity. Often there is an element of slapstick comedy, the central figure being an amiable rogue.

A word must be said about the many riddles and proverbs which form an essential part of the daily talk of the villagers. They reflect not only part of the folk philosophy, but also certain anxieties and goals. A great many riddles are of an obscene character, with the question being phrased to suggest sexual activities but with the correct answer being surprisingly harmless. These riddles are embarrassing because the person is made to believe that obscenity is involved in the answer also, and he usually prefers to claim ignorance. Then when told the answer, which is quite innocent, the person is likely to feel guilt for his imaginary interpretation. Such riddles are of interest because they evidently express many repressed sexual desires and fantasies, and also because they give some insight into a crude sexual symbolism existent in the language.

Besides this type of riddle, there are many that refer to food and the cooking or eating of it, reflecting once more the high emotional value of these elements. Most of the common proverbs and sayings express such thoughts as these: poor people have no luck; exterior appearance is all that counts; laziness is an obstacle to raising one's status; ignorance and credulity make fools of people; personality traits are all genetically inherited, etc.

In conclusion we can say that in its general themes and motifs the oral literature of the village presents a faithful image of the socio-psychological conditions we have observed so far in the local culture.

X

SUMMARY

WORLD VIEW, VALUES, AND PERSONALITY TYPES

IN the preceeding chapters we have presented a description of the general physical and sociological conditions under which individual and community life develops in Aritama. Although all these various aspects are subject to slow change in the course of time, they form a given situation into which the individual is born. But parallel to this physical and social framework into which the person enters at birth, there exists the metaphysical and ethical framework of the local culture, which, although also being modified by time, constitutes another fundamental dimension into which each individual is born. Before speaking then of the individual personality and of the changing institutions of which he is to become a member in the process of his education, we shall outline in brief the character of the value orientations that guide this process and that formulate the essential philosophy of life of the villagers.

The general concept of the universe is that it is a complex magical system into which man is born and in which he exists without ever being able to achieve security and peace. The community of the living and the individuals that constitute it are nothing but passing shadows, unwelcome guests in a world controlled by unknown and unknowable powers which are essentially hostile to mankind. The structure and the function of the universe are thought to be far beyond human experience and understanding, and all speculations as to its meaning and all efforts to dominate even the most insignificant aspect of it, are deemed idle.

It is taken for granted that man can never know the laws that govern life and the universe, because these laws themselves are thought to be inconsistent, to change in an arbitrary and unforseeable fashion. There are eclipses and earthquakes, droughts and tempests, landslides and epidemics; healthy people die suddenly while an ill person might live for many years; virtue is seldom rewarded and crime is seldom punished. These facts are thought to be ample proof that there is no order, no justice, no hope at all. People believe that there is no way to forestall disaster or to invite success.

The land itself is not considered to be one's own but to belong to the ancestors, to the spirits of the dead. The living have only a lease on it, a tenant's right which expires the moment an ancestral spirit feels slighted or forgotten. Only obligations are thought to have been inherited from the ancestors, only the duty to live life in their ever present shadow. The ancestors owned this land; they cleared it and planted it; they traced the trails and built the houses; they gave names to mountains and rivers. Their imprint is felt on everything and their ownership and control are believed to continue and to enchain their descendants forever in a web of obligations.

Nature, therefore, is always thought to be dangerous and animated by the presence of spirits, not only of the ancestral owners, but of chthonian beings, tree and water spirits, harmful animals, and evil winds. The safest thing is to stay at home, but should circumstances oblige a person to leave temporarily the relative security of house and village, it is thought advisable to use the open trails and fields and never to stray off into the underbrush or the forest, where all kinds of dangers might be lurking. Sun, moon, and stars, wind and rain, heat and cold, light and shadow—all are believed to have occasionally harmful powers over body and mind. The cool air near the river or the reflected heat from rocks or trails are thought to be dangerous, the same as the shadow of certain trees or the damp of the forest. Dangers are seen everywhere in nature, and to try to understand them or to overcome them would be considered as foolishness.

Why these things are the way they are, or the way they are conceived to be, is thought to be beyond man's understanding. Tradition says that these dangers do exist, and experience proves tradition right. This, then, is 'reality'.

Logical reasoning is rare. Supernatural, unknowable powers are supposed to control nature and life, and all man can do in order to survive is to avoid all occasions that, traditionally, spell danger. Causes are established on the basis of *post hoc, ergo propter hoc*; plurality of causes is doubted, and every phenomenon is rather believed to be due to one single specific cause. Few people will reason, 'If I do this, any number of things might happen' Rather they think, 'If I do this, then *that* will happen.' But if it does not happen so, there was not a fault in logic, but an error in action. The causal factor was not well defined, or the causal action was not carried out as it should have been. There is, therefore, no interest in experiment or in testing a new hypothesis.

But this kind of reasoning about cause and effect is admitted to have validity only within the local culture. A stranger from another village or town might see things in a quite different way and might commit actions without any danger which, if committed by a villager, would have dire results. He might be able to do things no one in the village ever dared or tried to do, but that does not mean that now anybody can do them. His 'reality' is different.

All attitudes toward life are eminently fatalistic. Every individual is believed to be born under a particular sign (*signio*), a certain star, which determines his existence in every detail. These concepts are continuously verbalized in such expressions as 'to fall to one's lot' (*tocar*) or 'to coincide' (*convenir*). The first verb refers to the speaker himself, as, for example, when saying, 'It fell to my lot to be ill' (*me tocó enfermarme*), or to others with whom one commiserates, 'He was rich but it fell to his lot to be poor now' (*Estaba rico pero le tocó quedar pobre*). The second verb often has a moralizing or spiteful and mischievous connotation: 'He fell ill? Well, he had it coming!' (i.e., fate's workings) (*Se enfermó? Pues, le convino!*).

However, a person's fate is believed to change sometimes for the better or for the worse, quite independently of the individual's conduct. Suddenly 'one's luck changes' (*la suerte de uno se compone*), and everything goes well, but then there come periods of ill fate (*estar en la de malas, venirle a uno la de malas*). As there is no escape from fate and predestination, it is thought useless to try to live according to certain norms or to make efforts to change one's lot. Individual responsibility, therefore, is not a recognized quality. The individual never believes that he himself could be responsible for his having failed in a certain endeavour, but will always blame fate for his failures.

Although the concept of fate is continuously referred to by people, on the narrow scene of everyday personal experience and frustration blame for failure is often put on society, on the neighbours, the family, the government, the climate, the land. But never would an individual think it possible that his own judgment or actions might have brought about a failure. Those who speak of Divine Providence will identify God and fate by saying, 'God is predestination' (*Dios es la predestinación*). It is God himself who is thought to cause man's failure; not as a trial or a punishment for evil deeds, but because God is conceived as a vengeful despot who 'prefers the rich' (*prefiere a los ricos*). But also the so-called rich fail sometimes in their efforts and in their lives. Then it is said, 'God protects the poor' (*Dios protege a los pobres*).

Life is conceived as a continuous struggle for food, health, and security, and the expression 'the struggle for life' (*la lucha por la vida*) is heard everywhere. However, the ultimate goal of life is to be respected (*ser respetado*), and all human activities are essentially oriented toward achieving this end. Leisure, capital, material progress, food, health, or whatever an individual may have made his ambition,

441

are really only means to this single aspiration in life: to be accepted by society; to be free of discrimination, persecution, and ridicule; to be respected.

To be respected means to be accepted as a 'civilized' person and to be attributed dignity in spite of skin color and poverty. All inner problems, all psychological tensions, indeed the whole process of individual life develop in this dimension, between the aspired goal of being respected and the ever-present fear of being taken for a backward and poor Indio.

There are minor goals but they are not ends to be achieved for themselves but are only means for the greater goal. To have a family, to have sons who help in the fields, to have less work and more food, better clothes, to travel, to find a suitable match, were ambitions most frequently stated, but it was always understood that all these minor ambitions had value only insofar as they would contribute to personal prestige. Achievement of the main goal depends, of course, upon individual fate. Some people, according to their character, will struggle all their lives to attain this goal; but some will tire and will abandon all hope of ever realizing it. They are the old, the embittered, the ones who know that their physical characteristics will never let them advance beyond a certain status. These people tend to return to an infantile goal conceived in terms of obliging others to care for them and feed them. They will continuously complain of illness, of mistreatment, of being a burden to their own families, only to shame or coax others into supporting them.

The prestige of being respected is gained mainly through authority and dominance over others. The desire to dominate is never openly expressed; as a matter of fact, any overt sign of it would be strongly condemned, but nevertheless it is a basic motivation which can be inferred from many ramifications of individual behaviour. All human motivations are believed to be essentially suspicious, and co-operation is never based upon mutual confidence, trust, or affection. On the contrary, every individual expects the worst from his fellow men, be they his brothers, parents, or children. Social unity is then based upon a relationship of dominion and submission. Every individual is subordinated to others, but dominates still others. This is verbalized continuously with the use of the verb 'to command' (*mandar*). In daily conversation people will say, 'I commanded to be sold rice' (*Mandé que me vendan arroz*) or 'I commanded to have my hair cut' (*Me mandé motilar*). On the other hand, one frequently hears phrases like 'Who commanded you to do this?' (*Quién te mandó hacer eso?*) or 'Who commands here, who gives orders here?' (*Quién manda aquí?*) or 'He commands to tell you . . .' (*El manda decirle . . .*). This concept of authority is transferred to nature, too. The male 'commands' over the females; certain trees 'command' over others, the same as do certain ceremonial sites, certain legendary Indian shamans, certain mysterious pools in the river, or certain evil winds. A wealthy person is said to have 'power' (*fuerza*), and stores are always evaluated according to their relative 'power', i.e., turnover.

We shall turn now to the problem of values. Most values are defined in terms of suitable behavior in interpersonal relations, and few if any limited to the individual's intellect or his own relationship with the universe and the supernatural. Although the various value categories are frequently expressed in the many 'dos' or 'don'ts' of child-training, schooling, and adult social intercourse, they are rarely phrased in a clear form and have to be inferred from observation, conversation, and overt behavior. There are, of course, individual differences in outlook, differences according to age, sex, status, and educational level, but as a whole the value system is remarkably uniform.

Ceremonial conduct patterns as demonstrated in politeness, greeting, and visiting are greatly emphasized. In connection with them, facial control is highly valued. Smiles, laughter, tears, rage, sadness, pain, or fear should never be shown, and to maintain a 'wooden face' (*cara de palo*) is a prerequisite for being considered a 'serious person' (*persona seria*), i.e., a dependable character. On the street people, especially men, look straight ahead or downward and cast only furtive glances sideward, while walking busily, in a purposeful way and with worried faces. This 'seriousness' and self-control is asked for in all dealings with others, be it the immediate family, the kin, or society at large. The correct phrasing of greetings and condolences, and fluency of expression (*saber expresarse bien*) are most desirable. It is 'formality' (*formalidad*) that is valued because only the 'formal person' (*la persona formal*) can hope to be respected.

To be approachable (*ser tratable*) is highly desirable, wherever all pretentiousness is abhorred. Generosity with food, in opposition to stinginess, is greatly prized, and a person who readily shares food with others will be appreciated by everyone. One could hardly say something worse about a person than 'He eats alone' (*el come solo*), meaning that he does not share everything he has. To be co-operative (*persona voluntaria*) is another high virtue. To be willing to lend a hand whenever others might need help, to take part in communal labor, to help a neighbor or a friend during illness or at the harvest time, are qualities that are greatly respected. Discretion and the willingness to keep a secret and to withhold information that might be harmful to others are similarly highly important qualities. But above all, respect for others, for their personal integrity and for their property, is the main virtue. To show disrespectful behavior toward persons of the same status level or to steal from them is forgivable, but the pretentious looking-down upon the poor and the ignorant is considered to be the most condemnable behavior.

A highly desirable quality but one which is seldom spoken of is 'purity' (*pureza*). In a sense, this quality cannot be attained but is an innate or charismatic state of mind. Purity is defined in terms of sincere altruism, of real generosity, unselfishness, and helpfulness. The term 'innocence' is used in the same sense when speaking of children or very ignorant persons. Honesty, on the other hand, is considered a good thing, but it is emphasized that it is difficult to achieve. Its real value lies rather in the eventuality that others will refer to the person in conversation as 'an honest man', a fact which means prestige, but otherwise it is a quality that is not an absolutely necessary requirement for being respected. Honesty is only worthwhile if it is ostentatious and is talked about. Intellectual skills, learning, esoteric knowledge in magic and religion, are thought desirable as long as they are believed to refer only to accustomed practices, but are feared as soon as the individual is suspected to acquire through them a certain influence over others. A person who knows a few prayers or who is skilful in setting bones rises in public esteem, but should his or her knowledge be suspected to be paired with magical practices that lie outside everyday experience, the person is likely to be considered a dangerous public enemy.

Productiveness is greatly esteemed as long as the person limits his efforts to meet the needs of his family, but should he go beyond that and begin to accumulate a surplus, criticism is bound to result. To be a good provider is a highly valued quality, but to work toward the possession of a small capital is interpreted as an intent to acquire power over others and is, therefore, resented.

In opposition to these valued qualities, there is a great number of attitudes that are considered as undesirable in a higher or lesser degree. In opposition to ceremonial behavior, self-control, and co-operativeness, there is aggressiveness in the physical sense. All fighting and brawling are emphatically condemned, and violent gestures or words are never found to be wholly justified. The destruction of other people's property is considered a serious crime, and even to chase away the neighbor's dog would be taken to be a manifestation of aggressive feelings against its owner. Envy is the great and common sin and is always paralleled or followed by Black Magic, aggression, and pretentiousness. Magical aggression is not so much feared for its consequences as for its being practiced at all, because it means that the aggressor does not 'respect' the victim. The same is true about theft, avarice, gossip, authoritarianism, envy, pretentiousness, or physical aggressiveness. That which really counts is not so much the damage done, but the 'disrespectful' component of such actions and attitudes. The offense does not consist in being victimized, but in being chosen a victim in the first place.

The concept of shamelessness (*sinvergüenza*) refers mainly to a person's unwillingness to mend his ways in connection with scandalous illicit love affairs or with habitual petty larceny. This quality is considered to be less condemnable in men than in women. Inquisitiveness, followed by envious and malicious gossip, is a greatly despised attitude. Inquisitiveness is indeed one of the worst qualities a person could have, and any attitude that could be interpreted as observant or watchful is condemned as prying (*velar*). A standard type of evasive answer is 'I haven't been curious' (*No he sido curioso*). One might ask about a person's name, health, a recently accomplished or a projected trip, but hardly more. As a general rule in conversation one should always refer rather to actions and not to motivations; one might ask, 'Did X come already'; but one should not ask, 'Why hasn't X come yet?' One should never ask *why* because it is disrespectful to do so. To ask about the state of one's affairs or to ask one's opinion on any subject or person is considered very bad behaviour.

All ostentatiousness is condemned. To speak in a loud voice, to wear unusual clothes, to be enthusiastic about something, to demonstrate interest or curiosity, to be emotional and affectionate, are all considered to be very unbecoming traits. Nothing personal should ever be praised. A person will never talk with pride of his possessions, family, children, or domestic animals because to do so would be an open invitation to be envied. It would be an offensive provocation by which the person gives to understand that he considers others so weak and inferior that their envy does not have to be feared. The only things one might occasionally praise are other people's possessions or achievements, but this should always be done in a perfunctory manner so as not to arouse distrust or give the impression that one is envious.

A person should never try to collect a debt and never, in any way, remind the debtor of his obligations by asking him to fulfil them. One has to wait until he is paid. Sometimes one might send an 'innocent' intermediary, such as a child or a complete stranger, but one should never try to collect personally and directly because this would mean that one does not respect the debtor. One should also never eat less than others, lest one be accused of being a miser (*miserable*), evil and avaricious. To eat less and worse than others causes strong criticism, but it is taken for granted that people will claim to eat more and better than anybody, although all know that this is not true.

It is necessary to distinguish here between attitudes that are considered undesirable and actions that are considered to be real 'sins' (*pecados*). To kill, to rob, and to practice Black Magic are sins. Some people, mainly the poor, will say that envy and pretentiousness are also sins, but others would not agree with this. Lying, adultery, and petty thefts are not believed to be sins and are not thought to have anything to do with morals at all. Nor are desertion of the home, sodomy, laziness, mistreatment of wife and children, or the bearing of false witness considered to be evil deeds in the sense of sins. But to steal food from another's field is a 'sin' the same as to be aggressive in public or to threaten one's fellow with magic.

The basic directives of valued behavior and character traits can be reduced to a series of proscriptions as follows: never practice aggressive magic, never try to surpass others openly; never tell strangers how much land you own; never contradict anybody except your immediate family; never expect any good from anyone; never believe what people tell you; never be aggressive or otherwise emotional outside your own home; never demonstrate hunger outside your own home; never accept sexual favors without paying for them; never tell others what you eat; never eat more or better or less than others; never mention dead people's names in a derogatory way.

The scheme in Table 41 outlines this system in its principal points.

TABLE 41

Valued	*Condemned*
Ceremonial behavior	Black Magic
Respect for others	Envy
Generosity with food	Physical aggression
Co-operation	Pretentiousness
Discretion	Authoritarianism
Honesty	Avarice
Dignity	Gossip
Self-control	Inquisitiveness
Fluency of expression	Theft
Purity	Shamelessness
Productiveness	Greed
Skills (religious, scientific)	Ignorance

It is obvious that most, if not all, values are defined in terms of interpersonal relations. There is little or no emphasis on what might be called 'Christian virtues' or on values defined in a wider social context, such as responsibility, citizenship, or patriotism. The character of the individual is judged in terms of how he behaves in society, not in terms of what kind of person he is. Intelligence, courage, initiative, loyalty, perseverance, optimism, religious devotion, or individual progress are, therefore, largely ignored as possible values, because the local society does not see any benefit for others in such qualities. A person's worth depends on his being a group-member, not on being an individual.

Summary

This emphasis on interpersonal relations reflects, of course, the basic problem of the whole cultural situation of the community. The valued or condemned attitudes mirror the deep anxieties felt by all its members: to be despised and slighted by others who, for one reason or the other, are more powerful, more influential, more 'civilized'.

Values define ideal behavior. In Aritama, as anywhere, there is a chasm between the ideal pattern and the actual behavior of people, but this chasm is not a very deep one. The goals formulated by the local culture are all attainable for most of its members.

The value system is a selective guide for life in society, but from it, again, people select and orient their lives according to certain values, while ignoring others. This possibility of individual selection from a set of values depends to a large degree upon the sanctions inflicted upon the deviant, but the intensity of this sanction varies according to the specific value that is disregarded. Any open ostentation of power and authority, the same as physical violence, is easily dominated. The habitual aggressor is simply overpowered, beaten, imprisoned, or even killed. From historical to present times there have been cases where reincident physical aggressors were murdered by the populace, or by known individuals who acted as public judges. On the other hand, aggressive or authoritarian people are likely to be shunned by everyone, and no co-operation whatsoever will be extended to them. They are unable to sell their products or to find hired labor or to establish credit. In this way, aggressiveness is curbed very efficiently and, in an overt physical form, is hardly said to exist in the community. Crime, in the sense of the legal code, does not exist in Aritama. Avarice and greed, on the other hand, are controlled by similar means, and economic collaboration, labor, and credit will be withheld. Shameless scandalous behavior between the sexes is also controlled by economic sanctions, and, as the case may be, by female rejection. But gossip, inquisitiveness, and envy are far more difficult to control. As a matter of fact, the problem of establishing the identity of the culprit makes it practically impossible to take direct action, and in this manner all measures of defense or control are left to the individual who, of course, is likely to repay like with like. These undesirable but almost uncontrollable forces of aggression are thus very frequent, as a matter of fact quite dominant, and represent an outlet for otherwise repressed aggressive tendencies. The crime of Black Magic is probably the most difficult to prove, but as it represents a powerful weapon in intra-village strife, it is widely committed. However, it is necessary to point out here that in reality there are probably very few people who know the traditional details of magical aggression and that the frequency of the practice is much exaggerated. But no matter if magic is practiced or only pretended to be practiced, the potential victim lives in great fear of it. Theft, the guilt of which can occasionally be established, is never controlled by physical aggression but rather by ridicule, verbal chastisement, and social stigma. People in real need care little for these consequences, and so petty thefts are frequent and often ignored entirely, at least as long as food is not involved. Selfishness and pretentiousness can, of course, be attributed to certain individuals or groups, but they are difficult to control, as only people of high social and economic status will demonstrate these attitudes. Although magic might be used to control such behavior, it is common.

Of valued attitudes it can be said that ceremonial behavior, self-control, and dignity are the outstanding characteristics of the individual, together with a certain generosity in sharing food with others. However, of what concerns discretion and respect for others, there is but little observable beneath the exterior façade of control and politeness. As one can judge from the ever-present gossip, inquisitiveness, and magical aggression, there is a wide gap between exterior make-believe and intimate hostility. Individual productiveness and spontaneous co-operation with others are also rare, as are absolute honesty, purity of mind (as defined above), or intellectual skill and abilities.

We can thus reduce this system to the general scheme presented in Table 42.

TABLE 42

Valued		Condemned	
Overtly Present	*Generally Absent*	*Covertly Present*	*Generally Absent*
Ceremonial behavior	Respect for others	Envy	Physical aggression
Food-sharing	Co-operation	Pretentiousness	Authoritarianism
Self-control	Discretion	Gossip	Avarice
Dignity	Honesty	Inquisitiveness	Shamelessness
Seriousness	Productiveness	Ignorance	Greed
	Purity	Petty thefts	
	Verbal fluency	Black Magic	
	Intellectual skills	Selfishness	

The principal feature of overt behavior is the extreme control the individual exercises over all his actions and words. Devoid of all spontaneity and warmth, of all intellectual curiosity and social grace, people display in public a suppressed, stylized, and stereotyped behavior, which in many cases turns into preoccupied bitterness, moodiness, and intolerance when they are in the intimate circle of their families. Quite often the social personality is maintained even in the home. Underneath this apparent indifference and equanimity, however, there are the confused anxieties of the mind that has not come to terms with life. There is an insistent defensiveness, a nagging necessity for prestige behavior, a deep despair of overcoming one's insufficiency and inferiority in front of the 'civilized', the sophisticated, the people from the lowlands.

The foregoing outline of value orientations establishes a basic framework delineating the limits within which personality development—as formulated by the local culture—takes place. The value system implies an ideal personality type, but next to it allowance is made for a certain selective range of configurations outside of which all behavior would be considered aberrant and undesirable. We shall try to trace these limits of permissibility and to describe, within them, the main characteristics of the desirable, normal, permissible, and rejectable personality configurations.

The *ideal* personality type is the humble, modest food-provider; the unpretentious and hard-working father, the submissive and loving mother, and the grateful child. In addition to his family and his kin, the person should readily co-operate with neighbor, friends, or any other member—or group of members—of the community. Although he may be authoritarian and paternalistic within the family, the person should accept willingly the authority of those whose knowledge, experience, or social status is superior to his. He should be generous and self-sacrificing in all interpersonal relations, absolutely trustworthy and dependable among kin and friends, and unpretentious but ever ready to give good advice or to lend a helping hand. He should be unobtrusive, serious, and silent, always keeping his emotions under control except in deep sorrow or great joy. He should be equanimous in accepting his fate as a humble peasant.

The *normal* type of personality, i.e., the one we believe to have met most frequently, is characterized by very different traits. By selecting some of the attributes that appear to be highly typical, we may describe this type as follows: The person is extremely controlled and rigid in his reactions to others, and the maintenance of satisfactory relations is very difficult. Authority figures are thought of realistically as irresponsible, unpredictable in their actions, and likely to be unjust and hostile. There is mistrust of all motivations in others, little submission, and never rebellion, but rather avoidance of all close relationships. Uncooperativeness and hostility are evident, but open outbursts of the latter are very rare and if they occur they are directed against inoffensive persons (women, children, old people, Indians), against animals, or against inanimate objects. Gloominess and cynical self-accusations are frequent. On the other hand, hostility and aggression are readily verbalized in malicious and envious gossip, but carefully hidden as far as Black Magic is concerned. Interpersonal relations are made dependent to a high degree upon food-sharing patterns. There is exaggerated concern with phenotype, dress, correct language, accompanied by fantasied achievements and pretentiousness. There is no spontaneity and all overt behavior is dominated by profound anxieties. Lack of public recognition, ill health through envious magic, and poverty through economic failure are constantly worried about.

Next to this personality type there exists another one which we shall call the *conservative* type. He is found mainly among the lomeros of Indian ancestry and among the old people of all strata. Those we have come to consider as representatives of this personality configuration show the following characteristics: close and stable personal relationships with few people of a similar type; a co-operativeness within the kin-group and an occasional disinterested generosity with outsiders; a respect for paternal authority but strong emotional bonds with mother figures; correct self-evaluation and realism as to the evaluation of one's own status, economic possibilities, and social prestige; an occasional cynicism and fatalistic bitterness, but without self-depreciating attitudes or self-pity; no ambitions for 'progress' and little repressed envy; secretiveness but not shame; a confidence in final 'justice'; a low anxiety level and low interest in magical aggression; and a marked emotional maturity and stability.

A third type would be the *progressive* personality. This configuration is exemplified by a number of placeros and by some of the younger people of all sections of the community. The main characteristics are self-control and timidity which easily turn into verbose self-assertion; security of position within one's own community and an insecurity outside it; good contact with others of the same type, although very competitive and critical; dominant, authoritarian, and tradition-flouting; inquisitive, open to change, and critical of village conditions; an economical and physical aggressiveness; a hedonistic, materialistic, and impulsive mentality. These are evidently the people who approach lowland Creole norms.

Both the conservative and the progressive types are permissible but always exposed to criticism by the majority. The former are blamed for being retrograde 'Indians' and the latter for being aggressive 'exploiters of the poor'. While the conservative type is accused of its apparent indifference or resistance to 'progress' and 'civilization', the progressive type is often suspected of representing political and government interests which are believed to be bent upon 'enslaving' the village. However, the progressive type is greatly envied because of his economic activity and status. He tends to become the focus of magical aggression and village gossip, and it seems that he serves quite frequently as a model in child-training in families where the normal and conservative types dominate.

There exist, of course, marginal types which are tolerated or ignored, but the ones we have tried to characterize here are the principal ones. Outside the range of permissibility are several types of personality configuration of which there are a few cases. There is the person who carries a chip on his shoulder and who is physically aggressive, authoritarian, a boisterous drunkard, liar, and a seducer. Even if he is a good provider and a generous spender, he is shunned and watched, and eventually eliminated from the community, even by use of force. Then there is the 'savage' (*salvaje*), who lives in isolation, does not care for exterior appearances, is stingy and unco-operative, uncouth in conversation and manners, and aggressive when approached. He is criticized, ridiculed, and excluded from the community. The same happens to the tradition-oriented, to the strict monogamist and moralist whose model is the old mission-educated generation. Then there is the pretentious and inquisitive type, the spinster, the arrogant and self-righteous, and the calculating egotist who always refuses to help but who lives at the expense of others, whom he tries to dominate by gossip. But all these types are rare. They are rejected, isolated, ignored, sometimes driven out of the village but more often leave on their own accord.

That these different personality types depend to a large degree upon differences in child-training patterns and that these patterns are varying from generation to generation in an accelerated rate is obvious. Of the generation educated by those who lived when the village was still culturally a relatively homogeneous unit, there still remain a number of individuals, and their influence in creating a conservative type of personality in their descendants can readily be observed. On the other hand, the varying composition of household units provides different frameworks for child-training. Children are brought up by their biological mothers, or surrogate mothers like aunts, grandmothers, nurses, or older siblings, and as their residence changes they are exposed to different modes of rearing. The depersonalization of relationships; the ambivalent perception of authority figures; the anxiety caused by hostility, envy, and prestige conflicts thus seem to lead necessarily to the inhibited, shut-in, and frozen type of personality which we have designated as normal. But the general trend, it seems, is toward a more aggressive self-assertion—aggressive in the sense of an outward projection of insecurity in the form of a more active participation in community affairs, politics, and economic efforts. The pent-up fear of being inferior is finding release in the mistrusted but secretly admired Creole norms where 'respect' is guaranteed regardless of phenotype or socioeconomic village status. In the same norms the predominantly negative value system of the villagers might also find the positive value of an integrated religion, a need which people furtively but frequently express when speaking of their conflicts.

THE CHANGING SCENE

In order to evaluate the present situation of culture change in Aritama, we must reach back once more into the sources and origins of community life in the Sierra Nevada and try to isolate some of the principal loci in which the major changes took place. If we look back upon the sequence of historical events through which the village has passed during the last 500 years, we discern in it four principal periods of accentuated culture contact and change, separated by periods of relative isolation and stability. These periods of change are the Spanish conquest of the sixteenth century, the missionary efforts of the middle of the eighteenth century, the colonizing period of the late nineteenth century, and the present.

During the period of the conquest the contact with the Spaniards produced many far-reaching changes which affected above all the political and economic institutions of aboriginal society. Although there seems to have been no violent conquest of the valley of Aritama, the defeat of the Tairona, the dissolution of their ancient village federations, and their subsequent flight to the mountain fastnesses influenced profoundly the inhabitants of the valley, even if they themselves were not directly involved in military action. To this was added the introduction of iron tools, new food plants, and the first contacts with a new administrative system. These changes, however, probably were not abrupt events but developed slowly, over many years. Geographically, the valley occupied a position that was of practically no interest to the military and economic aims of the conquerors. No *encomienda* system was established, no resident priests came, and there was no forced labor in mines or on plantations. One certainly cannot suppose that every man now had iron tools or sugar-cane fields and that the ecological balance was thus greatly changed all of a sudden. As a matter of fact archeological evidence shows, for example, that the early Spanish trade axes were of a very poor quality and were quite scarce relative to stone axes. And as, during the same period, maize cultivation provided the staple food, the new food plants could have been hardly more than welcome additions to the diet, but certainly not 'revolutionizing' factors. In any event, as soon as the military resistance of the Tairona had been broken, the Spaniards abandoned the Sierra Nevada again, and any contact that existed between the mountain Indians and the conquerors during this later part of the sixteenth century must have been a sporadic one with only the few Spanish settlements at the base of the massif. It seems that the inhabitants of the valley of Aritama were

452

then able to continue their old-accustomed ways and that tribal identity was largely preserved. For some two centuries (at least) life in the sparsely settled valley, which never appears to have formed an important part of the larger aboriginal culture, continued much as it had before, and there was plenty of time to integrate the new elements which arrived by a slow trickle, and not in a sudden rush. From this first period of contact, the Indian community survived well into the eighteenth century without major changes in its traditional culture.

The eighteenth century, however, was a period of change of a far deeper nature. In the first place, the establishment, in about 1750, of permanent mission centers in and around the Sierra Nevada, and their subsequent activity over the entire Indian territory, brought practically all aboriginal communities into more or less permanent and close contact with Christian ideology. The mission schools taught the catechism, and reading and writing, all in the Spanish language. Indian servants were taken into the houses of priests as well as of Spanish landowners and administrators of the lowlands. Sugar-cane production was put on a commercial basis, and it was probably at this time and in connection with this crop that such beasts of burden as donkeys, mules, and oxen were introduced among the Indians. The transportation of such Indian products as raw sugar, hammocks, potatoes, and citrus fruits—the latter introduced already in the period of the conquest—to the markets of the now rising lowland towns provided an occasion for contact which formerly had not existed. In the second place, the Spanish authorities now began to incorporate the Indian hamlets into the administrative structure of the vice-kingdom by appointing in each settlement a body of official representatives. In this way, Spanish legal procedure was definitely introduced and became from then on the basis for the solution of such problems as might arise regarding land tenure, inheritance, tributes, communal labor, and all matters of crime and delinquency as defined by the new lawgivers. It was during this period that, under the pressure of the ecclesiastical and civil authorities, the inhabitants of the village were obliged to live in a nucleated settlement, and it is most probable that wattle-and-daub constructions and square gable-roofed houses began to replace the round, cane-walled and conical-roofed Indian-type house. Spanish religious, political, and economic interests obliged the Indians to live in compact villages, and thus the scattered tribe became a village community. These changes, then, were profound and lasting. Much of the present-day culture of the village points to the strong influence of missionaries, administrators, traders, and colonizers during the eighteenth century: the architectural style of the chapels in the vicinity, the style of the wooden images of saints still preserved in them; the family names still in use and taken from those of prominent public servants active at that period in the Spanish administration; the

present use of certain units of measurement, of certain magical procedures, religious rituals, Spanish folk dances, games, and certain words
employed in everyday language. It was during this period that Western
civilization obtained a foothold among the Sierra Nevada tribes and
added religious, moral, legal, economic, medical, aesthetic, and recreational concepts to their traditional culture—all concepts which,
although often reinterpreted and transformed, are still readily recognizable today. But in spite of these evident changes and of the wider
reorientation of cultural development implied by them, Aritama continued in essence to be an Indian community, and as such it appears
in the early official records up to the first decade of the nineteenth
century.

There followed a period of two or three generations during which
this local cultural configuration continued apparently without further
marked changes. Untouched by the turmoil of the War of Independence,
the villagers carried the eighteenth-century tradition of Hispano-Indian
culture well into the second half of the nineteenth century. The missionaries and administrators, as well as their schools, were gone again.
There was misery and famine in the lowlands. Open civil war or sporadic
guerrilla warfare devastated the new republic, and Aritama led an
isolated life during those long and violent years. In part, there seems
to have occurred a certain reversion to the old tribal ways; not perhaps
as a reaction against Church and State but simply because the former
stimulus and coercion were now lacking and all decisions on the village
and community level had to be met by the inhabitants themselves,
without guidance or the possibility of appeal to a higher government
authority. It is also probable that the political violence which then
prevailed in the lowlands led to the partial decentralization of the
community, many members of which preferred to live again in their
fields in the mountain folds instead of in a village exposed to the attacks
of marauding soldiery. If, therefore, there was any specific outside
influence on the village during these years, it was mainly one of fear and
distrust of the lowlands.

The third period of intensified contact and subsequent culture change
began with the previously mentioned immigration of the lowland
peasantry early in the second half of the nineteenth century. There is no
need to repeat here what has already been said in previous chapters
about the socioeconomic changes set in motion by this immigration, so
we shall point out only a few of the major results. Although the missionaries and the schools had returned to Aritama once again, most
marked changes took place in the social and economic structure of the
community. The village became divided into the Loma and Plaza
barrios, into 'Spanish' and 'Indian' inhabitants. Cattle-breeding
and cash crop-raising—above all coffee-growing—influenced tre-

mendously all spheres of village life. But most important of all, the concubinage pattern and the growing mixed population led to a change in values, in motivations, in ambitions. It became shameful to be an 'Indian', biologically or culturally, and those whose phenotype or economic position allowed it began to strive for recognition as 'Spaniards'. It was at this time, therefore that a deep inner struggle began, the struggle for prestige, for 'respect', for equality with the lowland Creoles. This struggle has continued up to the present and is evidently far from having reached a phase approaching social integration.

In the late thirties and early forties of the present century, a new period of change made itself felt in the village. This time changes were brought about mainly by improved communications and the necessity for making use of them, under the pressure of new needs. In these years practically all of the lowland towns were connected by highways, and transportation by truck or bus became the rule. With it came the newspapers, the cinema, the loudspeakers, the travelers. And with them came party politics, commerical foods and textiles, fashions and furnitures, aluminum vessels and iron tools, barbed wire, dyes and paints, leatherwares, cosmetics, cheap rum, flashlights, Coca Cola, medicines, phonograph records of Mexican and Cuban music. This was 'progress'. Because of the monoply exercised by the store-owners of the village, as well as because of the increasing scarcity of nearby agricultural lands for daily food production, the population increase, the credit system, and the new labor problems, people were being forced to think not only in terms of the lowland markets but in terms of lowland Creole culture. A lowland-style Sunday suit, a handbag containing cosmetics, an umbrella, a colored kerchief, a patent-leather belt, aluminum kitchenware, kerosene lamps—they all became status symbols, everchanging, ever increasing in number and variety, ever to be bought anew.

There can be no doubt that the factor that has most strongly influenced the local culture during recent years is the replacement of subsistence farming by cash crops, cattle, and wage labor. The ready acceptance—even at the cost of great personal sacrifice—of the changes involved was due mainly to the circumstance that these activities provided money with which to buy the status symbols of Creole culture, which otherwise were unobtainable. In this manner, monetary gain was not invested so much in better living conditions but in prestige-carrying objects or practices, the only aim of which was to produce 'respect'. Appearance and form became of paramount importance, but behind this façade the inner struggle was steadily growing.

Throughout this study we have employed the term 'Creole culture', and we must refer briefly to this concept here. Accepting essentially

Gillin's[1] definition, we are inclined to see Latin-American civilization as a self-contained entity, apart from the mainstream of Western civilization. This separation, however, was a consequence of historical events which seem to be particularly evident in the case of Colombia. Three centuries of European colonialism; the long separation from the mother country, Spain—herself long isolated from the current followed by other Western nations; the racial mixture with its concommitant status-defining groupings; the economic dependence upon the United States; the substandard living conditions prevailing in most of the nation's territory—all these and many other no less important factors have given rise to a configuration of cultural patterns and attitudes which, although structurally similar to Western equivalents, have a very different ideological and emotional content. There is a basic homogeneity in 'Mestizo American' which, because of this sequence of historical experiences, often shows more parallels to modern conditions in Asia or Africa than to the Western world.

Although in Colombia African retentions are negligible, the Indian cultural tradition, or rather traditions, left an indelible imprint upon life—an influence which is apparent in many aspects of material culture, emotional responses, and mental processes. By the term 'Creole culture', then, we refer to this emerging civilization which steadily defines itself better and better, not so much in form, as in content. The general characteristics of this 'new' civilization have been described by many recent authors in a more or less adequate way, and we find that their basic formulations and conclusions are generally applicable to the Colombian scene. In the case of the Caribbean lowlands we are, of course, dealing with a subcultural variable, but the essential configuration of Creole culture is the same.

Returning again to Aritama, we find that, at present, Creole culture is dominant in the political, economic, and formal educational institutions and that it exercises a strong influence on family structure and kinship. In these institutions we can say that all—or almost all—individuals involved have adopted, successfully or not, lowland values. Even those individuals who have no cattle or cash crops and who are still subsistence farmers, who live in monogamous marriage, who do not educate their children in the schools, and do not have recourse to the established authorities in case of conflict, look at those values as a promise for the future, as a goal to be achieved by them or by their children. However, in a number of other institutional orders, the traditional local values prevail: religion, magic, science, aesthetics, and recreation. It is in these areas that differences are strongest and that

[1] John Gillin, *Moche: A Peruvian Coastal Community*, Institute of Social Anthropology Publication No. 3, Washington, D.C: The Smithsonian Institution, 1947.

subcultural variation is most marked, but before we turn to consider them in more detail, it is necessary to point out some significant traits of the manner in which the Creole-dominated institutions are functioning.

The form and general content of the Colombian political administrative system on the village level are well established. It is felt by all members of the community that there should be a government-appointed authority and a set of laws and rules to regulate village affairs; that there should be an authority '*pa' que respeten*' (so people will maintain respectful behavior), but that it should not make itself felt as long as it is agreed that there *is* respect. This does not mean that people feel the need for a paternalistic authority from which guidance, advice, and 'progress' are to be expected. What is expected from the representatives of the government is 'justice' in the settlement of a few quite specific conflicts. These conflicts are those in which strong prestige factors are involved and where 'justice', in terms of 'respect', coincides clearly with the law. On the other hand, there are those conflicts in which it is supposed that the law would be confused and not clearly coincident with the local concept of 'justice', and in these instances settlement is sought elsewhere, not from the civil authorities.

Both the prestige aspect and the types of conflict the settlement of which by the official authorities is expected or avoided, are quite characteristic of the transitional phase the village is passing through at present. The problems that are brought before the authorities are unlawful fencing-in of village plots, empty house lots, or unoccupied backyards; insults and offenses between immediate neighbors; fights between neighbors' children; theft of cattle. In all these situations open 'disrespectful' behavior is seen, and it is supposed that the law is quite clear in these matters. It is characteristic that mainly women will ask for the authorities' intervention, rarely men, except in the case of theft of cattle. Other types of conflicts in which the official authorities are *not* asked or wanted to interfere are property rights of arable land, fencing outside of the village, way and water rights, damage caused by fire or stray domestic animals, domestic quarrels between husband and wife, desertion, seduction, elopement, inheritance, debts, physical aggression, sorcery, and petty thefts. In all these the wronged person fears that—should he address the authorities—false testimony, envy, magical aggression, contradictory laws, and biased judges are likely to do more harm than good. In these cases of conflict, then, the political administration exercises little influence, and settlement is sought privately. The lowland Creoles would readily take such matters before the authorities, insists on their rights, and engage in long and complicated suits, but not the people in Aritama. There the law is thought to be too complex, too ambiguous, too little concerned with the fine balance of prestige and respect.

In any case, the influence of the political administration is weak. All government planning, community projects, municipal initiative, or political pressure is deeply resented and eyed with suspicion and fear. Nothing good is ever expected to come from the government, and its local representatives are recognized and submitted to only insofar as they are willing and able to maintain 'respect' for the individual's dignity. It may be added here that the lack of interest in party politics and world events is by no means a local characteristic, but rather a common attitude in the Caribbean regions of the country. Although we have said that in the political administrative order Creole culture is dominant in Aritama, it must be pointed out that this dominance refers only to the general acceptance of the system as a desirable control over certain forms of behavior in which local values coincide (or are thought to coincide) with national law and administrative usage.

In the economic order, adaptation to Creole practices and attitudes has been fairly complete. However, the credit system by which large groups of people are kept in debt by a handful of store-owners, the *peón-patrón* relationship described in Chapter VI, and the emphatic rejection of agricultural labor as an 'Indian' attitude are instead local phenomena. The first, i.e., the credit system, is very similar to the conditions encountered in contact situations between Creoles and tribal Indians, but is not at all the rule *within* small Creole communities. In labor relations all over the lowlands the 'respect' pattern between hired worker and employer is emphasized but not so strongly as in the case of Aritama. Among the Creoles equality in human dignity is asked for, but not equality of social status, as is often done in Aritama. The lowland peasant does not feel inferior by engaging in agricultural activities concerned with daily food production. He might prefer cash crops and cattle and he will, whenever possible, combine them with his daily subsistence activities, but he will not risk hunger by refusing to work the available land with his own hands. Again, the problem in Aritama is prestige behavior, the constant fear that any action might be taken for an 'Indian' attitude by others. Another local pattern consists in trying to control, or to avoid altogether, the economic influence of the lowland Creoles by magical practices of Indian tradition. It would not occur to the lowland people to make stone offerings to insure good sales or to celebrate rites to stop the construction of an approaching highway, but in Aritama such practices are common. The fact that the prices in the lowlands fluctuate and that road construction is often interrupted for lack of government funds, confirms local beliefs in the efficacy of magical practices in many instances. When, in the recent past, the first roofs of corrugated iron were introduced by some placeros, all sorts of evil consequences for their owners' health, crops, and domestic animals were prognosticated. Magical defenses against them were sought, and there was even a movement to force the owners of such roofs to return them to the lowlands where they had bought them. When the roofs stayed, some people abandoned the village and went to live in their fields, and it is said that they avoided looking back at the village from afar so as not to see the brilliant sun rays reflected by the roofs, which were thought to cause serious eye disease. A similar reaction was shown a few years before this event when aluminum kitchenware was first introduced. Such magical attitudes are not found any more in the the lowlands and are only characteristic of the local situation, of the envy and prestige patterns which are at once brought into play.

The placero-owned stores are, of course, major foci of Creole influence. Their owners are among the few, or rather are the only ones, who live on a Creole level. These stores dictate the prices of cash crops and all locally manufactured goods, as well as tastes and fashions in fabrics, cosmetics, combs, kerchiefs. It is the store-owner and his wife who advise the customer in the choice of color, style, and quality of dress, and it is he who prescribes commercial medicines or even gives injections. They are the first to criticize and ridicule people for being ill-dressed, in order to make them buy new clothes at their stores. The store-owner is a banker, pharmacist, family counselor, accountant, public scribe, and a news service. His wife is the one who introduces the new hairdo, the new soap or perfume, and the new style in dress. The store-owners can write to a government agency and ask for new seeds; they can ask for loans in a lowland town; they know lawyers and judges and can carry on suits; they can travel to buy and sell their wares—all this because their educational level enables them. Disliked and distrusted as they are because of imposing ever-new necessities and status requirements, they fulfil an important role in the change toward Creole values, and even if their main motivation is more often than not material gain, they frequently show a sincere concern for the 'progress' of the community, often more than do the official authorities or other leading families. However, the local stores have not yet become gathering places where people may come to discuss daily events of local or national importance, as is the custom in the lowlands. In this sense the stores are still isolated and their function is limited, but nonetheless their owners, clients, and wares are closely watched by all, and the appearance of a new item or a casual remark overheard while passing by may have, perhaps, a stronger influence than long conversations with a group of people.

If one would judge Aritama only by its little church, its processions with the patron saint or at Corpus Christi, its lay brotherhoods, baptismal records, or other exterior signs of Catholicism, one would easily believe that the village differs but very little from the great majority of Creole settlements all over the country. We have seen, however, that this is not so and that religious attitudes and practices are far from falling within the common range of Catholic dogma and usage. It is here, in the fields of religion and magic, especially in the ancestor cult and the stone offerings, that the Indian tradition is still dominant. In many magico-religious practices we can, of course, discern a number of traits of Mediterranean folk Catholicism of centuries ago, but the underlying premises and attitudes are still strongly Indian-oriented. Similar influences can also be observed in medical practices and in most concepts relating to the biological and natural sciences. Partly Indian and partly Mediterranean as a body of beliefs and practices, this complex differs considerably from the one found among the lowland Creoles for whom the Church and the Catholic religion form—in spite of materialism, moral laxity, and growing anticlericalism—an important focus of individual and community life. In the lowlands Mass, Confession, Communion, and prayer have an important meaning and function for most individuals. Holy Week and Christmas are still solemn occasions; parish priests are respected and are often leading influences in the material progress of their villages as well. But in Aritama the picture is very different indeed.

We have been generalizing but must now make use of concrete facts to show how some of these different concepts operate on the individual level. Changing institutions can be understood only in terms of the changing individuals who form them and who are, in turn, formed by them. It is on this personal, individual level that the whole drama takes place.

The search for identity and self-assertion in 'civilized', and therefore 'respected', Creole culture presupposes a reorientation of values and goals, emotional responses, and personality. To most people in Aritama, above all to the lomero majority, Creole orientation demands major psychological reformulations and a new structural and emotional balance. This balance has not yet been achieved, it seems. The way in which definite situations must be handled according to Creole patterns does not coincide with the personality type of most villagers. They lack the economic and social aggressiveness of the Creole, the rudeness behind which he hides his timidity, his verbal facility, easy courtesy, his calculated bragging, and his tearful sentimentality. Whereas the urban-oriented Creole projects his timidity outward and transforms it in his overt behavior into boisterous self-assertion, the people in Aritama inhibit all public and social expressions of this kind of self-assertion out of fear of showing themselves as 'Indians', unable to handle the situation in the manner they believe is expected of them. They try to solve the conflict by hidden magic and malicious gossip and by presenting to the outsider a wholly imaginary picture of local ways. But even this picture is not presented in a consistent and convincing fashion, and if the outsider sees through it there is no surprise or insistence but only gloomy self-accusation. Even among those people of the Plaza section who have assimilated Creole culture to a considerable degree, one finds this type of reaction. A person will say, for example, 'When I was little my grandmother told me that once upon a time people made offerings to their ancestors by wrapping powdered stones in corn husks' or another might say, 'In those old times people would "baptize" a new house and call an Indian shaman for this purpose'. If told quite bluntly that X made a stone offering to his ancestors only yesterday and that Y had his house 'baptized' by a shaman only last week, the reaction is never one of open anger or simulated disbelief but of confusion and shame. Of course, such things are not told to convince the outsider that these customs have disappeared long ago, but to demonstrate that the speaker, at least, holds them in contempt and does not engage in such practices. Day after day, in all contacts with people from the outside, these painfully humiliating experiences are repeated. There is the person who ridicules 'Indian superstitions' but refuses to touch an archeological object; the person who claims to be a practicing Catholic but who admits that he lives in concubinage and never goes to Mass; the person who boasts of being of lowland 'Spanish' origin but must admit to illegitimacy and illiteracy; the person who pretends to be only a casual visitor to the village, on his way back to a large city, but who on closer acquaintance turns out to be a native resident who has not left the village in years.

At the same time the fear of losing prestige leads to misunderstandings by which certain cultural elements of Old World origin begin to be considered as 'Indian' and therefore as 'ugly' and reprehensible. For example, because the lowland Creoles disparage the Indians for eating all the animal entrails and other internal organs, the people in Aritama have come to conclude that the liver also falls into this category of despicable 'Indian' foods and admit only shamefacedly that a number of people eat this organ boiled or fried. In the lowlands, however, liver is a common and well-liked dish, and nobody would associate this item with the Indians or a low social status. But people in Aritama do not know this, and many deprive themselves of this food for prestige reasons, to avoid being called 'tripe-eaters' by the Creoles. A similar confusion occurs with the Cucamba dancers. The placeros and a great many lomeros believe that these bird masks are an aboriginal pagan feature in the Corpus Christi fiesta, and several attempts have been made to suppress this dance as 'savage' and 'ugly'. When we told them that in reality the Cucambas represented symbolically St. John the Baptist and are part of an old Andalusian Catholic folk tradition, there was great surprise and relief and the dance became respectable again. Other examples are plentiful: the Latin expression *de jure* (as in, '*de jure* it has to be this way') is often heard in Aritama but is thought to be an 'ugly' Indian term. Leather sandals, straw hats of a certain type, certain styles of female dress such as the *chambrita*, are believed to be of Indian origin and are therefore criticized. But on the other hand, nobody would believe that the hammock, the dibbling-stick, the woven fiber bags, or the many starchy food plants are aboriginal elements. They are thought to have come directly from Spain and people will deny that they form part of an Indian heritage. There is then a selective process at work by which some replaceable elements are eliminated or reinterpreted while a nucleus of less replaceable and more basic elements is maintained and rationalized as of 'civilized' origin.

In the entire trend toward Creole culture the dominating motivation is not a higher standard of living but fear of being taken for an 'Indian', of being 'uncivilized' (*inculto*). And the dominating technique is not slow assimilation and reorientation of values, but rapid imitation of exterior forms. The inner conflicts caused by the incompatibility of patterns and by constant contradictions between private reality and public make-believe are manifest in the overall personality of the villagers. Their timidity and their deeply felt shame of it make them vacillate, in the extremity of humiliation, between aggressive self-assertion and a profound sense of inadequacy. But the level of ambition is high and, what is more, it is realistic. There is a growing tendency to teach children the basic values of Creole culture, but within the limits sets by phenotype and fate. They are not taught to aspire to great things, only to what is obtainable. People want to change and they strive to form part of a larger community, of a larger unit beyond the narrow limits of the village scene. They know that they still occupy a marginal position and that they are antiquated and 'strange' in the eyes of the lowlanders. But no one wants to defend this traditional culture, and no one insists in the validity of the old goals, except those whose Indian phenotype is a limiting factor and who are therefore the 'uncivilized' and 'unprogressive'.

There is a bitter irony in this situation. In reality, those despised as 'unprogressive Indians' stand ideologically closer to Western civilization than the local 'Spaniards' or the lowland Creoles. The conservative Indian peasant lives by a value system and demonstrates a personality type which are far more Western than the emerging Creole outlook on life. Among the former, their eighteenth-century Catholicism and their respect for due process of law, for family life, and village authority are in obvious opposition to the materialism of the average Creole, his hedonism, his disregard for law and authority, and his disrupted family life.

Summary

But neither can there be any doubt as to the final outcome. Not only Aritama but the whole of the Creole world, it seems, are steadily becoming less Western. There remain the institutional forms of Western civilization, but their contents are new, because their basic values and motivations are now those of a people to whom the human condition has a different meaning than it has to the West, than it had to their fathers, than it had to those who still were able to look upon their ancestors with legitimate pride. Aritama is only a pebble traveling in this stream, but it gives us perhaps a measure of the current.

Appendix

CURES FOR DISEASES

THE following specific treatments for different diseases and ailments can be considered as common practice. Alternative treatments are indicated by arabic numerals in brackets.

HEADACHE. (1) Poultice with boiled leaves of *matarratón* (*Gliricida sepium*). (2) Poultice with boiled leaves of *guandú* (*Cajanus indicus*). (3) Poultice with leaves of *yarumo* (*Cecropia* sp.). (4) Poultice with leaves of *verbena* (*Heliotropium indicum* L.). (5) Poultice with leaves of *bijo* (*Bursera tomentosa* [Jacq.] Tr. and Pl.). (6) Application of raisin from a *cascarrilla* tree (indet.). (7) Application of raisin from a *fraylejón* plant (*Espeletia* sp.). (8) Direct application of a *lirio* leaf (indet.), slightly warmed over a fire. (9) Direct application of a *chicorión* leaf (*Chaptalia nutans* [L] Polak), slightly warmed. (10) The leaves of a coffee plant are cut into small pieces, wrapped into a cloth, and applied to the head. (11) A 'hat' of the leaves of the *caranganito* plant (indet.) is fashioned, left to dry in the sun, sprinkled with rum, and then put on.

DISEASE OF THE EYES. (1) Against *ceguera* (conjunctivitis) the white interior part of a leaf of the *sábila* plant (*Aloe vulgaris*) is grated and mixed with cold water. A bit of refined sugar is added, and drops of the liquid are applied to the eyes. (2) The flower of a *pastelito* plant (*Commelina elegans* H.B.K.) is pressed, and the liquid is dripped into the eye. (3) The juice of the leaves of a *trupillo* tree (*Neltuma juliflora*) is mixed with human or goat's milk and applied to the eye. (4) For glaucoma equal parts of salt, refined sugar, and ground bark of the *malambo* tree (*Croton Malambo* Karst.) are mixed and applied. (5) The fruit of a plant called *ojito de sangre* (indet.) is cooked, and the water is used to wash the eyes. (6) The seeds of *zapotillo amarillo* (indet.) are put into alcohol for several days, and the eyes are washed with the liquid.

DISEASES OF THE EARS. (1) Against pains in the ears a small piece of fried shallot is introduced into them. (2) A few drops of human milk are used in the case of small infants. (3) The ground resin of the *fraylejón* plant (*Espeletia* sp.) is put on a bit of cotton and introduced into the ear. (4) Warm water sweetened with raw sugar is dripped into the ear.

NOSEBLEEDING. (1) A cold bath is taken early in the morning. (2) Leaves of the *matarratón* tree (*Gliricida sepium*) are rolled between the fingers and introduced into the nostrils. (3) Ground *matarratón* bark is sniffed.

TOOTHACHE. (1) Tobacco leaves are boiled for hours or days, and the thick juice is applied to the tooth. (2) A bit of raw sugar and a grain of salt are added to boiling water that is left to stand until cold and used to rinse the mouth. (3) The mouth is rinsed with rum. (4) A small wasp's nest of clay is diluted in rum, and a poultice is applied externally. (5) An *alhucema* flower (*Lavandula vera*) is rolled between the fingers and applied to the tooth. (6) Leaves of *alhucema* (*Lavandula vera*) are boiled, and a poultice is applied externally. (7) The upper fibrous part of a coconut is scraped and boiled, and the water is used to rinse the mouth. (8) A *creso* flower (indet.) is put on the aching tooth. (9) Tomato-plant shoots are boiled, and the water is used for rinsing the mouth. (10) *Llantén* leaves (*Plantago* spp.) are boiled for rinsing the mouth. (11) A few seeds of *Yerba mora* (*Solanum nigrum* L. var.) are put into a piece of cotton and burned before the open mouth of the patient. The smoke is supposed to kill the 'worms' that attack the tooth.

MOUTH INFECTIONS. The white interior part of a *sábila* leaf (*Aloe vulgaris*) is left to stand in rum for two days, after which the liquid is applied over the affected parts with a feather.

INFECTED CUTS AND SORES, etc. (1) The ground bark of the *yarumo* tree (*Cecropia* sp.) is mixed with a bit of salt and applied to the infected spot. (2) A small bit of a green banana of the *criollo* or *manzano* variety is mashed and some salt is added before applying the paste. (3) A small piece of the shell of a land turtle (*Testudo denticulata*) is burned and ground, mixed with water, and applied to the infected part. (4) A cigar is chewed and when thoroughly wet is applied. (5) Warm beeswax is applied so the 'cold' will not enter the infection. (6) The liquid raisin of the *bijo* tree (*Bursera tomentosa* [Jacq.] Tr. and Pl.) is applied. (7) Local infections behind the ears of infants are treated with a poultice made from the leaves of *contra de lobo* (*Salvia occidentalis* Swartz).

INFECTED THORNS OR SPLINTERS. (1) Salt is added to the bile of a cow, and the liquid is applied with a feather. A small, flat piece of wood is tied over the thorn or splinter and is supposed to 'extract' it. (2) Fat, salt, and raw sugar are mixed in equal parts and are slightly warmed before being applied to the spot.

INFECTED UMBILICUS OF NEWBORNS. (1) The seeds of a *dividivi* tree (*Libidibia coriara*) are ground, and the powder is applied. (2) The fine powdered earth which accumulates under the doorstep is applied.

BLEEDING WOUNDS. (1) Spiderwebs are applied. (2) The leaves of *siempreviva roja* (*Gomphrena* sp.) are boiled, and the water is applied in a poultice.

SKIN INFECTIONS. Against itch or mange ('*Sabrocita*') lukewarm water, wherein certain plants have been boiled, is applied: (1) *laurél* leaves (*Nectandra concinna* Nees); (2) leaves of *almácigo* (*Bursera Simaruba* Sarg.?); (3) leaves of the *guayaba* tree (*Psidium guajaba*); (4) leaves of the *albahaca* plant (*Ocimum micranthum* Willd.); leaves of the *guandú* tree (*Cajanus indicus*); leaves of *salva real* (indet.); (7) young leaves of the *quebracho* tree (*Astronium graveolens* Jacq.); (8) leaves of the *volador* plant (indet.) are warmed and applied directly. Against zona herpes the following are used: (1) ground green leaves of *yerba mora* (*Solanum nigrum* L. var.) mixed with rum, human milk, or with a child's urine are applied with a feather; (2) poultice of *lechoncito* leaves (indet.); (3) poultice of *creso* leaves (indet.). Against papiloma the following remedies are applied externally: (1) the sap of the papaya tree (*Carica papya*); (2) a piece of bark of the *ceiba* tree (*Ceiba pentandra*) is left to stand in cold water and then used as a poultice; (3) the fine powder which forms on a stone when sharpening a knife. To combat erysipelas a live toad is held for a while against the affected part and then hung by a hind leg until it dies.

BOILS. (1) A green leaf of chili pepper is covered with goat's fat and applied directly. (2) A poultice of leaves of *contra de lobo* (*Salvia occidentalis* Swartz). (3) Toasted ground fruits of *piñique-piñique* (*Rauwolfia hirsuta* Jacq.) mixed with alum. (4) *Creso* leaves (indet.) (5) Poultice of *chicorión* leaves (*Chaptalia nutans* [L.] Polak). (6) Iguana fat. (7) Human saliva, applied early in the morning before any food has been consumed. Against larger skin tumors, a *pichiguey* (*Melocactus violaceus* Pfeiff.?) is grated and applied with a few grains of salt.

RHEUMATISM. (1) The leaves of the *malanga* plant (*Xanthosoma sagittifolium*) are warmed over a fire, sprinkled with rum, and applied to the painful region. (2) Leaves of *mata andréa* (indet.) are used in the same way. (3) Leaves and stems of the *zarzaparilla* plant (*Gouania polygama* [Jacq.] Urban) are used as a poultice after boiling them. (4) The leaves of *abrazapalo* (indet.) are held for a moment over an open fire, sprinkled with rum, and applied while still warm.

COLDS. Infusions of the following boiled leaves are taken: (1) *romero* (*Rosmarinus officinalis*); (2) *tomillo* (*Thymus vulgaris*; (3) *borraja* (*Borrago officinalis*); (4) *guayabo blanco* (*Psidium guajaba*); (5) *bijo* (*Bursera tomentosa* [Jacq.] Tr. and Pl.); (6) *yarumo* (*Cecropia* sp.); (7) *salva real* (indet.); (8) combined leaves of *yarumo* (*Cecropia* sp.), *bijo* (*Bursera tomentosa* [Jacq.] Tr. and Pl.), *almácigo* (*Bursera Simaruba* Sarge.?), *verbena* (*Heliotropium indicum*), and *eucalipto* (*Eucalyptus* sp.); (9) combined leaves of *resfrío* (*Scleria hirtella* Sw.), *eucalipto* (*Eucalyptus*) and *quina* (*Cinchona* spp.); (10) combined leaves of *verbena* (*Heloitropium indicum*) and stems of *comino rústico* (*Pectis elongata* H.B.K.); (11) boiled bark of *bijo* (*Bursera tomentosa* [Jacq.] Tr. and Pl.); (12) bark of *almácigo* (*Bursera Simaruba* Sarg.?); (13) boiled stems of *comino rústico* (*Pectis elongata* H.B.K.); (14) boiled raisin of *arañagato* (indet).

FEVER. Infusions of the following boiled leaves or barks are taken: (1) *viravira* (*Achyrocline* sp.); (2) bark of *quina* (*Cinchona* sp); (3) bark *granada* (indet.); (4) roots of *guayacana* (indet.); (5) whole but very small plants of *tedé* (indet.). (6) Poultices of the leaves of *sábila* (*Aloe vulgaris*) mixed with a bit of baking soda. (7) Massages with a mixture of camphor and powdered quina bark in rum. (8) 'Shoes' of *matarratón* leaves (*Gliricida sepium*), with soles of sewn maize leaves; before they are put on they are heated over an open fire.

TORTICOLIS. (1) Massages with fat or oil. (2) The painful region is pinched repeatedly with a sharp splinter.

PAINS IN THE CHEST. One or two whites of egg are beaten and drunk.

PNEUMONIA. (1) Poultice of ground mustard seed. (2) Poultice of mashed leaves of *hojita de centella* (*Plumbago scandens*), generally combined with ground mustard seeds. (3) Leaves of *verbena* (*Heliotropium indicum*) are buried in hot ashes, ground, sifted and boiled. After mixing with a bit of table oil, teaspoonfuls are taken every hour.

ASTHMA. A small hole is drilled in a coconut, the milk is taken out, and the nut is filled with refined sugar. After being buried for one month, the white interior is eaten. Three coconuts have to be eaten in three different months.

DYSENTERY. (1) Pure lemon juice. (2) Lemon juice with refined sugar and some bicarbonate of soda. (3) Very hot water with plenty of salt. (4)

Diluted manioc starch made of unripe tubers. (5) Ground bark of *guácimo* (*Gauzuma ulmifolia* Lam. var.) (6) Infusions of *paja de limón* (*Cymbopogon citratus* [DC] Stapf.). (7) Ground cumin seed in boiled water.

STOMACH-ACHE. The following infusions are used: (1) *yerbabuena de mentol* (*Mentha piperita*); (2) flowers of *manzanilla* (*Matricaria chamomilla*); (3) *comino rústico* (*Pectis elongata* H.B.K.); (4) lemon juice with soda; (5) ginger root (*Zingiber officinale*).

CONSTIPATION. (1) A bit of red earth is excavated from beneath the hearth, boiled in water, sifted, and drunk. (2) An entire pod of *cañafistula* (*Cassia grandis*) is boiled and taken as an infusion. (3) The root of *mechoacán* (indet.) is dried, ground, and boiled as infusion. (4) Seeds of *piñoncito* (*Jatropha Curcas* L.) are dried, ground, and taken in lukewarm water.

VOMITING. The following infusions are used in order to stop vomiting: (1) *canela* (*Cinnamomum Zeylanicum* Bl.); (2) *valeriana* (*Valeriana* spp.); (3) *yerbabuena* (*Mentha piperita* L.). In order to induce vomiting the following are taken: (1) boiled roots of *lirio blanco* (indet.); (2) hot urine of an old man.

COLITIS. The following infusions are taken: (1) boiled bark of *guácimo* (*Guazuma ulmifolia* Lam. var.) with some sugar added; (2) fresh, grated *guácimo* bark, with sugar.

COLIC. Infusions of *siempreviva blanca* (*Gomphrena globosa* L.) are taken.

INTESTINAL PARASITES. The following infusions are used: (1) *paico* (*Chenopodium antihelminticm* L.); (2) a combination of *paico*, *yerbabuena* (*Mentha piperita* L.), and *verdolaga blanca* (indet.) in equal parts; (3) a few seeds of *almizclillo* (*Hibiscus abelmoschus* L.) and some garlic are put into a little cloth bag and carried around the neck. (4) Small children are buried up to the waist in sand and left for about one hour. (5) Older children wear a necklace of garlic for several days.

LIVER AILMENTS. The following infusions are used: (1) *sábila* (*Aloe vulgaris*) with some soda added; (2) boiled and sifted grass; (3) a leaf of the avocado tree is warmed and applied locally.

KIDNEY AILMENTS. A long strip of the leaf of a *tuna de España* (indet). is left to soak in water. This is beaten and the water is drunk.

IRREGULAR MENSTRUATION. The following infusions are taken: (1) *guácimo* (*Guazuma ulmifolia* Lam. var.); (2) *viravira* (*Achyrocline* sp.) combined with *romero* (*Rosmarinus officinalis*); (3) flowers of *siempreviva* (*Gomphrena* sp.). Against painful menstruation: (1) *viravira* (*Achyrocline* sp.), *romero* (*Rosmarinus officinalis*) and *borraja* (*Borrago officinalis*) are combined in an infusion; (2) flowers of *venturosa* (*Corchorus hirtus* L.) and mashed leaves of *piñuelo* (indet.); (3) shavings from the hoof of a tapir, taken in rum.

CHILDBIRTH. To accelerate birth the following infusions are taken: (1) rum with chili peppers; (2) *manzanilla* (*Matricaria chamomilla*); (3) mustard seed; (4) *yerbabuena* (*Mentha piperita* L.). The abdomen is massaged with fat or oil. In order to eject the afterbirth, vomitives are taken or an infusion of the roots of *yerbabuena* (*Mentha piperita* L.). In difficult cases the nest of a small parrot ('*cotorra*'), made of clay, is dissolved in water, boiled, sifted, and taken as an infusion. For several days after birth the following infusions are taken: (1) *viravira* (*Achyrocline* sp.); (2) whole plants of *pita mirial* (*Pedilanthus tithymaloides* [L.] Poit.).

ABORTIVES. In order to induce an abortion, the following infusions are taken: (1) *siempreviva roja* (*Gomphrena globosa* L.); (2) boiled sap of the papaya tree (*Carica papaya*); (3) boiled roots of the *ceiba* tree (*Ceiba pentandra*); (4) boiled roots of *barbasco* (indet.); (5) boiled roots of *platanito* (indet.); boiled roots of *maguey* (*Agave americana*). A very potent abortive is supposed to be the water in which the seed of an avocado has been boiled.

GONORRHEA. The following infusions are taken: (1) leaves and stems of *ojo de buey* (*Desmoncus* sp.), also used as a poultice; (2) leaves and flowers of *corzonera* (indet.), also a poultice; (3) boiled leaves and stems of the *malva* plant (*Malvastrum peruvianum*).

SYPHILLIS. (1) Plain water is left to stand in the sun, in a green or transparent bottle, and is then taken in small sips. (2) Infusions of the seeds of *ojito de sangre* (indet.).

SMALLPOX. The following poultices are applied: (1) leaves of *yerba india* (*Solanum nigrum* var.); (2) whole plants of *calentura vieja* (indet.).

SNAKEBITE. The following infusions are used: (1) roots of *piñique-piñique* (*Rauwolfia hirsuta* Jacq.), combined with *capitana* (*Aristolochia maxima* Jacq.), *bejuco de cadena* (indet.), *capitanita* (indet.), *guaco morado* or *blanco* (indet.), *torompita* (indet.), and *culantro* (*Coriandrum sativum* L.); (2) *escobita* (*Scoparia dulcis* L.); (3) *contrayerba* (*Dorstenia Contrajerva* L.). Other remedies consist in drinking immediately the bile of the snake or in applying externally half of the seed of *ojo de buey* (*Desmoncus* sp.), which is supposed to 'suck out the poison'.

INSECT BITES. Scorpion bites are treated with an infusion or poultice of shavings from the bark of a *malambo* tree (*Croton Malambo* Karst.). Against the rash produced by a centipede, a piece of cheese is applied. Tick bites are treated with drops of lemon juice. Against the bite of the 'white' spider, a piece of thinly cut sugar cane is applied, while against the bite of the *coralito* spider, the whole body is bathed with water wherein the following herbs have been boiled: *torompita* (indet)., stems of *yerba de paraco* (*Croton pedicellatus* H.B.K.), and the main fiber of a tobacco leaf. Immediately after the bath an infusion of *borraja* (*Borrago officinalis*) is taken. Infections caused by the bristles of certain caterpillars are treated with poultices and infusions of the leaves of the *malambo* tree (*Croton Malambo* Karst.). A general remedy for all insect bites consists in applying chewed tobacco to the bite, and in swallowing some of the juice. *Mastranto* leaves (*Hyptis suaveolens* [L.] Poit.) are put on the floor in order to keep fleas away.

BRUISES, FALLS, ETC. The following infusions are used: (1) *jarilla* (indet.); (2) coca leaves (*Erythroxylon coca*); (3) a green *totuma* fruit (*Crescentia cujete*) is hollowed out, water is poured into it, a bit of salt is added, and the liquid is left to stand overnight; in the morning it is drunk; (4) *Arnica* (*Trixis radialis* [L.] Ktze), also in poultice; (5) earth excavated from beneath the hearth, mixed with water, and with some salt added; also for poultices.

FRACTURES. (1) The sap of the *higuillo copey* tree (*Clusia* sp.) is applied. (2) The sap of the *higuito* tree (indet.) is mixed with the ground fruits of *mastuerzo* (*Lepidium bipinnatifidum* Dsv.?), and the paste is applied.

RACHITISM. A small *zanconcito* plant (*Elytraria imbricata* [Vahl] Pers.) is put into a bottle of rum, and the legs of the child are sprinkled with the liquid.

SHARP PAINS, 'AIRES', 'PUNZADAS', ETC. The following infusions are taken: (1) coca leaves (*Erythroxylon coca*); (2) *jarilla* (indet.); aniseed (*Pimpinella anisum* L.); (4) ginger root (*Zingiber officinale*), also in a bottle of rum. The following poultices are applied: (1) mashed leaves of *hoja de centella* (*Plumbago scandens* L.), combined with ground mustard seed; (2) ground ginger root.

HEART AILMENTS. The following infusions are taken: (1) coca leaves (*Erythroxylon coca*); (2) orange leaves; (3) roots of orange; (4) ginger root; (5) roots of *toronjil* (*Ocimum* sp.).

HICCUPS. (1) Smell of a *totumo* flower (*Crescentia cujete*). (2) Three sips of water. (3) A drink of very cold water. (4) Sudden fright. Small children are treated by placing a bit of damp cotton upon their forehead.

VARIA. The application of fresh leaves of *higuereto* (*Rhicinus communis* L.) on the breasts of a woman is supposed to produce abundant milk and to prevent sores during lactation. The leaves of *verbena* (*Heliotropium indicum* L.) are boiled together with goat's dung, and women suffering from abdominal pains after childbirth use the water for poultices. To make infants sleep, an infusion of lettuce leaves is given. Many pains are relieved by taking an infusion of the leaves of *alivia-dolor* (*Lantana* sp.). Sterility in men or women is said to be cured by eating, fried, the salted and dried bile of a *morrocoy* turtle (*Testudo denticulata*). To combat heartburn a bit of raw manioc is chewed.

INDEX

473

Drugs, commercial, 80, 132, 291, 294, 297, 310, 311, 312, 313, 459
Drums, 197, 198, 369, 374

Economics: general aspects of, 51, 261; history of, 50–51, 130, 132; household budgets, 240–44; *see also* Agriculture; Commerce and trade; Credit system; Food exchange; Industry
Educational theory, 77, 99, 102–3, 106, 107, 121, 122–23, 124–25
El Banco: town of, 3; Department of, 16
El Mamón, region of, 10
El Rosario, village of, 9
Elopement, 114, 162, 193
Encisco, Martín Fernández de, 6
Encomienda system, 6, 8, 129, 452
Envy, 136, 167, 278, 281, 282, 309, 331, 444; *see also* Interpersonal conflicts
Ethnographical setting, 3 ff.
Evil eye, 89, 122, 284, 285, 289, 293, 309, 372, 402–3, 427

Family: budgets, 239–44; historical development of, 129–33, 144 ff.; structure, 144 ff.; *see also* Concubinage; Conjugal union; Household; Interpersonal relations
Fatalism, 77, 94, 99, 259, 441–42
Fauna, local, 20, 229–31
Fear of darkness, 83, 90, 94, 95, 98, 102–3, 105, 192
Fences, 22, 203, 208, 233
Fiestas: cycle of, 343, 367 ff.; organization of, 368
Fines, 119, 245
Fire, sacredness of, 350, 394
Fishing, 53, 56, 230–31, 330
Fits, hysteroid or epileptoid, 47, 48, 189, 285, 302, 309, 333
Folk tales, 327, 433–37
Food: attitudes toward, 51, 57, 100, 217, 290–91, 313 ff.; availability and acquisition of, 50, 56, 57, 247, 313; classification of, 61 ff.; 313, 317–18, 321; daily consumption of, 66 ff.; expenditures for, 239–44; and health, 51, 91, 286, 290–91; nutrient composition of, 45, 72–76, 316–17, 320; preparation of, 58 ff., 74, 317; and prestige, 51, 65, 66, 71, 317, 321, 322, 327, 230; production of, 50, 51 ff.; 313, 314–15; quality and quantity of, 61 ff., 313, 314; rumors, 324–25, 326; scarcity of, 55, 56–57, 65, 223, 324–25; seasonal availability of, 55, 56, 57, 65, 71–72, 74, 324–26; storage of, 43, 58, 59, 60, 251; store-bought, 51, 55, 57, 72; substitutes, 55, 92; trade of, 50, 51, 56
Food exchange, patterns of, 91, 92, 164, 194, 247–54, 330
Food plants, cultivated, 50 ff., 52–53, 55 ff.
Franciscan order, 8, 13, 343
Free union: economic aspects of, 146–47, 160; factors in selection of consort in, 146, 160; historical aspects of, 145–46, 167; separation of, 145, 164; stability of, 146–47; 160, 163; *see also* Conjugal union; Family; Household; Social structure
Fright, magical, 418 ff.
Fruits: cultivated, 218–19; wild growing, 53–54, 56, 72, 104, 200
Fundación River, 9

Gambling, 196
Gangs, children's, 200–1
Garbage, disposal of, 43
Garden crops, 215–18
Genealogy, interest in, 167, 336
Genetic constitution, 12, 24–25
Geographical setting, 3 ff.; 19–20
Geophagy, 50, 302
Ghosts and apparitions; *see* Hallucinations
Gillin, John, 456 n.
Godparents; *see* Kinship; Ritual

Wake, 103, 171, 279, 378–82, 392, 401, 407
War of Independence, 8, 15, 180, 342
Water, storage and supply, 40, 43–43, 59
Wealth: concept of, 239; and food habits, 61 ff.; as status factor, 139, 141, 142
Weaning, 82–83, 90, 92, 323, 327
Weaving; *see* Industry
Winds: beliefs about, 41, 78, 281, 283, 309; prevailing, 4, 5, 19, 20, 41, 202, 203
Witchcraft; *see* Magic

Witches, 94, 300, 408–10, 422–25
Women: daily routine of, 60–61, 79, 162; ideal role of, 186; position of in family, 146, 157, 159–63, 185, 191; work of, 139, 146, 211, 231, 254, 255, 256, 263
Work: attitudes and patterns of, 259–66, 290; cycles of, 261–62; incentives to, 35, 261, 314; local definition of, 259, 314; and prestige, 259–66, 314; rhythm of, 266–71

Yuko, Indians, 12